FOUNDATION MATHEMATICA

FOR

ALL MATHEMATICS EXAMINATION

BY

JUDE NDUBUISI ONICHA

© JUDE M. N. ONICHA 2014

First Published 2014

VERY STRICT ANTI-PRIVACY MEASURES

All right reserved. No part of this publication may be reproduced or transmitted in any form or by any means, electronic or mechanical, including photocopy, recording or any information storage and retrieval system, without permission in writing from the author and copyright owner.

ISBN-13: 978-1500915278

For help, enquires, or bulk purchase of this book, contact the author on any of these addresses,

Email: kenonich@yahoo.com, amazon.com

Phone: 08168812939, 08029276704, 08028548254

Website: www.mmmiexamssolutions.com

Printed by Createspace, An Amazon.com Company

DEDICATION

To God Almighty

FORWARD

It is a known fact that Mathematics is the formidable foundation required for all fields.

The author's mathematical foundation is autochonous as reflected in the book. He calculates effortlessly, the way men breaths. He has made mathematics and effortless subject. It is a masterpiece. Anyone with a copy of this book is certain of performing exceedingly well in any mathematics examination.

Finally, posterity will thank him for having shown it that the authors before him did not know everything.

Engr J J Chikwe HND, B.Eng, M. Eng, Ph.D

Former Dean Faculty of Engineering

Yaba College of Technology

PREFACE

This book treats all topics designed by different examination bodies in the simplest possible form rather than a mere question and answer text.

The author has also researched deeply through many topics with ambiguous cases. His findings are put into use in the making of this book.

Students of Mathematics and Mathematics related courses in University, Polytechnic and Professional examination bodies will find Foundation Mathematica indispensible and highly rewarding.

The text is an exclusive work of the author and is open to any constructive criticism.

The author would like to duly acknowledge and profoundly thank the authors of the different text/materials used in the preparation of this manuscript. My inability to reach them should not be seen as a calculated intention.

Special thanks goes to Engr J J Chikwe for his immeasurable support, endless efforts in making these book a reality. May God bless you abundantly.

In particular, I wish to acknowledge and thank Oboh Emmanuel Ewariezi who was specially in charge of all diagrams and typing of this manuscript. Mr Ambrose Akinnodi for the finishing touches and professional advice that made this book a reality. James Obeahon for his relentless effort in making this work a topnotch quality.

I also thank every member of my family for their patience during this great task. May God bless you all!

Jude M N Onicha

CONTENTS

Chapter 1: Introduction to algebra 1

Algebraic terms and processes, Fraction, Word problems leading to fractions

Chapter 2: Number system 8

Definition, Conversion of number base, addition, subtraction, multiplication and division of number bases.

Chapter 3: Approximation of numbers 16

Definition, decimal place system, significant figures system, nearest values system, standard form system, errors,

Chapter 4: Indices 25

Indices, laws of indices, indicial equation.

Chapter 5: Logarithm 35

Principle of logarithm, Laws of logarithms, logarithmic equation.

Chapter 6: Surds 43

Rules of surd, similar surd, simplification of surd, Algebra of surds, Equality of surds.

Chapter 7: Change of subject of an equation 54

Definition, techniques of evaluation.

Chapter 8: Factorization 57

Definition, techniques of factorization, factorization of difference of two square, factorization of sum of two cube, factorization of difference of two cube, factorization of trinomial, factorization of difference of two fourth powers, factorization expressions containing more than four terms.

Chapter 9: Linear equation 61

Definition, method of solving a linear equation.

Chapter 10: Simultaneous equation 65

Definition, Methods of solving simultaneous equation, elimination method, substitution method, graphical method, word problem leading to simultaneous equation.

Chapter 11: Quadratic equation...78

Definition, methods of solving quadratic equation, completing the square, quadratic formula, nature of quadratic roots, forming a quadratic equation when the roots are given, Word problem leading to quadratic equation.

Chapter 12: Variation...92

Definition, types of variation, direct variation, inverse variation, joint variation, partial variation.

Chapter 13: Ratio, proportion and percentage...100

Definitions, applications of ratio and proportion, applications of percentage in change in quantities, decrease and increase, in mixtures, profit and loss sales, discount sales, commission, simple and compound Interest,

Chapter 14: Rate and rateable values..131

Speed, distance, time, work.

Chapter 15: Polynomials...143

Definition, Operation of polynomials, factor and remainder theorems,

Application of factor and remainder theorems in factorization of a polynomial,

Function notation.

Chapter 16: Algebraic fractions..153

Definition, Types of fractions, simplification of fractions, partial fraction.

Chapter 17: Inequality..161

Definition, Postulates of inequality, use of number line and cartesian graph, positivity and negativity of an expression, inequality with variables in the denominator, range of inequalities, quadratic inequalities, range of a function.

Chapter 18: Sequences..178

Definition, arithmetic progression, sum of an arithmetic progression, arithmetic mean, Geometric progression, sum of a geometric progression, summation to infinity, geometric mean, mixed series.

Chapter 19: Binary operation..203

Definition, interpretation and simplification of binary operation, operation and algebraic laws of binary operations, operation properties from tables.

Chapter 20: Parallel lines, angle sums..214
Definition, angles formed by two lines cut by a transversal, principles of parallel lines, triangles, terms associated with triangles, pythagorean theorem, applications of the pythagorean theorem, special right triangles, midpoint and median.

Chapter 21: Quadrilaterals...247

Definition, trapezoids/trapezium, parallelograms, special parallelograms, rhombus.

Chapter 22: Mensuration..259
Definition, types of shapes or figures, Area of various figures.

Chapter 23: Circle..287

Definition, circle principles, tangent principles, circles in varying relative positions, measurement of angles and arcs in a circle, similarity in circles

Chapter 24: Polygons..315
Definition, sum of the measures of the angles of a polygon, regular polygons, relationships of segment in regular polygons of 3, 4 and 6 sides, area of a regular polygon, ratio of segments and areas of regular polygons, relationship between circumference and area of a circle, length of an arc, area of a sector and a segment, areas of combined figures.

Chapter 25: Analytical geometry 1: straight line...337

Definition, distance between two points, midpoint of a line segment, gradient of a line, equation of a straight line, intersection of straight lines, collinear points, parallelism and perpendicularity of lines, angle between two lines, locus of points, area of any polygon.

Chapter 26: Analytical geometry 11: circle..354

Definition, general form of the equation of a circle, equation of the tangent, equation of point of intersection of a straight line and a cycle, equation for length of tangent to a circle from an external point, equation of a diameter, equation of circle given the coordinate of the end diameter, equation of a circle passing through three points,

Chapter 27: Conic section: Parabola...366

Definition, equation of a chord to a parabola, point of intersection of a line and a parabola, equation of tangent to the parabola, equation of chord to the parabola, equation of tangent and normal to the parabola, parametric equation of the parabola.

Chapter 28: Conic section: Ellipse..367

Definition, equation of a chord to a ellipse, point of intersection of a line and a ellipse, equation of tangent to the ellipse, equation of chord to the ellipse, equation of tangent and normal to the ellipse, parametric equation of the ellipse.

Chapter 29: Conic section: Hyperbola..376

Definition, equation of a chord to a hyperbola, point of intersection of a line and a hyperbola, equation of tangent to the hyperbola, equation of chord to the hyperbola, equation of tangent and normal to the hyperbola, parametric equation of the hyperbola, the rectangular hyperbola.

CHAPTER 30: Trigonometry...383

Definition, the trig ratios, trig ratio of acute angles, relationship between trigonometry ratios, trigonometry ratio of special acute angles, trigonometry ratio of negative angles, trigonometry ratio of obtuse and reflex angles, trigonometry ratio of allied angles, trigonometry value of compound angles, applications of compound angles, trigonometrical graph.

CHAPTER 31: Applications of trigonometry..**409**

Definition, Derivation of the sine and cosine rule, angle of elevation and depression, bearing,

CHAPTER 32: Calculus 1: Differentiation..**452**

Definition, methods of differentiation, applications of differentiation

CHAPTER 33: Calculus 2 : Integration..**473**

Definition, methods of integration, applications of integration,

CHAPTER 34: Set theory..**488**

Definition, forms of set, terms associated with set, deductions from a two set relationship, deductions from a three set relationship, four set relationship, set laws

CHAPTER 35: Probability..**506**

Definition, terms associated with probability, probability of coins, probability of dice, probability of cards, probability laws.

CHAPTER 36: Permutation and combination..**528**

Definition, techniques of permutation, combination, relationships between permutation and combination, laws of permutation and combination, formation of groups in combination

CHAPTER 37: The binomial theorem..**544**

Definition, expansion techniques, Pascal triangle, the binomial expansion formula

CHAPTER 38: Statistics..**549**

Definition, terms associated with statistics, representation of data, measures of central tendencies, ,mean, median, mode, measures of dispersion, variance, standard deviation,

CHAPTER 39: Probability distributions...**587**

Definition, terms associated with probability distributions, binomial distribution, Poisson distribution, normal distribution, normal curve.

CHARPTER 1   INTRODUCTION TO ALGEBRA

Algebra is a set with a defined binary operation. It is the unifying thread of all branch of mathematics.

Algebraic terms and processes

(i) Square of a number: This is simply the multiplication of a number by itself twice. e.g. Square of $9 = 9^2 = 9 \times 9 = 81$

(ii) Cube of a number: This is simply the multiplication of a number by its square. e.g. cube of $5 = 5^3 = 5 \times 5 \times 5 = 125$

(iii) Square root of a number: This is a number which when multiplied by itself two times gives a particular number e.g. Square root of $\overline{9} = \sqrt{9} = 3$ as $3 \times 3 = 9$

(iv) Cube root of a number: This is a number which when multiplied by itself three places gives a particular number e.g. Cube root of $\overline{27} = \sqrt{27} = 3$ as $3 \times 3 \times 3 = 27$

(v) Reciprocal of a number: This is simply the inverse of number. e.g. reciprocal of $\frac{3}{5}$ of $\frac{5}{3}$

(vi) Multiples: By multiples of a number we mean numbers that divide another without any remainder

(vi) Integer: An integer is any number that can be positive or negative including zero.

(vii) Factors of a number: These are possible multiplies that can be combined to produce a given number

($viii$) Perfect square: These are factors that can be expressed as even powers

e.g $12 = 2 \times 2 \times 2 \times 3 = 2^2 \times 3^1$

Hence, 2 is a perfect square as it has even power. 3 is not a perfect square as it has odd power.

(ix) Prime numbers/prime factors: These are positive integers greater than 1 that are divisible by 1 and themselves only. Examples of such numbers are 2, 3, 5, 7, 11,

(x) Lowest common multiple (L.C.M): This is the smallest (non--zero) number that is a multiple of two or more numbers.

(xi) Highest common factor (H.C.F): The highest common factor of two numbers is the largest whole number which is a factor of both.

HCF of 4 and 6 is gotten by

4 = 2 x 2

6 = 2 x 3

HCF = 2 x 2 x 3

(x) Fraction: A fraction is a part of a quantity. Any value less than 1 but positive is a fraction.

The general representation of a fraction is $\frac{a}{b}$ where a = numerator, b = denominator

If a > b it is an improper fraction

If a < b it is a proper fraction

Simplification of fraction

Fractions are easily simplified by application of BODMAS

Where BODMAS simply means Bracket, of, division, multiplication, addition and subtraction.

Applying BODMAS implies you bracket the first expression that comes first when either, ÷, × or + appear in an equation together.

BODMAS is not important if division and multiplication are the only operations present.

Word problem leading to fraction

When word problems are given, we simplify by obeying the rules of fraction

QUESTIONS

(**1.1**) Danielle ate $\frac{1}{4}$ of a bag of pop corn and gave $\frac{1}{6}$ of the remainder to Phil. How much of the original container was left.

Solution

Danielle ate = $\frac{1}{4}$, remaining $1 - \frac{1}{4} = \frac{3}{4}$

Phil got $\frac{3}{4} \times \frac{1}{6} = \frac{3}{24}$

Content remaining → $1 - \left[\frac{1}{4} + \frac{3}{24}\right]$ → $1 - \frac{9}{24} = \frac{5}{8}$

(1.2) If $\frac{3}{7}$ of a bucket can be filled in one minute. How long will it take to fill the rest of the bucket.

Solution

$\frac{3}{7}$ filled, remaining $1 - \frac{3}{7} = \frac{4}{7}$

$\frac{\frac{3}{7}}{\frac{4}{7}} = \frac{1 \text{ minute}}{x \text{ minute}}$ → $x = \frac{3}{7}x = \frac{4}{7}$ → $x = \frac{28}{21} = \frac{4}{3}$

(1.3) One half of the content of a container evaporates in one week and three-fourth of the remainder evaporates in the following week. At the end of two weeks, what fractional part of the original content remains?

Solution

First week = $\frac{1}{2}$, remaining $1 - \frac{1}{2} = \frac{1}{2}$

second week = $\frac{3}{4}$ of remainder → $\frac{3}{4} \times \frac{1}{2} = \frac{3}{8}$

Content remaining → $1 - \left[\frac{1}{2} + \frac{3}{8}\right]$ → $1 - \left[\frac{4}{8} + \frac{3}{8}\right] = \frac{1}{8}$

(1.4) Three men do a piece of work. The first does $\frac{7}{15}$, The second does $\frac{5}{6}$ of the remainder, while the third does the rest. If the rest done by the third person equals a score and a one–third of a dozen units. Find the whole piece of work.

Solution

First man = $\frac{7}{15}$, remaining $1 - \frac{7}{15} = \frac{8}{15}$

Second man does = $\frac{5}{6} \times \frac{8}{15} = \frac{4}{9}$, remaining $1 - \left[\frac{4}{9} + \frac{7}{15}\right] = \frac{135 - 60 - 63}{135} = \frac{12}{135} = \frac{4}{45}$

Third man does the rest = $\dfrac{4}{45}$

Since third man's portion equals a score and a dozen, we have $\dfrac{1}{3} \times 12 + 20 \to 24$

The whole piece of work is $\dfrac{45}{4} \times 24 = 270$.

(1.5) Find the reciprocal of $\dfrac{2/3}{\frac{1}{2}+\frac{1}{3}}$

Solution

$\dfrac{1}{2} + \dfrac{1}{3} \to \dfrac{3+2}{6} = \dfrac{5}{6}$

$\dfrac{2/3}{\frac{1}{2}+\frac{1}{3}} \to \dfrac{2/3}{5/6} = \dfrac{2}{3} \times \dfrac{6}{5} = \dfrac{4}{5}$ ∴ reciprocal $= \dfrac{5}{4}$

(1.6) The positive difference between $4\dfrac{5}{7}$ and $2\dfrac{1}{4}$ is greater than the sum of $\dfrac{1}{14}$ and $1\dfrac{1}{2}$ by?

Solution

Let the positive difference be greater than the sum by x

Difference → $4\dfrac{5}{7} - 2\dfrac{1}{4} \to \dfrac{33}{7} - \dfrac{9}{4} \to \dfrac{132 - 63}{28} = \dfrac{69}{28}$

Sum → $\dfrac{1}{14} + 1\dfrac{1}{2} \to \dfrac{1}{14} + \dfrac{3}{2} \to \dfrac{1+21}{14} = \dfrac{22}{14}$

As the difference is greater than the sum by x,

$\dfrac{69}{28} > \dfrac{22}{14} = X \to X = \dfrac{69}{28} - \dfrac{22}{14} \to \dfrac{69 - 44}{28} \to \dfrac{25}{28} = \dfrac{50}{56}$

(1.7) The sum of $3\dfrac{7}{8}$ and $1\dfrac{1}{3}$ is less than the negative difference between $\dfrac{3}{8}$ and $1\dfrac{2}{3}$ by ?

Solution

Let the sum be less than the negative difference by x

Sum → $3\dfrac{7}{8} + 1\dfrac{1}{3} \to \dfrac{31}{8} + \dfrac{4}{3} \to \dfrac{93 + 32}{24} = \dfrac{125}{24}$

Difference → $\dfrac{3}{8} - 1\dfrac{2}{3} \to \dfrac{3}{8} - \dfrac{5}{3} \to \dfrac{9 - 40}{24} = -\dfrac{31}{24}$

as the sum is less than the difference by x,

$\dfrac{125}{24} < -\dfrac{31}{24} = X \to X = \dfrac{-31}{24} - \dfrac{125}{24} \to \dfrac{-31 - 125}{24} \to \dfrac{-156}{24} = \dfrac{-26}{4} = -6\dfrac{1}{2}$

(1.8) A school canteen uses three identical buses and occupies $\frac{4}{5}$ of the seats. After $\frac{1}{4}$ of the passenger leave, the remaining passengers use only two of the buses. What fraction of the seats on the two buses is occupied?

Solution

Sits in 1 bus = x, sits in 3 buses = 3x

Sits occupied initially → $\frac{4}{5} \times 3x = \frac{12x}{5}$

When $\frac{1}{4}$ leaves, It remains $1 - \frac{1}{4}$ → $\frac{4-1}{4} = \frac{3}{4}$

Sits occupied finally = $\frac{3}{4} \times \frac{12x}{5}$ → $\frac{9x}{5}$

Fraction of sit occupied → $\frac{\frac{9x}{5}}{2x}$ → $\frac{\frac{9}{5}}{2} = \frac{9}{10}$

(1.9) Simplify $\dfrac{1\frac{1}{2}}{2 \div \frac{1}{4} \text{ of } 32}$

Solution

Applying BODMAS

$2 \div \frac{1}{4} \text{ of } 32$ → $2 \div \left(\frac{1}{4} \times 32\right)$ → $2 \div 8$ → $\frac{2}{8} = \frac{1}{4}$ → $\dfrac{1\frac{1}{2}}{\frac{1}{4}}$ → $\dfrac{\frac{3}{2}}{\frac{1}{4}}$ → $\frac{3}{2} \times \frac{4}{1} = 6$

(1.10) Simplify $2\frac{5}{11} - 1\frac{7}{8} \times \frac{6}{5}$

Solution

Applying BODMAS

$2\frac{5}{11} - 1\frac{7}{8} \times \frac{6}{5}$ → $2\frac{5}{12} - \left(1\frac{7}{8} \times \frac{6}{5}\right)$ → $\frac{29}{12} - \left(\frac{15}{8} \times \frac{6}{5}\right)$ → $\frac{29}{12} - \frac{9}{4}$ → $\frac{29-27}{12} = \frac{2}{12} = \frac{1}{6}$

(1.11) Simplify $3\frac{1}{3} - 1\frac{1}{4} \times \frac{2}{3} + 1\frac{2}{5}$

Solution

Applying BODMAS

$3\frac{1}{3} - 1\frac{1}{4} \times \frac{2}{3} + 1\frac{2}{5}$ → $3\frac{1}{3} - \left(1\frac{1}{4} \times \frac{2}{3}\right) + 1\frac{2}{5}$ → $\frac{10}{5} - \left(\frac{5}{4} \times \frac{2}{3}\right) + \frac{7}{5}$ = $\frac{10}{3} - \frac{5}{6} + \frac{7}{5}$

$= \frac{100 - 25 + 42}{30} = \frac{117}{30} \rightarrow 3\frac{27}{30} = 3\frac{9}{10}$

(1.12) Find the L.C.M of $a^2 + a - 6$, $2a^2 + 12a + 18$ and $3a - 6$

Solution

$a^2 + a - 6 \rightarrow a^2 + 3a - 2a - 6 \rightarrow a(a + 3) - 2(a + 3) \rightarrow (a - 2)(a + 3)$

$2a^2 + 12a + 18 \rightarrow 2a^2 + 6a + 6a + 18 \rightarrow 2a(a + 3) + 6(a + 3) \rightarrow (a + 3)(2a + 6)$

$2(a + 3)(a + 3)$

$3a - 6 \rightarrow 3(a - 2)$

$\therefore$ L.C.M $= 2 \times 3(a + 3)^2 (a - 2) \rightarrow 6(a + 3)^2 (a - 2)$

(1.13) Find the L.C.M of $2x - 2$ and $x^2 + x - 2$

Solution

$2x - 2 = 2(x - 1)$

$x^2 + x - 2 \rightarrow x^2 + 2x - x - 2 \rightarrow x(x + 2) - 1(x + 2) \rightarrow (x - 1)(x + 2)$

L.C.M $= 2, x - 1, x + 2 = 2(x - 1)(x + 2)$

(1.14) Find the H.C.F of $(2a - 3b)^2$, $4a^2 - 9b^2$ and $4a - 6b$

Solution

$(2a - 3b)^2 \rightarrow (2a - 3b)(2a - 3b)$

$4a^2 - 9b^2 \rightarrow (2a - 3b)(2a + 3b)$

$4a - 6b = \rightarrow 2(2a - 3b)$

H.C.F = common items = $(2a - 3b)$

(1.15) A fraction not in its lowest terms is equal to $\frac{3}{4}$, if the numerator of the fraction were doubled. It would be 34 greater than the denominator. Find the fraction

Solution

Let the fraction be $\frac{x}{y}$

Solution

Let the fraction be $\frac{x}{y}$

$\frac{x}{y} = \frac{3}{4}$ ....(i)

$2x = y + 34$ ...... (ii)

From (i) $4x = 3y \rightarrow y = \frac{4x}{3}$

Inserting into (ii) $2x = \frac{4x}{3} + 34 \rightarrow 2x - \frac{4x}{3} = 34 \rightarrow \frac{6x - 4x}{3} = 34$

$\frac{2x}{3} = 34 \rightarrow 2x = 102 \therefore x = 51$

$y = \frac{4x}{3} \rightarrow \frac{4 \times 51}{3} = 68$

$\frac{x}{y} = \frac{52}{68}$

(1. 16) $\frac{1}{4}$ of this year's senior have average above 90, $\frac{1}{2}$ of the remainder have averages between 80 and 90. What part of the senior class has averages below 80?

Solution

$\frac{1}{4}$ have average above 90

$\frac{1}{2}$ remainder is $\rightarrow \frac{1}{2} \times \frac{3}{4} = \frac{3}{8}$ have above 80 and 90

$\therefore \frac{1}{4} + \frac{3}{8} \rightarrow \frac{2 + 3}{8} = \frac{5}{8}$ have averages above 80

Those with average below 80 is

$1 - \frac{5}{8} = \frac{8 - 5}{8} = \frac{3}{8}$

CHAPTER 2 NUMBER SYSTEM

This is a system for expressing numbers of a given set by using digits or other symbols in a consistent manner.

Conversion of Number bases

(1) Conversion from base ten to base 2 or any other base: To do this we keep dividing the number to be converted by the base, writing the quotient (answer) and the remainder until the quotient is less than the base. The result is then written from the last quotient through to the first remainder

(2) Conversion from any other base to base 10: This is done by successive multiplication of each term in a number by the power of the base starting with power of zero.

(3) Conversion from one base to the other: This is done by converting to base 10 first and then from base 10 to the required base.

Addition of number bases

Here we write the remaining value when the number base or its multiple is taken from a number while the number of such base is transferred to another digit as a whole number e.g.

$$\begin{array}{r} 3\ 4 \\ \underline{8\ 9}_{10} \\ 1\ 2\ 3 \end{array}$$

In the addition above, $4 + 9 = 13 \rightarrow 10$ goes in $13 = 1$ Rm 3. Thus 3(the remainder) is written while 1 (the number of times it goes) found in the result is taken to the next digit. Also, $1 + 3 + 8 = 12 \rightarrow 10$ goes in $12 = 1$ Rm 2. Thus 2 is written while 1 is taken forward and as it does not meet any number, the result is also 1

Subtraction of number base

Here we proceed from the fact that when borrowing from one digit to the other the number is the same as the base number. e.g. subtracting 1 in a base ten system indicates 1 = 10 while in base six system, 1 = 6

Multiplication of number base

Here we proceed like the addition process by counting the number of base in a result before writing the remainder and transferring the whole number to the other digit

$$\begin{array}{r} 3\ 2 \\ \times\ \ \ 3 \\ \hline 2\ 2\ 2 \end{array}$$

$3 \times 2 = 6 \rightarrow 4$ goes in $6 = 1$ Rm 2

$3 \times 3 = 9$, $9 + 1$(number of times it goes) $= 10$
4 goes in $10 = (2)$ Rm 2

Division of number bases

Division is carried out by special technique, where we convert both the numerator and denominator to base 10 before proceeding.

QUESTIONS

(2.1) $P344_6 - 23P2_6$. Find P.
Solution

$$\begin{array}{r} P\ 3\ \ 4\ \ 4 \\ -\ 2\ 3\ \ P\ \ 2_6 \\ \hline 2\ \ P\ \ P\ \ 2 \end{array}$$

$4 - 2 = 2$, $4 - P = P \rightarrow 4 = 2P \therefore P = 2$
Taking 1 from 3 an adding to $4 \rightarrow 6 + 4 = 10$
$\therefore 10 - P = P \rightarrow 10 = 2P \therefore P = 5$
Since we have gotten two values of P, we now insert to test
From the operation given $3 - 3 = 0 = P$, thus $P \neq 2 \therefore P = 5$

(2.2) Evaluate $(20_3)^2 - (11_3)^2$ in base three.

Solution

$(20_3)^2 = $
```
   2 0
 x 2 0₃
   0 0
 1 1 0
 1 1 0 0
```

$(11_3)^2 = $
```
   1 1
   1 1₃
   1 1
 1 1
 1 2 1
```

$(20_3)^2 - (11_3)^2$ becomes

```
  1 1 0 1
-   1 2 1₃
    2 0 2
```

(2.3) If $(k2)_6 \times 3_6 = 3_5(k4)_5$. Find k.

Solution

$(k \times 6^1 + 2 \times 6^0) \times 3_6 = 3_5(k + 5^1 + 4 \times 5^0) \rightarrow (6k+2)3 = 3(5k+4)$

$6k + 2 = 5k + 4 \rightarrow 6k - 5k = 4 - 2 \therefore k = 2$

(2.4)
```
   4 2 4 3
 - 1 3 x 4₅
   y 3 4 4
```

Find x and y respectively in the subtraction above carried out in the base 5.

Solution

As 4 does not go in 3, 1 is taken from 4 on reaching the digit with 3 → 5 + 3 = 8

∴ 8 − 4 = 4

taking 1 from 2 to the remaining 3(4 becomes 3) → 5 + 3 = 8 ∴ 8 − x = 4 ∴ x = 4

1 from 4 to the remaining 1 gives 5 + 1 = 6

6 − 3 = 3

Remaining 3 − 1 = 2   ∴ x = 4, y = 2

(2.5) Convert 14_5 to base 8.

Solution

14_5 to base ten → $1 \times 5^1 + 4 \times 5^0$ → $5 + 4 = 9_{10}$

10

9_{10} to base eight →

```
8 | 9
8 | 1 Rm 1
  | 0 Rm 1
```

$14_5 = 11_8$

(2.6) Simplify $\left(\frac{1222}{10201}\right)_3$.

Solution

1222_3 to base 10 → $1 \times 3^3 + 2 \times 3^2 + 2 \times 3^1 + 2 \times 3^0 = 27 + 18 + 6 + 2 = 53$

10201_3 to base 10 → $1 \times 3^4 + 2 \times 3^2 + 0 \times 3^1 + 1 \times 3^0 = 81 + 18 + 1 = 100$

$\therefore \left(\frac{1222}{10201}\right)_3 = \left(\frac{53}{100}\right)_3 = 0.53_{10}$

0.53_{10} to base 3 =
```
    0 . 5 3
  x       3
  (1) . 5 9
          3
  (1) .  7 7
          3
  (2) .  3 1
```

$0.53_{10} = 0.112_3$

(2.7) Express 12.625_{10} in base two.

Solution

12.625_{10} in base two = 12_{10} in 2 + 0.625_{10} in 2

For numbers we use progressive division

For decimal we use progressive multiplication

```
2 | 12
2 | 6  Rm 0
2 | 3  Rm 0
2 | 1  Rm 1
  | 0  Rm 1
```

$$0.625$$
$$\underline{\times\quad 2}$$
$$1.250$$
$$\underline{\times\quad 2}$$
$$0.500$$

Combining both we have 1100.101_2

(2.8) What is the value of x if $(101)_x = 17$.
Solution
To base 10 → $1.x^2 + 0.x^1 + 1.x^0 = 17$ → $x^2 + 1 = 17$ → $x^2 = 16$ ∴ $x = 4$

(2.9) If $y = 23_5 + 101_3$. Find y leaving your answer in base two.
Solution
To base 10 → $23_5 + 101_3 = 2.5^1 + 3.5^0 + 1.3^2 + 0.3^1 + 1.3^0$ → $10 + 3 + 9 + 1 = 23$
23_{10} → To base 2

```
2| 23
2| 11  Rm 1
2|  5  Rm 1
2|  2  Rm 1
2|  1  Rm 0
    0  Rm 1
```

$23_{10} = 10111_2$

(2.10) Arrange in ascending order of magnitude 26_8, 36_7, 25_9.
Solution
Converting all to 10 we have
26_8 → $2 \times 8^1 + 6 + 8^0$ → $16 + 6 = 22_{10}$
36_7 → $3 \times 7^1 + 6 + 7^0$ → $21 + 6 = 27_{10}$
25_9 → $2 \times 9^1 + 5 \times 9^0$ → $18 + 5 = 23_{10}$
Ascending order implies from lowest to greatest = 26_8, 25_9, 36_7

(2.11) Two numbers 24_x and 31_y are equal in value when converted to base ten. Find the equation connecting x and y.

Solution

In base 10 → $24_x = 2(x^1) + 4(x^0) \to 2x + 4$

In base 10, $31_y = 3(y^1) + 1(y^0) \to 3y + 1$

Equal in value implies $2x + 4 = 3y + 1 \to 2x = 3y + 1 - 4$, $2x = 3y - 3$ or $2x = 3(y - 1)$

(2.12) If $12_e = X_7$, find X where e = 12.

Solution

To base 10, $12_{12} = X_7 \to 1 \times 12^1 + 2 \times 12^0 = x.(7^0) \to 12 + 2 = x$ ∴ $x = 14_{10}$

X_7 implies 14_{10} is in base 7

```
7 | 14
7 |  2  Rm 0
  |  0  Rm 2
```

$X_7 = 20_7$

(2.13) If 263 + 441 = 714, what number base has been used?

Solution

Let the base be y

$263_y + 441_y = 714_y$

Converting all to base ten

$(2 \times y^2 + 6 \times y^1 + 3 \times y^0) + (4 \times y^2 + 4 \times y^1 + 1 \times y^0) = (7 \times y^2 + 1 \times y^1 + 4 \times y^0)$

$2y^2 + 6y + 3 + 4y^2 + 4y + 1 = 7y^2 + y + 4$

$6y^2 + 10y + 4 = 7y^2 + y + 4 \to 6y^2 - 7y^2 = y - 10y + 4 - 4$

$-y^2 = -9n$ ∴ $n = 9$

(2.14) Find X if (X base 4)^2 = 100100 base 2.

Solution

(X base 4)$^2 \to (X_4)^2 = (X_4)(X_4) \to (X)(X)_4 = X^2{}_4$

$X^2{}_4 = 100100_2$

Converting to base 10

$X^2(4^0) = 1 \times 2^5 + 0 \times 2^4 + 0 \times 2^3 + 1 \times 2^2 + 0 \times 2^1 + 0 \times 2^0$

$X^2 = 32 + 4 = 36 \to X = \sqrt{36} = 6$ ∴ $X = 6_{10}$

To base 4

```
4 | 6
4 | 1  Rm 2
  | 0  Rm 1
```

∴ $X_4 = 12_4$

(2.15) If $2_9 \times (Y3)_9 = 3_5 \times (Y3)_5$. Find the value of Y.

Solution

Converting to base 10

$(2 \times 9^0) \times (Y.9^1 + 3 \times 9^0) = (3 \times 5^0) \times (Y.5^1 + 3.5^0)$

$(2)[(9Y) + 3] = 3(5Y + 9) \rightarrow 18Y + 6 = 15Y + 9 \rightarrow 18Y - 15Y = 9 - 6$

$3Y = 3 \therefore Y = 1$

(2.16) Evaluate $123_4 \times 1101_2$ leaving your answer in base five.

Solution

Converting to base 10

$123_4 \times 1101_2 \rightarrow (1 \times 4^2 + 2 \times 4^1 + 3 \times 4^0) \times (1 \times 2^3 + 1 \times 2^2 + 0 \times 2^1 + 1 \times 2^0)$

$(16 + 8 + 3) \times (8 + 4 + 0 + 1) \rightarrow (27)(13) = 351_{10}$

$351_{10} \rightarrow$ To base 5

5	351		
5	70	Rm	1
5	14	Rm	0
5	2	Rm	4
	0	Rm	2

$351_{10} = 2401_5$

(2.17) Divide 1324_8 by 20201_3 leaving your answer in binary numeral.
Solution
$1324_8 \rightarrow 1 \times 8^3 + 3 \times 8^2 + 2 \times 8^1 + 4 \times 8^0 \rightarrow 512 + 192 + 16 + 4 = 724$
$20201_3 \rightarrow 2 \times 3^4 + 0 \times 3^3 + 2 \times 3^2 + 0 \times 3^1 + 1 \times 3^0 \rightarrow 162 + 18 + 1 = 181$
$\therefore \frac{1324_8}{20201_3} = \frac{724}{181} = 4_{10}$

$4_{10} \rightarrow$ To base 2

$$\begin{array}{r|l} 2 & 4 \\ \hline 2 & 2 \text{ Rm } 0 \\ 2 & 1 \text{ Rm } 0 \\ & 0 \text{ Rm } 1 \end{array}$$

$$4_{10} = 100_2$$

CHAPTER 3 APPROXIMATION OF NUMBERS

Approximation is used for reducing numbers into values that can be easily handled. In other words it is an estimate of calculation. This can be done by

(*i*) Decimal place system (*ii*) Significant figures system (*iii*) Nearest values system (*iv*) Standard form system

(*i*) Decimal Approximation

This is an approximation that affects the elements after the decimal point only

To round off a decimal number to any place. Follow these rules

1. Keep all the digits to the left of the specified place
2. In that place, keep the digit if the next digits is < 5, and increase that digit by 1 if the next digit is ≥ 5[NOTE. 9 increased by 1 is 10 : put down the 0 and carry 1]
3. If there are still digits to the left of the decimal point, change them the 0's and eliminate the decimal point and everything that follows it.
4. If you are at or beyond the decimal point don't write any more digits.

For example

4.445 to 2 decimal places, we check the third i.e. 5. Therefore, 4.445 = 4.45

(*ii*) **Significant numbers**: This is a system of approximation where numbers are counted from the first non-zero element irrespective of the decimal point.

43.46 to 3 significant figures is 43.5

4445 to 3 sig fig = 4450

0.0348 to 1 sig fig = 0.03

(*iii*) **Nearest value system**: This refers to approximation based on measurement and specifications, that is units of measurements such whole number, hundreds digits, tens digit, units digit, tenth digit, hundredth digit etc

The approximation is done by considering the unit mentioned and the immediate unit as in general procedure.

Also note that the value immediately after the decimal point is tenth and not unit.

Thus before the decimal point (from left) we have unit, ten, hundred etc

After the decimal point (from right) we have tenth, hundredth etc

Also note the meaning of the following

Nearest km = nearest 1 km = nearest unit digit

Nearest 10km = nearest tens digit

Nearest 1000km = nearest thousand digits

For example

To correct 153.58 to nearest ten

    H   T   U

    1   5   3.58 → 150

To correct 657 to nearest hundred

    H   T   U

    6   5   7 → 700

To correcting 1.3462 to nearest hundredth

T   Tenth   Hundredth   Thousandth

1.   3   (4)   (6) 2 = 1.3500

1.35 to nearest hundredth

1444 km to nearest km → 144(4) to nearest km = 1444 km

1444km to nearest 10 km → nearest ten = 1440 km

1444km to nearest 100km → nearest hundred = 1400 km

6.4 s to nearest second → nearest 1s = nearest unit digit

6.4 s to nearest second = 6.0 s = 6s

(iv) Standard Form System

A number is said to be in standard form if it written in the form of $A \times 10^n$ where

A is a number between 1 and 10 and n is an integer

In shifting the point, the integer takes either positive or negative whole number. If the point is shifted backwards the power takes a positive sign and a negative sign when shifted forward.

Operation with standard form

For addition and subtraction you must make both powers the same

For division and multiplication you don't need to make both powers the same, just apply indices

Errors

This is the difference between a computed, estimated or measured value and the accepted true or theoretically correct value.

There are various types of errors; error from approximation is our interest here.

Maximum error = $\frac{1}{2} \times$ (digit)

Where digit is the digit occupied by the number.

Percentage error: This is the ratio of the error made to the original value.

Mathematically, Percentage error = $\frac{Error}{original\ values} \times 100$

Where, Error = Measurement – Actual value

QUESTIONS

(3.1). Express 49 to three significant figures.

Solution

49.0 in 3 significant figures

(3.2). Simplify $6.04 \times 10^8 + 2.63 \times 10^7$.

Solution

$6.04 \times 10^8 + 0.263 \times 10^8 = 6.303 \times 10^8$

(3.3). Simplify $9.32 \times 10^6 + 2.456 \times 10^4$.

Solution

$9.32 \times 10^6 + 0.02456 \times 10^6 = 9.3 \times 10^6$

(3.4). Simplify $5.8 \times 10^{16} \div 0.14 \times 10^{11}$.

Solution

$\frac{5.8}{0.14} \times 10^{16-11} = 4.14 \times 10^6$

(3.5). Arrange $\frac{3}{5}$, $\frac{9}{16}$, $\frac{34}{59}$ and $\frac{71}{97}$ in ascending order of magnitude

Solution

Convert the fraction to decimals;

$\frac{3}{5} = 0.6$, $\frac{9}{16} = 0.5625$, $\frac{34}{59} = 0.5763$, $\frac{71}{97} = 0.7320$

∴ The ascending order $= \frac{9}{16}, \frac{34}{59}, \frac{3}{5}, \frac{71}{97}$

(3.6). Find, correct to three significant figures, the value of $\sqrt{418330}$.

Solution

$\sqrt{418330} = 646.7878 = 647.00 = 647$

(3.7). When 423,890 is rounded off to the nearest thousand, how many digits will be changed?

Solution

423,890 = 424,000 = 3 digits [3,8,9]

(3.8). Evaluate correct to 4 decimal places 827.51 x 0.015.

Solution

827.51 x 0.15 = 12.41265 = 12.4127 to 4 decimal places

(3.9). Express 37.05 x 0.0042 in standard form.

Solution

37.05 x 0.0042 – 0.15561 = 1.5561 x 10^{-1}

(3.10). The diameter of a rod is measured as 23.40 cm to four significant figures. What is the maximum error in the measurement?

Solution

Diameter = 23.40

4th significant figure is 0 which occupies the hundredth digit.

Maximum error = $\frac{1}{2}$ x (digit) → $\frac{1}{2}$ x $\left[\frac{1}{100}\right]$ = 0.005

The measurement is thus 23.40 ± 0.005 while the error = 0.005

(3.11). Round off 3815.296 to the place indicated.

Solution

Round to Nearest	Procedure	Answer
Thousand	The digit in the thousand place is 3, since the next digit is 8 is ≥ 5, increase the 3 → 4; fill in the 3 places to the left the left of the decimal point with 0	4000
Hundred	The digit in the hundreds place is 8, keep everything to the left of it and keep the 8 since the next digit (1) is < 5, fill in 0's to the left of the decimal point	3800
Ten	The digit in the ten place is 1 keep everything to the left of it and increase the 1 to a 2 since the next digit (s) is ≥ 5, fill in 0 to the left of the decimal point	3820
One	The digit in the ones places is 5, keep everything to the left of it, and keep the 5 since the next digits (2) is < 5: there are no more places to the left of the	3815

	decimal points so stop.	
Tenth	The digit in the tenth place is 2, keep everything to the left of it, and increase the 2 to 3 since the next digit (9) is ≥ 5 you are beyond the decimal point, So stop	3815.3
Hundredth	The digit in the hundredth place is 9, keep everything to the left of it, and since the next digit (6) is > 5 increase 9 to 10 put the 0 and carry 1 into the tenths place :0.29 becomes 0.30. since you are beyond the decimal point stop	3815.30

(3.12). If $0.0000152 \times 0.00042 = A \times 10^B$, where $1 < A < 10$, find A and B.

Solution

$0.0000152 \times 0.00042 = (1.52 \times 10^{-5}) \times (4.2 \times 10^{-4}) = 6.384 \times 10^{-9}$

Comparing 6.384×10^{-9} with $A \times 10^B$

$A = 6.38$ and $B = -9$

(3.13). What is the difference between 0.007685 correct to three significant figures and 0.007685 correct to four places of decimal.

Solution

0.007685 to 3 significant figures = 0.00769

0.007685 to 4 decimal places = 0.0077

Difference = $0.0077 - 0.00769 = 0.0001 = 1 \times 10^{-5}$

(3.14). The power P required to move a load against a resistance R with velocity V is given in a suitable units by RV. If R = 500 and V = 30, each correct to 1 s.f, between what limits does P lie?

Solution

For R = 500 in 1 sig figure

First significant figure is 5 which occupies the hundred digit

Maximum error = $\frac{1}{2} x$ (digit) → $\frac{1}{2}$ x [100] = 50

R = 500 ± 50 = 450 & 550

For V = 30 in 1 sig. figure

1st sig. figure is 3 which occupies the ten digit position

Maximum error = $\frac{1}{2} x$ (digit) → $\frac{1}{2}$ x [10] = 5

∴ V = 30 ± 5 = 25 & 35

P = RV = (450 – 550)(25 – 35) = (11250 – 19250)

(3.15). A firm employs 130 men, and the average weekly wage per man is ₦ 34, correct to the nearest naira. What are the greatest and least possible weekly wage bills for that firm?

Solution

Weekly wage of 1 man = ₦34 .

Nearest Naira means nearest one naira i.e. unit digits

Maximum error = $\frac{1}{2} x$ (digit) → $\frac{1}{2}$ x [1] = 0.5

Weekly wage of 1 man = ₦ (34 ± 0.5)

130 x ₦ (34 ± 0.5) → 130(33.5 – 34.5) = (₦4355 - ₦4485)

(3.16). The base of a triangle is given as 8 cm and the area of the triangle is given as 30cm², each correct to 1 significant figures. Between what limits, correct to 2 significant figures does the height of the triangle lie?

Solution

A = 30 cm² (1 s.f)

1st significant figure is 3 which occupies the ten digit position

Error = ½ (10) = 5 ∴ A = (30 ± 5) or (25 – 35)

b = 8 cm (1 s.f)

1st significant figure is 8 which occupies the unit digit position.

Area of triangle = $\frac{1}{2}$ bh → h = $\frac{2A}{b}$ = $\left(\frac{2 \times A_{min}}{b_{max}} - \frac{2 \times A_{max}}{b_{min}}\right)$ = $\left(\frac{2 \times 25}{8.5} - \frac{2 \times 35}{7.5}\right)$

5.88 – 9.33 = 5.9 – 9.3 (2 sig. figures)

(3.17) Correct each of the number 59.81798 and 0.0746829 to three significant figures and multiply them, leaving your answer to three significant figures.

Solution

59.81798 = 59.8 , 0.0746829 = 0.0747

59.8 x 0.0747 = 4.46706 → 4.46706 = 4.47 (3 s.f)

(3.18) Area of the big square of a circle is 2 cm. a measurement error showed the radius to be 2.01cm. Find the percentage in the area of the circle.

Solution

r_1 = 2cm, r_2 = 2.01 cm

but $A = \pi r^2$ (for circle)

% error = $\frac{A_2 - A_1}{A_1}$ x 100 → $\frac{\pi r_2^2 - \pi r_1^2}{\pi r_1^2}$ → $\frac{r_2^2 - r_1^2}{r_1^2}$ x 100 → $\frac{(2.01)^2 - 2^2}{2^2}$ x 100

$\frac{4.0401 - 4}{4}$ x 100 = 1.0025%

(3.19) The population density of a village is 520 people per km². If the village estimated area of 3.4 km². Find its population to the nearest 100 people.

Solution

Population density = $\frac{population}{area}$ → Population = pop density x area = 520 x 3.4 km²

1768

Since the hundred digit is 7,

1768 = 1800 people

(3.20) Evaluate 2700000 x 0.03 ÷ 18000.

Solution

2700000 x 0.03 ÷ 1800 → 2700000 x $\frac{3}{100}$ x $\frac{1}{1800}$ → $\frac{27 \times 3}{18}$ → $\frac{3 \times 3}{2}$ = $\frac{9}{2}$ = 4.5

(3.21) Reduce each number to 2 significant figures and then evaluate $\frac{0.021741 \times 1.2047}{0.023789}$.

Solution

$\frac{0.022 \times 1.2}{0.024}$ = 1.1

(3.22) If a rod of length 250cm is measured as 255cm long in error. What is the percentage error in the measurement?

Solution

% error = $\frac{255 - 250}{250}$ x 100 → $\frac{50}{25}$ = 2

(3.23) Find correct to 3 decimal place $\frac{1}{0.05}$ ÷ $\frac{1}{5.005}$ − [(0.05 x 2.05)].

Solution

$\frac{1}{0.05}$ ÷ $\frac{1}{5.005}$ → $\frac{1}{0.05}$ x $\frac{5.005}{1}$ (0.05 x 2.05) → $\frac{5.005}{0.05}$ − (0.05 − 2.05) →

100.1 − (0.1025) = 99.998

CHAPTER 4   INDICES

These deals with numbers or quantities with exponents. The analyses and simplification depends on the basic interpretation and rules of indices as enumerated below.

Laws of indices

These are rules guiding the operation between numbers such as multiplication, division, power, change of base and etc. they are as enumerated below.
Product of powers with the same base: This is done by taking one of the bases and summing their exponents → $a^b \times a^c = a^{b+c}$

Division of numbers with the same base: This is done by taking one of the bases and subtracting their powers → $a^b \div a^c = \dfrac{a^b}{a^c} = a^{b-c}$

Number with double power: This is combining the powers using multiplication. Thus. $(a^b)^c = a^{bc}$

Numbers with powers and bracket

$(ab)^x = a^x \cdot b^x$

Number with zero power: This is taken as 1 i.e $a^0 = 1$, $50^0 = 1$

Number with a negative power: This is taken as the reciprocal of the result remaining when the negative sign is removed

$a^{-1} = \dfrac{1}{a^1} = \dfrac{1}{a}$

$2^{-2} = \dfrac{1}{2^2} = \dfrac{1}{2 \times 2} = \dfrac{1}{4}$

Number with fractional powers: This is simplified by taking the denominator of the fraction as the root and the numerator as the power of the result remaining.

$a^{b/c} = \left(\sqrt[c]{a}\right)^b$

$8^{\frac{2}{3}} = \left(\sqrt[3]{8}\right)^2 = (2)^2 = 4$

Note: when it is square root, it is written as $\sqrt{}$ without the two.

Thus, $4^{\frac{3}{2}} = (\sqrt{4})^3 = (2)^3 = 8$

Number with negative fractional power: This is simplified by combining the rules above

$a^{\frac{-b}{c}} = \dfrac{1}{(\sqrt[c]{a})^b}$

$27^{\frac{-2}{3}} = \dfrac{1}{(\sqrt[3]{27})^2} = \dfrac{1}{(3)^2} = \dfrac{1}{9}$

Also $\left(\dfrac{1}{\sqrt[y]{a}}\right)x$ can be rewritten as $\dfrac{1}{a^{\frac{x}{y}}} = a^{\frac{-x}{y}}$

Indicial equation

This refers to indices resulting to equation. It is also known as exponential equation. Therefore the rules of indices must be obeyed for correct evaluation.

Methods of solution

Indicial equations are evaluated by simply expressing both sides of the equation to have the same base or power e.g.

e.g. $3^x = 27 \rightarrow 3^x = 3^3 \therefore x = 3$ (as the base are equal)

They can also be evaluated by carrying out a reverse processes i.e carrying out the reverse process to an operation. e.g. square for square root and vice–versa, cube for cube root and vice–versa etc

e.g. $x^2 = 4 \rightarrow \sqrt{x^2} = \sqrt{4} \rightarrow x = \sqrt{4} = 2$

Powers are eliminated by multiplying all powers by the reciprocal of the available power. e.g. $x^2 = 4$, available power = 2, reciprocal = ½

$x^{2 \times 1/2} = 4^{\frac{1}{2}} \rightarrow x = (\sqrt{4})^1 = 2^1 = 2$

Questions

Solve for x or y in the following

(4.1). $3x^3 = 24$

Solution

Dividing both sides by 3

$x^3 = 8 \rightarrow x = 2$

(4.2). $5^{x+1} + 5^{x+1} = 150$

$5^x \cdot 5^1 + 5^x = 150 \rightarrow 5^x(5+1) = 150 \rightarrow 5^x \cdot 6 = 150$

$\therefore 5^x = \frac{150}{6} = 25 \rightarrow 5^x = 5^2 \therefore x = 2$

(4.3). $8^x = 0.25$

Solution

$8^x = \frac{25}{100} \therefore 8^x = \frac{1}{4} \rightarrow 2^{3x} = 2^{-2} \rightarrow 3x = -2 \rightarrow x = \frac{-2}{3}$

(4.4). $3x^{-2} = \frac{4}{27}$

Solution

$\frac{3}{x^2} = \frac{4}{27} \rightarrow 4x^2 = 3 \times 27 \rightarrow x = \sqrt{\frac{81}{4}} = \frac{9}{2}$

(4.5). $10^y \times 5^{2y-2} \times 4^{y-1}$

Solution

$10^y \times 5^{2y-2} \times 2^{2(y-1)} = 1 \rightarrow 10^y \times 5^{2y-2} \times 2^{2y-2} = 1 \rightarrow 10^y \times 10^{2y-2} = 1$

$10^{y+2y-2} = 10^0 \rightarrow 3y - 2 = 0 \rightarrow 3y = 2 \therefore y = {^2}/{_3}$

(4.6). $8x^{-2} = \frac{2}{25}$

Solution

$8 \times \frac{1}{x^2} = \frac{2}{25} \rightarrow \frac{8}{x^2} = \frac{2}{25} \rightarrow 2x^2 = 200 \rightarrow x^2 = 100 \rightarrow x = \sqrt{100} \therefore x = 10$

(4.7). $x^{\frac{2}{3}} = 9$

Solution

$x^{\frac{2}{3}} = 3^2$ multiply both powers by 3

$x^{\frac{2}{3} \times 3} = 3^{2 \times 3} \to x^2 = 3^6 \to x^2 = 729 \therefore x = 27$

(4.8). $9^{1+n} \times 3 = 27^{-n}$

Solution

$3^{2(1+n)} \times 3 = 3^{3(-n)} \to 3^{2+2n} \times 3^1 = 3^{-3n}$

$2 + 2n + 1 = -3n$ (dropping the base)

$3 = -3n - 2n \to 3 = -5n \therefore n = -{}^3/_5$

(4.9). Find x If ¼ of $16^{-2x+1} = 64$

Solution

$¼ \times 16^{-2x+1} = 64 \to \frac{16^{-2x+1}}{4} = 64 \to 16^{-2x+1} = 256 \to 4^{2(-2x+1)} = 4^4$

$2(-2n+1) = 4 \to -4n + 2 = 4 \to -4n = 4 - 2 \therefore n = -{}^2/_4 = -{}^1/_2$

(4.10). If $b^3 = a^{-2}$ and $C^{\frac{1}{3}} = a^{\frac{1}{2}} b$ obtain c in term of a.

Solution

For $b^3 = a^{-2}$, multiply both power by $\frac{1}{3}$

$\therefore b = a^{\frac{-2}{3}}$

$C^{\frac{1}{3}} = a^{\frac{1}{2}} b$ becomes $C^{\frac{1}{3}} = a^{\frac{1}{2}} \times a^{-2/3} \to C^{\frac{1}{3}} = a^{\frac{3-4}{6}} \to c = a^{\frac{-1}{6} \cdot 3} \therefore c = a^{-1/2}$

(4.11). $27^{\frac{x}{2}} = 3^{\frac{3}{4}} \times 9^{\frac{-1}{4}}$

Solution

$3^{3\left[\frac{x}{2}\right]} = 3^{3/4} \times 3^{2 \times \frac{-1}{4}} \to 3^{\frac{3x}{2}} = 3^{3/4} \times 3^{-\frac{2}{4}} \to \frac{3x}{2} = \frac{3}{4} - \frac{1}{2} \to \frac{3x}{2} = \frac{1}{4} \to (3x) \times 4 = 2$

$12x = 2 \therefore x = \frac{1}{6}$

(4.12). $5(2^{x-3}) = 160$

Solution

Dividing through by 5

$\frac{5(2^{x-3})}{5} = \frac{160}{5} \to 2^{x-3} = 32 = 2^5 \to x - 3 = 5 \therefore x = 8$

(4.13). $8^{2x} = 64 \times 4^{3y}$

$2^{3(2x)} = 2^6 \times 2^{2(3y)} \rightarrow 2^{3(2x)} = 2^{6+6y} \rightarrow 6x = 6+6y \therefore x = \frac{6+6y}{6} = 1+y$

(4.14). $(7^8 \times 7^9)^{10} = ?$

Solution

$[7^{8+9}]^{10} \rightarrow (7^{17})^{10} = 7^{170}$

(4.15). $5x = 40x^{-1/2}$

Solution

Dividing through by 5

$x = 8x^{-1/2}$

Dividing through by $x^{-1/2}$

$\frac{x}{x^{-1/2}} = 2^3 \rightarrow x^{1+\frac{1}{2}} = 2^3 \rightarrow x^{\frac{3}{2}} = 2^3 \rightarrow x = 2^2 \therefore x = 4$

(4.16). $x = 9\sqrt{9x^{1/2}}$

Solution

Square both sides

$x^2 = \left[9\sqrt{9x^{1/2}}\right]^2 \rightarrow x^2 = 9^2 \times 9x^{1/2} \rightarrow x^2 = 81 \times 9x^{\frac{1}{2}}$

$\frac{x^2}{x^{1/2}} = 81 \times \frac{9x^{1/2}}{x^{1/2}} \rightarrow x^{2-\frac{1}{2}} = 729 \rightarrow x^{\frac{3}{2}} = 729 \rightarrow x = (\sqrt[3]{729})^2 \rightarrow x = 9^2 = 81$

(4.17). $3x^{-2} = \frac{4}{27}$

Solution

$x^{-2} = \frac{4}{27} \times \frac{1}{3} \rightarrow \frac{1}{x^2} = \frac{4}{81} \rightarrow x^2 = \frac{81}{4} \rightarrow x = \sqrt{\frac{81}{4}} \therefore x = \frac{9}{2}$

(4.18). $\frac{(2.50 \times 10^4) \times (2.0 \times 10^{-3})}{12.5 \times 10^5}$

Solution

$\frac{25 \times 10^3 \times 2 \times 10^{-3}}{12.5 \times 10^5} \rightarrow \frac{50}{12.5} \times 10^{-5} \rightarrow 4 \times 10^{-5}$

(4.19). $\left[\frac{1}{x^{-2}} \times \frac{1}{y^2}\right]^{-1/2}$

Solution

$\left[\frac{x^2}{y^2}\right]^{-1/2} \rightarrow \sqrt{\frac{y^2}{x^2}} = \frac{y}{x}$

(4.20). Simplify $(3^{1+\sqrt{2}})^{1-\sqrt{2}}$

Solution

$(3^{1+\sqrt{2}})^{1-\sqrt{2}} \rightarrow (3^{(1+\sqrt{2})(1-\sqrt{2})}) \rightarrow 3^{1-2} \rightarrow 3^{-1} = \frac{1}{3}$

(4.21). Simplify $\frac{x^{-2}-y^{-2}}{x^{-1}-y^{-1}}$

Solution

$\frac{\frac{1}{x^2}-\frac{1}{y^2}}{\frac{1}{x}-\frac{1}{y}} = \frac{y^2-x^2}{x^2y^2} \times \frac{xy}{x+y} \rightarrow \frac{(y+x)(y-x)}{xy(x+y)} \rightarrow \frac{y-x}{xy}$

(4.22). Simplify $[x+(1+x^{-1})^{-1}]^{-1}$

Solution

$\left[x+\left[1+\frac{1}{x}\right]^{-1}\right]^{-1} \rightarrow \left[x+\left[\frac{x+1}{x}\right]^{-1}\right]^{-1} \rightarrow \left[x+\frac{x}{x+1}\right]^{-1} \rightarrow \left[\frac{x(x+1)+x}{x+1}\right]^{-1} \rightarrow \left[\frac{x^2+x+x}{x+1}\right]^{-1}$

$\left[\frac{x^2+2x}{x+1}\right]^{-1} \rightarrow \frac{1+x}{x(x+2)}$

(4.23). If $\frac{x}{y} = \frac{3}{5}$ then $\frac{x-3}{y-5}$?

Solution

$\frac{x}{y} = \frac{3}{5} \rightarrow y = \frac{5x}{3} \therefore \frac{x-3}{y-5} \rightarrow \frac{x-3}{\frac{5x}{3}-5} \rightarrow \frac{3(x-3)}{5x-15} \rightarrow \frac{3(x-3)}{5(x-3)} = \frac{3}{5}$

(4.24). $\frac{81^{3/4}-27^{1/3}}{3 \times 2^3}$

Solution

$\frac{(\sqrt[4]{81})^3 - (\sqrt[3]{27})^1}{3 \times 2^3} \rightarrow \frac{27-3}{24} \rightarrow \frac{24}{24} = 1$

(4.25). If $\frac{1}{a} = \frac{1}{b} + \frac{1}{c}$ and $b+c-k=0$.   Express a in term of b and k

Solution

From $b + c - k = 0 \rightarrow c = k - b$

Putting into the question

$\frac{1}{a} = \frac{1}{b} + \frac{1}{k-b} \rightarrow \frac{1}{a} = \frac{k-b+b}{b(k-b)} \therefore a = \frac{b(k-b)}{k}$

(4.26). Find the value of x for which $3^{2x} + 6(3^x) = 27$.

Solution

$(3^2)^2 + 6(3^x) = 27$ let $P = 3^x$

$P^2 + 6P - 27 = 0$

$P^2 + 9P - 3P - 27 = 0$ (factorizing)

$P(P+9) - 3(P-9) = 0 \rightarrow (P-3)(P-9) = 0 \rightarrow P - 3 = 0$ or $p + 9 = 0$

$P = 3$ or $P = -9$

recall

$P = 3^x \therefore 3^x = 3$ or $3^x = 9$

$3^x = 3^1$ or $3^x = -3^2 \therefore x = 1$

(4.27). Solve for x: $2^{2x} + 2^{x+1} - 8 = 0$.

Solution

$(2^x)^2 + 2^x \cdot 2^1 - 8 = 0$ let $2^x = P$

$P^2 + P \cdot 2 - 8 = 0 \rightarrow P^2 + 2P - 8 = 0 \rightarrow P^2 + 4P - 2P - 8 = 0 \rightarrow P(P+4) - 2(P+4) = 0$

$(P-2)(P+4) = 0 \rightarrow P - 2 = 0$ or $P + 4 = 0 \therefore P = 2$ or $P = -4$

recall $2^x = 2 \rightarrow 2^x = 2^1 \therefore x = 1$

(4.28). Solve $2^{m-n} = 32$, $3^{3n-m} = 27$.

Solution

$2^{m-n} = 2^5$, $3^{3n-m} = 3^3$

$m - n = 5$ ....(i)

$-m + 3n = 3$ ....(ii)

$2n = 8 \rightarrow n = 8/2 = 4$

put n = 4 in equation (i)

$m - 4 = 5 \therefore m = 9$

(4.29). Given that $3^{x-2y} = 3$, $5^{x-3y} = 25$. find 3^{x+y}.

Solution

$3^{x-2y} = 3 \rightarrow x + 2y = 1$

$5^{x-3y} = 5^2 \rightarrow x + 3y = 2$

x + 2y = 1 ....(i)

x + 3y = 2 ....(ii)

y = -1

put y = -1 into equation (i)

$x - 2(-1) = 1 \rightarrow x + 2 = 1 \therefore x = -1$

$\therefore 3^{x+y} = 3^{-1-1} \rightarrow 3^{-2} = 1/9$

(4.30). $5^{2x} + 1 = 26(5^{x-1})$.

Solution

$(5^x)^2 + 1 = 26(5^x) \cdot 5^{-1}$

Let P = 5^x

$P^2 + 1 = \frac{26(p)}{5} \rightarrow 5P^2 + 5 = 26p$

$5p^2 - 26P + 5 = 0 \rightarrow 5P(P-5) - 1(P-5) = 0 \rightarrow (5P-1)(P-5) = 0$

5P = 1 or P = 5 $\therefore$ P = $1/5$ or 5

From P = $5^x \rightarrow 5^x = 5$, x = 1

(4.31). $2^x + 32(2^{-x}) - 12 = 0$.

Solution

Let y = 2^x

$y + 32y^{-1} - 12 = 0 \rightarrow y - 12 + \frac{32}{y} \rightarrow y^2 - 12y + 32$

$y^2 - 8y - 4y + 32 = 0 \rightarrow y(y-8) - 4(y-8) \rightarrow (y-8)(y-4) \therefore y = 4 \text{ or } 8$

from $2^x = y$ if $y = 4 \rightarrow 2^x = 2^2 \therefore x = 2$

If $y = 8 \rightarrow 2^x = 2^3 \quad x = 3$

(4.32). Simplify the expression $\frac{1}{q^{-4k/3}} \times q^{-k/3}$.

Solution

$\frac{1}{q^{-4k/3}} \times q^{-k/3} \rightarrow q^{4k/3} \times q^{-k/3} \rightarrow q^{\frac{4k}{3} - \frac{k}{3}} \rightarrow q^{\frac{3k}{3}} = q^k$

(4.33). Simplify $\frac{6^{2n+1} \times 9^n \times 4^{2n}}{18^n \times 2^n \times 12^{2n}}$.

Solution

$\frac{(2 \times 3)^{2n+1} \times (3^2)^n \times (2^2)^{2n}}{(2 \times 3^2)^n \times 2^n \times (3 \times 2^2)^{2n}} \rightarrow$

$\frac{2^{2n+1} \times 3^{2n+1} \times 3^{2n} \times 2^{4n}}{2^n \times 3^n \times 2^n \times 3^{2n} \times 2^{4n}} \rightarrow \frac{2^{2n+1} \times 3^{2n+1}}{2^{n+n} \times 3^{2n}} \rightarrow \frac{2^{2n+1} \times 3^{2n+1}}{2^{2n} \times 3^{2n}} \rightarrow 2^{2n+1-2n} \times 3^{2n+1-2n} = 2 \times 3 = 6$

(4.34). The value of $16^{\frac{1}{8}}$ is?

Solution

$16^{\frac{1}{8}} = (\sqrt[8]{16})^1 \rightarrow (2^4)^{\frac{1}{8}} \rightarrow 2^{\frac{1}{2}} \rightarrow \sqrt{2}$

(4.35). Evaluate $(2^0 + 4^{-\frac{1}{2}})^2$.

Solution

$2^0 = 1, \; 4^{-\frac{1}{2}} = \frac{1}{4^{1/2}} = \frac{1}{\sqrt{4}} = \frac{1}{2}$

$(2^a + 4^{-\frac{1}{2}})^2 \rightarrow (1 + \frac{1}{2})^2 \rightarrow (1\frac{1}{2})^2 \rightarrow \left[\frac{3}{2}\right]^2 = 9/4$

(4.36). Simplify $\sqrt[3]{\frac{27a^{-9}}{8}}$.

Solution

$$\sqrt[3]{\frac{27a^{-9}}{8}} \rightarrow \frac{3a^{-3}}{2} \rightarrow \frac{3}{2a^3}$$

(4.37). If $2^m = 4x$ and $2^w = 8x$. What is m in terms of w?

Solution

$2^m = 4x$ ……(i)

$2^w = 8x$ …….(ii)

Multiplying (i) by 2

$2(2^m) = 2(4x) \rightarrow 2^{m+1} = 8x$

$w = m + 1 \rightarrow m = w - 1$

(4.38). Evaluate $\frac{2^2 + 3^2}{5^2} + \frac{1}{10}$.

Solution

$$\frac{4+9}{25} + \frac{1}{10} \rightarrow \frac{13}{25} + \frac{1}{10} \rightarrow \frac{26+5}{50} = \frac{31}{50}$$

(4.39). If x is a fraction which ranges $\frac{1}{4}$ to $\frac{1}{2}$ and y is a fraction which ranges from $\frac{3}{4}$ to $\frac{11}{12}$. What is the maximum value of $\frac{x}{y}$?

Solution

Making x bigger and y smaller i.e $\frac{1}{2} > \frac{1}{4}$ for x and $\frac{3}{4} < \frac{11}{12}$ for y

$$\frac{x}{y} \rightarrow \frac{\frac{1}{2}}{\frac{3}{4}} \rightarrow \frac{1}{2} \times \frac{4}{3} = \frac{2}{3}$$

CHAPTER 5 LOGARITHM

Principal of logarithm

According to John Napier. The logarithm of a number to a given base is the power to which the base must be raised to obtained the numbers

The theory of logarithms is quite different from common or natural logarithm.

Theory of logarithm is based on bases order than base 10

Laws of logarithms

Logarithm rules: These are rules guiding the operation between numbers such as multiplication, division, power, change of base and etc. they are as enumerated below.

1. Addition law: This states that when two logarithm are added the result is the log of the product of the numbers to a common bases.

$$\log_a x + \log_a y = \log_a xy$$
$$\log_a 2 + \log_a 3 = \log_a 2 \times 3 = \log_a 6$$

2. Subtraction law: This state that when two logarithms are subtracted the number of the log been subtracted is used as the divisor.

$$\log_a x - \log_a y \rightarrow \log_a \frac{x}{y}$$

$$\log_a 10 - \log_a 2 = \log_a \frac{10}{2} = \log_a 5$$

3. Power law: When a number is raised to a power in logarithm. The power multiplies the logarithm itself.

$$\log_a x^p = p \log_a x$$
$$\log_a 5^2 = 2 \log_a 5$$

4. Power of the base law: This states that if the base of a logarithm is raised to a given power, the reciprocal of the power is used to multiply the logarithm.

$$\log_{a^b} k = \frac{1}{b} \log_a k$$
$$\log_{a^2} 7 = \frac{1}{2} \log_a 7$$

5. Power of the base, Power of the number law: this states that the power of the number and power of the base are used to form a factor, provided the number and the base are equal.

$$\log_{a^k} a^l = \frac{l}{k}$$

$$\log_{2^3} 2^4 = \frac{4}{3}$$

6. Logarithms equal to its own base law: this states that if the number and the base is equal the result is 1.

$$\log_a a = 1$$

$$\log_2 2 = 1$$

7. Logarithm of 1 to any base law, this state that the logarithm of 1 to any base is 0

$$\log_a 1 = 0$$

$$\log_7 1 = 0$$

8. Reciprocal law: This states that if the reciprocal of logarithm is required then the number and base must interchange position

$$\log_x a = \frac{1}{\log_a x}$$

$$\log_x 2 = \frac{1}{\log_2 x}$$

9. Transformation law: This states that if the same subtraction is being carried out in a fraction the result is -1 when there is difference in direction.

$$\frac{\log x - \log y}{\log y - \log x} = -1$$

$$\frac{\log 2 - \log 3}{\log 3 - \log 2} = -1$$

10. Change of base law: This states that if the change of base is required then the basic must be the number itself all in commonbasic

$$\log_a x = \frac{\log_n x}{\log_n a}$$

$$\log_4 2 = \frac{\log 2}{\log 4} = \frac{\log 2}{\log_2 2} = \frac{\log 2}{2\log 2} = 1/2$$

11. $\log_{mn} x = \dfrac{\log_n x}{1+ \log_n m}$

Special simplification techniques. The logarithm of a number can be easily handled by expressing both the number and the base as powers and taking the fraction of the powers when the bases are counter-balanced.

$\log_2 8 = \log_2 2^3 \rightarrow 3 \log_2 2 = 3$

Also $\log_2 8$ can be written as $\log_{2^1} 2^3$ and as the bases cancel each other,

The ratio of power $= \dfrac{3}{1} = 3$

Note: that the logarithm is related to exponential function such as

$a^x = y$ we can use logarithm to define the above relation as

a = base, x = is the power to which the base must be raised to have the number

$\log_a N = x \quad \therefore \quad N = a^x$

Questions

Evaluate the following

(5.1). $\log_3 3 + \log_3 9$.

Solution

$\log_3 3 \times 9 \rightarrow \log_3 27 \rightarrow \log_3 3^3 = 3\log_3 3 = 3$

(5.2). $\log_2 28 - \log_2 14$.

Solution

$\log_2 \dfrac{28}{14} = \log_2 2 = 1$

(5.3). $\log_2 8^3$.

Solution

$3\log_2 8 \rightarrow 3\log_3 2^3 \rightarrow 3 \times 3\log_2 2 \rightarrow 3 \times 3 = 9$

(5.4). $\log_{81} 9^{\frac{1}{2}}$.

Solution

½ log₉² 9 → $\frac{1}{2} \times \frac{1}{2}$ log₉ 9 = ¼

(5.5). log₂₃ 16 .

Solution

log₂₃ 2⁴ → 4/3

(5.6). $\log_{9^{\frac{1}{2}}} 27$.

Solution

$\log_{9^{\frac{1}{2}}} 3^3$ → 3 log₃ 3 = 3

(5.7). log₁₆ 4 .

Solution

log₂⁴ 2² → $\frac{2}{4} \times \frac{\log 2}{\log 2} = \frac{1}{2}$

(5.8). log₄ 8 .

Solution

log₂² 2³ → $\frac{3}{2} \times \frac{\log 2}{\log 2}$ = 3/2

(5.9). $\frac{\log 16}{\log 32}$.

Solution

$\frac{\log 2^4}{\log 2^5}$ → $\frac{4}{5} \times \frac{\log 2}{\log 2}$ = 4/5

(5.10). log₈ 14 − log₈ 7.

Solution

$\frac{\log \frac{14}{7}}{\log_2 3}$ = 1/3

(5.11). log₄ 32 + log₄ 2.

Solution

log₄ 32 x 2 → log₄ 64 → log₄ 4³ = 3

(5.12). $6\log_4 8 - \log_4 32$.

Solution

$6\log_{2^2} 2^3 - \log_{2^2} 2^5 \rightarrow \frac{18}{2} - \frac{5}{2} = \frac{13}{2}$

(5.13). $\log_{49} 343$.

Solution

$\log_{7^2} 7^3 \rightarrow \frac{3}{2} \times \frac{\log 7}{\log 7} = \frac{3}{2}$ or $1\frac{1}{2}$

(5.14). $\log_5 62.5 - \log_5 0.5$.

Solution

$\log_5 \frac{625}{10} - \log_5 \frac{5}{10} \rightarrow \log_5 \frac{625}{5} = 12$

(5.15). $2\log 5 + \log 36 - \log 9$.

Solution

$\log \frac{25 \times 36}{9} \rightarrow \log_{10} 100 = 2$

(5.16). Without using tables, find the numerical value of $\log_7 49 + \log_7\left(\frac{1}{7}\right)$.

Solution

$\log_7 49 + \log_7\left(\frac{1}{7}\right) \rightarrow \log_7\left[49 \times \frac{1}{7}\right] \rightarrow \log_7 7 = 1$

(5.17). Simplify $\log_{10} a^{\frac{1}{3}} + \frac{1}{4}\log_{10} a - \frac{1}{12}\log_{10} a^7$.

Solution

$\log_{10} a^{\frac{1}{3}} + \frac{1}{4}\log_{10} a - \frac{1}{12}\log_{10} a^7 \rightarrow \log_{10}\left[\frac{a^{\frac{1}{3}} + a^{\frac{1}{4}}}{a^{\frac{7}{12}}}\right] \rightarrow \log\left[\frac{a^{\frac{7}{12}}}{a^{\frac{7}{12}}}\right] = \log_{10} 1 = 0$

(5.18). Simplify $\log_m A - \log_m B - \log_m C$.

Solution

$\log_m A - \log_m B - \log_m C \rightarrow \log_m (A/B) - \log_m C \rightarrow \log_m\left(\frac{\frac{A}{B}}{C}\right) = \log_m\left(\frac{A}{BC}\right)$

(5.19). Find x, if $\log_9 x = 1.5$.

Solution

$\log_9 x = 1.5 \rightarrow x = 9^{1.5} \rightarrow 9^{15/10} \rightarrow 9^{3/2} \rightarrow (\sqrt{9})^3 \rightarrow (3)^3 = 27$

(5.20). If $\log_8 N = \frac{r}{2}$, $\log_2 (2N) = S$ and $S - r = 4$, find N.

Solution

From $S - r = 4 \to S = 4 + r$......(i)

From $\log_8 N = \frac{r}{2} \to N = 8^{\frac{r}{2}}$

$\log_2(2N) = \log_2 2\left(8^{\frac{r}{2}}\right) \to \log_2 2\left(2^{3\frac{r}{2}}\right) \to \log_2 2\left(2^{\frac{3r}{2}}\right) \to \log_2\left(2^{1+\frac{3r}{2}}\right)$

$\to 1 + \frac{3r}{2} \log_2 2 = 1 + \frac{3r}{2}$

Since $\log_2 (2N) = S \to 1 + \frac{3r}{2} = S = 4 + r \to \frac{3r}{2} - r = 4 - 1 = 3$

$\frac{r}{2} = 3 \therefore r = 2(3) = 6$

$N = 8^{\frac{r}{2}} = 8^{\frac{6}{2}} = 8^3 = 512$

(5.21). Given $\log_{10} Y = 2$, $\log_{10} 2x = 1$. Evaluate $\frac{\log_{10} \sqrt{Y}}{3x}$.

Solution

From $\log_{10} (2x) = 1 \to 2x = 10^1 \to x = 5$

$\frac{\log_{10} \sqrt{Y}}{3x} \to \frac{\log_{10} Y^{\frac{1}{2}}}{3x} \to \frac{\frac{1}{2}\log_{10} Y}{3x} \to \frac{\frac{1}{2}(2)}{3(5)} = \frac{1}{15}$

(5.22). Simplify $\frac{\log_{10} 8 - \log_{10} 4}{\log_{10} 4 - \log_{10} 2}$.

Solution

$\log_{10} 8 - \log_{10} 4 \to \log_{10}\left(\frac{8}{4}\right) = \log_{10} 2$

$\log_{10} 4 - \log_{10} 2 \to \log_{10}\left(\frac{4}{2}\right) = \log_{10} 2$

$\therefore \frac{\log_{10} 8 - \log_{10} 4}{\log_{10} 4 - \log_{10} 2} = \frac{\log_{10} 2}{\log_{10} 2} = 1$

(5.23). Find the value of the product of $\log_2 3 \cdot \log_3 4 \cdot \log_4 5 \cdot \log_5 6 \cdot \log_6 7 \cdot \log_7 8$

Solution

Converting all to base 2, we have

$\log_2 3 \cdot \dfrac{\log_2 4}{\log_2 3} \cdot \dfrac{\log_2 5}{\log_2 4} \cdot \dfrac{\log_2 5}{\log_2 4} \cdot \dfrac{\log_2 6}{\log_2 5} \cdot \dfrac{\log_2 7}{\log_2 6} \cdot \dfrac{\log_2 8}{\log_2 7}$

$\log_2 8 = \log_2 2^3 = 3\log_2 2 = 3$

(5.24). Find the value of $\log_{12} 7$ approximately.

Solution

$\log_{12} 7 = \dfrac{\log_{10} 7}{\log_{10} 12} \rightarrow \dfrac{0.8451}{1.0792} = 0.7831$

(5.25). Find n if $\log_2 4 + \log_2 7 - \log_2 n = 1$.
Solution

Since all are in base two, $1 = \log_2 2$

$\therefore \log_2 4 + \log_2 7 - \log_2 n = \log_2 2 \rightarrow \log_2 4 + \log_2 7 - \log_2 2 = \log_2 n$

$\log_2 \left[\dfrac{4 \times 7}{2}\right] = \log_2 n \rightarrow \log_2 14 = \log_2 n \rightarrow n = 14$

(5.26). Write the equation $2\log_2 x - x\log_2(1+y) = 3$ in a form not involving logarithm.

Solution

Since the numbers are all in base 2 $\rightarrow 3 = 3\log_2 2$

$2\log_2 x - x\log_2(1+y) = 3\log_2 2 \rightarrow \log_2 x^2 - \log_2(1+y)^x = \log_2 2^3 = \log_2 8$

$\dfrac{x^2}{(1+y)^x} = 8 \therefore x^2 = 8(1+y)^x = x$

(5.27). If $\log_2 x + \log_4 x + \log_{16} x = \dfrac{21}{4}$, find x.

Solution

Reducing all logarithms to base 2

$$\log_4 x = \frac{\log_2 x}{\log_2 4} \rightarrow \frac{\log_2 x}{\log_2 2^2} \rightarrow \frac{\log_2 x}{2\log_2 2} = \frac{\log_2 x}{2}$$

$$\log_{16} x = \frac{\log_2 x}{\log_2 16} \rightarrow \frac{\log_2 x}{\log_2 2^4} \rightarrow \frac{\log_2 x}{4\log_2 2} = \frac{\log_2 x}{4}$$

$$\therefore \log_2 x + \log_4 x + \log_{16} x \rightarrow \log_2 x + \frac{1}{2}\log_2 x + \frac{1}{4}\log_2 x$$

$$\log_2 x + \log_2 x^{\frac{1}{2}} + \log_2 x^{\frac{1}{4}} = \frac{21}{4} \rightarrow \log_2\left(x \cdot x^{\frac{1}{2}} \cdot x^{\frac{1}{4}}\right) = \frac{21}{4}$$

$$\log_2\left(x^{\frac{7}{4}}\right) = \frac{21}{4} \rightarrow x^{\frac{7}{4}} = 2^{\frac{21}{4}} \rightarrow x^{\frac{7}{4} \cdot \frac{4}{7}} = 2^{\frac{21}{4} \cdot \frac{4}{7}} \rightarrow x = 2^3 = 8$$

(5.28). Given that $10^x = 0.2$ and $\log_{10} 2 = 0.3010$, find x.

Solution

Given $10^x = 0.2$, taking log of both side to base 10

$$\log_{10} 10^x = \log_{10} 0.2 \rightarrow x \log_{10} 10 = \log_{10}\left[\frac{2}{10}\right] \rightarrow x = 0.3010 - 1.000 = -0.6990$$

CHAPTER 6 SURD

This is mathematics of root numbers or elements e.g. $\sqrt{7}, \sqrt{x}$ etc.

Rules of surds

(1) $\sqrt{a} + \sqrt{b} \neq \sqrt{a+b}$

(2) $\sqrt{a} \times \sqrt{b} = \sqrt{ab}$

(3) $\sqrt{a} - \sqrt{b} \neq \sqrt{a-b}$

(4) $\sqrt{\dfrac{a}{b}} = \dfrac{\sqrt{a}}{\sqrt{b}}$

Similar surds

Surds are said to be similar if they are in the same basic form. That is the number under the root sign of both surds are the same. For example $a\sqrt{n}$ and $b\sqrt{n}$ are similar surds.

Simplification of surds

This is simply the reduction to basic form. That is the number under the radicand is not a perfect square.

Algebra of surds

(1) Addition and subtraction

This is only possible if the surds are similar. That is we combine roots of similar numbers or elements.

Multiplication: It based on multiplication rule as annotated earlier; $\sqrt{a} \times \sqrt{b} = \sqrt{a \times b}$

Division: This brings about rationalization of surds

Rationalization of an expression in form of $\dfrac{a}{\sqrt{b}}$

Here we simply multiply the top and bottom by the bottom and evaluate.

$\dfrac{a}{\sqrt{b}} \times \dfrac{\sqrt{b}}{\sqrt{b}} \rightarrow \dfrac{a\sqrt{b}}{\sqrt{b \times b}} = \dfrac{a\sqrt{b}}{b}$

Rationalization of an expression in form of $\frac{\sqrt{a}}{\sqrt{b}+1}$

Here we multiply the top and bottom by the conjugate of the surd in the denominator.

Conjugate surd: This is defined as a fractional surd expression with opposite sign to the one given. e.g. conjugate of $c+\sqrt{d}$ is $c-\sqrt{d}$

Thus to evaluate $\frac{\sqrt{a}}{\sqrt{b}+1}$ we have

$$\frac{\sqrt{a}}{\sqrt{b}+1} = \frac{\sqrt{a}}{\sqrt{b}+1} \times \frac{\sqrt{b}-1}{\sqrt{b}-1}$$

The denominator of the above expression is evaluated by

$(\sqrt{b}+1)(\sqrt{b}-1) = (\sqrt{b})^2 - \sqrt{b} + \sqrt{b} - 1 = (\sqrt{b})^2 - (1)^2 = b - 1$ which is not a surd. Thus the product of a surd and its conjugate is not a surd.

Equality of surds

If $(\sqrt{a}+\sqrt{b})$ is squared we have

$(\sqrt{a}+\sqrt{b})^2 = a + b + 2\sqrt{ab}$

If $(\sqrt{a}-\sqrt{b})$ is squared we have

$(\sqrt{a}-\sqrt{b})^2 = a + b - 2\sqrt{ab}$

From the above analysis, it implies we can find the positive square root of a surd. Also note that a is greater than b.

QUESTIONS

Simplify the following

(6.1). $\sqrt{18}$

Solution

$\sqrt{18} = \sqrt{9 \times 2} = \sqrt{9} \times \sqrt{2} = 3\sqrt{2}$

(6.2). $\sqrt{8}$

Solution

$\sqrt{8} = \sqrt{4 \times 2} = \sqrt{4} \times \sqrt{2} = 2\sqrt{2}$

(6.3). $2\sqrt{50}$

Solution

$2\sqrt{50} \rightarrow 2\sqrt{25 \times 2} \rightarrow 2 \times 5 \times \sqrt{2} = 10\sqrt{2}$

(6.4). $3\sqrt{28}$

Solution

$3\sqrt{28} \rightarrow 3\sqrt{4 \times 7} \rightarrow 3 \times 2 \times \sqrt{7} \rightarrow 6 \times \sqrt{7} = 6\sqrt{7}$

(6.5). $\sqrt{44}$

Solution

$\sqrt{44} \rightarrow \sqrt{4 \times 11} \rightarrow 2\sqrt{11}$

(6.6). $\sqrt{108}$

Solution

$\sqrt{108} \rightarrow \sqrt{9 \times 4 \times 3} \rightarrow 3 \times 2\sqrt{3} = 6\sqrt{3}$

(6.7). $\sqrt{x^2 y}$

Solution

$\sqrt{x^2 y} = \sqrt{x^2} \times \sqrt{y} = x\sqrt{y}$

(6.8). $5\sqrt{63}$

Solution

$5\sqrt{63} \rightarrow 5\sqrt{9 \times 7} \rightarrow 5 \times 3\sqrt{7} = 15\sqrt{7}$

(6.9). $\sqrt{72}$

Solution

$\sqrt{72} \rightarrow \sqrt{9 \times 8} \rightarrow \sqrt{9 \times 4 \times 2} \rightarrow 3 \times 2\sqrt{2} = 6\sqrt{2}$

(6.10). $\sqrt{10800}$

Solution

$\sqrt{10800} \rightarrow \sqrt{108 \times 100} \rightarrow \sqrt{9 \times 4 \times 3 \times 100} \rightarrow 3 \times 2 \times 10\sqrt{3} = 60\sqrt{3}$

(6.11). $\sqrt{32} + 3\sqrt{8}$

Solution

$\sqrt{32} + 3\sqrt{8} \rightarrow \sqrt{16 \times 2} + 3\sqrt{4 \times 2} \rightarrow 4\sqrt{2} + 6\sqrt{2} = 10\sqrt{2}$

(6.12). $7\sqrt{3} - \sqrt{75}$

Solution

$7\sqrt{3} - \sqrt{75} \rightarrow 7\sqrt{3} - \sqrt{25 \times 3} \rightarrow 7\sqrt{3} - 5\sqrt{3} = 2\sqrt{3}$

(6.13). $\sqrt{28} - 5\sqrt{7}$

Solution

$\sqrt{28} - 5\sqrt{7} \rightarrow \sqrt{4 \times 7} - 5\sqrt{7} \rightarrow 2\sqrt{7} - 5\sqrt{7} \rightarrow -3\sqrt{7}$

(6.14). $\sqrt{11} + \sqrt{44} - \sqrt{99}$

Solution

$\sqrt{11} + \sqrt{44} - \sqrt{99} \rightarrow \sqrt{11} + \sqrt{4 \times 11} - \sqrt{9 \times 11} \rightarrow 1\sqrt{11} + 2\sqrt{11} - 3\sqrt{11} \rightarrow$

$(1 + 2 - 3)\sqrt{11} = 0$

(6.15). $\sqrt{18} - \sqrt{32} + \sqrt{50}$

Solution

$\sqrt{18} - \sqrt{32} + \sqrt{50} \rightarrow \sqrt{9 \times 2} - \sqrt{16 \times 2} + \sqrt{25 \times 2} \rightarrow 3\sqrt{2} - 4\sqrt{2} + 5\sqrt{2}$

$(3 - 4 + 5)\sqrt{2} = 4\sqrt{2}$

(6.16). $3\sqrt{27} - \sqrt{48} - 2\sqrt{75} + \sqrt{108}$

Solution

$3\sqrt{27} - \sqrt{48} - 2\sqrt{75} + \sqrt{108} \rightarrow 3\sqrt{9 \times 3} - \sqrt{16 \times 3} - 2\sqrt{25 \times 3} + \sqrt{36 \times 3}$

$3 \times 3\sqrt{3} - 4\sqrt{3} - 2 \times 5\sqrt{3} + 6\sqrt{3} \rightarrow (9 - 4 - 10)\sqrt{3} + 6\sqrt{3} = \sqrt{3}$

(6.17). $5\sqrt{12} + 4\sqrt{12} - 3\sqrt{18} + 2\sqrt{75}$

Solution

$5\sqrt{12} + 4\sqrt{12} - 3\sqrt{18} + 2\sqrt{75} \rightarrow 5\sqrt{4 \times 3} + 4\sqrt{4 \times 3} - 3\sqrt{9 \times 2} + 2\sqrt{25 \times 3} \rightarrow$

$10\sqrt{3} + 8\sqrt{3} - 9\sqrt{2} + 10\sqrt{3} \rightarrow 28\sqrt{3} - 9\sqrt{2}$

(6.18). $5\sqrt{18} - 3\sqrt{72} + 4\sqrt{50}$

Solution

$5\sqrt{18} - 3\sqrt{72} + 4\sqrt{50} \rightarrow 5\sqrt{9 \times 2} - 3\sqrt{36 \times 2} + 4\sqrt{25 \times 2} \rightarrow$

$5 \times 3\sqrt{2} - 3 \times 6\sqrt{2} + 4 \times 5\sqrt{2} \rightarrow 15\sqrt{2} - 18\sqrt{2} - 20\sqrt{2} = 17\sqrt{2}$

(6.19). $\frac{2\sqrt{14} \; x \; 3\sqrt{21}}{7\sqrt{24} \; x \; 2\sqrt{98}}$

Solution

$\frac{2\sqrt{14} \; x \; 3\sqrt{21}}{7\sqrt{24} \; x \; 2\sqrt{98}} \rightarrow \frac{6\sqrt{14 \; x \; 21}}{14\sqrt{24 \; x \; 98}} \rightarrow \frac{6\sqrt{7 \; x \; 2 \; x \; 7 \; x \; 3}}{14\sqrt{8 \; x \; 3 \; x \; 49 \; x \; 2}} \rightarrow \frac{6\sqrt{49 \; x \; 2 \; x \; 3}}{14\sqrt{16 \; x \; 49 \; x \; 3}} \rightarrow \frac{6 \; x \; 7 \; x \sqrt{2} \; x \sqrt{3}}{14 \; x \; 4 \; x \; 7 \; x \sqrt{3}} = \frac{3\sqrt{2}}{28}$

(6.20). $\frac{1}{\sqrt{2} + \sqrt{5}}$

Solution

$\frac{1}{\sqrt{2} + \sqrt{5}} = \frac{1}{\sqrt{2} + \sqrt{5}} \; x \; \frac{\sqrt{2} - \sqrt{5}}{\sqrt{2} - \sqrt{5}} \rightarrow \frac{\sqrt{2} - \sqrt{5}}{(\sqrt{2})^2 + (\sqrt{5})^2} \rightarrow \frac{\sqrt{2} - \sqrt{5}}{2 - 5} \rightarrow \frac{\sqrt{2} - \sqrt{5}}{-3} \rightarrow \frac{-\sqrt{2} + \sqrt{5}}{3} = \frac{\sqrt{5} - \sqrt{2}}{3}$

(6.21). $\frac{5\sqrt{7} - 7\sqrt{5}}{\sqrt{7} - \sqrt{5}}$

Solution

$$\frac{5\sqrt{7}-7\sqrt{5}}{\sqrt{7}-\sqrt{5}} = \frac{5\sqrt{7}-7\sqrt{5}}{\sqrt{7}-\sqrt{5}} \times \frac{\sqrt{7}+\sqrt{5}}{\sqrt{7}+\sqrt{5}} \to \frac{5\sqrt{49}+5\sqrt{35}-7\sqrt{35}-7\sqrt{25}}{(\sqrt{7})^2-(\sqrt{5})^2} \to \frac{(5 \times 7)+5\sqrt{35}-7\sqrt{35}-(7 \times 5)}{7-5}$$

$$\to \frac{35-2\sqrt{35}-35}{2} \to \frac{-2\sqrt{35}}{2} = -\sqrt{35}$$

(6.22). $\frac{1}{3+\sqrt{5}} - \frac{1}{3-\sqrt{5}}$

Solution

$$\frac{1}{3+\sqrt{5}} - \frac{1}{3-\sqrt{5}} \to \frac{(3-\sqrt{5})-(3+\sqrt{5})}{(3+\sqrt{5})(3-\sqrt{5})} \to \frac{3-\sqrt{5}-3-\sqrt{5}}{(3)^2-(\sqrt{5})^2} \to \frac{-2\sqrt{5}}{9-5} \to \frac{-2\sqrt{5}}{4} = \frac{-1\sqrt{5}}{2}$$

(6.23). $4 - \frac{1}{2-\sqrt{3}}$.

Solution

$$\frac{4}{1} - \frac{1}{2-\sqrt{3}} \to \frac{4(2-\sqrt{3})-1}{(2-\sqrt{3})} \to \frac{8-4\sqrt{3}-1}{(2-\sqrt{3})} \to \frac{7-4\sqrt{3}}{2-\sqrt{3}} \to \frac{7-4\sqrt{3}}{2-\sqrt{3}} \times \frac{2+\sqrt{3}}{2+\sqrt{3}}$$

$$\frac{14+7\sqrt{3}-8\sqrt{3}-4\sqrt{9}}{(2)^2-(\sqrt{3})^2} \to \frac{14+7\sqrt{3}-8\sqrt{3}-(4 \times 3)}{4-3} \to \frac{14-\sqrt{3}-12}{1} = 2-\sqrt{3}$$

(6.24). $\frac{\sqrt{1+x}+\sqrt{x}}{\sqrt{1+x}-\sqrt{x}}$

Solution

$$\frac{\sqrt{1+x}+\sqrt{x}}{\sqrt{1+x}-\sqrt{x}} \to \frac{\sqrt{1+x}+\sqrt{x}}{\sqrt{1+x}-\sqrt{x}} \cdot \frac{\sqrt{1+x}+\sqrt{x}}{\sqrt{1+x}+\sqrt{x}} \to \frac{(\sqrt{1+x})^2+(\sqrt{x})\sqrt{1+x}+(\sqrt{x})\sqrt{1+x}+(\sqrt{x})^2}{(\sqrt{1+x})^2-(\sqrt{x})^2}$$

$$\frac{(1+x)+2\sqrt{x}\sqrt{1+x}+x}{(1+x)-x} \to \frac{1+x+2\sqrt{x}\sqrt{1+x}+x}{1+x-x} = \frac{1+2x+2\sqrt{x(1+x)}}{1}$$

(6.25). $\left(\frac{1}{\sqrt{5}+\sqrt{3}} - \frac{1}{\sqrt{5}-\sqrt{3}}\right) \times \frac{1}{\sqrt{3}}$.

Solution

$$\frac{1}{\sqrt{5}+\sqrt{3}} - \frac{1}{\sqrt{5}-\sqrt{3}} \to \frac{(\sqrt{5}-\sqrt{3})-(\sqrt{5}+\sqrt{3})}{(\sqrt{5}+\sqrt{3})(\sqrt{5}-\sqrt{3})} \to \frac{\sqrt{5}-\sqrt{3}-\sqrt{5}-\sqrt{3}}{(\sqrt{5})^2-(\sqrt{3})^2} \to \frac{-2\sqrt{3}}{5-3} \to \frac{-2\sqrt{3}}{2} \to -\sqrt{3}$$

$$\therefore \left(\frac{1}{\sqrt{5}+\sqrt{3}} - \frac{1}{\sqrt{5}-\sqrt{3}}\right) \times \frac{1}{\sqrt{3}} = -\sqrt{3} \times \frac{1}{\sqrt{3}} = -1$$

(6.26). Find the value of x if $(x+4)^{1/2} - (x-1)^{1/2} = 1$.

Solution

$(x+4)^{1/2} - (x-1)^{1/2} = \sqrt{(x+4)} - \sqrt{(x-1)} \rightarrow (\sqrt{x+4} - \sqrt{x-1}) = 1$

Squaring both sides

$(x+4) + (x-1) - 2\sqrt{(x+4)(x-1)} = 1$

$2x + 3 - 1 = 2\sqrt{(x+4)(x-1)} \rightarrow 2x + 2 = 2\sqrt{(x+4)(x-1)}$

$x + 1 = \sqrt{(x+4)(x-1)} \rightarrow (x+1)^2 = (x+4)(x-1) \rightarrow x^2 + 2x + 1 = x^2 + 3x - 4$

$1 + 4 = 3x - 2x \rightarrow x = 5$

(6.27). If $x = 3 - \sqrt{3}$, find $x^2 + \frac{36}{x^2}$.

Solution

$x^2 = (3 - \sqrt{3})^2 = 3^2 - 6\sqrt{3} + (\sqrt{3})^2 \rightarrow 9 - 6\sqrt{3} + 3 = 12 - 6\sqrt{3}$

$\frac{36}{x^2} \rightarrow \frac{36}{12 - 6\sqrt{3}} \rightarrow \frac{36}{6(2 - \sqrt{3})} \rightarrow \frac{6}{2 - \sqrt{3}} \cdot \frac{2 + \sqrt{3}}{2 + \sqrt{3}} = \frac{6(2+\sqrt{3})}{2^2 + (\sqrt{3})^2} = \frac{6(2+\sqrt{3})}{4-3} = 6(2 + \sqrt{3}) = 12 + 6\sqrt{3}$

$x^2 + \frac{36}{x^2} = 12 - 6\sqrt{3} + 12 + 6\sqrt{3} = 24$

(6.28). Find the square root of $49 - 12\sqrt{5}$

Solution

$49 - 12\sqrt{5} = a + b - 2\sqrt{ab} \rightarrow a + b = 49$ .....(i)

$-2\sqrt{ab} = -12\sqrt{5} \therefore \sqrt{ab} = 6\sqrt{5}$ squaring both sides gives

$ab = 180$ ....(ii)

From (i) $a = 49 - b$, inserting into (ii)

$(49 - b)b = 180 \rightarrow 49b - b^2 = 180 \rightarrow b^2 - 49b + 180 = 0 \rightarrow$

$b^2 - 45b - 4b + 180 = 0 \rightarrow b(b - 45) - 4(b - 45) = 0 \rightarrow (b - 4)(b - 45)$

a = 45 , b = 4

$49 - 12\sqrt{5} = \sqrt{a} - \sqrt{b} \rightarrow \sqrt{45} - \sqrt{4} \rightarrow \sqrt{9 \times 5} - 2 \rightarrow 3\sqrt{5} - 2$

(6.29). Find the square-root of $170 - 20\sqrt{30}$

Solution

a + b = 170 ....(i)

$2\sqrt{ab} = 20\sqrt{30} \rightarrow \sqrt{ab} = 10\sqrt{30} \rightarrow ab = 100(30)$

ab = 3000 ....(ii)

From (i) b = 170 – a

Putting into (ii)

$a(170 - a) = 3000 \rightarrow 170a - a^2 = 30000 \rightarrow a^2 - 170a + 3000 = 0$

$(a - 150)(a - 20) = 0 \rightarrow a = 150, b = 20$

$\sqrt{(170 - 20\sqrt{30})} = \sqrt{150} - \sqrt{20} \rightarrow \pm(\sqrt{25 \times 6} - \sqrt{4 \times 5}) \rightarrow \pm(5\sqrt{6} - 2\sqrt{5})$

$\sqrt{(170 - 20\sqrt{30})} = (5\sqrt{6} - 2\sqrt{5}) \text{ or } -(5\sqrt{6} - 2\sqrt{5})$

$(5\sqrt{6} - 2\sqrt{5}) \text{ or } (-5\sqrt{6} + 2\sqrt{5}) \therefore (5\sqrt{6} - 2\sqrt{5}) \text{ or } (2\sqrt{5} - 5\sqrt{6})$

(6.30). Find the square roots of $8 + 2\sqrt{15}$

Solution

$\sqrt{(8 + 2\sqrt{15})} = \pm\sqrt{(a+b) + 2\sqrt{ab}} = (\sqrt{a} + \sqrt{b})$

a + b = 8 ....(i)

$2\sqrt{ab} = 2\sqrt{15} \rightarrow \sqrt{ab} = \sqrt{15} \rightarrow ab = 15$

$ab = 15$ ....(ii)

From (i) b = 8 – a, inserting into (ii)

$a(8 – a) = 15 \rightarrow 8a – a^2 = 15 \rightarrow a^2 – 8a + 15 = 0 \rightarrow (a – 5)(a – 3) = 0 \therefore a = 5$ or 3

$\sqrt{(8 + 2\sqrt{15})} = (\sqrt{5} + \sqrt{3})$

(6.31). Find the positive square of $50 + 10\sqrt{21}$

Solution

$\sqrt{50 + 10\sqrt{21}} = \pm\sqrt{(a + b) + 2\sqrt{ab}} = +(\sqrt{a} + \sqrt{b})$

$a + b = 50$ .... (i)

$2\sqrt{ab} = 10\sqrt{21} \rightarrow \sqrt{ab} = 5\sqrt{21} \rightarrow ab = 525$ .... (ii)

Putting (i) in (ii)

$a(50 – a) = 525 \rightarrow 50a – a^2 = 525 \rightarrow a^2 - 50a + 525 = 0 \rightarrow (a – 35)(a – 15) = 0$

a = 35, b = 15

$\sqrt{(50 + 10\sqrt{21})} = \sqrt{35} + \sqrt{15}$

(6.32). Find the positive square root of $15 - 2\sqrt{26}$

Solution

$\sqrt{(15 – 2\sqrt{26})} = \sqrt{(a + b) – 2\sqrt{ab}} = \sqrt{a} – \sqrt{b}$

a + b = 15 ....(i)

$2\sqrt{ab} = 2\sqrt{26} \rightarrow ab = 26$

From (i) b = 15 – a put in (ii)

$a(15 – a) = 26 \rightarrow 15a – a^2 = 26 \rightarrow a^2 – 15a + 26 = 0 \rightarrow (a – 13)(a - 2) = 0$

a = 13, or a = 2 $\therefore a = 13, b = 13$

51

$$\sqrt{(15 - 2(\sqrt{26})} = (\sqrt{13} - \sqrt{2})$$

(6.33). If $(m\sqrt{2} + n)^2 = 34 - 24\sqrt{2}$, find m and n

Solution

$$(m\sqrt{2} + n)^2 = 34 - 24\sqrt{2} \rightarrow (m\sqrt{2} + n) = \sqrt{(34 - 24\sqrt{2})}$$

from $\sqrt{(a + b + 2\sqrt{ab})} = \sqrt{a} + \sqrt{b}$

a + b = 34......(i)

$2\sqrt{ab} = -24\sqrt{2} \rightarrow \sqrt{ab} = -12\sqrt{2} \rightarrow ab = 144(2) = 288$ ....(ii)

From (i) b = 34 – a, put into (ii)

a(34 – a) = 288 $\rightarrow$ 34a – a² = 288 $\rightarrow$ a² - 34a + 288 = 0 $\rightarrow$ (a – 16)(a – 18) = 0

a = 16 or 18

$\sqrt{a} + \sqrt{b} = \sqrt{16} + \sqrt{18} = 4 + 3\sqrt{2}$ or $- 4 + -3\sqrt{2} \rightarrow -4 - 3\sqrt{2}$

Comparing we have

For $3\sqrt{2} + 4 = m\sqrt{2} + n$ ∴ m = 3, n = 4

For $-3\sqrt{2} - 4$ with $m\sqrt{2} + n$ ∴ m = -3, n = - 4

(6.34). $5(\sqrt{1.6} + \sqrt{0.4})$

Solution

$$5\left[\sqrt{\frac{16}{10}} + \sqrt{\frac{4}{10}}\right] \rightarrow 5\left[\frac{4}{\sqrt{10}} + \frac{2}{\sqrt{10}}\right] \rightarrow 5\left[\frac{4+2}{\sqrt{10}}\right] \rightarrow 5\left[\frac{6}{\sqrt{10}}\right] \rightarrow 5\left[\frac{6}{\sqrt{10}}\right] \times \frac{\sqrt{10}}{\sqrt{10}}$$

$= 3\sqrt{10}$

(6.35). $4\sqrt{\frac{1}{32}} - 2\sqrt{\frac{1}{8}} + 3\sqrt{\frac{1}{2}}$

Solution

$4\dfrac{\sqrt{1}}{\sqrt{32}} - 2\dfrac{\sqrt{1}}{\sqrt{8}} + 3\dfrac{\sqrt{1}}{\sqrt{2}} \rightarrow 4\dfrac{\sqrt{1}}{\sqrt{16 \times 2}} - 2\dfrac{\sqrt{1}}{\sqrt{4 \times 2}} + 3\dfrac{\sqrt{1}}{\sqrt{2}} \rightarrow 4\dfrac{\sqrt{1}}{4\sqrt{2}} - 2\dfrac{\sqrt{1}}{2\sqrt{2}} + 3\dfrac{\sqrt{1}}{\sqrt{2}}$

$\dfrac{1}{\sqrt{2}} - \dfrac{1}{\sqrt{2}} + \dfrac{3}{\sqrt{2}} \rightarrow \dfrac{1}{\sqrt{2}} \times \dfrac{\sqrt{2}}{\sqrt{2}} - \dfrac{1}{\sqrt{2}} \times \dfrac{\sqrt{2}}{\sqrt{2}} + \dfrac{3}{\sqrt{2}} \times \dfrac{\sqrt{2}}{\sqrt{2}} \rightarrow \dfrac{\sqrt{2}}{2} - \dfrac{\sqrt{2}}{2} + \dfrac{3\sqrt{2}}{2} = \dfrac{3\sqrt{2}}{2}$

(6.36). $\sqrt[3]{(64r^{-6})^{\frac{1}{2}}}$

Solution

$\sqrt[3]{\sqrt{(64r^{-6})}} \rightarrow \sqrt[3]{8r^{-3}} \rightarrow \sqrt[3]{8} \times \sqrt[3]{r^{-3}} \rightarrow 2 \times r^{-3 \times 1/3} \rightarrow 2r^{-1} = \dfrac{2}{r}$

CHAPTER 7   CHANGE OF SUBJECT OF AN EQUATION

This deals with the techniques of expressing a variable in terms of the other. In order to change the subject of a formula we treat the formula like an equation and the new subject as the unknown. All the rules of algebra must be obeyed. It is imperative to always take the variable to be made the subject to the positive side.

Note: Brackets are cleared by expansion.

Fractions are cleared by multiplying through by the Lcm.

Root signs are cleared by multiplying both sides by the reciprocal of the available power.

QUESTIONS

(7.1). Make c the subject of expression in $a(b+c) + \frac{5}{d} - 2 = 0$

Solution

$a(b+c) + \frac{5}{d} - 2 = 0 \rightarrow a(b+c) = 2 - \frac{5}{d} \rightarrow b + c = \frac{2}{a} - \frac{5}{ad}$

$c = \frac{2}{a} - \frac{5}{ad} - b = \frac{2d - 5 - abd}{ad}$

(7.2). Make c the subject of the formula in $V = 1 - \frac{a}{5}\left(b + \frac{3}{7}c\right)$

Solution

$\frac{a}{5}\left(b + \frac{3c}{7}\right) = (1-V) \rightarrow a\left(b + \frac{3c}{7}\right) = 5(1-V) \rightarrow b + \frac{3c}{7} = \frac{5(1-V)}{a}$

$\frac{3c}{7} = \frac{5(1-V)}{a} - b \rightarrow 3c = 7\left[\frac{5(1-V)}{a} - b\right] \rightarrow c = \frac{7}{3}\left[\frac{5(1-V)}{a} - b\right]$

Multiplying the numerator and denominator by -1, we have,

$c = \frac{-1}{-1} \cdot \frac{7}{3}\left[\frac{5(1-V)}{a} - b\right] = \frac{7}{-3}\left[\frac{-5(1-V)}{a} + b\right]$

$c = -\frac{7}{3}\left[\frac{5(V-1)}{a} + b\right]$

(7.3). Make v subject of the formula $S = \sqrt{\frac{6}{v} - \frac{w}{2}}$

Solution

$$S = \sqrt{\frac{6}{v} - \frac{w}{2}}$$

Squaring both sides, we have,

$$S^2 = \frac{6}{v} - \frac{w}{2} \rightarrow S^2 + \frac{w}{2} = \frac{6}{v} \rightarrow v\left(S^2 + \frac{w}{2}\right) = 6 \rightarrow \frac{v(2S^2 + w)}{2} = 6$$

$$v(2S^2 + w) = 12 \rightarrow v = \frac{12}{2S^2 + w}$$

(7.4). Make y the subject of the formula in $z = x^2 + \frac{1}{y^3}$

Solution

$$z - x^2 = \frac{1}{y^3} \rightarrow y^3(z - x^2) = 1 \rightarrow y = \sqrt[3]{\frac{1}{z-x^2}} = \frac{1}{(z-x^2)^{1/3}}$$

(7.5). Make t the subject of the equation

$$\frac{av}{1-v} = \sqrt[3]{\frac{2v+t}{a+2t}}$$

Solution

$$\left[\frac{av}{1-v}\right]^3 = \frac{2v+t}{a+2t} \rightarrow (2v+t)(1-v)^3 = (a+2t)(a^3v^3)$$

$$2v(1-v)^3 + t(1-v)^3 = a^4v^3 + 2ta^3v^3$$

$$2v(1-v)^3 - a^4v^3 = 2ta^3v^3 - t(1-v)^3$$

$$2v(1-v)^3 - a^4v^3 = t[2a^3v^3 - (1-v)^3] \rightarrow t = \frac{2v(1-v)^3 - a^4v^3}{2a^3v^3 - (1-v)^3}$$

(7.6). The solution of the quadratic equation $bx^2 + cx + a = 0$ is given by?

Solution

In this case. a = b, b = c, c = a

From $x = \frac{-b \pm \sqrt{b^2 - 4ac}}{2a}$

$$\therefore x = \frac{-c \pm \sqrt{c^2 - 4.b.a}}{2.b} = \frac{-c \pm \sqrt{c^2 - 4ab}}{2b}$$

(7.7). Make t the subject of formular $s = ut + \frac{1}{2}at^2$

Solution

$\frac{1}{2}at^2 + ut - s = 0$

Thus a = ½ a, b = u , c = s

From $x = \frac{-b \pm \sqrt{b^2 - 4ac}}{2a}$

$t = \frac{-u \pm \sqrt{u^2 - 4 \cdot \frac{1}{2}a \, x \, -s}}{2\frac{1}{2}a} \rightarrow \frac{-u \pm \sqrt{u^2 + 2as}}{a} \rightarrow t = \frac{1}{a}\left[-u \pm \sqrt{u^2 + 2as}\right]$

(7.8). Make x the subject of the relation in $\frac{1+ax}{1-ax} = \frac{p}{q}$

Solution

$q(1+ax) = p(1-ax) \rightarrow q + qax = p - pax \rightarrow qax + pax = p - q \rightarrow$
$x(aq + ap) = p - q \rightarrow x = \frac{p-q}{a(q+p)}$

(7.9). Express r in terms of p and q in $\frac{p}{\sqrt{2}} = \sqrt{\frac{r}{r+q}}$

Solution

$\frac{p^2}{2} = \frac{r}{r+q} \rightarrow 2r = p^2 r + p^2 q \rightarrow 2r - p^2 r = p^2 q \rightarrow r(2 - p^2) = p^2 q$

$\therefore r = \frac{p^2 q}{2 - p^2}$

(7.10). Given that $m = \frac{wd}{4}\left[l - \frac{d}{2}\right]$ make l the subject of the relation.

Solution

$4m = wd\left[l - \frac{d}{2}\right] \rightarrow \frac{4m}{wd} = l - \frac{d}{2} \rightarrow l = \frac{4m}{wd} + \frac{d}{2}$

CHAPTER 8 FACTORIZATION

This is the process of finding the factors of algebraic expression arising from expansion.

An instruction often attached to question on factorization is ''Factorize completely''.

It implies factorize "to the very last stage"

This process involves techniques under the following sub-topics.

(*i*) Factorization of difference of two squares

(*ii*) Factorization of trinomials

(*iii*) Factorization of sum of two cubes

(*iv*) Factorization of difference of two cubes

(*v*) Factorization of sum of two fourth powers

(*vi*) Factorizing expressions containing more than four terms

It is important to note that the items on the left hand side of all listed below are the identity of the various cases of factorization so little transformation to this standard notation may be required while those on the right hand side are the steps to the solution.

(*i*) Factorization of difference of two squares

The general identity of a difference of two squares is

$a^2 - b^2 = (a-b)(a+b)$

(*ii*) Factorization of sum of two cubes

$a^3 + b^3 = (a+b)(a^2 - ab + b^2)$

(*iii*) Factorization of difference of two cubes

$a^3 - b^3 = (a-b)(a^2 + ab + b^2)$

(*iv*) Factorization of difference of two fourth powers

$a^4 - b^4 = [a^2]^2 - [b^2]^2 = (a^2 - b^2)(a^2 + b^2)$

(v) Factorization of trinomials

A trinomial is a three term algebraic expression in the form of $ax^2 + bx + c = 0$

where a = first term, b = middle term and c = constant term.

Apply the following steps

(i) Multiply c with ax^2 to get acx^2

(ii) Find a pair of factors which when multiplied gives

acx^2 and which when added together gives the middle term bx

(iii) Replace the middle term with these two factors in the question given and factorize

(vi) Factorizing expressions containing more than four terms

Apply the following steps

(i) If the expression contains a term with a power of 2 then there is presence of a trinomial. Simply separate the trinomial from the monomial and binomial.

(ii) Factorize the trinomial separately

(iii) Combine the factorizations together

QUESTIONS

Factorize the following completely.

(8.1). $a^2 - 9$.

Solution

From $a^2 - b^2 = (a-b)(a+b)$

$a^2 - 3^2 = (a+3)(a-3)$

(8.2). $16x^2 - y^2$.

Solution

$(4x)^2 - (3y)^2 = (4x+3y)(4x-3y)$

(8.3). $k^2 - (m-n)^2$

Solution

$k^2 - (m-n)^2 \rightarrow [(k + (m-n)(k - (m-n)] \rightarrow (k + m - n)(k - m + n)$

(8.4). $16(m-n)^2 - 25(p-q)^2$

Solution

$4^2(m-n)^2 - 5^2(p-q)^2 \rightarrow [4(m-n)]^2 - [5(p-q)]^2$

$[4(m-n) + 5(p-q)][4(m-n) - 5(p-q)] \rightarrow$

$[4m - 4n + 5p - 5q][4m - 4n - 5p + 5q]$

(8.5). $\dfrac{4ay - 6by}{6ax - 9bx}$

Solution

$\dfrac{2y(2a - 3b)}{3x(2a - 3b)} = \dfrac{2y}{3x}$

(8.6). $7 - 63x^2$

Solution

$7(1 - 9x^2) \rightarrow 7(1^2 - (3x)^2) \rightarrow 7[(1 + 3x)(1 - 3x)]$

(8.7). $x^2 + ax + 4x + 3a + 3$

Solution

$(x^2 + 4x + 3) + (ax + 3a) \rightarrow x^2 + 3x + x + 3 + (ax + 3a)$

$x(x + 3) + 1(x + 3) + a(x + 3) \rightarrow (x + 3)[x + 1 + a]$

(8.8). $p^2 - 4p + 4 - q^2$

Solution

$p^2 - 2p - 2p + 4 - q^2 \rightarrow p(p - 2) - 2(p - 2) - q^2 \rightarrow (p - 2)^2 - q^2$

$(p - 2 + p)(p - 2 - q)$

(8.9). $x^2 + 7x + xy + 12 + 4y$

Solution

$7x + 12 + xy + 4y \rightarrow x^2 + 3x + 4x + 12 + xy + 4y \rightarrow$

$x(x + 3) + 4(x + 3) + y(x + 4) \rightarrow (x + 4)(x + 3) + y(x + 4)$

$(x + 4)[x + 3 + y]$

(8.10). $a^2 + 2a + 1 - ax - x$

Solution

$a^2 + a + a + 1 - x(a + 1) \rightarrow a(a + 1) + 1(a + 1) - x(a + 1)$

$(a + 1)[a + 1 - x)]$

(8.11). $x^2 - 5x + 6$

Solution

$x^2 \times 6 = 6x^2$, -3x and -2x are the factors

$x^2 - 3x - 2x + 6 \rightarrow x(x - 3) - 2(x - 3) \rightarrow (x - 2)(x - 3)$

(8.12). $x^2 - 8x - 20$

Solution

$x^2 \times 20 = -20x^2$, -10x and +2x are the factors

$x^2 - -10x + 2x + 6 \rightarrow x(x - 10) + 2(x - 10) \rightarrow (x + 2)(x - 10)$

(8.13). Simplify $\dfrac{x - y}{x^{1/3} - y^{1/3}}$

Solution

$\dfrac{x - y}{x^{1/3} - y^{1/3}} = \dfrac{[x^{1/3}]^3 - [y^{1/3}]^3}{x^{1/3} - y^{1/3}} \rightarrow \dfrac{(x^{1/3} - y^{1/3})(x^{2/3} + x^{1/3} y^{1/3} + y^{2/3})}{x^{1/3} - y^{1/3}}$

$(x^{2/3} + x^{1/3} y^{1/3} + y^{2/3})$

(8.14). Factorize $64h^3 + 27$

Solution

$64h^3 + 27 = (4h)^3 + 3^3 \rightarrow (4h + 3)[(4h)^2 - 4h \cdot (3) + 3^2] = (4h + 3)(16h^2 - 12h + 9)$

CHAPTER 9 LINEAR EQUATION

This an equation in which the highest power of the variable is one (1). An example of such an equation is the equation of a straight line. y = mx + c

The question should be interpreted carefully for correct evaluation.

QUESTIONS

(9.1). A mother is 3 times as old as her daughter in 12 yrs time; she will be twice as old. How old is the mother now.

Solution

Let the daughters age now be x yrs

Mother age now = $3x$ years

In 12 years time

Daughter age will be $(x + 12)$ yrs

Mothers age will be = $(3x + 12)$

Since mother's age = 2 x daughter's age → $(3x + 12) = 2(x + 12)$

3x + 12 = 2x + 24 → x = 12

∴ mother's age = 3x = 3 x 12 = 36yrs

(9.2). The sum of four consecutive numbers is 90. Find the numbers

Solution

For four consecutive numbers → $x + x + 1 + x + 2 + x + 3 = 90$

4x = 90 – 6 = 84 ∴ $x = 21$

∴ *The numbers are* 21, 22, 23, 24

(9.3). Divide 104 into two parts, so that one part is $\frac{3}{5}$ of the other part

Solution

Let the larger number be x

Let the smaller number be $\frac{3x}{5}$

$\frac{3x}{5} + \frac{x}{1} = 104 \rightarrow \frac{3x+5x}{5} = 104 \rightarrow \frac{8x}{5} = 104 \rightarrow 8x = 520 \therefore x = 65$

The other part is $\frac{3x}{5} = \frac{3 \times 65}{5} = 39$

Check: 39 + 65 = 104

(9.4). Add the same number to the numerator and denominator of $\frac{3}{18}$. If the resulting fraction is $\frac{1}{2}$. The number added is?

Solution

Let the number added by x, then

$\frac{3+x}{18+x} = \frac{1}{2} \rightarrow 2(3+x) = 18 + x \rightarrow 6 + 2x = 18 + x \rightarrow 2x - x = 18 - 6 = 12$

(9.5). A man and wife went to buy an article costing $400. The woman did 10% of the cost and the man 40% of the remainder. How much did they have altogether?

Solution

Cost of an article = $400

Amount with the woman = 10% of the cost = $\frac{10}{100} \times 400 = \$40$

Amount remaining = $400 - $40 = $360

Amount with the man = 40% of the remainder $\rightarrow \frac{40}{100} \times 360 = \$144$

Amount with both of them = $40 + $14 = $ 184

(9.6). A man spent $\frac{1}{10}$ of his monthly salary on rent and $\frac{2}{3}$ of the remainder on household needs. If $135.00 is left, how much is his monthly salary?

Solution

Let the man's salary be x

$\frac{1}{10}$ of the salary on rent = $\frac{1}{10} x$

Remainder = $\frac{10}{10}x - \frac{1}{10}x = \frac{9x}{10}$

$\frac{2}{3}$ of the remainder on household needs $= \frac{2}{3} \times \left(\frac{9x}{10}\right) = \frac{6x}{10}$

$x - \left(\frac{6x}{10} + \frac{x}{10}\right)$

$\frac{1}{3}$ of the remainder is left $= \frac{1}{3}\left(\frac{9x}{10}\right) = \frac{3x}{10}$

i.e $\frac{3x}{10} = 135$, $x = \frac{1350}{3} = \$450$

the monthly salary is $450

(9.7). Three boys shared some oranges. The first received $\frac{1}{3}$ of the oranges. The second received $\frac{2}{3}$ of the remainder. If the third boy received the remainder 12 oranges. How many oranges did they share?

Solution

Let the total oranges be T

the 1st received $\frac{1}{3}T$

remainder $\rightarrow$ T $- \frac{1}{3}$T $= \frac{2}{3}$T

The 2nd received $\frac{2}{3}$ of the remainder $\rightarrow \frac{2}{3} \times \left(\frac{2}{3}T\right) = \frac{4}{9}T$

The 3rd received $\frac{1}{3}$ of the remainder $\rightarrow \frac{1}{3} \times \left(\frac{2}{3}T\right) = \frac{2T}{9} = 1 - \left(\frac{1}{3} + \frac{4}{9}\right) = 1 - \frac{7}{9}$

$\left(\frac{2}{9}T\right) = 12$, $\therefore$ T $= \frac{12 \times 9}{2} = 54$

(9.8). Three children shared a basket of mangoes in such a way that the first child took ¼ and the second ¾ of the remainder. What fraction of the mangoes did the third take?

Solution

Let the total number of mangoes to be shared be T

1st = ¼ T

Remainder $\rightarrow$ T $- \frac{1}{4}$T $= \frac{3}{4}$T

$2^{nd} \rightarrow \frac{3}{4}$ of the remainder $= \frac{3}{4}\left(\frac{3T}{4}\right) = \frac{9T}{16}$

3rd will take ¼ of the remainder $= \frac{1}{4}\left(\frac{3T}{4}\right) = \frac{3T}{16}$

(9.9). John gives one third of his money to Janet who had $105.00. He then finds that his money is reduced to one-fourth of what Janet now has. Find how much money john had at first.

Solution

Let John's money be x

When John gives $\frac{1}{3}x$ of his money to janet, this is $\frac{1}{3}x$ he is left with $\frac{2x}{3}$

Janet now have $\left(\frac{1}{3}x + \$105\right)$

$\frac{2x}{3} = \frac{1}{4}\left(\frac{1}{3}x + \$105\right) \rightarrow \frac{2x}{3} = \frac{1}{12}x + 26.25 \rightarrow \frac{2x}{3} - \frac{1x}{12} = 26.25$

$\frac{8x - x}{12} = 26.25 \rightarrow \frac{7x}{12} = 26.25 \rightarrow x = \frac{12 \times 26.25}{7} = \$45$

CHAPTER 10 SIMULTANEOUS EQUATION

This is a system of equations in two or more unknown variables.

The following methods can be used to solve simultaneous equation, if the examiner does not specify the method to be used

1. Matrix method, 2. Substitution method, 3. Elimination method, 4. Graphical method

Graphical solution: This is done by sketching the graphs of the equations given and determining the co-ordinates of the point of intersection.

Solve: $x + 2y = 4$, $x - 3y = 8$ graphically.

Solution

For the first equation

$x + 2y = 4$. when $x = 0 \to 2y = 4 \to y = 2$. when $y = 0 \to x = 4$

For the second equation

$x - 3y = 8$. when $x = 0 \to -3y = 8 \to y = -8/3$. When $y = 0 \to x = 8$

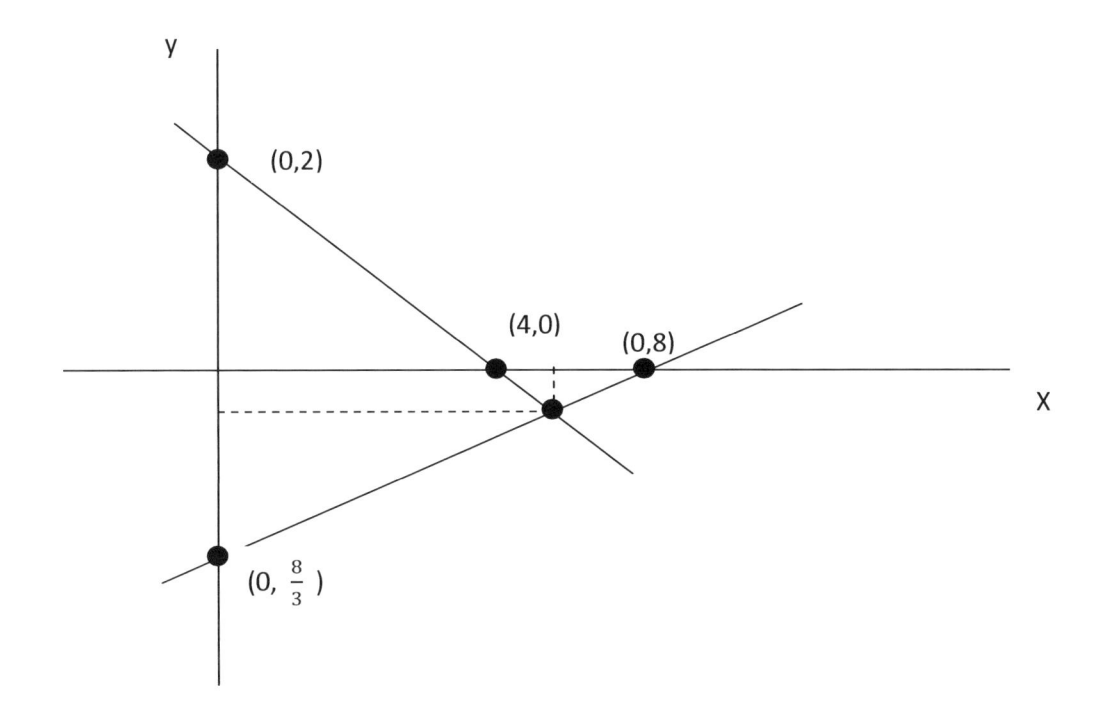

Substitution method

Here we make one of the unknown variable subject of the formula and substitute in the second equation.

Solve the given pair of equations using substitution method

(i) $x + 2y = 5$, $x + 3y = 8$

$x + 2y = 5$ ……….(i)

$x + 3y = 8$……….. (ii)

From (ii)

$x = 8 - 3y$ insert into equation (i)

8 - 3y + 2y = 5 → $-y = 5 - 8 = -3$ → $y = 3$

insert into (i)

$x + 2y = 5$ → $x + 2(3) = 5$ → $x + 6 = 5$ → x = -1

$\therefore x = -1$, $y = 3$

(ii) Solve $2x + y = 7$, $3x - 2y = 3$

$2x + y = 7$ ………..(i)

$3x - 2y = 3$ ………..(ii)

From (i) $y = 7 - 2x$

put into equation (ii)

$3x - 2(7 - 2x) = 3$

3x - 14 + 4x = 3 → 7x = 3 + 14 → $x = {}^{17}/_7$

Put x into equation (i)

$2x + y = 7$ → $2\left[\frac{17}{7}\right] + y = 7$ → $\frac{34}{7} + y = 7$ → $y = 7 - \frac{34}{7}$ → $\frac{49-34}{7} = \frac{15}{7}$

$\therefore x = \frac{17}{7}$ $y = \frac{15}{7}$

Elimination method

This involves elimination of one of the variable in order to find the other.

(i) Make the co-efficient of the same variable in the two equation equal.

(ii) Add the two equation if the sign are different.

(iii) Subtract one equation from the other if the sign are the same.

Solve the given pair of equations using elimination method.

(i) $x + 2y = 5$, $x + 3y = 8$

$x + 2y = 5$ ....(i)

$x + 3y = 8$ ....(ii)

multiply equation (i) by 3 and (ii) by 2

$3x + 6y = 15$ ....(iii)

$2x + 6y = 16$ ....(iv)

Subtracting: x = -1

put x = 1 into equation 1

$-1 + 2y = 5$ → $2y = 5 + 1$ ∴ $y = 3$

(ii) Solve $2x + y = 7$, $3x - 2y = 3$

$2x + y = 7$ ....(i)

$3x - 2y = 3$ ....(ii)

Multiply equation (i) by 2 and (ii) by 1

$4x + 2y = 14$ ....(iii)

$3x - 2y = 3$ ....(iv)

Adding : $7x = 17$ ∴ $x = \frac{17}{7}$

Put value of x into (i)

$2\left[\frac{17}{7}\right] + y = 7$ → $\frac{34}{7} + y = 7$ → $y = 7 - \frac{34}{7}$ → $\frac{49 - 34}{7} = \frac{15}{7}$

$\therefore x = \frac{17}{7} \quad y = \frac{15}{7}$

Thus, irrespective of the method the same answer is gotten.

Now we consider the various cases in which simultaneous equation question can be given.

Case 1: When three expressions are equated

Solve: 4x - 3 = 3x + y = 2y + 5x - 12

Solution

Here we simply equate the first two and last two expressions to get what we need.

4x - 3 = 3x + y → 4x – 3x = y + 3

$x - y = 3$ ....(i)

2y + 5x - 12 = 3x + y → 2y – y + 5x – 3x = 12

$y + 2x = 12$ ....(ii)

$x - y = 3$ ....(i)

$\underline{2x + y = 12}$ ....(ii)

Adding: $3x = 15 \therefore x = 5$

Putting x = 5 into equation (i)

$5 - y = 3 \rightarrow -y = -2 \therefore y = 2$

Case 2: When fraction with letter numerator question is given

Solve: $\frac{x}{2} + \frac{y}{4} = \frac{1}{2}$, $\frac{x}{3} - \frac{4}{5} = \frac{1}{9}$

Solution

To solve clear fraction

$\frac{x}{2} + \frac{y}{4} = \frac{1}{2}$

$\frac{x}{3} - \frac{4}{5} = \frac{1}{9}$

2x + y = 2 ....(i)

15x – 9y = 5 ....(ii)

Multiply equation (i) by 9 and (ii) by 1

18x + 9y = 18 …………..(iii)

15x – 9y = 5 …………..(ii)

Adding: $33x = 23 \therefore x = \frac{23}{33}$

Putting x = $\frac{23}{33}$ into equation (i)

y = 2 – 2x → $y = 2 - 2\left[\frac{23}{33}\right]$ → $2 - \frac{46}{33} = \frac{66-46}{33} = \frac{20}{33}$

Case 3: When fraction with letter denominator question is given

Solve: $\frac{2}{x} - \frac{3}{y} = 2$, $\frac{4}{x} + \frac{3}{y} = 10$

Solution

Here we transform the question to our own taste.

$2(1/x) - 3(1/y) = 2$ ……………(i)

$4(1/x) + 3(1/y) = 10$ …………….(ii)

$6\left[\frac{1}{x}\right] = 12$ → $\frac{1}{x} = 2 \therefore x = \frac{1}{2}$

Put x = $1/2$ in equ (i)

$2\left[\frac{1}{\frac{1}{2}}\right] - 3\left[\frac{1}{y}\right] = 2 \rightarrow 4 - 3\left[\frac{1}{y}\right] = 2 \rightarrow -3\left[\frac{1}{y}\right] = -2$

$\therefore x = 1/2, \quad y = 3/2$

OR

Let $\frac{1}{x} = P$ and $\frac{1}{y} = Q$

$\therefore \frac{2}{x} - \frac{3}{y} = 2 \rightarrow 2\left(\frac{1}{x}\right) - 3\left(\frac{1}{y}\right) = 2 \rightarrow 2P - 3Q = 2 \dots\dots(i)$

$\frac{4}{x} + \frac{3}{y} = 10, \ 4\left(\frac{1}{x}\right) + 3\left(\frac{1}{y}\right) = 10 \rightarrow 4P + 3Q = 10 \dots\dots(ii)$

Adding: $6P = 12$ ∴ $x = \frac{1}{P} = \frac{1}{2}$

Substituting P in (i) → $2(2) - 3Q = 2$ → $4 - 3Q = 2$ → $3Q = 2$ → $Q = \frac{2}{3}$ ∴ $y = \frac{1}{Q} = \frac{3}{2}$

∴ $(x, y) = \left(\frac{1}{2}, \frac{3}{2}\right)$

Case 4: **If the unknown variables are raised to power of negative unity**

Solve: $2m^{-1} - 3n^{-1} = 4$, $4m^{-1} - n^{-1} = 1$

Solution

Ignore all negative power and re-state when you get the answer.

$2m - 3n = 4$

$4m - n = 1$

Multiply equation (ii) by 3

$2m - 3n = 4$

$12m - 3n = 3$

Adding: $14m = 7$ → $m = \frac{1}{2}$ → $m^{-1} = 2$

Put $m = \frac{1}{2}$ into (i)

$2\left[\frac{1}{2}\right] - 3n = 4$ → $-3n = 4 - 1 = 3$ ∴ n = -1 → $n^{-1} = 1$

It is important to note that the question requires us to solve for m^{-1} and n^{-1} respectively not for m and n!

Case 5: **When the question is given in decimal**

Solve $0.5x - 0.3y = 1.65$, $0.7x + 0.2y = 0.14$

Solution

We simply shift the points

$5x - 3y = 16.5$…………(i)

$7x + 2y = 1.4$…………..(ii)

Multiply equation (i) by 2 and (ii) by 3

10x – 6y = 33 ………………..(iii)

21x + 6y = 4.2 ……………..(iv)

Adding: 31x = 37.2 → $x = 1.2$

Put x = 1.2 into equation (i)

7x + 2y = 1.4 → 7(1.2) + 2y = 1.4 → 8.4 + 2y = 1.4 → 2y = 1.4 – 8.4 → 2y = -7.0

y = $-7/2$

Case 6: When it is given in indicial form

Solve: $2^{x+y} = 32$, $3^{3y-x} = 27$

Solution

Here we solve by obeying rules of indices

$2^{x+y} = 2^5$ ………(i)

$3^{3y-x} = 3^3$ ………(ii)

x + y = 5   …………..(i)

- x + 3y = 3 …………..(ii)

4y = 8 → y = 2

Put y = 2 in equation (i)

x + y = 5 → x = 5 – 2

∴ x = 3, y = 2

Case 7: When it is given in form of Logarithm

$\log_x 27 + \log_y 4 = 5$, $\log_x 27 - \log_y 4 = 1$

Solution

Here we solve by obeying rules of logarithm

$\log_x 27 + \log_y 4 = 5$ …………(i)

$\log_x 27 - \log_y 4 = 1$……………..(ii)

Adding: $2\log_x 27 = 6 \to \log_x 27 = 3 \to \log_x 3^3 = 3 \to 3^x = 3^3 \therefore x = 3$

Put x = 3 into equation (i)

$\log_3 27 + \log_y 4 = 5 \to \log_3 3^3 + \log_y 4 = 5$

$3 + \log_y 4 = 5 \to \log_y 4 = 5 - 3 \to \log_y 2^2 = 2 \to 2^2 = 2^y \therefore y = 2$

Case 8: When it is given in a diagram.

What is the length of the shaped diagonal also calculate its area.

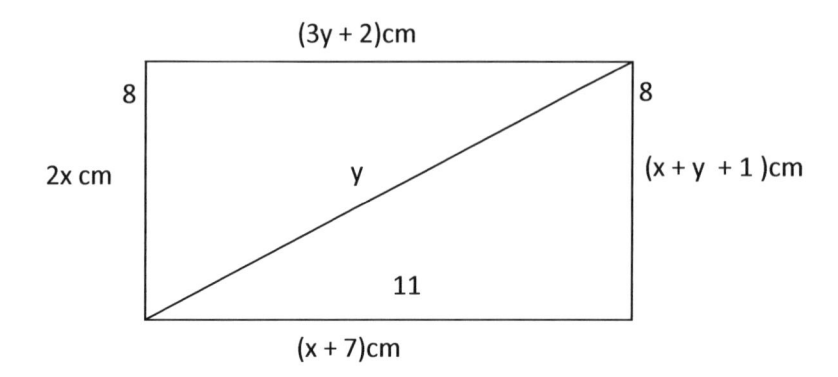

```
              (3y + 2)cm
        8 ┌─────────────┐ 8
          │           ╱ │
   2x cm  │         ╱   │  (x + y + 1 )cm
          │       y     │
          │     ╱       │
          │   ╱     11  │
          └─────────────┘
              (x + 7)cm
```

Solution

The characteristics of the diagram reveals the solution

$x + 7 = 3y + 2 \to x - 3y = 2 - 7 \to x - 3y = -5$ ………..(i)

$2x = x + y + 1 \to x - y = 1$ ………..(ii)

$x - 3y = -5$

$\underline{x - y = 1}$

$-2y = -6 \therefore y = 3$

Put y = 3 into (ii)

$x - y = 1 \to x = 1 + y \to x = 1 + 3 = 4$

By Pythagoras theorem

$y^2 = 8^2 + 11^2 \to 64 + 121 = 185 \to y = \sqrt{185} = 14\text{cm}$

Area = L x B = 8 x 11 = 88cm^2

Case 8. When quadratic equation is given

Solve : $x^2 + y^2 = 13$, $\quad 3x^2 - 2y^2 = -6$

Solution

Here do not treat it as one linear one quadratic.

$x^2 + y^2 = 13$ …………..(i)

$3x^2 - 2y^2 = -6$ …………..(ii)

Multiply (i) by 2 and (ii) by 1

$2x^2 + 2y^2 = 26$ …………(iii)

$3x^2 - 2y^2 = -6$ …………(iv)

Adding: $5x^2 = 20 \rightarrow x^2 = 4 \rightarrow x = \sqrt{4} \therefore x =$

Put $x = 2$ into equation (i)

$x^2 + y^2 = 13 \rightarrow 2^2 + y^2 = 13 \rightarrow y^2 = 13 - 4 = 9 \rightarrow y = \sqrt{9} \therefore y = 3$

Case 9: When it is given in form of word problem.

Word problem leading to simultaneous equation

In this situation, two letters are used to represent the variables. Interpret the question as given by the examiner

(**10. 1**). The cost of 12kg of apples and 24kg of oranges is #43,200. The cost of 24kg of apple and 12kg of oranges is #3600. Find the unit cost of apple and orange.

Solution

Let the unit cost of apple be a

Let the unit cost of orange be g

$12a + 24g = 43200$ ………….(i)

$24a + 12g = 3600$ ……………(ii)

Multiply equation (i) by 2 and (ii) by 1

24a + 48g = 86400 ....(iii)

24a + 12g = 3600 ....(iv)

Subtracting: 36g = 50400 → g = 1400

Put g into (i)

$12a + 24 \times 1400 = 43200$ → $12a + 33600 = 43200$ → $12a = 9600$ ∴ a = 800

∴ Unit cost of orange = #1400, unit cost of apple = #800

(10.2). A number is made up of two digits; the sum of the numbers is 11. If the digits are interchanged the original number is greater by 9. Find the original number.

Solution

Let the digits of the original number be x and y. Interpreting carefully we have.

$x + y = 11$ ....(i)

$xy = yx + 9$ ....(ii)

∴ $xy - yx = 9$ → $(10x + y) - (10y + x) = 9$ → $10x + y - 10y - x = 9$ → $9x - 9y = 9$

$x - y = 1$ ....(iii)

Solving (i) and (iii)

$x + y = 11$

$x - y = 1$

Adding: $2x = 12$ ∴ $x = 6$

From $x + y = 11$ → $6 + y = 11$ ∴ $y = 5$

∴ The no is 56

(10.3). 7 liters of petrol and 4 liters of diesel cost $255 altogether. One liter of petrol cost $5 more than a liter of diesel. Find the cost of 1500cm^3 of petrol and 2500cm^2.

Solution

7P + 4d = 255.........(i)

P − d = 5 ....(ii)

multiplying equation (i) by 1 and (ii) by 4

7P + 4d = 255 ....(iii)

4P − 4d = 20 ....(iv)

Adding: $11P = 275$ → $P = 25$

Put P = 25 into (iv)

4(25) - 4d = 20 → 100 - 20 = 4d → $80 = 4d$ ∴ $d = 20$

Since 1 litre = 1dm³ = 1000cm³

1500cm³ of Petrol $= \frac{1500 \times 25}{1000}$ = $50

2500cm³ of diesel $= \frac{2500 \times 20}{1000}$ = $50

(10. 4). Find a two digit number such that 2 times the ten digit is three less than thrice the unit digit and four times the number is 99 greater than the number obtained by reversing the digits.

Solution

Let the ten digit be = x , Let the unit digit be = y

2x = 3y – 3

2x – 3y = - 3 ....(i)

Also

4xy = yx + 99

$4(10x + y) = (10y + x) + 99$ → 40x + 4y - x – 10y = 99 → $39x - 6y = 99$ ....(ii)

Multiply (i) by 2 and (ii) by 3

4x – 6y = - 6 ....(iii)

39x - 6y = 99 ....(iv)

Subtracting: $-35x = -105$ ∴ $x = 3$

Put x = 3 into (iii)

$4(3) - 6y = -6$ → 12 – 6y = - 6 → 12 + 6 = 6y → 1 8 = 6 y ∴ $y = 3$
∴ *The number is* 10(x) + y → 10(3) + 3 = 33

(10.5). Evaluate

ax + by = c

dx + ey = f

multiply (i) by e and (ii) by b

aex + bey = ce
bdx + bey = bf
aex − bdx = ce − bf
x[ae − bd] = ce − bf

$$x = \frac{ce - bf}{ae - bd}$$

putting x into (b)

$$a\left[\frac{ce - bf}{ae - bd}\right] + by = c$$

$$\frac{ace - abf}{ae - bd} + by = c \rightarrow by = c - \frac{ace - abf}{ae - bd} \rightarrow by = \frac{c[ae - bd] - [ace - abf]}{ae - bd}$$

$$by = \frac{[ae^2 - bcd] - [ace - abf]}{ae - bd} \rightarrow \frac{ac^2 - bcd - ace + abf}{ae - bd} \rightarrow \frac{ac(c - e) + b(af - cd)}{e(a - d)}$$

$$\therefore y = \frac{ac(c - e) + b(af - cd)}{be(a - d)}$$

(10.6). Find a two digit number such that three times the tens digits is 2 less than twice the units digit, and twice the units digit, and twice the number is 20 greater than the number obtained by reversing the digits.

Solution

Let the digits of the original number be x and y. Interpreting carefully we have

Three times the tens digits = 3x

Twice the units digit = 2y

As three times the tens digits is less → 2y − 3x = 2 ………..(i)

Original number = xy → x(10) + y(1) = 10x + y

Twice the number = 2xy → 2(10x + y) → 20x + 2y

Reversing the digit, the number = $y(10) + x(1)$ → $10y + x$

As twice the number is greater

$(20x + 2y) - (10y + x) = 20$ → $20x + 2y - 10y - x = 20$ → $19x - 8y = 20$ (ii)

Combining (i) and (ii) we have;

$2y - 3x = 2$ ………..(i)

$-8y + 19x = 20$ ……….(ii)

on multiplying (i) and (ii) by 8 and 2 respectively

$16y - 24x = 16$

$\underline{-16y + 38x = 40}$

Adding: $14x = 56$ → $x = 4$

Put x in (i): $2y - 3(4) = 2$ → $2y - 12 = 2$ → $2y = 14$ ∴ $y = 7$

$(x,y) = (4,7)$. The number is 47

CHAPTER 11 QUADRATIC EQUATIONS

This is an equation in which the highest power of the variable is two (2).

The general identity of a quadratic equation is $ax^2 + bx + c$ where

c = constant term, b = middle term, a = first term

Methods of solution

1. **Factorization**: This has been treated under factorization of trinomials.

2. **Completing the square:** This means completing the square for an incomplete algebraic expression having a variable with highest power of 2

How to complete the square

1. Identify the co-efficient of the letter not squared

2. Divide the co-efficient of the letter not squared by 2

3. Squared the result and add to the original question

At this point two questions can be asked

(i) What must be added to make a perfect square: The answer to this question is the step 3

(ii) Complete the square: Factorize the answer of the last step i.e step (i) above

3. **Formula method**: Every quadratic equation is solvable by using the quadratic formula given by.

$$x = \frac{-b \pm \sqrt{b^2 - 4ac}}{2a}$$

It is important to chose the values of a, b and c carefully.

4. **Graphical Method**: This is done by sketching the graph of the function on x-y plane and identifying the points where the curve produced cuts the x- axis e.g.

x = -a or b

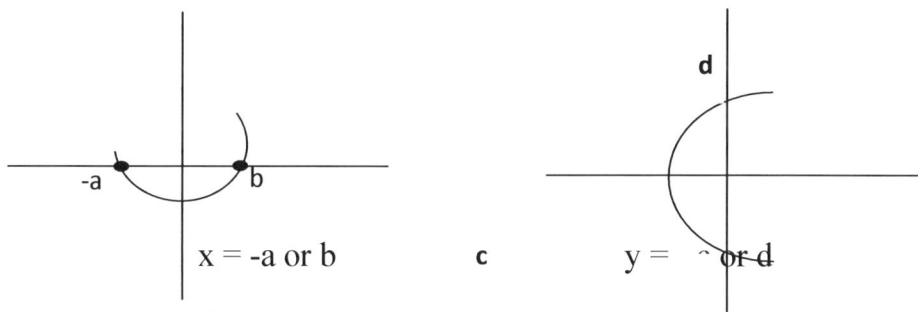

y = c or d

Nature of quadratic roots

The type of root formed by a quadratic equation depends on the value of the discriminant

D = $b^2 - 4ac$

Quadratic roots can be real, equal or imaginary

Real roots

For real roots $b^2 > 4ac$ and positive. The curve also cuts the x-axis at only one point.

Equal roots

It holds when adding a number to make a perfect or complete square.

For equal roots $b^2 - 4ac = 0$. The curve also cuts the x-axis.

Imaginary or complex roots

For imaginary roots $b^2 < 4ac$

The curve does not cut the x-axis.

Sum and product of roots

Given $ax^2 + bx + c = 0$, $x = \dfrac{-b \pm \sqrt{b^2 - 4ac}}{2a}$

i.e $x = \dfrac{-b + \sqrt{b^2 - 4ac}}{2a}$ or $x = \dfrac{-b - \sqrt{b^2 - 4ac}}{2a}$

sum of roots = $\dfrac{(-b + \sqrt{b^2 - 4ac}) + (-b - \sqrt{b^2 - 4ac})}{2a}$ → $\dfrac{(-b + \sqrt{b^2 - 4ac}) - b - \sqrt{b^2 - 4ac}}{2a}$

$-\dfrac{2b}{2a} = -\dfrac{b}{a}$

Product of roots = $\dfrac{(-b + \sqrt{b^2 - 4ac})}{2a} \cdot \dfrac{(-b - \sqrt{b^2 - 4ac})}{2a} = \dfrac{b^2 + b\sqrt{b^2 - 4ac} - b\sqrt{b^2 - 4ac} - (\sqrt{b^2 - 4ac})^2}{4a^2}$

$\dfrac{b^2 - (b^2 - 4ac)}{4a^2}$ → $\dfrac{b^2 - b^2 + 4ac}{4a^2}$ → $\dfrac{4ac}{4a^2}$ → $\dfrac{4 \cdot a \cdot c}{4 \cdot a \cdot a} = \dfrac{c}{a}$

How to form a quadratic equation when the roots are given

This can be done by using the expression below.

$x^2 - x(sum\ of\ root) + (product\ of\ roots)$

Word problem leading to quadratic equation

Here represent the variable with the smaller magnitude with a letter and interpret the question.

The following solved question illustrates how to interpret word problem leading to quadratic equation.

QUESTIONS

(11.1). The solution of the equation $x^2 - 2x = 8$ is ?

Solution

From $x^2 - 2x = 8 \rightarrow x^2 - 2x - 8 = 0 \rightarrow x^2 - 4x + 2x - 8 = 0 \rightarrow x(x-4) + 2(x-4) = 0$

$(x+2)(x-4) = 0 \rightarrow x+2 = 0$ or $x-4 = 0 \rightarrow x = -2$ or $x = 4$

(11.2). Find the roots of the equation $10x^2 - 13x - 3 = 0$.

Solution

$10x^2 - 15x + 2x - 3 = 0 \rightarrow 5x(2x-3) + 1(2x-3) = 0 \rightarrow (5x+1)(2x-3) = 0$

$5x + 1 = 0$ or $2x - 3 = 0 \rightarrow 5x = -1$ or $2x = 3$

$x = -1/5$ or $x = 3/2$

(11.3). Solve the equation $x^2 + 6x - 2 = 0$

Solution

By formula, $a = b, b = 6, c = -2$

$x = \dfrac{-b \pm \sqrt{b^2 - 4ac}}{2a} \rightarrow \dfrac{-6 \pm \sqrt{6^2 - 4 \times 3 \times -2}}{2 \times 3} \rightarrow \dfrac{6 \pm \sqrt{36 + 24}}{6} \rightarrow \dfrac{-6 \pm \sqrt{60}}{6} \rightarrow \dfrac{-6 \pm \sqrt{4 \times 15}}{6} \rightarrow$

$\dfrac{-6 \pm 2\sqrt{15}}{6} \rightarrow \dfrac{2(-3 \pm \sqrt{15})}{6} \rightarrow \dfrac{-3 \pm \sqrt{15}}{3} \rightarrow \dfrac{-3}{3} \pm \dfrac{\sqrt{15}}{3} = -1 \pm \dfrac{\sqrt{15}}{3}$

(11.4). The set of values x and y which satisfies the equation $x^2 - y - 1 = 0$ and $y - 2x + 2 = 0$ is?

Solution

From $y - 2x + 2 = 0 \rightarrow y = 2x - 2$

Substitute in $x^2 - y - 1 = 0 \rightarrow x^2 - (2x - 2) - 1 = 0 \rightarrow x^2 - 2x + 2 - 1 = 0$

$x^2 - 2x + 1 = 0 \rightarrow x^2 - x - x + 1 = 0 \rightarrow x(x - 1) - 1(x - 1) = 0 \rightarrow (x - 1)(x - 1) = 0$

$x - 1 = 0$ or $x - 1 = 0 \rightarrow x = 1$ or $x = 1 \rightarrow x = 1$ twice

from $y = 2x - 2 \rightarrow y = 2(1) - 2 = 2 - 2 = 0$

$\therefore (x, y) = (1, 0)$

(11.5). Solve the equation $y - 11\sqrt{y} + 24 = 0$

Solution

Let $\sqrt{y} = x$, $\therefore y = x^2$

$y - 11\sqrt{y} + 24 = 0$ becomes $x^2 - 11x + 24 = 0 \rightarrow (x - 8)(x - 3) = 0 \rightarrow x = 8$ or 3

As $y = x^2 \rightarrow y = 8^2$ or $3^2 = 64$ or 9

(11.6). Solve the equation $(\log_y x)^2 - 6\log_2 x + 9 = 0$

Solution

Let $\log_3 x = y$

$y^2 - 6y + 9 = 0 \rightarrow (y - 3)(y - 3) = 0 \rightarrow y - 3 = 0$ or $y - 3 = 0$

$y = 3$ or $y = 3$, $y = 3$ twice

From $\log_3 x = y \rightarrow \log_3 x = 3 \rightarrow x = 3^3 = 27$

(11.7). If $9^{(x - \frac{1}{2})} = 3^{x^2}$, find the value of x.

Solution

$3^{2(x - \frac{1}{2})} = 3^{x^2} \rightarrow 2x - 1 = x^2$ or $x^2 - 2x + 1 = 0 \rightarrow (x - 1)(x - 1) = 0$

x = 1 twice

(11.8). Find the value of x if $3^{x^2-1} = \frac{27}{3^{-3x}}$

Solution

$3^{x^2-1} = \frac{3^3}{3^{-3x}} \rightarrow 3^{x^2-1} = 3^{3+3x}$

$x^2 - 1 = 3 + 3x \rightarrow x^2 - 3x - 1 - 3 = 0 \rightarrow x^2 - 3x - 4 = 0$

$(x-4)(x+1) = 0 \rightarrow x - 4 = 0$ or $x + 1 = 0 \rightarrow x = 4$ or $x - 1$

(11.9). If $3^{2y} + 6(3^y) = 27$ find y.

Solution

$(3^y)^2 + 6(3^y) = 27$

If $A = 3^y$

$A^2 + 6A = 27 \rightarrow A^2 + 6A - 27 = 0 \rightarrow (A-3)(A+9) = 0 \therefore A = 3 \text{ or } -9$

$3^1 = 3^y$ and $-9 = 3^y$

$-9 = 3^y$ cannot be expressed

$\therefore y = 1$

(11.10). What are the values of y which satisfy the equation $9^y - 4 \times 3^y + 3 = 0$.

Solution

$(3^2)^y - 4 \times 3^y + 3 = 0$

If $A = 3^y \rightarrow A^2 - 4A + 3 = 0 \rightarrow (A-1)(A-3) = 0$

From $A = 3^y$, $1 = 3^y$ and $3 = 3^y$

$3^0 = 3^y$ and $3^1 = 3^y$

$\therefore y = 0 \text{ and } y = 1$

(11.11). Factorize; $6^{2x+1} + 7(6^x) - 5$

Solution

$6^{2x+1} = 6^{2x}.6^1 = (6^x)^2.6^1 = 6(6^x)^2$

$\therefore 6(6^x)^2 + 7(6^x) - 5$

Let 6^x be A $\to$ $6A^2 + 7A - 5$ $\to$ $(3A + 5)(2A - 1)$

Putting the value of A $\to$ $[3(6^x) + 5][2(6^x) - 1]$

(11.12). Solve for x if $25^x + 3(5^x) = 4$.

Solution

$(5^x)^2 + 3(5^x) = 4$

Let $y = 5^x$ $\to$ $y^2 + 3y = 4$ $\to$ $y^2 + 3y - 4 = 0$ $\to$ $(y-1)(y+4) = 0$ $\to$ y = 1 or y = -4

From $y = 5^x$ $\to$ $1 = 5^x$ or $-4 = 5^x$ $\to$ $5^0 = 5^x$ or $-4 = 5^x$

$-4 = 5^x$ cannot be expressed

$\therefore x = 0$

(11.13). The sum of two number is 8, their product is 15, find the two positive numbers.

Solution

Let the smaller number be x, bigger number = x – 8

Product of numbers = 15

$x(x - 8) = 15$ $\to$ $x^2 - 8x = 15$ $\to$ $x^2 - 5x - 3x + 15 = 0$ $\to$ $x(x - 5) - 3(x - 5) = 0$

$(x - 3)(x - 5) = 0$ $\to$ x = 3 or x = 5

The two positive number are 3 and 5

(11.14). The perimeter of a rectangular lawn is 32m while the area is $6cm^2$. Find the breadth of the lawn.

Solution

Perimeter = 2(L + B) → 2(L + B) = 32 → L + B = 16 → L = 16 – B

Since Area = L x B → (16 – B)B = 60 → 16B – B^2 = 60

-B^2 + 16B - 60 = 0 → B^2 - 16B + 60 = 0

factorizing B^2 – 10B – 6B – 60 = 0 → B(B – 10) -6 (B – 10) = 0

(B - 6) = 0 or (B -10) = 0 → B = 10 or B = 6

Breadth = 6m

(11. 15). The sum of ages of a mother and daughter is 44yrs , Three years ago, the product of their ages was 192. How old is the daughter now?

Solution

Let the ages of daughter be x , Mother's age = (44 – x)yrs

Three years ago

Daughter age was (x – 3) yrs

Mothers age was (44 – x – 3) yrs = (41 – x) yrs

Product of age = 192

(x – 3)(41 – x) = 192 → x^2 - 41x + 3x -123 =192 → x^2 - 41x + 3x -123 -192 = 0

x^2 - 44x – 315 = 0   factorizing

x^2 - 35x – 9x + 315 = 0 → x(x – 35) - 9(x – 35) = 0

(x - 35) (x – 9) → x = 35 or x = 9

Ages of daughter = 44 – 35 = 9

(11. 16). A trade spent $550 on certain article each costing $2x – 28. Find the no of articles.

Solution

The unit cost of given in term of x , we assume that the no of article is x

Unit con of article = $\frac{550}{x}$

$\frac{1 \text{ article}}{x \text{ article}} = \frac{2x-28}{550}$ → x(2x – 28) = 550 x 1 → $2x^2 – 28x = 550$

$2x^2 – 28x - 550 = 0$

Divided by 2 → $x^2 - 14x - 275 = 0$

Factorizing $x^2 – 25x + 11x \_ 275 = 0$ → x(x – 25) + 11(x -25) = 0

(x - 25) = 0 or (x + 11) = 0

∴ x = 25   x = - 11

number of article are 25

(11. 17). James walked advance of 10km at an average speed of xkm/h John walks the same distance at (x – 1) km/h. If the difference in their time is 30min. fine the value of x.

Solution

T = $\frac{Distance}{speed}$

Time used by James = $\frac{10}{x}$, Time used by John = $\frac{10}{x-1}$

Difference in time = 30 min/hr = $\frac{30}{60}$ = ½

$\frac{10}{x} - \frac{10}{x-1} = \frac{1}{2}$

lcm = 2x(x – 1)

10(2x) - 20 (x - 1) = 1 (x) (x - 1)

20x – 20x + 20 = x(x – 1) → 20 = $x^2 – x$ → x^2 - x – 20 = 0 → x (x + 4) -5 (x -4) = 0

(x – 4)(x – 5) → x + 4 = 0 or   x – 5 = 0 → x = - 4   or x = 5

(11. 18). A two digit number is such that its ten digit is greater than its unit digit by 4. The two digit number is less than four times the product of the digits by 11. Find the number.

Solution

The general identity of any two digit number is *xy* where x represent the tenth digit and y represent the unit digit

Mathematically

$xy = 10x + y$, and y = y

Interpreting carefully we have $x = y + 4$ and $xy = 4xy - 11$

From $xy = 4xy - 11 \to 10x + y = 4xy - 11 \to 10(y+4) + y = 4(y+4)y - 11$

$10y + 40 + y = 4y^2 + 16y - 11 \to 4y^2 + 5y - 51y = 0$

$4y^2 + 17y - 12y - 51 = 0 \to (4y + 17)$ or $(y - 3) = 0$

$\therefore y = 3$, $x = y + 4 = 7$. $\therefore xy = 73$

(11.19). A student bought some mangoes for #21.60 if she had paid 24k less for each mango, she could have brought three more mangoes. How many mangoes did she buy?

Solution

$100k = \#1 \therefore \#21.60 = 2160k$

Old number of mangoes = x

Old price $= \frac{2160}{x}$

New number of mangoes = x + 3

New price of mangoes $= \frac{2160}{x} - 24$

New price $= \frac{2160}{x+3}$

$\frac{2160}{x} - 24 = \frac{2160}{x+3} \to \frac{2160}{x} - \frac{2160}{x+3} = 24$

$2160(x+3) - 2160(x) = 24(x)(x+3) \to 2160x + 6480 - 2160x = 24x^2 + 72x$

$6480 = 24x^2 + 72x \to 24x^2 + 72x = 6480 \to x^2 + 3x - 270 = 0$

$(x + 18)(x - 15) = 0 \to x + 18 = 0$ or $x - 15 = 0$

x = -18 or x = 15

No of mangoes bought = 15

(11.20). The ages of Tosan and Isa differs by 6 and the product of their ages is 187, write their ages in the form (x, y) where x > y.

Solution

Let Tosan's age be x and Isa's age be y

x – y = 6   (i) where x > y

xy = 187

From (i) → x = 6 + y

Put in (ii) → (6 + y)y = 187 → 6y + y² = 187 → y² + 6y – 187 = 0

$(y - 11)(y + 17) = 0$ → $y - 11 = 0 \; or \; y + 17 = 0$

y = 11 or y = -17

As ages cannot be negative, y = 11, x = 17
(x,y) = (17,11)

(11.21). Find the positive number n, such that thrice its square is equal to twelve times the number.

Solution

Thrice the square of the number = 3n²

Twelve times the number = 12n

∴ $3n^2 = 12n$ → n = 4

(11.22). If the price of oranges was raised by 1/2k per oranges the number of oranges a customer can buy for ₦2.40 will be less by 16. What is the present price of oranges?

Solution

Let the initial price per orange be P

number of oranges bought be n

Thus total cost or price = pn = ₦2.40 = 240k ………(i)

When the price per orange becomes P + ½
n becomes (n – 16)

Total cost becomes (P + ½)(n – 16) = 240 ……(ii)

From (i) $n = \left(\frac{240}{p}\right)$

Putting into (ii)

pn – 16p + ½ n – 8 = 240

$240 - 16p + \frac{1}{2}\left(\frac{240}{p}\right) - 8 = 240$

-16p² + 120 – 8p = 0 → 16p² + 8p - 120 = 0 → 2p² + p – 15 = 0

2p = -6 or 2p = 5 → $p = -3 \; or \; p = \frac{5}{2}$

(**11.23**). If the quadratic function $3x^2 - 7x + R$ is a perfect square, find R.

Solution

Comparing $3x^2 - 7x + R$ with $ax^2 + bx + c = 0$

a = 3, b = -7, c = R

for perfect square b² = 4ac → $c = \frac{b^2}{4a}$

$(-7)^2 = 4(3)(R) \rightarrow 49 = 12R \; \therefore \; R = \frac{49}{12}$

(**11.24**). What value of g will make the expression $4x^2 - 18xy + g$ a perfect square.

Solution

$4x^2 - 18xy + g \rightarrow 4x^2 - 18y(x) + g$

a = 4, b = -18y, c = g

for perfect square b² = 4ac → $c = \frac{b^2}{4a}$

$(-18y)^2 = 4(4)(g) \rightarrow 324y^2 = 16g \rightarrow g = \frac{324y^2}{16} = \frac{81y^2}{4}$

(**11.25**). Find the possible values of the constant m, for which the equation $x^2 - 4x + 1 = m(x - 4)$ has equal roots.

Solution

From $x^2 - 4x + 1 = m(x - 4) \rightarrow x^2 - 4x + 1 = mx - 4m \rightarrow x^2 - 4x - mx + 1 + 4m = 0$

$x^2 - (4 + m)x + (1 + 4m) = 0$

for equal roots b² = 4ac → $[-(4 + m)]^2 = 4(1)(1 + 4m)$

$(4 + m)^2 = 4(1 + 4m) \rightarrow 16 + 8m + m^2 = 4 + 16m \rightarrow m^2 - 8m + 12 = 0$

$(m - 6)(m - 2) = 0 \therefore m = 6 \text{ or } 2$

(11.26). Find the sum of roots of the equation

$\frac{1}{2}x^2 - 7x + 4 = 0$

Solution

From the equation, $a = \frac{1}{2}$, $b = -7$, $c = -4$

$\text{Sum} = -\frac{b}{a} = -\frac{7}{\frac{1}{2}} = 7(2) = 14$

(11.27). If α and β are the roots of the indicial equation $2^{2x-3} = 9(2^x) - 1$. Find $(\alpha + \beta)$.

Solution

$2^{2x+3} = 9(2^x) - 1 \rightarrow 2^{2x} \cdot 2^3 = 9(2^x) - 1 \rightarrow (2^x)^2(2^3) = 9(2^x) - 1$

$(2^x)^2 8 = 9(2^x) - 1$

Let $2^x = y \rightarrow y^2(8) = 9y - 1 \rightarrow 8y^2 - 9y + 1 = 0 \rightarrow (y - 1)(8y - 1) = 0$

$y = 1 \text{ or } y = \frac{1}{8}$

from $2^x = y$

$2^x = 1$ and $2^x = \frac{1}{8}$

$2^x = 2^0$ and $2^x = 2^{-3}$

$x = 0$ and $x = -3$

Sum of roots are $0 + 3 = -3$

(11.28). If α and β are the roots of the equation $3x^2 + 5x - 2 = 0$ find the value of $\frac{1}{\alpha} + \frac{1}{\beta}$.

Solution

$a = 3, b = 5, c = -2$

$$\alpha + \beta = -\frac{b}{a} = -\frac{5}{3}, \quad \alpha\beta = \frac{c}{a} = -\frac{2}{3}$$

$$\frac{1}{\alpha} + \frac{1}{\beta} = \frac{\alpha + \beta}{\alpha\beta} = \frac{\frac{5}{3}}{\frac{-2}{3}} = -\frac{5}{3} \times \frac{3}{-2} = \frac{5}{2}$$

(11.29). Find the quadratic equation in m whose roots are -3/4 and 4/3

Solution

m = -3/4 and m = 4/3 ∴ (m + ¾) and (m - 4/3)

(m + ¾)(m - 4/3) → (4m + 3)(3m − 4) = 0 → $12m^2 - 16m + 9m - 12 = 0$

$12m^2 - 7m - 12 = 0$

(11.30). If α and β are the roots of $4x^2 + 5x - 3 = 0$. Find the equation whose roots are $-\frac{3}{\alpha}$ and $-\frac{3}{\beta}$.

Solution

$4x^2 - 5x - 3 = 0$, a = 4, b = 5, c = -3

$$\alpha + \beta = -\frac{b}{a} \to -\frac{5}{4}, \quad \alpha\beta = \frac{c}{a} \to -\frac{3}{4}$$

For equation with roots, $-\frac{3}{\alpha}$ and $-\frac{3}{\beta}$

$x^2 - x(sum\ of\ root) + (product\ of\ roots)$

Sum $= -\frac{3}{\alpha} + -\frac{3}{\beta} \to \frac{-3\beta + (-3\alpha)}{\alpha\beta} \to \frac{-3(\beta + \alpha)}{\alpha\beta} = \frac{-3(-5/4)}{-3/4}$

Product $= -\frac{3}{\alpha} \cdot -\frac{3}{\beta} \to \frac{9}{\alpha\beta} \to \frac{9}{-3/4} \to 9 \times \frac{4}{-3} = -12$

using $x^2 - x(sum\ of\ root) + (product\ of\ roots) \to x^2 + 5x - 12 = 0$

(11.31). The sum of the root of a quadratic equation is 5/2 and the product of its root is 4. The quadratic equation is?

Solution

Sum = 5/2, product = 4

The equation is $x^2 - \frac{5x}{2} + 4 = 0 \rightarrow 2x^2 - 5x + 8 = 0$

(**11.32**). The quadratic equation whose roots are $1 - \sqrt{13}$ and $1 + \sqrt{13}$ is?

Solution

Sum of roots = $(1 - \sqrt{13}) + (1 + \sqrt{13}) = 2$

Product of roots = $(1 - \sqrt{13})(1x \sqrt{13}) \rightarrow 1^2 - (\sqrt{13})^2 \rightarrow 1 - 13 = -12$

$x^2 - 2x + -12 = 0$ or $x^2 - 2x - 12 = 0$

Chapter 12 VARIATION

This deals with the relationship that exists between two quantities or two more quantities.

Types of variation

(*i*) Direct variation (*ii*) Inverse variation (*iii*) Joint variation (*iv*) Partial variation

When solving questions on variation, the first thing to do is to determine the constant of proportionality.

Direct variation

This occurs when one variable increases and the other variable increases with equal proportion or means increase. An example is Charles law.

Inverse variation

This occurs when one variable is increasing and the other is decreasing. An example Boyle's law.

Joint variation

This exists if the relation involves two or more variables.

Partial variation

This refers to variation in two parts. One is partly constant and the other is not. Two constants must be introduced in the variation.

Questions

(12. 1). If the resistance to the motion of an object varies directly as the square of the speed. Write the law governing the relationship, resistance in Newton while speed in km/h given that a resistance is 600N when speed is 200km/h calculate (i) Speed when the resistance is 337.5N (ii) Resistance given that the speed is 32km/h.

Solution

Let resistance be R and speed be V

$R \alpha V^2 \rightarrow R = kV^2$

$600 = k \times 20^2 \rightarrow 600 = k \times 400 \rightarrow K = \frac{600}{400} = \frac{3}{2}$

$R = \frac{3v^2}{2}$ is the law governing them

when R = 337.5N

$R = \frac{3v^2}{2} \rightarrow \frac{337}{1} = \frac{3v^2}{2} \rightarrow 3V^2 = \frac{2 \times 337.5}{3}$

$V^2 = 225 \therefore V = \sqrt{225} = 15 \text{kmh}^{-1}$

When V = 32 → R = $\frac{3 \times 32^2}{2} = 3 \times 16 \times 32 = 1536N$

(12.2). P varies directly as the square of Q. If P = 3 when Q = 2, find q when P is 6.

Solution

p α q² → p = kq² ∴ 3 = k × 2² ∴ k = $\frac{3}{4}$

p = $\frac{3}{4}q^2$ Law governing them

To get q when P is 6 → 6 = $\frac{3}{4} \times q^2$ → $\frac{24}{3} \times q^2$ → q² = 8 → q = $\sqrt{2.8}$

(12.3). If M varies directly as cube of N and M = 3 while N = 2. Find M when N is 4.

Solution

M α N² → M = kN² → k = $\frac{m}{N^3}$ = $^3/_8$

∴ M = $^3/_8 \times 4^3$ = $^3/_8 \times 64$ = 24

(12.4). The electrical resistance of a wire varies inversely as the square of the radius. If the resistance is 0.24Ω (ohms) when the radius is 0.5. find the resistance when the radius is 0.04cm.

Solution

Let resistance be R and radius be r

R α $\frac{1}{r^2}$ → R = $\frac{k}{r^2}$

$0.24 = \frac{k}{0.5^2}$ → k = 0.24 × 0.25 ∴ k = 0.06

when r is 0.04, R = $\frac{k}{r^2}$ $\frac{0.06}{0.04 \times 0.04}$ = $\frac{6}{4 \times 0.04}$ = $\frac{600}{16}$ = 37.50Ω

(12.5). If A varies inversely as the forth root of b and A = 3 when B = 16 find B when A = 16.

Solution

$A \alpha \dfrac{1}{\sqrt[4]{B}} \rightarrow A = \dfrac{k}{\sqrt[4]{B}} \rightarrow k = A \times \sqrt[4]{B}$

when $A = 3$ and $B = 16 \rightarrow k = 3 \times \sqrt[4]{16} = 3 \times 2 = 6$

$A = \dfrac{6}{\sqrt[4]{B}}$ is the relationship between A and B.

When $A = 16$, $B = ? \rightarrow 16 = \dfrac{6}{\sqrt[4]{B}} \rightarrow \sqrt[4]{B} = \dfrac{6}{16} = \dfrac{3}{8} \rightarrow B = \left[\dfrac{3}{8}\right]^4 \rightarrow = {}^{81}/_{4096}$

(12.6). If n varies inversely as $\dfrac{kv}{k+v}$ and it is equal to 16 when $k = 4$, $v = 8$. Find the relationship between k, v, n.

Solution

$n \alpha \dfrac{1}{\frac{kv}{k+v}} \rightarrow n = C \times \dfrac{k+v}{kv}$ c = proportionality constant

$16 = C \times \dfrac{4+8}{4 \times 8} \rightarrow 16 = C \times \dfrac{12}{32} \rightarrow C = \dfrac{16 \times 32}{12}$

$n = \dfrac{128}{3} \dfrac{k+v}{kv}$ is the relationship between k, v and n

(12.7). If $v \alpha \sqrt{d}$ and $\sqrt{v} = 4$ when $d = 64$. Find d in term of its related letters.

Solution

$v \alpha \sqrt{d} \rightarrow v = k\sqrt{d}$

$\sqrt{v} = 4 \therefore v = 16, d = 64 \therefore \sqrt{d} = 8$

$16 = k \times 8 \rightarrow k = \dfrac{16}{8} = 2$

$V = 2\sqrt{d}$ is the relationship between them

finding d in term of related letters

$V = k\sqrt{d} \rightarrow \sqrt{d} = \dfrac{v}{k} \rightarrow d = \dfrac{v^2}{k^2} = \dfrac{v^2}{4}$

(12.8). If A varies inversely as the $\sqrt[3]{b}$ and $A = 1$ when $b = 64$. find b when $a = 6$

Solution

$A \alpha \dfrac{1}{\sqrt[3]{b}} \rightarrow A = \dfrac{k}{\sqrt[3]{B}} \rightarrow 1 = \dfrac{k}{\sqrt[3]{64}} \therefore k = 4$

$6 = \dfrac{4}{\sqrt[3]{B}} \rightarrow \sqrt[3]{B} = \dfrac{4}{6} \therefore B = \dfrac{64}{216} = \dfrac{8}{27}$

(12. 9). The number of telephone call N between two A and B varies directly as the population P_A, P_B in A and B respectively and inversely as the square of the distance between A and B. Give the equation representing this relation.

Solution

$N \alpha \frac{P_A P_B}{D^2} \rightarrow N = k \frac{P_A P_B}{D^2}$

(12. 10). What is the relationship between x and y if $x \alpha \sqrt{y}$ and $x = {}^9/_2$ when y = 9.

Solution

$x \alpha y \rightarrow x = k\sqrt{y} \rightarrow k = \frac{x}{\sqrt{y}} = \frac{{}^9/_2}{3} \rightarrow k = {}^9/_2 \cdot {}^1/_3 = {}^3/_2$

$x = {}^3/_2 \sqrt{y}$

(12. 11). V varies jointly as the square of x and inversely to y. If V = 18 when x = 3 and y = 4. Find V when x = 6 and y = 9.

Solution

$V \alpha x^2 \alpha \frac{1}{y} \rightarrow V = k\frac{x^2}{y} \rightarrow 18 = k\frac{9}{4} \quad \therefore k = 8$

Law governing them $V = 8\frac{x^2}{y}$

Finding V $\rightarrow V = 8 \times \frac{6^2}{9} = 32$

(12. 12). Suppose t varies inversely as S, S varies directly as the square of L and t = 1 when L = 3. Find t when $L = \frac{1}{3}$.

Solution

$t \alpha \frac{1}{s} \rightarrow t = \frac{k}{s}$ (k is of proportionality)

$s \alpha l^2 \rightarrow s = cl^2$ (c is constant of proportionality)

Combining $\therefore t = \frac{k}{cl^2} \rightarrow 1 = \frac{k}{c} \times \frac{1}{9} \rightarrow \frac{k}{c} = 9$

Law governing them $t = 9\frac{1}{l^2}$

When $L = \frac{1}{3} \rightarrow t = 9 \times \frac{1}{\left[\frac{1}{3}\right]^2} \quad \therefore t = 81$

(12.13). y varies inversely as cube of x and x varies directly as the square of z. Find the relationship between y and z if P is the constant of variation.

Solution

$y \: \alpha \: \frac{1}{x^3} \rightarrow y = \frac{k}{x^3}$ (k is constant of proportionality)

$x \: \alpha \: z^2 \rightarrow x = cz^2$ (c is constant of proportionality)

Combining $\therefore \: y = \frac{k}{[cz^2]^3} \rightarrow y = \frac{k}{c^3 z^6} \rightarrow y = p \: x \: \frac{1}{z^6}$

(12.14). If a is jointly proportional to the cube of b and the fifth power of c. In what ratio is a decreased or increased when b is increased by 200% and c is reduced by 50%.

Solution

For old a $\rightarrow \: a \: \alpha \: b^3 c^5 \rightarrow a = kb^3 c^5$ Old b = b, Old c = c

New b $\rightarrow \frac{300b}{100} = 3b$, New c $= \frac{50c}{100} = \frac{1}{2}c$

$\therefore$ New a $\rightarrow \: a = kb^3 c^5 \rightarrow k(3b)^3 \: (1/2)^5 \rightarrow k\frac{27 b^3 c^5}{32}$

Change in a is $\rightarrow \frac{new \: a}{old \: a} = k\frac{27 b^3 c^5}{32} \div kb^3 c^5 \rightarrow 27 : 32$

It is important to note that only the ratio was asked! If percentage increase/decrease was required then it would be

$\frac{27}{32} \: x \: 100 = 84\% \rightarrow 100 - 84 = 16\%$.

(12.15). Q is jointly proportional to the cube of x and fourth power of y. If x is halved and y is doubled, then the value of Q is?

Solution

$Q \: \alpha \: x^3 y^4 \rightarrow Q = kx^3 y^4$

When x is halved new x is $\left[\frac{1}{2} x\right]^3 = \frac{1}{8} x^3$, When y is doubled new y is $[2y]^4 = 16y^4$

Change in Q is $\rightarrow \frac{new \: Q}{old \: Q} \rightarrow \frac{k \frac{1}{8} x^3 \: x \: 16 y^4}{k x^3 y^4} = \frac{16}{8} = 2 : 1$

(12.16). X is proportional to y and y is inversely to z. If x is increased by 20% and y is decreased by 50%. What is the percentage decrease or increase?

Solution

$x \alpha y$, $y \alpha \frac{1}{z}$ → $x = k\frac{y}{z}$ .....(1)

When x is increased by 20%, new x is → $x = \frac{120}{100}x = 1.2x$

When y is decreased by 50%, new y is → $y = \frac{50}{100}y = 0.5y$

From (i) $z = k\frac{y}{x}$ → $k\frac{0.5y}{1.2x} = \frac{5}{12}\frac{ky}{x}$

%increase or decrease = $100 - \frac{new\ z}{old\ z} \times 100$ → $100 - \frac{\frac{5\ ky}{12\ x}}{\frac{ky}{x}} \times 100$ → $100 - 41.66 = 58.3\%$

(12.17). The cost of a conference party for a group of participant is partly constant and partly varies inversely as the number of participants. If the cost is 850 when there are 17 participants and 550 when there are 11 participants. Find the cost when there are 20 participants.

Solution

Let C represents cost of conference party

Let N represents number of participants

$C = a + b\frac{1}{N}$ (where a and b are constants)

$850 = a + b\frac{1}{17}$ → $14450 = 17a + b$ ....(i)

$550 = a + b\frac{1}{11}$ → $6050 = 11a + b$ ....(ii)

$17a + b = 14450$

$\underline{11a + b = 6050}$

6a = 8400 ∴ $a = 1400$

Putting a = 1400 in (i) → $14450 = 17 \times 1400 + b$ → $14450 - 23800 = b$ ∴ $b = -9350$

Cost of 20 participants $c = 1400 + (-93500)\frac{1}{20} = 932.5$

(12.18). A tennis club has a machine which serves ball to practicing players. The machine serves the ball at a speed which is constant and partly varies as the time of flight of the balls. When the ball has been travelling for $1/2$ seconds, its speed reaches 128km/hr. When it has been travelling for $1/6$ seconds, its speed is 46km/hr. Find the speed of the ball when it has been travelling for $1/3$ seconds.

Solution

Let s represents cost of conference party

Let t represents number of participants

$S = a + bt$ (where a and b are constants)

$128 = a + \frac{1}{2}b \rightarrow 256 = 2a + t$ ....(i)

$46 = a + \frac{1}{6}b \rightarrow 276 = 6a + b$ ....(ii)

Multiplying (i) by 3 and (ii) by 1

$6a + 3b = 768$

$\underline{6a + b = 276}$

$2b = 492 \therefore b = 246$

Putting b = 246 in (i) $\rightarrow 256 = 2a + 246 \rightarrow 260 - 246 = 2a \therefore a = 5$

Speed when it has been travelling for $1/3$ seconds

$S = 5 + \frac{246}{3} = 87 km/hr$

(12.19). The resistance to the motion of a vehicle is partly constant and partly varies as s^2. At 30km/hr the resistance is 496Newton and at 50km/hr the resistance is 656km/hr. Find the resistance at 60km/hr.

Solution

Let R represents resistance

$R = a + bS^2$

$496 = a + b(30)^2 \rightarrow 496 = a + 900b$ ....(i)

$656 = a + b(50)^2 \rightarrow 656 = a + 2500b$ ....(ii)

$160 = 1600b \therefore b = 0.1$

Put b = 0.1 into (ii) $\rightarrow 656 = a + 2500(0.1) \therefore a = 406$

Finding R when s = 60

$R = a + bS^2 \rightarrow R = 406 + 0.1 \times 3600 = 766 Newton$

(12.20). The time(t) taken to sink a swimming pool varies partly as the depth(d) and partly as the square of the depth where n and k are constants respectively. What is the depth in terms of other variables.

Solution

$t = dn + kd^2$ (where n and k are constants)

$kd^2 + dn - t = 0$ solving the quadratic equation

$d = \dfrac{-n \pm \sqrt{n^2 - 4k(-t)}}{2k} = \dfrac{-n \pm \sqrt{n^2 + 4kt}}{2k}$

(12.21). The time taken for a committee meeting is partly constant and partly varies as the square of number of men present. If there are 120 men the meeting last for 56mins but with 20men it takes exactly 2hrs. How long will it last if there are 16 men.

Solution

Let t represents time

Let N represents number of men

$t = a + bN^2$ (where a and b are constants)

56 = a + b (12)² → 56 = a + 144b ....(i)

120 = a + b (20)² → 120 = a + 400b ....(ii)

64 = 256b ∴ b = 0.25

Put b = 0.25 into (i) → 56 = a + 144(0.25) ∴ a = 20

Finding t when N = 60

$t = a + bN^2 \rightarrow t = 20 + 0.25 \times 16^2$ 84mins = 1.4hrs

CHAPTER 13 RATIO, PROPORTION AND PERCENTAGE

Ratio are used to compare quantities by division, thus the ratio of two quantities is the first divided by the second. They are expressed (i) using a colon, as in 3:4 (ii) using "to" as in 35 to 7.

Proportion: This is an equality of two ratios. Thus 2:5 = 4:10 is a proportion.

The forth term of a proportion is the fourth proportional to the other three taken in order. Thus in 2 : 3 = 4 : x. x is the fourth proportion to 2, 3, and 4.

The means of a proportion are its middle terms, that is, its second and third terms.

Thus in a : b = c : d, the means are b and c.

The extremes of a proportion are its outside terms, that is, its first and fourth terms.

Thus in a : b = c : d, the extremes are a and d.

If the two means of a proportion are the same, either mean is the mean proportional between the first and fourth terms. Thus in 9:3 = 3:1, 3 is the mean proportional between 9 and 1

Also note that If A: B = 4 : 8

The part in A is 4 out of the total which is (4 + 8) = 12

Thus, $A = \frac{4}{12}T$, $B = \frac{8}{12}T$, where T = Total

Proportion principles

1. In any proportion, the product of the means equals the product of the extremes

Thus if a : b = c : d → ad = bc

2. If the product of two numbers equals the product of two other numbers, either pair may be made the means of a proportion and the other pair may be made the extremes

Thus if $3x = 5y$ → $x: y = 5: 3 \; or \; y: x = 3: 5 \; or \; 3: y = 5: x \; or \; 5: x = 3: y$

Applications of ratio and proportion

Ratio and proportion find application in sharing of items:

Percentage: means the proportion of quantity as a fraction of hundred. Thus it is interpreted as the ratio of quantities multiplied by 100.

For example 2 can be expressed as a percentage of 5 simply by

Percentage = $\frac{2}{5} \times 100 = 40\%$

Applications of percentage

1. **Change in quantities**

Here we focus our attention on how to interpret statements on % increase or decrease

A sentence, increase by 15% is interpreted as $\frac{115x}{100}$

A sentence, decrease by 15% is interpreted as = $\frac{85x}{100}$

Where x = original quantity before increment or decrement

2. **% Decrease or Increase**

Since change in quantity (Increase or Decrease) is given by = $\frac{New}{Old} \times \frac{100}{1}$

% Decrease or Increase = 100 – (Increase or Decrease)

3. **In Mixtures**

Every question on mixtures is solvable by applying the approach below

Formula	x	y	Amount of y
Original			
Added			
New	Total		Total

4. **Profit and loss sales**

These are outcomes from business transactions.

Cost price: This is the amount a good is bought by a seller (CP)

Selling price: This is the amount a good is sold by a seller (SP) or the amount a good is bought by a customer.

Profit: This is made when a good is sold above its cost price.

Loss: is the shortage made when a good is sold below its cost price.

Profit percent: This is the ratio of profit to the cost price.

Loss percent: This is the ratio of loss to the cost price.

Mathematically the following holds,

Profit = SP – CP

Loss = CP – SP

Profit /gain % = $\frac{Profit}{CP}$ % = $\frac{SP-CP}{CP} \times \frac{100}{1}$

Loss % = $\frac{Loss}{CP}$ % = $\frac{CP-SP}{CP} \times \frac{100}{1}$

Sp = $\left(\frac{100 + profit}{100}\right) \times Cp$

Sp = $\left(\frac{100 - Loss}{100}\right) \times Cp$

The last two gives the relationship between CP and SP when profit and loss are given in percentage respectively.

5. Discount Sales

Discount: This is the preference reduction given to the cash sale of goods. It is always expressed as a percentage of the marked price.

Cash SP = Marked price - Discount (Marked Price) = $[1 - D]mp$

6. Commission: This is a form of payment to an agent for services rendered.

Mathematically,

Amount Earned (Total income) = Commission x Sales + Amount Paid (Salary)

7. Simple and Compound Interest

Simple Interest: Interest on a fixed principal which is paid at definite interval of time e.g. monthly, half yearly or yearly. Thus the principal and interest remains constant for equal intervals of time.

Interest, $I = P \times R\% \times T = \frac{p \times R \times T}{100} = \frac{PRT}{100}$

Amount at the end of an interval is given by

$A = P + I = P + PR\% + T = P(1 + R\% \, T)$

Compound interest: Is the interest on a constantly changing principal. The interest and principal change continuously as the interval of time change

$A = P(1 + R\%)^n$

Depreciation $A = P(1 - R\%)^T$

QUESTIONS

(13.1). At a selling price of $273 a refrigerator yield a 30% profit on the cost. What selling price will yield a 10% profit on the cost?

Solution

$Sp = \frac{(100 + profit)}{100} \times cp \rightarrow 273 = \frac{130}{100} cp \rightarrow cp = 210$

When profit = 10%

$sp = \frac{[100 + profit]}{100} \times cp \rightarrow \frac{110}{100} \times 210 = 111 \times 210 = \$231$

(13.2). A certain radio costs a merchant $72. At what price must the merchant sell this radio in order to make a profit of 20% of the selling price?

Solution

$Sp = x$, $Cp = 72$, Profit $= \frac{20}{100} \times Sp = \frac{20x}{100} = 0.2x$

Profit = Sp – Cp $\rightarrow$ 0.2x = Sp – 72 $\rightarrow$ 0.2x – x = -72 $\rightarrow$ -0.8x = - 7.2 $\therefore x = \frac{72}{0.8} = \$90$

(13.3). A store sells a watch for a profit 25 percent of the cost. What percent of the selling price is the profit?

Solution

Profit $= \frac{25}{100} \times Cp = 0.25cp$

From Profit = Sp – Cp → 0.25cp = Sp – cp → Sp = 0.025cp + cp = 1.25cp

What percent of SP = Profit implies

$\frac{x}{100} \times sp = profit$ → $\frac{x}{100} \times 1.25cp = 0.25cp$ → 1.25x = 25 ∴ x = $\frac{25}{1.25}$ = 20%

(13.4). Ray sold his suits for $160.00 and trousers $96.00. He made a profit of 20% on his trousers and took a 10% loss on his suits. He ended up with a ?

Solution

For the trousers

sp = $\frac{(100 + profit)}{100} cp$ → 96 = $\frac{(100 + 20)}{100} cp$ → Cp = $\frac{100 \times 96}{120}$ = $\frac{5 \times 96}{6}$ = 80

Profit = Sp – Cp → 96 – 80 = 16

For the suits

sp = $\frac{(100 - Loss)}{100} cp$ → 160 = $\frac{(100 - 10)}{100} cp$ → Cp = $\frac{100 \times 160}{90}$ = $\frac{100 \times 16}{9}$ = 177.7

Loss = cp – sp → 177.7 – 160 = 17.7

Trousers = $16 profit, suits = $17.7 Loss

∴ 17.7 – 16 = 1.78 loss

(13.5). A dealer sells a car for $1540 at a profit of 40%. Express his profit as a percentage of the selling price.

Solution

Sp = $\frac{(100 + profit)}{100} cp$ → 1540 = $\frac{(140)}{100} Cp$ → Cp = $\frac{1540 \times 100}{140}$ = $1100

Profit as % of Sp = $\frac{rofit \%}{Sp}$ → $\frac{(Sp - Cp)}{Sp} \times 100$ = $\frac{(1540 - 1100)}{1540} \times 100$ = $\frac{440}{1540} \times 100$

= $28\frac{4}{7}$

(13.6). A dealer buys 30 phones, all at the same price. He sells 20 of them at a profit of 16% and has to sell the remaining 10 at a loss of 40%. What is his percentage profit?

Solution

Cost Price of each x

Total CP = 30x

For those he made profit

CP of 20 of them = 20x

$Sp = \frac{(100 + 16)}{100} 20x = \frac{116 \times 20x}{100} = 23.2x$

For those he made loss

CP of 10 of them = 10x

$Sp = \frac{(100 - 4)}{100} \times 10x \rightarrow \frac{96 \times 10x}{100} = 9.6x$

$Total\ S.p = 23.2x + 9.6x = 32.8x$

$Total\ C.p = 30x$

$profit = SP - CP = 32.8x - 30 = 2.8x$

$profit\ \% = \frac{(sp - cp)}{cp} \times 100\% = \frac{2.8x}{30x} \times 100 = 9\frac{1}{3}\%$

(13.7). Dennis sold his house to Smith at a profit of 10%, smith sold it to Robinson at a gain of 5%, Robinson paid $1240 more for the house than Dennis paid. What did Dennis pay?

Solution

Let A = Dennis, B = Smith, C = Robinson

	A	B	C
Cp	x	$\frac{110x}{100}$	$\frac{105}{100} \times \frac{110x}{100}$
Sp	$\frac{110x}{100}$	$\frac{105}{100} \times \frac{110x}{100}$	

105

From R = 1240 + Dennis

$$\frac{105}{100} x \frac{110x}{100} = 1240 + x \rightarrow \frac{1155}{1000} = 1240 + x \rightarrow 1.15x = 1240 + x$$

$$1.15x - x = 1240 \rightarrow 0.15x = 1240 \therefore x = \frac{1240}{0.15} = \$8000$$

(13.8). A wholesaler sells goods to a retailer at a profit of $33\frac{1}{3}$%. The retailer sells to the customer at a profit of 50%. Express the price the customer paid as a percentage of the cost to the wholesaler.

Solution

	W	R	C
Cp	x	$\frac{400x}{300}$	$\frac{150}{100} x \frac{400x}{300}$
Sp	$\frac{400x}{300}$	$\frac{150}{100} x \frac{400x}{300}$	

Since $\frac{150}{100} x \frac{400x}{300} \rightarrow \frac{60x}{30} = \frac{6x}{3}$

% of $\frac{Customer}{wholesaler} = \frac{\frac{6x}{3}}{x} x \frac{100}{1} \rightarrow \frac{6x}{3} x \frac{1}{x} x \frac{100}{1} = \frac{600}{3} = 200\%$

(13.9). Last year Jose sold a painting for $2000. If he made a 25% profit on the sale. How much had he paid for the painting?

Solution

$$Sp = \frac{(100+25)}{100} \times cp \rightarrow 2000 = \frac{125}{100} Cp \rightarrow Cp = \frac{2000 + 100}{125} = 1,600$$

(13.10). If a sweater sells $48, after a 25% markdown, what was it is original price

Solution

$$Sp = [1 - D]Cp \rightarrow 48 = \left[1 - \frac{25}{100}\right] x\ cp$$

$$48 = \left[1 - \frac{1}{4}\right] cp = \frac{3}{4} cp \rightarrow cp = \frac{48 \times 4}{3} = \$64$$

(13.11). A hardware store is selling a lawnmower for $300. If the store makes a 25% profit on the sale, what is the store's cost for the lawn owner?

Solution

$$S.p = \left[\frac{100 + PROFIT}{100}\right] CP \rightarrow 300 = \left[\frac{100 + 25}{100}\right] cp \rightarrow cp = \frac{300 \times 100}{125} = \$240$$

(13.12). A retailer marked up the cost of a coat by 20% when she first displayed it in her store after several weeks she reduced the selling price of the coat by 25%. If the retailer originally paid $50 for the coat, what will be her loss on the coat at the final price.

Solution

Marked up = $Sp = \frac{120x}{100}$, $Cp = \$50$

$sp = \frac{120}{100} x\ 50 = \$60$

New SP is reduced by 25% = $\frac{75}{100}$ x old sp = $\frac{75}{100}$ x 60 = $\frac{75 \times 3}{5}$ = 45

Final loss = New SP – Old SP = 45 – 50 = $5

(13.13). The annual profit of a transport business was divided between two partners A and B in the ratio 3: 5. If B received $3000 more than A, the total profit was.

Solution

let the total profit = $ x

A : B = 3 : 5

A gets $\frac{3x}{5}$, B gets $\frac{5x}{8}$

Since B is $ 3000 more than A

$\frac{5}{8} = \frac{3}{8} + 3000 \rightarrow \frac{5x}{8} - \frac{3x}{8} = 3000 \rightarrow \frac{2x}{8} = 3000 \therefore x = \frac{3000 \times 8}{2} = \$12000$

(13.14). Three people share an inheritance in the ratio 2: 3 : 4 and the share of the person who receives most is $ 5,000. The share of the person next to him is $1250 more than the third person. How much does the third person receive?

Solution

Sharing ratio = 2: 3 : 4, the share = x

Person that receives most = $\frac{4x}{9}$ = $5,000 → x = $\frac{9 \times \$5,000}{4}$ = $\frac{45,000}{4}$ = $ 11250

Person next to him → $\frac{3x}{9}$ = $\frac{3}{9}$ x 11250 = $3750

Since second person share is = 1250 + third person's share

3750 = 1250 + third person's share

Third person's share = 3750 – 1250 = $2500

(13.15). The size of a quantity first doubles and then increases by a further 16%. After a short time its size decreases by 16%. What is the net increase in size of the quantity?

Solution

Let the original quantity be x = $\frac{100x}{100}$ = 100% x

When doubled, it is 2x = $\frac{200x}{100}$ = 200%x

When increased further by 16%, it becomes $\frac{216x}{100}$ or 216% x

When it decreased by 16%, it becomes $\frac{200x}{100}$ or 200% x

Net increase in size = 200 – 100 = 100%

(13.16) Father reduced the quantity of food bought for the family by 10% when he found that the cost of living had increased by 15%. Thus, the fractional increase the family food bill is now?

Solution

Let x quantity be bought at y per unit. Total cost = xy.

When x is reduced by 10%, it becomes $\frac{90x}{100}$

When y is increased by 15%, it becomes $\frac{115y}{100}$

Total cost = $\left(\frac{90x}{100}\right)\left(\frac{115y}{100}\right) = \frac{10350xy}{10000} = 1.035xy$

Increase in the cost = $1.035xy - xy = 0.035 \rightarrow \frac{35}{1000} = \frac{7}{200}$

(13.17). Factory P produces 20,000 bags of cement per day while factory Q produces 15,000 bags per day, if P reduces production by 5% and Q increases production by 5%. Determine the effective loss in the number of bags produced per day by the two factories.

Solution

P = 20,000 bags per day, Q = 15,000 bags per day

Total bags produced = 35,000

If P reduces production by 5% P will produce $\frac{95}{100} \times 20,000 = 19,000$

If Q increases production by 5%, Q will produce $\frac{105}{100} \times 15,000 = 15750$

Total production now = 19000 + 15750 = 34750

Loss in production = 35000 – 34750 = 250

(13.18). If the length of a square is increased by 20% while its width is decreased by 20% to form a rectangle. What is the ratio of the area of the rectangle to the area of the square?

Solution

Let the initial length be L and initial width be L

New length = $\frac{120L}{100}$, new width = $\frac{80L}{100}$

Area of rectangle = LB = $\left(\frac{120L}{100}\right)\left(\frac{80L}{100}\right) = \frac{96L^2}{100}$

Area of square = L x L = L^2

Ratio of area of rectangle to square = $\dfrac{\frac{96L^2}{100}}{L^2} = \dfrac{96}{100} = \dfrac{24}{25} = 24:25$

(13.19). If 3 gallon of spirit containing 20% water is added to 5 gallons of another spirit containing 15% water, what percentage of the mixture is water?

Solution

gallons	Water	
3	20% x 3	0.6 gallons
5	15% x 5	0.75 gallons
8		1.35 gallons

% of water in mixture = $\dfrac{1.35}{8} \times 100 = \dfrac{135\%}{8} = 16\dfrac{7}{8}\%$

(13.20). A baking recipe calls for 2.5kg of sugar and 4.5kg of flour. With this recipe some cakes were baked using 24.5kg of sugar and flour. How much sugar was used?

Solution

sugar	flour	Mixture
2.5	4.5	24.5 kg

Sugar = $\left[\dfrac{2.5}{2.4+2.5}\right] 24.5 = \dfrac{2.5}{7.0} \times 24.5 = 8.75$ kg

(13.21). After getting a rise of 15%, a man's new monthly salary $ 345. How much per month did he earn before the increase?

Solution

Let the old salary be x

With rise of 15%, new salary $\dfrac{115x}{100} = \$345 \rightarrow x = \dfrac{\$345 \times 100}{115} = \$300$

(13.22). A worker's present salary is $24000 per annuum. His annual increment is 10% of his basic salary. What would be his annual salary at the beginning of the third year?

Solution

Present basic salary = $24,000 (salary per annum)

Annual increment = 10% of basic = $\frac{10}{100} \times 24000$ = $2400

At the beginning of the second year, the salary will be increased by N2400

At the beginning of the second year the salary = $ 24,000 + $ 2,400 = $ 26,400

At the beginning of the third year, the salary will be increased by $\frac{10}{100} \times 26,400$ = $ 2640

At the beginning of the third year the salary = $26,400 + $2,640 = $29,040

(13.23). A man's initial salary $40.00 a month and increases after each period of six months by $36.00. Find his salary in the eight month of the third year.

Solution

Initial salary = $ 540

8th month of the third year is between 2 ½ and 3rd year

Period	Salary
0 – 6 month	540
6mth – 1st year	+ 36
1st yr – 1 ½ yr	+36
1 ½ yr – 2yr	+36
2yr – 2 ½ yr	+36
2 ½ yr – 3yr	+36
Total	$720

(13.24). Peter's weekly wages are $20.00 for the first 20 weeks and $36.00 for the next 24 weeks. Find his average weekly wage for the remaining 8 weeks of the year, if his average weekly wage for the whole year is $30.00.

Solution

With weekly wage = $ 20

For 20 weeks, the wage = $20 x 20 = $400

With weekly wage = $36

For 24 weeks, the wages = $ 36 x 24 = $864

Let the weekly, the wage = x(8) = $8x

But average weekly wage for the whole year is equal to

$\frac{Total\ wages}{Total\ no.of\ weeks}$ → $\frac{400 + 864 + 8x}{52} = \$30$ → $1264 + 8x = \$30 \times 52 = \$1560$

$8x = \$(1560 - 1264) = \$296$ → $x = \frac{\$296}{8} = \$37$

(13.25). A man is paid r naira per hour for normal work and double rate for overtime. If he does a 35-hour week which includes q hours of overtime, what is his weekly earning in naira?

Solution

Normal work = r naira per hour, Overtime = 2r naira per hour

Total time spent = 35 hrs, Overtime = q

∴ Normal work time = (35 − q) hr

Weekly earnings = r(35 − q) + 2r(q) = r(35 − q + 2q) = r(35 + q)

(13.26). Last year, James start up company showed a profit of $20,000. This year, the same company showed a profit of $25,000. If his company shows same percent increase in the coming year, what will that profit be?

Solution

Last year profit =20,000, this year profit = 25,000

Next year profit = ?

Since increase is same we find it

% increase → $\frac{(25000 - 20000)}{20000}$ → $\frac{5000}{2000} = \frac{5}{20} = \frac{1}{4}$

Anticipated increase = %increase x last profit = $\frac{1}{4} \times 25{,}000 = 6250$

Next profit = Anticipated increase + last profit → 6250 + 25000 = $31,250

(13.27). A gallon of water is added to 6 quarts of a solution that is 50% acid. What percent of the new solution is acid?

Solution

1 gallon = 4 quart

Formula	Quartz	Acid	Amount of Acid
Original	6	$\frac{50}{100} \times 6$	3
Added	4	0	0
New	10		3

% of new = $\frac{3}{10} \times 100 = 30\%$

(13.28). A 15-gallon mixture of 20% alcohol has 5 gallon of water added to it. The strength of the mixture as a percents approximately?

Solution

Formula	Gallon	Alcohol	Amount of Alcohol
Original	15	$\frac{50}{100} \times 15$	3
Added	5	0	0
New	20		3

% $of\ new = \frac{3}{20} \times 100 = 15\%$

(13.29). If 5 pound of raisens that cost $1.00per pound are mixed with 2 pounds of almonds that cost $2.40 per pound. What is the cost per pound of the resulting mixture?

Solution

Formula	Raisins	Almond	Amount of Acid
Original	2	4.8	4.8
Added	5	5	5
New	7		9.8

Cost of pound = $\frac{9.8}{7}$ = $1.40

(13.30.) A 50 litre solution of alcohol and water is 5 percent alcohol. If 1 ½ litres of alcohol and 8 ½ litres of water are added to the solution; what percent of the solution produced is alcohol?

Solution

Formula	Water	Alcohol	
Original	50	$\frac{5}{100}$ x 50	$\frac{25}{10}$
Added	$\frac{17}{2}$	$\frac{3}{2}$	$\frac{3}{2}$
New	58.5		4.0

% of new = $\frac{4}{58.5} \times \frac{100}{1} = 6\frac{2}{3}$ %

(13.31). A sales person receives a salary of $100 a week and a commission of 5% on all sales. What must be the amount of sales for a week in which the sales person's total weekly income is $360?

Solution

Amount earned = Commission x sale + Amount

$360 = \frac{5}{100} \times sales + 100 \rightarrow 360 - 100 = 0.05 sales \rightarrow 260 = 0.05 sale$ ∴ Sales = $5,200

(13.32). How many dollars does a sales person earn on a sale of s dollar at a commission of r%?

Solution

Amount earned = Commission x sales + Amount paid

$A = \frac{r}{100} \times s = \frac{rs}{100}$

(13.33). Bill delivers newspaper for a dealer and keeps 8% of all money collected. One month he was able to keep $16. How much did he forward to the newspaper?

Solution

Amount = commission x sales

$16 = \frac{8}{100} \times s \rightarrow 1600 = 8s \rightarrow sales = 200$

Amount paid = Sales - Amount earned = 200 – 16 = $184

(13.34). A brush salesman earns $5,000 salary each month plus 10 percent commission on the value of his sales. If he earned $20,000 last month, what was the total value of his sales?

Solution

$20,000 = \frac{10 \times sales}{100} + 5000 \rightarrow 15,000 = 0.1s \rightarrow sales = \frac{15000}{0.1} = 150,000$

(13.35) Jim receives a commission of 25% for every $20.00 worth of merchandise he sells. What percent is his commission?

Solution

1$ = 100cent

$\frac{1\$}{x\ \$} = \frac{100\ cent}{25\ cent} \rightarrow x = \frac{25}{100} = 0.25\$$

Amount earned = commission x sale → $0.25 = commission x 20

Comm. $= \frac{0.25}{20} = \frac{25}{2000} = 1\frac{1}{4}\%$

(13.36). Divide a line of length 60 cm into three parts whose ratios are 3: 7: 10

Solution

Let the parts be A, B and C. Total ratio = 3 + 7 + 10 = 20

A = $\frac{3}{20}$ x 60 = 9cm, B = $\frac{7}{20}T = \frac{7}{20}$ x 60 = 21 cm, C = $\frac{10}{20}$ x 60 = 30 cm

(13.37). Given that a:b = 1:3 and b: c = 2:3. What is a:b:c ?

Solution

$\frac{a}{b} = \frac{1}{3}$ and $\frac{b}{c} = \frac{2}{3}$

$$\frac{a}{c} = \frac{a}{b} \times \frac{b}{c} \rightarrow \frac{1}{3} \times \frac{2}{3} = \frac{2}{9} \text{ or } a:c = 2:9$$

(13.38). The sides of a triangle are in the ratio 4 : 7 : 8 and its perimeter is 38 cm. find the sides.

Solution

The total sum of sides = perimeter

total ratio = 4 + 7 + 8 = 19

Thus the sides of a triangle take the proportion

4 : 7 : 8 from 38 cm

1st side : $\frac{4}{19} \times 38 = 8 \, cm$, 2nd side : $\frac{7}{19} \times 38 = 14 \, cm$

3rd side : $\frac{8}{19} \times 38 = 16 \, xm$

(13.39). Alice deserves twice as much marks as Brenda and Brenda deserves half as many marks as Catharine. How many does each receive when their total marks are 125?

Solution

Alice deserves twice as many marks as Brenda means

A : B = 2 : 1

Brenda deserves half as many marks as Catharine means

B : C = 1 : 2

Since B is equal already

Combining the ratio, we have; A : B : C = 2 : 1 : 2

Thus A gets $\frac{2}{6} \times 125 = 50$, B gets $\frac{1}{5} \times 125 = 25$, C gets $\frac{2}{5} \times 125 = 50$

(13.40). Divide $22000 between six people so that five of them get twice the sixth person

Solution

Let the people be A, B, C, D, E, and F

Thus A: B: C: D: E: F = 2: 2: 2: 2: 2: 1

Total ratio is = 11

Thus A will get $\frac{2}{11} \times \$22000 = \$4000$

A = B = C = D = E = $ 4000 each

F will get $\frac{1}{11} \times \$22000 = \$2000$

(13.41). A man bought a car for $800 and sold it for $640. Find his loss percent

Solution

Loss = Cp – Sp → 800 – 640 = 160

Loss percent = $\frac{Cp - Sp}{Cp} = \frac{160 \times 100}{800} = 20\%$

(13.42). A dealer sells an article costing $5 at a gain of 12 ½ %. Find the selling price.

Solution

SP = $\left[\frac{100 + Profit}{100}\right] \times Cp \rightarrow \left[\frac{100 + {}^{25}/_2}{100}\right] \times 5 \rightarrow \left[\frac{200 + 25}{200}\right] \times 5 = \$5.63$

(13.43). A dealer gains $4 when he sells an article to gain 8%. What is the selling price?

Solution

Sp = $\left(\frac{100 + 8}{100}\right) \times 4 \rightarrow = \frac{108}{100} cp$

Profit = SP − CP → 4 = $\frac{108}{100} cp - cp$ → 4 = 1.08 cp − cp → Cp = $\frac{4}{0.08}$ = $50

SP = Profit - Cp = $50 + 4 = $54

(13.44). A sells to B at a gain 20%, B sells to C at a price a paid. What does B lose as a percentage?

117

Solution

	A	B	C
Cp	x	$\frac{120}{100}x$	
Sp	$\frac{120}{100}x$ (to B)	x what A paid (to C)	

B losses = c.p − s.p → $\frac{120x}{100} - x = \frac{20}{100}x$

Loss percent = $\frac{loss}{C.p} \times 100$ → $\frac{\frac{20x}{100}}{\left(\frac{120}{100}\right)x} \times 100$ → $\frac{20}{100} \times \frac{100}{120} \times 100 = \frac{100}{6} = 16\frac{2}{3}$

(13.45). P sold his bicycle to Q at a profit of 10%. Q sold it to R for $ 209.00 at a loss of 5%. How much did the bicycle cost?

Solution

	P	Q	R
Cp	x	$\frac{110}{100}x$	
Sp	$\frac{110}{100}x$ (to Q)	$\frac{95}{100}\left(\frac{110x}{100}\right)$	

Since $\frac{95}{100}\left(\frac{110x}{100}\right) = \$209.00$ → x = $\frac{\$209 \times 100 \times 100}{95 \times 110}$ = $200

(13.46). Audu bought an article for $50,000 and sold it to femi at a loss of x%. femi later sold the article to Oche at a profit of 40%. If Femi made a profit of $10,000. Find the value of x.

Solution

Audu's CP = $50,000

Audu's SP → Sp = $\frac{(100 - loss)}{100} \times cp$ → $\left(\frac{100 - x}{100}\right) \times 50,000$

118

Femi's CP = (100 – x) 500

Femi's SP: → $Sp = \frac{140}{100} x\, cp$ → $\frac{140}{100}(100-x)500 = (100-x)700$

Profit made by Femi → $profit = sp - cp$ → $10000 = 700(100-x) - 500(100-x)$

$10000 = (100-x)200$ → $100 - x = 50$ ∴ $x = 50$

(13.47). When a dealer sells a bicycle for $81, he makes a profit of 8%. What did he pay for the bicycle?

Solution

SP = $81, profit = 8%

$Sp = \frac{108}{100} Cp = 81$ → $Cp = 81 \times \frac{100}{108} = \$75$

(13.48). By selling an article for $45.00, a man makes a profit of 8% for how much should he have sold it order to make a profit of 32%.

Solution

Selling an article for $45.00, profit = 8%

$Sp = 45 = \frac{108}{100} Cp$ → $Cp = \frac{45 \times 100}{108}$

To make a profit of 32% → $Sp = \frac{132}{100} Cp$ → $\frac{132}{100} \times \frac{4500}{108} = \$55$

(13.49). By selling 20 oranges for $1.35 a trader makes a profit 8%. What is his percentage gain or loss if he sells the same 20 oranges for $1.10?

Solution

Selling 20 oranges for $1.35 at a profit of 8% → $Sp = \frac{108}{100} CP = \$1.35$

$Cp = \frac{1.35 \times 100}{108} = \$1.25$

Selling 20 oranges for $1.10 is a loss as Sp < Cp

loss % = $\frac{loss}{Cp} \times 100 = \frac{1.25 - 1.10}{1.25} \times 100 = \frac{0.15}{1.25} \times 100 = 12\%$

(13.50) A trader gives a discount of 12% on the marked price of an article. If a customer pays $1760.00 for the article, what marked price of the article?

Solution

Cash sp = (1 – D)mp → 1760 = (1 – 0.12)mp → 1760 = 0.88mp → mp = 2000

(13.51). A shopkeeper marks his goods to gain 20%. He allows 5% discount for cash. Find his percentage profit when he sells in cash

Solution

Marking goods to gain 20% implies $Sp = \frac{120}{100}Cp$

Allowing 5% discount on cash sale, $Sp = \frac{115}{100}Cp$

Selling in cash, the percentage profit $= \frac{115}{100}Cp - Cp = 15\%$

(13.52). Find the simple interest on $340.$62\frac{1}{2}$ in 3 years at 4 ½ % per annum.

Solution

$R = 4\frac{1}{2}\% = \frac{9}{2}\% = \frac{9}{200}$ ∴ I = P x R% x T → $340.625 \times \frac{9}{200} \times 3 = \$45.98$

(13.53). A man invested a sum of $280.00 partly at 5% and partly at 4%. If the total interest is $12.80 per annum. Find the amount invested at 5%.

Solution

5% + 4% = $280 …………..(i)

Let the amount invested at 5% be x

From (i) the amount invested at 4% will be (280 – x)

Interest at 5% → $\frac{PRT}{100} = \frac{x(5)}{100} = \frac{5x}{100}$

Interest at 4% → $\frac{PRT}{100} = (280 - x)\frac{4}{100} = \frac{1120 - 4x}{100}$

Total interest = $\frac{5x}{100} + \frac{1120 - 4x}{100} = \$12.80$ → $5x + 1120 - 4x = \$1280$

x = \$1280 - \$1120 = \$160

(13.54). Find the sum of money which yields \$7.15 simple interest in 4 years at $2\frac{3}{4}\%$ per annum.

Solution

I = \$7.15, T = 4 years, R = $2\frac{3}{4}\% = \frac{11}{4}\%$

I = P x R% x T → P = $\frac{1}{R\% \times T} = \frac{\$7.15}{\frac{11}{400} \times 4} = \frac{\$7.15}{0.11} = \$65$

(13.55). At what rate would a sum of \$100.00 deposited for 5yrs raise an interest of \$ 7.50.

Solution

P = \$ 100, T = 5yrs, I = \$7.50

R% = $\frac{1}{PT}$ → $\frac{7.50}{100 \times 5}$ → $\frac{7.50}{500} = 0.015$ → R = 0.015 x 100 = 1.5% = 1 ½ %

(13.56). If \$225.00 yields \$27.00 in x years simple interest at the rate of 4% per annum. Find x.

Solution
P = \$225, I = \$27, T = x, R = 4%

$I = \frac{PRT}{100}$ → $27 = 225\frac{4}{100}.x$ → $x = \frac{27 \times 100}{225 \times 4}$ → $\frac{2700}{900} = 3yrs$

(13.57) A man invests a sum of money at 4% per annum simple interest. After 3yrs, the principal amount to \$7,000.00. Find the sum invested.

Solution

Principal = P, R = 4%, T = 3 yrs, A = \$7,000

$A = P + I = P\left(1 + \frac{RT}{100}\right)$ → $7000 = P\left(1 + \frac{4 \times 3}{100}\right)$ → $7000 = P(1 + 0.12)$

$7000 = 1.12p \rightarrow p = \frac{7000}{1.12} = \$6250$

(13.58). Find the simple interest rate per cent per annum at $ 1000 accumulates to $1240 in 3 years.

Solution

P = $1000, A = $1240, T = 3yrs

$A = P + I = P\left(1 + \frac{RT}{100}\right) \rightarrow 1240 = 1000\left(1 + \frac{R \times 3}{100}\right)$

$1.24 = 1 + \frac{3R}{100} \rightarrow \frac{3R}{100} = 1.24 - 1 = 0.24 \rightarrow R = \frac{0.24 \times 100}{3} = 8\%$

(13.59). Oke deposited $800.00 in the bank at the rate of 12 ½ % simple interest. After some time the total amount was one and half times the principal. For how many years was the money left in the bank.

Solution

$P = \$800, R = 12\frac{1}{2}\% = \frac{25}{2}\% = \frac{25}{200}, A = 1\frac{1}{2}P = \frac{3}{2}P$

$A = P + I = P\left(1 + \frac{RT}{100}\right) \rightarrow \frac{3P}{2} = P\left(1 + \frac{25T}{200}\right)$

$1.5 = 1 + 0.125T \rightarrow 0.125T = 1.5 - 1 \rightarrow T = \frac{0.5}{0.125} = 4yrs$

(13.60). How long will it take a sum money increased 5% per annum simple interest to increase in value to 40%.

Solution

For the money to have increased by 40%, A = 140%P, R = 5%

From $A = P\left(1 + \frac{RT}{100}\right) \rightarrow \frac{140P}{100} = P\left(1 + \frac{5T}{100}\right) \rightarrow 1.4 = 1 + 0.05T$

$0.05T = 1.4 - 1 = 0.04 \rightarrow T = \frac{0.4}{0.05} = 8 \; years$

(13.61). A sum of money invested at 5% per annum simple interest amount to $282.20 after 3 years. how long will it take the same sum to amount to $ 434.00 at 7 ½ % per annum simple annum?

Solution

Let P be invested at 5%, A = $285.20, T = 3yrs

$$A = P\left(1 + \frac{RT}{100}\right) \rightarrow 285.20 = P\left(1 + \frac{5 \times 3}{100}\right) = P\left(1 + \frac{15}{100}\right) = P(1.15)$$

$$P = \frac{285.20}{1.15} = \$248$$

investing the same sum ($ 248) to produce $434.00

$$R = 7\frac{1}{2}\% = \frac{15}{2}\% = \frac{15}{200}$$

$$434 = 248\left(1 + \frac{15 \times T}{200}\right)$$

$$\frac{434}{248} = 1 + 0.075T \rightarrow 1.75 = 1 + 0.075T \rightarrow 0.075T = 1.75 - 1 \rightarrow 0.075T = 0.75$$

$$T = \frac{0.75}{0.075} = 10$$

(13.62). Musa burrow $10.00 at 2% per month simple interest and repays $8.00 after 4 months. How does he still owe?

Solution

P = $10, R = 3%, T = 4months

$$I = \frac{PRT}{100} \rightarrow \frac{10 \times 2 \times 4}{100} \rightarrow \frac{80}{100} = \$0.08$$

Amount at the end of 4 months = P + I = $10.00 + $0.8 = $10.80

If he pays $8.00 at the end of the end of the 4 months, he will be owing (10.80 – 8.00) = 2.80

(13.63). Find the nearest dollar the amount of $100 invested at 4% per annum compound interest after 20 years.

Solution

P = $100, R = 4%, n = 20

$$A = P(1 + R\%)^n \rightarrow A = 100(1 + 4\%)^{20} \rightarrow 100(1 + 0.04)^{20} = 100(1.04)^{20}$$

A = $219.11

(**13.64**). Find the compound interest on $200 in 3 years at 4% per annum.

Solution

$A = P(1 + R)^n \rightarrow A = 200(1 + 4\%)^3 = 200(1 + 0.04)^3 = \$224.97$

For compound interest, $I = A - P \rightarrow \$224.97 - \$200 = \$24.97$

(**13.65**). How long would it take a sum of money to double itself 5% per annum compound interest?

Solution

With $A = 2P$

$A = P(1 + R\%)^n \rightarrow 2P = P(1 + R\%)^n \rightarrow 2 = (1 + 5\%)^n \rightarrow 2 = (1 + 0.05)^n$

$2 = 1.05^n \rightarrow \log 2 = n \log 1.05 \rightarrow n = \frac{\log 2}{\log 1.05} \rightarrow \frac{0.3010}{0.0212} = 14.20$

n = 14 years   (to nearest years)

(**13.66**). $1860 is invested for 2 years at 5% per annum compound interest. Find how much more profitable it would be have the interest added half yearly, rather than annually?

Solution

P = $1860

When interest is added half yearly, for two years, n = 4, R = 2.5%

$A = P(1 + R)^n \rightarrow 1860(1 + 2.5\%)^4 \rightarrow 1860(1 + 0.025)^4 \therefore A = 1860(1.025)^4 = \$2053.09$

When interest is added annually, for two years, n = 2, R = 5%

$A = P(1 + R\%)^n \rightarrow 1860(1 + 5\%)^2 \rightarrow 1860(1 + 0.05)^2 \therefore A = 1860(1.05)^2 = \$2050.65$

Profit = $2053.09 - $2050.65 = $2.44

(**13.67**). The population of a town increase by 4% each year. If the population at one census is 42500, what will it be at the next census, 4 years later?

Solution   R = 4%, P = 42500, n = 4

$A = P(1 + R\%)^n \to (1 + 4\%)^4 = 42500(1 + 0.04)^4 = 42500(1.04)^4$

$42500(1 + 0.04)^4 = 49719$

(13.68). A small factory which originally cost $6920 is depreciated at the end of each year at the rate of 5% based on the book value at the beginning of each year. What is the book value of the factory at the beginning of the fifteenth year to the nearest naira.

Solution

P = $6920, R% = 5, n = 15

$A = P(1 - R\%)^n \to 6920(1 - 5\%)^{15} \to 6920(1 - 0.05)^{15} \to 6920(0.95)^{15} = \$3206$

(13.69). If the radius of a circle is diminished by 20% the area is diminished by?

Solution

If r diminishes by 20%, New $r = \frac{80r}{100} = 0.8r$

Area of a circle $= \pi r^2$

decrease $= \frac{New}{Old} \times \frac{100}{1} \to \frac{\pi(0.8r)^2}{\pi r^2} \times \frac{100}{1} = \frac{\pi \times 0.64 r^2}{\pi r^2} \times \frac{100}{1} = 64\%$

% Decrease $= 100 - 64\% = 36\%$

(13.70). If the radius of a circle is decreased by percent in its area decreased?

Solution

Decrease in radius $= \frac{90r}{100} = 0.9r$

Area of a circle $= \pi r^2$

decrease $= \frac{New}{Old} \times \frac{100}{1} \to \frac{\pi(0.9r)^2 r^2}{\pi r^2} \times \frac{100}{1} = 0.9r$

Area or a circle $= \pi r^2$

Decrease in Area $= \frac{\pi(0.9)^2 r^2}{\pi r^2} \times \frac{100}{1} = 81$

%Decrease $= 100 - 81 = 19\%$

(13.71). A cube has an edge which is four include is increased by 25%. Then the volume is increased by approximately by?

Solution

Increase in length $= \frac{125L}{100} = 1.25L$

Volume of a cube $= L^3$

Increase in volume $= \frac{New}{Old} \times \frac{100}{1} \rightarrow \frac{(0.8L)^3}{L^3} \times \frac{100}{1} = (1.25)^3 = 1.953 \times 100$

% Increase $= 100 - 195 = 95\%$

(13.72). What is 10% of $\frac{1}{3}x$ if $\frac{2x}{3}$ is 10% of 60?

Solution

If $\frac{2x}{3} = \frac{10}{100} \times 60 \rightarrow \frac{2x}{3} = \frac{600}{100} \rightarrow \frac{2x}{3} = 6 \rightarrow 2x = 18 \rightarrow x = 9$

10% of $\frac{1}{3}x \rightarrow \frac{10}{100} \times \frac{x}{3} \rightarrow \frac{10}{100} \times \frac{9}{3} = \frac{30}{100} = 0.3$

(13.73). A college graduate goes to work for x dollar per week. After several months the company gives all the employees a 10% pay cut. A few months later the company gives the employee a 10% raise. What is the college graduate's new salary?

Solution

Salary $= x$

10% $pay\ cut = \frac{90x}{100}$

10% $pay\ raise = \frac{110x}{100}$

$\therefore \frac{90x}{100} \times \frac{110x}{100} = 0.99x$

(13.74). If the base of a rectangle is increased by 30% and the altitude is decreased by 20% the area is increased by?

Solution

Increased in breadth $= \frac{130B}{100} = 1.3B$

126

Decrease in length = $\frac{80L}{100} = 0.8L$

Increase in Area = $\frac{1.3B \times 0.8L}{B \times L} \times \frac{100}{1} = 1.04 \times 100 = 104$

% increase = $100 - 104 = 4\%$

(13.75). If the radius of a circle is increased by 10%, the area of the circle is increased by?

Solution

$Increase\ in\ radius = \frac{110r}{100} = 1.1r$

$Area\ of\ a\ circle = \pi r^2$

New area = $\pi(1.1)^2 = 1.21\pi r^2$

Increase in area = $\frac{New}{Old} \times 100 = \frac{1.21\pi r^2}{\pi r^2} \times \frac{100}{1} = 121$

Increase = $100 - 121 = 21\%$

(13.76). What percent of a is b?

Solution

$\frac{x}{100} \times a = b \quad \rightarrow \quad ax = 100b \quad \rightarrow \quad x = \frac{100b}{a}$

(13.77). In May, carter's appliances sold 40 washing machine. In June, the store sold 50 washing machines. What is the percent of increase in the number of washing machine sold?

Solution

$\frac{increase}{old} \times \% \quad \rightarrow \quad \frac{80-40}{40} \times 100 = 100\%$

(13.78). What percent of a half dollar is a penny, a nickel, and a done?

Solution

$\frac{x}{100} \times 50 = 16 \quad \rightarrow \quad 50x = 10 \times 100 \quad \rightarrow \quad x = \frac{10 \times 100}{50} = 32\%$

(13.79). If a increased by 25% and b is decreased by 25%, the resulting numbers will be equal. what is the ratio of a to b?

Solution

Increase in a = $\frac{125a}{100}$ = 1.25a

Decrease in b = $\frac{75b}{100}$ = 0.75b

1.25b = 0.75a

Dividing both sides by 1.25 gives

$\frac{1.25a}{1.25} = \frac{0.75b}{1.25} \rightarrow a = \frac{0.75b}{1.25} \rightarrow \frac{a}{b} = \frac{0.75}{1.25} = \frac{75}{125} = \frac{3}{5}$

(13.80). What percentage of 50 is b?

Solution

$\frac{x}{100} \times 50 = b \rightarrow 50x = 100b \rightarrow x = \frac{100b}{50} \quad x = 2b$

(13.81). If a = 2b, $\frac{1}{2}b = c$, and 4c = 3d find $\frac{d}{a}$?

Solution

From = a = 2b $\rightarrow b = \frac{a}{2}$

From $\frac{1}{2}b = c \rightarrow \frac{1}{2}\left(\frac{a}{2}\right) = c \rightarrow \frac{a}{4} = c$

From 4c = 3d $\rightarrow 4\left(\frac{a}{4}\right) = 3d \rightarrow a = 3d$

Dividing the last expression by 3

$\frac{a}{3} = d \quad \therefore \frac{d}{a} = \frac{1}{3}$

(13.82). If the diameter of a circle increased by 50 percent by what percent will the area of the circle increase?

Solution

Old D = D, New D = $\frac{150}{100} D = 1.5D$

128

Area $= \pi r^2 = \dfrac{\pi D^2}{4}$

$\dfrac{New}{Old} \times 100 = \dfrac{\frac{\pi(1.5D)^2}{4}}{\frac{\pi D^2}{4}} = \dfrac{\frac{\pi 2.25 D^2}{4}}{\frac{\pi D^2}{4}} \; x \dfrac{100}{1} = 2.25 \times 100 = 225$

% increase $= 100 - 225 = 125\%$

(13.83). A price rise by 10% one year and by 20% the next. What is the combined % increase?

Solution

% increase $= \dfrac{110x}{100} = 1.1x = \dfrac{New}{Old} \times 100 = \dfrac{1.1x}{x} \times 100$

$Next \to \dfrac{120x}{100} = 12x \to \dfrac{1.2x}{x} \times 110 = 132$

Total $= 132 - 100 = 32\%$

(13.84). The volume of a cylinder whose height is 4 and whose radius is 2 is how many times the volume of a cylinder whose height is 2 and whose radius is 4?

Solution

$V_1 = \pi r^2 h = \pi(2^2)4 = 16\pi$

$V_2 = \pi r^2 h = \pi(4^2)2 = 32\pi$

$\dfrac{V_1}{V_2} = \dfrac{16\pi}{32\pi} = \dfrac{1}{2}$

(13.85). Let a and b be positive numbers such that a% of a% of b equals c. if a^2% of b equals kc. What is the value of k?

Solution

$$\frac{a}{100} \times \frac{a}{100} \times b = \frac{a^2 b}{100 \times 100} = c \ \ldots\ldots (i)$$

If kc = a^2% of b = $\frac{a^2 b}{100}$

Inserting into (i)

$$\frac{a^2 b}{100 \times 100} = c \ \rightarrow\ \frac{a^2 b}{100} \times \frac{1}{100} = c \ \rightarrow\ \frac{kc}{100} = c$$

kc = 100c ∴ $k = 100$

CHAPTER 14 RATE AND RATEABLE VALUES

Time rate: This is the amount of a quantity in a unit time

Mathematically, the relation holds

$$Speed = \frac{distance}{time}$$

The term ''same route'' implies same distance

Work = distance

Work and Time

The number of workers is directly proportional to the quantity of work done and inversely proportional to the time taken i.e W α N $\propto$ 1/T

Mathematically, $\frac{M_1 T_1}{W_1} = \frac{M_2 T_2}{W_2}$

M = men, W = work/job, T = time take/ no of days

When people work together, the following relationship holds

When 2 people work together the time taken to do the job together is given by

$$T_{AB} = \frac{product}{sum\ of\ product\ of\ any\ two} = \frac{T_A \times T_B}{T_A + T_B}$$

When 3 people work together the time taken to do the job together is given by

$$T_{ABC} = \frac{product}{sum\ of\ product\ of\ any\ two} = \frac{T_A \times T_B \times T_C}{T_A \times T_B + T_A \times T_C + T_B \times T_C}$$

QUESTIONS

(14.1). A motorist drives 80 miles to her destination at an average speed of 40mph and makes the return trip at an average rate of 30mph. the average speed in mph for the entire trip is?

Solution

Going $\rightarrow D = 60\ mile, s = 40mph \rightarrow t_1 = \frac{60}{40} = \frac{3h}{2}$

Coming $\rightarrow D = 60\ mile, s = 30mph \rightarrow t_2 = \frac{60}{30} = 2hr$

Average speed $= \frac{Total\ distance}{Total\ time} = \frac{60+60}{\frac{3}{2}+2} = \frac{120}{\frac{7}{2}} \rightarrow \frac{120}{1} \times \frac{2}{7} = \frac{240}{7} = 34\frac{2}{7}\ mph$

(14.2). A train running between two towns arrives at its destination 10 min late when it goes 40 mph and 16 min late. When it goes 30 mph. the distance between the towns is?

Solution

When you arrive late, you use additional time.

Let the two town be A → B

$S_1 = 40$ mph, $D_1 = x$, $t_1 = (t+10)$min $= \left(\frac{t+10}{60}\right)$ hrs

$S = \frac{D}{T} \rightarrow D_1 = s \times t = \left(\frac{t+10}{60}\right) \times 40 = x$

$4t + 40 = 6x$ ....(i)

$S_2 = 30$mph, $D_2 = x$, $t_2 = (t+16)$min $= \left(\frac{t+16}{60}\right)$ hrs

$D_2 = s \times t = \left(\frac{t+16}{60}\right) \times 30 = x$

$3t + 48 = 6x$ .... (ii)

Re-arranging (i) and (ii)

$4t - 6x = -40$ .... (i)

$3t - 6x = -48$ .... (ii)

$t = -40 - (-48) = 8$ ∴ $t = 8$hrs

put $t = 8$ into (i) → $4(8) - 6x = -4$ → $32 + 40 = 6x$ → $72 = 6x$ → $x = \frac{72}{6} = 12\ mile$

(14.3). A man travels a distance of 20 mile at 60 mph and return over the same route at 40mph. what is his average rate for the round trip in mph.

Solution

$D_1 = 20$, $S_1 = 60$mph → $t_1 = \frac{20}{60} = \frac{1}{3}$

$D_2 = 20$, $S_2 = 40$mph → $t_2 = \frac{20}{40} = \frac{1}{2}$

$$average\ speed = \frac{Total\ distance}{Total\ time} = \frac{20+20}{\frac{1}{3}+\frac{1}{2}} = \frac{\frac{40}{5}}{\frac{5}{6}} = \frac{40}{1} \times \frac{6}{5} = \frac{240}{5} = 48mph$$

(14. 4). A motorist drives 90 mile at an average speed of 50mph and returns at an average speed of 50mph and returns at an average speed of 60 mph. what is her average speed in mph for the entire trip?

Solution

$D_1 = 90$, $s_1 = 50mph \rightarrow t_1 = \frac{90}{50} = \frac{9}{5}$

$D_2 = 90$, $s_2 = 60mph \rightarrow t_2 = \frac{90}{60} = \frac{9}{6}$

$$Average\ Speed = \frac{Total\ distance}{Total\ Time} = \frac{90+90}{\frac{9}{5}+\frac{9}{6}} = \frac{180}{\frac{99}{30}} \rightarrow \frac{180}{1} \times \frac{30}{99} = 54.5\ mph$$

(14. 5). A man travels 320 mile in 8 hours. If he continue at the same rate, how many miles will he travel in the next 2hours?

Solution

$d_1 = 320$, $t_1 = 5hrs$, $s_1 = \frac{D_1}{t_1} = \frac{320}{8} = 40$

$d_2 = ?$, $s_2 = 40$, $t_2 = 2hr$

$D_2 = s_2 \times t_2 = 40 \times 2 = 80$ mile

(14. 6). If a train covers 14mile in 10 minutes, what is the rate of the train in mph.

Solution

$60\ min = 1hr \rightarrow x = \frac{10}{60} = \frac{1}{6}$

$S = \frac{D}{T} \rightarrow \frac{14}{\frac{1}{6}} \rightarrow 14 \times 6 = 84\ mph$

(14. 7). John always jog, to school at a speed of 6km/h and walks home alone the same route at a speed of 3km/h. if he spends exactly one hour total travelling both ways. How many kilometers is his school from his home?

Solution

$s_1 = 6km/hr$, $d_1 = x$, $t_1 = \frac{D_1}{S_1} = \frac{x}{6}$

$s_2 = 3$km/hr, $d_2 = x$, $t_2 = \frac{d_2}{s_2} = \frac{x}{3}$

$t_1 + t_2 = \frac{x}{6} + \frac{x}{3} = 1 \rightarrow \frac{x+2x}{6} = 1 \rightarrow 3x = 6 \therefore x = 2$

(14.8). At a speed of 48 mile per hour. How many minutes will be required to do 32 miles?

Solution

$\frac{48\ mile}{32\ mile} = \frac{1\ hr}{x\ hr} \rightarrow x = \frac{32}{48} hr = \frac{2h}{3}$

$\frac{60\ minute}{x\ minute} = \frac{1\ hr}{\frac{2}{3}hr} \rightarrow x = \frac{60 \times 2}{3} = 40\ min$

(14.9). Mark drove to a meeting at 60m/h returning over the same route. He encountered heavy traffic and drove at only 40m/hr. If the returning took 1 hour longer, how many miles did he drive each way?

Solution

$s_1 = 60$m/h, $d_1 = 60x$, $t_1 = x$, $s_2 = 40$m/hr, $t_2 = x + 1$, $d_2 = 40(x + 1)$

Same route implies same distance

$d_1 = d_2 \rightarrow 60x = 40(x + 1) \rightarrow 60x = 40x + 40 \rightarrow 60x - 40x = 40$

$20x = 40 \rightarrow x = \frac{40}{20} = 2$

$d_1 = 60x = 60 \times 2 = 120$, $d_2 = 40(x+1) = 40(3) = 120$

$d_1 = d_2 = 120$

(14.10). Joy driver to work in 40min. she takes the same route to return home her average speed on the trip home is half as her average speed on the trip to work, how much time does she spend on the round trip?

Solution

$S_W = \frac{d_W}{t_W} = \frac{x}{40}$, $t = 40, D = x$

$S_H = \frac{1}{2} S_W \rightarrow \frac{1}{2}\left[\frac{x}{40}\right] = \frac{x}{80} = \frac{d_H}{t_H}$

Total time = *Time* $_{Home}$ + *Time* $_{work}$ = 40 + 80 = 120

(14.11). John drove for h hours at a constant rate of r mile per hour. How many miles did she go during the final 20 minutes of her drive?

Solution

$\frac{60 \text{ min}}{20 \text{ min}} = \frac{1 \text{ hr}}{x \text{ hr}} \rightarrow x = \frac{20}{60} = \frac{1}{3} hr$

$S = \frac{D}{T} \rightarrow D = s \times t = r \times \frac{1}{3} = \frac{r}{3} \ m/hr$

(14.12). To get to a business meeting, Joan drives m mile in h hours, and arrived ½ hour early. At what rate should she have driven to arrive exactly on time?

Solution

Exactly On time = Time she drove + Time she arrive = $h + \frac{1}{2}$

Rate = speed = $\frac{D}{T} = \frac{m}{h + \frac{1}{2}} = \frac{m}{\frac{2h+1}{2}} = \frac{2m}{2h+1}$

(14.13). The distance between Ali's house and college is exactly 135 mile. If she drove $\frac{2}{3}$ of the distance in 135 minute. What was her average speed in mile per hour?

Solution

Distance = $\frac{2}{3} \times 135 = 90 \ mile$

$\frac{60 \text{ min}}{135 \text{ min}} = \frac{1 \text{ hr}}{x \text{ hr}} \rightarrow x = \frac{135}{60} = 2.25 \ hr$

$S = \frac{D}{T} = \frac{90}{2.25} = 40 mph$

(14.14). A car going 40mph set out on an 80 mile trip at 9AM. Exactly 10 minutes later, a second car left from the same place and followed the same route. How fast in m/hr was the second car going if it caught up with the first car at 10.30 a.m.

Solution

1st car, S = 40, t = [10.20 – 9.00] → s_1 = 40, t_1 = 1.30 min

$\frac{60 \text{ min}}{30 \text{ min}} = \frac{1 \text{ hr}}{x \text{ hr}} \rightarrow x = \frac{30}{60} = \frac{1}{2} hr$

1hr: 30min = 1 + 0.5 = 1.5hrs

$s_1 = 40$, $t_1 = 1.5$hrs, $d_1 = 40 \times 1.5 = 60$ mile

2nd car: $t_2 = (10.30 - 9.10) = $ 1hr: 20 min

$\frac{60 \text{ min}}{20 \text{ min}} = \frac{1 \text{ hr}}{x \text{ hr}} \rightarrow x = \frac{20}{60} = \frac{1}{3} hr$

1hr: 20 min = 1 + 0.33 = 1.33hr

$s_2 = \frac{d_2}{t_2} = \frac{60}{1.33} = 45 \ m/hr$

(14.15). Henry drove 100m to visit a friend. If he had driven 8 mile faster than he did; he would have arrived in $\frac{5}{6}$ of the time he actually took. How many minutes did the trip take.

Solution

$d_1 = 100$, $s_1 = x$, $t_1 = \frac{d_1}{s_1} = \frac{100}{x}$

$d_2 = 100$, $s_2 = x + 8$, $t_2 = \frac{100}{x+8}$

$\frac{5}{6} x \left(\frac{100}{x}\right) = \frac{500}{6x} \rightarrow \frac{500}{6x} = \frac{100}{8+x}$

$40000 + 500x = 600x \rightarrow 40000 = 600x - 500x = 100 \rightarrow x = \frac{4000}{100} = 40 mph$

$t_1 = \frac{d_1}{s_1} = \frac{100}{40} = 2.5hrs$

$\frac{60 \text{ min}}{x \text{ min}} = \frac{1 \text{ hr}}{2.5 \text{ hr}} \rightarrow x = 60 \ x \ 2.5 = 150 \ mins$

$t_2 = \frac{d_2}{s_2} = \frac{100}{48} = 2.1hr$

$\frac{60 \text{ min}}{x \text{ min}} = \frac{1 \text{ hr}}{2.1 \text{ hr}} \rightarrow x = 60 \ x \ 2.1 = 125 \ mins$

(14.16). If Henry drove 198km between 10:00 am and 1.40pm. What was his average speed in km/hr?

Solution

10am – 1.40pm = 3hr : 40min

$\frac{60 \text{ min}}{40 \text{ min}} = \frac{1 \text{ hr}}{x \text{ hr}} \rightarrow x = \frac{40}{60} = 0.6 \, hr$

3hr : 40min = 3hr + 0.6hr = 3.6hrs

Average speed = $\frac{Dist}{Time} = \frac{198}{3.6} = 55 km/hr$

(14.17). If a woman runs a kilometer in 3 minute and a train is moving at 80km/h. if the woman and train both decreases their speed by 5%. Express the speed of the woman now as a percentage of new speed of the train?

Solution

$d_1 = 1, t_1 = 3\text{min} = \frac{3}{60} \, hr = \frac{1}{20} \, hr, \; s_1 = \frac{1}{\frac{1}{20}} = 20$

Woman decrease in speed $\rightarrow \frac{95}{100} \times 20 \rightarrow \frac{95}{5} = 19$

Train decrease in speed $\rightarrow \frac{95}{100} \times 80 \rightarrow \frac{95}{5} \times 4 = 76$

% Expression $\rightarrow \frac{19}{76} \times \frac{100}{1} = 25\%$

(14.18). How many minutes did John take, driving at 20 m/hr to go the same distance that Mary took 30 minutes to drive at 60m/h.

Solution

$mary \rightarrow s_1 = 60, t_1 = 30, d_1 = 60 \times 30 = 1800$

John $\rightarrow s_2 = 20, t_2 = ? \; d_1 = 1500$

$t_2 = \frac{d_2}{s_2} = \frac{1800}{20} = 90$

(14.19) Gilda drove 650 mile at an average speed of 50m/hr. how many m/hr faster would she have had to drive in order for the trip to have taken 1 hour less.

Solution

$D_1 = 650, S_1 = 50, t_1 = \frac{D_1}{S_1} = \frac{650}{50} = 13 hrs$

For the trip to be 1hr less

$t_2 = 12, D_2 = 650$

$$S_2 = \frac{d_2}{t_2} = \frac{650}{12} = 54\frac{1}{6} m/hr$$

mile per hour faster = $54\frac{1}{6} - 50 = 4\frac{1}{6} faster$

(14.20). 5 men can complete a job in 4 days. In how many days can 10 men working at ¼ of the previous rate complete the Job?

Solution

Men working at ¼ of the previous men or 1 previous man = 4(new men)

∴ 5 *previous men* = 5 x 4(*new men*) = 20 *new men*

$M_1T_1 = M_2T_2$ → 20 x 4 = 10 x 1 → x = 8 days

(14.21). Three men cab do a piece of job for 12 days. If two of the men work twice as fast as the third, how long would it take one of the faster men to do the job?

Solution

Two faster men working twice the third man or 1 man (third man) = ½ (the faster men)

3 men = 2 faster + third man = 2 + ½ = 2 ½ faster men

Thus, 2 ½ faster men use 12 days, 1 faster man will use y days

From $M_1T_1 = M_2T_2$ → $2\frac{1}{2} \times 12 = 1 \times y$ → $y = \frac{5}{2} \times 12 = 30\ days$

(14.22). Tunde and Shola can do a piece of work in 18 days. Tunde can do it alone in x days, whilst Shola takes 15 days to do it alone. Determine an equation satisfied by x?

Solution

Time for both = $\frac{product\ of\ seperate\ times}{sum\ of\ seperate\ times}$ → $18 = \frac{x(x+15)}{x+(x+15)}$ → $18 = \frac{x(x+15)}{2x+15}$

$x(x+15) = 18(2x+15)$ → $x^2 + 15x = 36x + 720$ → $x^2 - 21x - 270 = 0$

(14.23). A can build wall in 9 days and B the same length in 12 days. They work together for 4 days, and then B is moved to another job. How long does it take A to finish the wall alone?

Solution

$T_A = \frac{1}{9}$, $T_B = \frac{1}{12}$ → $T_A + T_B = \frac{1}{9} + \frac{1}{12} = \frac{7}{36}$

Work done together = Rate x time = $\frac{7}{36} x\ 4 = \frac{28}{36}$

Work undone = $1 - \frac{28}{30} = 6 = \frac{5}{36}$

$T_A = \frac{\frac{8}{36}}{\frac{1}{9}} = 2$

(14.24). Three laborers could each do a certain job in 10, 7 ½ and 6 days respectively, if working alone. How long will they take working together?

Solution

T_1 = 10 days, t_2 = 7½ = 7.5 days, T_3 = 6 days

Time together = $\frac{product}{sum\ of\ product\ of\ any\ two}$

Product = 10 x 7.5 x 6 = 450

Sum = (10 + 7 ½) + (10 x 6) + (7 ½ x 6) → 75 + 60 + 45 = 180

T = $\frac{450}{180} = 2.5\ days = 2\frac{1}{2}\ days$

(14.25). A completes a job in 10 days while B does it in 15 days. When A, B and C worked together, the job was completed in 4 days. If C worked alone, how many days will it take to complete the job?

Solution

T_A = 10 days, T_B = 15 days, T_c = ? , T_{ABC} = 4 days

$T_{ABC} = \frac{product}{sum\ of\ product\ of\ any\ two}$ → $4 = \frac{10\ x\ 15\ x\ T_C}{10(15) + 10(T_C) + 15(T_C)} = \frac{150\ T_C}{150 + 25T_C}$

$150T_C = 4(150 + 25T_C)$ → $150T_C = 600 + 100T_C$ → $150T_C - 100T_C = 600$

$50T_C = 600$ → $T_C = \frac{600}{50} = 12\ days$

(14.26). A man drove 4hrs in a certain speed. He then doubled his speed and drove for another 3hrs altogether he covered 600km. At what speed did he drive for the last 3hrs.

Solution

Let the man drive for 4hrs at a speed of x

Speed $= \frac{distance}{time} \rightarrow d = s \times t = x(4) = 4x$

For another 3hrs at a speed of 2x, $s = \frac{D}{T} \rightarrow 2x = \frac{D}{3} \rightarrow d = 2x(3) = 6x$

Total distance = 4x + 6x = 600 km $\rightarrow$ 10x = 600 $\therefore$ x = 60

For the last 3 hrs, the speed = 2x = 2(60) = 120km/h

(14.27). A train moves from P to Q at an average speed of 90km/h and immediately returns from Q to P through the same route at an average speed of 45km/h. find the average speed for the entire journey.

Solution

From P to Q, distance = x, speed = 90km/h

From Speed $= \frac{dist}{time} \rightarrow t_1 = \frac{dist}{speed} = \frac{x}{90}$

From Q to P, distance = x, speed = 45km/h, $t_2 = \frac{x}{45}$

Total distance travelled = x + x = 2x

Total time taken = $t_1 + t_2 = \frac{x}{90} + \frac{x}{45} = \frac{x + 2x}{90} = \frac{3x}{90}$

Average speed $= \frac{Total\ distance}{total\ time} = \frac{2x}{3x/90} = 2x \cdot \frac{90}{3x} = 60 km/h$

(14.28). A car travels from Calabar to Enugu, a distance of p with an average speed of U km/h and continues to Benin, a distance of q km, with an average speed of Wkm/h. find its average speed from Calabar to Benin.

Solution

From Calabar to Enugu, distance = P, speed = U km/h

time taken $= \frac{dist}{Speed} = \frac{P}{U}$

From Enugu to Benin, distance = q, speed = w

time taken $= \frac{dist}{Speed} = \frac{q}{W}$

From Calabar to Benin: Total distance = p + q

Total time = $\frac{p}{U} + \frac{q}{W} = \frac{Wp + qU}{UW}$

Average speed from Calabar to Benin = $\frac{Total\ distance}{Total\ time} = \frac{p+q}{\frac{Wp+qU}{UW}} = p + q\left(\frac{UW}{Wp+qU}\right)$

(14.29). A man runs a distance of 9km at a constant speed for the first 4km and then 2km/h faster for the rest of distance. The whole run takes him one hour. His average speed for the first 4km is?

Solution

For the first 4km, speed = x, $time = \frac{distance}{speed} = \frac{4}{x}$

Rest distance (9 – 4) = 5km, speed = (x + 2), $time = \frac{dist}{speed} = \frac{5}{x+2}$

$total\ time = \frac{4}{x} + \frac{5}{x+2} = 1hr \rightarrow \frac{4(x+2)+5x}{x(x+2)} = 1$

$4x + 8 + 5x = x^2 + 2x \rightarrow 9x + 8 = x^2 + 2x \rightarrow x^2 - 7x - 8 = 0 \rightarrow x = 8$ or -1, x = 8

(14.30). On each market day. Mrs Bassey walks to the marker from her home at a steady speed. This journey normally takes her 2hrs to complete. She finds, however that by increasing her usual speed by 1km/h, she can save 20 minutes. Find her usual speed in km/h

Solution

For a distance of x, time = 2hrs, speed = $\frac{x}{2}$

When speed = $\left(\frac{x}{2} + 1\right)$, time = (2hr – 20mins)

$speed = \frac{distance}{time} \rightarrow \frac{x}{2} + 1 = \frac{x}{1hr\ 40min} \rightarrow \frac{x}{2} + 1 = \frac{x}{1\frac{40}{60}hr} = \frac{x}{1\frac{2}{3}hr} = \frac{x}{\frac{5}{3}hr} = \frac{3x}{5}$

Multiply both sides by *l.c.m* of 2 and 5

$10\left(\frac{x}{2} + 1\right) = 10\left(\frac{3x}{5}\right) \rightarrow 5x + 10 = 6x \rightarrow 6x - 5x = 10 \therefore x = 10$

Her usual speed = $\frac{x}{2} = \frac{10}{2} = 5km/h$

(14.31). Two cars x and y start at the same point and travel towards a point P which is 150km away. If the average speed of y is 60km/hr and x arrives at P 25 minutes earlier than y. what is the average speed of x.

Solution

Average speed of y $= \frac{150}{t} = 60 km/hr \rightarrow t = \frac{150}{60} = 2.5h$

Time taken by x = 25 min earlier than y $\rightarrow$ 2hr 30 min – 25 min = 2hr 5min

Average Speed of x $= \frac{150}{2\ hr\ 5min} = \frac{150}{2\frac{5}{60}} = \frac{150}{\frac{125}{60}} = \frac{150 \times 60}{125} = 7$

CHAPTER 15 POLYNOMIALS

Polynomials are expression with ascending or descending powers of variable which do not include negative powers.

Thus the following are polynomials:

$x + 2 \rightarrow x^1 + 2x^0$

$3x^2 + 4x - 8 \rightarrow 3x^2 + 4x^1 - 8x^0$

Thus the following are not polynomials with reasons annotated:

$x + 2 + \frac{5}{x} \rightarrow x + 2x^0 + 5x^{-1}$ (negative power)

$\text{Log}(2x + 3)$ (because of the logarithm)

$\sqrt{x^3 + 2x^2 + 5x} \rightarrow (x^3 + 2x^2 + 5x)^{1/2}$ (because of the square root)

$2^{x^2 + 4x}$ because it is a power of 2

Operation of Polynomials

The following operations are possible with polynomials

Addition, subtraction, multiplication, Division, Factors and remainder theorem, Factorization and roots of equations

Addition and Subtraction

For addition and subtraction, we just combine variables with the "same powers"

Division

(i) Here divide the first term of the divided by the first term of the divisor to obtain the first term of the quotient.

(ii) Multiply each term of the divisor by the first term of the quotient and write below the first two terms of the dividend

(iii) Subtract the product obtained in the second step from the first two terms of the dividend and add the next term of the dividend

(iv) Use the result of (iii) above as a new dividend and repeat steps (i) to (iii)

The process continues until division is no longer possible.

We therefore define a polynomial as:

$Polynomial = Qoutient \times divisor + Remainder$

Multiplication

Here simply use easy term in the first bracket to multiply each term of the other bracket and collect like terms.

Factor and Remainder Theorems

These are theorems deduced from division of polynomials for the purpose of determining the remainder when a division operation is given.

Remainder Theorem

This states that if polynomial f(x) is divided by x + a or x − a, the remainder is f(-a) or f(a) respectively. This theorem is applied to cases where only remainder is required.

Factor Theorem

This states that if the remainder when the polynomial f(x) is divided by $mx \pm a$ is zero, then $mx \pm a$ is a factor of f(x).

Application of factor and remainder theorems

1. **Factorization of a polynomial**

To factorize a polynomial such as $x^3 + x^2 - 6x + 4$
Simply look for factors (including the negative factors) of the constant term which is 4
e.g. factors of 4 are 1, 2, 4, (-1), (-2), (-4)
Substitute these factors and into the given question and solve, if the answer is equal to zero then it is a factor.

2. **Function Notation**
A function is a rule of correspondence that associates to each element x in X a unique element y in Y i.e f : X → Y

Evaluation of functional notations
(i) If two function of the same letter are given, then their values are equated and simplified where necessary before substitution.
e.g. If f(x) and f(y) are given, then x = y

(ii) Functions of different letters are combined as composite functions e.g. functions like f(x) and g(x) can be combined as fg(x) or fog(x), gf(x) or gof(x) etc

The combined function is simplified by separating the function with different bracket so that the rule or relationship under each function can be satisfied e.g.
Fg(x) or fog(x) = F[g(x)] i.e solving g(x) and using it as a component of f
gof(x) = g[f(x)] i.e. solving f(x) and using it as a component of g

3. Inverse of a function: To determine the inverse of a given function. Do the following
(i) Replace the given function f(x) with another alphabet say y
(ii) Solve for x
(iii) Replace y with x

Questions

(15.1). Given $P_1 = 2 + 3x - 5x^2 + 7x^3 - 4x^4$, $P_2 = 4 - 5x + 6x^2 + 3x^3 - 8x^4$
Find $P_1 \times P_2, P_1 + P_2, P_1 - P_2$.

Solution

$P_1 + P_2 = 2 + 4 + 3x - 5x - 5x^2 + 6x^2 + 7x^3 + 3x^3 - 4x^4 - 8x^4$

$6 - 2x + x^2 + 10x^3 - 12x^4$

$P_1 - P_2 = 2 - 4 + 3x + 5x - 5x^2 - 6x^2 + 7x^3 - 3x^3 - 4x^4 + 8x^4$

$-2 + 8x - 11x^2 + 4x^3 + 4x^4$

$P_1 \times P_2 = (2 + 3x - 5x^2 + 7x^3 - 4x^4)(4 - 5x + 6x^2 + 3x^3 - 8x^4)$

$8 - 10x + 12x^2 + 6x^3 - 16x^4 + 12x - 15x^2 + 18x^3 + 9x^4 - 24x^5 - 20x^2 + 25x^3 - 30x^4 - 15x^5 + 40x^6 + 28x^3 - 35x^4 + 42x^5 + 21x^6 - 56x^7 - 16x^4 + 20x^5 - 24x^6 - 12x^7 + 32x^8$

$\rightarrow 8 + 2x - 23x^2 + 77x^3 - 88x^4 + 23x^5 + 37x^6 - 68x^7 + 32x^8$

(15.2). If $P_1 = (2x + 4)$, $P_2 = 4x^2 - 3x$, find (i) $P_1 + 3P_2$ (ii) $2P_1 - P_2$.

Solution

$P_1 + 3P_2 \rightarrow (2x + 4) + 3(4x^2 - 3x) \rightarrow (2x + 4) + 12x^2 - 9x \rightarrow 12x^2 + 2x - 9x + 4$

$= 12x^2 - 7x + 4$

$2P_1 - P_2 = 2(2x + 4) - (4x^2 - 3x) \rightarrow 4x + 8 - 4x^2 + 3x \rightarrow -4x^2 + 4x + 3x + 8$

$= -4x^2 + 7x + 8.$

(15.3). Divide $x^3 + 3x^2 - 4x + 2$ by $x - 1$

Solution

$\dfrac{x^2 + 3x^2 - 4x + 2}{x - 1}$

$$\begin{array}{r} x^2 + 4x \quad \leftarrow quotient \\ x-1\overline{\smash{)}x^3 + 3x^2 - 4x + 2} \\ \underline{x^3 - x^2} \\ 4x^2 - 4x \\ \underline{4x^2 - 4x} \\ +2 \leftarrow remainder \end{array}$$

(15.4). Divide $x^3 - 2x^2 + 5x + 8$ by $x - 2$.

Solution

$\dfrac{x^3 - 2x^2 + 5x + 8}{x - 2} =$

$$\begin{array}{r} x^2 + 5 \\ x-2\overline{\smash{)}x^3 - 2x^2 - 5x + 8} \\ \underline{x^3 - 2x^2} \\ 5x + 8 \\ \underline{5x - 10} \\ +18 \end{array}$$

(15.5). Find the quotient and remainder when $3x^3 + 6x^2 - 5x - 6$ is divided by $x^2 - 3x + 1$.

Solution

$$x^2 - 3x + 1 \overline{\smash{\big)}\begin{array}{l} 3x+15 \\ \hline 3x^3 + 6x^2 - 5x - 6 \\ \underline{3x^3 - 9x^2 + 3x} \\ 0 + 15x^2 - 8x - 6 \\ \underline{15x^2 - 45x + 15} \\ 0 - 37x - 21 \end{array}}$$

(15.6). Divide $a^{3x} - 26a^{2x} + 156a^x - 216$ by $a^{2x} - 24a^x + 108$

Solution

$$a^{2x} - 24a^x + 108 \overline{\smash{\big)}\begin{array}{l} a^x - 2 \\ \hline a^{3x} - 26a^{2x} + 156a^x - 216 \\ \underline{a^{3x} - 24a^{2x} + 108a^x} \\ 0 - 2a^{2x} + 48a^x - 216 \\ \underline{-2a^{2x} + 48a^x - 216} \\ 0 \quad + 0 \quad + 0 \end{array}}$$

(15.7). Find the quotient and remainder when $2 + 3x - 5x^2 + 7x^3 - 4x^4$ is divided by $4 - 5x + 6x^2 + 3x^3 - 8x^4$

Solution

$$4 - 5x + 6x^2 + 3x^3 - 8x^4 \overline{\smash{\big)}\begin{array}{l} \frac{1}{2} \\ \hline 2 + 3x - 5x^2 + 7x^3 - 4x^4 \\ 2 - \frac{5}{2}x + 3x^2 + \frac{3}{2}x^3 - 4x^4 \\ 0 + \frac{11}{2}x - 8x^2 + \frac{11}{2}x^3 \end{array}}$$

(15.8). Divide the expression $x^3 + 7x^2 - x - 7$ by $-1 + x^2$
Solution

$$x^2 - 1 \overline{\smash{\big)}\begin{array}{l} x + 7 \\ \hline x^3 + 7x^2 - x - 7 \\ \underline{x^3 \qquad\quad - x} \\ 7x^2 \quad - 7 \\ \underline{7x^2 \quad - 7} \end{array}}$$

(15. 9). Find the remainder when $3x^3 + x^2 + 24$ is divided by $x + 2$.
Solution
From $x + 2 = 0 \rightarrow x = -2$
$R = f(-2) = 3(-2)^3 + (-2)^2 + 24 = -24 + 4 + 24 = 4$

(15. 10). Find the values of a and b if the expression $x^3 + ax^2 + bx - 4$ is exactly divisible by $x^2 - 4$.
Solution
$f(x) = x^3 + ax^2 + bx - 4$
$x^2 - 4 = 0 \rightarrow x^2 - 2^2 = 0 \rightarrow (x-2)(x+2) = 0 \rightarrow x = 2$ or -2
$R = f(2) = 2^3 + a(2)^2 + b(2) - 4 \rightarrow 8 + 4a + 2b - 4 \rightarrow 4a + 2b + 4$
$R = f(-2) = (-2)^3 + a(-2)^3 + b(2) - 4 \rightarrow -8 + 4a - 2b - 4 \rightarrow 4a - 2b - 12$

Combining then Adding   combining then subtracting
$4a + 2b = -4$ $4a + 2b = -4$
$4a - 2b = 12$ $4a - 2b = 12$
$8a = 8 \therefore a = 1$ $4b = -16 \therefore b = -4$

(15. 11). If $(x + 2)$ and $(x - 1)$ are factors of the expression $lx^3 + 2kx^2 + 24$ find the values of l and k.
Solution
From $(x + 2) = 0$ and $(x - 1) = 0 \rightarrow x = -2$ or $x = 1$
For $x = -2$
$f(-2) = l(-2)^3 + 2k(-2)^2 + 24 \rightarrow -8l + 8k + 24 = 0 \rightarrow 8l - 8k = 24 \rightarrow l - k = 3$

For $x = 1$
$f(1) = l(1)^3 + 2k(1)^2 + 24 \rightarrow l + 2k + 24 = 0 \rightarrow l + 2k = -24$

Combining
$l - k = 3$ (i)
$l + 2k = -24$ (ii)
$-3k = 27 \rightarrow k = -\frac{27}{3} = -9$
Put $k = -9$ in (i) $l - (-9) = 3 \rightarrow l + 9 = 3 \therefore l = -6$
$\therefore l = -6, k = -9$

(15. 12). If $(x - 2)$ and $(x + 1)$ are factors of $x^3 - 3x - 2 = 0$ find the third factor.
Solution
For x^3, "at most" 3 factors are expected
$\therefore x^3 - 3x - 2 = (x - 2)(x + 1)(a + b)$
$x^3 = x.x.a$ and $-2 = 2.1.b$
$a = \frac{x^3}{x^2} = x$ and $b = -\frac{2}{-2} = 1$

148

∴ the third factor = (x + 1)

(15.13). If $(x - 2)$ and $(x + 1)$ are factors of $x^3 + px^2 + qx + 1$ what is the sum of p and q?
Solution
From $x - 2 = 0$ ∴ $x = 2$
$2^3 + p(2)^2 + q(2) + 1 \rightarrow 8 + 4p + 2q + 1 \rightarrow 4p + 2q = -9$
From $x - 1 = 0$ ∴ $x = -1$
$(-1)^3 + p(-1)^2 + q(-1) + 1 \rightarrow -1 + p - q + 1 \rightarrow p - q = 0$

$4p + 2q = -9$
$p - q = 0$
$4p + 2q = -9$
$2p - 2q = 0$
$6P = -9$ ∴ $p = -\frac{3}{2}$
Put $p = -\frac{3}{2}$ in (i) $q = -\frac{3}{2}$

$p + q \rightarrow \frac{-3}{2} + \frac{-3}{2} \rightarrow \frac{-6}{2} = -3$

(15.14). Factorize $3x^3 + 4x^2 - 13x + 6$ completely, given that $x - 1$ is a factor.
Solution
Factors of 6 are 1, -1, 2, -2, 3, -3, 6, -6.
From $f(x) = 3x^3 + 4x^2 - 13x + 6$
$f(-3) = 3(-3)^3 + 4(-3)^2 - 13(-3) + 6 \rightarrow -81 + 36 + 39 + 6 = 0$
∴ $(x + 3)$ is a factor.
1, -3 and 2/3 gives zero when substituted into $3x^3 + 4x^2 - 13x + 6$
$3x^3 + 4x^2 - 13x + 6 = (x - 1)(x + 3)(3x - 2)$

(15.14). If one factor $x^3 - 8^{-1}$ is $x - 2^{-1}$, the other factor is?
Solution
$x^3 - 8^{-1} \rightarrow x^3 - (2^3)^{-1} \rightarrow x^3 - (2^{-1})^3 \rightarrow (a - b)(a^2 + ab + b^2)$
$(x - 2^{-1})[x^2 + x \cdot 2^{-1} + (2^{-1})^2] \rightarrow (x - 2^{-1})(x^2 + 2^{-1}x + 4^{-1})$
Thus, the other factor is $x^2 + 2^{-1}x + 4^{-1}$

(15.15). Factorize $x^3 + x^2 - 6x + 4$.
Solution
Factors of 4 are 1, -1, 2, -2, 4, -4
$f(x) = x^3 + x^2 - 6x + 4$
Only $f(1) = 0$ i.e
$f(1) = 1^3 + 1^2 - 6(1) + 4 = 1 + 1 - 6 + 4 = 0$, $x - 1$ is a factor
Hence, the polynomial is divided by the available factor to determine the other factor.

$$\begin{array}{r}
x^2 + 2x - 4 \\
x-1 \overline{\smash{\big)}\, x^3 + x^2 - 6x + 4}\\
\underline{x^3 - x^2}\\
2x^2 + 6x\\
\underline{2x^2 + 6x}\\
-4x + 4\\
\underline{-4x + 4}
\end{array}$$

The factors are $(x-1)(x^2 + 2x - 4)$

(15.17). Solve the equation $x^3 - 5x^2 - x + 5 = 0$.
Solution
Factors of 5 are 1, -1, 5 and -5
$f(1) = 1^3 - 5(1) - 1 + 5 = 1 - 5 - 1 + 5 = 0$ $\therefore (x - 1)$ is a factor
$f(5) = 5^3 - 5(5)^2 - 5 + 5 = 125 - 125 - 5 + 5 = 0$ $\therefore (x - 5)$ is a factor
$\therefore x^3 - 5x^2 - x + 5 = (x - 1)(x - 5)(x + 1)$
i.e $(x - 1)(x - 5)(x + 1) = 0$
$x - 1 = 0$ or $x - 5 = 0$ or $x + 1 = 0$
$x = 1$ or $x = 5$ or $x = -1$

(15.18). If $f(x) = 2x^2 - 5x + 3$, find $f(x + 1)$
Solution
$x = x + 1$
$f(x + 1) = 2(x + 1)^2 - 5(x + 1) + 3 \rightarrow 2(x^2 + 2x + 1) - 5(x + 1) + 3$
$2x^2 + 4x + 2 - 5x - 5 + 3 = 2x^2 - x$

(15.19). If $g(Y) = \frac{Y-3}{11} + \frac{11}{Y^2-9}$ what is $g(Y + 3)$?
Solution
$Y = Y + 3$
$g(Y + 3) = \frac{(Y+3)-3}{11} + \frac{11}{(Y+3)^2 - 9} \rightarrow \frac{Y}{11} + \frac{11}{Y^2 + 6Y + 9 - 9} = \frac{Y}{11} + \frac{11}{Y^2 + 6Y} = \frac{Y}{11} + \frac{11}{Y(Y+6)}$

(15.20). If a function is defined by f(x + 1) = 3x² – x + 4 find f(0).
Solution
Equating: x + 1 = 0 → x = - 1
$f(x + 1) = 3x^2 - x + 4$ → $f(0) = 3(-1)^2 - (-1) + 4$ → 3 + 1 + 4 = 8

(15.21). If f(x) = 2(x – 3)² + 3(x – 3) + 4 and g(y) = $\sqrt{5 + y}$ find g[f(3)] and f[g(4)].
Solution
f(x) = 2(x – 3)² + 3(x – 3) + 4
f(3) = 2(3 – 3)² + 3(3 – 3) + 4 = 4
g[f(3)] = g[4]
from g[y] = $\sqrt{5 + y}$ → $g[4] = \sqrt{5 + 4} = \sqrt{9} = 3$
∴ $g[f(3)] and f[g(4)] = 3$ and 4

(15.22). Two functions f and g, defined on the set of real numbers are given as f(x) = 3x – 2 and g(x) = 4x + k. find the value of the constant k for which gf(x) = fg(x).

Solution

gf(x) = g[f(x)] = g[3x – 2] = 4(3x - 2) + k

fg(x) = f[g(x)] = f[4x + k] = 3(4x + k) – 2

12x – 8 + k = 12x + 3x – 2, 3k –k = 12x- 12x - 8+ 2

(15.23). If f(x) = x² – 3x + 2 and g(x) = x – 1, for call x ε R, find the value of x for which fg(x) = 0.

Solution

fg(x) = f[g(x)] → f(x – 1) = (x – 1)² – 3(x – 1) + 2 = 0 → x² – 2x + 1 – 3x + 3 + 2 = 0

x² - 5x + 6 = 0 → (x -2)(x – 3) = 0 ∴ x = 2 or 3

(15.24). If f(x) = $\frac{4x - 3}{2x + 5}$ Find $f^{-1}(x)$.
Solution

From f(x) = $\frac{4x - 3}{2x + 5}$ → y = $\frac{4x - 3}{2x + 5}$ → $4x - 3 = y(2x + 5)$ → $4x - 3 = 2xy + 5y$
$4x - 2xy = 5y + 3$ → $x(4 - 2y) = 5y + 3$ → $x = \frac{5y + 3}{4 - 2y}$
Replacing y with x, $f^{-1}(x) = \frac{5x + 3}{4 - 2x}$

(15.24). If $f(x) = \frac{4x-3}{2x+5}$ Find $f^{-1}(x)$.

Solution

From $f(x) = \frac{4x-3}{2x+5} \rightarrow y = \frac{4x-3}{2x+5} \rightarrow 4x-3 = y(2x+5) \rightarrow 4x-3 = 2xy+5y$
$4x - 2xy = 5y + 3 \rightarrow x(4-2y) = 5y+3 \rightarrow x = \frac{5y+3}{4-2y}$

Replacing y with x, $f^{-1}(x) = \frac{5x+3}{4-2x}$

(15.25). If $f(x) = 3x + 4$ Find $f^{-1}(x)$

Solution

From $f(x) = \frac{4x-3}{2x+5} \rightarrow y = 3x + 4 \rightarrow x = \frac{y-4}{3}$

Replacing y with x, $f^{-1}(x) = \frac{x-4}{3}$

CHAPTER 16 ALGEBRAIC FRACTIONS

Algebraic fractions can be rational or irrational.

Types of fractions
(i) *Rational* Fractions: are the ones with defined denominator. i.e where the denominator is not equal to zero.
(ii) Irrational fractions: are the ones with zero denominators. Hence they are said to be undefined

Simplification of Irrational fraction:
Irrational fractions are called undefined fractions. Thus a given fraction can be said be undefined or irrational by simply equating its denominator to zero.

Simplification of rational Fraction
Rational faction is simplified by linear combination and factorization and by partial fraction.

Simplification of rational fraction by linear combination and factorization
Here we simply find the LCM of the expression and evaluate. The L.C.M must be selected carefully using the technique below
Note The L.C.M is
(i) The product of denominators when the denominators are different
(ii) One of the denominators when the denominators are the same
(iii) The greatest multiple when one denominator is a multiple of the other

Simplification of rational fraction by partial fraction: Partial fraction is a fraction consisting of one or more parts obtained from a fraction that cannot be further simplified by factorization or the use of L.C.M. we simplify them by using the following techniques

(i) Linear factor in denominator: Consider the expression $\dfrac{-1-5x}{(x+2)(1-x)}$

A linear equation is an equation of the form y = mx + c where m and c are constants
Whenever such is given we just transform the question to

$\dfrac{-1-5x}{(x+2)(1-x)} = \dfrac{A}{(x+2)} + \dfrac{B}{(1-x)}$ and solve for A and B

(ii) Unfactorisable second degree factor in the denominator: Consider $\dfrac{3x^2-2x+1}{(x+1)(x^2-2x-1)}$

unfactorisable second degree means a quadratic factor i.e $x^2 - x - 1$ that is not factorisable. Whenever such is given we just transform the question to

153

$$\frac{3x^2 - 2x + 1}{(x+1)(x^2 - 2x - 1)} = \frac{A}{(x+1)} + \frac{Bx + C}{(x^2 - 2x - 1)}$$ and solve for a, b and c.

(*iii*) Repeated factors in the denominator: Consider the expression $\frac{2x^2 - 3x - 1}{(x+2)(x-1)^2}$

Repeated factors imply there is a multiple of the other.

Whenever such is given we just transform the question to
$$\frac{2x^2 - 3x - 1}{(x+2)(x-1)^2} = \frac{A}{(x+2)} + \frac{B}{(x-1)} + \frac{C}{(x-1)^2}$$ and solve for a, b and c.

Questions

(16.1). For what values of x is $\frac{2x+5}{2x^2 - 7x - 4}$ undefined?

Solution
It is undefined when the denominator is zero.
$2x^2 - 7x - 4 = 0 \rightarrow 2x^2 - 8x + x - 4 = 0 \rightarrow 2x(x-4) + 1(x-4) = 0$
$2x + 1 = 0$ or $x - 4 = 0 \rightarrow x = -1/2$ or $x = 4$

(16.2). The function $\frac{2x^3 - 3x - 1}{mx - 6}$ is undefined at the point x = 4 find the value of m.

Solution
It is undefined when the denominator is zero at x = 4
From $mx - 6 = 0 \rightarrow m(4) - 6 = 0 \therefore m = 6/4 = 3/2$ or 1.5

(16.3). Resolve $\frac{3x - 19}{(x-3)(x+2)}$ into partial fraction.

Solution
$$\frac{3x - 19}{(x-3)(x+2)} = \frac{A}{(x-3)} + \frac{B}{(x+2)}$$

Multiplying both sides by the Lcm
$3x - 19 = A(x + 2) + B(x - 3)$
Setting $x + 2 = 0, x = -2$
$3(-2) - 19 = 0 + B(-2 - 3) \rightarrow -6 - 19 = -5B \therefore B = \frac{-25}{-5} = 5$
Setting $x - 3 = 0, x = 3$
$3(3) - 19 = A(3 + 2) + 0 \rightarrow -10 = 5A \therefore A = \frac{-10}{5} = -2$

$$\therefore \frac{3x - 19}{(x-3)(x+2)} = \frac{-2}{(x-3)} + \frac{5}{(x+2)}$$

(16.4). Resolve $\dfrac{x-7}{(x-1)(x+2)}$ into partial fraction.

Solution

$$\dfrac{x-7}{(x-1)(x+2)} = \dfrac{A}{(x-1)} + \dfrac{B}{(x+2)}$$

Multiplying both sides by the Lcm
$x - 7 = A(x+2) + B(x-1)$

Setting $x + 2 = 0$, $x = -2$
$-2 - 7 = 0 + B(-2-3) \to -9 = -3B \therefore B = \dfrac{-9}{-3} = 3$

Setting $x - 1 = 0$, $x = 1$
$1 - 7 = A(1+2) + 0 \to -6 = 3A \therefore A = \dfrac{-6}{3} = -2$

$\therefore \dfrac{x-7}{(x-1)(x+2)} = \dfrac{-2}{(x-1)} + \dfrac{3}{(x+2)}$

(16.5). Resolve $\dfrac{3x^2 - 2x + 1}{(x+1)(x^2 - 2x - 1)}$ into partial fraction.

$$\dfrac{3x^2 - 2x + 1}{(x+1)(x^2 - 2x - 1)} = \dfrac{A}{(x+1)} + \dfrac{Bx + C}{(x^2 - 2x - 1)}$$

Multiplying both sides by the Lcm
$3x^2 - 2x + 1 = A(x^2 - 2x - 1) + (Bx + C)(x+1)$
Setting $x + 1 = 0$, $x = -1$
$3(-1)^2 - 2(-1) + 1 = A((-1)^2 - 2(-1) - 1) + 0 \to 6 = 2A \therefore A = 3$

Set $x = 0$
$3(0)^2 - 2(0) + 1 = 3((0)^2 - 2(0) - 1) + (B(0) + C)(0+1)$
$1 = -3 + c \to c = 4$

Set $x = 1$
$3(1)^2 - 2(1) + 1 = 3((1)^2 - 2(1) - 1) + (B+4)(1+1) \to 2 = -6 + 2B + 8$

$2 + 6 - 8 = 2B \therefore B = 0$

(16.6). Resolve $\dfrac{1}{x^3 - 1}$ into partial fraction.

Solution

$\dfrac{1}{x^3 - 1^3} = \dfrac{1}{(x-1)(x^2 + x + 1)} \therefore \dfrac{1}{x^3 - 1} = \dfrac{1}{(x-1)(x^2 + x + 1)}$

$$\frac{1}{x^3-1} = \frac{A}{(x-1)} + \frac{Bx+C}{(x^2+x+1)}$$

Multiplying both sides by the Lcm

$1 = A(x^2 + x + 1) + (Bx + C)(x - 1) \rightarrow 1 = Ax^2 + Ax + A + Bx^2 - Bx + Cx - C$

$1 = (A + B)x_2 + (A + C - B)x + A - C$

Comparing co-efficient
A + B = 0 ....(i)
A + C – B = 0 ....(ii)
A – C = 1 ....(iii)

From (i) A = -B inserting into (ii)
A + C – (-A) = 0 → 2A + C = 0
$\qquad\qquad\qquad$ A – C = 1
$\qquad\qquad\qquad$ 3A = 1 ∴ $A = \frac{1}{3}$

From A – C = 1 → $C = A - 1 \rightarrow \frac{1}{3} - 1 = -\frac{2}{3}$

Since A = -B → $B = -\frac{1}{3}$

$$\frac{1}{x^3-1} = \frac{A}{(x-1)} + \frac{Bx+C}{(x^2+x+1)} \rightarrow \frac{\frac{1}{3}}{(x-1)} + \frac{-\frac{1}{3}x - \frac{2}{3}}{(x^2+x+1)} \rightarrow \frac{1}{3}\left[\frac{1}{x-1} - \frac{x+2}{(x^2+x+1)}\right]$$

(16.7). Resolve $\frac{3x^2 - 2x - 1}{(x+2)(x-1)^2}$ into partial fraction.

Solution

$$\frac{3x^2 - 2x - 1}{(x+2)(x-1)^2} = \frac{A}{(x+2)} + \frac{B}{(x-1)} + \frac{C}{(x-1)^2}$$

$3x^2 - 2x - 1 = A(x - 1)^2 + B(x - 1)(x + 2) + C(x + 2)$

Setting x – 1 = 0, x = 1
$3(1)^2 - 2(1) - 1 = C(1 + 2) \rightarrow 0 = 3C$ ∴ C = 0
Setting x + 2 = 0, x = -2

$3(-2)^2 - 2(-2) - 1 = A(-2-1)^2 \rightarrow 15 = 9A$ ∴ $A = \frac{15}{9} = \frac{5}{3}$

Setting x = 0

$3(0)^2 - 2(0) - 1 = \frac{5}{3}(0-1)^2 + B(0-1)(0+2) \rightarrow -1 = \frac{5}{3} - 2B$ ∴ $B = \frac{-8}{-6} = \frac{4}{3}$

$$\frac{3x^2-2x-1}{(x+2)(x-1)^2} = \frac{5}{3(x+2)} + \frac{4}{3(x-1)} + \frac{0}{(x-1)^2}$$

(16.8). Simplify $\frac{3}{2x-1} + \frac{2-x}{x-2}$

Solution

$\frac{3}{2x-1} + \frac{2-x}{x-2} \rightarrow \frac{3(x-2)+(2-x)(2x-1)}{(2x-1)(x-2)} \rightarrow \frac{3x-6+4x-2-2x^2+x}{(2x-1)(x-2)} \rightarrow \frac{-2x^2+8x-8}{(2x-1)(x-2)} =$
$\frac{-(2x^2-8x+8)}{(2x-1)(x-2)} \rightarrow \frac{-2(x^2-4x+4)}{(2x-1)(x-2)} \rightarrow \frac{-2(x-2)(x-2)}{(2x-1)(x-2)} \rightarrow \frac{-2(x-2)}{2x-1} = \frac{-2x+4}{2x-1} = \frac{4-2x}{2x-1}$

(16.9). Simplify $\frac{1}{x^2+5x+6} + \frac{1}{x^2+3x+2}$

Solution

$\frac{1}{x^2+5x+6} + \frac{1}{x^2+3x+2} \rightarrow \frac{1}{(x+3)(x+2)} + \frac{1}{(x+1)(x+2)} \rightarrow \frac{(x+1)+(x+3)}{(x+3)(x+2)(x+1)} = \frac{2x+4}{(x+3)(x+2)(x+1)}$
$\frac{2(x+2)}{(x+3)(x+2)(x+1)} = \frac{2}{(x+3)(x+1)}$

(16.10). Simplify $\frac{x+2}{x+1} - \frac{x-2}{x+2}$

Solution

$\frac{x+2}{x+1} - \frac{x-2}{x+2} \rightarrow \frac{(x+2)(x+2)-(x-2)(x+1)}{(x+1)(x+2)} \rightarrow \frac{x^2+4x+4-(x^2+x-2x-2)}{(x+1)(x+2)}$
$\frac{x^2+4x+4-x^2-x+2x+2)}{(x+1)(x+2)} = \frac{5x+6}{(x+1)(x+2)}$

(16.11). Simplify $\frac{x^2+y^2+xy}{x+y} - \frac{x^2+y^2-xy}{x-y}$

Solution

$\frac{x^2+y^2+xy}{(x+y)} - \frac{x^2+y^2-xy}{(x-y)} \rightarrow \frac{(x-y)(x^2+y^2+xy) - (x+y)(x^2+y^2-xy)}{(x+y)(x-y)}$

$\frac{(x^3-y^3)-(x^3+y^3)}{(x+y)(x-y)} = \frac{x^3-y^3-x^3-y^3}{(x+y)(x-y)} = \frac{-2y^3}{x^2-y^2} = \frac{2y^3}{y^2-x^2}$

(16.12). Simplify $\frac{x-7}{x^2-9} \times \frac{x^2-3x}{x^2-49}$

Solution

$\frac{x-7}{x^2-9} \cdot \frac{x^2-3x}{x^2-49} \rightarrow \frac{x-7}{x^2-3^2} \cdot \frac{x(x-3)}{x^2-7^2} \rightarrow = \frac{x-7}{(x-3)(x+3)} \cdot \frac{-x(x-3)}{(x-7)(x+7)} = \frac{x}{(x+3)(x+7)}

157

(16.13). Simplify $\dfrac{1-x^2}{x-x^2}$, where $x \neq 0$

Solution

$\dfrac{1-x^2}{x-x^2} \to \dfrac{1^2 - x^2}{x(1-x)} \to \dfrac{(1-x)(1+x)}{x(1-x)} = \dfrac{(1+x)}{x}$

(16.14). Simplify $\dfrac{(4-a^2)(a^2+4a+3)}{(a^2-9)(a^2-a-2)}$

Solution

$\dfrac{(4-a^2)(a^2+4a+3)}{(a^2-9)(a^2-a-2)} \to \dfrac{(2-a)(2+a)[(a+1)(a+3)]}{(a+3)(a-3)[(a-2)(a+1)]} \to \dfrac{-(-2+a)(2+a)}{(a-3)(a-2)} \to \dfrac{-(a-2)(2+a)}{(a-3)(a-2)} = \dfrac{-(2+a)}{(a-3)}$

(16.15). Simplify $\dfrac{(2m-u)^2 (m+2u)^2}{5m^2 - 5u^2}$

Solution

$\dfrac{(2m-u)^2(m+2u)^2}{5m^2-5u^2} \to \dfrac{(4m^2-4mu+u^2)-(m^2-4mu+4u^2)}{5(m^2-u^2)} \to \dfrac{3m^2-3u^2}{5(m-u)(m+u)}$

$\dfrac{3(m^2-u^2)}{5(m-u)(m+u)} \to \dfrac{3(m-u)(m+u)}{5(m-u)(m+u)} = \dfrac{3}{5}$

(16.16). Simplify $\dfrac{x^2-1}{x^3-2x^2-x-2}$.

Solution

$x^2 - 1 = x^2 - 1^2 = (x-1)(x+1)$
For $x^3 + 2x^2 - x - 2$
Factors of 2 are 2, -2, 1, -1
Let $f(x) = x^3 + 2x^2 - x - 2$
$f(1) = 1 + 2 - 1 - 2 = 0$ i.e $(x-1)$ is a factor
$f(-2) = -8 + 8 + 2 - 2 = 0$ i.e $(x+2)$ is a factor
$\therefore x^3 - 2x^2 - x - 2 = (x-1)(x+2)(x+1)$
$\dfrac{x^2-1}{x^3-2x^2-x-2} = \dfrac{(x-1)(x+1)}{(x-1)(x+2)(x+1)} = \dfrac{1}{(x+2)}$

(16.17). Resolve $\dfrac{x^2+3x+2}{x+1}$ into partial fraction.

Solution

$$\begin{array}{r} x+2\\ x+1{\overline{\smash{\big)}\,x^2+3x+2}}\\ \underline{x^2+x}\\ 2x+2\\ \underline{2x+2}\\ \end{array}$$

$\therefore \dfrac{x^2+3x+2}{x+1} = (x+2)$ no remainder

(**16.18**). Evaluate $\frac{x^3 + 2x^2 - 8x + 7}{x^2 + 4x - 3}$

Solution

$$\begin{array}{r}
x - 2 \\
x^2 + 4x - 3 \overline{\smash{\big)}\,x^3 + 2x^2 - 8x + 7}\\
\underline{x^3 + 4x^2 - 3x}\\
-2x^2 - 5x + 7\\
\underline{-2x^2 - 8x + 6}\\
3x + 7
\end{array}$$

$\frac{x^3 + 2x^2 - 8x + 7}{x^2 + 4x - 3} = (x - 2) + \frac{3x + 7}{x^2 + 4x - 3}$

(**16.19**). $\frac{4x^2 - 2x - 3}{(x-2)(x-1)^2} = \frac{3}{(x-2)} + \frac{4}{(x+1)} + \frac{C}{(x+1)^2}$ find c.

Solution
$4x^2 - 2x - 3 = 3(x+1)^2 + 4(x+1)(x-2) + c(x-2)$
Setting x = 0
$4(0)^2 - 2(0) - 3 = 3(0+1)^2 + 4(0+1)(0-2) + c(0-2)$
$-3 = 3 - 8 - 2c \therefore c = \frac{-2}{2} = -1$

(**16.20**). Find P if $\frac{x-3}{(1-x)(x+2)} = \frac{P}{(1-x)} + \frac{Q}{(x+2)}$

Solution
$P = \frac{x-3}{x+2}$ with $1 - x = 0$ or $x = 1$

$\therefore P = \frac{1-3}{1+2} = \frac{-2}{3}$

(**16.21**). If $\frac{3x^2 - 7}{x^3 - 2x^2 - 8x} = \frac{7}{8x} + \frac{P}{x+4} + \frac{Q}{x-2}$, find P + Q.

Solution
$P = \frac{3x^2 - 7}{8x(x-2)}$ where $x + 4 = 0$ or $x = -4$

$P = \frac{3(-4)^2 - 7}{8(-4)(-4-2)} = \frac{48-7}{-32(-6)} = \frac{41}{192}$

$Q = \frac{3x^2 - 7}{8x(x+4)}$ where $x - 2 = 0$ or $x = 2$

$Q = \frac{3(2)^2 - 7}{8(2)(2+4)} = \frac{12-7}{16(6)} = \frac{5}{96}$

$P + Q \rightarrow \frac{41}{192} + \frac{5}{96} \rightarrow \frac{41+10}{192} = \frac{51}{192}$

(16.22). Resolve $\frac{4x-1}{2x^2 - 5x + 2}$ into partial fraction.

Solution

$2x^2 + 5x + 2 \rightarrow 2x^2 + 4x + x + 2 \rightarrow 2x(x+2) + 1(x+2) = (2x+1)(x+2)$

$\therefore \frac{4x-1}{2x^2 + 5x + 2} = \frac{4x-1}{(2x+1)(x+2)} = \frac{A}{2x+1} + \frac{B}{x+2}$

Where $A = \frac{4x-1}{x+2}$ and $2x + 1 = 0$ or $x = -\frac{1}{2}$

$A = \frac{4\left(-\frac{1}{2}\right) - 1}{-\frac{1}{2} + 2} \rightarrow \frac{-2-1}{3/2} \rightarrow \frac{-3}{3/2} \rightarrow -3 \times \frac{2}{3} = -2$

$B = \frac{4x-1}{2x+1}$ and $x + 2 = 0$ or $x = -2$

$B = \frac{4(-2) - 1}{2(-2) + 1} \rightarrow \frac{-8-1}{-4+1} \rightarrow \frac{-9}{-3} = 3$

$\therefore \frac{4x-1}{2x^2 + 5x + 2} = \frac{-2}{2x+1} + \frac{3}{x+2}$ or $\frac{3}{x+2} - \frac{2}{2x+1}$

(16.23). Given that $\frac{6x + P}{2x^2 + 7x - 15} = \frac{4}{x+5} - \frac{2}{2x-3}$ find the value of the constant P.

Solution

$4 = \frac{6x + P}{2x - 3}$ where $x + 5 = 0$ or $x = -5$

i.e $4 = \frac{6(-5) + P}{2(-5) - 3} \rightarrow \frac{-30 + P}{-10 - 3} = \frac{-30 + P}{-13}$

$-30 + P = 4(-13) \rightarrow -30 + P = -52$
$P = -52 + 30 = -22$

CHAPTER 17   INEQUALITIES

Inequalities are symbols or signs used for combining elements in arithmetic operation instead of equality sign. The symbols and their interpretation is given below.

$>$ = greater than
$\geq$ = greater than or equal to
$\not>$ = not greater than
$<$ = less than
$\leq$ = less than or equal to
$\not<$ = not less than

Postulates of inequality

(1) If a > b

Adding a positive number x to both sides gives: a + x > b + x , a – b > 0 e.g. if 5 > 4

5 + 3 > 4 + 3 → 8 > 7

5 – 4 > 0 → 1 > 0

Multiplying both sides by a positive number x gives: ax > bx

e.g. if 5 > 4

5(2) > 4(2) → 10 > 8

Multiplying both sides by a negative number x gives: ax < bx

e.g. given 5 > 4

5(-2) < 4(-2) → -10 < - 8

(2) If a < b

Multiplying both sides by a negative number x gives: ax > bx

e.g. given 5 < 6

5(-3) > 6 (-3)   → -15 > - 18

Multiplying both sides by a positive number x gives: ax < bx

e.g. given 5 < 6

$5(3) < 6(3) \to 15 < 18$

(3) If $a > b$ and a and b are both positive. the following holds

(i) $a^2 > b^2, a^3 > b^3 \ldots$

(ii) $\frac{1}{a} < \frac{1}{b}, \frac{1}{a^2} < \frac{1}{b^2}$

(4) If $a > b \to a - b$ is positive

If $a < b \to a - b$ is negative

If $a > b$ and $c > d$ then the following holds

(i) $ac > bd$ (ii) $a + c > b + d$ (iii) $\frac{a}{d} > \frac{b}{c}$

e.g. given $5 > 4$ and $7 > 6$

$5(7) > 4(6) \to 35 > 24$

$5 + 7 > 4 + 6 \to 12 > 10$

$\frac{5}{6} > \frac{4}{7}$

If $a > b$ and $b > c$ then $a > c$

$9 > 8$ and $8 > 5$ then $9 > 5$

Magnitude and inequality

If $|a| = b \to a = b$ or $a = -b$

If $|a| < b \to -b < a < b$

If $|a| > b \to a < -b$ or $a > b$

Inequality between 0 and 1

For any number $0 < x < 1$

(i) $\sqrt{x} > x$

E.g. $\sqrt{\frac{3}{4}} > \frac{3}{4}$

(ii) $\frac{1}{x} > x$ infact $\frac{1}{x} > 1 \to \frac{1}{0.2} > 0.2 > 1$

(iii) $x^2 < x$

e.g. Given $(0.2)^2 < 0.2 \rightarrow 0.04 < 0.2$

(iv) Multiplying by any positive number a to x gives: $xa < a$

E.g. Given $0 < x < 1$, multiplying by $19 \rightarrow 0.85 \times 19 < 19$

(v) Raising the number to powers if $m > n > 1 \rightarrow$ then

If $m > n > 1 \rightarrow$ then $x^m < x^n < x$

$\left(\frac{1}{2}\right)^5 < \left(\frac{1}{2}\right)^5 < \frac{1}{2}$

Product of Numbers

If the product of two or more numbers is zero at least one of them must be zero.

If $ab = 0$, then $a = 0$ or $b = 0$

If $xyz = 0$, then $x = 0$ or $y = 0$ or $z = 0$

If the product of two numbers is > 0 then either both numbers are positive or both are negative.

E.g. If $ab > 0$ then: a = positive, b = positive

or a = negative, b = negative

Operations with inequality

(1) Use of number line and Cartesian graph
Number line: Is a line with an arrow signifying the direction of the numbers that satisfy the given inequality. It is important to note that an arrow with empty circle illustrates $(>)$ or $(<)$ while an arrow with a shaded circle illustrates $(\geq)$ or $(\leq)$.
Also, an arrow pointing to the left indicates less than $(<)$ while the one pointing to the right indicates greater than $(>)$

○———▶ = >

◀———○ = <

●———▶ = ≥

◀———● = ≤

Thus,

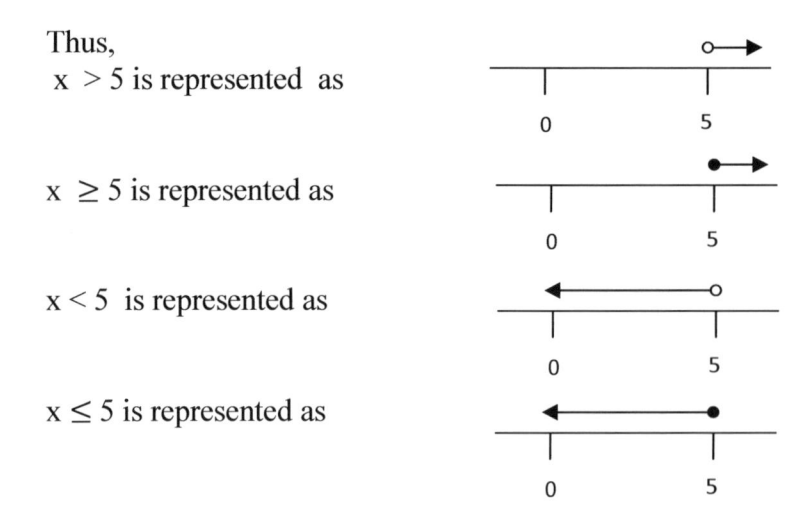

x > 5 is represented as

x ≥ 5 is represented as

x < 5 is represented as

x ≤ 5 is represented as

Cartesian Graph: This is the process of shading a portion of a graph where shaded area is used to distinguish between the required inequality and the opposite end at the equality region.
The equality region also called boundary line is denoted by full line or broken line.
The full line is used when either ≥ *or* ≤ is involved
The broken or dotted line is used when < or > is involved
Note: That area to the left or below a line represents less than while area to the right or above represents greater than.

For Cartesian Graph

If ≥ or ≤ is given, use full line

If < or > is given, use broken line

_____ full

---------------------- broken

The illustrations below annotates how to use a Cartesian graph.

If x > 4 is given, we shade one side of x = 4 with dotted line.

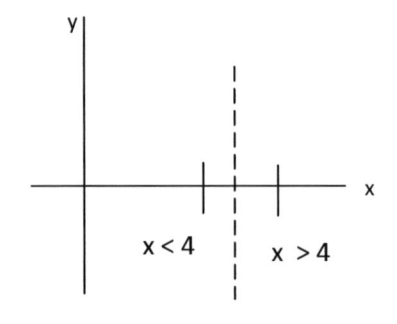

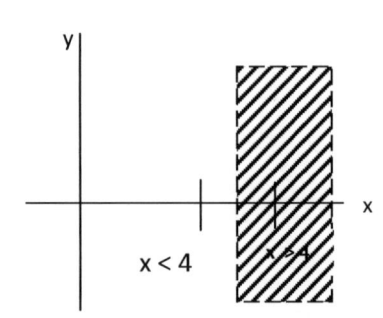

If x ≥ 4 is given, we shade one side of x = 4 with full line since ≥ is given.

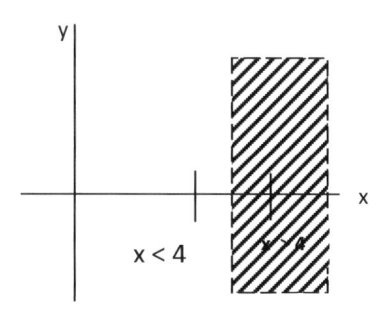

If y > 2 is given, we shade one side of y = 2 denoted by dotted line.

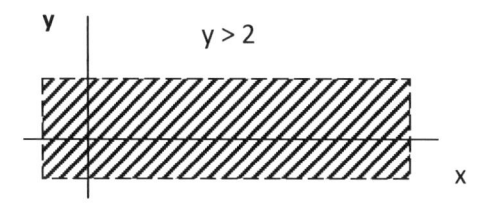

If y > x is given, we shade one side of y = x denoted by dotted line. Line y = x is drawn by assuming values based on the equation.

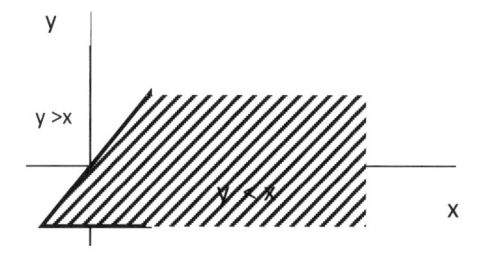

If x + y ≥ 5 is given, we determine the respective values of x and y by inserting 0.

Thus, from x + y = 5. when x = 0, y = 5, y = 0, x = 5

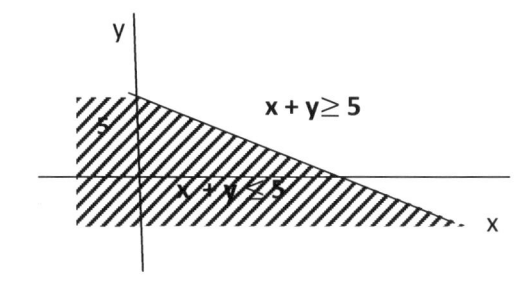

(2) Complete solution: This is the combination of solutions of inequalities in a single form. We obtain a complete solution when the inequalities can meet when represented on a number line.

Given x < 4   and x > 2

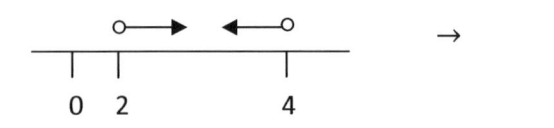

Thus from x < 4 and x > 2

x > 2 can be written as 2 < x and also x < 4

∴ $2 < x < 4$

(3) Incomplete solution: This is the combination of solutions of inequalities in separate form. This occurs when the inequalities cannot meet when represented on a number line.

Given, x > 4 and x < 2

Since x > 4 and x < 2 can never meet when drawn on a number line, there is no complete solution.

(4) Positivity and Negativity of an expression

For positivity of an expression combine with greater than zero i.e > 0

For negativity of an expression combine with less than i.e < 0

(5) Inequality with variables in the denominator

To evaluate, cross multiply and solve. To get the final answer between the two (> > signs) take the bigger value while between the two (< < signs) take the lesser value. If the signs are opposite like > and < take the first i.e greater than.

(6) Range of Inequalities

Range of inequalities is the value between which the solution of inequalities lie or cannot lie. It lies within the value if a complete solution is obtained. It does not lie within the value if the solution is incomplete.

(7) To solve simultaneous equation in form of inequalities

Solve by elimination by making co-efficient equal to get the unknowns.

(8) Determining the answer of a quadratic inequalities

After factorization, to determine the final answer take the smaller values determine this by putting x = 0 in the factorized value with the inequality sign given, while the bigger value is used when the inequality sign have been reversed.

(9) Determining the range of a function, highest possible value

Substitute the two limits given into the question. The limit is small → highest of the two answers gotten.

QUESTIONS

(17.1). If a and b are negative and c is positive which of the following is (are) true?

(i) $a - b < a - c$ (ii) $\frac{1}{a} < \frac{1}{c}$ (iii) if $a < b$ then $\frac{a}{c} < \frac{b}{c}$

Solution

a = negative, b = negative, c = positive

∴ b < c

Also a < c

from $b < c \rightarrow -b > -c$ (multiply by – 1)

adding a to both sides

$a - b > a - c$

(ii) From $a < b$ dividing by c

$\frac{a}{c} < \frac{b}{c}$

(iii) b = negative so $\frac{1}{b}$ = negative

c = positive so $\frac{1}{c}$ = positive

$\frac{1}{a} < \frac{1}{c}$

(ii) and (iii) are true

(**17.2**). If $ab > 0$ and $a < 0$ which of the following is negative?

(i) b (ii) $-b$ (iii) $-c$ (iv) $(a-b)$ (v) $-(a+b)$

Solution

From $a < 0$

Since a = negative , b = negative

B is the correct

(**17.3**). If $0 < a < b < 1$ which of the following is (are) true?

(a) $a - b$ is negative (b) $\frac{1}{ab}$ is positive (c) $\frac{1}{b} - \frac{1}{a}$ is positive

Solution

since $a < b$ → $a - b <$ is negative (True)

since a and b are positive

a x b = ab = positive (True)

from $\frac{1}{b} - \frac{1}{a} = \frac{a-b}{ab} = \frac{-ve}{+ve}$ (false)

I and II only are true

(**17.4**). For how many positive integer a is it true that $a^2 \leq 2a$?

Solution

Since a = positive, $\frac{a^2}{a} \leq \frac{2a}{a}$ → $a \leq 2$

$a \leq 2$ → 1 or 2. 2 integers.

(**17.5**). Which of the following statements is (are) true? (i) $-2^{10} > 0$ (ii) $-(-2^{10}) > 0$

(iii) $2^{10} - (-2)^{10} > 0$

Solution

(i) $-2^{10} = -2^{10} < 0$ → false

(ii) $-(-2^{10}) = -2^{10} < 0$ → false

(iii) $2^{10} - (-2)^{10} = 2^{10} - 2^{10} = 0$ → false

None

(17.6). If P and Q are primes greater than 2 which of the following must be true?

(i) $p + q =$ even (ii) $pq =$ odd (iii) $p^2 - q^2 =$ even

Solution

All prime number greater than 2 are odd so p and q are odd

odd + odd = even (i) true

odd x odd = Odd (ii) true

$(odd)^2 - (odd)^2 =$ even (iii) true

All true

(17.7). If $-7 \leq x \leq 7$ and $0 \leq y \leq 12$. What is the greatest possible value of $y - x$.

Solution

making y large as possible and x small as possible

$y - x = 12 - -7 = 19$

(17.8). If $0 < x < 1$, the correct lists in increasing order is?

(a) $\sqrt{x}$, x, x^2 (B) x^2, x, $\sqrt{x}$ (c) x^2 $\sqrt{x}$, x (D) x, x^2, $\sqrt{x}$ (E) x, $\sqrt{x}$, x^2

Solution

x^2, x, $\sqrt{x}$

(17.9). The solution set of the inequality $3x + 6 \geq 18$ is?
Solution
From $3x + 6 \geq 18$ → $3x \geq 18 - 6$ → $3x \geq 12$ → $x \geq 4$

(17.10). Solve the inequality $5x + 7 \leq 6(x + 3)$

169

Solution

$5x + 7 \leq 6x + 18 \rightarrow 6x + 18 \geq 5x + 7 \rightarrow 5x - 6x \leq 18 - 7 \rightarrow 6x - 5x \geq 7 - 18$

$- x \leq 11 \rightarrow x \geq -11$ (by multiplying through by -1)

(17.11). Find the range of the values of x for which $\frac{4}{x} > 3$.

Solution

Cross multiplying we have the possible cases

If $x > 0$, x is positive, $4 > 3x \rightarrow 3x < 4 \rightarrow x < 4/3$

If $x < 0$, x is negative. $4 < 3x \rightarrow 3x > 4 \rightarrow x > 4/3$

From the first condition, $x > 0, x < 4/3 \rightarrow 0 < x < 4/3$

From the second, $x < 0$ and $x > 4/3$ there is no complete solution. thus the range is as given by the first condition i.e $0 < x < 4/3$.

(17.12). Simplify $\frac{4}{x} > -2$.

Solution

From $\frac{4}{x} > -2 \rightarrow 4 > -2x$

If $x > 0$, x is positive, $4 > - 2x \rightarrow - 2x < 4 \rightarrow 2x > - 4 \rightarrow x > - 2$

If $x < 0$, x is negative, $4 < - 2x \rightarrow - 2x > 4 \rightarrow 2x < - 4 \rightarrow x < - 2$

Between $x > 0$ and $x > -2$, $x > 0$ is taken

Between $x < 0$ and $x < -2$, $x < -2$ is taken

The value for the inequality is therefore $x > 0$ or $x < -2$

(17.13). What are the values that satisfy the inequality?

$\frac{y-1}{y-4} > 0$

Solution

Considering the denominator : $y - 4 = 0, y = 4$

If $y > 4, y - 4$ is positive, $y - 1 > (y - 4)0 \rightarrow y - 1 > 0 \rightarrow y > 1$

Between $y > 4$ and $y > 1$, $y > 4$ is taken

Between $y < 4$ and $y < 1$, $y < 1$ is taken

Thus the solution is $y > 4$ or $y < 1$

y is not between 1 and 4.

(17.14). Solve the inequality $\frac{4}{x-3} > 1$.

Solution

From $\frac{4}{x-3} > 1 \rightarrow 4 > 1(x-3)$

Considering the denominator $x - 3 = 0$, $x = 3$

If $x > 3$, $x - 3$ is positive, $4 > 1(x - 3) \rightarrow x - 3 < 4 \rightarrow x < 7$

If $x < 3$, $x - 3$ is negative, $4 < 1(x - 3) \rightarrow x - 3 > 4 \rightarrow x > 7$

From condition (i) we have $x > 3$ and $x < 7$ i.e $3 < x < 7$

For condition (ii) we have $x < 3$ and $x > 7$ which is not true.

∴ The true solution is $3 < x < 7$.

(17.15). Simplify $\frac{x+5}{1-x} \leq 3$.

Solution

From $\frac{x+5}{1-x} \leq 3 \rightarrow x + 5 \geq 3(1 - x)$

When $1 - x = 0$, $x = 1$

If $x > 1$, $1 - x$ is negative

$x + 5 \geq 3(1 - x) \rightarrow x + 5 \geq 3 - 3x \rightarrow x + 3x \geq 3 - 5 \rightarrow 4x \geq -2 \therefore x \geq -1/2$

If $x < 1$, $1 - x$ is positive

$x + 5 \leq 3(1 - x) \rightarrow x + 5 \leq 3 - 3x \rightarrow x + 3x \leq 3 - 5 \rightarrow 4x \leq -2 \therefore x \leq -1/2$

From condition (i) $x > 1$ and $x \geq -½$, $x > 1$ is taken

From condition (ii) $x < 1$ and $x \leq -½$, $x \leq -½$ is taken

∴ The solution is $x > 1$ or $x \leq -1/2$.

(17.16). What is the range of values for t if $\frac{3t}{4} - \frac{t}{5} + 3 > \frac{t}{2}$?

Solution

$\frac{3t}{4} - \frac{t}{5} + 3 > \frac{t}{2}$

Multiplying throughout by $l.c.m$

171

$20\frac{(3t)}{4} - 20\frac{(t)}{5} + 20(3) > 20\frac{(t)}{2}$ → $15t - 4t + 60 > 10t$
$15t - 4t - 10t > -60$ → $t > -60$

(17.17). Find all real numbers x which satisfy the inequality $\frac{1}{3}(x+1) - 1 > \frac{1}{5}(x+4)$.

Solution

From $\frac{1}{3}(x+1) - 1 > \frac{1}{5}(x+4)$

Multiply throughout by $l.c.m$

$15 \cdot \frac{1}{3}(x+1) - 15 \cdot \frac{(1)}{3}(x+4)$ → $5(x+1) - 15 > 3(x+4)$ → $5x + 5 - 15 > 3x + 12$
→ $5x - 3x > 12 + 15 - 5$ → $2x > 22$ ∴ $x > 11$

(17.18). Find the range of the function $\frac{x+1}{4}$ for $0 \leq x \leq 3$.

Solution

With $x = 0$ → $\frac{x+1}{4}$ → $\frac{0+1}{4} = \frac{1}{4}$

With $x = 3$ → $\frac{x+1}{4}$ → $\frac{3+1}{4}$ → $\frac{4}{4} = 1$

range is from $\frac{1}{4}$ to 1

(17.19). Find the highest possible value of $\frac{4}{1-x^2}$ for $0 \leq x \leq 3$.

Solution

With x = 0 → $\frac{4}{1-x^2}$ → $\frac{4}{1-0^2}$ → $\frac{4}{1} = 4$

With x = 3 → $\frac{4}{1-x^2}$ → $\frac{4}{1-3^2}$ → $\frac{4}{1-9}$ → $\frac{4}{-8} = -\frac{1}{2}$

Thus, the highest possible value is 4.

(17.20). Find the range of values if x and y for the inequalities.

$2x + y < 5$, $x + 2y < -2$

Solution

Multiplying both equations by 1 and 2, we have,

$2x + y < 5$ ....(i)
$2x + 4y < -4$ ......(ii)
Subtracting: $-3y < 9$ → $-y < 3$ → $y > -3$
Multiplying both equations by 2 and 1, we have

$4x + 2y < 10$ ....(i)
$x + 2y < -2$ ......(ii)

172

subtracting: $3x < 12 \rightarrow x < 4$

thus, the range is $x < 4$ and $y > -3$

(17.21). Find the range values that satisfy the inequality $x^2 - x \leq 6$.

Solution

$x^2 - x \leq 6 \rightarrow x^2 - x - 6 \leq 0 \rightarrow (x-3)(x+2) \leq 0$

$x - 3 \leq 0$ and $x + 2 \geq 0 \rightarrow x \leq 3$ and $x \geq -2 \rightarrow x \leq 3$ and $-2 \leq x$

$-2 \leq x \leq 3$

i.e x lies between -2 and 3

(17.22). Solve the inequality $(x-4)(x-6) > 0$.

Solution

$x - 6 > 0$ or $x - 4 < 0 \rightarrow x > 6$ or $x < 4$

i.e x cannot lie between 4 and 6

(17.23). Find the range of values of x for which $(2x-1)(x+3) > 0$.

Solution

$(2x-1)(x+3) > 0 \rightarrow 2x - 1 > 0$ or $x + 3 < 0 \rightarrow x > 1/2$ or $x < -3$

$-3 > x > 12$

(17.24).

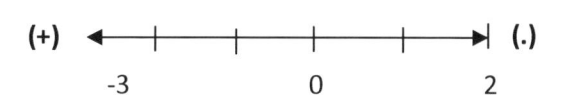

The inequality which represents any point x on the number line shown above is?

Solution

The arrow combines the number from -3 to $+2$ with 2 inclusive as it is shaded.

Thus the inequality is $-3 < x \leq 2$

(17.25). Find the inequality which represents the shaded portion in the diagram below.

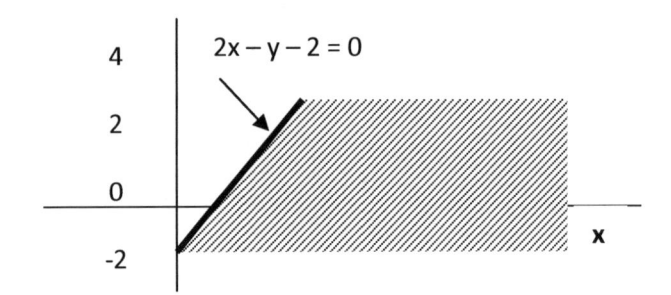

Solution

Since the line is also thick and full and the shaded portion is less than zero. the shaded portion is $2x - y - 2 \leq 0$

(17.26). Find the range of values of x for which $3x^2 + 10x - 8 \leq 0$.

Solution

$3x^2 + 10x - 8 \rightarrow 3x^2 + 12x - 2x - 8 \rightarrow 3x(x+4) - 2(x+4) \rightarrow (3x-2)(x+4)$

$(3x - 2)(x + 4) \leq 0 \rightarrow 3x - 2 \leq 0 \text{ or } x + 4 \geq 0$

$x \leq \frac{2}{3}$ or $x \geq -4 \rightarrow -4 \leq x \leq 2/3$ (x lies between -4 and 2/3)

(17.27). Determine the real number x satisfying $x\left(\frac{3}{x} + x\right) > 2$.

Solution

From $x\left(\frac{3}{x} + x\right) > 2 \rightarrow (3 + x^2) > 2x$

$x > 2$ and $3 + x^2 < 2x \rightarrow x^2 - 2x + 3 < 0$

The real number satisfying it is $x > 2$

(17.28). For what range of values of x is $2x^2 - 11x + 12$ positive?

Solution

For positivity $\rightarrow x > 0$

$2x^2 - 11x + 12 > 0 \rightarrow 2x^2 - 8x - 3x + 12 > 0 \rightarrow 2x(x-4) - 3(x-4) > 0 \rightarrow$

$(2x - 3)(x - 4) > 0$

$\therefore x - 4 > 0 \text{ and } 2x - 3 < 0 \rightarrow x > 4 \text{ and } 2x < 3 \quad x > 4 \text{ and } x < 3/2$

(**17.29**). What range of values of x is $3x^2 + 7x + 2$ negative?

Solution

For negativity → x < 0 is used

$3x^2 + 7x + 2 < 0$ → $3x^2 + 6x + x + 2 < 0$ → $3x(x+2) + 1(x+2) < 0$

$3x + 1 < 0$ → $x + 2 > 0$ → $x < -\frac{1}{3}$ or $x > -2$

Combining we get $-2 < x < -1/3$

(**17.30**). Find the range of values of x for which $\frac{1}{x} > 2$ is true.

Solution

The possible cases are
when x > 0, x is positive → $1 > 2x$ → $2x < 1$ → $x < \frac{1}{2}$
when x < 0, x is negative → $1 < 2x$ → $2x > 1$ → $x > 1/2$
from the first condition, x > 0 and x < 1/2, 0 < x < 1/2

(**17.31**). If x is negative, what is the range of values of x within which $\frac{x+1}{3} > \frac{1}{x+3}$

Solution

If x > -3, x + 3 is positive. → $(x+1)(x+3) > 3$ → $x^2 + 4x + 3 > 3$ →

$x^2 + 4x + 3 - 3 > 0$ → $x^2 + 4x > 0$ → $x(x+4) > 0$ → x > 0 or x + 4 < 0 → x < -4

x > -3, x < -4 and x > 0 are not true

If x < -3, x + 3 is negative, thus $(x+1)(x+3) < 3$ → $x^2 + 4x + 3 < 3$ →

$x^2 + 4x + 3 - 3 < 0$ → $x^2 + 4x < 0$ → $x(x+4) < 0$ → x < 0 or x + 4 > 0 → x > -4

-4 < x < -3

(17.32). Which of the values of the variables (a) x = 0 (b) x = -3 (c) x = 9, satisfy the inequalities?

$$0 < \frac{x+3}{x-1} \leq 2$$

Solution

with $x = 0 \rightarrow \frac{x+3}{x-1} \rightarrow \frac{3}{-1} = -3 \therefore 0 < -3 \leq 2$

Since 0 is not less than – 3, this is false

With $x = -3 \rightarrow \frac{x+3}{x-1} \rightarrow \frac{-3+3}{-3-1} = 0 \therefore 0 < 0 \leq 2$

Since 0 is not less than 0 and ≤ 2, this is false

With $x = 9 \rightarrow \frac{x+3}{x-1} \rightarrow \frac{9+3}{9-1} \rightarrow \frac{12}{8} = \frac{3}{2} = 1.5$

i.e $0 < 1.5 \leq 2$

Since $1.5 \neq 2$, this is false

None correct.

(17.33). List all the integers values of x satisfying the inequality $-1 < 2x - 5 \leq 5$.

Solution

$-1 < 2x - 5 \rightarrow 2x - 5 > -1 \rightarrow 2x > -1 + 5 \rightarrow 2x > 4 \rightarrow x > 2$

$2x - 5 \leq 5 \rightarrow 2x \leq 5 + 5 \rightarrow 2x \leq 10 \rightarrow x \leq 5$

since $x > 2$ but less and equal to 5 : the numbers are 3, 4, 5

(17.34). Find the range of values of x where $x^2 - x < 2$.

Solution

$x^2 - x < 2 \rightarrow x^2 - x - 2 < 0 \rightarrow (x-2)(x+1) < 0 \rightarrow x - 2 < 0$ and $x + 1 > 0$

$x < 2$ and $x > -1 \rightarrow x < 2$ and $-1 < x$

$-1 < x < 2 \rightarrow 2 > x > -1$

(17.35). What can be deduced about x in the inequality $(3x - 1)(x + 2) > 0$.

Solution

$(3x - 1)(x + 2) > 0$

$3x - 1 > 0$ or $x + 2 < 0$ → $x > 1/3$ or $x < -2$

as x cannot be greater than 1/3 and be less than - 2, x cannot lie between -2 and -1/3.

(17.36). The solution to the equation $x^2 + 2x - 3 < 0$ is?

Solution

$x^2 + 3x - x - 3 < 0$ → $x(x + 3) - 1(x + 3) < 0$ → $(x - 1)(x + 3) < 0$

$(x - 1) < 0 \ (x + 3) > 0$ → $x < 1 \text{ or } x > 3$ → $-3 < x < 1$

CHAPTER 18   SEQUENCES

A sequence is a succession of terms in such a way that the terms are related to one another according to a well defined rule.

Terms associated with sequence

(i) Finite sequence: This is one with a defined first and last term.

(ii) Infinite sequence: This is one that continues indefinitely.

(iii) Series: This is the sum of terms of a sequence.

(iv) Finite series: This is one with a defined first and last term.

(v) Infinite series: This is one that continues indefinitely.

(vi) Arithmetic progression: This is a sequence with a common difference between the participating elements.

(vii) Geometric progression: This is a sequence with a common ratio between the participating elements.

($viii$) Mixed series: This refers to the mixture of geometric progression and arithmetic progression.

(ix) Further Sequence: These are sequences or series with no common difference or common ratio. They are evaluated by analyzing the relationship between the participating elements.

Arithmetic Progression

The general form of an arithmetic progression is given by

$$T_1 \quad T_2 \quad T_3 \quad T_4 \quad T_5 \quad T_n$$
$$a \quad a+d \quad a+2d \quad a+3d \quad a+4d \quad a+(n-1)d$$

It follows that the common difference in an AP is given by

$$d = T_2 - T_1, T_3 - T_2, T_n - T_{n-1}$$

Sum of terms in an Arithmetic progression

When the sequence is infinite, sum is given by

Sn = $\frac{n}{2}[2a + (n-1)d]$

When the sequence is finite, sum is given by

$$S_n = \frac{n}{2}(a + l)$$

L = last term, a = first term, d = common differences,

ARITHMETIC MEAN

Let a,b,c represent three consecutive terms in an A.P e.g. 4, 8, 12

8 – 4 = 4 and 12 – 8 = 4

$\therefore$ b - a = c – b $\rightarrow$ b + b = a + c $\rightarrow$ 2b = a + c $\rightarrow$ b $= \frac{a+c}{2}$

Geometric sequence or Progression

The general form of a geometric progression is given by

T_1	T_2	T_3	T_4	T_5	T_n
a	ar	ar^2	ar^3	ar^4	ar^{n-1}

It follows then that the common ratio r is equal to $\frac{ar}{a} = \frac{ar^2}{ar} = \frac{ar^3}{ar^2} = r$

Sum of a Geometric progression

Summation is given by

$$S_n = \frac{a(1 - r^n)}{1 - r} \quad \text{when r < 1}$$

$$S_n = \frac{a(r^n - 1)}{r - 1} \quad \text{when r > 1}$$

Summation to infinity of a Geometric progression

When number of terms to be added is not given and the magnitude of the common ratio is less than 1.

$$S_n = \frac{a}{1 - r}$$

GEOMETRIC MEAN

Let a, b, c represent three consecutive terms of a GP e.g. 2,6,18 or 3, 9, 27

$\frac{6}{2} = \frac{18}{6}$

$\frac{b}{c} = \frac{c}{b} \rightarrow b^2 = a \times c \rightarrow b = \pm\sqrt{ac}$

MIXED SERIES

A mixed series can be represented diagrammatical as shown with the algebraic operation used written below the line.

	T_1	T_2	T_3	T_4	T_5
AP	a	$a+d$	$a+2d$	$a+3d$	$a+4d$
GP	a	ar	ar^2	ar^3	ar^4

In solving problems of this nature, the rules of geometric progression and arithmetic progression must be obeyed.

QUESTIONS

(18.1). Find the sum of numbers between 1 to 50 that are divisible by 5.

Solution

5, 10, 15, 20, 25, ... 50

$a = 5, d = 5, L = 50, n = ?$

$T_n = a + (n-1)d \rightarrow 50 = 5 + (n-1)5 \rightarrow 50 - 5 = (n-1)5 \rightarrow \frac{45}{5} = \frac{(n-1)5}{5} \rightarrow 9 = n - 1 \therefore n = 10$

$S_n = \frac{n}{2}(a+L) \rightarrow \frac{n}{2}[5+50] \rightarrow \frac{10}{2}[55] = 275$

(18.2). The 28th term of an A.P is -5. Find the common difference if its first term is 31.

Solution

$a = 31, d = ?, T_{28} = -5$

$T_n = a + (n-1)d \rightarrow T_{28} = 31 + (28-1)d \rightarrow -5 = 31 + (27)d \rightarrow -5 - 31 = 27d$

$d = \frac{-36}{27} = \frac{-4}{3}$

(18.3). If 8, x, y, z and 20 are in an A.P. Find x, y and z.

Solution

T_1	T_2	T_3	T_4	T_5
8	x	y	z	20

$T_5 = a + (n - 1)d \rightarrow 20 = 8 + 4d \rightarrow 4d = 20 - 8 \therefore d = \frac{12}{4} = 3$

$T_2 = a + (n - 1)d \rightarrow 8 + (1)d \rightarrow 8 + 1 \times 3 = 11$

$T_3 = a + (n - 1)d \rightarrow 8 + (2)d \rightarrow 8 + 2 \times 3 = 14$

$T_4 = a + (n - 1)d \rightarrow 8 + 3(d) \rightarrow 8 + 3 \times 3 = 17$

(18.4). a,b,c are three consecutive terms of an AP whose sum is 21. Find the product of the terms if a : c = 6:1.

Solution

First term = a = a

Second term = b = a + d

Third term = c = a + 2d

$a + b + c = 21 \rightarrow a + a + d + a + 2d = 21 \rightarrow 3a + 3d = 21 \rightarrow a + d = 7$ ……….. (i)

also from $\frac{c}{a} = \frac{6}{1} \rightarrow \frac{a}{a+2d} = \frac{6}{1} \rightarrow 6a + 12d = a \rightarrow 5a + 12d = 0$ ……..(ii)

solving (i) and (ii) simultaneously

multiply (i) by 12

5a + 12d = 0

<u>12a + 12d = 84</u>

- 7a = 84 $\rightarrow$ a = 12

a + d = 7 $\rightarrow$ 12 + d = 7 $\therefore$ d = - 5

with a = 12, b = 7, c = 2 $\rightarrow$ $\therefore$ abc = 168

(18.5).

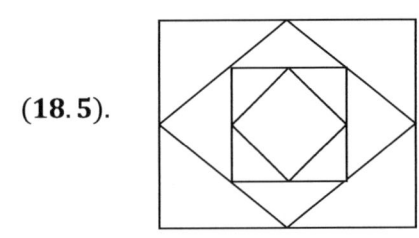

Find the perimeter of the nth square if we continue to form square by joining the midpoint of the sides of each square to form another square.

Solution

$a = x, r = \frac{1}{2}$

$T_n = ar^{n-1} \rightarrow (4x) x \left(\frac{1}{2}\right)^{n-1} \rightarrow (4x) x \, 2^{1-n}$

(18.6). When a ball drops on the floor, it always rebound a distance equal to 2/3 of the height it fell. If the original height was hm (a) how high will it rise after the 5th bounce (b) Assuming the height is 486m, calculate the height of the 5th bounce.

Solution

$T_1 = hm, \, T_2 = \frac{2}{3} x \, h = \frac{2h}{3}, \, T_3 = \frac{4h}{9}, \, r = \frac{T_2}{T_1} = \frac{2}{3}$

$T_n = ar^{n-1} \rightarrow T_5 = h \, x \left[\frac{2}{3}\right]^{5-1} \rightarrow h \, x \left[\frac{2}{3}\right]^4 \rightarrow \frac{16}{81} h$

$T_5 = h \, x \, \frac{81}{16} \rightarrow 486 \, x \, \frac{81}{16} \rightarrow 6 \, x \, 16 = 96 \, m$

(18.7). If x + 1, x + 3, and x + 7 are consecutive terms of an GP. Find the seventh term.

Solution

$T_1 = x + 1, \, T_2 = x + 3, \, T_3 = x + 7$

$\therefore r = \frac{x+3}{x+1} = \frac{x+7}{x+3} \rightarrow (x+3)(x+3) = (x+1)(x+7) \rightarrow x^2 + 3x + 3x + 9 = x^2 + 7x + x + 7 \rightarrow$

$x^2 + 6x + 9 = x^2 + 8x + 7 \rightarrow 8x - 6x = 9 - 7 \rightarrow 2x = 2 \therefore x = 1$

$T_1 = a = x + 1 = 1 + 1 = 2, \, r = \frac{x+3}{x+1} = \frac{1+3}{1+1} = \frac{4}{2} = 2$

$\therefore T_n = ar^{n-1} \rightarrow T_7 = 2 \, x \, 2^6 \rightarrow 2^{1+6} = 2^7$

(18.8). What term of the G.P $\frac{1}{2}, \frac{3}{4}, \frac{9}{4}, \ldots$ is $3^9 \, x \, 2^{-10}$?

Solution

$a = T_1 = \frac{1}{2}$, $T_3 = \frac{9}{4}$, $r = \frac{3}{4} \times \frac{2}{1} = \frac{3}{2}$

$T_n = ar^{n-1} \rightarrow 3^9 \times 2^{-10} = \frac{1}{2} \times \left[\frac{3}{2}\right]^{n-1} \rightarrow 3^9 \times 2^{-10} \times 2^1 = \left[\frac{3}{2}\right]^{n-1}$

$3^9 \times 2^{-10+1} = \left[\frac{3}{2}\right]^{n-1} \rightarrow 3^9 \times 2^{-9} = \left[\frac{3}{2}\right]^{n-1} \rightarrow \left[\frac{3}{2}\right]^9 = \left[\frac{3}{2}\right]^{n-1}$

$9 = n - 1 \rightarrow n = 10$

(18.9). A GP of positive terms and an AP have the same first term. The sum of their first term is 3. The sum of their second terms is $1\frac{3}{2}$ and the sum of their third term is 6. Find the sum of their 5th term.

Solution

For mixed series

	T_1	T_2	T_3	T_4	T_5
AP	a	$a+d$	$a+2d$	$a+3d$	$a+4d$
GP	a	ar	ar^2	ar^3	ar^4
	3	$\frac{3}{2}$	6		

$2a = 3$ | $a + d + ar = \frac{3}{2}$ | $a + 2d + ar^2 = 6$

$a = \frac{3}{2}$ | $\frac{3}{2} + d + \frac{3r}{2} = \frac{3}{2}$ | $\frac{3}{2} + 2d + \frac{3r^2}{2} = 6$

| $3 + 2d + 3r = 3$ | $3 + 4d + 3r^2 = 12$

| $2d + 3r = 0$ | $4d + 3r^2 = 9$

From column II $\rightarrow$ $2d = -3r \rightarrow d = \frac{-3r}{2}$ ....(i)

Put value of d into column III $\rightarrow$ $4\left[\frac{-3r}{2}\right] + 3r^2 = 9 \rightarrow -6r + 3r^2 - 9 = 0$

$3r^2 - 6r - 9 = 0 \rightarrow r^2 - 2r - 3 = 0 \rightarrow (r-3)(r+1) = 0 \therefore r = 3$ or -1

Put r in equation (i) $d = \frac{-9}{2}$

Sum of 5th term = $a + 4d + ar^4 \to \frac{3}{2} + 4\left[\frac{-9}{2}\right] + \frac{3}{2} \times 81 = \frac{3}{2} - 18 + \frac{243}{2} = 105$

(18.10). An AP and G.P have the same first term. Corresponding term of the progression are now added together to give the series 4 + 13 + 30. Find the two possible linear sequence.

Solution

This is a mixed series

	T_1	T_2	T_3
AP	a	$a+d$	$a+2d$
GP	a	ar	ar^2
	4	13	30

$2a = 4$ | $a + d + ar = 13$ | $a + 2d + ar^2 = 30$

$a = 2$ | $2 + d + ar = 13$ | $2 + 2d + 2r^2 = 30$

    | $d + 2r = 11$ | $d + r^2 = 14$

$d + r^2 = 14$ ....(i)

$d + 2r = 11$ ....(ii)

Subtracting: $r^2 - 2r = 3$

$r^2 - 2r - 3 = 0 \to (r - 3)(r + 1) = 0 \to r = 3$ or -1

when $r = 3 \to d = 11 - 2r \to 11 - 6 = 5$

when $r = -1 \to d = 11 - 2r \to 11 - 2(-1) \to 11 + 2 = 13$

possible linear sequence is AP: $a, a+d, a+2d$

For d = 13, a + d → 2 + 13 = 15, a + 2d → 2 + 2(13) = 28

For d = 5, a + d → 2 + 5 = 7, a + 2d → 2 + 2(5) = 12

possible A.P are 2, 7, 12 or 2, 15, 28

(**18.11**). The first, third and ninth term of an A.P are the first three terms of a G.P. If the nth term of the A.P = 14. Calculate the (i) 20th term of the AP (ii) the sum of the first 7 terms of the G.P.

Solution

a, a + 2d, a + 8d = a, ar, ar^2

a = a, a + 2d = ar, a + 8d = ar^2 , a + 6d = 14

a(r -1) = 2d → a = $\frac{2d}{r-1}$

(**18.12**). The sum of the first two terms of a G.P is P and the sum of the last two term is q. If the GP has n terms the common ratio is?

Solution

From $T_n = ar^{n-1}$

a + ar = p → a (1 + r) = p .... (i)

$ar^{n-2} + ar^{n-1} = q$ → $ar^{n-2}(1+r) = q$ …………..(ii)

Dividing (ii) by (i) → $r^{n-2} = \frac{q}{p}$ → $r = \left[\frac{q}{p}\right]^{\frac{1}{n-2}} = \sqrt[n-2]{\frac{q}{p}}$

(**18.13**). To what value does the sum 20 + 124 + $36/5$ + …… tends to infinity.

Solution

a = 20, r = $12/20$ = $3/5$

$\infty = \frac{a}{1-r}$ → $\frac{a}{1-\frac{3}{5}}$ → $\frac{20}{\frac{2}{5}}$ = 50

(**18.14**). The sum to infinity of a GP is $2/3$ and the first term is $1/12$, find the common ratio.

Solution

$\infty = 2/3$, a = $1/12$, r = ?

$\infty = \frac{a}{1-r}$ → $\frac{2}{3} = \frac{\frac{1}{12}}{1-r}$ → $\frac{2}{3}(1-r) = \frac{1}{12}$ → $2(1-r) = \frac{1}{4}$ → $1-r = \frac{1}{8}$ → r = $1 - \frac{1}{8} = \frac{7}{8}$

(**18.15**). The sum of infinity of the series $x + x^3 + x^5$ ….. is $3/8$. Find the value of x.

185

$r = \dfrac{x^3}{x} = x^2$, $a = x$, $\alpha = 3/8$

$\dfrac{3}{8} = \dfrac{x}{1-x^2} \rightarrow 8x = 3 - 3x^2 \rightarrow 8x = 3(1 - x^2) \rightarrow 3x^2 + 8x - 3 = 0$

$3x^2 + 9x - x - 3 = 0 \rightarrow 3x(x + 3) - 1(x + 3) = 0 \rightarrow 3x - 1 = 0$ or $x + 3 = 0$

$3x = 1$ or $x = -3 \rightarrow x = \dfrac{1}{3}$ or $x = -3$

(18. 16). If The sum of infinity of a GP is twice the first term find the common ratio.

Solution

$\alpha = \dfrac{a}{1-r} \rightarrow 2a = \dfrac{a}{1-r} \rightarrow 2a(1-r) = a \rightarrow 1 - r = \dfrac{a}{2a} \rightarrow 1 - r = \dfrac{1}{2} \rightarrow r = 1 - \dfrac{1}{2} \therefore r = ½$

(18. 17). Find the sum of infinity of $1 + \dfrac{1}{\sqrt{2}} + \dfrac{1}{2} + \ldots$

$\alpha = ?$ $a = 1, r = \dfrac{\frac{1}{\sqrt{2}}}{\sqrt{2}} = \dfrac{1}{2}$

$\infty = \dfrac{1}{1 - \frac{1}{\sqrt{2}}} \rightarrow \dfrac{1}{\frac{\sqrt{2}-1}{\sqrt{2}}} \rightarrow \dfrac{\sqrt{2}}{\sqrt{2}-1} \rightarrow \dfrac{\sqrt{2}}{\sqrt{2}-1} \times \dfrac{\sqrt{2}+1}{\sqrt{2}+1} = \dfrac{2+\sqrt{2}}{2-1} = 2 + \sqrt{2}$

(18. 18). Find the sum to infinity of $1 + \tan 30^0 + \tan^2 30^0 + \tan^3 30^0$

Solution

$r = \tan 30$, $a = 1$ $\alpha = ?$

$\alpha = \dfrac{1}{1 - \tan 30} \rightarrow \dfrac{1}{1 - \frac{1}{\sqrt{3}}} \rightarrow \dfrac{1}{\frac{\sqrt{3}-1}{\sqrt{3}}} = \dfrac{\sqrt{3}}{\sqrt{3}-1} \rightarrow \dfrac{\sqrt{3}}{\sqrt{3}-1} \times \dfrac{\sqrt{3}+1}{\sqrt{3}+1} \rightarrow \dfrac{3+\sqrt{3}}{3-1} = \dfrac{3+\sqrt{3}}{2}$

(18. 19). The first winner in a lottery gets $2000 while subsequent winners get $50 less than the preceding winner. The winner in the 20th position gets?

Solution

2000, 1950, 1900, 1850, … $d = -150$, $a = 2000$

$T_{20} = a + 19d \rightarrow 2000 + 19(-50) = \$1050$

(18. 20). The first term of an AP is 19. If the difference between the third and sixth term is 18. The tenth term is?

Solution

a = 19

$T_3 = a + 2d \rightarrow 19 + 2d$, $T_6 = a + 5d \rightarrow 19 + 5d$

$T_6 - T_3 = (19 + 5d) - (19 + 2d) = 18 \rightarrow 3d = 18 \therefore d = 6$

$T_{10} = a + 9d \rightarrow 19 + 9(6) = 73$

(18.21). A reception hall is arranged such that the first row contains 10 seats and each successive row has two more seats that the preceding row. The total number of seats in the first twelve rows is?

Solution

10 + 12 + 14 + ….

$S_n = \frac{n}{2}[2a + (n-1)d] \rightarrow \frac{12}{2}[2(10) + (12 - 1)2] \rightarrow 6[20 + (11 \times 2)] = 252$

(18.22). What pattern does each of the following sequence follows and give their next 2 terms.

(a) 0, 1, 1 , 2, 3, 5, 8... (b) 1, 8, 27, 64, ... (c) a, a + d, a + 2d

Solution

(*i*) 0, 1, 1 , 2, 3, 5, 8... The sequence is obtained by adding two successive term to obtain the next term

5 + 8 = 13, 13 + 8 = 21 ∴ 0, 1,1, 2 , 3 ,5 , 8, 13 ,21

(*ii*) By indices $1^1, 2^3, 3^3, 4^3$ means each terms is the cube of successive natural number.

(*iii*) By adding [d] to the preceding term.

(18.23). The sum of the first three terms of an AP is -18. The third term is half the seventh term. Find the sum of the first four terms of the progression.

Solution

$Sn = \frac{n}{2}[2a + (n-1)d] \rightarrow \frac{3}{2}[2a + (3-1)d] \rightarrow = \frac{3}{2}(2a + 2d) = -18 \rightarrow 3(a + d) = -18$

a + d = - 6 …….(i)

$T_3 = a + 2d$, $T_7 = a + 6d$

$\frac{a+6d}{2} = a + 2d \rightarrow a + 6d = 2a + 4d \rightarrow a - 2d = 0$ ....(ii)

Solving (i) and (ii) simultaneously

2a + 2d = -12
a – 2d = 0
3a = -12 → a = - 4
a + d = - 6 → - 4 + d = - 6 → d = - 6 + 4 = -2
$S_4 = \frac{n}{2}[2a + (n-1)d] \rightarrow \frac{4}{2}[2(-4) + (4-1)-2] \rightarrow 2[-8-6] = -28$

(18.23). The second term of a G.P is 9, and the seventh term is $\frac{1}{27}$. Find the common ratio.

Solution

$T_2 = ar = 9, \quad T_7 = ar^6 = \frac{1}{27}$

$\frac{ar^6}{ar} = \frac{\frac{1}{27}}{9} \rightarrow ar^5 = \frac{1}{27} \times \frac{1}{9} \rightarrow r^5 = \frac{1}{3^3}\frac{1}{3^2} \rightarrow r^5 = \frac{1}{3^5} \rightarrow r^5 = 3^{-5} \rightarrow r = \sqrt[5]{3^{-5}} = \frac{1}{3}$

(18.24). Given that r is the common ratio and d is the common difference where 2, x, 18 .. are respectively a geometric progression and arithmetic progression then the ratio r : d is?
Solution

For AP d is gotten from x – 2 = 18 – x → 2x = 20 ∴ x = 10

For GP r is given by $\frac{x}{2} = \frac{18}{x} \rightarrow x^2 = 36 \therefore x = 6$

Thus AP = 2, 10, 18, GP = 2, 6, 18

∴ $r : d = 3 : 8$

(18.25). In a family, the ages of children arranged from the youngest to the oldest are 2, 6, y, 14, z and x. if the sequence of age is an arithmetic progression. What is the ratio of z : y?

Solution

Given 2, 6, y, 14, x

d is gotten from 6 – 2 = y – 6 → 4 = y – 6 ∴ y = 10

Hence the A.P becomes

2, 6, 10, 14

Similarly 14 – 10 = z – 14 ∴ z = 18

z : y = 18 : 10 → 9 : 5

(18.26). What is the eleventh term of the sequence 9.3, 3.7, 3.1, 2.5 ?

Solution

a = 4.3, d = - 0.6

T_{11} = a + 10d → 4.3 + 10(- 0.6) → 4.3 – 0.7 = 1.7

(18.27). Find the value of r if $\log_{10}r + \log_{10}r^2 + \log_{10}r^4 + \log_{10}r^8 + \log_{10}r^{16} + \log_{10}r^{32} = 63$.

Solution

$\log_{10}[r + r^2 + r^4 + r^8 + r^{16} + r^{32}] = 63$

$\log_{10}r^{63} = 63 \rightarrow r^{63} = 10^{63}$ ∴ r = 10

(18.28). If p, 6, r and 48 are consecutive terms of a GP find the value of p + q + r.

Solution

$\frac{6}{p} = \frac{q}{6}, \frac{r}{q} = \frac{q}{6}, \frac{48}{r} = \frac{r}{q}$

$pq = 36$ .... (i) $q^2 = 6r$ .... (ii) $r^2 = 48q$ ....(iii)

From (ii) r = $\frac{q^2}{6}$

inserting into (iii)

$\frac{q^4}{36} = 48q \rightarrow q^4 = 36 \times 48q \rightarrow q^3 = 1728 \rightarrow q = \sqrt[3]{1728} = 12$

from (i) pq = 36 → 12p = 36 ∴ p = 3

since r = $\frac{q^2}{6} \rightarrow \frac{12 \times 2}{6} = 24$

p + q + r = 3 + 12 + 24 = 39

(18.29). In the series 3, 7, 12, 18, 25 … the 9th term is ?

Solution

This is an AP with no common difference.

7 - 3 = 4, 12 – 7 = 5, 18 – 12 = 6, 25 – 18 = 7

The differences are 4, 5, 6, 7, 8, 9 in that order.

Therefore, the series line 3, 7, 12, 18, 25, 33, 42, 52, 63

(18.30). In an A.P, the sum of the first 8th term is 164 and the sum of the next 6th term is 333. Find the A.P.

Solution

For the first 8 term

$S_8 = \frac{8}{2}[2a + (8-1)d] \rightarrow 164 = 4[2a + 7d] \rightarrow 2a + 7d = 41$ ....(i)

Sum of the next 6th term,

n = 8 + 6 = 14, S_n 164 + 333 = 497

$497 = \frac{14}{2}[2a + (14-1)d] \rightarrow 497 = 7(2a + 13d) \rightarrow 2a + 13d = 71$......(ii)

Bringing together
2a + 7d = 41
2a + 13d = 7
  - 6d = - 30 → d = 5
Put d = 5 into (i)
2a + 7(5) = 41 → 2a + 35 = 41 → 2a = 41 – 35 = 6 ∴ a = 3

From Tn = a + (n - 1)d

$T_1 = a$, $T_2 = a + d$, $T_3 = a + 2d$

AP = 3, 8, 13 ....

(18.31). How many terms of the AP 3, 7, 11… must be added together to produce a total of 300?

Solution

$S_n = \frac{n}{2}[2a + (n-1)d] \rightarrow 360 = \frac{n}{2}[2 \times 3 + (n-1)4] \rightarrow 300 = \frac{n}{2}[6 + 4n - 4]$

$300 = \frac{n}{2}[2 + 4n] \rightarrow 300 = 2n^2 + n \rightarrow 2n^2 + n - 300 = 0$

$2n^2 + 25n - 24n - 300 = 0 \rightarrow n(2n + 25) - 12(2n + 25) = 0 \rightarrow (2n - 25)(n - 12) = 0$

n = 12 or $-23/2$ ∴ n = 12

(18.32). Find the sum of the series 50 + 32 + 34 + …… + 148

Solution

$T_{148} = a + 147d \rightarrow 148 = 50 + (n - 1)2 \rightarrow 148 = 50 + 2n - 2 \rightarrow 148 = 48 + 2n$

$100 = 2n \therefore n = 50$

From $S_n = \frac{n}{2}[a + l] \rightarrow \frac{50}{2}[50 + 148] \rightarrow 25[198] = 4950$

(18.33). S_n is the sum of the first n terms of a series given by $S_n = n^2 - 1$. Find the nth term.

Solution

$S_n = n^2 - 1$

$S_1 = 1^2 - 1 = 0, \qquad S_2 = 2^2 - 1 = 3, \qquad S_3 = 3^2 - 1 = 8$

$T_1 = S_2 - S_1 \rightarrow 3 - 0 = 3$

$T_2 = S_3 - S_2 \rightarrow 8 - 3 = 5$

$T_3 = S_4 - S_3 = 15 - 8 = 7$

From this a = 3, d = 2

$T_n = a + (n - 1)d \rightarrow 3 + (n - 1)2 \rightarrow 3 + 2n - 2 = 2n + 1$

(18.34). Find the next two terms of the sequence $\frac{1}{1}, \frac{3}{2}, \frac{7}{5}, \frac{17}{12}, \ldots\ldots$

Solution

It is clear that the sum of the numerator and denominator gives the denominator of the next and sum of the two consecutive denominator gives the numerator of the second

thus

$\frac{1}{1}, \frac{3}{2}, \frac{7}{5}, \frac{17}{12}, \frac{41}{29}, \frac{99}{70}$

(18.35). If the sum of the 8th and 9th term of an A.P is 72 and the 4th term is -6. Find the common difference.

Solution

$T_8 + T_9 = 72 \rightarrow a + 7d + a + 8d = 72$

$2a + 15d = 72 \ldots\ldots$ (i)

a + 3d = - 6   ……..(ii)

multiply (ii) by 5 and (i) by 1

2a + 15 d = 72
5a + 15d = -30
-3a = 102 → a = -34
Put a into (ii)
a + 3d = - 6 → - 34 + 3d = - 6 → 3d = - 6 + 34 = 28 ∴ d = $\frac{28}{3}$

(18.36). Write $0.0\dot{6}$ as a proper fraction in its lowest term.

Solution

$0.0\dot{6} = \frac{6}{100} + \frac{6}{1000} + \frac{6}{10000}$

$a = \frac{6}{100},\ r = \frac{6}{1000} \div \frac{6}{100} = \frac{1}{10}$

$\alpha = \frac{a}{1-r} \to \frac{\frac{6}{100}}{1-\frac{1}{10}} = \frac{\frac{6}{100}}{\frac{10-1}{10}} \to \frac{\frac{6}{100}}{\frac{9}{10}} \to \frac{6}{100} \times \frac{10}{9} \to \frac{6}{90} = \frac{1}{15}$

(18.37). Express $0.\dot{4}\dot{5}$ as fraction in it is lowest term.

Solution

$0.\dot{4}\dot{5} = 0.454545 \ldots\ldots$

$0.\dot{4}\dot{5} = \frac{45}{100} + \frac{45}{10000} + \frac{45}{100,000} + - - -$

$a = \frac{45}{100},\ r = \frac{45}{10000} \div \frac{45}{100} = \frac{1}{100}$

$\alpha = \frac{a}{1-r} \to \frac{\frac{45}{100}}{1-\frac{1}{100}} \to \frac{\frac{45}{100}}{\frac{100-5}{100}} \to \frac{\frac{45}{100}}{\frac{99}{100}} \to \frac{45}{100} \times \frac{100}{99} \to \frac{45}{99} = \frac{5}{11}$

(18.38). Find the sum of the first twenty terms of the A.P $\log a,\ \log a^2,\ \log a^3$.

Solution

$a = \log a,\ d = \log a^2 - \log a \to 2\log a - \log a \to \text{Log } a [2 - 1]$

$S_{20} = \frac{n}{2}[2a + (n-1)d] \to S_{20} = \frac{20}{2}[2\log a + 19 \text{Log} a]$

$S_{20} = 10[21 \log a] \to 210 \log a \to \text{Log } a^{210}$

(18.39). The sum of the first three terms of a G.P is half its sum to infinity. Find the positive common ratio of the progression.

Solution

$$a + ar + ar^2 = \frac{1}{2}\left[\frac{a}{1-r}\right]$$

$a(1 + r + r^2) = \frac{a}{2(1-r)}$ → $2(1-r)(1+r+r^2) = 1$ → $(2-2r)(1+r+r^2) = 1$

$2 - 2r + 2r^2 - 2r - 2r^2 - 2r^3 = 2r^3 = 1$

$r^3 = \frac{1}{2}$ → $r = \sqrt[3]{\frac{1}{2}} = \frac{1}{\sqrt[3]{2}}$

(18.40). If the mean of a series of number is 20 are their sum is 160. How many number are in the series?

Solution

$\bar{x} = \frac{\sum x}{n}$ → $20 = \frac{160}{n}$ ∴ $n = \frac{160}{20} = 8$

(18.41). The number missing in the series 2, 6, 12, 20, ?, 24, 56, 72 is?

Solution

6 – 2 = 4,   12 – 6 = 6,   20 – 12 = 8

Hence difference increase by 2

30 - 20 = 10 ∴ The missing no is 30

(18.42). How many terms of the series 3, - 6, +12, - 24 +… are needed to make a total of $1 - 2^8$?

Solution

$\frac{-6}{3} = -2$, $\frac{12}{-6} = -2$, ∴ $r = -2$

$S_n = \frac{a(1-r^n)}{1-r}$ → $\frac{3[1-(-2)^n]}{1--2} = 1 - 2^8$ → $\frac{3[1-(-2)^n]}{3} = (1-(-2)^n) = 1 - 2^8$ ∴ $n = 8$

(18.43). The first term of sequence I is 2 and subsequent term is 2 more that the preceding term. The first term of sequence II is 2 and each subsequent term is two times the preceding term. Find ratio of 32nd term of sequence II to the 32 term or sequence I?

Solution

Sequence I = 2, 4, 6, 8, 10 → $T_n = 2n$ ∴ $T_{32} = 2(32) = 64$

Sequence II = 2, 4, 8, 16, 32 $T_n = 2^n$ ∴ $T_{32} = 2^{32} = 64$

$\frac{Sequence\ II}{Sequence\ I} = \frac{2^{32}}{64} = \frac{2^{32}}{2^6} = 2^{26}$

(18.44). The nth term of a sequence is given by $3 \times 2^{n-2}$ write down the first three terms.

Solution

Tn = 3 x 2^{n-2} → T_1 = 3 x 2$^{1-2}$ → 3 x 2^{-1} = $\frac{3}{2}$

T_2 = 3 x 2$^{2-2}$ → 3 x 2^0 = 3 , T_3 = 3 x 2$^{3-2}$ → 3 x 2^1 = 6

The first three terms are 3/2, 3, 6

(18.45). Find the series of the first six terms of $2^n + 4n^2$.

Solution

Tn = $2^n + 4n^2$

$T_1 = 2^1 + 4(1)^2 = 6$, $T_2 = 2^2 + 4(2)^2 = 20$, $T_3 = 2^3 + 4(3)^2 = 44$

$T_4 = 2^4 + 4(4)^2 = 80$, $T_5 = 2^5 + 4(5)^2 = 132$, $T_6 = 2^6 + 4(6)^2 = 208$

Sum of series = 6 + 20 + 44 + 80 + 132 + 208

(18.46). Find the sum of the series of $n^2 + 5n$ up to the 4th term.

Solution

Tn = $n^2 - 5n$

$T_1 = 1^2 + 5(1) = 6$, $T_2 = 2^2 + 5(2) = 14$, $T_3 = 3^2 + 5(3) = 24$

$T_4 = 4^2 + 5(4) = 36$

Sum of series = 6 + 14 + 24 + 36 = 80

(18.47). Given the series 16 + 9 + 2 + ……. Find the sum of the first twenty terms.

Solution

$S_n = \frac{n}{2}[2a + (n-1)d]$ → $S_{20} = \frac{20}{2}[2(16) + (20-1)(-7)]$ → $10[32 + (19)(-7)]$

$10[32 - 133]$ → $10[101]$ = 1010

(18.48). The ninth and twenty second term of an AP are 29 and 55 respectively. Find the sum of its 60 terms.

Solution

T_9 → a + 9d = 29   ……(i)

T_{22} → a + 22d = 55 ……..(ii)

  13d = 26 ∴ d = 2

Put d in (i)
a + 8d = 29 → a + 16 = 29 → a = 29 – 16 = 13

$S_n = \frac{n}{2}[2a + (n-1)d]$ → $\frac{60}{2}[2(13) + 59 \times 2]$ → $30[26 + 118]$ → 30 x 144 = 4320

(18.49). The 16th terms of an AP is 93, given that its common difference is 6. Find the first and 28th term.

Solution

T_{16} = a + (n – 1)d → 93 = a + (16 – 1)6 → 93 = a + 90 → a = 93 – 90 = 3

T_{28} = a + 27d → 3 + 27(6) → 3 + 162 = 165

(18.50). The sum of the first 16th term is - 504 while the sum of its first nine terms is -26. Find the 16th term.

Solution

When n = 16, S_n = 504

$S_n = \frac{n}{2}[2a + (n-1)d]$

$S_{16} = \frac{16}{2}[2a + (16-1)d] = 504$ → $8[2a + 15d] = 504$ → $2a + 15d = \frac{-504}{8}$

2a + 15d = - 63 …………….(i)

195

When n = 9, S_n = -126

$S_n = \frac{9}{2}[2a + 8d] - 126 \to a + 4d = \frac{-126}{9}$

a + 4d = - 14 ....(ii)

Bringing together

2a + 15d = - 63 ....(i)

a + 4d = -14....................(ii)

Multiply (ii) by 2

2a + 8d = -28

Subtract (ii) from (iii)

$7d = -35 \to d = \frac{-35}{7} = -5$

putting d into equation (ii)

a + 4(-5) = - 14 → a - 20 = - 14 → a = 20 - 14 = 6

$S_{30} = \frac{30}{2}[2(6) + 29(-5)] \to 15(12 - 145) \to 15 \times (-132) = -1995$

(18.51). Find the two possible value of P if P - 3, 3P + 5 and 18P – 5 are three consecutive term of a GP.

Solution

P – 3, 3P + 5, 18P + 5

$\frac{3p+5}{p-3} = \frac{18p-5}{3p+5} \to (3P+5)(3P+5) = (P-3)(18P-5) \to 9P^2 + 15P + 15P + 25 = 18P^2 - 5P - 54P + 15 \to 9P^2 + 30P + 25 = 18P^2 - 59P + 15 \to 18P^2 - 9P^2 - 59P - 30P + 15 - 25 = 0$

$9P^2 - 89P - 10 = 10 \to (9P^2 - 90P) + (1P - 10) = 0 \to 9P(P - 10) + 1(P - 10) = 0 \to (9P + 1)(P - 10) = 0$

9P = - 1 or P = 10 ∴ $P = \frac{-1}{a}$ or 10

(18.52). Given that 443 is the nth term of the arithmetical progression 5 + 8 + 11 + . , find n.

Solution

a = 5, d = 8 – 5 = 3, nth term = 443

nth term = a + (n – 1) d

443 = 5 + (n - 1)3 → 443 – 5 = (n – 1)3 → 438 = (n -1) 3 → 146 = n – 1

∴ $n = 146 + 1 = 147$

(18.53). Find the first term of the sequence x + 1, 3x – 18, 2x – 1, ……… if this sequence is an arithmetic progression.

Solution

From x + 1, 3x – 18, 2x – 1

d = (3x – 18) – (x + 1) → 3x – 18 – x – 1 = 2x – 19

also d = (2x – 1) – (3x – 18) → 2x – 1 – 3x + 18 = - x + 17

equating ∴ 2x – 19 = -x + 17 → 2x + x = 17 + 19 → 3x = 36 ∴ x = 12

∴ first term = (x + 1) = 12 + 1 = 13

(18.54). If the 6th term of an arithmetic progression is 11 and the first term is 1. Find the common difference.

Solution

1st term = 1, 6th term = 11

a + 5d = 11 → 1 + 5d = 11 → 5d = 11 – 1= 10 ∴ d = 2

(18.55). The 4th term of an AP is 13 while the 10th term is 31. Find the 21st term.

Solution

4th term = 13 →   a + 3d = 13   ......(i)

10th term = 31   → a + 9d = 31   ....(ii)

                       6d = 18 ∴ d = 3

Substituting d = 3 into (i)

a + 3(3) = 13 → a + 9 = 13 → a = 13 – 9 = 4

21st term → a + 20d → 4 + 20(3) → 4 + 60 = 64

(18.56). Find the sum of the 20 term of an arithmetic progression whose first term is 7 and last term is 117.

Solution

a = 8, l = 117, n = 20

$S_n = \frac{n}{2}(a+l) = \frac{20}{2}(7+117) = 10(124) \therefore S_n = 1240$

(18.57). Find the sum of the first 21 terms of the progression -10, -8, -6, …..

Solution

a = -10, d = - 8 – (- 10) = - 8 + 10 = 2, n = 21

$\therefore S_n = \frac{n}{2}[2a + (n-1)d] = \frac{21}{2}[2(-10) + (21-1)2]$

$S_n = \frac{21}{2}[-20 + (20)2] \to \frac{21}{2}(-20+40) \to \frac{21}{2} \cdot 20 = 210$

(18.58). Find the sum of the first twenty terms of the arithmetic progression log a, log a^2, log a^3.

Solution

a = log a, d = log a^2 – log a = 2log a – log a = log a, n = 20

$S_n = \frac{n}{2}[2a+(n-1)d] \to \frac{20}{2}[2(\log a) + (20-1)\log a]$

= 10(2loga + 19 log a) → 10(21 loga) → 210 log a = log a^{210}

(18.60). An arithmetic progression has a first term 11 and fourth term 32. The sum of the first ninth term is?

Solution

a = 11, n = 9

a + 3d = 32 → 11 + 3d = 32 → 3d = 32 – 11 = 21 → 3d = 21 ∴ d = 7

$S_n = \frac{n}{2}[2a+(n-1)d] \to \frac{9}{2}[2(11)+(9-1)7] \to \frac{9}{2}[22+8(7)] \to \frac{9}{2}(22+56)$

$\frac{9}{2}(78) = 351$

(18.61). A man is able to save $50.00 of his salary in a particular year. After this, every year he saved $20.00 more than the preceding year. How long does it take him to save $4,370?

Solution

Since the man save $50.00 at first and increases this by $20.00 every year, the problem is an Arithmetic progression saving $4,370 means summing all the savings together.

a = $50.00, d = $20.00

$S_n = \frac{n}{2}[2a + (n-1)d] \rightarrow 4370 = \frac{n}{2}[2(50) + (n-1)20]$

$8740 = n[100 + 20(n-1)] \rightarrow 8740 = 100n + 20n(n-1) \rightarrow 8740 = 100n + 20n^2 - 20n$

$20n^2 + 80n - 8740 = 0 \rightarrow n^2 + 4n - 437 = 0 \rightarrow n = \frac{-4 \pm \sqrt{4^2 - 4 \times 1 \times -437}}{2 \times 1} \rightarrow \frac{-4 \pm \sqrt{16 + 1748}}{2} \rightarrow$

$\frac{-4 \pm \sqrt{1764}}{2} \rightarrow \frac{-4 \pm 42}{2} = \frac{38}{2} = 19$

(18.62). Find the eleventh term of the progression 4, 8, 16, ……

Solution

$\frac{8}{4} = 2, \frac{16}{8} = 2 \therefore r = 2$

$T_{11} = ar^{10} \rightarrow 4(2)^{10} \rightarrow 2^2 \times 2^{10} \rightarrow 2^{2+10} = 2^{12}$

(18.63). The sum of the positive odd integers less than 50 is ?

Solution

Positive odd integers are positive odd whole numbers these are: 1,3,5, ……. 49

Number of positive odd integers = 25

a = 1, d = 3 – 1 or 5 – 3 = 2, n = 49

$\therefore S_n = \frac{25}{2}(1 + 49) \rightarrow \frac{25}{2}(50) = 625$

(18.64). If the nth term of a sequence U₁, U₂, U₃ …….. is 2n – 1. Find the sum of its first eight terms.

Solution

Nth term = 2n – 1

1ˢᵗ term = 2(1) – 1 = 2 – 1 = 1

2ⁿᵈ term = 2(2) – 1 = 4 – 1 = 3

3ʳᵈ term = 2(3) – 1 = 6 – 1 = 5

3 – 1 = 5 – 3 = 2 = common difference implies an A.P

Sum of A.P = $\frac{n}{2}[(2a + (n-1)d]$

$S_n = \frac{8}{2}[2(1) + (8-1)2] = 4[2 + (7)2] \to 4(2 + 14) = 4 \times 16 = 64$

(18.65). If k +1, 3k – 1, 3k + 1 are three consecutive terms of a geometric progression. Find the possible values of the common ratio.

Solution

For consecutive term in G.P,

$r = \frac{2k-1}{k+1}$ or $\frac{3k+1}{2k-1}$

$\therefore \frac{2k-1}{k+1} = \frac{3k+1}{2k-1} \to (2k-1)(2k-1) = (k+1)(3k+1)$

$(2k-1)^2 = (k+1)(3k+1) \to 4k^2 - 4k + 1 = 3k^2 + k + 3k + 1$

$4k^2 - 3k^2 - 4k - 4k + 1 - 1 = 0 \to k^2 - 8k = 0$

$k(k-8) = 0 \to k = 0$ or $k - 8 = 0 \to k = 0$ or $k = 8$

When k = 0 or 8 $\to r = \frac{2k-1}{k+1} = \frac{2(0)-1}{0+1}$ or $\frac{2(8)-1}{8+1}$

$r = \frac{0-1}{0+1}$ or $\frac{16-1}{8+1} \to r = \frac{-1}{1}$ or $\frac{15}{9} \to r = -1$ or $5/3$

(18.66). The sum of n terms of a G.P is $10 - \frac{5}{2^{n-1}}$ find (i) sum of first four terms, (ii) Fourth term.

Solution

$S_n = 10 - \frac{5}{2^{n-1}} \to S_4 = 10 - \frac{5}{2^{4-1}} \to 10 - \frac{5}{2^3} \to 10 - \frac{5}{8} = 9\frac{3}{8}$

4th term $= S_4 - S_3 = \left(10 - \frac{5}{2^{4-1}}\right) - \left(10 - \frac{5}{2^{3-1}}\right) \to 10 - \frac{5}{2^3} - 10 + \frac{5}{2^2} \to \frac{5}{2^2} - \frac{5}{2^3}$

$= \frac{5}{4} - \frac{5}{8} = \frac{10-5}{8} = \frac{5}{8}$

(18.67). The common ratio of a Gp is negative. The fifth term is $\frac{48}{625}$ and the third term is $\frac{12}{25}$. Calculate the first term and the common ratio respectively.

Solution

200

5th term = ar^4 = $ar^2 \cdot r^2 = \frac{48}{625}$ ....(i)

3rd term = $ar^2 = \frac{12}{25}$ ....(ii)

Substituting (ii) in (i)

$\left(\frac{12}{25}\right) r^2 = \frac{48}{625} \rightarrow r^2 = \frac{48}{625} \times \frac{25}{12} = \frac{4}{25}$

$r = \pm\sqrt{\frac{4}{25}}, \quad r = \pm\frac{2}{5}, \quad r = \frac{-2}{5}$ (as r is negative)

Substituting r in (ii), $a\left(\frac{-2}{5}\right)^2 = \frac{12}{25}$

$\frac{4a}{25} = \frac{12}{25}, \quad a = \frac{12}{25} \cdot \frac{25}{4} = 3$

$a = 3, r = -\frac{2}{5}$

(18.68). What is the sum to infinity of the progression $1 - \frac{1}{2} + \frac{1}{4}$ ....

Solution

$a = 1, \quad r = -½$

$S_\infty = \frac{a}{1-r} \rightarrow \frac{1}{1--\frac{1}{2}} \rightarrow \frac{1}{1+\frac{1}{2}}$

(18.69). Evaluate $\left[\frac{1}{2} - \frac{1}{4} - \frac{1}{8} - \frac{1}{16} + \cdots\right] - 1$.

Solution

$a = ½ \quad r = -¼ \div ½ = -½$

$S_\infty = \frac{a}{1-r} \rightarrow \frac{\frac{1}{2}}{1--\frac{1}{2}} \rightarrow \frac{\frac{1}{2}}{1+\frac{1}{2}} \rightarrow \frac{\frac{1}{2}}{\frac{3}{2}} \rightarrow \frac{1}{2} x \frac{2}{3} \rightarrow \frac{1}{3} - 1 = \frac{-2}{3}$

(18.70). The Sum to infinity of G.P is 99. Find its First term, if the common ratio is $\frac{-2}{3}$.

Solution

$S_\infty = \frac{a}{1-r} \rightarrow 99 = \frac{a}{1-\frac{2}{3}} \rightarrow 99 = \frac{a}{\frac{1}{3}} \rightarrow 99 = 3a \therefore a = 33$

(18.71). Two G.P equal sum to infinity. Then, first term are 80 and 25 respectively. If the common ratio of the former is $\frac{4}{5}$ what is of the common ratio of the later.

Solution

$S_{\infty 1} = S_{\infty 2} \rightarrow = \frac{80}{1-\frac{4}{5}} = \frac{25}{1-r} \rightarrow 5(80 - 80r) = 25 \rightarrow 80 - 80r = \rightarrow 80r = 75$

$r = \frac{75}{80} = \frac{15}{16}$

(18.72). Find the formula for the nth term 12, 5, -2. Hence find the 50th term.

Solution

$T_n = a + (n-1)d \rightarrow 12 + (n-1) - 7 \rightarrow 12 - 7n + 7 \rightarrow 19 - 7n \therefore T_n = 19 - 7n$

$\therefore T_{50} = 19 - 7(50) = 19 - 350 = -331$

(18.73). The sum of the 3rd and 7th terms of an A.P is 38 and the 9th term is 37, Find the A.P.

Solution

$a + 2d + a + 6d = 38 \rightarrow 2a + 8d = 38 \rightarrow a + 4d = 19$

for the 9th term $\rightarrow a + 8d = 37$

$2a + 8d = 38$
$\underline{a\ \ + 8d = 37}$
$a\ \ \ \ \ \ \ \ = 1$

put a = 1 in (ii) $\rightarrow 1 + 8d = 37 \rightarrow 8d = 36 \rightarrow d = 36/8 = 9/2 + 4/2 = 5\frac{1}{2}$

(18.74). If the tenth term of an AP is double the second term. Find the eight term given that the first term is root of forty-nine.

Solution

$a = \sqrt{49} \rightarrow a + 9d = 2(a + d) \rightarrow 7 + 9d = 2(7 + d) \rightarrow 7 + 9d = 14 + 2d \rightarrow 9d - 2d = 14 - 7$

$\rightarrow 7d = 7 \therefore d = 1.$

CHAPTER 19 BINARY OPERATIONS

Is the combination of two or more elements or numbers according to a given rule or equation. It usually identified by their signs or symbols such as O, Δ, ☐ etc.

Interpretation and Simplification

Operations are simplified by equating or substituting values when similar or equal operations are given. Only operations with similar signs or symbols can be equated.

Operation and Algebraic Laws of Binary operations

(*i*) Commutativity: A binary operation on a set S is commutative if for every a, b ϵ S, a * b = b * a.

thus for commutativity we test with two elements

(*ii*) Associativity: A binary operation on a set S is associative if for every a, b, c ϵ S, a * (b * c) = (a * b) * c

It implies that associativity will only come in when three variables are involved.

Note:

1. The operation of addition and multiplication are both commutative and associative i.e
3 + 5 ≡ 5 + 3   (addition commutative)

5 x 4 ≡ 4 x 5   (multiplication commutative)

2 + (3 + 6) ≡ (2 + 3) + 6 (addition associative)

3 x (4 x 2) ≡ (3 x 4) x 2 (multiplication associative)

2. The operation of division and subtraction are neither commutative nor associative i.e 3
- 5 ≠ 5 + 3   (subtraction not commutative)

$\frac{8}{4} \neq \frac{4}{8}$ (division not commutative)

2 - (3 - 6) ≠ (2 − 3) − 6 (addition not associative)

$$\frac{\left[\frac{8}{4}\right]}{2} \neq \frac{8}{\left[\frac{4}{2}\right]}$$ (division not associative)

(***iii***) **Distributivity**: A binary operation between two operator * and O distributes if

a * (b O c) = (a * b) O (a * c)

(***iv***) **Closure**: An operation * is said to be closed on a set S if for every a, b ϵ S, a * b ϵ S. Thus an operation is closed if the resulting combination is the same in nature with the original elements. e.g.

If odd numbers are combined under an operation to give odd number.

Rational numbers combined to give a rational number.

Examples of closed operations include ;

Addition of whole number to give a whole number   4 + 3 = 7
Addition of even numbers to give an even number   2 + 4 = 6

(***v***) **Identity**: Let the set (S,*) be a binary operation. An element e of S is called the identity element if for every a ϵ S, a * e = a.

In operation an identity is represented by letter e and also combined with another element to produce the same element.

for simplification, the second term or element in an operation is substituted for identity.

(***vi***) **Inverse element:** can also be regarded as a element to be combined with another to produce an identity.

i.e a * a^{-1} = e where a^{-1} = inverse of a $\therefore$ a * Δ = e

Note: Identity element must be known before solving for inverse element.

To solve for identity substitute Δ for the second element of the given operation.

Operation properties from Tables

The above properties of binary operation can also be obtained from a module table. It is of paramount importance to obey the rules before a decision is made.

QUESTION

(19.1). If a * b = 2ab + a, find 2 * 3

Solution

a * b = 2 * 3 ∴ a = 2, b = 3

∴ 2ab + a = 2(2)(3) + 2 = 14

(19.2). If a * b = +$\sqrt{ab}$, evaluate 2 * (12 * 27).

Solution

Treat the bracket first

a * b = 12 * 27

12 * 27 = +$\sqrt{12(27)}$ → +$\sqrt{324}$ = 18

∴ 2 * (12 * 27) = 2 * 18

a * b = 2 * 18 → 2 * 8 = +$\sqrt{2(18)}$ = $\sqrt{36}$ = 6

(19.3). A binary operation * is defined over R, the same real numbers such that x * y = x^2 + 2y. Find x = 4 and y = 3.

Solution

x = 4, y = 3

x * y = 4^2 + 2(3) = 16 + 6 = 22

(19.4). If x * y = 1 * 5, find x + 2y * 3y.

Solution

From x * y = 1 * 5, x = 1, y = 5

∴ x + 2y = 1 + 2(5) → 1 + 10 = 11

3y = 3(5) = 15

i.e x + 2y * 3y = 11 * 15

(19.5). If m * n = m² + n² + 2mn, find the value of m * 10 when m = 5.

Solution

From m * n = m * 10 where m = 5

∴ $m * n = 5 * 10 \rightarrow m = 5, n = 10$

Substituting

5 * 10 = 5² + 10² + 2 x 5 x 10 = 25 + 100 + 100 = 225

(19.6). If x * y = x + y – 3xy, what is the value of x if x * 2 = -13 ?

Solution
Equating x * y and x * 2 → x = x and y = 2 from x * y = x + y – 3xy

x * 2 = x + 2 – 3 (x) (2)

Also x * 2 = -13

-13 = x + 2 – 6x → 6x – x = 2 + 13 → 5x = 15 ∴ x = 3

(19.7). If x * y = xy + x + y, solve the equation (x * 3) + (2 * x) = 40.

Solution
The equation to be solve has y = 3 and y = 2

x * y = xy + x + y

when y = 3 → x * y = x(3) + x + 3 → 3x + x + 3 = 4x + 3

when y = 2 → 2 * x = 2(x) + x + 2 → 3x + 2

since (x * 3) + (2 * x) = 40

(4x + 3) + (3x + 2) = 40 → 4x + 3x + 3 + 2 = 40 → 7x + 5 = 40

$7x = 40 - 5 = 35 \quad \therefore x = \frac{35}{7} = 5$

(19.8). A binary operation * is defined on a set of real numbers by x * y = x^y for all real values of x and y. If x * 2 = x, find the possible values of x.

Solution

Comparing x * y and x * 2, x = x and y = 2

Also from x * y = x^y and x * 2 = x

x^y = x → ∴ x^2 = x → x^2 – x = 0 → x(x – 1) = 0 → x = 0 or x – 1 = 0

x = 0 or x = 1

(19.9). The binary operation * is defined by x * y = xy – y – x for all real values x and y if x * 3 = 2 * x, find x.

Solution

x * y = xy – y – x

x * 3 = x(3) – 3 – x = 3x – 3 – x = 2x – 3

2 * x = 2(x) – x – 2 = 2x – x – 2 = x – 2

As x * 3 = 2 * x → 2x – 3 = x – 2 → 2x – x = - 2 + 3 ∴ x = 1

(19.10).

Mod 10	2	4	6	8
2	4	8	2	6
4	8	6	4	2
6	2	4	6	8
8	6	2	8	4

The multiplication table has module 10 on the set S = [2, 4. 6, 8] find the inverse of 2.

Solution

A condition for identity is a * e = a

The only number from the table satisfying such condition is 6

2 mod 6 gives 2 i.e identity e = 6

A condition for inverse is a * Δ = e

As 8 and 2 are combined to give 6, they are inverse of each other

∴ the inverse of 2 is 8.

(19.11).

⊕	0	1	2	3	4	5
0	0	1	2	3	4	5
1	1	2	3	4	5	0
2	2	3	4	5	0	1
3	3	4	5	0	1	2
4	4	5	0	1	2	3
5	5	0	1	2	3	4

In table P ⊕ K is defined as what remains of the sum of P and K when divided by 6. What is identity element?

Solution

A condition for identity is a * e = a

The only number from the table satisfying such condition is 0

i.e 1 ⊕ 0 = 1 or 5 ⊕ 0 = 5

(19.12). A binary operation * on a set = {a, b, c, d, e} is defined by the entries in the table below:

■	a	b	c	d	e
a	e	c	a	b	d
b	d	e	b	a	c
c	a	b	c	d	e
d	c	a	d	e	b
e	b	d	e	c	a

What is the identity element of the set of the set under the operation?

Solution

for identity a * e = a

since all given are letters, we carefully test with the rule

From the table a* a = e, a* b = c, a * c = a

c is the identity element

208

(**19.13**).

*	a	b	c	d
a	d	c	b	a
b	c	a	d	b
c	b	d	a	c
d	a	b	c	d

using the operation table given, find the identity element under the operation *.

Solution

a * d = a , b * d = b

∴ the identity element = d

(**19.14**).

⊗	p	q	r	s
p	r	p	r	p
q	p	q	r	s
r	r	r	r	r
s	q	s	r	q

The identity element with respect to the multiplication shown in the table is?

Solution

p ⊗ q = p , s ⊗ q = s

∴ the identity element = q

(**19.15**). Which of the properties of binary operation does not hold for the operation table;

209

■	1	-1	i	-i
1	1	-1	i	-i
-1	-1	1	-i	i
i	i	-i	-1	1
-i	-i	i	1	-1

Solution

Communtativity : holds as -1 * 1 = 1 * -1

Associativity holds as the identity = 1

Identity = 1 as i * 1 = i

Closure: holds as the entries in the table are with the top values

∴ The property that does not hold is consistency

(19.16). A binary Operation * is defined on R, on the set of real numbers, by x * y = $\frac{x+y}{2}$, for all x, y ϵ R. If (2 * P) * 7 = 5, find P.

Solution

From $x * y = \frac{x+y}{2}$

$2 * P = \frac{2+P}{2}$

$(2 * P) * 7 = \frac{2+P}{2} * 7$

from $x * y = \frac{x+y}{2}$

$\frac{2+P}{2} * 7 = \frac{\frac{2+P}{2}+7}{2} = \frac{1}{2}\left(\frac{2+p}{2} + 7\right)$

as (2 * P) * 7 = 5 → $\frac{1}{2}\left(\frac{2+P}{2} + 7\right) = 5$

$\frac{2+p}{2} + 7 = 10$, $2 + P + 14 = 20$

P + 16 = 20, P = 20 − 16 = 4

(19.17). If p * q = 2pq, what property holds for the operation?

Solution

p * q = 2pq, q * p = 2pq = 2pq

Since p * q = q * p, it is commutative

(19.18). A binary operation * is defined on set R of real numbers by a * b = $a^2 + b^2$ – ab for all a, b ϵ R, which binary operation is/are true of operation 2* (-4) * 1?

Solution

a * b = $a^2 + b^2$ – ab

2 * (- 4) can be [2 * (-4)] * 1 or 2 * [(-4) * 1]

2 * - 4 = $2^2 + (-4)^2$ - 2(-4) = 4 + 16 + 8 = 28

∴ [2 * (-4)] * 1 = 28 * 1 = $28^2 + 1^2$ – 28(1) → 784 + 1 – 28 = 757

Inspecting the reverse i.e 1 * [(-4) * 2]

- 4 * 2 = $(-4)^2 + 2^2$ – (-4)2 = 16 + 4 + 8 = 28

1* [-4 * 2] = 1 * 28 = 1^2 + 28 – 1(28) → 1 + 784 – 28 = 757

∴ the operation is commutative.

(19.19). If operation * and O are defined as p * q = x + 3, p * r = 4 x and a O b = 2a + b, find p * (p O r) for a distributive operation.

Solution

For a distributive operation. p * (q O r) = (p * q) O (p * r)

using a O b = 2a + b

(p * q) O (p * r) = 2(p * q) + (p * r) → 2(x + 3) + (4x) = 2x + 6 + 4x

(19.20). Given two binary operations a ~ b = a + b – ab , a . b = a – b + ab

Evaluate (3.2) ~ (2. 3)

211

Solution

From $a \cdot b = a - b + ab$

$1.2 = 3 - 2 + 3(2) = 3 - 2 + 6 = 7$

$1.3 = 2 - 3 + 2(3) = 2 - 3 + 6 = 5$

$(3.2) \sim (2.3) = 7 \sim 5$, from $a \sim b = a + b - ab$

$\therefore 7 \sim 5 = 7 + 5 - 7(5) = 7 + 5 - 35 = -23$

(19.21). Two binary operations $\cdot$ and $\otimes$ are defined as $m \cdot n = mn - n - 1$ and $m \otimes n = mn + n - 2$ for real numbers m, n. find the value of $3 \otimes (4.5)$.

Solution

From $m \cdot n = mn - n - 1 \rightarrow 4.5 = 4(5) - 5 - 1 \rightarrow 20 - 5 - 1 = 14$

$\therefore 3 \otimes (4.5) = 3 \otimes 14$

But $m \otimes n = mn + n - 2$

$3 \otimes 14 = 3(14) + 14 - 2 = 42 + 14 - 2 = 54$

(19.22). An operation O is defined over the set of real number by $x \, O \, y = x + y + x^2 y$. find the identity element.

Solution

For identity, $a * e = a$

$x \, O \, e = x + e + x^2 e \rightarrow x = x + e + x^2 e \rightarrow x - x = e + x^2 e \rightarrow 0 = e(1 + x^2)$

$e = \dfrac{0}{1 + x^2} = 0$

(19.23). If z is the integers and * is an expression defined by $a * b = a + b + 1$ on z. find the identity element.

Solution

For identity, $a * e = a$

$a * e = a + e + 1 = a \rightarrow e = a - a - 1 = -1$

212

(19.24). Find the inverse of a real number y under the operation a * b = 4ab.

Solution

For identity $a * e = 4ae = a \rightarrow e = \frac{a}{4a} = \frac{1}{4}$

For inverse $a * \Delta = e$

$a * b = 4ab \rightarrow a * \Delta = 4a\Delta = e = \frac{1}{4}$

$4a\Delta = \frac{1}{4} \rightarrow \Delta = \frac{1}{4} \cdot \frac{1}{4a} = \frac{1}{16a} = \frac{1}{16y}$

(19.25). An operation * is defined on the set of real numbers y x* y = x + y – 2xy. If the identity element is 0 find the inverse of element P under *.

Solution

With $e = 0$

For inverse $a * \Delta = e \rightarrow x * \Delta = x + \Delta - 2x\Delta = e = 0$

$0 = p + p^{-1} - 2p.p^{-1}$

$\Delta(1 - 2x) = -x \rightarrow \Delta = \frac{-x}{1-2x}$ multiplying top and bottom by -1

$\frac{-(-x)}{-(1-2x)} = \frac{x}{-1+2x} \quad \frac{p}{2p-1}$

(19.26). The operation * is defined on the set R of real numbers by $a*b = a + b + \frac{ab}{2}$ for all a, b ε R. Is the operation associative?

Solution

$a * (b * c) = (a * b) * c \rightarrow 2 * (3 * 5) = (2 * 3) * 5$

$2 * (3 * 5) = 2 * \left[3 + 5 + \frac{3 \times 5}{2}\right] \rightarrow 2 * 15.5 \rightarrow 2 + 15.5 + \frac{2 \times 15.5}{2} = 33.$

$(2 * 3) * 5 = \left[2 + 3 + \frac{2 \times 3}{2}\right] * 5 \rightarrow 8 * 5 \rightarrow 8 + 5 + \frac{8 \times 5}{2} = 33$

Hence it is associative.

213

CHAPTER 20   PARALLEL LINES, ANGLE SUMS

Definitions

Parallel lines are straight lines which lie in the same plane and do not intersect .
The symbol for parallel is ∥; thus *AB ∥ CD* it read "line AB is parallel to line CD" in diagrams arrow are used to indicate that line are parallel.

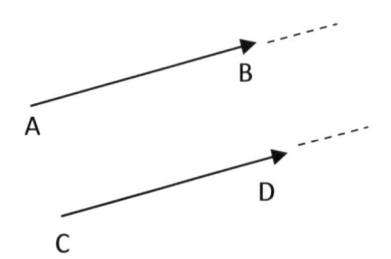

Transversal: This is a line that cuts across two or more lines.
Thus $\overleftrightarrow{EF}$ is a transversal of AB and CD as shown below:

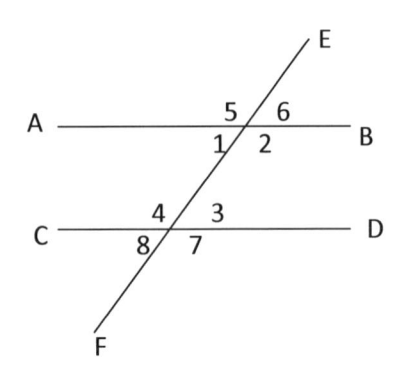

Interior angles: This are the angles formed between the two lines cut by a transversal.

Exterior angles: This are the angles formed outsides the lines cut by a transversal.

Thus, in the diagram above eight angles are formed (four interior angles
∠1, ∠2, ∠3, ∠4 *and* four exterior angles ∠5, ∠6, ∠7, ∠8).

∴ *When a transversal cuts a parallel line* Four acute angles and four obtuse angles are produced.

Angles formed by two lines cut by a transversal

1. Corresponding angles: These are angles on the same side of the transversal and on the same side of the line i.e the two angles are both of the right of the transversal and both below the lines as shown below.

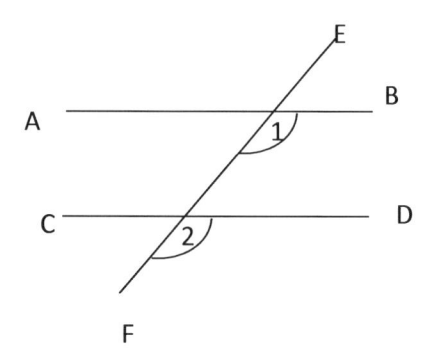

Thus ∠1 *and* ∠2 are corresponding angles of AB and CD cut by transversal EF.

Also close observation of the diagram above show that the sides of two corresponding angles from a capital F in varying positions as shown below:

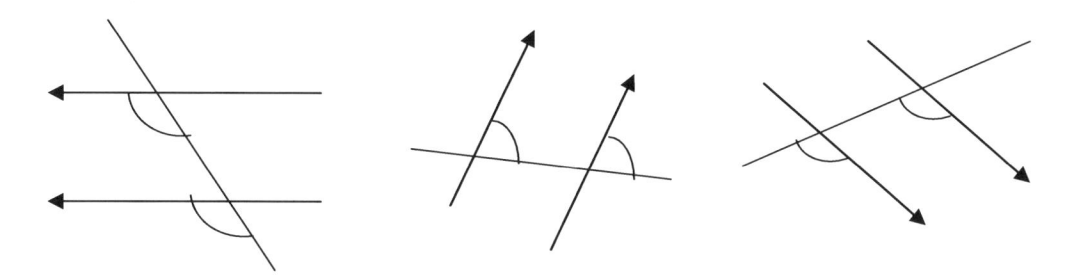

Hence, to identify a corresponding angle look for the letter F in any position.

2. Alternative interior angles: These are nonadjacent angles between the two lines and on opposite sides of the transversal.

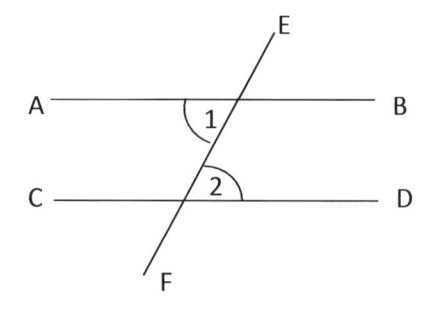

Thus ∠1 *and* ∠2 are alternative interior angles of AB and CD cut by EF.

Also close observation of the diagram above show that the sides of two alternative interior angles from a capital Z or N in varying positions, as shown below:

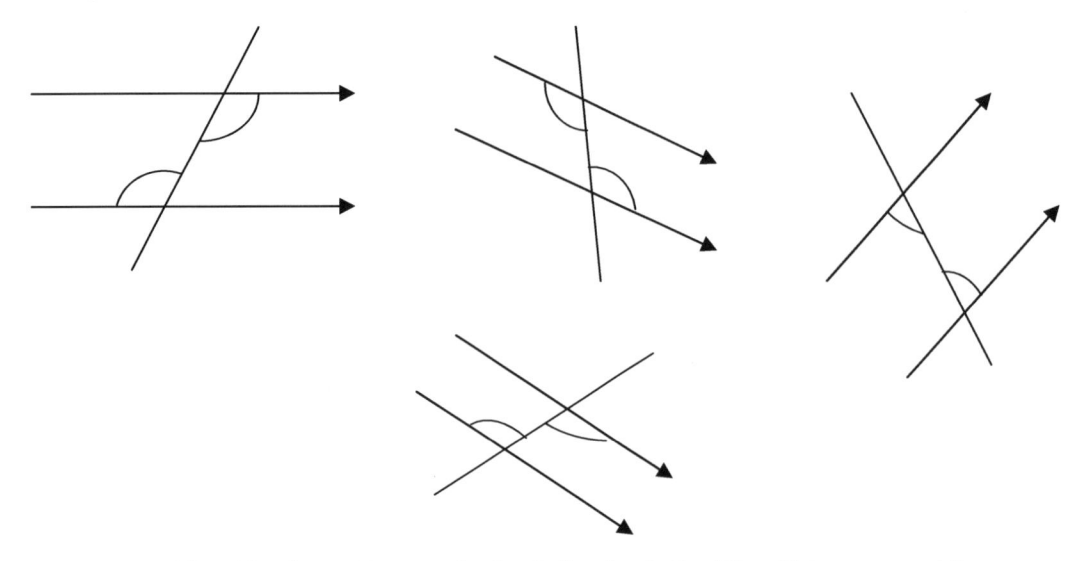

In summary: to identify alternating angle, look for the letter N or Z in any position.

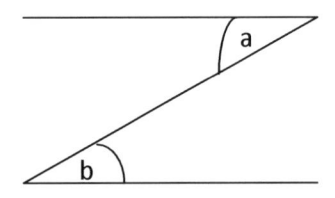

Where $a = b$

3. Adjacent angels: These are angles placed side by side or with a common vertex when drawn. Adjacent angles on the same side of a transversal which can be readily located by noting the capital U formed by their sides.

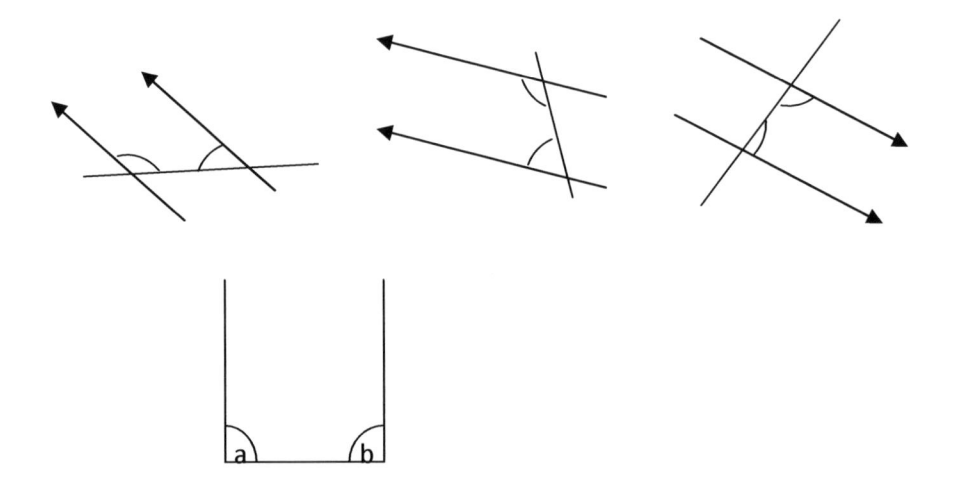

since supplementary angles add up to 180

∴ *for* Interior angles: $a + b = 180$

Principles of Parallel lines

Principle 1: Through a given point not on a given line, one and one line can be drawn parallel to a given line (parallel line postulate).

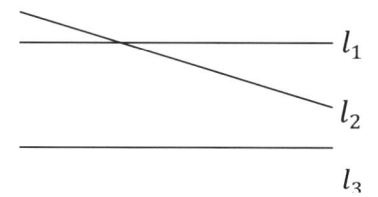

Thus in the diagram above either l_1 or l_2 but not both may be parallel to l_3

Principle 2: Two lines are parallel if a pair of corresponding angles are congruent.

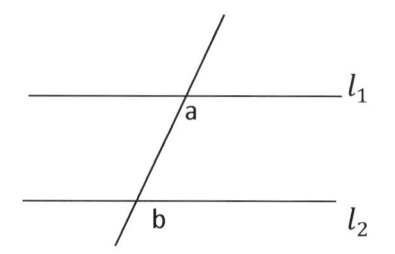

Thus in the diagram above $l_1 \parallel l_2$ *if* $\angle a \cong \angle b$

Principle 3: Two lines are parallel if a pair of alternate interior angles are congruent.

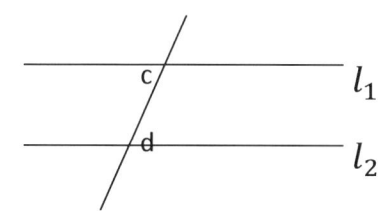

Thus in the diagram above $l_1 \parallel l_2$ *if* $\angle c \cong \angle d$

Principle 4: Two lines are parallel if a pair of interior angles on the same side of a transversal is supplementary.

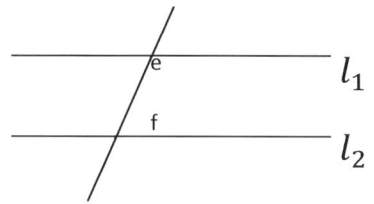

Thus in the diagram above $l_1 \parallel l_2$ if $\angle e \cong \angle f$ are supplementary

Principle 5: Lines are parallel if they are perpendicular to the same line (perpendicular to the same line are parallel).

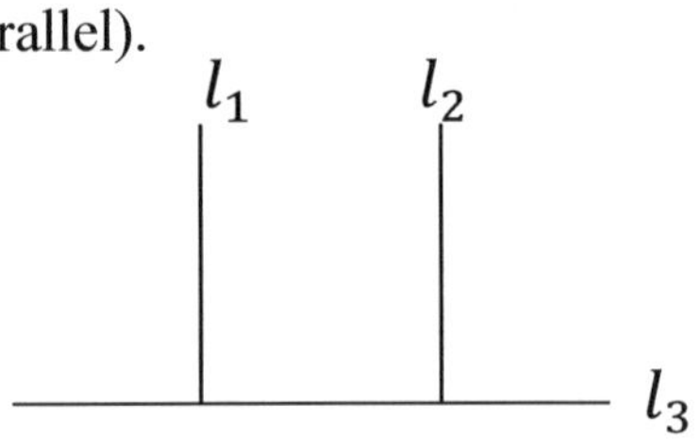

Thus $l_1 \parallel l_2$ if l_1 and l_2 are each perpendicular to l_3

Principle 6: Lines are parallel if they are parallel to the same line, (parallels to the same line are parallel).

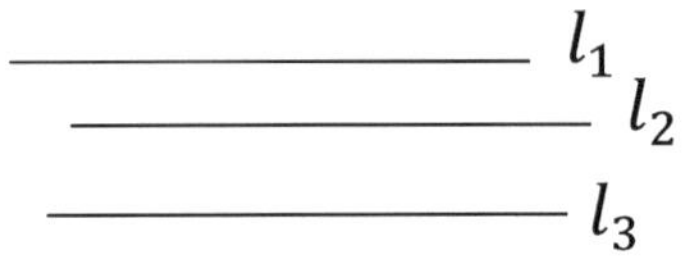

Thus, in the diagram above $l_1 \parallel l_2$ if l_1 and l_2 are each parallel to l_3

Principle 7: If two lines are parallel, each pair of corresponding angles are congruent. (Corresponding angles of parallel lines are congruent).

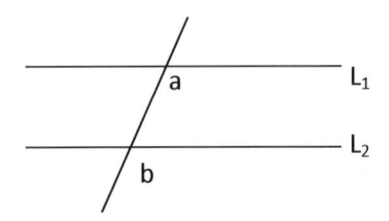

Thus, in the diagram above if $l_1 \parallel l_2$ then $\angle a \cong \angle b$

Principle 8: If two lines are parallel, each pair of alternate interior angle are congruent. (Alternate interior angles of parallel lines are congruent).

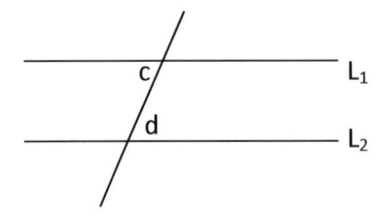

Thus, in the diagram above if $l_1 \parallel l_2$ then $\angle c \cong \angle d$

Principle 9: If two lines are parallel, each pair of interior angles on the same side of the transversal are supplementary.

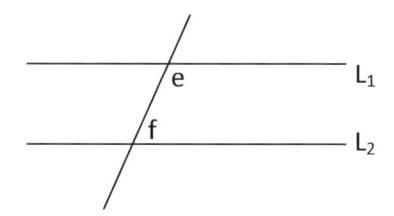

Thus, in the diagram above if $l_1 \parallel l_2$ then $\angle e \cong \angle f$ are supplementary

Principle 10: If lines are parallel, a line perpendicular to one of them is perpendicular to the others also.

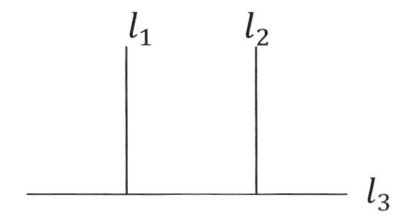

Thus, in the diagram above if $l_1 \parallel l_2$ and $l_3 \perp l_1$, then $l_3 \perp l_2$

Principle 11: If lines are parallel, a line parallel to one of them is parallel to the others also.

Thus if $l_1 \parallel l_2$ and $l_3 \parallel l_4$ then $l_3 \parallel l_2$

Principle 12: If the sides of two angles are respectively parallel to each other, the angles are either congruent or supplementary.

Thus, in the diagram above if $l_1 \parallel l_3$ and $l_2 \parallel l_4$ then $\angle a \cong \angle b$ and $\angle a \cong \angle c$ are supplementary.

TRIANGLES

This is a polygon with three edges and three vertices.

Classification of triangles

(*i*) Right angle triangle: This is a triangle with one of its angles equal to $90°$.

(*ii*) Pythagoras triplet: This is a right angle triangle with the sides in the ratio 3:4:5

(*iii*) Isosceles triangle: This is a triangle with two sides equal.

(*iii*) Equilateral triangle: This is a triangle with all three sides equal.

(*iii*) Scalene triangle: This is a triangle with no sides equal.

Terms associated with triangles

(**1**) Congruency: Triangles are said to be congruent if they have the same size and shape. It deals with pair of triangles embedded or separated.

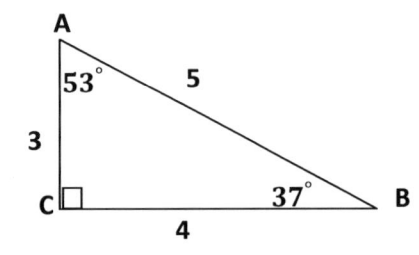

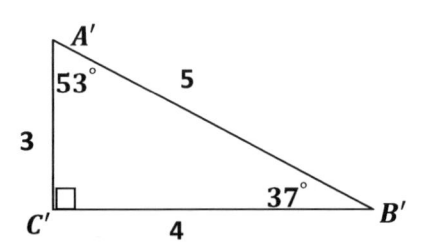

In the diagram above $\triangle ABC = \triangle A'B'C'$ are congruent triangles. Thus, ABC and $A'B'C'$ have congruent corresponding sides ($AB = A'B'$, $BC = B'C'$, and $AC = A'C'$) and congruent corresponding angles ($\angle A \cong \angle A'$, $\angle B \cong \angle B'$, and $\angle C \cong \angle C'$).

Principles of Congruent triangles

Principle 1: If three sides of one triangle are congruent to three sides of another, then the triangle are congruent. This is also known as (s.s.s ≅ s.s.s).

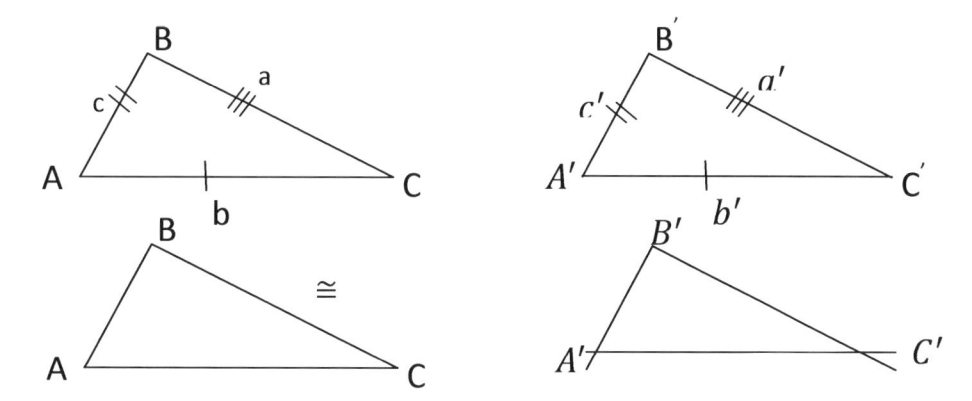

From the diagram above, thus if $a \cong a', b \cong b'$ and $c \cong c'$ then $\triangle ABC = \triangle A'B'C'$

Principle 2: If two sides and the included angle of one triangle are congruent to the corresponding parts of another, then the triangles are congruent. This is also known as (s.a.s ≅ s.a.s).

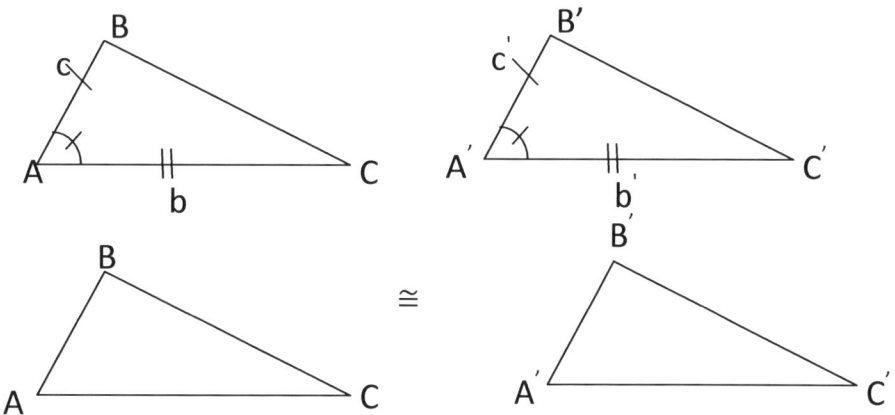

From the diagram above, thus $b \cong b', c \cong c'$ and $\angle A \cong \angle A'$ then $\triangle ABC = \triangle A'B'C'$

Principle 3: If two angles and the included side of one triangle are congruent to the corresponding part of another, then the triangle are congruent. This is also known as (a.s.a ≅ a.s.a).

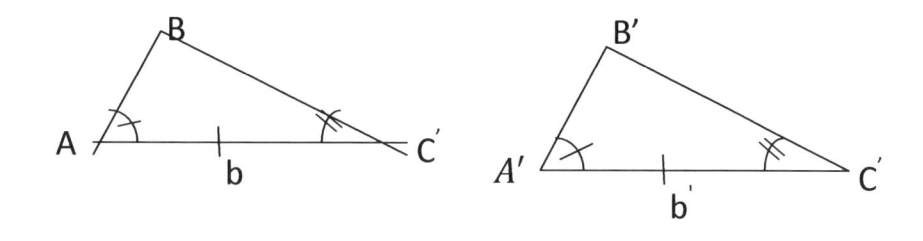

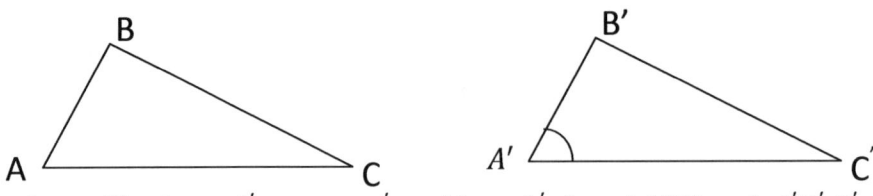

From the diagram above, if $\angle A \cong \angle A', \angle c \cong \angle c'$ and $b \cong b'$ then $\triangle ABC = \triangle A'B'C'$

(2) Pythagorean Theorem

This states that in a right triangle, the square of the length of the hypotenuse equal the sum of the squares of the lengths of the legs.

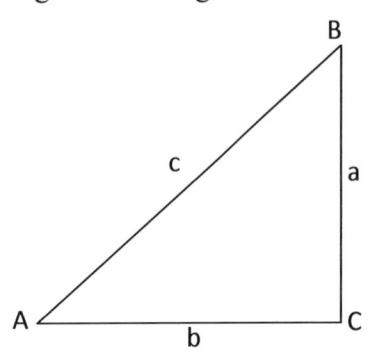

In the diagram above c, a and b are the three sides of a triangle ABC with

c = hypotenuse (longest side), a = opposite and b = adjacent

Mathematically, $c^2 = a^2 + b^2$

Applications of the Pythagorean Theorem

(i) Determining the types of triangles: Pythagorean theorem can be used to determine the type of triangle given:

If $c^2 = a^2 + b^2$ → Right triangle.

If $c^2 \neq a^2 + b^2$ → Not a right triangle.

If $c^2 < a^2 + b^2$ → Acute triangle.

If $c^2 > a^2 + b^2$ → obtuse triangle.

(ii) Isosceles triangle: For an isosceles triangle that is right handed, the altitude h of the triangle bisects the base.

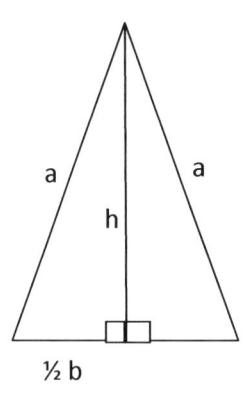

Thus, by Pythagoras → $a^2 = h^2 + \left[\frac{1}{2}b^2\right]$

(*iii*) Rhombus: For a rhombus that is right handed, the diagonals are perpendicular bisectors of each other.

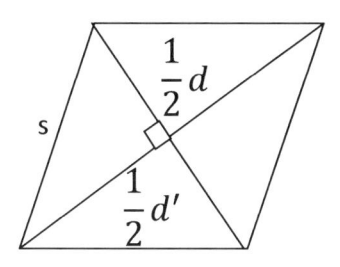

Thus, by Pythagoras → $s^2 = \left(\frac{1}{2}d\right)^2 + \left(\frac{1}{2}d'\right)^2$

(*iv*) Trapezoid: For a trapezoid that is right handed, we have a rectangle and triangles attached to each other.

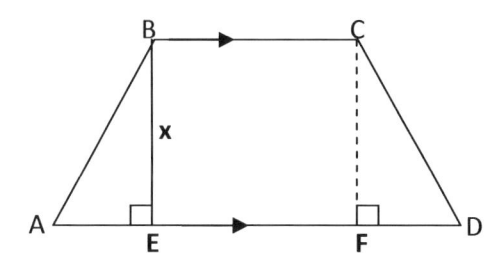

With $EF = BC$

Thus, by Pythagoras → $BE^2 = BA^2 - AE^2$

(3) Special right triangles: These are right triangles with some regular feature that makes calculations on such triangles easier. They include:

(*i*) 30^0- 60^0-90^0 Triangle: This is one-half an equilateral triangle.

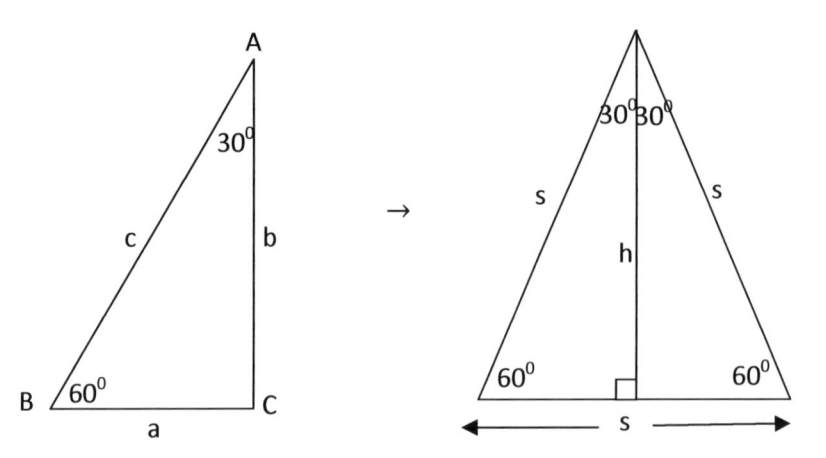

In right $\triangle ABC$ $a = \frac{1}{2}c$

Thus in a 30^0- 60^0-90^0 triangle, the following holds

The ratio of the sides a:b:c is given by $x : x\sqrt{3} : 2x$

The leg opposite the 30^0 angle is given by $\frac{Hypotenus}{2}$

The leg opposite the 60^0 angle is given $\frac{Hypotenus \; x \; \sqrt{3}}{2}$

The altitude in an equilateral triangle, trapezoid (isosceles) forms a 30^0-60^0-90^0 triangle and it is given by : Altitude $= \frac{Hypotenus \; x \; \sqrt{3}}{2}$

(*ii*) 45^0-45^0-90^0 Triangle: This one-half a square.

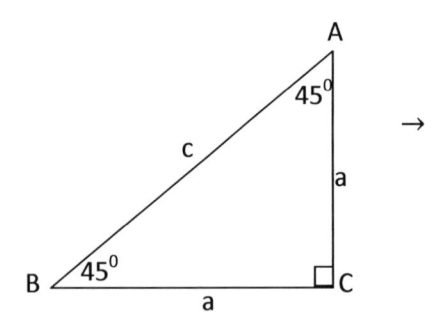

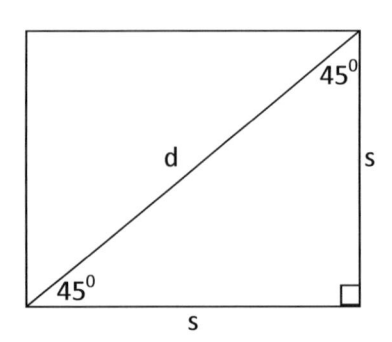

224

In right triangle ABC, $c^2 = a^2 + a^2 \rightarrow c = a\sqrt{2}$.

Thus in a 45^0-45^0-90^0 triangle, the following holds

The ratio of the sides a:a:c is given by $x:x:x\sqrt{2}$

Each leg is given by $\dfrac{\text{Hypotenus x } \sqrt{2}}{2}$

Hypotenuse is given leg x $\sqrt{2}$

The diagonal in a square forms a 45^0-45^0-90^0 triangle and it is given by

Diagonal = Side x $\sqrt{2}$

Note: If the hypotenuse of a right triangle is twice the length of one of the legs there, it's a 30-60-90 and that leg is 60°

In all right angle triangle. You can use [the two legs other than the hypotenuse) as a base and altitude.

The sum of the lengths of any two sides of a triangle is greater than the length of the third side.

The difference between the lengths of any two sides of a triangle is less than the length of the third side.

If the positions of the angles are reversed, reverse the formula.

(4) **Sum of the measures of the angles of a triangle**

The following principles states the angle sum principles:

Principle 1: The sum of the measures of the angles of a triangle equals the measure of a straight angle or 180^0.

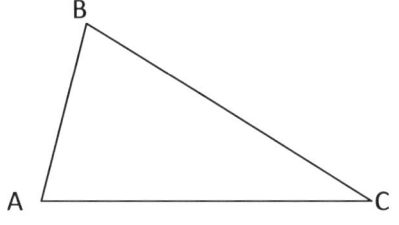

Thus in $\triangle ABC \rightarrow m\angle A + m\angle B + m\angle C = 180^o$

Principle 2: If two angle of one triangle are congruent respectively to two angles of another triangle, the remaining angles are congruent.

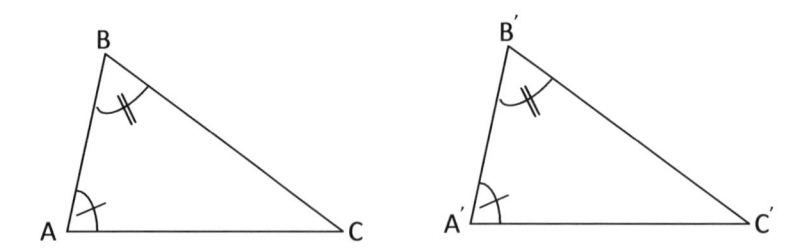

Thus in $\triangle ABC$ and $\triangle A'B'C'$ if $\angle A \cong \angle A'$ and $\angle B \cong \angle B'$, then $\angle C \cong \angle C'$

Principle 3: The measure of each exterior angle of a triangle equals the sum of the measures of its two nonadjacent interior angles.

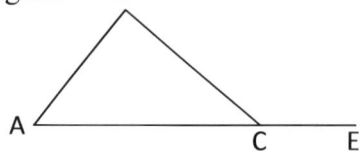

Thus in $\triangle ABC \rightarrow m\angle A + m\angle B = m\angle ECB$

Principle 4: The sum of the measures of the exterior angles of a triangle equals 360^0

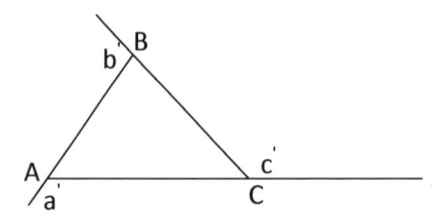

Thus $in \triangle ABC \rightarrow m\angle a' + m\angle b' + m\angle c' = 360^0$

Principle 5: The measure of each angle of an equilateral triangle equals 60^0,

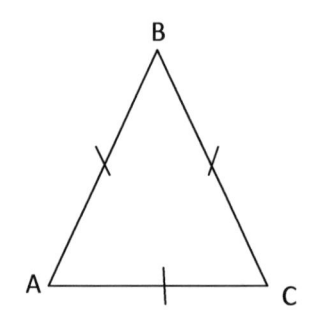

Thus *in* △ABC → $m\angle A = 60°$, $m\angle B = 60°$ and $m\angle C = 60°$

Principle 6: The acute angles of a right triangle are complementary.

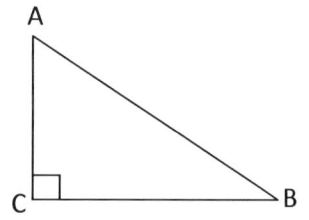

Thus in right △ABC if $m\angle C = 90°$, then $m\angle A + m\angle B = 90°$

Principle 7: The measure of each acute angle of an isosceles right angle equals to $45°$

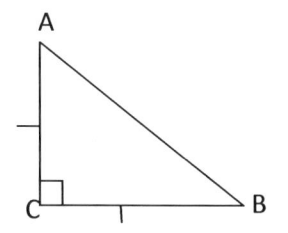

Thus in isosceles right △ABC if $m\angle C = 90°$, then $m\angle A = 45°$ and $m\angle B = 45°$

Principle 8: A triangle can have no more than one obtuse angle.

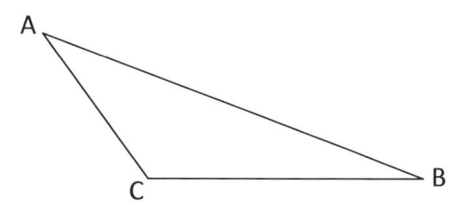

Thus in obtuse △ABC if $\angle C$ is obtuse, then $\angle A$ and $\angle B$ cannot be obtuse angles.

Principle 9: Two angles are supplementary if their sides are respectively perpendicular to each other.

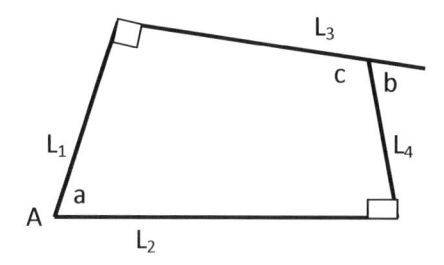

227

Thus if $l_1 \perp l_2$ and $l_2 \perp l_4$ → $\angle a \cong \angle b,$ and a and $\angle c$ are supplementary.

Principle 10: The sum of the measures of the angles of a quadrilateral equals $360°$

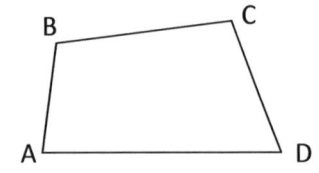

Thus in quadrilateral ABCD → $m\angle A + m\angle B + m\angle C + m\angle D = 360°$

Note: Properties of parallel apply to triangles once you spot any of them, use them.

(5) Midpoint and median

Terms associated with midpoint and median of triangles:

(i)   Median: This is a line that divides one side of a triangle into two equal parts from the edge or vertex.

(ii)   Centroid: This is a point where two medians meet.

(iii)   Altitude: This is a line drawn from an edge or a vertex perpendicular to any side of a triangle.

(iv)   Orthocentre: This is a point where the altitude meets.

(iv)   Circumcentre: This is a point where the perpendicular bisectors of the sides of a triangle meet.

(v)   Incentre: This is a point where the internal bisectors of the sides of a triangle meet.

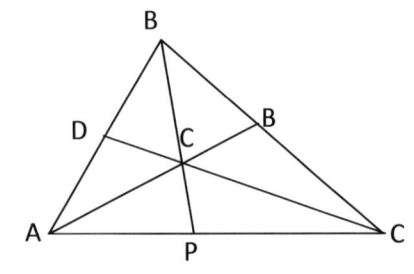

AB and CD = median, C = Centroid

Midpoint and median principle of triangles

Principle 1: If a line is drawn from the midpoint of one side of a triangle and parallel to a second side, then it passes through the midpoint of the third side.

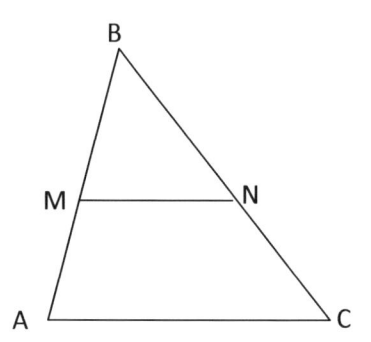

In the diagram above (∆ABC) if M is the midpoint of $\overline{AB}$ and $\overline{MN} \parallel \overline{AC}$, then N is the midpoint of $\overline{BC}$.

∴ $MN = \frac{1}{2}AC$

Principle 2: If a line joins the midpoints of two sides of a triangle, then it is parallel to the third side and its length is one-half the length of the third side.

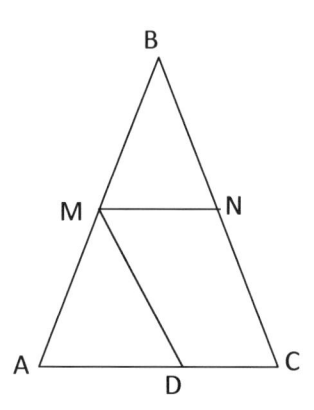

In the diagram above, if M and N are the midpoint of $\overline{AB}$ and $\overline{BC}$, then $\overline{MN} \parallel \overline{AC}$.

$MN = \frac{1}{2}AC, MD = \frac{1}{2}BC$

Principle 3: The length of the median to the hypotenuse of a right triangle equals one-half the length of the hypotenuse.

In the right ∆ABC if $\overline{CM}$ is the median to hypotenuse $\overline{AB}$, then $CM = \frac{1}{2}AB$.

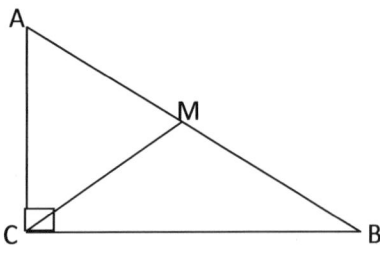

$CM = \frac{1}{2}AB \ldots \ldots \ldots \ldots \ldots (i)$

$CM = AM \ldots \ldots \ldots \ldots \ldots (ii)$

$CM = BM \ldots \ldots \ldots \ldots \ldots (iii)$

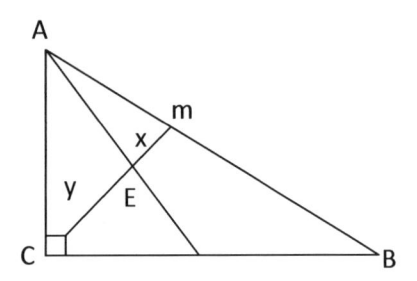

$x = \frac{1}{3}CM, \quad y = \frac{2}{3}cm, \quad CM = \frac{1}{2}AB$

Principle 4: The median of a triangle meet in a point which is two-third of the distance from any vertex to the midpoint of the opposite side.

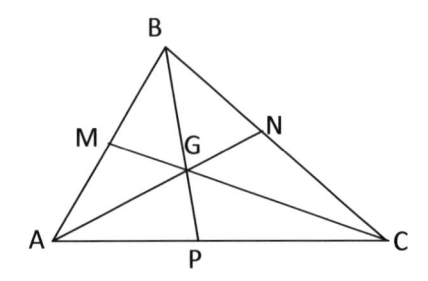

In the diagram above, $\overline{AN}, \overline{BP}$ and $\overline{CM}$ are median of $\triangle ABC$ they meet in a point G, which is two-thirds of the distance from A to N, B to $P,$ and C to M.

QUESTIONS

Find x and y in the diagrams below:

(20.1).

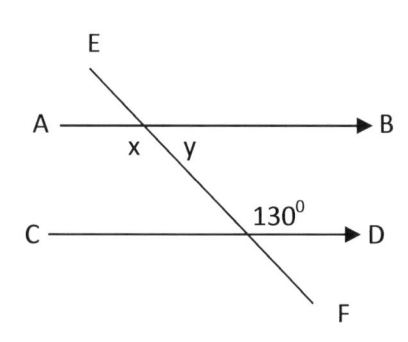

Solution

To find x, observe that a letter Z is on the diagram ∴ $x = 130^0$ or apply principle 8. To find y, observe that a letter U is on the diagram ∴ $y = 180^0 - 130^0 = 50$.

(20.2).

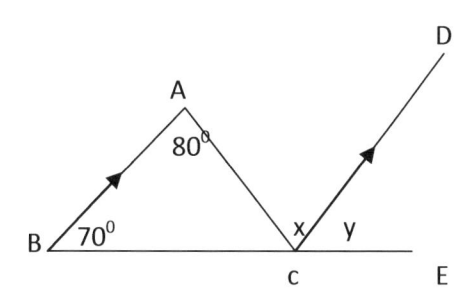

Solution

To find x, observe that a letter Z is on the diagram ∴ $x = 80^0$ or apply principle 8. to find y, from principle 7, $y = 70^0$

(20.3).

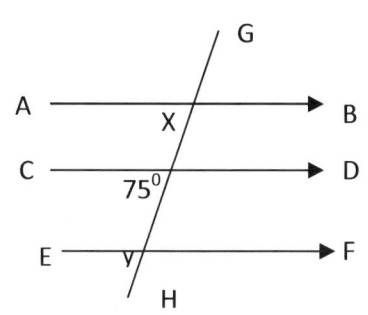

Solution

To find x, observe that a letter F is on the diagram ∴ $x = 75^0$ or apply principle 7, to find y observe that a letter U is on the diagram ∴ $y = 180^0 - 75^0 = 105^0$ or apply principle 9.

(20.4).

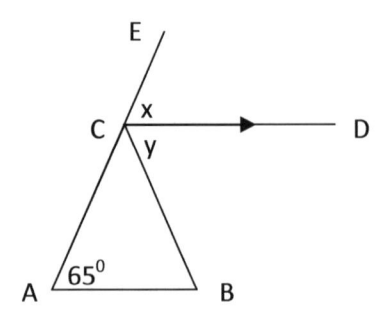

Solution

To find x apply principle 7 ∴ $x = 65°$, To find y, observe that a letter Z is on the diagram ∴ $x = 65^0$ or apply principle 8.

(20.5).

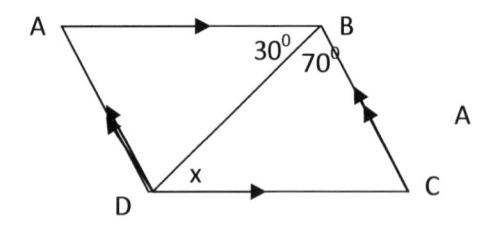

Solution

To find x, observe that a letter Z is on the diagram ∴ $x = 30^0$ or apply principle 8. To find y observe that a letter U is on the diagram.

∴ $y = 180^0 - (30^0 + 70^0) = 80°$ or apply principle 9.

(20.6).

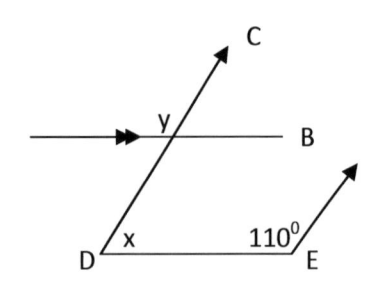

Solution

To find y observe that a letter U is on the diagram ∴ x = $180^0 - 110^0$ = 70 (principle 9), y = 110 (principle 12).

(20.7).

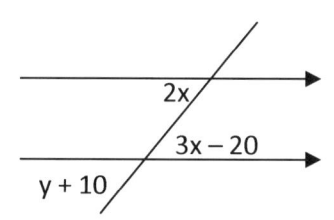

Solution

From principle 8 or Z → 3x − 20 = 2x → x = 20^0

From principle 7 or F → y + 10 = 2x → y +10 = 40 → y = 30^0

(20.8).

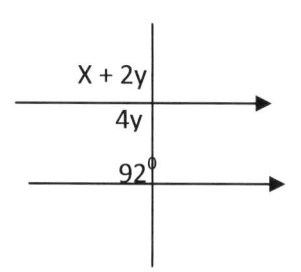

Solution

From principle 9 or U → 4y + 92 = 180 → 4y = 180 − 92 = 88 → y = 22^0

From principle 7 or F → x + 2y = 92 → x + 44 = 92 → x = 48^0

(20.9).

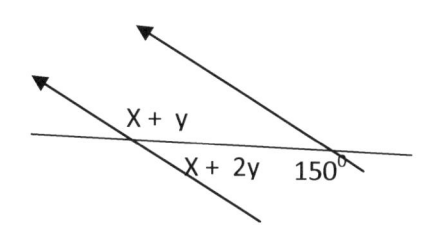

Solution

For the letter U → x + y = 150 …..(i)

For angle on a straight line → x + y + x − 2y = 180 → 150 + x − 2y = 180

233

$x - 2y = 30$ ∴ $150 - y - 2y = 30 \rightarrow 150 - 3y = 30 \rightarrow 3y = 120$

y = 40^0

from (i) $x + 40 = 150 \rightarrow x = 110^0$

(20.10).

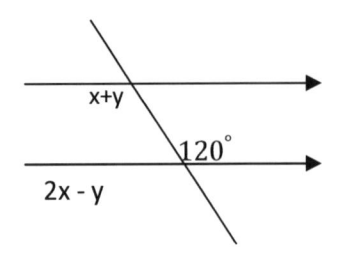

Solution

For the letter F → $x + y = 2x - y \rightarrow y + y = 2x - x$ ∴ $2y = x$

For the letter Z $120 = x + y \rightarrow 120 = 2y + y = 3y$ ∴ $y = 40$, ∴ $x = 80$

(20.11).

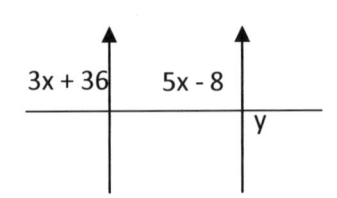

Solution

For the letter F → $5x - 8 = 3x + 36 \rightarrow 5x - 3x = 42$ ∴ $x = 22$

(20.12).

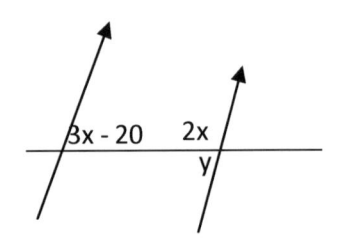

Solution

For the letter U → $3x - 20 = 2x \rightarrow 3x - 2x = 20$ ∴ $x = 20$

For the letter Z → $3x - 20 = y \rightarrow 3(20) - 20 = y \rightarrow 60 - 20 = y$ ∴ $y = 40$

(**20.13**).

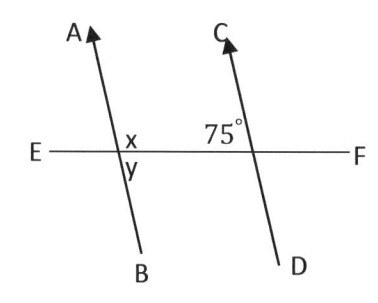

Solution

For the letter U → x + 75 = 180 → $x = 180 - 75 = 105$

For the letter Z → $y = 75$

(**20.14**).

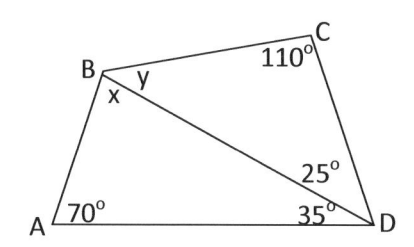

Solutions

From property 1 → x + 35 + 70 = 180 → x = 75°

Also y + 110 + 25 = 180 → y = 45°

(**20.15**).

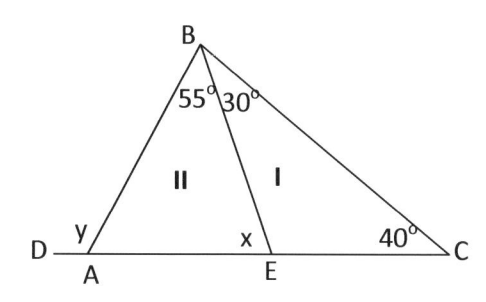

Solutions

x is external angle $of\ \Delta I \therefore x = 30 + 40 = 70^o$

y is external $angle\ of\ \Delta ABC \therefore y = m\angle B + 40 \rightarrow 85 + 40 = 125^o$

(20.16).

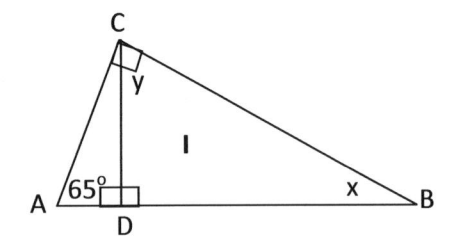

In $\triangle ABC$, by property 6, $x + 65 = 90 \rightarrow x = 25°$

In $\triangle I$, by property 6 $\rightarrow$ $x + y = 90 \rightarrow 25 + y = 90 \rightarrow y = 65°$

(20.17).

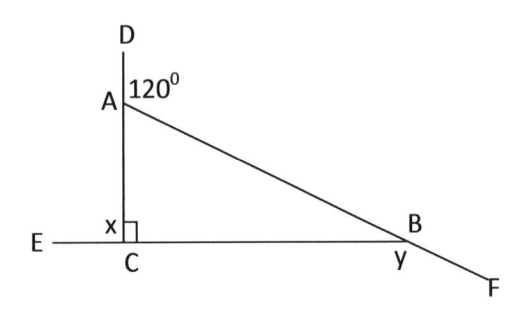

Solutions

With $\overleftrightarrow{DC} \perp \overleftrightarrow{EB}$ $\therefore x = 90$

By principle 4 $\rightarrow$ $x + y + 120 = 360 \rightarrow 90 + y + 120 = 360°$

$y = 150°$

(20.18).

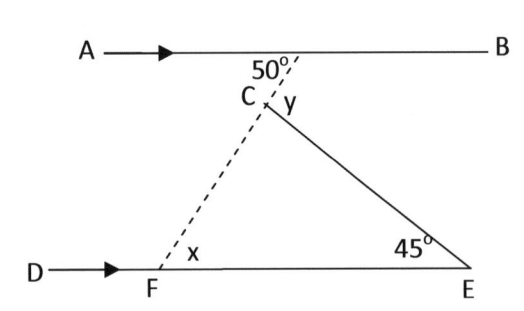

Solution

Spot the letter Z or since $\overleftrightarrow{AB} \parallel \overleftrightarrow{DE}$ $\therefore x = 50$

from principle 3 $\rightarrow y = x + 45 \rightarrow y = 50 + 45 = 95°$

(20.19).

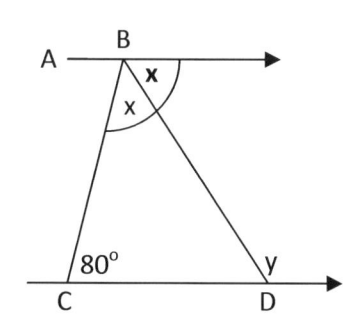

Spot the letter U or since $\overleftrightarrow{AB} \parallel \overleftrightarrow{CD} \rightarrow 2x + 80 = 180 \rightarrow 2x = 100 \therefore x = 50°$

from property 3 $\rightarrow y = x + 80 \therefore y = 50 + 80 = 130°$

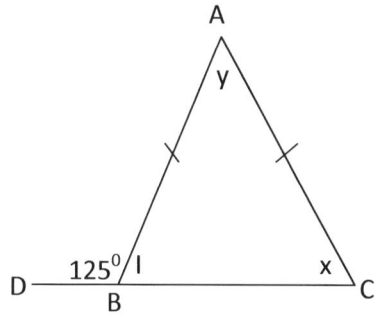

(20.20).

For isosceles triangle that it not right handed. The two angles at the bottom are always equal i.e $\overline{AB} \cong \overline{AC} \therefore \angle 1 \cong \angle x$

$125 = x + y$ ………(i)

since x = 1 *we have from principle 1* $\rightarrow x + x + y = 180 \rightarrow x + 125 = 180 \therefore x = 55°$

also from principle 1 $\rightarrow x + x + y = 180 \rightarrow 2x + y = 180 \rightarrow 110 + y = 180 \therefore y = 70°$

(20.21).

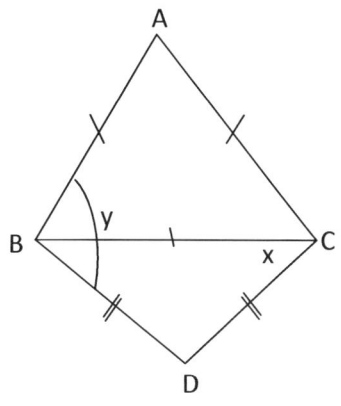

237

Solution

The top triangle is an equilateral. $\therefore$ by principle 5, $m\angle ABC = 60$

The bottom triangle is an acute $\therefore$ by principle 7 $m\angle CBD = 45°$

Also by Property 7, x = 45°

$y = 60 + 45 = 105°$

(20.22).

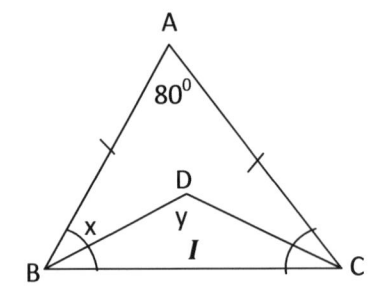

In the diagram above $\overline{BD}$ bisects $\angle B$, $\overline{CD}$ bisects $\angle C$. Find x and y.

Solution

$\overline{AB} \cong \overline{AC} \therefore \angle ABC \cong \angle ACB$

$2x + 80 = 180 \therefore x = 50°$

In ΔI by property 1 $\rightarrow \frac{1}{2}x + \frac{1}{2}x + y = 180 \rightarrow x + x + 2y = 2(180)$

$2x + 2y = 2(180) \rightarrow 2(x+y) = 2(180) \therefore x + y = 180$

$50 + y = 180 \therefore y = 130°$

(20.23).

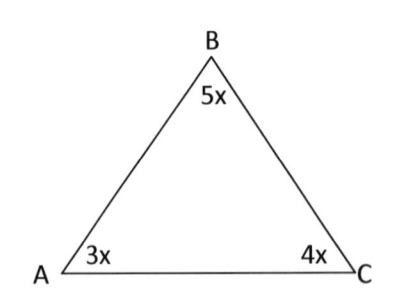

238

Find the measure of each angle of a triangle if its angle measures are in the ratio of 3:4:5.

Solution

With sum of angles = 180

$3x + 4x + 5x = 180 \rightarrow 12x = 180 \therefore x = 15$.

$\therefore 3x = 45, 4x = 60$ and $5x = 75$. The angles are $45^0\ 60^0\ 75^0$

(20.24).

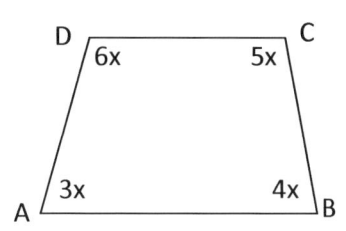

Find the measure of each angle of a quadrilateral if its angle measures are in the ratio of 3:4:5:6.

Solution

With sum of angles = 360

$3x + 4x + 5x + 6x = 360 \rightarrow 18x = 360 \therefore x = 20$.

$\therefore 3x = 60, 4x = 80, 5x = 100, 6x = 120$. The angles are $60°, 80°, 100°, 120°$

(20.25).

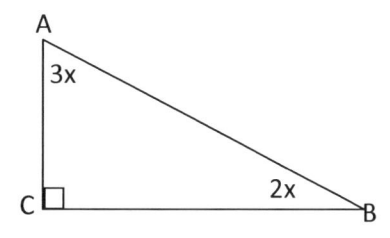

Find the measure of each angle of a of a right triangle if the ratio of the measures of its acute angles is 2:3.

Solution

With sum of angles = 90

$2x + 3x = 90 \rightarrow 5x = 90 \rightarrow x = 18$

239

∴ 2x = 36, 3x = 54. The angles are 36° 54° 90°

(20.26).

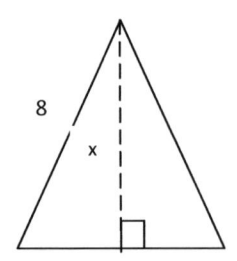

Find x if the triangle above is equilateral.

Solution

The altitude in an equilateral triangle forms a 30^0-60^0-90^0

$x = \frac{8 \times \sqrt{3}}{2} = 4\sqrt{3}$

(20.27).

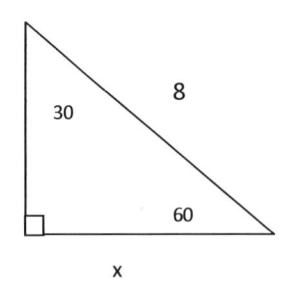

Find x in the triangle above.

Solution

For a 30^0-60^0-90^0 triangle

$x = \frac{8}{2} = 4$

(20.28).

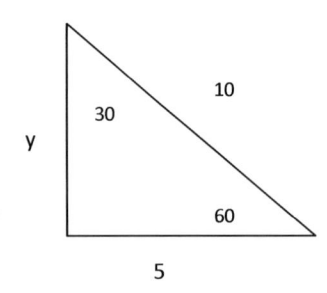

Find y in the triangle above

Solution

For a 30^0-60^0-90^0 triangle

$y = \frac{10 \times \sqrt{3}}{2} = 5\sqrt{3}$

(20.29).

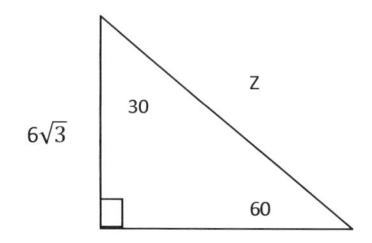

Solution

For a 30^0-60^0-90^0 triangle

$6\sqrt{3} = \frac{z\sqrt{3}}{2} \rightarrow z = 12$

(20.30).

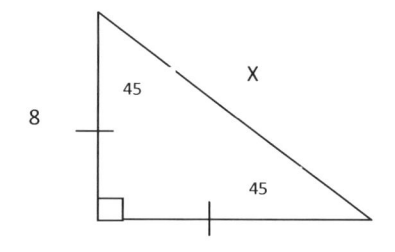

Solution

For a 45^0-45^0-45^0 triangle

Hypotenuse = leg x $\sqrt{2}$ $\rightarrow$ $8\sqrt{2}$

(20.31).

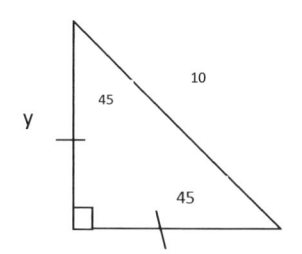

Solution

For a 45^0-45^0-45^0 triangle

$\text{Leg} = \dfrac{\text{Hypotenus} \times \sqrt{2}}{2} \rightarrow y = \dfrac{10 \times \sqrt{2}}{2} = 5\sqrt{2}$

(20.32).

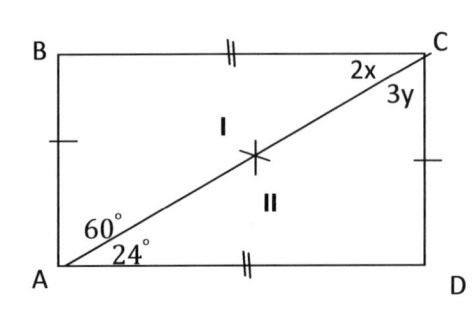

Solution

By congruency: $\triangle I \cong \triangle II \rightarrow 2x = 24 \rightarrow x = 12$ also $3y = 60 \rightarrow y = 20$.

(20.33)

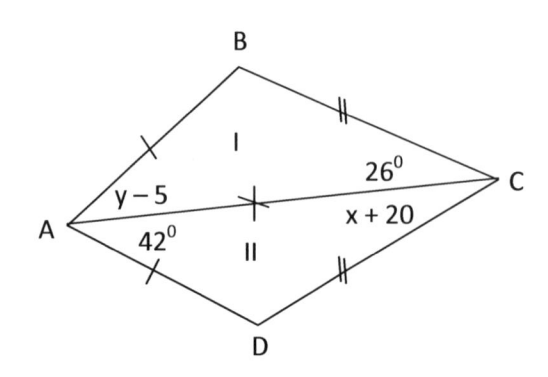

Solution

By congruency: $\triangle I \cong \triangle II \rightarrow x + 20 = 26 \therefore x = 6$ also $y - 5 = 42 \therefore y = 47$

(20.34).

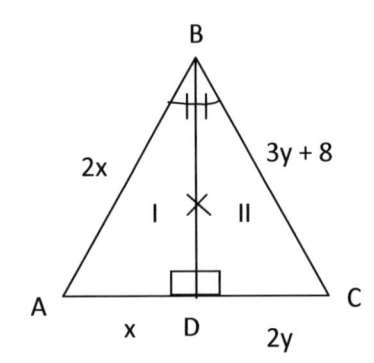

Solutions

By congruency: $\triangle I \cong \triangle I \rightarrow x = 2y$ also $2x = 3y + 8$. Substituting $2(2y) = 3y + 8 \rightarrow 4y - 3y = 8$ $y = 8$. Then $x = 2y = 16$

(20.35).

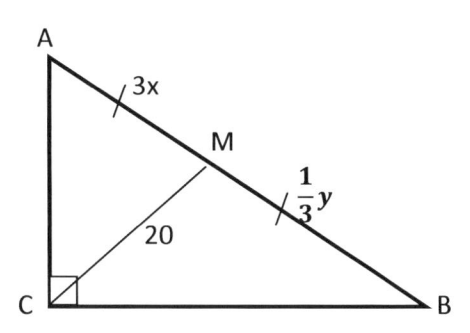

$CM = AM = BM$

$20 = 3x \rightarrow x = \frac{20}{3}$

$\frac{1}{3}y = 20 \rightarrow y = 3 \times 20 = 60$

(20.36).

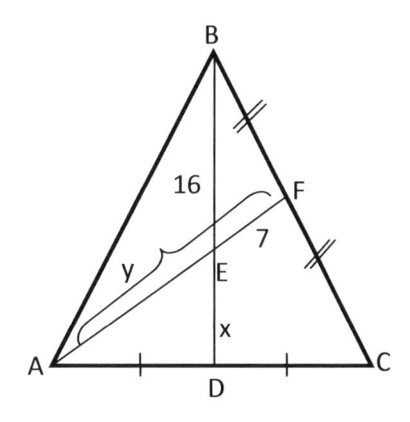

Solution

$AE = 3EF$, $DE = \frac{1}{2}BE$

$\therefore x = \frac{1}{2}(16) = 8$, $y = 3(7) = 21$

243

(**20.37**).

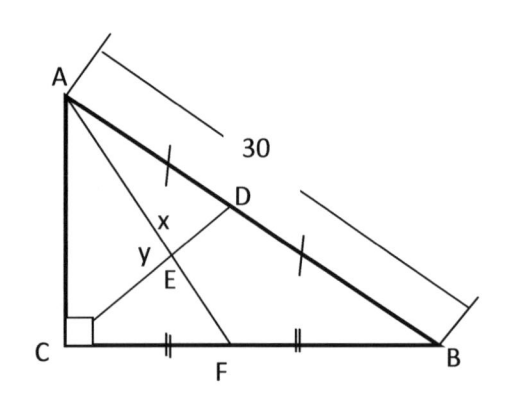

Solution

$CD = \frac{1}{2}AB \rightarrow \frac{1}{2}(30) = 15$

$x = \frac{1}{3}CD \rightarrow \frac{1}{3}(15) = 5$

$y = \frac{2}{3}CD \rightarrow \frac{2}{3}(15) = 10$

(**20.38**).

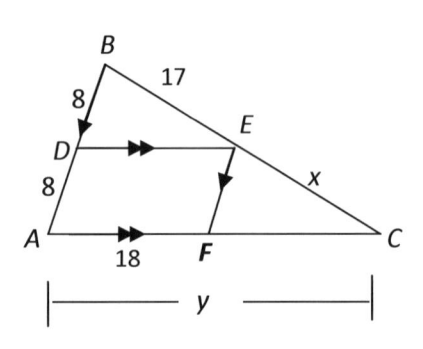

Solution

Here AD = BD, BE = CE $\rightarrow$ $x = 17$ and $y = 36$

(**20.39**).

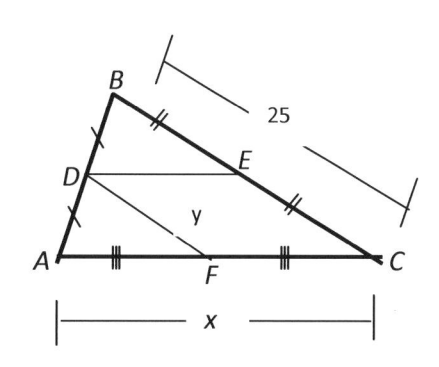

Solution

$DF = \frac{1}{2}BC \rightarrow y = \frac{1}{2}(25) = 12\frac{1}{2}$

$DE = \frac{1}{2}AC \rightarrow 12 = \frac{1}{2}(x) \therefore x = 24$

CHAPTER 21   QUADRILATERALS

These are figures with four sides. They include trapezium, rectangle, square, parallelogram, rhombus and kite.

We now treat each of them in details.

(1) TRAPEZOIDS/TRAPEZIUM

This is a quadrilateral having two and only two parallel sides with the following

Base: These are its parallel sides

Leg: This is its non parallel sides.

Median: This is the line segment joining the midpoints of its legs

An isosceles trapezoid is a trapezoid whose legs are congruent.

The base angles of a trapezoid are the angles at the ends of its longer base

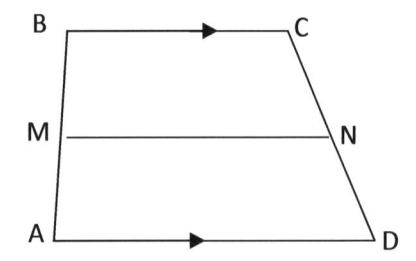

In the trapezoid ABCD $\overline{AD}$ and $\overline{BC}$ = bases, $\overline{AB}$ and $\overline{CD}$ = legs

Also If M and N are midpoints, then $\overline{MN}$ is the median of the trapezoid.

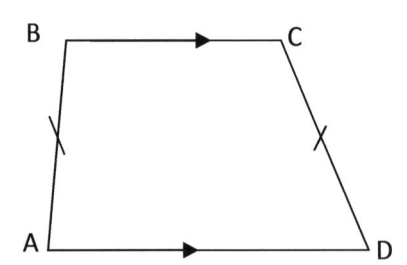

In the isosceles trapezoid ABCD, $\overline{AB} = \overline{CD}$.

∠A nad ∠D are the base angle of isosceles trapezoid ABCD

For isosceles trapezoid identified with the mark \ / , just equate the two bottom i.e A = D

For non - isosceles trapezoid the sum of the legs equals 180

Median in trapezoids

In trapezoids, the median is parallel to its bases, and its length is equal to one half of the sum of their length.

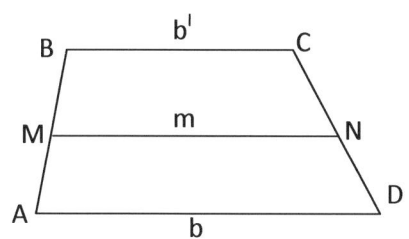

Thus if m is the median of trapezoid ABCD then $m \parallel \overline{AD}, m \parallel \overline{BC}$

$\therefore MN = m = \frac{1}{2}(b + b')$

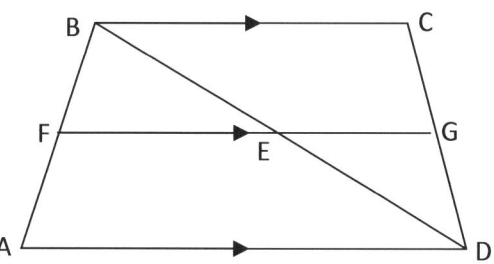

For the trapezoid above,

BE = ED

GC or GD = $\frac{1}{2}$ CD

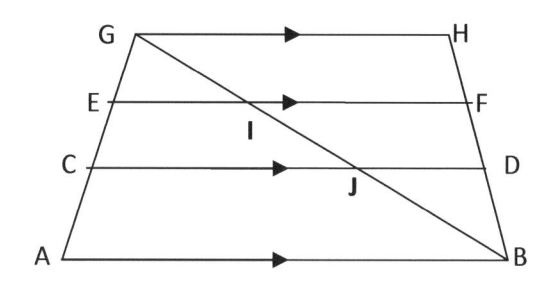

For the trapezoid above,

AC = CE = EG

BD = DF = FH

(2) PARALLELOGRAMS

This is a quadrilateral whose opposite sides are parallel. They are identified easily by the symbol ▱

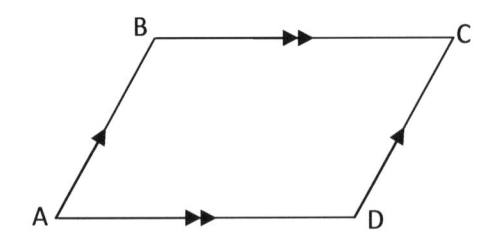

thus in ▱ABCD above $\overline{AB} \parallel \overline{CD}$ in $\overline{AD} \parallel \overline{BC}$

Properties of parallelograms

Principle 1: The opposite sides of a parallelogram are parallel.

Principle 2: The opposite sides of a parallelogram are congruent

Thus in ▱ABCD $\overline{AB} \cong \overline{CD}$ and $\overline{AD} = \overline{BC}$

Principle 3: The opposite angles of a parallelogram are congruent.

Thus in ▱ABCD, $\angle A \cong \angle C$ and $\angle B \cong \angle D$

Principle 4: The consecutive angles of a parallelogram are supplementary

Thus in ▱ABCD, $\angle A$ is a supplement of both $\angle B$ and $\angle D$

Principle 5: A diagonal of a parallelogram divides it into two congruent triangles.

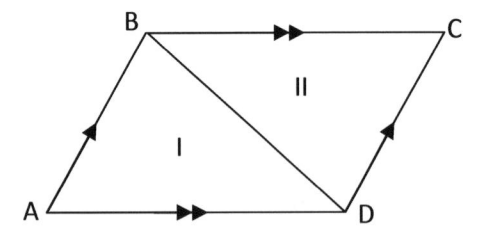

Since $\overline{BD}$ is a diagonal of ▱ABCD. $\Delta I \cong \Delta II$

Principle 6: The diagonals of a parallelogram bisect each other

248

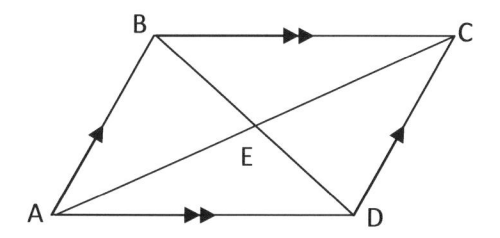

Thus in ▱ABCD $\overline{AE} \cong \overline{EC}$ and $\overline{BE} \cong \overline{ED}$

In summary, whenever ▱ ABCD is given use this to solve always!

A = C

B = D   ………(i)

B + C = 180

A + D = 180 …….(ii)

BC = AD ……….(iii)

AB = CD ……….(ii)

Special parallelograms

These are rectangles, rhombuses and squares. Each of these may be defined as a parallelogram, as follows:

1. A rectangle is an equiangular parallelogram
2. A rhombus is an equilateral parallelogram
3. A square is an equilateral and equiangular parallelogram. Thus a square is both a rectangle and rhombus.

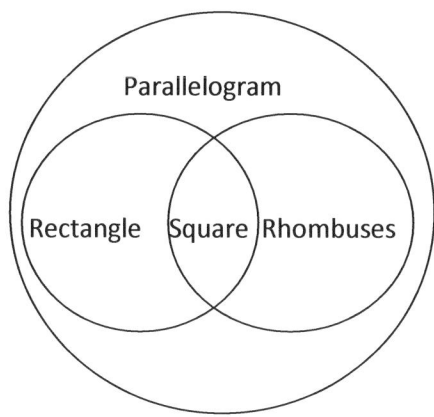

The relationship among the special parallelogram is annotated above.

Note the following

1. Since every rectangle and every rhombus must be a parallelogram the circle for the set of rectangles and the circle for the set of rhombuses must be inside the circle for the set of parallelogram.
2. Since every square is both a rectangle and a rhombus, the overlapping shaded section must represent the set of squares

Principle involving properties of the special parallelograms

Principle 1: A rectangle, rhombus, or square has all the properties of a parallelogram

Principle 2: Each angle of a rectangle is a right angle.

Principle 3: The diagonals of a rectangle are congruent.

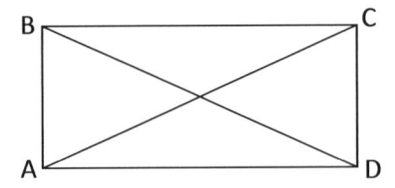

Thus in rectangle ABCD above $\overline{AC} \cong \overline{BD}$.

Principle 4: All sides of a rhombus are congruent.

Principle 5: The diagonals of a rhombus are perpendicular bisectors of each other.

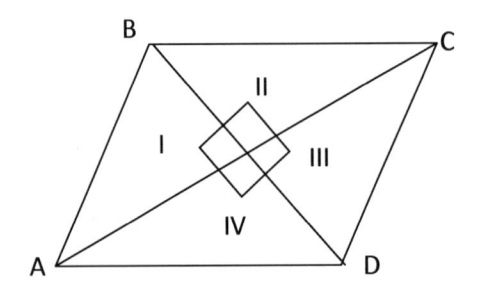

250

Thus in rhombus ABCD above $\overline{AC} \cong \overline{BD}$ are $\perp$ bisector of each other.

Principle 6: The diagonals of a rhombus bisect the vertex angles.

Thus in rhombus ABCD, $\overline{AC}$ bisect $\angle A$ and $\angle C$

Principle 7: The diagonals of rhombus form four congruent triangles

Thus in rhombus ABCD, $\Delta I \cong \Delta III = \Delta IV$.

Principle 8: A square has all the properties of both rhombus and the rectangle

By definition, a square is both a rectangle and a rhombus.

Diagonal properties of parallelogram, rectangle, rhombuses and squares

Diagonal properties	Parallelogram	Rectangles	Rhombus	Square
Diagonal bisect each other	✓	✓	✓	✓
Diagonal are congruent		✓		✓
Diagonal are perpendicular			✓	✓
Diagonal bisect vertex angles			✓	✓
Diagonals from 2 pairs of congruent triangles	✓	✓	✓	✓
Diagonal from 4 congruent triangles			✓	✓

QUESTIONS

In each of the following find the value of x and y.

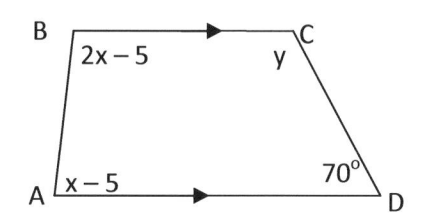

(**21.1**).

B ──→ C, 2x − 5, y, 70°, A, x − 5 ──→ D

Solution

For trapezoid (non-isosceles) sum of the legs equals 180

Since $\overline{AD} \parallel \overline{BC} \rightarrow (2x - 5) + (x + 5) = 180 \rightarrow 3x = 180 \therefore x = 60$

251

Also y + 70 = 180 → y = 110

(21.2).

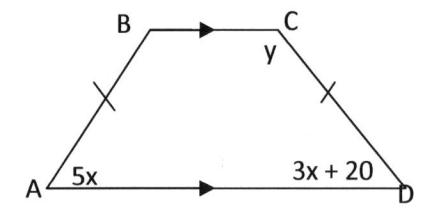

Solution

For isosceles trapezoid $\angle A \cong \angle D$ → $5x = 3x + 20$ → $2x = 20$ ∴ $x = 10$

Since $\overline{BC} \parallel \overline{AC}$ → $y + (3x + 20) = 180$ → $y + 50 = 180$ ∴ $y = 130$

(21.3).

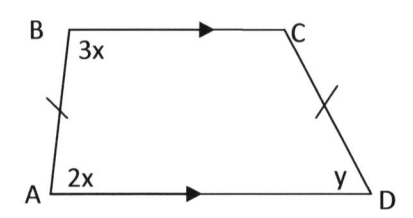

Solution

Since $\overline{BC} \parallel \overline{AD}$ → $3x + 2x = 180$ ∴ $x = 36$

For isosceles trapezoid $\angle D \cong \angle A$, $y = 2x$ → $y = 2(36) = 72$

(21.4).

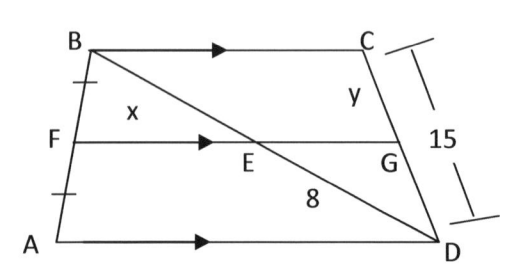

Solution

With $BE = ED$ and $GC = \frac{1}{2}CD, x = 8$ and $y = 7\frac{1}{2}$

(21.5).

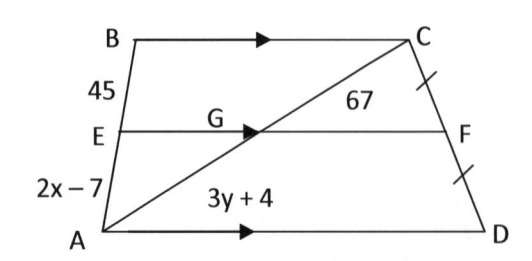

252

Solution

With $BE = EA$, $2x - 7 = 45$ → $2x = 52$ ∴ $x = 26$

$CG = AG$, → $3y + 4 = 67$ → $3y = 63$ ∴ $y = 21$

(21.6).

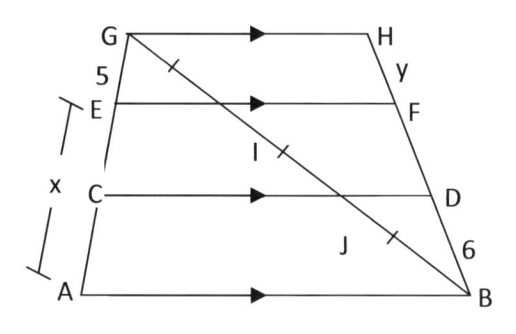

Solution

With $AC = CE = EG$ and $HF = FD = DB$, $x = 10$ and $y = 6$

(21.7).

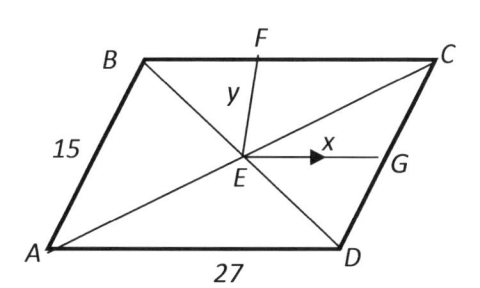

Solution

$x = \frac{1}{2}(AD)$ → $\frac{1}{2}(27) = 13\frac{1}{2}$

$y = \frac{1}{2}(AB)$ → $\frac{1}{2}(15) = 7\frac{1}{2}$

(**21.8**).

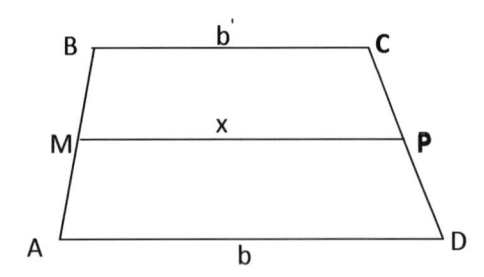

If $\overline{MP}$ is the median of trapezoid $ABCD$. Find x if $b = 20$ and $b' = 28$

Solution

$x = \frac{1}{2}(b + b')$ → $m = \frac{1}{2}(20 + 28)$ ∴ $x = 24$

(**21.9**). Assuming ABCD is a rhombus, Find x and y

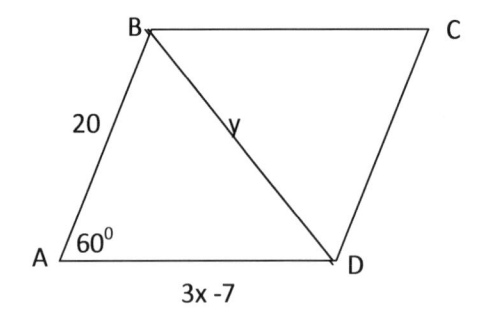

Solution

Equating the shape $<$ i.e
$\overline{AB} \cong \overline{AD}$ → $3x - 7 = 20$ ∴ $x = 9.$ $since\ \triangle ABD\ is\ equiangular\ and\ so\ y = 20$

(**21.10**).

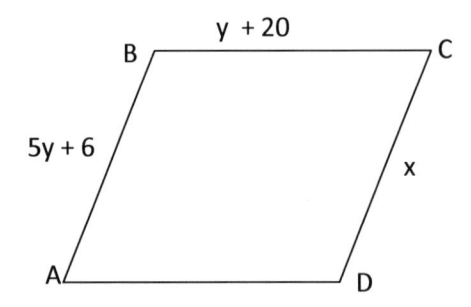

254

Solution

Since $\overline{BC} \cong \overline{AB} \to 5y + 6 = y + 20 \to y = 3\frac{1}{2}$.

since $\overline{CD} \cong \overline{BC} \to x = y + 20 \to x = 23\frac{1}{2}$

(**21.11**).

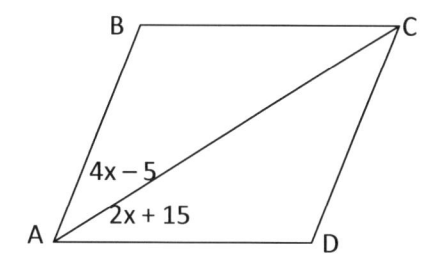

Solution

Since $\overline{AC}$ bisect $\angle A, 4x - 5 = 2x + 15 \to x = 10.$ hence $2x + 15 = 35$

$m\angle A = 2x = 2(35) = 70°$.

$\angle B$ and $\angle A$ are supplementary $\therefore y + 70 = 180 \to y = 100$

(**21.12**).

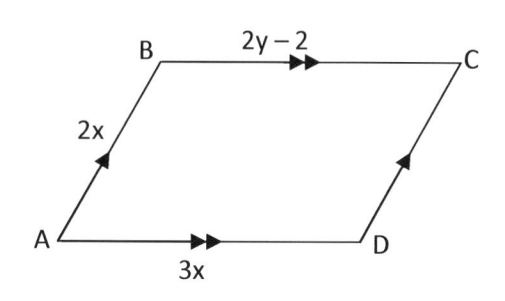

Perimeter = 40

ABCD is a parallelogram find x and y.

Solutions

BC = AD = 3x and CD = AB = 2x,

$2(2x + 3x) = 40 \to 10x = 40 \therefore x = 4$

255

(21.13).

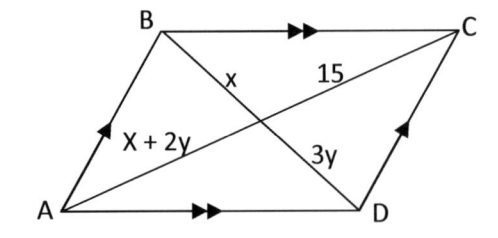

ABCD is a parallelogram find x and y.

Solution

x + 2y = 15, also x = 3y → 3y + 2y = 15 ∴ y = 3, from x = 3y, x = 9

(21.14).

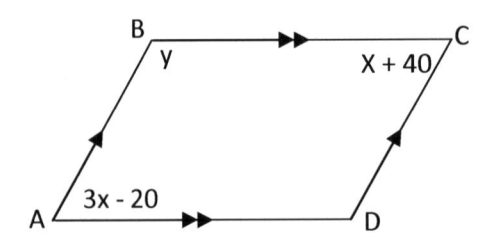

ABCD is a parallelogram find x and y.

Solution

3x − 20 = x + 40 → 2x = 60 ∴ x = 30

Also y + (x + 40) = 180 → y + (30 + 40) = 180 ∴ y = 110

256

CHAPTER 22 MENSURATION

Mensuration is the branch of mathematics which deals with the study of Geometric shapes, their area, volume and related parameters.

Terms associated with mensuration

1. Area: This is the product of one side and the thickness. i.e Area =
Length x breadth , Length x height or length x thichness

2. Volume: This is the product of area and thickness.

$Volume = Area\ x\ Thickness$

3. Density is a ratio of mass of a body to its volume

$\text{Density} = \frac{\text{mass}}{\text{Volume}}$

4. Perimeter is the distance round an object i.e the sum of all possible sides surrounding an object.

5. Quadrilaterals: Figures with four sides. Examples include: rectangle and square, parallelogram and rhombus and trapezium

6. Polygons Figures with many sides. Example include: square, equilateral triangle, pentagon (5 sides) etc

Types of Shapes or Figures

Plane shapes: These are objects or shapes with two sides. They are also called two dimensional figures. Examples are: triangle, quadrilaterals, polygon, circles.

Solid Shapes: These are objects with three sides (length, breadth and height). They are also called three dimensional figures. Examples are cuboid, cube, prism, cylinder, cone, frustum, sphere, and pyramids.

Composite shapes: Shape obtained by merging two or more of plane and solid shapes together.

(1) SQUARE: A square unit is the surface enclosed by a square whose side is 1 unit as shown below. The area of a closed plane figure, such as a polygon, is the number of square unit contained in its surface.

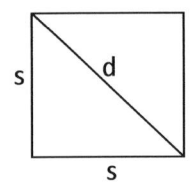

From the diagram above the following holds.

Area = S^2 = L x L = L^2 = $\frac{(Diagonal)^2}{2}$

Perimeter = L + L + L + L = 4L

Length of a square = $\sqrt{Area}$ = $\frac{Diagonal}{2}$ x $\sqrt{2}$

Diagonal = Length x $\sqrt{2}$

(2) RECTANGLE

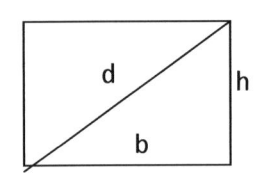

From the diagram above, the following holds.

d^2 = $b^2 + h^2$

Area = L x B

Perimeter = L + B + L + B = 2L + 2B = 2(L + B)

Volume of a rectangle = Length x width x height

(3) Parallelogram

The area of a parallelogram equals the product of the length of a side and the length of the altitude to that side.

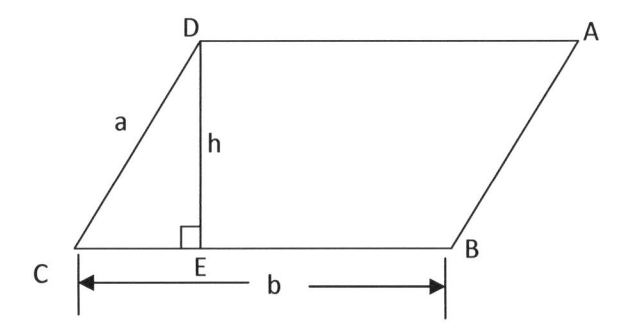

Thus in the parallelogram above ABCD

A = bh

When two sides a, b and the angle between them is θ is given as shown below

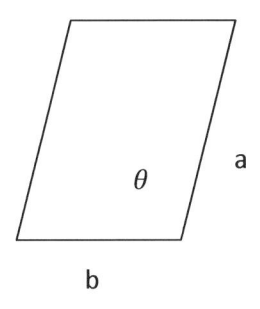

Area of a parallelogram is given by

A = absin θ = 2 x Area of triangle

(4) Trapezoid

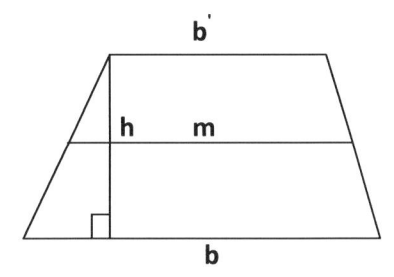

The area of a trapezoid equals one-half the product of the length of its altitude and the sum of the length of its base or equals the product of the length of its altitude and median.

Since $A = \frac{1}{2}h(b+b')$ and $m = \frac{1}{2}(b+b')$, $A = hm$

$A = \frac{1}{2}h(b+b') = hm$

(5) Equilateral triangle

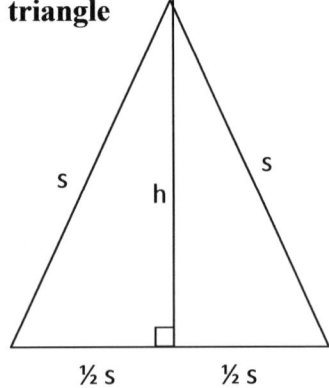

For an equilateral triangle whose side has length s

Here $A = \frac{1}{2}bh$, where $b = s$ and $h^2 = s^2 - \left(\frac{1}{2}s\right)^2 = \frac{3}{4}s^2$ or $h = \frac{1}{2}s\sqrt{3}$

∴ $A = \frac{1}{2}bh = \frac{1}{2}s(\frac{1}{2}s\sqrt{3}) = \frac{1}{4}s^2\sqrt{3}$.

For an equilateral triangle whose altitude has length h.
Here $A = \frac{1}{2}bh$, where $b = s$ and $h = \frac{1}{2}s\sqrt{3}$ or $s = \frac{2h}{\sqrt{3}}$

∴ $A = \frac{1}{2}bh = \frac{1}{2}sh = \frac{1}{2}(\frac{2h}{\sqrt{3}})h = \frac{1}{3}h^2\sqrt{3}$

Perimeter = 3s

(6) Triangle

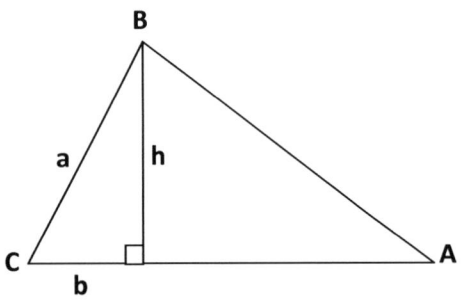

The area of a triangle equal one-half product of the length of a side and the length of the altitude to that side.

$A = \frac{1}{2}bh$

When two sides a, b, and the angle between a and b is given, Area of a triangle becomes $A = \frac{1}{2}ab\sin\theta$

260

From Hero's formula, Area of a triangle is given

$$A = \sqrt{s(s-a)(s-b)(s-c)}$$

where $s = \frac{a+b+c}{2}$ where a, b, c are the sides of the triangle

If no side of a triangle is parallel to either axis, the formula $A = \frac{1}{2}bh$ is no longer applicable

If the triangle is enclosed in a rectangle whose sides are parallel to the axes as shown below

The area of the triangle can be found from the areas of the figures so formed :

area (ΔABC) = area(rectangle ADEF) – [area(ΔABD) + $area(\Delta BCE)$ + $area(\Delta ACF)$].

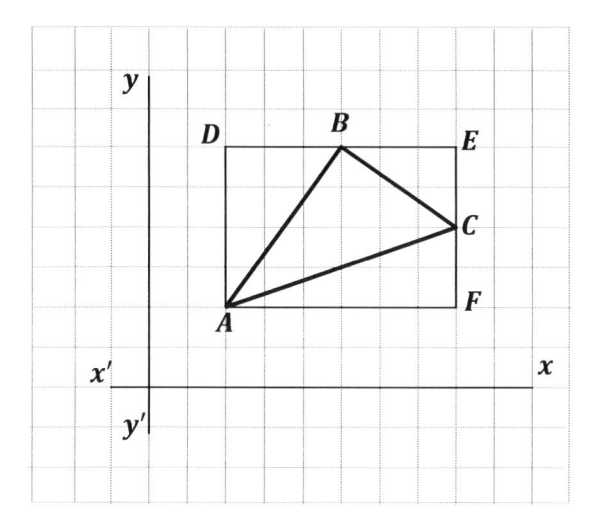

If a trapezoids whose bases are parallel to the y-axis is formed by dropping perpendiculars to the x-axis as shown below

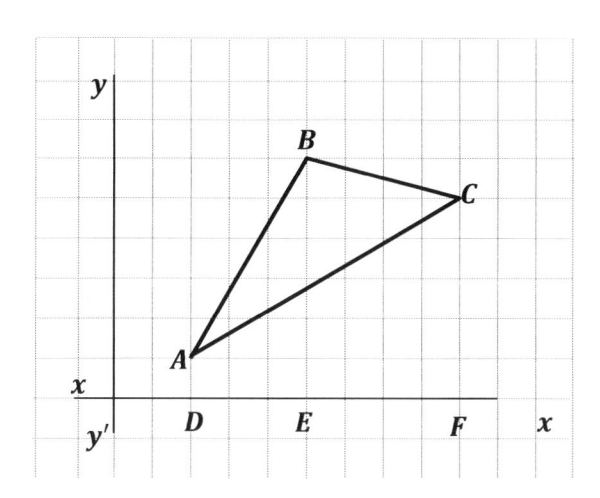

261

Area(△ABC) =
area(trapezoid ABED) + area(trapezoid BEFC) − area(trapezoid DFCA)

(7) Rhombus. This is a figure in which all sides are equal and with acute or obtuse angles.

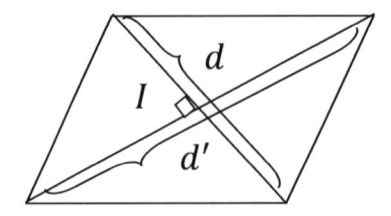

The area of a rhombus equals one-half the product of the length of its diagonals. From the diagram above, each diagonal is the perpendicular bisector of the other, the area of triangle I is $\frac{1}{2}\left(\frac{1}{2}d\right)\left(\frac{1}{2}d'\right) = \frac{1}{8}dd'$. Thus the area of the rhombus which consist of four triangles congruent to △I is $4\left(\frac{1}{8}dd'\right)$

$$A = \frac{1}{2}dd'$$

(8) Cuboid: A cuboid has two opposite sides and equal.

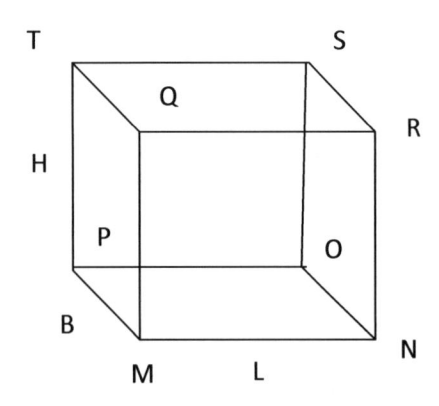

For a cuboid, Total surface area consists of

(i) Top and bottom = LB + LB = 2LB
(ii) Front and back = LH + LH = 2LH
(iii) Left and Right side = HB + LB = 2BH

Total surface area = 2LB + 2BH + 2LH = 2(LB + BH + LH)

Volume of cuboid = Length x breadth x height

Length of diagonal of cuboid = $\sqrt{l^2 + b^2 + h^2}$

(9) Cube

A cube has 12 edges with all sides equal.

Longest diagonal of a cube = $\sqrt{3}$ L

Total surface area = 2(L.L + L.L + L.L) = 2(L² + L² + L²) = 2(3L²) = 6L²

Volume of cube = L x L x L = L³

(10) Prism: This is a shape produce by cutting a cuboid into two along the diagonal

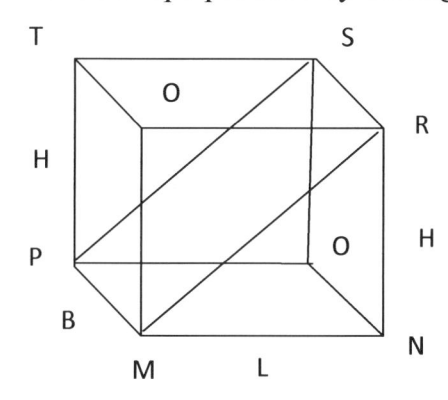

From the above diagram MPSRON is a prism

For the triangular prism MPSRON

Volume = Area of the triangular base x height = volume of half a cuboid =

½ (L x B x H) = $\left[\frac{1}{2}LH\right]B$

Total surface area: Area of half a cuboid + area of the cutting plane = (LB + BH + LH) + BH

Surface area of triangular prism= (Perimeter of base x height) + (2 x area of triangle)

Surface area of polygonal prism = (Perimeter of base x height) + (area of polygonal base x 2)

Lateral surface area of a prism = Perimeter of base x height

Volume of a prism can be taken as area of 1 triangle x distance between two triangles

(11) Cylinder: This is a figure with a curved face and two circular faces at the top and bottom. The distance between the circular faces is called height when the cylinder stands vertically and length when placed horizontally. Thus L = H

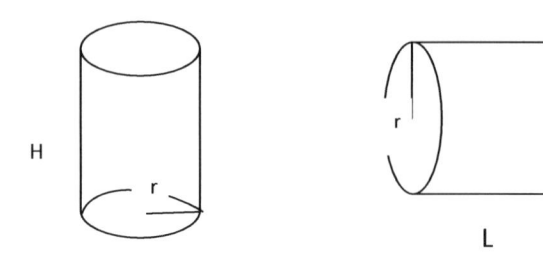

Generally, Curved surface area = $2\pi rh$ and Area of top = area of bottom = πr^2

Closed cylinder is one with two ends closed, for such cylinder the following holds

Total surface area = $2\pi rh + \pi r^2 + \pi r^2 = 2\pi rh + 2\pi r^2 = 2\pi(h + r)$

Open cylinder is one with one end closed, for such cylinder

Total surface area = $2\pi rh + \pi r^2 = \pi r(2h + r)$

Volume of cylinder = area of base x height = $\pi r^2 \cdot h = \pi r^2 h$

(12) Cone: This is a figure formed by folding a sector along its radius.

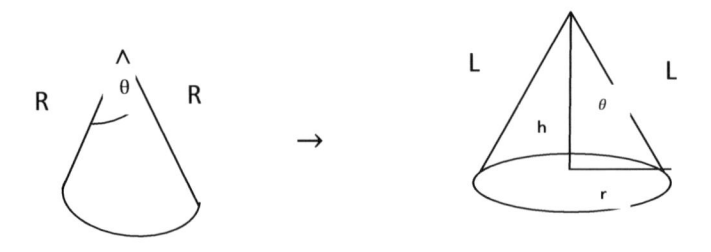

For a cone, the length of arc (from sector) is equal to the base circumference of the base circumference of the cone

Also the radius of sector = slant height of the cone R = L

$$\frac{\theta}{360} \times 2\pi R = 2\pi r \rightarrow r = \frac{\theta}{360} \times R$$

Also from the diagram, $L^2 = h^2 + r^2$ (by Pythagoras's)

The vertex or apex angle called vertical angle of cone is 2a and $\tan a = \frac{r}{h}$ or $\sin a \frac{r}{L}$ Where r = radius of cone, L = slant length

Area of base of a cone = πr^2
Curved surface area of cone = $\pi r L$

Total surface area = curved surface area + base area = $\pi r L \times \pi r^2$

Volume of a cone = $\frac{1}{3}$(base area) x height = $\frac{1}{3}\pi r^2 h$

(13) Pyramid: This is a figure with a common point called vertex or apex, through which lines are drawn to the edges of the base. There are various types of Pyramids named according to the bases i.e A pyramid on a circular base is called a circular pyramid or cone. The following will be considered

Right square pyramid: This is the case if a = length of base, b = length of equal side of the isosceles triangle forming the slanting face.

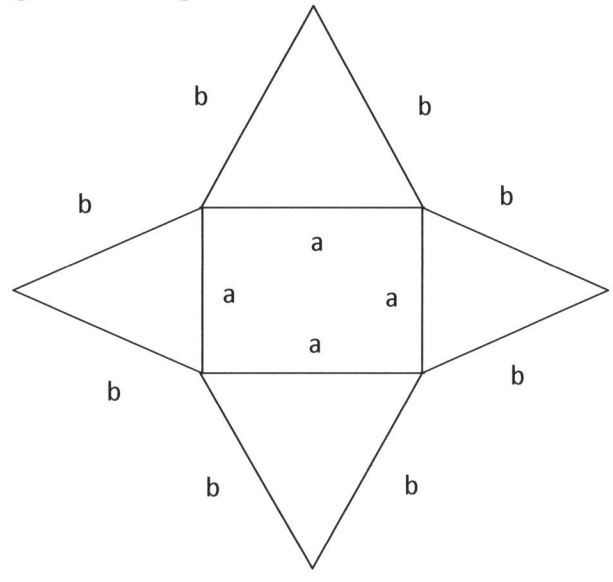

Surface area = $a\sqrt{4b^2 - a^2}$

Volume = $\frac{1}{2}$ (base area) x height = $\frac{1}{2}$ x L x B x h

Square pyramid (Johnson Pyramid):

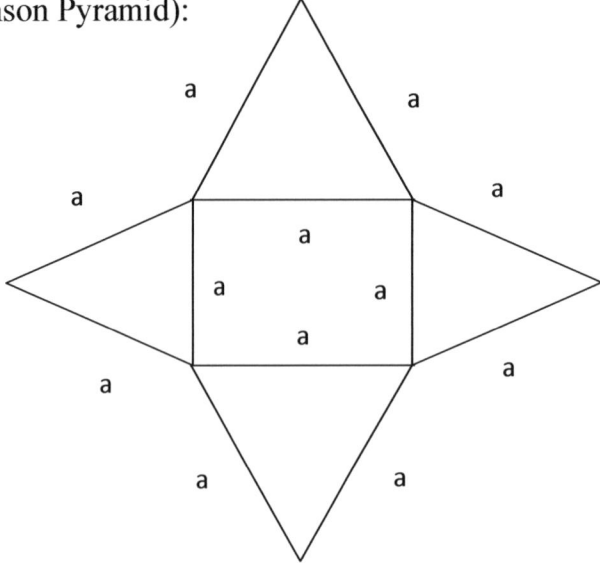

Total surface area = $\frac{\sqrt{2}}{6}$ x a^3

Volume = $(1 + \sqrt{3})$ x a^2

Square pyramid (Normal): This is the case if a = length of square base and h = height of the pyramid

Total surface area = $a^2 + a\sqrt{a^2 + (2h)^2}$

Volume = $\frac{1}{3}a^2 h$

(14) Sphere: A sphere is a solid bounded by all points that are given at given distance from a fixed point (the centre). Thus a sphere is greater than a circle which deals with the locus if a single point. Example is the earth.

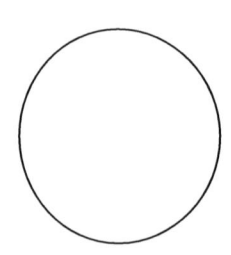

266

Area of sphere = $4\pi r^2$

volume of sphere = $\frac{4}{3}\pi r^3$

(15) Hemisphere: This is obtained by splitting a sphere in two.

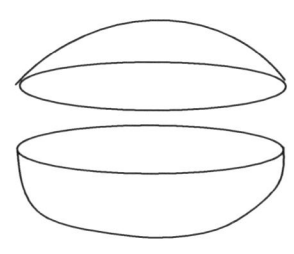

Hemisphere

Curved surface area of hemishpere = $2\pi r^2$

Total surface area of hemishpere = $3\pi r^2$

volume of hemisphere = $\frac{2}{3}\pi r^3 = \frac{1}{12}\pi d^3$

(16) Frustum: This is obtained when part of a pyramid is a cut away.

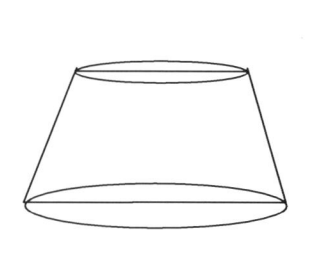

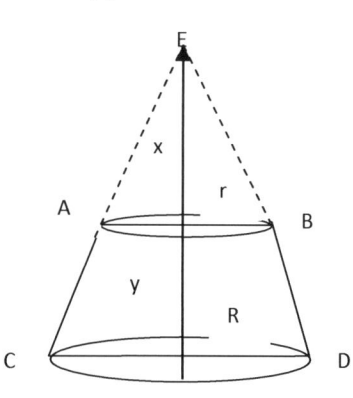

Considering the diagram above, cone EAB is produced from ECD.

Height of cone EAB = x, the radius = r

Height of cone ECD = x + y, the radius = R

267

By similarity → $\dfrac{x}{x+y} = \dfrac{r}{R} = \dfrac{EB}{ED}$

Curved surface area = Area of big cone – area of small cone = πRL – πrl = π(RL – rl)

Volume of frustum = volume of big cone – volume of small cone = $\frac{1}{3}$πR²H – $\frac{1}{3}$πr²h = $\frac{1}{3}$π(R²H – r²h)

Composite Shaped, similar Figures

A composite shape is a solid formed when two or more simple shapes are combined. the area of volume is found by adding the respective area or volume as shown below;

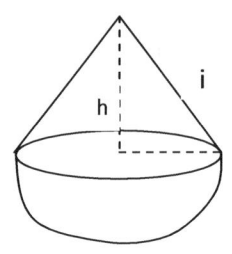

Total surface area = Area of cone + Area of hemisphere = $\pi r l + 2\pi r^2$

Volume = volume of cone + volume of hemisphere = $\frac{1}{3}\pi r^2 h + \frac{2}{3}\pi r^3$

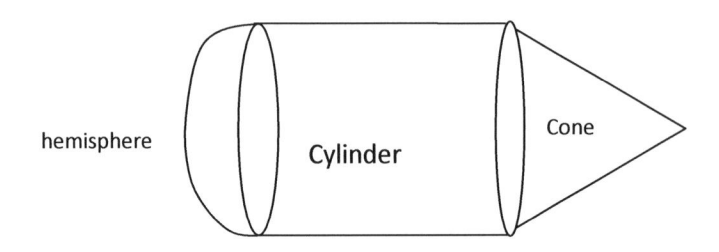

Total surface area = πrl² + πr² + 2πr²

volume = $\frac{2}{3}\pi r^3 + \pi r^2 h + \frac{1}{3}\pi r^2 h$

Comparing Areas of similar polygons

The area of similar polygon are to each other as the square of any two corresponding segment. Thus,

$$\frac{A_1}{A_2} = \left(\frac{s_1}{s_2}\right)^2 = \left(\frac{p_1}{p_2}\right)^2 = \left(\frac{m_1}{m_2}\right)^2 = \left(\frac{D_1}{D_2}\right)^2$$

Where p is perimeter, m is median, s is side and d is diameter

QUESTIONS

(22.1). Find the area of a parallelogram if the area is represented by $x^2 - 4$, the length of a side is $x^2 + 4$, and the length of the altitude to that side by $x - 3$

Solution

$A = x^2 - 4,\ b = x + 4,\ h = x - 3$

$A = bh \rightarrow x^2 - 4 = (x+4)(x-3) \rightarrow x^2 - 4 = x^2 - x - 12 \therefore x = 8\ A = x^2 - 4 = 64 - 4 = 60$

(22.2). In parallelogram, find the length of the altitude if the area is 54 and the ratio of the altitude to the base is 2:3

Solution

Let $h = 2x, b = 3x$.

$A = bh \rightarrow 54 = (3x)(2x) = 6x^2 \rightarrow 9 = x^2 \therefore x = 3$

(22.3). Find the length of a rectangle if the base has length 15 and the perimeter is 50

Solution

P = 50, b = 15

Perimeter = 2b + 2h $\rightarrow$ 50 = 2(15) + 2h $\rightarrow$ h = 10

A = bh = 15(10) = 150

(22.4). Find the area of a rectangle if the altitude has length 10 and the diagonal has length 26.

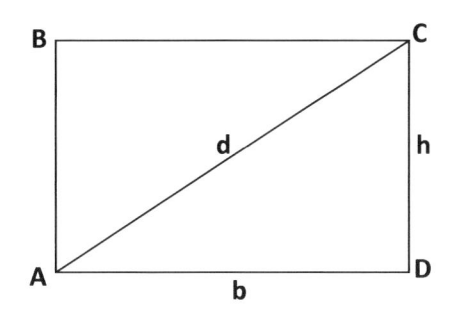

Solution

d = 26, h = 10.

In right $\triangle ACD, d^2 = b^2 + h^2 \rightarrow 26^2 = b^2 + 10^2 \therefore b = 24$

A = bh = 24(10) = 240.

(22.5). Find the length of the base and altitude of rectangle if its area is 70 and its perimeter is 34.

Solution

P = 2b + 2h → 34 = 2(b + h) → h = 17 – b.

A = bh → 70 = b(17 – b) → 70 = 17b – b² → b² – 17b + 70 = 0 ∴ b = 7 or 10.

From h = 17 – b putting both values of b gives h = 10 or 7

(22.6). Find the area of a square whose perimeter is 30.

Solution

$P = 4s = 30 \rightarrow s = 7\frac{1}{2}, \quad A = s^2 = \left[7\frac{1}{2}\right]^2 = 56\frac{1}{4}$

(22.7). Find the area of a square if the radius of the circumscribed circle is 10.
Solution

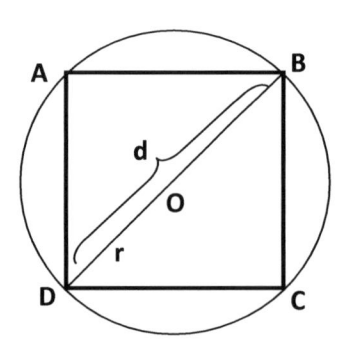

$r = 10, d = 2r = 2(10) = 20$

$A = \frac{1}{2}d^2 \rightarrow \frac{1}{2}(20)^2 = 200$

(22.8). Find the side and the perimeter of a square whose area is 20.

Solution

$A = s^2 = 20 \rightarrow s = \sqrt{20}$. Perimeter = 4s = 4 x $\sqrt{20}$ = $8\sqrt{5}$

(22.9) Find the number of square inches in a square foot.

Solutions.

From $A = s^2$, 1ft = 12 in $\rightarrow$ 1ft² = 1ft x 1ft = 12 in x 12 in = 144 in².

(22.10) The area of the triangle below is ?

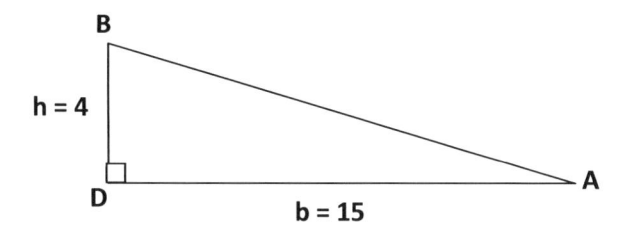

Solution

Here b = 15 and h = 4 Thus A = ½ bh = ½ (15)(4) = 30

(22.11). Find the area of an equilateral triangle whose perimeter is 24

Solution

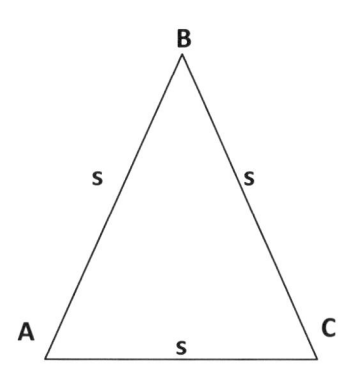

$P = 3s \rightarrow 24 = 3s \therefore s = 8$

$A = \frac{1}{4}s^2\sqrt{3} = \frac{1}{4}(64)\sqrt{3} = 16\sqrt{3}$

(22.12). Find the area of a rhombus in which the shorter diagonal has length 12 and an angle measure 60^0.

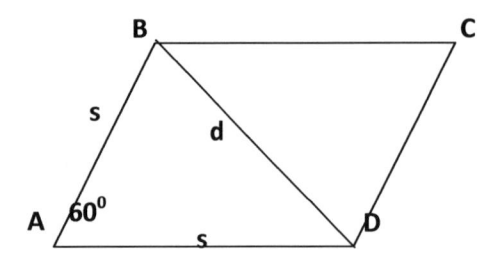

Solution

$m\angle A = 60, \Delta ADB$ is equilateral and $s = d = 12$.

Area of the rhombus is twice the area of ΔADB. Hence $A = 2\left[\frac{1}{2}s^2\right]\sqrt{3} = 72\sqrt{3}$.

(22.12) Find the area of a regular hexagon with a side of length 6.

Solution

Area of polygon = area of equilateral triangle x no of sides

$6 x \left(\frac{1}{4}s^2\right)\sqrt{3} = 6\left(\frac{1}{4}\right)(36\sqrt{3}) = 54\sqrt{3}$

(22.12). Find the area of a trapezoid if the base has length 7.3 and 2.7, and the altitude has length 3.8.

Solution

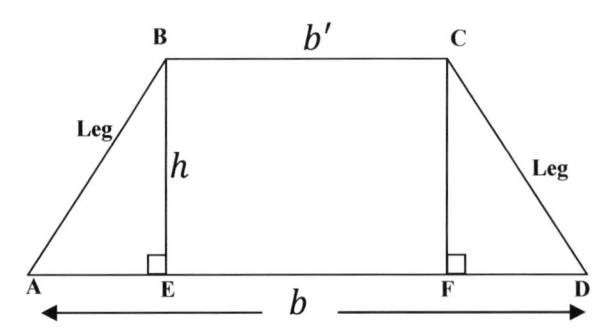

$b = 7.3, \ b' = 2.7, h = 3.8$

$A = \frac{1}{2}h(b + b') \rightarrow \frac{1}{2}(3.8)(7.3 + 2.7) = 19$

(22.13) Find the area of an isosceles trapezoid if the base has length 22 and 10, and the legs have length 10.

Solution

Here $b = 22$, $b' = 10$, $AB = 10$. since $EF = b'$ and $AE = \frac{1}{2}(22 - 10) = 6$

(22.14). Find the bases of an isosceles trapezoid if the area is $52\sqrt{3}$, the altitude has length $4\sqrt{3}$, and each leg has length 8.

Solution

$AE = \sqrt{(AB)^2 - h^2} \rightarrow \sqrt{64 - 48} = 4$
$FD = AE = 4$ and $b' = b - (AE + FD) = b - 8$.

From $A = \frac{1}{2}h(b + b') \rightarrow 52\sqrt{3} = \frac{1}{2}4\sqrt{3}(2b - 8) = \frac{1}{2}4\sqrt{3}.2(b - 4)$

∴ $13 = b - 4$ ∴ $b = 17$.

Then $b' = b - 8 = 17 - 8 = 9$

(22.15). Find the area of a rhombus if one diagonal has length 30 and a side has length 17.

Solutions:

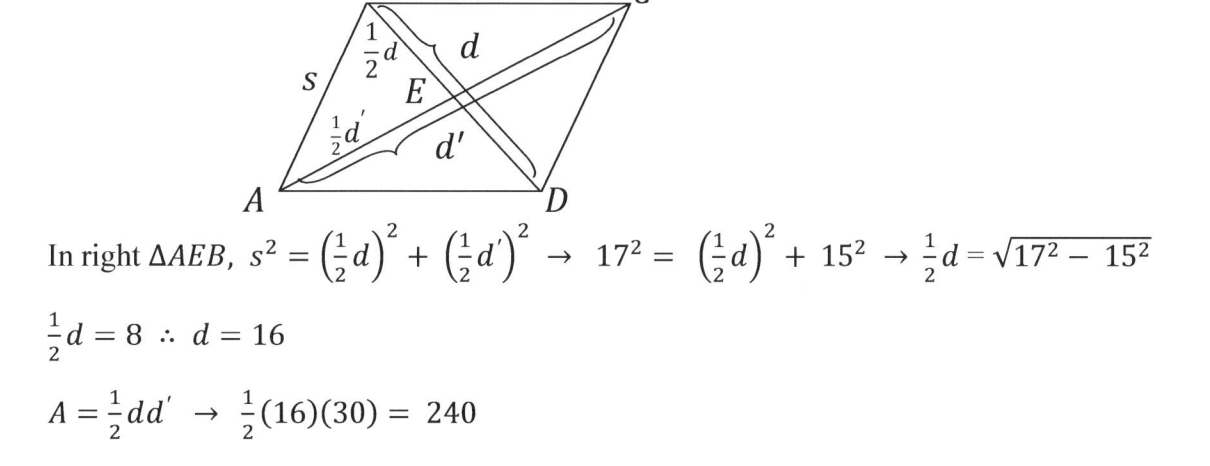

In right $\triangle AEB$, $s^2 = \left(\frac{1}{2}d\right)^2 + \left(\frac{1}{2}d'\right)^2 \rightarrow 17^2 = \left(\frac{1}{2}d\right)^2 + 15^2 \rightarrow \frac{1}{2}d = \sqrt{17^2 - 15^2}$

$\frac{1}{2}d = 8$ ∴ $d = 16$

$A = \frac{1}{2}dd' \rightarrow \frac{1}{2}(16)(30) = 240$

(22.16) Find the length of a diagonal of a rhombus if the other diagonal has length 8 and the area of the rhombus is 52.

Solution

Here $d' = 8$, $A = 52$.

From $A = \frac{1}{2}dd' \rightarrow 52 = \frac{1}{2}(d)(8) \therefore d = 13$.

(22.17)

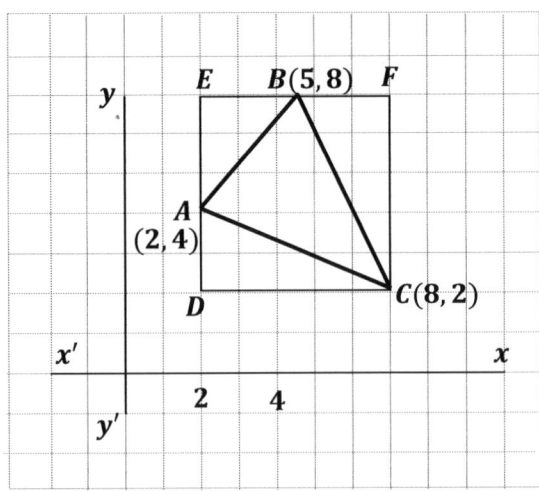

Find the area of $\triangle ABC$ whose vertices are A(2,4), B(5,8) and C(8,2)

Solutions

For triangle enclosed in a rectangle we apply

Area of rectangle $DEFC = bh = 6(6) = 36.$ then

Area of $\triangle DAC = \frac{1}{2}bh = \frac{1}{2}(4-2)(8-2) = \frac{1}{2}(2)(6) = 6$

Area of $\triangle ABE = \frac{1}{2}bh = \frac{1}{2}(5-2)(8-4) = \frac{1}{2}(3)(4) = 6$

Area of $\triangle BCF = \frac{1}{2}bh = \frac{1}{2}(8-5)(8-2) = \frac{1}{2}(3)(6) = 9$

area $\triangle ABC = area(DEFC) - area(\triangle DAC + \triangle ABE + \triangle BCF) =$

$36 - (6 + 6 + 9) = 15$

(22.18).

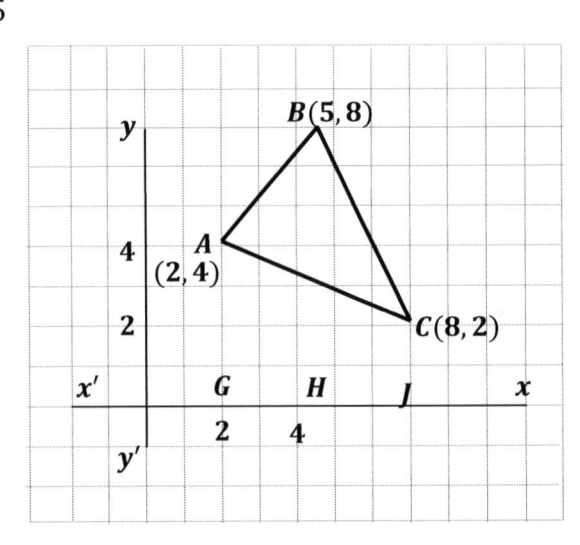

Find the area of $\triangle ABC$ whose vertices are A(2,4), B(5,8) and C(8,2)

Solution

For triangle forming a trapezoid we apply

Area of trapezoid $ABHG = \frac{1}{2}h(b + b') = \frac{1}{2}(3)(4 + 8) = 18$

Area of trapezoid BCJH $= \frac{1}{2}(3)(2 + 8) = 15$

Area of trapezoid ACJG $= \frac{1}{2}(6)(2 + 4) = 18$

area $(\triangle ABC) = area(ABHG) + area(BCJH) - area(ACJG) = 18 + 15 - 18 = 15$.

(22.19) Find the ratio of the areas of two similar triangles if the ratio of the length of two corresponding sides is 3:5.

Solutions

$\frac{A_1}{A_2} = \left(\frac{s_1}{s_2}\right)^2 \rightarrow \left[\frac{3}{5}\right]^2 = \frac{9}{25}$

(22.20). Find the ratio of the areas of two similar triangles if their perimeters are 12 and 7.

Solutions

$\frac{A_1}{A_2} = \left(\frac{p_1}{p_2}\right)^2 \rightarrow \left[\frac{12}{7}\right]^2 = \frac{144}{49}$

(22.20) Find the ratio of the length of a pair of corresponding sides if the ratio of the areas is 4 : 9.

Solution

$\left(\frac{s_1}{s_2}\right)^2 = \frac{A_1}{A_2} \rightarrow \left(\frac{s_1}{s_2}\right)^2 = \frac{4}{9} \rightarrow \frac{s_1}{s_2} = \frac{2}{3}$

(22.21). Find the ratio of the corresponding medians if the areas are 250 and 10.

Solutions

$\left(\frac{m_1}{m_2}\right)^2 = \frac{A_1}{A_2} \rightarrow \left(\frac{m_1}{m_2}\right)^2 = \frac{250}{10} \rightarrow \frac{m_1}{m_2} = 5$

(22.22). The area of two similar polygons is 80 and 5. If a side of the smaller polygon has length 2, find the length of the corresponding side of the larger polygon.

Solution

$\left(\frac{s_1}{s_2}\right)^2 = \frac{A_1}{A_2} \rightarrow \left(\frac{s_1}{2}\right)^2 = \frac{80}{5} = 16 \rightarrow \frac{s_1}{2} = 4 \therefore s_1 = 8$

(22.23). The corresponding diagonals of two similar polygons have length 4 and 5. If the area of the larger polygon is 75, find the area of the smaller polygon.

Solutions

$\frac{A_1}{A_2} = \left(\frac{D_1}{D_2}\right)^2 \rightarrow \frac{A}{75} = \left(\frac{4}{5}\right)^2 \rightarrow A = 75 \times \left(\frac{16}{25}\right) = 48$

(22.24).

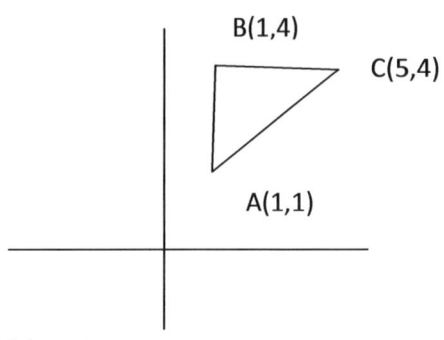

What is the length of side AC?

Solution

A(1,1), B(1,4), C = (5,4)

Comparing AB we see that AB = [4 – 1] = 3

BC we see that BC = [5 – 1] = 4

$AC^2 = 3^2 + 4^2 = 9 + 16 = 25 \rightarrow AC = 5$

(22.25). What is the greatest straight line distance between two vertices (corners) of a cube whose sides are 2239 cm long.

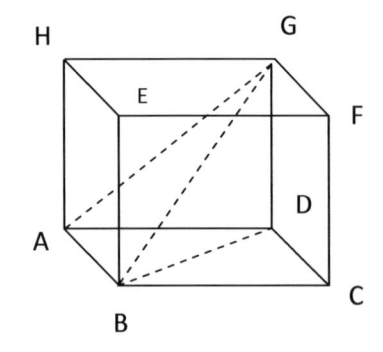

Solution

A, B, C, D, E, F, G, H are the vertices

Greatest straight line = longest diagonal BG

From the diagram ΔBDG and ΔBCD are right angle triangle

Thus by Pythagoras $BG^2 = BD^2 + GD^2$

$BD^2 = 2339^2 + 2239^2 \rightarrow 2239(2239 + 2239) = 2239 \times 4478$

$BD = \sqrt{2239 \times 4478} \rightarrow \sqrt{2239 \times 2 \times 2239} = 2239\sqrt{2}$

From $BG^2 = BD^2 + GD^2$

$BG^2 = (2239\sqrt{2})^2 + 2239^2 \rightarrow (2239^2 \times 2) + 2239^2 \rightarrow 2239^2 (2 + 1) \rightarrow 2239^2 \times 3$

$BG = \sqrt{2239^2 \times 3} \rightarrow 2239\sqrt{3}$

(22.26). A cuboid has a diagonal of length 9 cm and a square base of side 4 cm. what is its length?

Solution

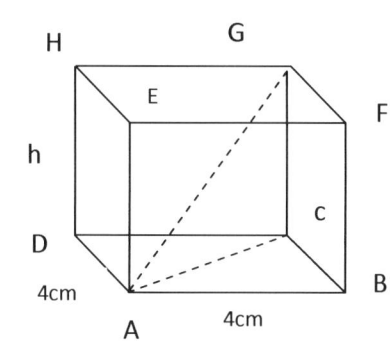

Longest diagonal = AG = 9cm

But $AC^2 = 4^2 + 4^2 \rightarrow 2(4^2)$ ∴ $AC = 4\sqrt{2}$

Also $AG^2 = AC^2 + CG^2 \rightarrow 9^2 = (4\sqrt{2})^2 + h^2 \rightarrow 81 = 16 \times 2 + h^2 = 32 + h^2$

$h^2 = 81 - 32 = 49$ ∴ $h = \sqrt{49} = 7cm$

(22.27).

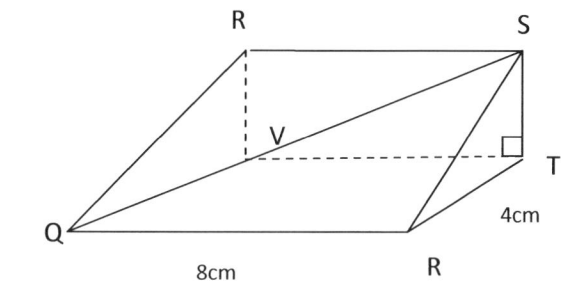

277

What is the volume of the regular three dimensional figure above?

Solution

For the triangle RST, RS = QR = 5cm, RT = 4cm

$ST^2 = RS^2 - RT^2 \rightarrow ST = \sqrt{RS^2 - RT^2} = \sqrt{5^2 - 4^2} = \sqrt{25 - 16} = \sqrt{9} = 3$

Volume of prism = (Area of 1 triangle) x distance between two triangles

(½ x 4 x 3) x 48 = 48 cm³

(22.28). A solid cylinder of radius 3 cm has a total surface area of $36\pi cm^2$. Find its height?

Solution

r = 3 cm, T.S.A = 36π

Total surface area = $2\pi r^2 + 2\pi rh = 36\pi$

$2\pi r^2 + 2\pi rh = 36 \rightarrow r^2 + rh = 18 \rightarrow 3^2 + 3h = 18 \rightarrow 9 + 3h = 18 \therefore h = 9/3 = 3cm$

(22.29). The area of the curved surface of the cone generated by the sector of a circle of radius 6 cm and arc length 22 cm is ?

Solution

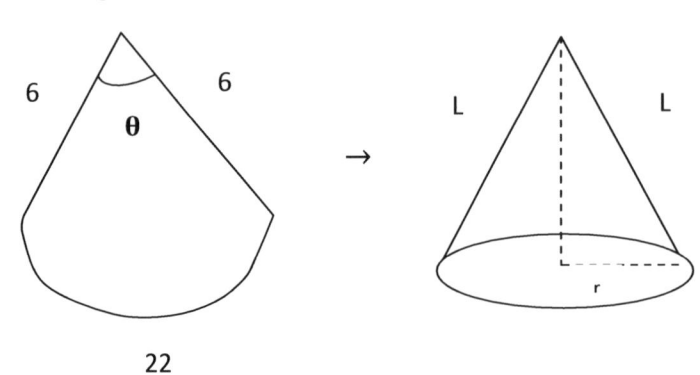

Arc length = $\frac{\theta}{360} \times 2\pi R \rightarrow 22 = \frac{\theta}{360} \times 2\pi(6) \therefore \frac{\theta}{360} = \frac{22}{12\pi}$

Radius of a cone = $\frac{\theta}{360} \cdot r$

Curved surface area of cone = $\pi rl \rightarrow \pi \cdot \frac{\theta}{360} \cdot r \cdot l \rightarrow \pi \times \frac{22}{12\pi} \times 6 \times 6 = 66$ cm²

(22.30). Find the area of the curved surface of a cone whose base radius is 6cm and whose height is 8 cm. (Take = π = 22/7)

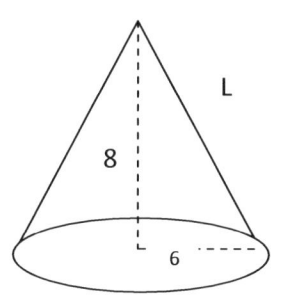

Solution

By Pythagoras's → L² = 8² + 6² → L² = 64 + 36 = 100 ∴ L = $\sqrt{100}$ = 10Cm

Curved surface area = $\pi r l$ → $\frac{22}{7}$ x 6 x 10 = 188.57cm²

(22.31).

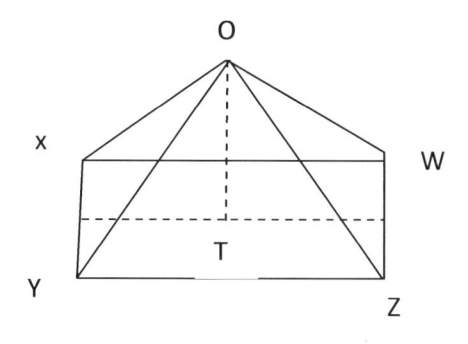

OXYZW is a pyramid with a square base such that
OX = OY = OZ = OW = 5 cm and XY = XW = YZ = WZ = 6cm. Find the height OT.

Solution

Base is square XWYZ

(ZX)² = 6² + 6² → 36 + 36 = 72 → ZX = $\sqrt{72}$ = $6\sqrt{2}$

ZT = $\frac{1}{2}$ZX → $\frac{1}{2}$ x $6\sqrt{2}$ = $3\sqrt{2}$

From triangle OTZ, TZ = $3\sqrt{2}$, OZ = 5 cm

OT² = OZ² − TZ² → 5² - $(3\sqrt{2})^2$ → 25 - 18 ∴ $OT = \sqrt{7}$

(22.32). The area of a circular plate is one sixteenth the surface area of ball, if the area of the plate is given as Pcm², then the radius of ball is?

Solution

Plate is circular, Ball is a sphere

Area of circle = πr^2, Area of a sphere = $4\pi R^2$

Area of circle = $\frac{1}{16}$ Area of a sphere → $P = \frac{1}{16}(4\pi R^2)$ → $16P = 4\pi R^2$

$4P = \pi R^2$ → $R = \sqrt{\frac{4P}{\pi}} = 2\sqrt{\frac{P}{\pi}}$

(22.33). A steel bar of radius 1 cm is dropped into a cylinder of radius 2 cm and height 4 cm. if the cylinder is now filled with water, what is the volume of the water in the cylinder?

Solution

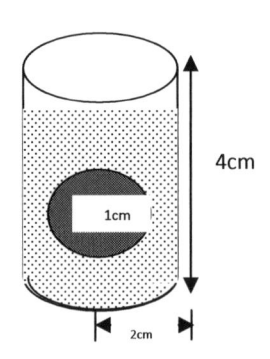

Volume of cylinder = $\pi r^2 h$ → $\pi \times 2^2 \times 4 = 16\pi cm^3$

Volume of steel ball = $\frac{4}{3}\pi \times 1^3$ → $\frac{4}{3}\pi \ cm^3$

$V = 16\pi - \frac{4\pi}{3}$ → $\frac{48\pi - 4\pi}{3} = \frac{44\pi}{3}$

(22.34). The square base of a pyramid of side 3 cm has height 8cm. If the pyramid is cut into two part by a plane parallel to the base midway between the base and the vertex, the volumes of the two section are?

Solution

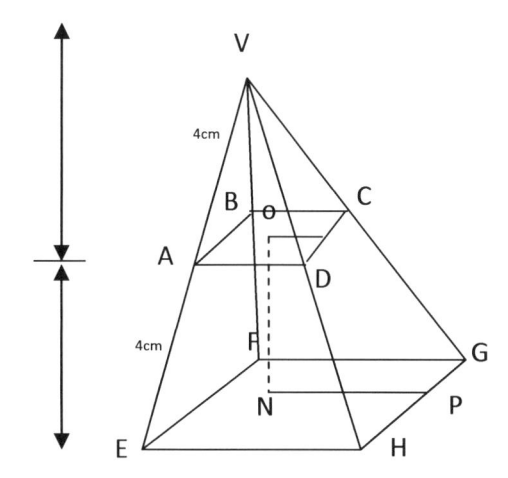

By similarity $\frac{VO}{x} = \frac{VN}{NP} \rightarrow \frac{4}{x} = \frac{8}{1.5} \rightarrow x = \frac{4 \times 1.5}{8} = 0.75$

∴ AD = 2 x 0.75 = 1.5 m

Volume of VABCD = $\frac{1}{3}$ (base area) x height → $\frac{1}{3}$ (1.5 x 1.5) x 4 = 3cm³

Volume of VEFGH = $\frac{1}{3}$ (base area) x height → $\frac{1}{3}$ (3 x 3) x 8 = 24cm³

Volume of ABCDEFGH is (24 – 3) = 21cm³

The volumes are 3cm³ and 21 cm³

(22.35).

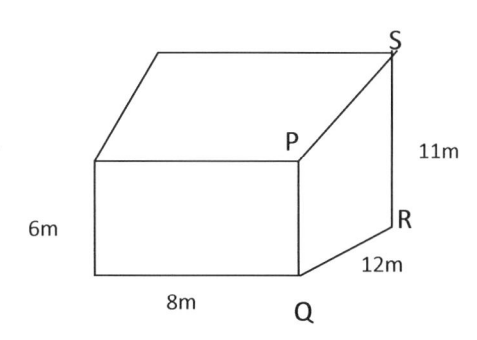

The figure is a solid with trapezium PQRS as its uniform cross section. Find its volume.

Solution

Volume = cross sectional area x distance apart

Volume = $\frac{1}{2}$(a + b)h x 8 → $\frac{1}{2}$(6 + 11)12 x 8 = $816 m^3$

(22.36) A rectangular lawn has an area of 1815 square yards if its length is 50 metres. Find its width in metres given that 1 metre equals 1.1 yards

Solution

$\frac{1m}{50m} = \frac{1.1 \; yards}{x \; yards}$ → $x = 50 \times 1.1 = 55 yards$

Area = L x B = 1815 square yards

Width = B = $\frac{1815}{L} = \frac{1815}{55} = 33 yards$

Since the answer must be in meters, we convert

$\frac{1m}{x \; m} = \frac{1.1 \; yards}{33 \; yards}$ → X = $\frac{33 \times 1m}{1.1} = \frac{330}{11} = 30$ m

(22.37). A pyramid is constructed on a cuboid. The number of edges on the combined figure is?

Solution

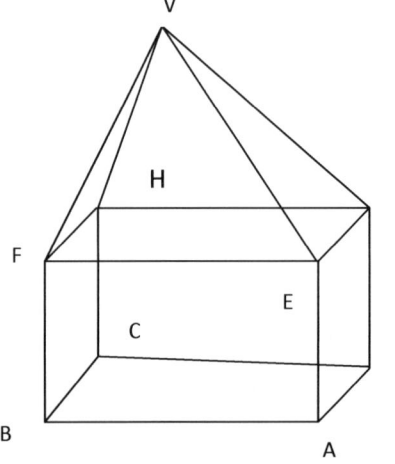

Edges are lines that join any two points

For cuboid, we have GH, GD, BC …….. = 12

For pyramid, we have VG, VE, VH, VF = 4

Total Edges = 12 + 4 = 16

282

(22.38). A solid sphere of radius 4 cm has a mass of 64kg. What will be the mass of a shell of same metal whose internal and external radii are 2 cm and 3 cm respectively?

Solution

From Volume of sphere $= \frac{4}{3}\pi r^3 \rightarrow v = kr^3$

$k = \frac{V_1}{V_2} = \left(\frac{r_1}{r_2}\right)^3 \rightarrow \frac{m_1}{m_2} = \left(\frac{r_1}{r_2}\right)^3$

$\frac{m_1}{m_2} = \frac{r_1^3}{R^3 - r^3} \rightarrow m_2 r_1^3 = m_1(R^3 - r^3) \rightarrow m_2(4^3) = 64(3^3 - 2^3) \rightarrow$

$64m_2 = 64(27 - 8) = 64 \times 19 \therefore m_2 = 19 \text{kg}$

(22.39). The area of a square i1 144sq cm, Find the length of its diagonal.

Solution

Length of diagonal = Length x $\sqrt{2} \rightarrow \sqrt{144} \times \sqrt{2} = 12\sqrt{2}$

(22.40). A square has a diagonal of x units. If the diagonal is increased by 2units. What is the length of the side of the new square?

Solution

Length $= \frac{diagonal}{2} \times \sqrt{2} \rightarrow \frac{(x+2)}{2} \times \sqrt{2}$

(22.41). Find the surface area of the figure shown below.

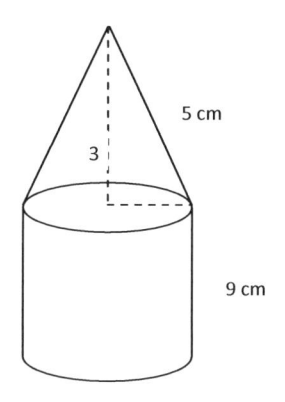

5 cm

3

9 cm

Solution

Radius of the cone is gotten from Pythagoras theorem. $r = \sqrt{5^2 - 3^2} = 4cm$

Total curved surface area = curved surface of cone + curved surface of cylinder

$\pi r l + 2\pi r h \rightarrow (\pi \times 4 \times 5) + (2\pi \times 4 \times 9) \rightarrow 20\pi + 72\pi = 92\pi$

(22.42). Find the volume of the figure below.

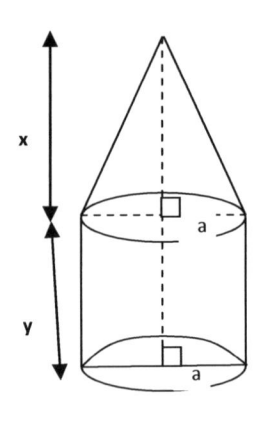

Solution

Total volume = Volume of cone + Volume of cylinder $\rightarrow \frac{1}{3}\pi r^2 h_1 + \pi r^2 h_2$

with $h_1 = x, h_2 = y$

Volume = $\frac{1}{3}\pi a^2 x + \pi a^2 y$

(22.43).

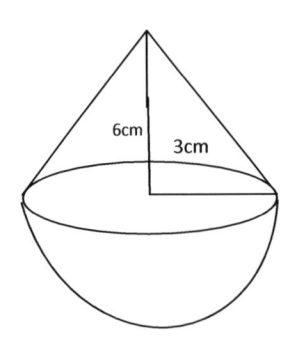

In the figure above, a solid consists of a hemisphere surrounded by a right circular cone of radius 3.0 cm and height 6.0cm. Find the volume of the solid.

Solution

Volume of solid = volume of cone + volume of hemisphere → $\frac{1}{3}\pi r^2 h + \frac{2}{3}\pi r^3$

With radius of cone = radius of hemisphere

Volume of the solid = $\frac{1}{3}\pi r^2(h + 2r)$ → $\frac{1}{3}\pi \times 3^2[6 + (2 \times 3)]$ → $3\pi(6 + 6)$ → $3\pi(12) = 36\pi$

(22.44)

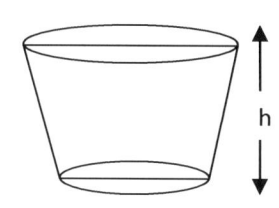

In frustum of a cone shown, the top diameter is twice the bottom diameter. If the height of the frustum is hcm. Find the height of the cone.

Solution

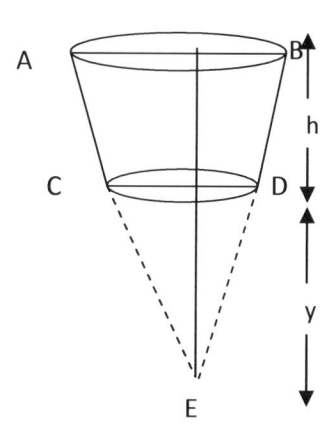

Let diameter of the bottom = d, diameter of the top = 2d

Thus cones ABE and CDE are produced

By similarity → $\frac{2d}{d} = \frac{h+y}{y}$ → $\frac{2}{1} = \frac{h+y}{y}$ → $2y = h + y$ → $2y - y = h$ ∴ $y = h$

y = h implies the height of the small cone is the same as that of a frustum

∴ Height of the complete cone = $h + h = 2h$

(22.45).

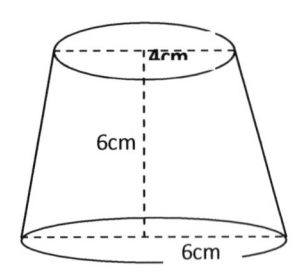

Find the curved surface area of the frustum in the above.

Solution

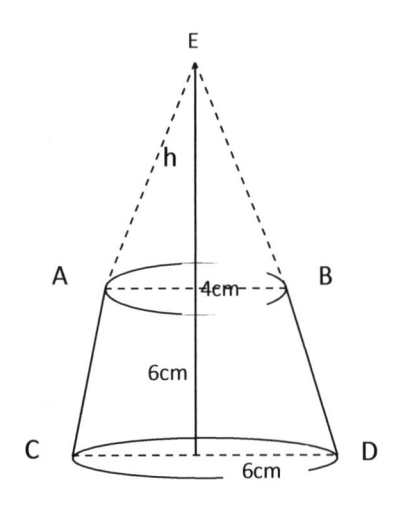

From the diagram, by similarity → $\frac{h}{4} = \frac{h+6}{6}$ → 6h = 4(h + 6) = 4h + 24

6h – 4h = 24 → 2h = 24 ∴ h = 12

Also, $EB^2 = h^2 + 4^2$ → $12^2 + 4^2$ → 144 + 16 = 160 ∴ $EB = \sqrt{360} = 6\sqrt{10}$

C.S.A of frustum = area of big cone – area of small cone → $\pi RL - \pi rl = \pi(RL - rl)$

C.S.A = $\pi[(6 \times 6\sqrt{10}) - (4 \times 4\sqrt{10})]$ → $\pi(36\sqrt{10} - 16\sqrt{10}) = \pi(20\sqrt{10})$

CHAPTER 23 CIRCLE

A circle is the set of all points in a plane that are at the same distance from a fixed point called the center.

Terms associated with the circle.

(i) The circumference of a circle is the distance around the circle. It contains 360^0.

(ii) Radius of a circle is a line segment joining the center to a point on the circle.

Note: since all radii of a given circle have the same length, we may at times use the word radius to mean the number that is "the length of the radius."

(iii) Central angle: This is an angle formed by two radii

(iv) Arc: This is a continuous part of a circle. The symbol for arc is ⌒ .

(vi) Semicircle: This is an arc measuring one-half the circumference of a circle.

(vii) Minor arc: This is an arc that is smaller than a semi circle.

($viii$) Major arc: This is an arc that is greater than a semicircle. Three letters are needed to indicate a major arc.

(ix) Chord: This is a line segment joining two points of the circumference.

(x) Diameter: This is a chord through the center.

(xi) Sector: This is an arc bounded by two radii.

(xii) Segment: This is a part of a circle bounded by a chord and its arc.

($xiii$) Minor segment: This is the smaller of the two segments.

(xiv) Secant: This is a line that intersects the circle at two points.

(xv) Tangent: This is a line that touches the circle at one and only one point no matter how far produced.

(xvi) Inscribed polygon: This is a polygon all of whose sides are chords of a circle.

(*xvii*) Circumscribed circle: This is a circle passing through each vertex of a polygon

(*xviii*) Circumscribed polygon: This is a polygon all whose sides are tangent to a circle.

(*xix*) Inscribed circle: This is a circle to which all the sides of a polygon are tangents.

(*xx*) Equal circles: Two circles are equal if their radii are equal in length.

(*xxi*) Congruent circles: Two circles are congruent circles if their radii are congruent.

(*xxii*) Two arcs are congruent if they have equal degree measure and length.

Diagrammatic representation of the above terms.

Line across a circle can either be chord, tangent, secant, diameter or radius. The diagram below annotates this lines.

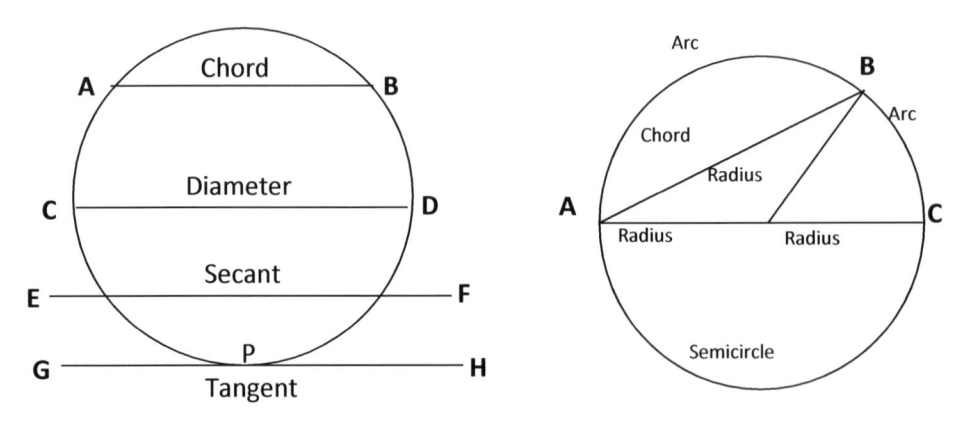

Thus in the first figure above (left) $\overline{CD}$ is a diameter of circle o, $\overleftrightarrow{EF}$ is a secant, $\overleftrightarrow{GH}$ is a tangent to the circle at P, P is the point of contact or the point of tangency.

Thus in the second figure above (right) $\widehat{BC}$ is a minor arc, $\widehat{BAC}$ is a major arc, $\overline{AC}$ is a chord.

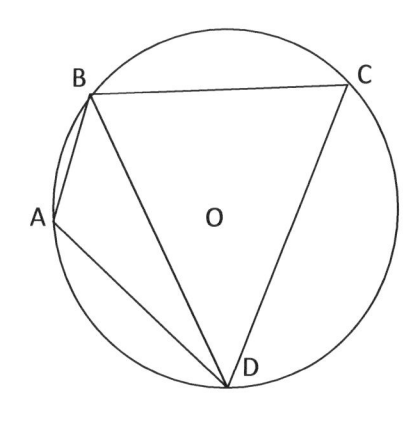

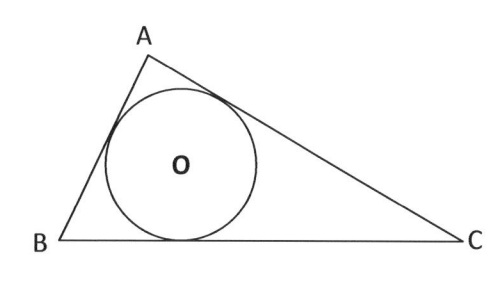

Circumscribed circle

Circumscribed polygon

Inscribed Polygons

Inscribed Circle

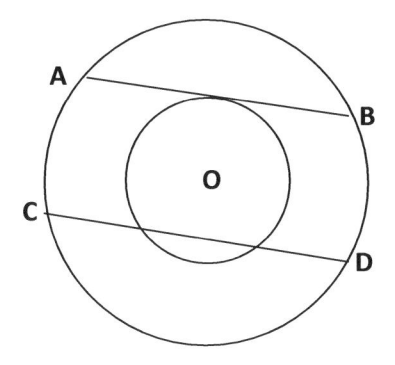

Concentric Circle

Thus the two circles shown above are concentric circles. $\overline{AB}$ is a tangent of the inner circle and a chord of the outer one. $\overline{CD}$ is a secant of the inner circle and a chord of the outer one.

All the above terms have been fused in a single diagram as annotated below

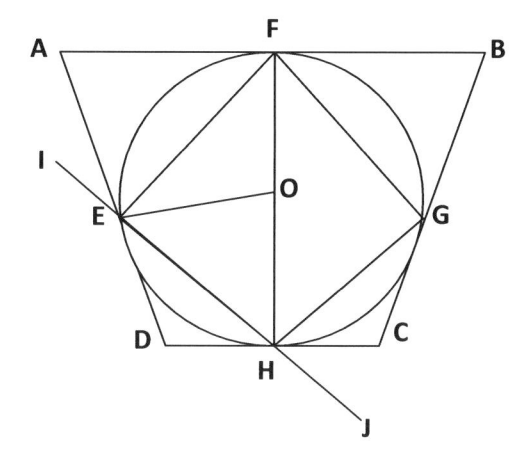

289

Where,

$\overline{OE}$ = Radius, $\overline{FG}$ = Chord, $\overline{FH}$ = Diameter, $\overline{CD}$ = Tangent

$\overline{IJ}$ = Secant, $\widehat{EF}$ = Minor arc, $\widehat{FGH}$ = Semicircle, $\widehat{FEG}$ = Major arc

∠EOF = Central angle, Circle O about EFGH = Circumscribed circle

Circle O about ABCD = Inscribed Circle, Quadrilateral EFGH = Inscribed Polygon

Quadrilateral ABCD = Circumscribed Polygon

Circle principles

Here we state the principles of circle. We use the notation m$\overline{AC}$ to denote "measure of arc $\overline{AC}$"

Principle 1: A diameter divides a circle into two equal parts.

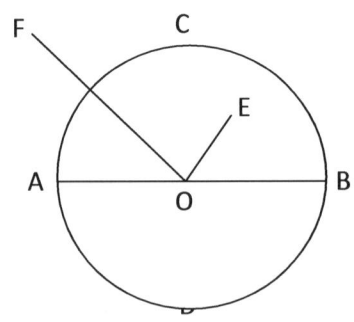

The diameter $\overline{AB}$ divides circle O above into two equal semicircles namely, $\widehat{ACB}$ and $\widehat{ADB}$.

Principle 2: if a chord divides a circle into two equal parts, then it is a diameter. (this is the converse of principle 1.)

Thus from the above diagram if $\widehat{ACB} = \widehat{ADB}$ then $\overline{AB}$ is a diameter.

Principle 3: A point is outside, on, or inside a circle according to whether its distance from the center is greater than, equal to or smaller than the radius.

Thus F is outside circle O in Figure above since FO is greater in length that radius. E is inside circle O since $\overline{EO}$ is smaller in length than a radius.

Principle 4: Radii of the same or congruent circle are congruent

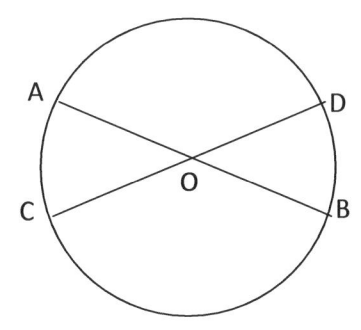

Thus in circle O of the figure above $\overline{OA} \cong \overline{OC}$

Principle 5: Diameters of the same or congruent circle are congruent.

Thus in circle O of the figure above $\overline{AB} \cong \overline{CD}$

Principle 6: in the same or congruent circles, congruent central angles have congruent arcs

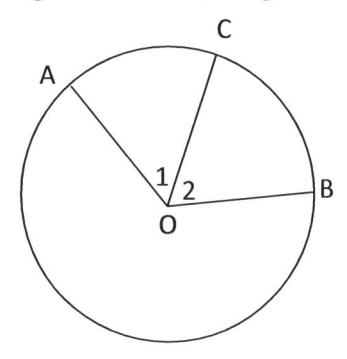

Thus in circle O above if $\angle 1 \cong \angle 2,$ then $\widehat{AC} \cong \widehat{CB}$

Principle 7: in the same or congruent circle, congruent arcs have congruent central angles (this is the converse of principle 6.)

Thus in circle O above if $\widehat{AC} \cong \widehat{CB}$ then $\angle 1 \cong \angle 2$

Principle 8: In the same or congruent circles, congruent chords have congruent arcs.

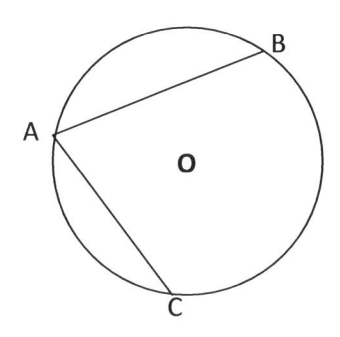

Thus in circle O above if $\overline{AB} \cong \overline{AC}$, then $\widehat{AB} \cong \widehat{AC}$

Principle 9: In the same or congruent circles, congruent arcs have congruent chords. (this is the converse of principle 8.)

Thus in circle O above if $\widehat{AB} \cong \widehat{AC}$ then $\overline{AB} \cong \overline{AC}$

Principle 10: A diameter perpendicular to a chord bisect the chord and its arcs

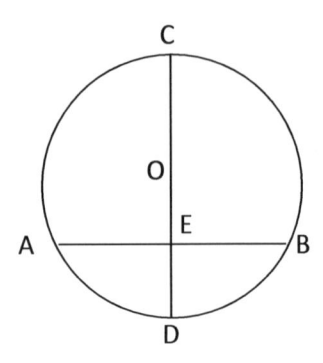

Thus in circle O above if $\overline{CD} \perp \overline{AB}$, then $\overline{CD}$ bisect $\overline{AB}, \widehat{AB}$ and $\widehat{ACB}$.

Principle 11: A perpendicular bisector of a chord passes through the center of the circle.

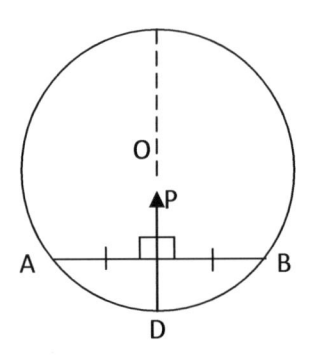

Thus in circle O above if $\overline{PD}$ is the perpendicular bisector of $\overline{AB}$, then $\overline{PD}$ passes through center O.

Principle 12: In the same or congruent circles, congruent chords are equally distant from the center.

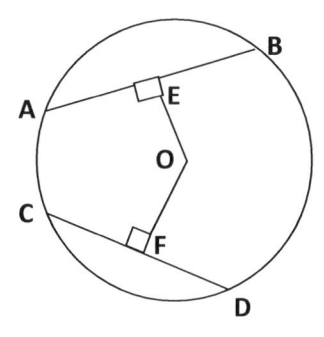

Thus in circle O above if $\overline{AB} \cong \overline{CD}$, if $\overline{OE} \perp \overline{AB}$ and if $\overline{OF} \perp \overline{CD}$ then $\overline{OE} \cong \overline{OF}$.

Principle 13: In the same or congruent circles, chords that are equally distant from the center are congruent. (this is the converse of principle 12.)

Thus in circle O above If $\overline{OE} \cong \overline{OF}$, $\overline{OE} \perp \overline{AB}$ and $\overline{OF} \perp \overline{CD}$ then $\overline{AB} \cong \overline{CD}$

Tangents

The length of a tangent from a point to a circle is the length of the segment of the tangent from the given point to the point of tangency. Thus PA is the length of the tangent from P to circle O in the fig below.

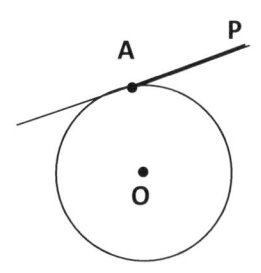

Tangent principles

Principle 1: A tangent is perpendicular to the radius drawn to the point of contact.

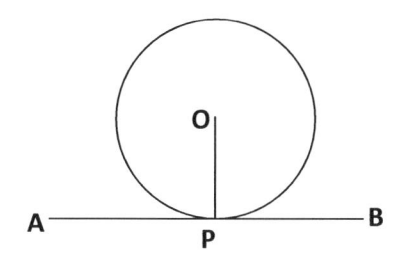

Thus if $\overleftrightarrow{AB}$ is a tangent to circle O at P in the figure above and $\overline{OP}$ is drawn, then $\overline{AB} \perp \overline{OP}$

Principle 2: A line is tangent to a circle if it is perpendicular to a radius at its outer end

Thus if $\overleftrightarrow{AB} \perp$ radius $\overline{OP}$ at P in the figure above then $\overleftrightarrow{AB}$ is tangent to circle O.

Principle 3: A line passes through the center of a circle if it is perpendicular to a tangent at its point of contact.

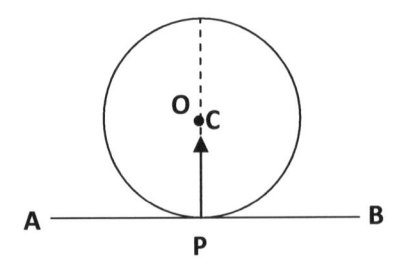

Thus if $\overleftrightarrow{AB}$ is a tangent to circle O at P in the figure above and $\overline{CP} \perp \overleftrightarrow{AB}$ at P, then $\overline{CP}$ extended will pass through the center O

Principle 4: Tangent to a circle from an outside point are congruent

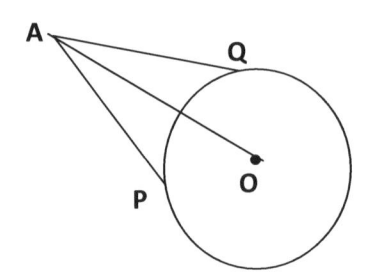

Thus if $\overline{AP}$ and $\overline{AQ}$ are tangent to circle O at P and Q in the Fig above, then $\overline{AP} \cong \overline{AQ}$

∴ Always equate the letters on each side of the shape "<" no matter how it is turned.

Principle 5: The segment from the center of a circle to an outside point bisects the angle between the tangents from the point to the circle.

Thus $\overline{OA}$ bisect $\angle PAQ$ in the figure above if $\overline{AP}$ and $\overline{AQ}$ are tangents to circle O

Two circles in varying relative positions

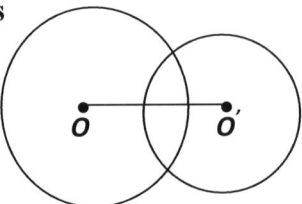

The line of centers of two circles is the line joining their centers. Thus $\overline{OO'}$ is the line of center of circles O and O' in the figure above. Now we consider various ways two circles can be connected

(i) Two circles touching externally

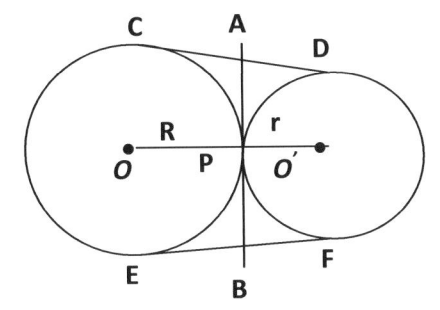

Circle O and O' in Fig above are tangent externally at P. $\overleftrightarrow{AB}$ is the common internal tangents of both circles. $\overleftrightarrow{AB}$ bisect each of the common external tangent, $\overline{CD}$ and $\overline{EF}$. The line of centers OO' passes through P, is perpendicular to $\overleftrightarrow{AB}$, and is equal in length to the sum of the radii $R + r$.

$OO' = R + r$

(ii) Two circles touching internally

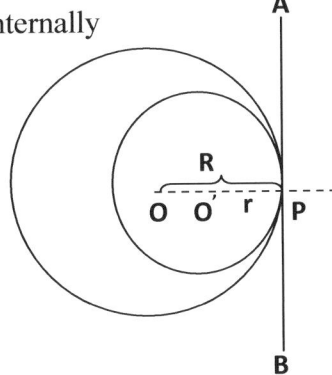

Circle O and O' in the figure above are tangent internal at P, $\overleftrightarrow{AB}$ is the common external tangent of both circles. The line of center OO' if extended passing through P, is perpendicular to $\overleftrightarrow{AB}$ and is equal in length to the difference of the radi, $R + r$

$OO' = R - r$

295

(*iii*) **Circles with the same centre:** For circles with same centre, length of their line of centers *OO' is given by*

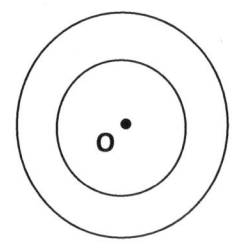

$OO' = 0$

(*iv*) **Circles separated by a distance:** In this case the length of their line of centers *OO' is given by*

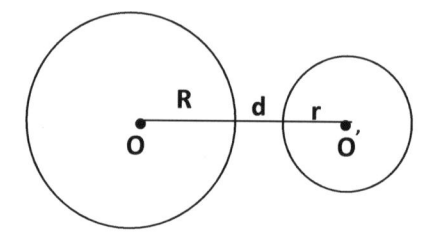

$OO' = R + d + r$

(*v*) **Overlapping circles**

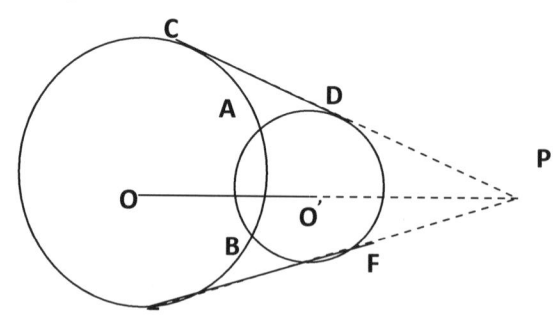

Circle O and O' in the figure above overlap. Their common chord is $\overline{AB}$. If the circle are unequal, their (equal) common external tangents $\overleftrightarrow{CD}$ and $\overleftrightarrow{EF}$ meet at P. the line of center $\overline{OO'}$ is the perpendicular bisector of $\overline{AB}$ and, if extended, passes through P

(*vi*) **Circle outside each other**

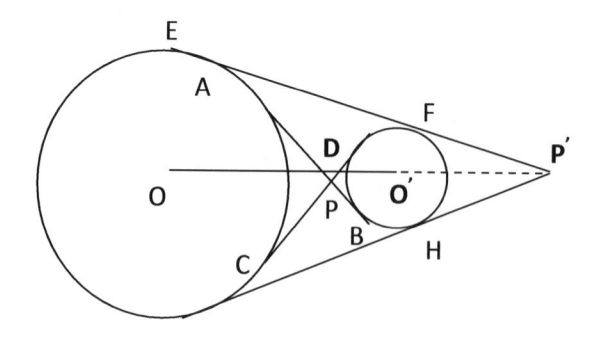

296

Circle O and O' in figure above are entirely outside each other. The common internal tangents $\overline{AB}$ and $\overline{CD}$, meet at P. if the circles are unequal, their common external tangents, $\overline{EF}$ and $\overline{GH}$, if extended, meet at P'. The line of center $\overline{OO'}$ passes through P and P'

MEASUREMENT OF ANGLES AND ARCS IN A CIRCLE

Before stating the angle-measurement principles two important terms must be defined.

(*i*) A central angle is measured by its intercepted arc. The symbol $\stackrel{\circ}{=}$ may be used to mean "is measure by" (This is so because an angle cannot equal an arc)

(*ii*) An inscribed angle is an angle whose vertex is on the circle and whose sides are chords.

Angle-measurement principles

Principle 1: A central angle is measured by its intercepted arc.

Principle 2: An inscribed angle is measure by one-half its intercepted arc.

Principle 3: in the same or congruent circles, congruent inscribed angles have congruent intercepted arcs.

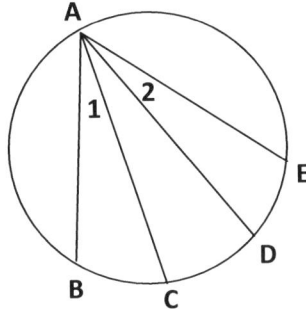

Thus in the figure above if $\angle 1 \cong \angle 2$ then $\widehat{BC} \cong \widehat{DE}$

Principle 4: In the same or congruent circles, inscribed angle having congruent intercepted arc are congruent. (this is the converse of principle 3)

Thus in the figure above if $\widehat{BC} \cong \widehat{DE}$, then $\angle 1 \cong \angle 2$

Principle 5: Angles inscribed in the same or congruent arcs are congruent

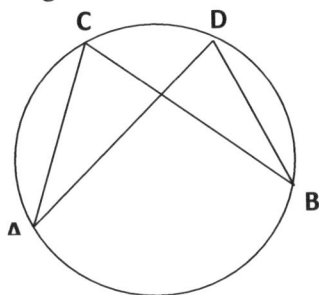

Thus in the figure above if ∠C and ∠D are inscribed in $\overset{\frown}{ACB}$, then ∠C ≅ ∠D

Principle 6: An angle inscribed in a semicircle is a right angle

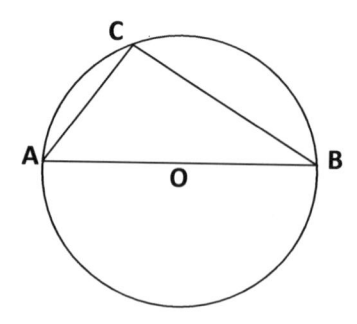

Thus in the figure above, since ∠C is inscribed in semicircle $\overset{\frown}{ACD}$, $m\angle C = 90°$

Principle 7: Opposite angles of an inscribed quadrilateral are supplementary

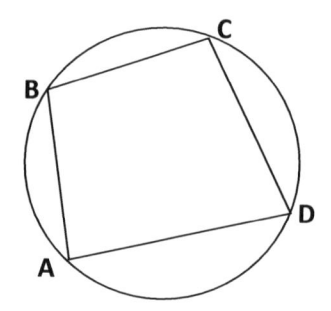

Thus in the figure above, if ABCD is an inscribed quadrilateral, ∠A is the supplement of ∠C

Principle 8: Parallel lines intercept congruent arcs on a circle.

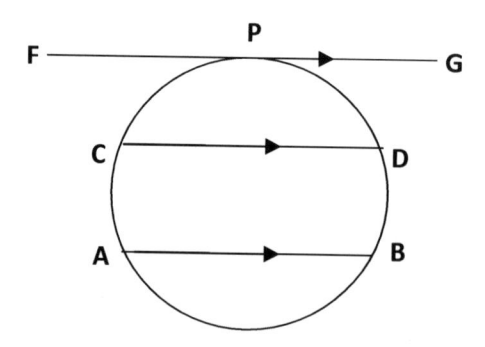

Thus in the figure above, if $\overline{AB} \parallel \overline{CD}$, then $\overset{\frown}{AC} \cong \overset{\frown}{BD}$, If tangent $\overleftrightarrow{FG}$ is parallel to $\overline{CD}$ then $\overset{\frown}{PC} \cong \overset{\frown}{PD}$

Principle 9: An angle formed by a tangent and a chord is measured by one half its intercepted arcs.

Principle 11: An angle formed by two secants intersecting outside a circle is measured by one-half the difference of the intercepted arc.

Principle 12: An angle formed by a tangent and a secant intersecting outside a circle is measured by one-half difference of the intercepted arcs

Principle 13: An angle formed by two tangents intersecting outside a circle is measured by one-half the difference of the intercepted arcs.

Analysis of Angle-measurement principles

There are various ways question can be presented; we therefore apply the above principles to various cases and provide useful deductions.

Principle 9 deals with tangent and chords.

(i) One tangent and one chord

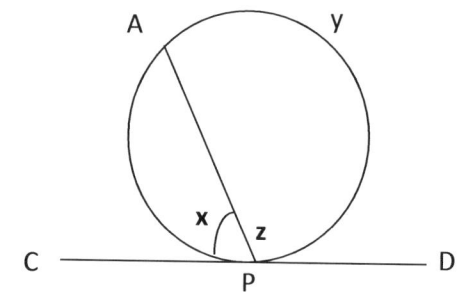

$x + z = 180 \ldots\ldots (i)$

$\angle z \stackrel{\circ}{=} \frac{1}{2}\hat{y} \ldots\ldots (ii)$

(ii) One tangent and two equal chords

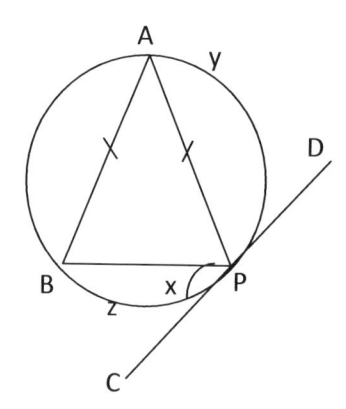

$AB = AP$

$AB + AP + \hat{z} = 360$ ....(ii)

Since $AB = AP \to 2AB + \hat{z} = 360$ ....(iii)

$\angle x \stackrel{\circ}{=} \frac{1}{2}\hat{z}$ ..... (iii)

(***iii***) One tangent and non equal chords

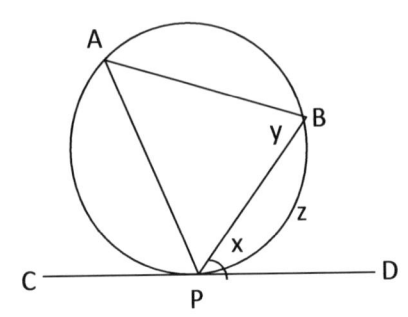

$\angle y \stackrel{\circ}{=} \frac{1}{2}\widehat{AP}$ ..... (i)

$AB + AP + \hat{z} = 360$ ....(ii)   Note AB ≠ AP

$\angle x \stackrel{\circ}{=} \frac{1}{2}\hat{z}$ ..... (iii)

Principle 10 deals with two chords intersecting internally

(***i***) **Two chords intersecting**

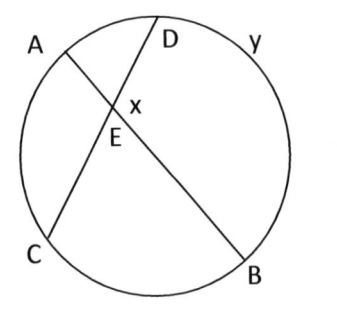

$\angle x \stackrel{\circ}{=} \frac{1}{2}(\widehat{AC} + \hat{y})$

(ii) Two chords intersect forming a quadrilateral

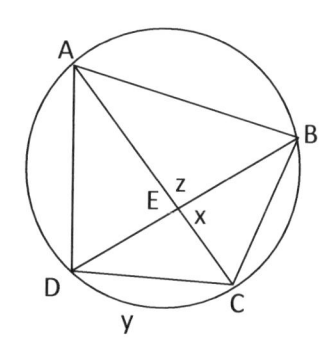

$\angle z \stackrel{\circ}{=} \frac{1}{2}\left(\widehat{AB} + \widehat{CD}\right) \equiv \angle z \stackrel{\circ}{=} \frac{1}{2}\left(\widehat{AB} + \hat{y}\right) \ldots \ldots (i)$

$z + x = 180 \ldots \ldots (ii)$

(iii) Two chords intersect forming a quadrilateral

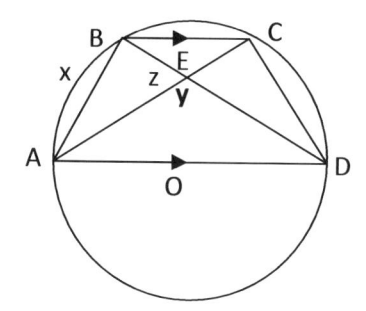

$\angle z \stackrel{\circ}{=} \frac{1}{2}\left(\widehat{AB} + \widehat{CD}\right) \equiv \angle z \stackrel{\circ}{=} \frac{1}{2}\left(\hat{x} + \widehat{CD}\right) \ldots \ldots (i)$

$\widehat{AB} = \widehat{CD} \ldots \ldots (ii)$

$Z + y = 180 \ldots \ldots (iii)$

$\angle z \stackrel{\circ}{=} \frac{1}{2}(2\widehat{AB}) \ldots \ldots (iv)$

Principle 11 to 13 deals with secant and tangent

(i) One tangent and one secant

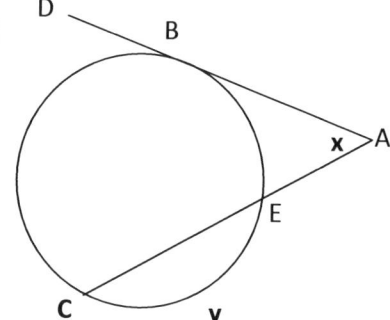

301

$\angle x \stackrel{\circ}{=} \frac{1}{2}[\widehat{BC} - \widehat{BE}] \dots\dots (i)$

$\widehat{BC} + \widehat{BE} + \hat{y} = 360 \dots\dots\dots (ii)$

(ii) For two tangents

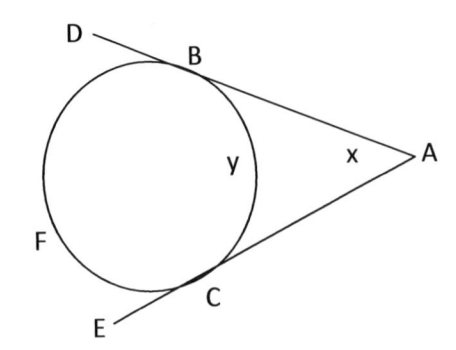

$\angle x \stackrel{\circ}{=} \frac{1}{2}[\widehat{BFC} - \hat{y}] \dots (i)$

$\frac{1}{2}[\widehat{BFC} + \hat{y}] = 180 \equiv [\widehat{BFC} + \hat{y}] = 360 \dots\dots (ii)$

$\angle x \stackrel{\circ}{=} \frac{1}{2}[\widehat{BFC} - \hat{y}] \dots\dots (iii)$

(iii) For two secants without an intersecting cords

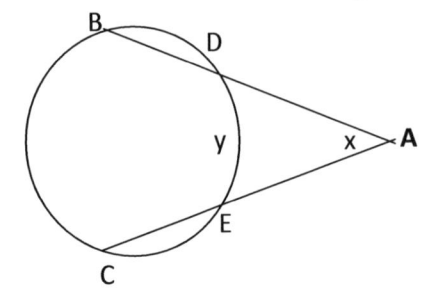

$\angle x \stackrel{\circ}{=} \frac{1}{2}(\widehat{BC} - \hat{y})$

Where $\angle x$ is the angle formed at point of intersection of the two secants.

(iv) For two secants with an intersecting cords

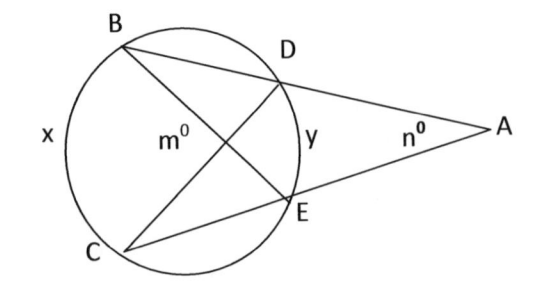

302

$\angle x \stackrel{\circ}{=} \frac{1}{2}(\widehat{BC} + \hat{y})$ ....(i)

$\angle x \stackrel{\circ}{=} \frac{1}{2}(\widehat{BC} - \hat{y})$ ....(ii)

Where $\angle x$ in (i) is angle at the intersecting chords (m⁰)

Where $\angle x$ in (ii) is angle at the intersecting secants (n⁰)

Solve both equations simultaneously to get values of x and y

(v) Two tangent s and chords

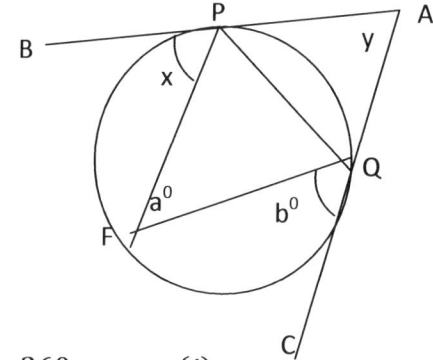

$\widehat{BFC} + \hat{y} = 360$ ....(i)

$\angle x = \frac{1}{2}[\widehat{BFC} - \hat{y}]$ ....(ii)

Apply principle 2 to determine any missing arc i.e $\angle a^o = \frac{1}{2}\widehat{PQ}$

Similarity in circles

Principle 1: If two secants intersect outside a circle, the product of the length of one of the secants and its external segment equals the product of the length of the other secant and its external segment.

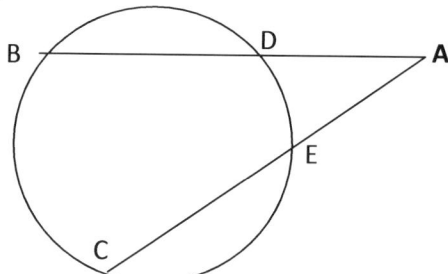

Thus in the diagram above $AB \times AD = AC \times AE$

Principle 2: If two chords intersect within a circle, the product of the length of the segment of one chord equal the product of the lengths of the segment of the other.

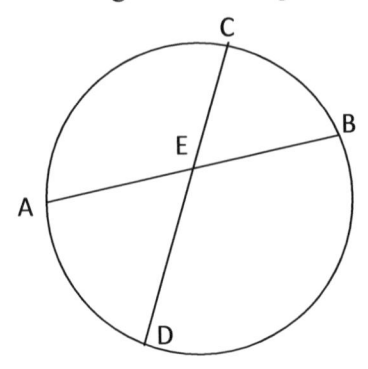

Thus in the diagram above, $AE \times EB = CE \times ED$

Principle 3: If a tangent and a secant intersect outside a circle, the tangent is the mean proportional between the secant and its external segment.

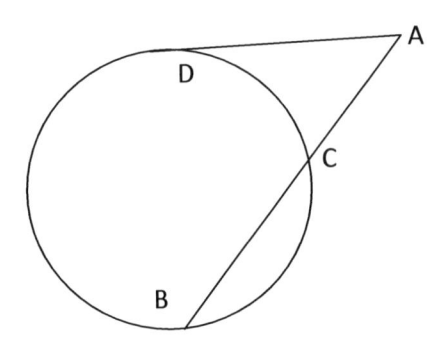

Thus in the diagram above if DA is a tangent, then $\dfrac{AB}{AD} = \dfrac{AD}{AC}$

QUESTIONS

(23.1).

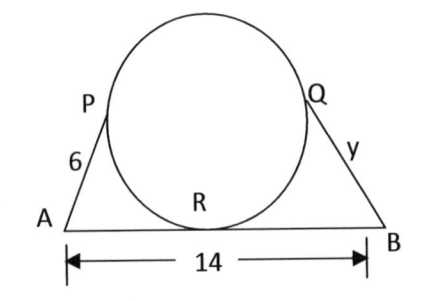

In the figure above $\overline{AP}$, $\overline{BQ}$ and $\overline{AB}$ are tangents. Find y

Solution

equating the shape ''<'' we have

$AB = AR + RB \ldots\ldots (i)$

$PA = AR = AR = RB = BQ \ldots\ldots (ii)$

$AR = 6 \text{ and } RB = y$

$from\ (i)\ RB = AB - AR = 14 - 6 = 8 \therefore y = RB = 8$

(23.2).

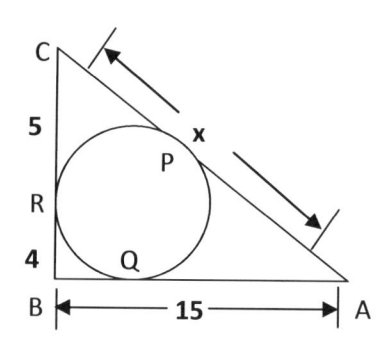

$\triangle ABCD$ in the figure is circumscribed. find x.

Solution

equating the shape ''<'' we have

$RC = PC, RB = QB$

$AP = AQ \ldots\ldots\ldots (i)$

$AB = QB + AQ \qquad \ldots\ldots (ii)$

$PC = 8, QB = 4$

From (ii) $AQ = AB - QB = 15 - 4 = 11$.

$\therefore x = AP + PC = 11 + 8 = 19$

(23.3).

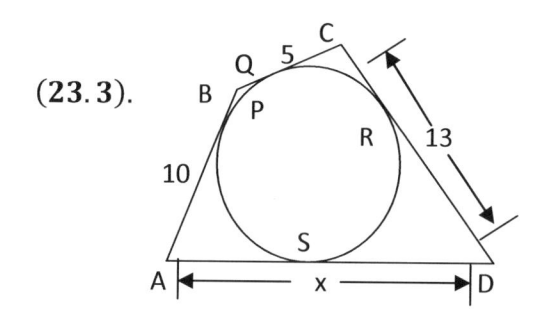

305

Quadrilateral ABCD in the figure above is circumscribed. Find x.

Solutions

$AP = AS, SD = RD \ldots\ldots (i)$

$CD = RD + CR \ldots\ldots (ii)$

$CR = QC$

$AD = AS + SD \ldots\ldots (iii)$

$AS = 10, CR = 5$

$RD = CD - CR = 13 - 5 = 8. \therefore x = AS + SD = 10 + 8 = 18$

(23.4). Two circle have radii of 9 and 4 respectively. Find the length of their line of centers under the following conditions (a) If the circle are tangent externally. (b) if the circle are tangent internally. (c) if the circles are concentric, if the circle are 5 unit apart

Solution

Let $R = radius\ of\ the\ larger\ cirlce,\ r = radius\ of\ smaller\ circle$ #

$(a)\ OO' = R + r = 9 + 4 = 13$

$(b)\ OO' = R - r = 9 - 4 = 5$

$(c)\ OO' = R + d + r = 9 + 5 + 4 = 18$

(23.5).

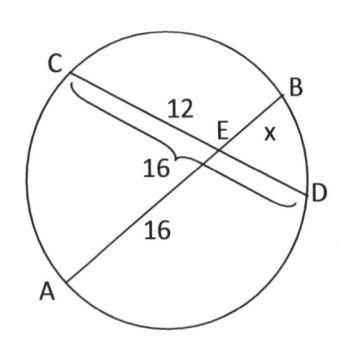

Find x if the two chords intersect.

Solution

$AE \times EB = CE \times ED \rightarrow 16x(x) = 12 \times 4 \therefore x = \frac{12 \times 4}{16} = 3$

(23.6).

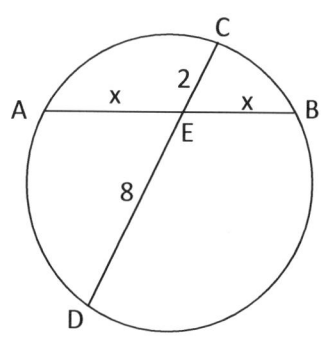

Find x if the two chords intersect

Solution

$AE \times EB = CE \times ED \rightarrow (x)x(x) = 2 \times 8 \rightarrow x^2 = 16 \rightarrow x = \sqrt{16} = 4$

(23.7).

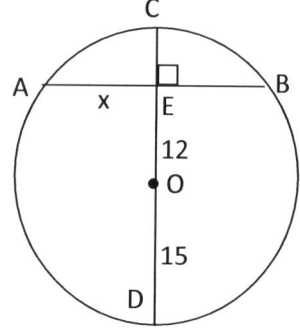

In the diagram above $diameter\ CD \perp AB$, find the value of x.

Solution

Here $AE = EB$, and CE = 3

$AE \times EB = CE \times ED \rightarrow (x) \times (x) = 3 \times 27 \rightarrow x^2 = 81 \rightarrow x = \sqrt{81} = 9$

(23.8).

307

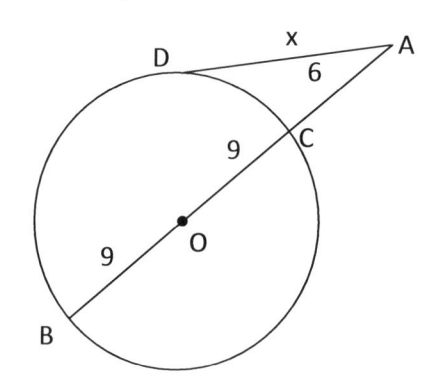

Find x in the diagram above

Solution

$\frac{AB}{AD} = \frac{AD}{AC} \rightarrow \frac{24}{x} = \frac{x}{6} \rightarrow 24 \times 6 = x^2 \rightarrow x = \sqrt{24 \times 6} \rightarrow \sqrt{144} = 12$

(23.9).

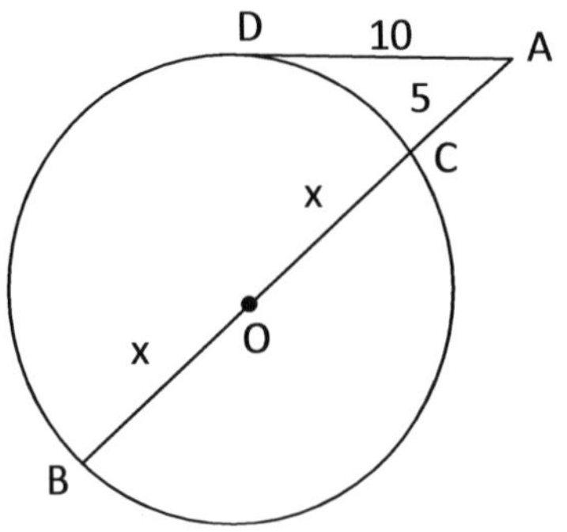

Solution

$\frac{AB}{AD} = \frac{AD}{AC} \rightarrow \frac{2x+5}{10} = \frac{10}{5} \rightarrow (2x+5)5 = 100 \rightarrow 10x + 25 = 100 \therefore x = 7\frac{1}{2}$

(23.10).

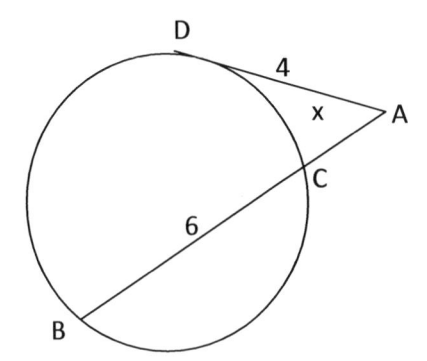

Find the value of x in the figure above.

Solution

$\frac{AB}{AP} = \frac{AP}{AC} \rightarrow \frac{6+x}{4} = \frac{4}{x} \rightarrow (6+x)x = 16 \rightarrow x^2 + 6x - 16 = 0 \rightarrow (x+8)(x-2) = 0 \rightarrow x = 2$

(23.11).

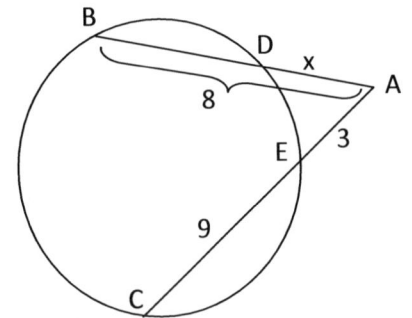

308

Find the value of x in the figure above.

Solution

$AB \times AD = AC \times AE \rightarrow 8 \times (x) = 12 \times 3 \rightarrow x = \frac{12 \times 3}{8} \therefore x = 4\frac{1}{2}$

(23.12).

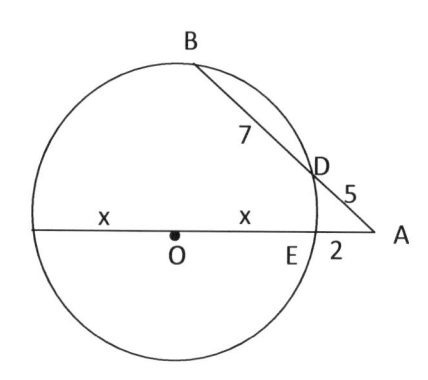

Find the value of x in the figure above.

Solution

$AB \times AD = AC \times AE \rightarrow 12 \times 5 = (2x + 2) \times 2 \rightarrow 60 = 4x + 4$

$60 - 4 = 4x \therefore x = \frac{56}{4} = 14$

Chapter 24 POLYGONS

These are figures with many sides and with all the sides equal examples include square, equilateral triangle etc

A circle may be regarded as a regular polygon having infinite number of sides.

Terms associated with polygons

(*i*) Regular polygon: This is an equilateral (all sides have the same length) and equiangular (all angles are equal in measure) polygon.

(*ii*) Irregular polygon: This is a polygon that does not have all sides equal and all angles equal.

(*iii*) Convex polygon: A polygon is convex if some angles are different from the other equal angles and none of the interior angles is greater than $180°$.

(*iv*) Re-entrant polygon: A polygon is re-entrant if some angles are different from the other equal angles and at least one of the interior angles is greater than $180°$.

Names of polygons according to the number of sides

Number of sides	Polygon	Number of Sides	Polygon
3	Triangle	8	Octagon
4	Quadrilateral	9	Nonagon
5	Pentagon	10	Decagon
6	Hexagon	12	Dodecagon
7	Heptagon	n	n-gon

Sum of the measures of the angles of a polygon

Sum of measures of interior angles of a polygon of n sides = $(n - 2)180°$

Sum of measures of exterior angles of a polygon of n sides = $360°$

If a regular polygon of n sides has an interior angle of measure i and an exterior angle of measure e

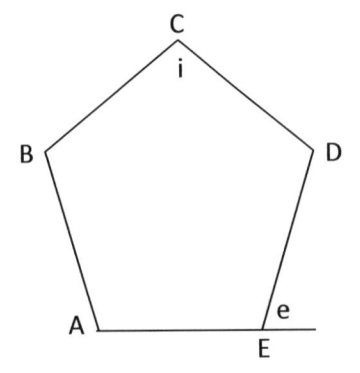

310

$$i = \frac{180(n-2)}{n}, \quad e = \frac{360}{n}$$

$$\therefore \quad i + e = 180$$

REGULAR POLYGONS

A regular polygon is an equilateral (all sides have the same length) and equiangular (all angles are equal in measure) polygon.

Terms associated with regular polygon

(*i*) Center: The center of a regular polygon is the common center of its inscribed and circumscribed circle.

(*ii*) Radius: This is a segment joining its center to any vertex. A radius of a regular polygon is also a radius of the circumscribed circle.

(*iii*) Center angle: This is an angle included between two radii drawn to successive vertices.

(*iv*) Apothem: This is a segment from its center perpendicular to one of its sides. An apothem is also a radius of the inscribed circle.

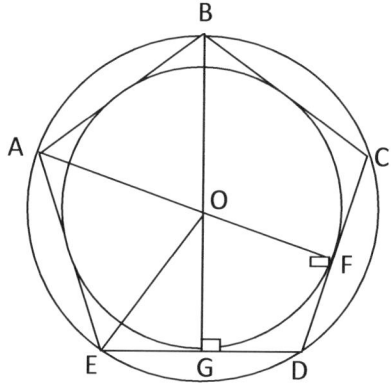

The diagram above shows a regular pentagon where

O = center, OA and OB = $radii$, $\angle AOB$ = central angle, OG and OF = apothems

$AB = BC = CD = DE = EA$ and $m\angle A = m\angle B = m\angle C = m\angle D = m\angle D = m\angle E$

For a regular polygon of n sides

Perimeter = number of sides x length = ns

Each central angle c measures $\dfrac{360^o}{n}$

Each interior angle i measures $\dfrac{(n-2)180^o}{n}$

Each exterior angle e measures $\dfrac{360^o}{n}$

Relationships of segment in regular polygons of 3, 4 and 6 sides

For a regular polygon with three, four or six sides, special right triangles are formed when the apothem r and a radius R terminating in the same side are drawn. We know consider each of them

(1) Equilateral triangle

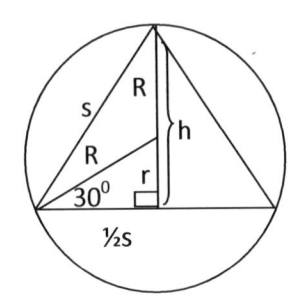

In an equilateral triangle a 30°-60°-90° triangle is obtained. The relationship between the lengths of the sides and radii is given by

$s = R\sqrt{3}, \quad h = r + R$

$r = \dfrac{1}{2}h, \quad R = \dfrac{2}{3}h, \quad r = \dfrac{1}{2}R$

(2) Square

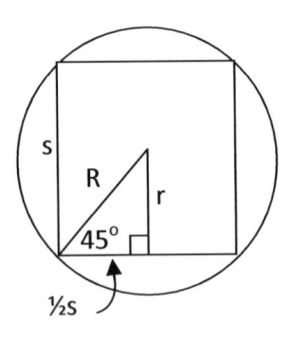

In the case of the square we obtain a 45°-45°-90° triangle, and we have

$S = R\sqrt{2}, \quad r = \dfrac{1}{2}s = \dfrac{1}{2}R\sqrt{2}$

(3) Hexagon

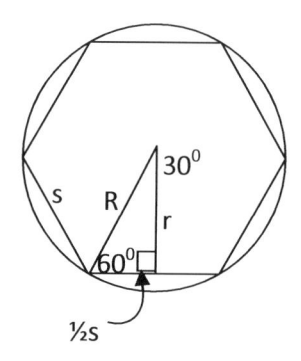

In a hexagon a 30^0-60^0-90^0 triangle is obtained. The relationship between the lengths of the sides and radii is given by

S = R   and $r = \frac{1}{2}R\sqrt{3}$

Area of a regular polygon

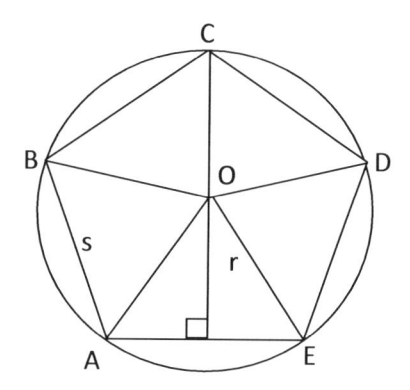

From the diagram above, by drawing radii we divide a regular polygon of n sides and perimeter P = ns into n triangles, each of area $\frac{1}{2}rs$. Hence, area is given by

$A = \frac{1}{2}nsr = \frac{1}{2}pr$

Thus, the area of a regular polygon equals one-half the product of its perimeter and the length of its apothem.

Ratio of segments and areas of regular polygons

Since corresponding segment of regular polygons having the same number of sides are in proportion where "segments" here includes sides, perimeters, radii or circumferences of circumscribed or inscribed circles, and such

Mathematically,

$S_1 : S_2 = P_1 : P_2 = r_1 : r_2$

Also areas of regular polygons having the same number of sides are to each other as the squares of the lengths of any two corresponding segment.

Mathematically.

$\frac{A_1}{A_2} = \left(\frac{S_1}{S_2}\right)^2$

Circumference and area of a circle

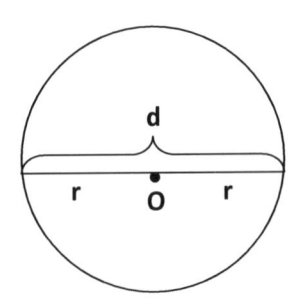

Circumference of a circle is given by $C = 2\pi r = \pi D$

Area of a circle is given by $A = \frac{1}{2}pr \rightarrow \frac{1}{2}Cr \rightarrow \frac{1}{2}(2\pi r)(r) = \pi r^2$

$\pi = \frac{C}{D} \rightarrow$

The following holds $\frac{D_1}{D_2} = \frac{C_1}{C_2}$, $\frac{A_1}{A_2} = \left(\frac{D_1}{D_2}\right)^2$, $\frac{A_1}{A_2} = \left(\frac{C_1}{C_2}\right)^2$

Where D = diameter, C = circumference, A = Area

For circumscribed (outside) $C = 2\pi R$, $A = \pi R^2$

For inscribed (inside) $C = 2\pi r$, $A = \pi r^2$

R = circumscribed, r = inscribed

Length of an arc, area of a sector and a segment.

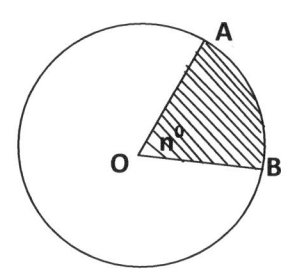

In the diagram above the shaded section of circle O is a sector i.e sector OAB.

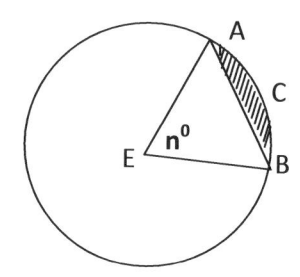

In the diagram above the shaded section of circle E is minor segment ACB.

Length of an arc $= \dfrac{n}{360} \times circumference\ of\ circle = \dfrac{n}{360} \times 2\pi r = \dfrac{\pi n r}{180}$

Area of a sector $= \dfrac{n}{360} \times area\ of\ circle = \dfrac{n}{360} \times \pi r^2$

Making Area of a sector subject gives

$\dfrac{Area\ of\ a\ sector\ of\ n^o}{Area\ of\ the\ circle} = \dfrac{lenght\ of\ an\ arc\ of\ measure\ n^o}{circumference\ of\ the\ circle} = \dfrac{n}{360}$

Note: If a regular polygon is inscribed in a circle the area of segment is given by

$Area\ of\ segment = \dfrac{Area\ of\ sector - Area\ of\ triagle\ formed}{no\ of\ sides}$

Otherwise,

Area of segment = Area of sector − Area of triagle formed

Areas of combined figures

The areas of combined figures are determined by calculating the individual areas and then adding or subtracting as required.

If the figure is enclosed we add to get the area

If the figure is not enclosed we subtract to get the area

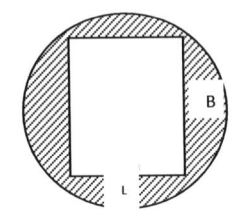

Shaded area = Area of circle - Area of rectangle = $\pi r^2 - (L \times B)$

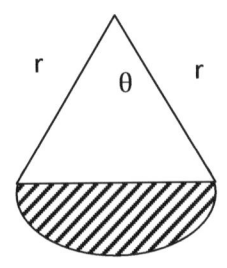

Shaded area = Area of sector − Area of triangle = $\frac{\theta}{360} \times \pi r^2 - \frac{1}{2} b \times h$

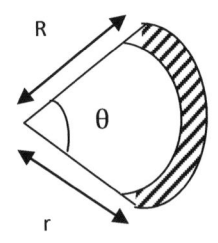

Shaded area = Area of a big sector − Area of small sector = $\frac{\theta}{360} \times \pi R^2 - \frac{\theta}{360} \times \pi r^2$

$= \frac{\theta}{360} \times \pi(R^2 - r^2)$

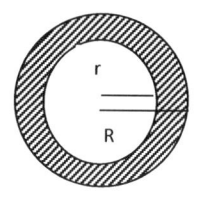

Shaded area = Area of big circle – Area of small circle = $\pi R^2 - \pi r^2 = \pi(R^2 - r^2)$

QUESTIONS

(24. 1). Find the sum of the measures of the interior angles of a polygon of 9 sides (express your answer in straight angles and in degrees)

Solution

In straight angles, S = n – 2 → 9 – 2 = 7 straight angles

In degrees, $m\angle S = n(n-2)180$ → $(9-2)(180) = 1260°$

(24. 2). Find the number of sides a polygon has if the sum of the measures of the interior angle is 3600°

Solution

In degrees, S = (n – 2)180 → 3600 = (n - 2)180 ∴ n = 22

(24. 3). Is it possible to have a polygon the sum of whose angle measures is 1890°?

Solution

1890 = (n – 2)180 → n = 12 ½.

A polygon cannot have 12 ½ sides.

(24. 4). Find the length of a side s of a regular pentagon if the perimeter p = 35.

Solution

From $p = ns$ 35 = 5s ∴ s = 7

(24. 5). Find the length of the apothem of a regular pentagon if the radius of the inscribed circle is 21.

Solution

Since an apothem r is a radius of the inscribed circle, it has length 21.

(24.6). In a regular polygon of five sides, find the measures of the central angle c, the exterior angle e, and the interior angle i.

Solution

$n = 5 \rightarrow m\angle c = \frac{360}{n} = \frac{360}{5} = 72°$

$m\angle e = \frac{360}{5} = 72°$

From $i + e = 180 \rightarrow m\angle i = 180 - m\angle e = 108°$

(24.7). Find each interior angle measure of a regular polygon having 9 sides

Solution

$n = 9 \rightarrow m\angle i = \frac{(n-2)180}{n} = \frac{(9-2)180}{9} = 140$

(24.8). Find the number of sides a regular polygon has if each exterior angle measures $5°$

Solution

With e = 5 $\rightarrow 5 = \frac{360}{n} \rightarrow 5n = 360 \therefore n = 72$

(24.9). Find the number of sides of a regular polygon has if each interior angle measure in 165°.

Solution

with $i = 165 \rightarrow i + e = 180 \rightarrow 165 + e = 180 \therefore e = 15$

Also from e = $\frac{360}{n} \rightarrow 15 = \frac{360}{n} \therefore n = 24$

(24.10). Find each interior angle measure of a quadrilateral if its interior angles are represented by $x + 10, 2x + 20, 3x - 50, and\ 2x - 20$

Solution

Sum of the measures equals $360°$

$(x + 10) + (2x + 20) + (3x + 50) + 2x - 20) = 360$

$8x - 40 = 360 \therefore x = 50$ Thus, $x + 10 = 60; 2x + 20 = 120; 3x + 50 = 100; 2x - 20 = 80$. Each interior measures $60°, 120°, 100°, 80°$

(24.11). Find each interior measure of a quadrilateral if its interior angles are represented if its exterior angles are in the ratio of $2: 3: 4: 6$

318

Solution

Sum of the measures equals 360^0

$2x + 3x + 4x + 6x = 360 \rightarrow 15x = 360 \therefore x = 24.$

Each exterior measures $48°, 72°, 96°, 144°$

(24.12). In a regular hexagon find the length of the side and apothem if the radius is 12.

Solution

$R = 12, s = R = 12$ and $r = \frac{1}{2}R\sqrt{3} = 6\sqrt{3}$

(24.13). Find the radius and length of the apothem if the side has length 8.

Solution

$s = 8, R = s = 8$ and $r = \frac{1}{2}R\sqrt{3} = 4\sqrt{3}$

(24.14). In a square find the length of the side and apothem if the radius is 16.

Solution

with $R = 16$, $s = R\sqrt{2} = 16$ and $r = \frac{1}{2}s \rightarrow \frac{1}{2}(R\sqrt{2}) = 8\sqrt{2}$

(24.15). Find the radius and the length of the apothem if a side has length 10.

Solution

With $s = 10, r = \frac{1}{2}s \rightarrow \frac{1}{2}(10) = 5,$ and $R = \frac{s}{\sqrt{2}} = \frac{1}{2}s\sqrt{2} = 5\sqrt{2}.$

(24.16). In an equilateral triangle, find the length of the radius, apothem, and side if the altitude has length 6

Solution

With $h = 6, r = \frac{1}{3}h \rightarrow \frac{1}{3}(6) = 2; R = \frac{2}{3}h \rightarrow \frac{2}{3}(6) = 4$

$s = R\sqrt{3} = 4\sqrt{3}$

(24.17). In an equilateral triangle, find the lengths of the side, apothem, and altitude if the radius is 9.

Solution

With $R = 9, s = R\sqrt{3} = 9\sqrt{3}; r = \frac{1}{2}R \rightarrow \frac{1}{2}(9) = 4\frac{1}{2};$

$h = \frac{3}{2}R \rightarrow \frac{3}{2}(9) = 13\frac{1}{2}$

(24.18). Find the area of a regular hexagon if the length of the apothem is $5\sqrt{3}$.

Solution

Length of apothem = Length of Altitude.

$A = \frac{h^2}{3} \times \sqrt{3} \times no\ of\ side \rightarrow \frac{(5\sqrt{3})^2}{3} \times \sqrt{3} \times 6 \rightarrow \frac{25 \times 3 \times \sqrt{3} \times 6}{3} = 6 \times 25 \times \sqrt{3} = 150\sqrt{3}$

(24.19). A regular hexagon is constructed inside a circle of diameter 12cm. The area of the hexagon is?

Solution

$Area = 6 \times \frac{6^2}{4} \times \sqrt{3} = 54\sqrt{3}$

(24.20). A regular polygon of (2k + 1) sides has $140°$ as the size of each interior angle. Find k.

Solution

$nx = (n-2)180 \rightarrow (2k+1)140 = (2k+1-2)180 \rightarrow$

$280k + 140 = 360k + 180 - 360 \rightarrow 280k - 360k = -140 + 180 - 360 \rightarrow -80k = -320 \therefore k = 4$

(24.21). If three angles of a quadrilateral are $(3y - x - z)°, (3x)°, (2z - 2y - x)°$. Find the fourth angle in terms of x, y and z.

Solution

Let the fourth angle be t

$3y - x - z + 3x + 2z - 2y - x + t = 360 \rightarrow t = 360 - y - x - z$

(24.22). In a regular polygon of n sides, each interior angle is $144°$. Find n

Solution

$nx = (n-2)180 \rightarrow 144n = (n-2)180 \rightarrow 144n = 180n - 360 \rightarrow 360 = 36n \therefore n = 10$

(24.23). Find the number of sides of a regular polygon whose interior angle is twice the exterior angle.

Solution

Interior → $x = \dfrac{180(n-2)}{n}$, Exterior → $x = \dfrac{360}{n}$

Interior angle = 2 x Exterior

Equating, $\dfrac{180(n-2)}{n} = 2\left[\dfrac{360}{n}\right]$ → $\dfrac{180n - 360}{n} = \dfrac{720}{n}$ → $180n - 360 = 720$

$180n = 1080$ ∴ $n = 6$

(24.24). The sum of the interior angle of a pentagon is 6x + 6y. Find y in term of x.

Solution

6x + 6y = 180(5 - 2) = 180 x 3 = 540 → $6(x + y) = 540$ → $x + y = 9$

$y = 90 - x$

(24.25). If two regular polygons having the same number of sides, find the ratio of the length of the apothems if the perimeter are in the ratio 5:3

Solution

$r_1 : r_2 = P_1 : P_2$ → 5 : 3

(24.26). If two regular polygons have the same number of sides, find the length of a side of the smaller if the lengths of the apothem are 20 and 50 and a side of the larger has length 32.5

Solution

$S_1 : S_2 = r_1 : r_2$ → $S_1 : 32.5 = 20:50$ → $S_1 = \dfrac{20 \times 32.5}{50} = 13$

(24.27). If two regular polygons have the same number of sides, find the ratio of the areas if the lengths of the sides are in the ratio of 1:5.

Solution

$\dfrac{A_1}{A_2} = \left(\dfrac{S_1}{S_2}\right)^2$ → $\dfrac{A_1}{A_2} = \left(\dfrac{1}{5}\right)^2 = \dfrac{1}{25}$

(24.28). If two regular polygons have the same number of sides, find the area of the smaller if the sides have length 4 and 12 and the area of the larger is 10,260.

Solution

$$\frac{A_1}{A_2} = \left(\frac{S_1}{S_2}\right)^2 \rightarrow \frac{A_1}{10,260} = \left(\frac{4}{12}\right)^2 \rightarrow A_1 = \frac{10,260 \times 16}{144} = 1140$$

(24.29). In a circle find the circumference and area if the radius is 6

Solution

With $r = 6$. $C = 2\pi r = 12\pi$ and $A = \pi r^2 = 36\pi = 36(3.14) = 113$

(24.30). In a circle find the radius and area if the circumference 18π

Solution

$from\ C = 2\pi r \rightarrow 18\pi = 2\pi\ \therefore\ r = 9.\ thus\ A = \pi r^2 \rightarrow 81\pi = 254$

(24.31). In a circle find the radius and circumference if area is 144π

Solution

$A = \pi r^2 \rightarrow 144\pi = \pi r^2\ \therefore\ r = 12,\ Also\ C = 2\pi r = 24\pi = 75$

(24.32). If the circumferences of two circles are in the ratio of 2:3, find the ratio of the diameters and the ratio of the areas.

Solution

$\frac{D_1}{D_2} = \frac{C_1}{C_2} \rightarrow \frac{2}{3}$ Also $\frac{A_1}{A_2} = \left(\frac{C_1}{C_2}\right)^2 \rightarrow \frac{A_1}{A_2} = \left(\frac{2}{3}\right)^2 = \frac{4}{9}$

(24.33). If the areas of two circles are in the ratio 1:25, find the ratio of the diameters and the ratio of the circumferences.

Solution

$\frac{A_1}{A_2} = \left(\frac{D_1}{D_2}\right)^2 \rightarrow \frac{1}{25} = \left(\frac{D_1}{D_2}\right)^2 \rightarrow \frac{D_1}{D_2} = \frac{1}{5}$

Also $\frac{D_1}{D_2} = \frac{C_1}{C_2} \rightarrow \frac{1}{5} = \frac{C_1}{C_2}$

(24.34).

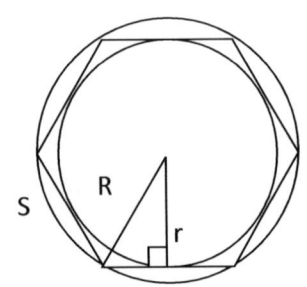

Find the circumference and area of the circumscribed circle and inscribed circle of a regular hexagon whose side has length 8

Solution

For the circumscribed use R and inscribed we use r. whose relations have been discussed earlier.

Here $R = s = 8$

From $C = 2\pi R \rightarrow 2\pi(8) = 16\pi, A = \pi R^2 = 64\pi, r = \frac{1}{2}R\sqrt{3} = 4\sqrt{3}$.

$\therefore C = 2\pi r = 8\pi\sqrt{3}$ and $A = \pi r^2$

(**24.33**).

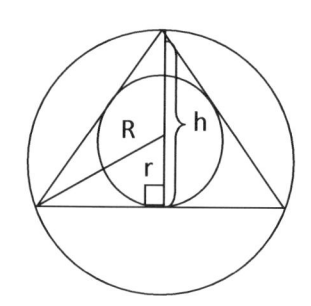

Find the circumference and area of the circumscribed circle and inscribed circle of an equilateral triangle whose altitude has length $9\sqrt{3}$.

Solution

Here $R = \frac{2}{3}h = 6\sqrt{3}$.

$C = 2\pi R \rightarrow 2\pi(6\sqrt{3}) = 12\pi\sqrt{3}, A = \pi R^2 \rightarrow \pi(6\sqrt{3})^2 = 108\pi$

$r = \frac{1}{3}h \rightarrow \frac{1}{3}(9\sqrt{3}) = 3\sqrt{3}$

$C = 2\pi r \rightarrow 6\pi\sqrt{3}$ and $A = \pi r^2 = 27\pi$

(**24.34**). Find the length of a 36 arc in a circle whose circumference is 45π

Solution

$n = 36, C = 2\pi r = 45\pi$

$l = \dfrac{n}{360} \times 2\pi r \rightarrow \dfrac{36}{360} \times 45\pi = \dfrac{9}{2}\pi$

(24.35). Find the radius of a circle if a 40 arc has a length of 4π

$l = 4\pi, n = 40$

$l = \dfrac{n}{360} \times 2\pi r \rightarrow 4\pi = \dfrac{40}{360} \times 2\pi r \rightarrow r = 18$

(24.36). Find the area of A of a 300^0 sector of a circle whose radius is 12.

Solution

$n = 300, r = 12$

$A = \dfrac{n}{360} \times \pi r^2 \rightarrow \dfrac{300}{360} \times 144\pi = 120\pi$

(24.37). Find the measure of the central angle of a sector whose area is 6π if the area of the circle is 9π.

Solution

$\dfrac{Area\ of\ sector}{Area\ of\ circle} = \dfrac{n}{360} \rightarrow \dfrac{6\pi}{9\pi} = \dfrac{n}{360} \rightarrow n = 240^0.$

(24.38). Find the radius of a circle if an arc of length 2π has a sector of area 10π

Solution

$\dfrac{Length\ of\ arc}{circumference} = \dfrac{area\ of\ sector}{area\ of\ circle} \rightarrow \dfrac{2\pi}{2\pi r} = \dfrac{10\pi}{\pi r^2} \rightarrow r = 10$

(24.39). Find the area of a segment if its central angle measures 60^0 and the radius of the circle is 12.

Solution

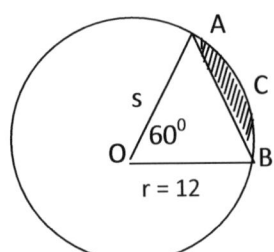

For central angle, radius = r

Given $n = 60, r = 12$

Area of sector $OAB = \frac{n}{360} \times \pi r^2 \rightarrow \frac{60}{360} \times 144\pi = 24\pi$

Area of equilateral $\Delta OAB = \frac{1}{4}s^2\sqrt{3} \rightarrow \frac{1}{4}(144)\sqrt{3} = 36\sqrt{3}$

Area of segment = Area of sector − Area of triangle formed

∴ Area of segment ACB = $24\pi - 36\sqrt{3}$

(24.40). Find the area of a segment it its central angle measures 90^0 and the radius of the circle is 8.

Solution

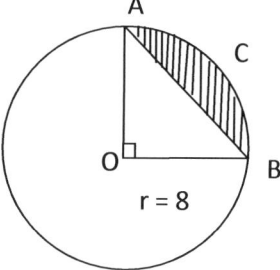

For central angle, radius = r = 8, $n = 90$, triangle formed is right angled

Area of sector $\Delta OAB = \frac{n}{360} \times \pi r^2 \rightarrow \frac{90}{360} \times 64\pi = 16\pi$

Area of right $\Delta OAB = \frac{1}{2}bh \rightarrow \frac{1}{2}(8)(8) = 32$

Area of segment = Area of sector − Area of triagle formed

Area of segment ACB = $16\pi - 32$.

(24.41). Find each segment formed by an inscribed equilateral triangle if the radius of the circle is 8.

Solution

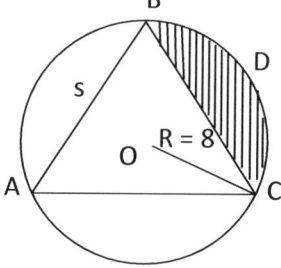

For non-central angle, radius = R = 8, triangle formed is equilateral

With s = $R\sqrt{3} = 8\sqrt{3}$

Area of ΔABC is $\frac{1}{4}s^2\sqrt{3} \rightarrow \frac{1}{4}(8\sqrt{3})^2 . \sqrt{3} = 48\sqrt{3}$

325

Area of circle O = πR^2 → $\pi(8^2) = 64\pi$

Area of segment = $\dfrac{Area\ of\ sector\ -\ Area\ of\ triagle\ formed}{no\ of\ sides}$

Area of segment BDC = $\dfrac{1}{3}(64\pi - 48\sqrt{3})$

(24.42).

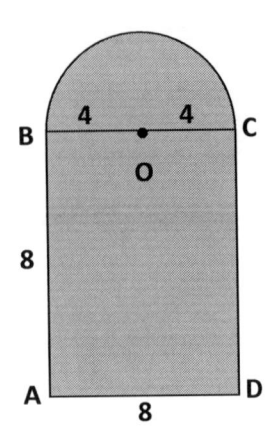

The shaded area in the figure above equals?

Solution

Shaded area = Area of square + Area of semicircle

$l^2 + \dfrac{1}{2}\pi r^2$ → $8^2 + \dfrac{1}{2}(16\pi)$ → $64 + 8\pi$

(24.43). In the figure below, the area of the shaded segment is?

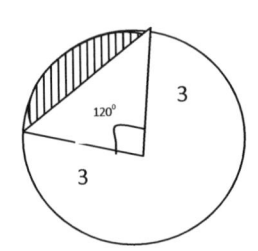

Solution

Area of sector = $\dfrac{\theta}{360} \times \pi r^2$ → $\dfrac{120}{360} \times \pi(3^2) = 3\pi$

Area of triangle = $\dfrac{1}{2}ab\sin\theta$ → $\dfrac{1}{2} \times 3 \times 3 \sin 120$ → $\dfrac{9}{2}\sin 60$ → $\dfrac{9}{2} \cdot \dfrac{\sqrt{3}}{2} = \dfrac{9\sqrt{3}}{4}$

Area of sector – Area of triangle

∴ Area of shaded segment = $3\pi - \dfrac{9\sqrt{3}}{4} = 3\left(\pi - \dfrac{3\sqrt{3}}{4}\right)$

(24.44). What is the area between two concentric circles of diameters 26cm and 20 cm?

Solution

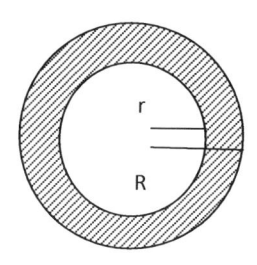

D = 26 cm, R = 13 cm, d = 20 cm, r = 10 cm

Area = area of big circle – area of small circle → $\pi R^2 - \pi r^2 = \pi(R^2 - r^2)$

Area = $\pi(13^2 - 10^2)$ → $\pi(169 - 100) = 69\pi$

(24.45).

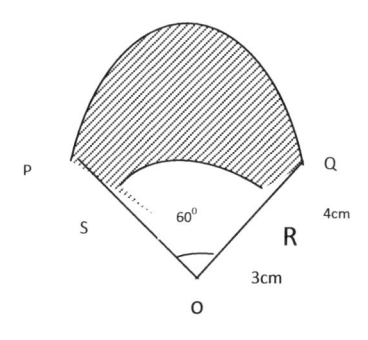

The figure is a sector of two concentric circles centre O. QR = 4cm, RO = 3cm and angle SOR = 60^0. Calculate the area of the shaded portion

Solution

radius of small sector = OR = 3cm

radius of big sector = OQ = 3 + 7 = 7cm

∴ Area of shaded portion = $\frac{\theta}{360} \times \pi R^2 - \frac{\theta}{360} \times \pi r^2$ → $\frac{60}{360} \times \pi(7^2 - 3^2)$

$\frac{1}{6}\pi(49 - 9)$ → $\frac{1}{6}\pi \times 40 = \frac{20\pi}{3}$ cm^2

(24.46).

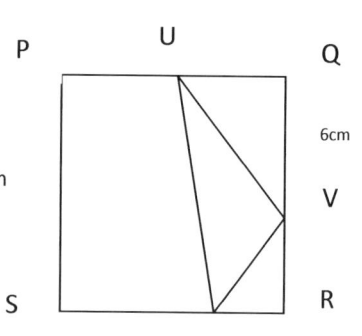

327

In figure, PQRS is a square of side 8 cm. what is the area of triangle UVW?

Solution

SW = 8 – 2 = 6cm, PU = 8 – 4 = 4cm, VR = 8 – 6 = 2cm

Area of square = 8 x 8 = 64 cm²

Area of PUWS = area of trapezium → ½ (PU + SW)PS → ½ (4 + 6) 8 = 40 cm²

Area of triangle QUV = ½bh → ½ x 4 x 6 = 12cm²

Area of triangle VWR = ½bh → ½ x 2 x 2 = 2cm²

Area of triangle UVW = Area of square – Area PUWS – Area QUV – Area VWR

Area or triangle UVW = 64 – 40 – 12 – 2 = 10cm²

(24.47). A rectangular picture 6 cm by 8cm is enclosed by a frame ½ cm wide. Calculate the area of the frame.

Solution

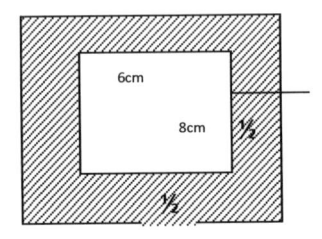

Length of the frame = 8 + ½ + ½ = 9cm

Breadth of the frame = 6 + ½ + ½ = 7 cm

Total area(frame + picture) = L x B = 9 x 7 = 63cm²

Area of picture only = 6 x 8 = 48 cm²

Since Total Area = Area of frame + Area of picture

∴ Area of frame = 63 − 48 = 15cm²

(24.48). If a circular paper disc trimmed in such a way that its circumference is reduced in the ratio 2: 5, in what ratio is the surface area reduced?

Solution

$\frac{A_1}{A_2} = \left(\frac{C_1}{C_2}\right)^2 \rightarrow \frac{A_1}{A_2} = \left(\frac{2}{5}\right)^2 = \frac{4}{25}$

$A_1 : A_2 = 4 : 25$

(24.49).

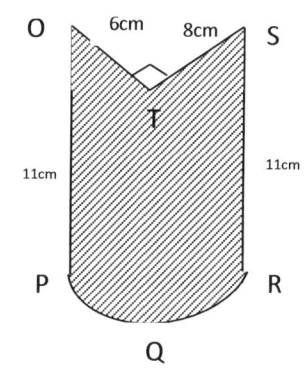

In figure above, PQR is a semicircle, calculate the area of the shaded region.

Solution

We simply complete the diagram as shown

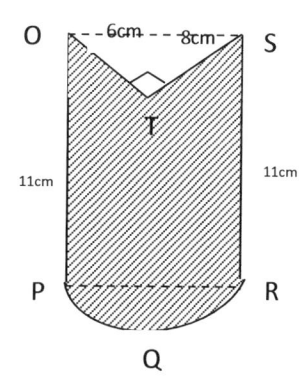

By Pythagoras's $OS^2 = 6^2 + 8^2 \rightarrow OS = \sqrt{36 + 64} = \sqrt{100} = 10 cm$

Area of the rectangle = $l \times b \rightarrow$ 11 x 10 = 110

329

Area of the triangle = $\frac{1}{2}$ bh → $\frac{1}{2}$ x 8 x 6 = 24cm²

Shade area in rectangle = area of rectangle – area of triangle = 110 – 24 = 86

Area of semicircle = $\frac{1}{2}\pi r^2$ = $\frac{1}{2}\pi\left[\frac{d}{2}\right]^2$ → $\frac{\pi d^2}{8}$ → $\frac{22}{7}$ x $\frac{10^2}{8}$ = $\frac{22}{7}$ x $\frac{100}{8}$ = $\frac{275}{7}$

Total Shaded area = 86 + $39\frac{2}{7}$ = $125\frac{2}{7}$ cm²

(24.50). Two distinct sectors in the same circle, subtending 100⁰ and 30⁰ respectively at the centre of the circle. Their corresponding arcs are in the ratio?

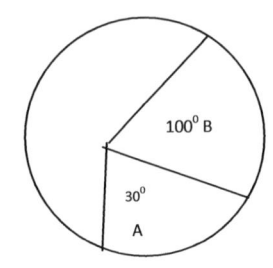

In B, arc length = $\frac{\theta}{360}$ x 2πr → $\frac{100}{360}$ x 2πr = $\frac{10}{18}\pi r$

In A, arc length = $\frac{\theta}{360}$ x 2πr → $\frac{30}{360}$ x 2πr = $\frac{\pi r}{6}$

Ratio of arc B to A → $\frac{10\pi r}{18}$: $\frac{\pi r}{6}$ → 60πr : 18πr = 10 : 3

(24.51).

In the figure, PQRS is a rectangle. If the shaded area is 72 sq cm. Find h

Solution

Area of rectangle PQRS = L x B → 2h x 3h = 6h²

Area of the unshaded rectangle = (3h – 2)(2h – 4)

Shaded area = Area of rectangle PQRS – Area of unshaded part

330

$72 = 6h^2 - (3h-2)(2h-4) \rightarrow 72 = 6h^2 - (6h^2 - 12h - 4h + 8)$

$72 = 6h^2 - 6h^2 + 12h + 4h - 8 \rightarrow 72 = 16h - 8 \rightarrow 16h = 72 + 8 = 80$

$\therefore$ $h = \frac{80}{16} = 5$cm

CHAPTER 25 ANALYTICAL GEOMETRY 1: STRAIGHT LINE

This is an aspect of Geometry that deals with points and lines joining them. The position of a point in a plane is given by its coordinates (x, y). The x-coordinate is called abscissa and the y-coordinate ordinate.

(1) Distance between two points in an euclidean plane

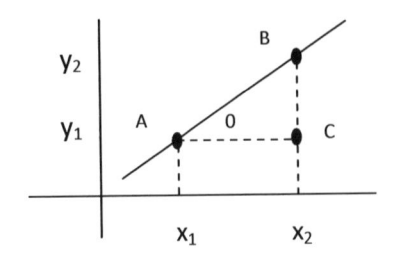

Given two points A (x_1, y_1) and B (x_2, y_2) in the x-y coordinate axis, the distance between the two points is derived as follows

By applying Pythagoras theorem to the right angle triangle above (ABC), we obtain $AB^2 = AN^2 + BN^2$

With $BC = y_2 - y_1$ and $AC = x_2 - x_1$

Distance between A and B = length $AB = (x_2 - x_1)^2 + (y_2 - y_1)^2$

$$\therefore AB = \sqrt{(x_2 - x_1)^2 + (y_2 - y_1)^2}$$

(2) Distance from the origin

From the above analysis, it follows that the distance between the origin (0,0) and the point (x_1, y_1) is $\sqrt{x_1^2 + y_1^2}$

(3) Midpoint of a line segment:

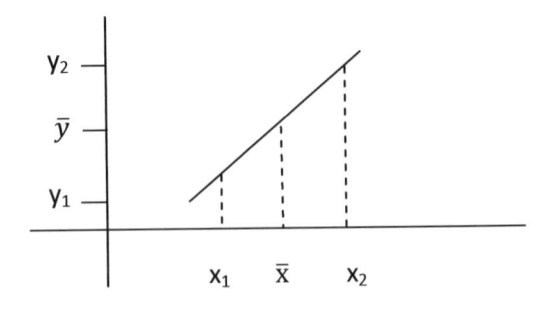

From the diagram above $\bar{y}$ and $\bar{x}$ are midpoints of the line joining the points

∴ Midpoint $= M(\bar{x}, \bar{y}) = \left[\dfrac{x_1 + x_2}{2}, \dfrac{y_1 + y_2}{2}\right]$

(4) Gradient of a line

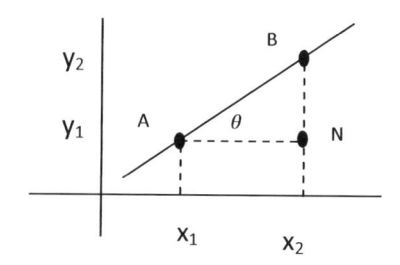

From the diagram above Gradient of a line is defined as $\dfrac{\text{change in y}}{\text{change in x}}$

∴ Gradient or slope (m) $= \dfrac{BN}{AN} = \dfrac{y_2 - y_1}{x_2 - x_1} = \tan\theta$

Hence, the slope or gradient can also be regarded as the tangent of the inclination angle to the horizontal. If $\tan\theta$ is negative, it implies that the gradient is negative.

(5) Equation of a straight line: Equation of a straight line can be found given necessary conditions, they include

(i) Gradient / intercept form: This is given by $y = mx + c$

where m = gradient, c = intercept on y axis

or $y = mx$ when there is no intercept on y-axis

Graphical representation of both equation is as shown

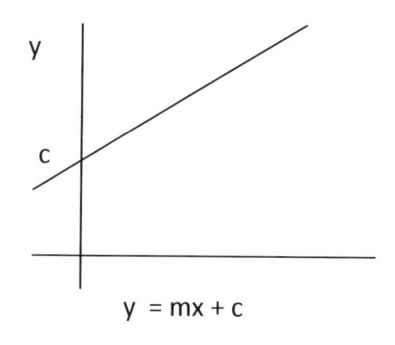

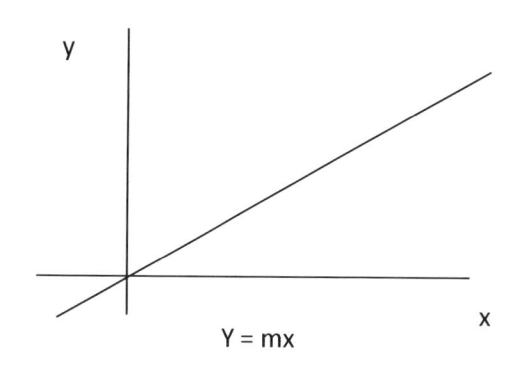

(*ii*) Gradient and a point on a line: When a point (x_1, y_1) and gradient is given, it becomes $y - y_1 = m(x - x_1)$

(*iii*) Gradient and two points on a line: When two points (x_1, y_1) and (x_2, y_2) and gradient are given. In this case, we transform the equation of a straight line to

$$y - y_1 = \frac{y_2 - y_1}{x_2 - x_1}(x - x_1)$$

Note: Under examination condition do not bother solving as…

The equation of a line passing through two points (x_1, y_1) and B (x_1, y_2) is equal to x_1

The equation of a line passing through two points (x_1, y_1) and B (x_2, y_1) is equal to y_1

(*iv*) Intercept and angle of slope: With the intercept on the y-axis and angle of slope given, the equation becomes

$$y = x\tan\theta + x$$

(*v*) Double intercept form: When the intercepts on the two axes are given. In this case from $ax + by - ab = 0$

dividing through by ab gives $\frac{ax}{ab} + \frac{by}{ab} = \frac{ab}{ab}$

$$\therefore \frac{x}{b} + \frac{y}{a} = 1$$

Where b = intercept on x-axis, a = intercept on y-axis

(*vi*) Intercept and angle of slope

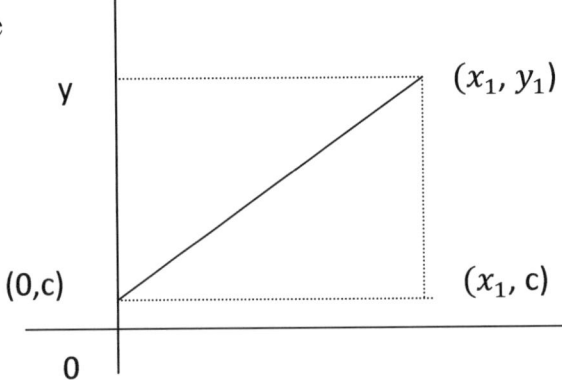

From the diagram $m = \frac{y_1 - c}{x_1 - 0} = \frac{y_1 - c}{x_1}$

$\frac{y - y_1}{x - x_1} = \frac{y_1 - c}{x_1}$

(6) Intersection of straight lines

To get the point of intersection between two lines simply solve the given equations simultaneously.

(7) Collinear points: Three or more points are collinear when they lie on the same line. To test for collinearity, the gradients between adjacent pair of points are found.

Also if the three points are collinear, then the area of the triangle is zero.

(8) Parallelism and perpendicularity of lines: The conditions for parallelism and perpendicularity is given by

Parallelism: $m_1 = m_2$

Perpendicularity: $m_1 m_2 = -1$

(9) Distance of a point from a straight line:

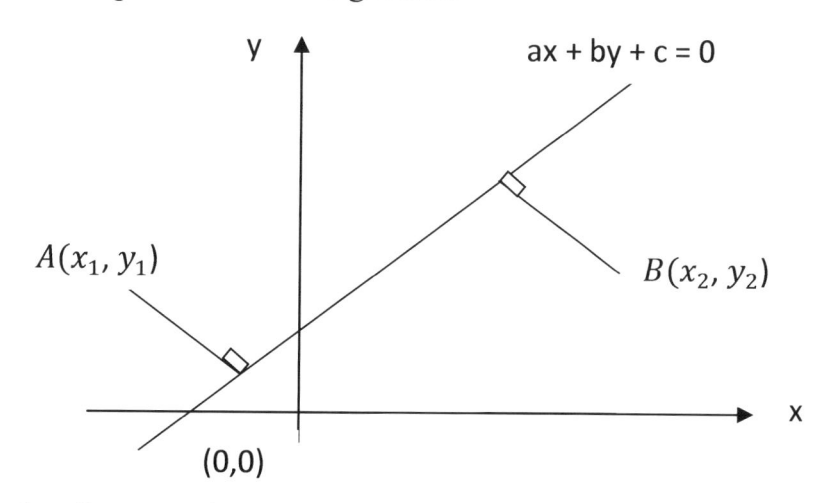

Perpendicular distance of a point (x_1, y_1) from a line $ax + by + c = 0$ is given by

$d = \frac{ax_1 + by_1 + c}{\pm\sqrt{a^2 + b^2}}$

Note: The sign of the root is same as the sign of the constant term (c)

If the distance from the origin to a straight line is required, set $(x_1, y_1) = (0,0)$.

If the distance is found to be zero, then the point is said to lie on the line

Two points are said to be on the same side of the line if the sign of the distance obtained with one point is the same with that of another given point

Two points are said to be on the opposite side of the line if the sign of the distance obtained with one point is not the same with that of another given point.

If the distance between two straight lines is required, the difference between the distances from the origin is calculated.

(10) Angle between two lines: The angle between two lines $y_1 = m_1 x + c$ and $y_2 = m_2 x + c$ is given by

$$tan\theta = \left|\frac{m_2 - m_1}{1 + m_2 m_1}\right|$$

Where m_2 and m_1 are the gradients of the two lines

(11) Locus of points: The path traced out by a moving point P in a plane is usually determined by the relationship that exists between its x and y coordinates. Such a path gives the locus of the point.

Given two points A (x_1, y_1) and B (x_2, y_2) the equation of the perpendicular bisector of the line AB is given by

$$(x - x_1)^2 + (y - y_1)^2 = (x - x_2)^2 (y - y_2)^2$$

(12) Division of a line into a given ratio

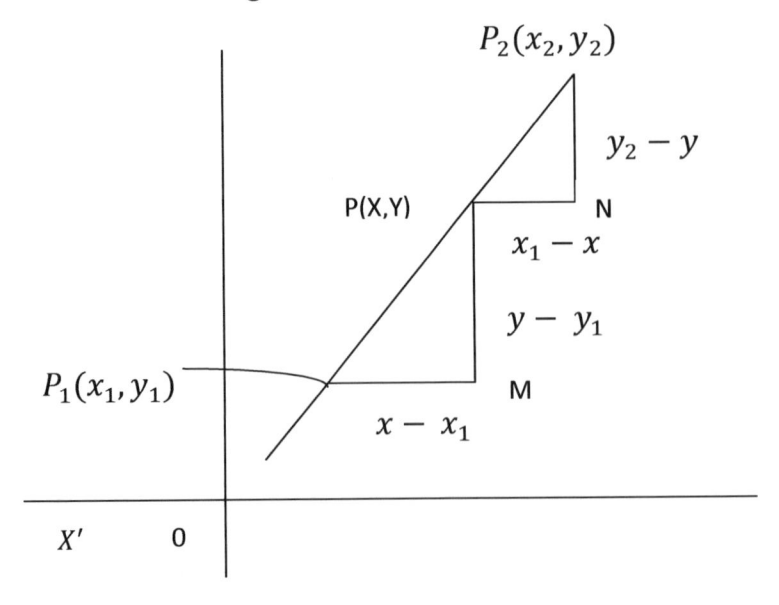

The coordinate of the point(x, y) which divides a line joining (x_1, y_1) and (x_2, y_2) in the ratio m: n is given by

$$(x, y) = \left[\frac{mx_2 + nx_1}{m + n}, \frac{my_2 + ny_1}{m + n}\right]$$

(13) Area of any polygon whose vertices are given: For any polygon whose vertices are given as $(x_1, y_1), (x_2, y_2), (x_3, y_3), (x_4, y_4) \ldots (x_n, y_n)$. The area can be found from

$$A = \frac{1}{2}\begin{bmatrix} x_1 & y_1 \\ x_2 & y_2 \\ x_3 & y_3 \\ x_3 & y_3 \\ \cdot & \cdot \\ \cdot & \cdot \\ x_1 & y_1 \end{bmatrix} \rightarrow \frac{1}{2}[x_1y_2 - x_2y_1 + x_2y_3 - x_3y_2 + x_3y_1 - x_1y_3 \ldots]$$

Note: This formula gives the area if and only if the vertices are arranged in an anticlockwise manner.

QUESTIONS

(25. 1). Determine whether the points (3, -1) and (2, 4) are on the same side of the straight line $y = 2x - 6$ and determine their respective distances.

Solution

From $y = 2x - 6 \rightarrow 2x - y - 6 = 0$ ∴ a = 2, b = -1, c = -6

For (3, -1) → x = 3, y = -1

From $d = \frac{ax_1 + by_1 + c}{\sqrt{a^2 + b^2}} \rightarrow \frac{2(3) + -1(-1) + -6}{\sqrt{2^2 + (-1)^2}} \rightarrow \frac{6 + 1 - 6}{\sqrt{5}} \rightarrow \frac{-1}{\sqrt{5}} \rightarrow \frac{-1}{\sqrt{5}} \cdot \frac{\sqrt{5}}{\sqrt{5}} = \frac{-\sqrt{5}}{5}$

For (2, 4) → x = 2, y = 4

$d = \frac{2(2) + -1(4) + -6}{-\sqrt{2^2 + (-1)^2}} \rightarrow \frac{4 - 4 - 6}{-\sqrt{5}} \rightarrow \frac{-6}{-\sqrt{5}} \rightarrow \frac{6}{\sqrt{5}} \cdot \frac{\sqrt{5}}{\sqrt{5}} = \frac{6\sqrt{5}}{5}$

With d_1 negative and d_2 positive, the points are on the opposite side of the straight line

(25. 2). Find the perpendicular distance between the point (-3, 7) and the line joining the points (2, -4) and (-6, 2).

Solution

For line joining the points (2, -4) and (-6, 2)

From $y - y_1 = \frac{y_2 - y_1}{x_2 - x_1}(x - x_1) \rightarrow y - -4 = \frac{2-(-4)}{-6-2}(x-2)$

$y + 4 = \frac{-6}{8}(x - 2) \rightarrow 8(y + 4) = -6(x - 2) \rightarrow 8y + 32 = -6x + 12$

$6x + 8y + 32 - 12 = 0 \rightarrow 6x + 8y + 20 = 0$

The distance between the point (- 3, 7) and $6x + 8y + 20 = 0$ is given by

$d = \frac{ax_1 + by_1 + c}{\pm\sqrt{a^2 + b^2}} \rightarrow \frac{6(-3) + 8(7) + 20}{+\sqrt{6^2 + 8^2}} \rightarrow \frac{-18 + 56 + 20}{\sqrt{100}} = \frac{58}{10}$

(25.3). Find the distance between the two parallel lines.

$3x - 4y + 12 = 0$ and $3x - 4y + 2 = 0$

Solution

This is found as the difference between the distances from the origin

$3x - 4y + 12 = 0$ from the origin (0, 0)

$d_1 = \frac{3(0) + -4(0) + 12}{+\sqrt{3^2 + 4^2}} = \frac{12}{\sqrt{25}} = \frac{12}{5}$

$3x - 4y + 2 = 0$ from the origin (0, 0)

$d_2 = \frac{3(0) + -4(0) + 2}{+\sqrt{3^2 + 4^2}} = \frac{2}{\sqrt{25}} = \frac{2}{5}$

distance between $3x - 4y + 12 = 0$ and

$3x - 4y + 2 = 0$ is $\frac{12}{5} - \frac{2}{5} = \frac{10}{5} = 2$

(25.4). What are the co-ordinates of the point x that divides the line segment PQ internally in the ration 3 : 2 where P is (-1, -1) and Q is at (-3, -4) ?

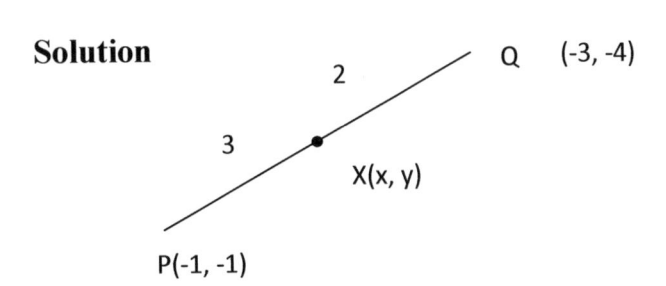

Solution

$$X(x,y) = \frac{3(-3,-4)+2(-1,-1)}{3+2} \rightarrow \frac{(-9-12)+(-2,-2)}{5} \rightarrow \frac{(-11,-14)}{5} = \left(-\frac{11}{5}, -\frac{14}{5}\right)$$

(25.5). What is the equation of the perpendicular bisector of the line segment through the points (a, 6) and (a, 8)?

Solution

Perpendicular bisector is a locus of a point which moves so that it is equidistant from two given points

thus, if C is point between A and B, then

AC = CB

∴ for A(a, 6), (Cx, y), B (a, 8)

$(x-a)^2 + (y-6)^2 = (a-x)^2 + (8-y)^2$

$x^2 - 2ax + a^2 + y^2 - 12y + 36 = a^2 - 2ax + x^2 + 64 - 16y + y^2$

$-12y + 16y + 36 - 64 = 0 \rightarrow 4y - 28 = 0 \quad y - 7 = 0$

(25.6). $3y = 4x - 1$ and $ky = x + 3$ are equations of two straight lines. If the two lines are perpendicular to each other, find k

Solution

From $3y = 4x - 1 \rightarrow y = \frac{4x}{3} - \frac{1}{3}, \quad m_1 = \frac{4}{3}$

From $ky = x + 3 \rightarrow y = \frac{1x}{k} + \frac{3}{k} \quad m_2 = \frac{1}{k}$

For perpendicularity, $m_1 m_2 = -1$

$\frac{4(1)}{3k} = -1, \rightarrow k = \frac{-4}{3}$

(25.7) The midpoint of the segment of the line y = 4x + 3 which lies between the x-axis and the y-axis is.

Solution

From y = 4x + 3 when x = 0 → y = 3 when y = 0 → x = -3/4

Mid point = $\frac{-3/4}{2}, \frac{3}{2}$ → $\left(\frac{-3}{8}, \frac{3}{2}\right)$

(25.8) The angle between the positive horizontal axis and a given line is 135^0. Find the equation of the line if it passes through the point (2, 3)

Solution

Gradient = tan θ → tan 135^0 → tan (180 – 135) → - tan 45^0

with point (2,3)

From y – y_1 = m(x – x_1)

y – 3 = -1(x – 2) → y – 3 = - x + 2 → y + x = 2 + 3 ∴ y + x = 5

(25.9) Find the distance between points Q(4,3) and the point common to the lines.

2x – y = 4 and x + y = 2

Solution

From x + y = 2 → y = 2 – x

Inserting into 2x – y = 4

2x – 2 + x = 4 → 3x = 6 ∴ x = 2

Substituting x in 2x – y = 4 → 2(2) – y = 4 → 4 – y = 4

Thus, the distance between (4, 3) and (2, 0) is given by

d = $\sqrt{(2-4)^2 + (0-3)^2}$ → $\sqrt{4+9}$ = $\sqrt{13}$

(25.10) If the distance between the points (x, 3) and (-x, 2) is 5. Find x.

Solution

d = $\sqrt{(-x-x)^2 + (2-3)^2}$ = 5 → $(-2x)^2 + (-1)^2 = 5^2$

$4x^2 + 1 = 25$ → $4x^2 = 25 - 1$ → $x^2 = 6$ ∴ x = $\sqrt{6}$

(25.11). Find the equation of the locus of a point which moves so that it is always at a distance of 2 units from the line 5x + 12y – 2 = 0.

Solution

The locus is a line parallel to the given line

For parallel line $m_1 = m_2$

$2 = \frac{5x+12y-2}{\sqrt{5^2+12^2}} \rightarrow 2 = \frac{5x+12y-2}{\pm 13} \rightarrow 5x+12y-2 = \pm 26$

5x + 12y - 2 = 26 or 5x + 12y – 2 = - 26

5x + 12y – 2 – 26 = 0 or 5x + 12y – 2 + 26 = 0

∴ 5x + 12y − 28 = 0 or 5x + 12y + 24 = 0

(25.12). Find the equation of a line which is parallel to x + 2y -4 = 0 and passes through point (4, -3).

Solution

From x + 2y – 4 = 0 $\rightarrow$ 2y = - x + 4 $\rightarrow$ $y = \frac{-x}{2} + 2$ ∴ $m = \frac{-1}{2}$

A line with $m = \frac{-1}{2}$ and passes through (4, -3)

From $y - y_1 = m(x - x_1)$ $\rightarrow$ $y - -3 = -\frac{1}{2}(x-4)$ $\rightarrow$ $-2(y+3) = x-4$

- 2y – 6 = x – 4 $\rightarrow$ x + 2y – 4 + 6 = 0 ∴ x + 2y + 2 = 0

(25.13). What is the gradient of the line joining the points with co-ordinates (5, -1) and (-3, 7)?

Solution

$m = \frac{y_2 - y_1}{x_2 - x_1} \rightarrow \frac{7--1}{-3-5} \rightarrow \frac{7+1}{-8} = -1$

(25.14). What is the distance between the points (3, -2) and (8,10).

Solution

$$d = \sqrt{(x_2 - x_1)^2 + (y_2 - y_1)^2} \rightarrow \sqrt{(8-3)^2 + (10--2)^2}$$

$$\sqrt{5^2 + 12^2} \rightarrow \sqrt{25 + 144} \rightarrow \sqrt{169} = 13$$

(25.14). The midpoint of the line joining the points x(4,2) and y(-5, 0) is.

Solution

Mid point $= (\bar{x}, \bar{y}) = \left(\frac{x_1+x_2}{2}, \frac{y_1+y_2}{2}\right)$

$(\bar{x}, \bar{y}) = \left(\frac{4+-5}{2}, \frac{2+0}{2}\right) \rightarrow \left(-\frac{1}{2}, \frac{2}{2}\right) = \left(-\frac{1}{2}, 1\right)$

(25.15). Given that the line $ax + 4y - 5 = 0$ is perpendicular to the line $4x - 2y + 6 = 0$, find the value of a.

Solution

From $ax + 4y - 5 = 0 \rightarrow 4y = -ax + 5 \rightarrow y = -\frac{ax}{4} + \frac{5}{4} \therefore m = -\frac{a}{4}$

From $4x - 2y + 6 = 0 \rightarrow 2y = 4x + 6 \rightarrow y = 2x + 3 \therefore m = 2$

For perpendicularity, $m_1 m_2 = -1 \rightarrow -\frac{a}{2}(2) = -1 \therefore a = 2$

(25.16). The equation of a straight line with gradient $\frac{1}{3}$ which passes through the point (1, 2) is?

Solution

From $y - y_1 = m(x - x_1) \rightarrow y - 2 = \frac{1}{3}(x - 1) \rightarrow 3(y - 2) = x - 1$

$3y - 6 = x - 1 \rightarrow x - 3y + 5 = 0$

(25.17). The intercept which the line $2x - 3y - 5 = 0$ makes with the y-axis is of length?

Solution

From $2x - 3y - 5 = 0 \rightarrow 3y = 2x - 5 \rightarrow y = \frac{2x}{3} - \frac{5}{3}$

Comparing with $y = mx + c$ ∴ The intercept (c) $= -\frac{5}{3}$

Length of c = $|c| = \frac{5}{3}$

(25.18). What is the equation of line which makes intercepts of 2 and 3 on the x and y axes respectively?

Solution

For double intercepts, $\frac{x}{a} + \frac{y}{b} = 1$

∴ $\frac{x}{2} + \frac{y}{3} = 1 \rightarrow 6\left(\frac{x}{2}\right) + 6\left(\frac{y}{3}\right) = 6(1) \rightarrow 3x + 2y = 6$

(25.19).

The equation of the line in the graph is?

Solution

For double intercepts $\frac{x}{a} + \frac{y}{b} = 1 \rightarrow \frac{x}{3} + \frac{y}{4} = 1$

$12\left(\frac{x}{3}\right) + 12\left(\frac{y}{4}\right) = 12(1) \rightarrow 4x + 3y = 12$ ∴ $3y = -4x + 12$

(25.20). If M(4,Q) is the midpoint of the line joining L(P, -2) and N(Q.P) find the values of p and q.

Solution

Midpoint of L(P, - 2) and N(Q, P) = $\left(\frac{P+Q}{2}, \frac{-2+P}{2}\right)$

343

But midpoint = (4,8)

$\frac{P+Q}{2} = 4$ and $\frac{-2+p}{2} = q$

From both equations

P + q = 8 ......(i)
P – 2q = 2 ....(ii)
3q = 6 → q = 2
From (i) p + 2 = 8 → p = 8 – 2 = 6
∴ (p, q) = (6, 2)

(25.21). Find the equation of line through the point (1, 2) and parallel to the line 4x – y = 2.

Solution

From 4x – y = 2 → y = 4x – 2 ∴ m = 4

For parallelism, $m_1 = m_2 = m$

∴ gradient of the line through the point (1,2) is 4

From $y - y_1 = m(x - x_1)$ → y - 2 = 4(x – 1) → y – 2 = 4x – 4 → y – 4x – 2 + 4 = 0

∴ y – 4x + 2 = 0

(25.22). Find the equation of the line through (1, 1) perpendicular to 2x – 3y = 4.

Solution

From 2x – 3y = 4 → 3y = 2x + 4 → $y = \frac{2x}{3} - \frac{4}{3}$ ∴ $m = \frac{2}{3}$

For perpendicularity $m_1 m = -1$ → $m_1 = -\frac{1}{m} = -\frac{1}{\frac{2}{3}} = -\frac{3}{2}$

The gradient of the line with point (1,1) is $-\frac{3}{2}$

From $y - y_1 = m(x - x_1)$ → $y - 1 = -\frac{3}{2}(x - 1)$ → 2y – 2 = - 3x + 3

2y + 3x = 3 + 2 → 2y + 3x = 5

(25.23). If the vertices of a triangle PQR are P(2,3), Q(4,7) and R(-2, 1), find the gradient of the altitude to the side QR.

Solution

Gradient = $m = \dfrac{y_2 - y_1}{x_2 - x_1}$

For side QR → $m = \dfrac{1 - 7}{-2 - 4} = \dfrac{-6}{-6} = 1$

Altitude to the side QR is a line perpendicular to QR.

Thus for perpendicularity $mm_2 = -1$

$m_2 = \dfrac{-1}{m} = \dfrac{-1}{1} = -1$

(25.24). Find the equation of the line perpendicular to $2y + 3x - 4 = 0$ and passes through the point (2, -5).

Solution

From $2y + 3x - 4 = 0$ → $2y = -3x + 4$ → $y = \dfrac{-3}{2}x + 2$ ∴ $m = \dfrac{-3}{2}$

For perpendicularity $m \cdot m_2 = -1$

$m_2 = \dfrac{-1}{m} = \dfrac{-1}{-3/2} = \dfrac{2}{3}$

The line thus has gradient $\dfrac{2}{3}$ and passes through (2, -5)

From $y - y_1 = m(x - x_1)$ → $y - -5 = \dfrac{2}{3}(x - 2)$ → $3y + 15 = 2x - 4$

$3y - 2x + 15 + 4 = 0$ → $3y - 2x + 19 = 0$

(25.25). What is the perpendicular distance of a point (2, 3) from the line $2x - 4y + 3 = 0$?

Solution

$(x_1, y_1) = (2,3)$, $(a, b) = (2, -4)$

$d = \dfrac{ax_1 + by_1 + c}{\sqrt{a^2 + b^2}}$ → $\dfrac{2(2) + -4(3) + 3}{\sqrt{2^2 + (-4)^2}}$ → $\dfrac{4 - 12 + 3}{\sqrt{20}}$ → $\dfrac{-5}{\sqrt{20}}$ → $\dfrac{-5}{\sqrt{20}} \cdot \dfrac{\sqrt{20}}{\sqrt{20}} = \dfrac{-5\sqrt{4 \times 5}}{20}$

345

$$\frac{-5 \times 2\sqrt{5}}{20} = \frac{-\sqrt{5}}{2}$$

The distance is $\frac{\sqrt{5}}{2}$ from the line opposite to it

(25.26). Find the coordinate of the points at which lines $4y = 3x + 2$ and $8y = 9x - 5$ intersect.

Solution

For intersection, solve both equations simultaneously. This gives $(x, y) = 3, 2\frac{3}{4}$

(25.27). Two perpendicular PQ and QR intersect at (1, -1). If the equation of PQ is $x - 2y + 4 = 0$, Find the equation of QR.

Solution

From $x - 2y + 4 = 0 \rightarrow 2y = x + 4 \rightarrow y = \frac{1}{2}x + 2$

For PQ, $m = \frac{1}{2}$

As QR is perpendicular to PQ $m_1 m_2 = -1$ holds

$m_2 = -\frac{1}{m_1}$ $\therefore m(QR) = \frac{-1}{1/2} = -2$

The equation thus passes through (1, -1) and $m = -2$

$y - y_1 = m(x - x_1) \rightarrow y - -1 = -2(x - 1) \rightarrow y + 1 = -2x + 2$

$2x + y + 1 - 2 = 0 \rightarrow 2x + y - 1 = 0$

(25.28). The distance between (a + b, a - b) and (b - a, a + b) is ?

Solution

$d = \sqrt{[(a + b) - (b - a)]^2 + [(a - b) - (a + b)]^2}$

$\sqrt{(a + b - b + a)^2 + (a - b - a - b)^2} \rightarrow$

$\sqrt{(2a)^2 + (-2b)^2} \rightarrow \sqrt{4a^2 + 4b^2} \rightarrow \sqrt{4(a^2 + b^2)} = 2\sqrt{(a^2 + b^2)}$

(25.29). A line passes through the point (3, 8) and makes an intercept of -2 with the y-axis. Find its equation.

Solution

For intercept and a point on the line

$\frac{y-y_1}{x-x_1} = \frac{y_1-c}{x_1} \rightarrow \frac{y-8}{x-3} = \frac{8-c}{3} = \frac{10}{3} \rightarrow 3(y-8) = 10(x-3) \rightarrow 3y = 10x - 6$

(25.30). Find the equation which makes angle 45° with the positive horizontal axis and passes through the point (-1, 5).

Solution

For angle of slope and a point on the line

$\frac{y-y_1}{x-x_1} = m = \tan\theta \rightarrow \frac{y-5}{x--1} = \tan 45° = 1 \rightarrow y - 5 = x + 1 \rightarrow y = x + 6$

(25.31). $X(2,5), Y(-1,-3)$ and $Z(5,3)$ are vertices of a triangle. If M is the midpoint of YZ, determine the equation of XM.

Solution

With M equals to midpoint of YZ

$M(YZ) = \left[\frac{x_1+x_2}{2}, \frac{y_1+y_2}{2}\right] \rightarrow \frac{-1+5}{2}, \frac{-3+3}{2} \rightarrow [2,0]$

To determine the equation XM we have $X(2,5)$ and $(2,0)$

The equation of a line passing through two points (x_1,y_1) and B (x_1,y_2) is equal to x_1

The equation of the line is 2.

Note: solving with $y - y_1 = \frac{y_2-y_1}{x_2-x_1}(x - x_1)$ still gives 2

(25.32). A line AB joins two points with coordinates (-2, 1) and (4, - 5). Find the coordinate of a point P from A which divides AB into a ratio 2:1

Solution

$P(x,y) = \left[\frac{2(4)+1(-2)}{2+1}, \frac{2(-5)+1(1)}{2+1}\right] \rightarrow \left[\frac{6}{3}, \frac{-9}{3}\right] = (2,-3)$

347

(25.33) The angle between two lines L_1 and L_2 is $45°$. If the slope m_1 of L_1 is $\frac{2}{3}$. Determine the slope of m_2 of L_2.

Solution

From $\tan\theta = \left|\frac{m_2 - m_1}{1 + m_2 m_1}\right| \rightarrow \tan 45° = 1 = \frac{m_2 - \frac{2}{3}}{1 + \frac{2}{3}m_2} \rightarrow 1 + \frac{2}{3}m_2 = m_2 - \frac{2}{3}$

$1 + \frac{2}{3} = m_2 - \frac{2}{3}m_2 \rightarrow \frac{5}{3} = \frac{3m_2 - 2m_2}{3} = \frac{m_2}{3} \rightarrow m_2 = \frac{15}{3} = 5$

(25.34). Find the area of a pentagon whose vertices are (-5, -2), (-2, 5), (2, 7), (5, 1) and (2, -4).

Solution

$A = \frac{1}{2} \begin{bmatrix} -5 & -2 \\ -2 & 5 \\ 2 & 7 \\ 5 & 1 \\ 2 & -4 \\ -5 & -2 \end{bmatrix} \rightarrow$

$\frac{1}{2}[(-5)(5) - (-2)(-2) + (-2)(7) - (2)(5) + (2)(1) - (7)(5) + (5)(-4) - (2)(1) + (2)(-2) - (-5)(-4)] = -66\text{units}$

CHAPTER 26 ANALYTICAL GEOMETRY 11: CIRCLE

A circle is represented by an equation of the second degree in two variables.

A circle is said to be complete if its centre and radius are known.

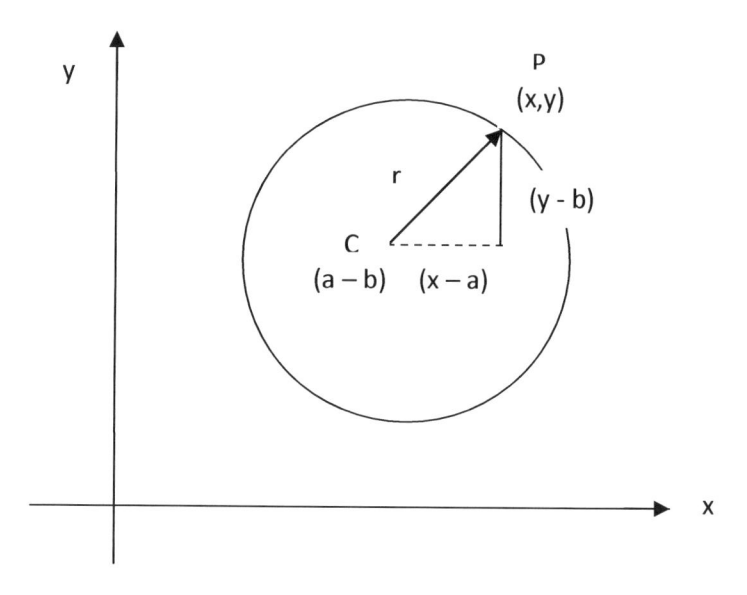

Consider the diagram above with $C(a, b) = $ *centre of the circle of radius r* and $P(x, y) = $ *point on the circle.*

The distance between the point with given coordinate is given by

$$r = \sqrt{(x_2 - x_1)^2 + (y_2 - y_1)^2}$$

with $x_1 = a$, $y_1 = b$, $x_2 = x$ and $y_2 = y$, $r = \sqrt{(x_2 - x_1)^2 + (y_2 - y_1)^2}$ becomes

$$d = \sqrt{(x - a)^2 + (y - b)^2}$$

Expanding we have

$$r^2 = (x - a)^2 + (y - b)^2 \rightarrow x^2 + y^2 - 2ax - 2by + a^2 + b^2 - r^2 = 0$$

This can be written as

$$x^2 + y^2 + 2gx + 2fy + c = 0$$

Where $g = -a$, $f = -b$, $c = a^2 + b^2 - r^2$

Also from $x^2 + y^2 + 2gx + 2fy + c = 0$

If D = 2g and E = 2f,

$x^2 + y^2 + 2gx + 2fy + c = 0 \rightarrow x^2 + y^2 + Dx + Ey + c = 0 \rightarrow x^2 + Dx + y^2 + Ey + c = 0$

Solving by completing the square

$x^2 + Dx + y^2 + Ey + c = 0 \rightarrow x^2 + Dx + \frac{D^2}{4} + y^2 + Ey + \frac{E^2}{4} = \frac{D^2}{4} + \frac{E^2}{4} - c \rightarrow$

$\left[x + \frac{D}{4}\right]^2 + \left[y + \frac{E}{4}\right]^2 = \frac{D^2 + E^2 - 4C}{4}$

Thus, the radius of the circle is given by $r = \frac{1}{2}\sqrt{D^2 + E^2 - 4C}$ with

Centre given by $\left[-\frac{D}{4}, -\frac{E}{4}\right]$

We therefore make the following deductions

(i) If $D^2 + E^2 - 4C > 0$, the circle is real

(ii) If $D^2 + E^2 - 4C < 0$, the circle is imaginary

(iii) If $D^2 + E^2 - 4C = 0$, the radius circle is zero

(1) When the centre and radius is given

Solve with $r^2 = (x - a)^2 + (y - b)^2$ and expand to get the general form of the equation of a circle given by $x^2 + y^2 + 2gx + 2fy + c = 0$

(2) When it is given in the general form

Use $r = \frac{1}{2}\sqrt{D^2 + E^2 - 4C}$ to get the radius and compare the given equation with the general form to get the centre

(2) When centre is the origin i.e (a = b = 0)

Here equation becomes $x^2 + y^2 = r^2$

(3) Equation of the tangent at the point (x_1, y_1) on the circle $x^2 + y^2 + 2gx + 2fy + c = 0$

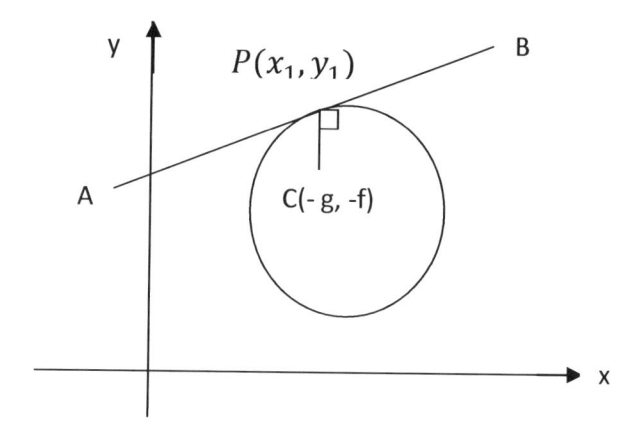

Consider the tangent AB of the circle above where $P(x_1, y_1)$ is the point both on the circle and on the tangent AB. If C is the center of the circle, PC is perpendicular to AB thus, $\therefore$ gradient of AB x gradient of PC = -1 $from$ $(m_1 m_2 = -1)$

Slope of PC $= \frac{y_1 + f}{x_1 + g}$, Slope of AB $= -\frac{x_1 + g}{y_1 + f}$

Equation of line AB is $\frac{y - y_1}{x - x_1} = -\frac{x_1 + g}{y_1 + f} \rightarrow (y - y_1)(y_1 + f) = -(x - x_1)(x_1 + g)$

$yy_1 + yf - y_1^2 - y_1 f = -[xx_1 - x_1^2 + gx - gx_1]$

$xx_1 + yy_1 + gx + fy = x_1^2 + y_1^2 + gx_1 + fy_1$

Adding $gx_1 + fy_1 + c$ to both sides

$xx_1 + yy_1 + gx + fy + gx_1 + fy_1 + c = x_1^2 + y_1^2 + gx_1 + fy_1 + gx_1 + fy_1 + c$

$xx_1 + yy_1 + gx + fy + gx_1 + fy_1 + c = x_1^2 + y_1^2 + 2gx_1 + 2fy_1 + c$

With the point (x_1, y_1) lying on the giving circle $x_1^2 + y_1^2 + 2gx_1 + 2fy_1 + c = 0$

$\therefore xx_1 + yy_1 + g(x + x_1) + f(y + y_1) + c = 0$

Close observation shows that the above equation is tantamount with the equation

$x^2 + y^2 + 2gx + 2fy \equiv x(x) + y(y) + g(x + x) + f(y + y)$

i.e putting one $x = x_1$ and one $y = y_1$ to obtain

$xx_1 + yy_1 + g(x + x_1) + f(y + y_1) + c = 0$

$\therefore$ we can differentiate the general equation of a circle implicitly to get the equation.

(4) Equation of point of intersection of a straight line and a cycle: Like with two lines, equation of point of intersection of a circle and a straight line is obtained by solving both equations simultaneously. Thus,

Straight → $y = mx + c$ ....(i)

Circle → $x^2 + y^2 + 2gx + 2fy + c = 0$ ....(ii)

By substitution

$x^2 + (mx + c)^2 + 2gx + 2f(mx + c) + c = 0$

$x^2 + m^2x^2 + 2mxc + c^2 + 2gx + 2fmx + 2fc + c →$

$(1 + m^2)x^2 + 2(g + mf + mc)x + c^2 + 2fc + c = 0$

This can be written as $Ax^2 + Bx + c = 0$

Where $A = 1 + m^2$, $B = 2(g + mf + mc)$, $C = c^2 + 2fc + c$

Like with all quadratic equations the equation above possesses either of the following roots

(i) Real root: In this case $B^2 > 4AC$ and the straight line and the circle cut at two distinct places

(ii) Imaginary root: In this case $B^2 < 4AC$ and the straight line and the circle do not cut at all

(iii) Equal root: In this case $B^2 = 4AC$. This is the point of intersection

$B^2 = 4AC$ → $[2(g + mf + mc)]^2 = 4(1 + m^2)(c^2 + 2fc + c)$

$4[(g + mf + mc)]^2 = 4(1 + m^2)(c^2 + 2fc + c)$

$[(g + mf + mc)]^2 = (1 + m^2)(c^2 + 2fc + c)$

∴ The condition that the line $y = mx + c$ be a tangent to the circle when the circle passes through the origin i.e $x^2 + y^2 = r^2$ is given by..

At origin, $g = f = 0$, $c = r^2$

From the last expression $m^2c^2 = 1 + m^2(c^2 - r^2) = c^2 + c^2m^2 - r^2 - r^2m^2$

$c^2 = r^2(1 + m^2)$ → $c = \sqrt{r^2(1 + m^2)} = \pm r\sqrt{(1 + m^2)}$

Hence y = mx $\pm r\sqrt{(1 + m^2)}$ are tangent to the circle $x^2 + y^2 = r^2$ for all value of m

(5) Equation for length of tangent to a circle from an external point

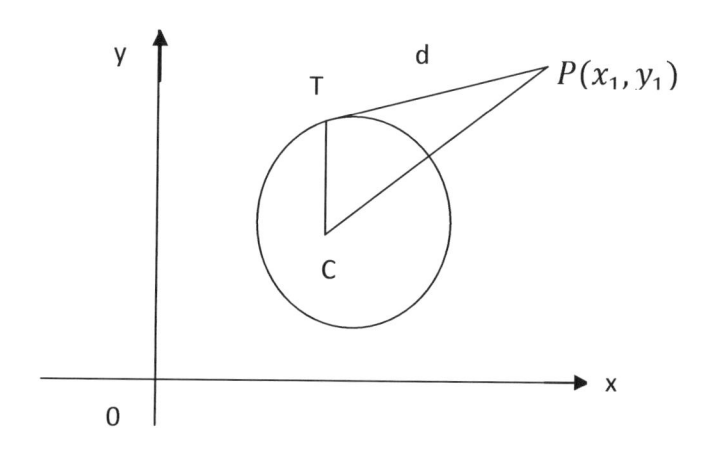

Consider the diagram above with circle of centre (-g,-f), CT is radius of the circle, PT is tangent to the circle.

By Pythagoras

$CT^2 + TP^2 = CP^2 \rightarrow TP^2 = CP^2 - CT^2 = (x_1 + g)^2 + (y_1 + f)^2 - (g^2 + f^2 - C)$

$x_1^2 + y_1^2 + 2gx_1 + 2fy_1 + g^2 + f^2 - g^2 - f^2 + c$

$TP^2 = x_1^2 + y_1^2 + 2gx_1 + 2fy_1 + c$

Thus close observation shows that the above equation is tantamount with the equation

$x^2 + y^2 + 2gx + 2fy + c \equiv x(x) + y(y) + 2g(x) + 2f(y) + c$

i.e putting $x = x_1$ and $y = y_1$ to obtain

$TP^2 = x_1^2 + y_1^2 + 2gx_1 + 2fy_1 + c$

∴ we substitute the given points in the circle equation to obtain the length.

(6) Equation of a radius of line is given by $\frac{y - y_1}{x - x_1}$

(7) Equation of a diameter is given by $\frac{y - y_1}{x - x_1} = \frac{y_2 - y_1}{x_2 - x_1}$

(8) Equation of circle given the coordinate of the end diameter is given by

$m_1 m_2 = -1 \rightarrow \dfrac{y - y_1}{x - x_1} \times \dfrac{y - y_2}{x - x_2} = -1$

(9) For a circle passing through three points $A(x_1, y_1)$, $B(x_2, y_2)$ and $C(x_3, y_3)$.

The equation can be found by solving the equations

$x_1^2 + y_1^2 + 2gx_1 + 2fy_1 + c = 0$

$x_2^2 + y_2^2 + 2gx_2 + 2fy_2 + c = 0$

$x_3^2 + y_3^2 + 2gx_3 + 2fy_3 + c = 0$

for g, f and c respectively and substituting into the general equation.

Note: The equation of a circle is a 2nd degree equation in x and y and there is no xy term in the equation.

QUESTIONS

(26.1). Write the equation of a circle with centre (3, -2) and radius of 7 units.

Solution

$a = 3, b = -2, f = 2, g = -3, r = 7$ and $c = 3^2 + (-2)^2 - 7^2 \rightarrow 9 + 4 - 49 = -36$

$x^2 + y^2 + 2gx + 2fy + c = 0 \rightarrow x^2 + y^2 + 2(-3)x + 2(2)y - 36 = 0$

$x^2 + y^2 - 6x + 4y - 36 = 0$

(26.2). Find the coordinate of the centre and the radius of the circle with equation.

$x^2 + y^2 - 6x + 4y - 36 = 0$.

Solution

Comparing with general form

$x^2 + y^2 - 2ax - 2by + a^2 + b^2 - r^2 = 0$

$a = \dfrac{6}{2} = 3, b = -2$

$a^2 + b^2 - r^2 = -36 \rightarrow 3^2 + 2^2 - r^2 = -36 \rightarrow 9 + 4 - r^2 = -36 \therefore r = \pm 7$

a = 1, g = -1

(26.3). Find the equation of the circle with centre (7, - 6) which touches the line with the equation 3x - 4y + 5 = 0.

Solution

Compare 3x - 4y + 5 = 0 with y = mx + c → $y = \frac{3x}{4} + \frac{5}{4}$ ∴ $m_1 = \frac{3}{4}$

Since the line is perpendicular to the radius $m_1 m_2 = -1$

$m_2 = -\frac{1}{m_1}$ → $-\frac{1}{\frac{3}{4}} = -\frac{4}{3}$

Equation of radius of line is given by $m = \frac{y - y_1}{x - x_1}$ → $\frac{y + 6}{x - 7} = -\frac{4}{3}$

$-4x + 28 = 3y + 18$ → $4x + 3y - 10 = 0$

(26.4). Find the equation of the circle with centre (3, -2) touching the line x + y - 3 = 0.

Solution

x + y - 3 → $y = 3 - x$

Comparing with y = mx + c ∴ $m = -1$

Since the line is perpendicular to the radius $m_1 m_2 = -1$

$m_2 = -\frac{1}{m_1}$ → $\frac{-1}{-1} = 1$

From $y - y_1 = m(x - x_1)$ → y - - 1 = 1(x - 3) → y + 2 = x - 3 ∴ $y = x - 5$

Solving both equations simultaneously we have

$y = x - 5$ .... (i)

$y = x + 3$ ..... (ii)

2y = - 2 ∴ $y = -1$

Inserting $y = -1$ into (i)

$y = x - 5$ → $-1 = x - 5$ ∴ $x = 4$

$r = \sqrt{(x_2 - x_1)^2 + (y_2 - y_1)^2} \to \sqrt{(3-4)^2 + (2--1)^2} = \sqrt{2}$

$\therefore r = \sqrt{2}$, b = -2, f = 2, a = 3, g = -3, $c = a^2 + b^2 - r^2 \to 3^2 + 2^2 - (\sqrt{2})^2 = 11$

The equation of the circle is $x^2 + y^2 + 2(-3)x + 2(2)y + 11 = 0$

$x^2 + y^2 - 6x + 4y + 11 = 0$

(26.5). The equation of a circle is $x^2 + y^2 - 8x + 4y + 15 = 0$. Find (i) The coordinate of the centre (ii) Its radius (iii) The equation of the tangent to the circle at the point (2, -3).

Solution

$x^2 + y^2 - 8x + 4y + 15 = 0 \to x^2 + y^2 + 2gx + 2fy + c = 0$

Comparing we have a = 4, g = -4, b = -2, f = 2

$c = a^2 + b^2 - r^2 \to 4^2 + (-2)^2 - 15 \to 20 - 15 = 5 \therefore r = \sqrt{5}$

(i) Coordinate of the centre = (4, -2)

(ii) The radius = $\sqrt{5}$

(iii) $x_1 = 2, y_1 = -3, x_2 = 4, y_2 = -2$

$\frac{y - y_1}{x - x_1} = \frac{y_2 - y_1}{x_2 - x_1} \to \frac{y - (-3)}{x - 2} = \frac{-2 - (-3)}{4 - 2} \to \frac{y + 3}{x - 2} = \frac{1}{2} \to \frac{y + 3}{x - 2} = -\frac{2}{1}$

$-2x + 4 = y + 3 \to y + 2x = -1$

(26.6). The equation of the tangent to a circle at P(x,y) is $2x - 3y + 1 = 0$. If the centre of the circle is (-1, 4). Find the coordinate of P and the equation of the circle.

Solution

$2x - 3y + 1 = 0 \to 3y = 2x + 1 \to y = \frac{2x}{3} + \frac{1}{3} \therefore m = \frac{2}{3}$

Since the line is perpendicular to the radius $m_1 m_2 = -1$

$m_2 = -\frac{1}{m_1} \to \frac{-1}{\frac{2}{3}} = -\frac{3}{2}$

356

From $y - y_1 = m(x - x_1) \rightarrow y - 4 = -\frac{3}{2}(x + 1) \rightarrow 2y - 8 = -3x - 3$

Solving both equations simultaneously we have

$3y - 2x = 1 \ldots (i)$

$\underline{2y + 3x = 5 \ldots (ii)}$

Making one variable equal

$6y - 4x = 2 \ldots (i)$

$\underline{6y + 9x = 15 \ldots (ii)}$

$\qquad 13x = 13 \quad \therefore \quad x = 1$

$3y - 2(1) = 1 \rightarrow 3y = 3 \quad \therefore y = 1$

(26.7) Calculate the centre and radius of the circle $x^2 + y^2 - 6x - 8y + 5 = 0$.

Solution

$x^2 + y^2 - 6x - 8y + 5 \rightarrow x^2 - 6x + 9 + y^2 - 8y + 16$

$(x - 3)^2 + (y - 4)^2 = 20 \rightarrow \sqrt{20} = \sqrt{10 \times 2} = 2\sqrt{5}$

$\therefore centre = (3, 4)$, radius $= 2\sqrt{5}$

(26.8). Write the equation of a circle with centre (2, 3) and radius of 5 units.

Solution

$a = 2, b = 3, f = -3, g = -2, r = 5$ and $c = 2^2 + 3^2 - 5^2 \rightarrow 4 + 9 - 25 = -12$

$x^2 + y^2 + 2gx + 2fy + c = 0 \rightarrow x^2 + y^2 + 2(-2)x + 2(-3)y - 12 = 0$

$x^2 + y^2 - 4x - 6y - 12 = 0$

(26.9). The end points of a circle have coordinates (2, 3) and (5, -6). Find the equation of the corresponding circle.

Solution

$m_1 m_2 = -1 \rightarrow \dfrac{y - y_1}{x - x_1} \times \dfrac{y - y_2}{x - x_2} = -1 \rightarrow \dfrac{y - 3}{x - 2} \times \dfrac{y - -6}{x - 5} = -1$

$\dfrac{y^2 + 3y - 18}{x^2 - 7x + 10} = -1 \rightarrow y^2 + 3y - 18 = -(x^2 - 7x + 10)$

$x^2 + y^2 - 7x + 3y - 8 = 0$

(26.10). Find the equation of the circle which passes through the points (6, 1)(3, 2) and (2, 3).

Solution

For point 1 $\rightarrow x_1^2 + y_1^2 + 2gx_1 + 2fy_1 + c = 0 \rightarrow 36 + 1 + 12g + 2f + c = 0$

For point 2 $\rightarrow x_2^2 + y_2^2 + 2gx_2 + 2fy_2 + c = 0 \rightarrow 9 + 4 + 6g + 4f + c = 0$

For point 2 $\rightarrow x_3^2 + y_3^2 + 2gx_3 + 2fy_3 + c = 0 \rightarrow 4 + 9 + 4g + 6f + c = 0$

$12g + 2f + c = -37$ ....(i)

$6g + 4f + c = -13$ ....(ii)

$4g + 6f + c = -13$ ....(iii)

Equation i – ii $\rightarrow 6g - 2f = -24$ ....(iv)

Equation ii – iii $\rightarrow 2g - 2f = 0$ ......(v)

$\qquad\qquad\qquad\quad 4g = -24 \therefore g = -6$

Putting $g = -6$ *into equation* (iv)

$6(-6) - 2f = -24 \rightarrow -36 - 2f = -24 \rightarrow -2f = 12 \therefore f - 6$

From (ii) $\rightarrow 6g + 4f + c = -13 \rightarrow 6(-6) + 4(-6) + c = -13$

$-36 - 24 + c = -13 \rightarrow -60 + c = -13 \therefore c = 47$

The equation is $x^2 + y^2 - 12x - 12y + 47 = 0$

(26.11). For the circle whose equation is $x^2 + y^2 - 3x + 5y - 14 = 0$, find the coordinates of the centre and the radius.

Solution From $x^2 + y^2 - 12x - 12y + 47 = 0$

$2gx = -3x \to 2g = -3 \therefore D = 2g = -3$

$2fy = 5y \to 2f = 5 \therefore E = 2f = 5$

$r = \frac{1}{2}\sqrt{D^2 + E^2 - 4C} \to \frac{1}{2}\sqrt{(-3)^2 + (5)^2 - 4(-14)} = \frac{3\sqrt{10}}{2}$

$2gx = -3x \therefore g = -\frac{3}{2}$

$2fy = 5y \therefore f = \frac{5}{2}$

Centre $= \left[\frac{3}{2}, -\frac{5}{2}\right]$

(26.12). Determine the constant k so that $x^2 + y^2 - 8x + 10y + k = 0$ is the equation of a circle whose radius is 7.

Solution

$r = \frac{1}{2}\sqrt{D^2 + E^2 - 4C} \to 7 = \frac{1}{2}\sqrt{(-8)^2 + (10)^2 - 4(k)} \to$

$14 = \sqrt{64 + 100 - 4k} \to (14)^2 = 164 - 4k \to 196 - 164 = 32 = -4k \therefore k = -8$

(26.13). Find the equation of the tangent to the circle $x^2 + y^2 + 3x - 3y - 38 = 0$ at point (-7, -2).

Solution

Differentiating $x^2 + y^2 + 3x - 3y - 38 = 0$ implicitly we have

$2x + 2y\frac{dy}{dx} + 3 - 3\frac{dy}{dx} = 0 \to 2y\frac{dy}{dx} - 3\frac{dy}{dx} = -2x - 3 \to$

$\frac{dy}{dx}[2y - 3] = 2x - 3 \to \frac{dy}{dx} = \frac{-(2x+3)}{2y-3}$

Inserting the values of x and y gives

$\frac{dy}{dx} = \frac{-(2x+3)}{2y-3} \to -\frac{[2(-7)+3]}{[2(-2)-3]} \to -\frac{11}{7}$

From $y - y_1 = m(x - x_1)$ → $y - -2 = -\frac{11}{7}(x - -7)$ → $y + 2 = -\frac{11}{7}(x + 7)$

$7y + 11x - 91 = 0$

(26.14) Find the equation of the tangents to the circle $x^2 + y^2 = 289$ which are parallel to the line $8x - 15y = 0$.

Solution

From $8x - 15y = 0$ → $15y = 8x$ → $y = \frac{8}{15}x$ ∴ $m = \frac{8}{15}$

$x^2 + y^2 = 289$ → $x^2 + y^2 = 17^2$

From $y = mx \pm r\sqrt{(1 + m^2)}$ → $\frac{8}{15}x + 17\sqrt{\left[1 + \frac{8^2}{15^2}\right]}$ → $\frac{8}{15}x + 17\sqrt{\left[\frac{15^2 + 8^2}{15^2}\right]}$

$\frac{8}{15}x \pm 17\sqrt{\left[\frac{225 + 64}{15^2}\right]}$ → $\frac{8}{15}x \pm 17\sqrt{\left[\frac{289}{15^2}\right]}$ → $\frac{8}{15}x \pm 17\sqrt{\left[\frac{17^2}{15^2}\right]}$

$\frac{8}{15}x \pm 17\left[\frac{17}{15}\right]$ → $\frac{8}{15}x \pm \frac{289}{15}$ ∴ $y = 8x \pm 289$

(26.15) Find the length of the tangent from (-5, 1) to the circle $x^2 + y^2 - 4x + 6y - 3 = 0$.

Solution

The phrase ''from'' implies from an external point, substituting the giving point into

$x^2 + y^2 - 4x + 6y - 3 = 0$ → $d^2 = (-5)^2 + (1)^2 - 4(-5) + 6(1) - 3 = 0$

$d^2 = 25 + 1 + 20 + 6 - 3 = 49$ ∴ $d = 7$

CHAPTER 27   CONIC SECTION: PARABOLA

Parabola is the locus of a point that moves in a plane so that its distance from a fixed point (focus) in the plane is equal to its distance from a fixed line (directrix) in the plane.

Terms associated with a parabola

Vertex: This is a point in which the curve cuts its axis of symmetry.

Latus rectum: This is the chord through a focus parallel to the conic section directrix.

Eccentricity: This is a measure of the deviation of a conic section from being circular. For a parabola e = 1.

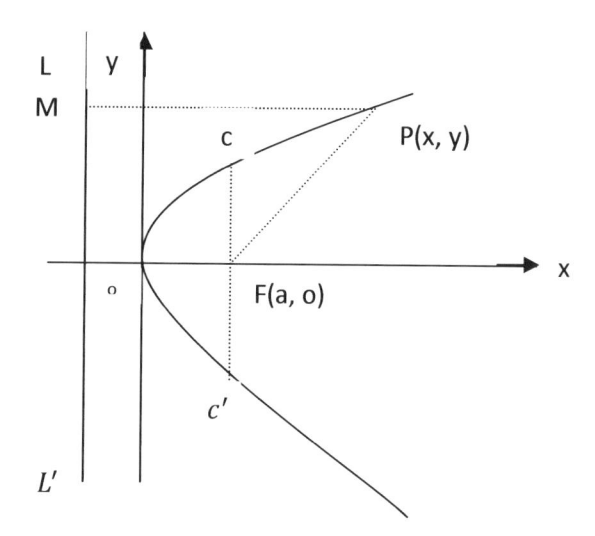

Consider the diagram above where F = fixed point (focus), LL' = fixed line (directrix). If the distance from the focus to the directrix is 2a and the coordinate of F being (a, 0) then the equation of the directrix is x + a = 0.

$$\therefore \sqrt{(x-a)^2 + (y-0)^2} = x + a \rightarrow x^2 - 2ax + a^2 + y^2 = x^2 + 2ax + a^2$$

$$y^2 = 4ax$$

The above deduction was for symmetry about the positive x-axis.

For symmetry about the negative x-axis $y^2 = -4ax$

For symmetry about the y-axis we have $x^2 = \pm 4ay$

(1) Equation of a parabola given the vertex and its focus

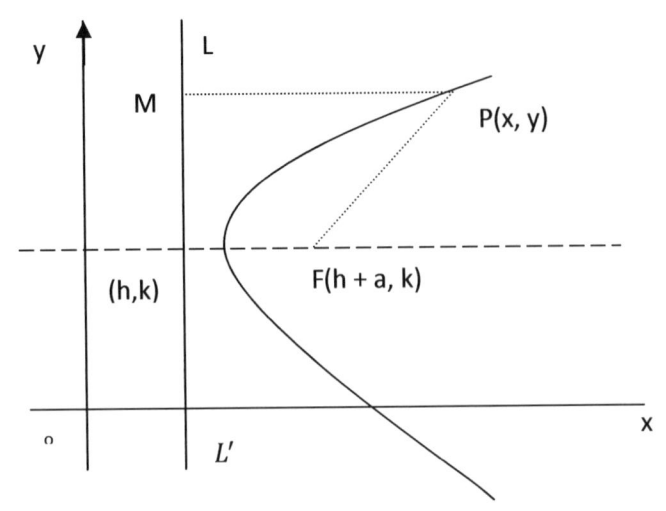

Consider the parabola above with vertex at (h, k), axis parallel to the x-axis, and focus at a distance a to the right of the vertex. The equation of the directrix, parallel to the y-axis and at a distance 2a to the left of the focus is x = h − a.

With PF = PM, equation $\sqrt{(x - a)^2 + (y - 0)^2} = x + a$ becomes

$\sqrt{(x - h - a)^2 + (y - k)^2} = x - h + a$

Recall that the expansion of $(a - b - c)^2 = [(a - b) - c]^2 \rightarrow (a - b)^2 - 2(a - b)c + c^2$

Applying this to the above equation and evaluating yield

$y^2 - 2ky + k^2 = 4ax - 4ah \rightarrow (y - k)^2 = 4a(x - h)$
$\therefore (y - k)^2 = 4a(x - h)$

Depending on the location of the focus, other standard forms of the equation of a parabola given the vertex and its focus are

$(y - k)^2 = -4a(x - h)$

$(x - h)^2 = 4a(y - k)$

$(x - h)^2 = -4a(y - k)$

Expanding the above equation results in equation of the form $y = ax^2 + bx + c$ or

$x = ay^2 + by + c$

(2) Equation of a chord to a parabola

The equation of a chord to the parabola $y^2 = 4ax$ can be found by

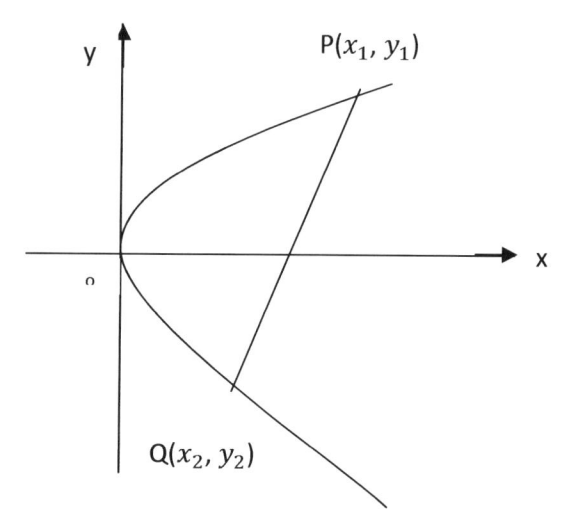

Considering the diagram above. Let P(x_1, y_1), Q(x_2, y_2) be two points on the parabola. The gradient of PQ is given by

Gradient $= \dfrac{y - y_1}{x - x_1} = \dfrac{y_2 - y_1}{x_2 - x_1} = m$

Since (x_1, y_1) and (x_2, y_2) are on the parabola from $y^2 = 4ax$ we have $y_1^2 = 4ax_1$ and $y_2^2 = 4ax_2$

$y_2^2 - y_1^2 = 4a(x_2 - x_1) \rightarrow (y_2 + y_1)(y_2 - y_1) = 4a(x_2 - x_1) \rightarrow$

$\dfrac{(y_2 - y_1)}{(x_2 - x_1)} = \dfrac{4a}{(y_2 + y_1)} = m \rightarrow y_2 - y_1 = \dfrac{4a}{(y_2 + y_1)}(x_2 - x_1)$

Which can be written as $y - y_1 = \dfrac{4a}{(y_2 + y_1)}(x - x_1)$

Putting $y_2 = y_1$ and $x_2 = x_1$

$y - y_1 = \dfrac{4a}{(y_2 + y_1)}(x - x_1) \rightarrow y - y_1 = \dfrac{4a}{2y_1}(x - x_1) = \dfrac{2a}{y_1}(x - x_1) \rightarrow$

$y_1(y - y_1) = 2a(x - x_1) \rightarrow yy_1 - y_1^2 = 2a(x - x_1)$

Inserting the value of y_1^2

$yy_1 - y_1^2 = 2a(x - x_1) \rightarrow yy_1 - 4ax_1 = 2ax - 2ax_1$

$\therefore yy_1 = 2a(x + x_1)$

(3) Point of intersection of the line y = mx + c and the parabola $y^2 = 4ax$

For intersection we simply solve both equations simultaneously

y = mx + c ....(i)

$y^2 = 4ax$.......(ii)

By substitution $(mx + c)^2 = 4ax \rightarrow m^2x^2 + 2mxc + c^2 = 4ax$

$m^2x^2 + 2mxc + c^2 - 4ax = 0 \rightarrow m^2x^2 + (2mc - 4a)x + c$

Like with all quadratic equations the equation above possesses either of the following roots

(i) When the line y = mx + c cuts the parabola $y^2 = 4ax$ at two distinct points, the root of the above equation is real.

$b^2 > 4ac \rightarrow (2mc - 4a)^2 > 4(m^2)c \rightarrow 4m^2c^2 - 16mac + 16a^2 > 4m^2c^2$

$-16mac > -16a^2 \rightarrow 16mac > 16a^2 \rightarrow m > \dfrac{a}{c}$

(ii) When the line y = mx + c does not cuts the parabola $y^2 = 4ax$, the root of the above equation is imaginary.

$b^2 < 4ac \rightarrow (2mc - 4a)^2 < 4(m^2)c \rightarrow 4m^2c^2 - 16mac + 16a^2 < 4m^2c^2$

$-16mac < -16a^2 \rightarrow 16mac < 16a^2 \rightarrow m < \dfrac{a}{c}$

(iii) When the line y = mx + c is tangent to the parabola, the roots are coincident.

$b^2 = 4ac \rightarrow (2mc - 4a)^2 = 4(m^2)c \rightarrow 4m^2c^2 - 16mac + 16a^2 = 4m^2c^2$

$-16mac = -16a^2 \rightarrow 16mac = 16a^2 \rightarrow m = \dfrac{a}{c}$

$\therefore$ For all values of m the line y = mx + $\dfrac{a}{m}$ is a tangent to the parabola $y^2 = 4ax$

(4) Equation of tangent to the parabola $y^2 = 4ax$

This can also be gotten from $yy_1 = 2a(x + x_1)$

(4) Equation of normal to the parabola $y^2 = 4ax$

From $y^2 = 4ax$, differentiating implicitly we have

$2y \frac{dy}{dx} = 4a \rightarrow \frac{dy}{dx} = \frac{2a}{y} = \frac{2a}{y_1}$

Since the tangent at the point (x_1, y_1) is perpendicular to the normal

$m_1 m_2 = -1 \rightarrow \frac{y - y_1}{x - x_1} \times \frac{y_2 - y_2}{x_2 - x_1} = -1 \rightarrow \frac{y - y_1}{x - x_1} \times \frac{dy}{dx} = -1 \rightarrow \frac{y - y_1}{x - x_1} \times \frac{2a}{y_1} = -1$

$\rightarrow \frac{y - y_1}{x - x_1} = \frac{-y_1}{2a} \rightarrow 2a(y - y_1) = -y_1(x - x_1)$

$\therefore 2ay - 2ay_1 = x_1 y_1 + y_1 x$

QUESTIONS

(27.1). Find the equation of the tangent to the parabola $y^2 = 16x$ at the point $(1, -4)$

Solution

Comparing with the general equation, $4a = 16 \rightarrow a = 4$

From $yy_1 = 2a(x + x_1) \rightarrow (-4)y = 2(4)[x + 1] \rightarrow -4y = 8x + 8$

$4y + 8x + 8 = 0$

(27.2). Find the equation of the normal to the parabola $y^2 = 12x$ at point $(3, 6)$

Solution

Comparing with the general equation, $4a = 12 \rightarrow a = 3$

From $2ay - 2ay_1 = x_1 y_1 + y_1 x \rightarrow$

$2(3)y - 2(2)6 = (3)6 + 6x \rightarrow 6y - 36 = 18 + 6x \rightarrow 6y = 6x + 54$

$\therefore y = x + 9$

(27.3). Determine the equation of the parabola with its focus at the point (6, - 2), and whose directrix $x - 2 = 0$.

Solution

From $\sqrt{(x - a)^2 + (y - 0)^2} = x + a$

Inserting the points, we have

$\sqrt{(x - 6)^2 + (y - -2)^2} = x - 2 \rightarrow (x - 6)^2 + (y - -2)^2 = (x - 2)^2$

$x^2 - 12x + 36 + y^2 + 4y + 4 = x^2 - 4x + 4 \rightarrow y^2 + 4y - 8x + 36 = 0$

(27.4). Determine the equation of the parabola with his vertex at (3, 2) and its focus at (5, 2).

Solution

From $(y - k)^2 = 4a(x - h) \rightarrow (y - 2)^2 = 4(2)(x - 3) \therefore y^2 - 4y - 8x + 28 = 0$

CHAPTER 28 CONIC SECTION: ELIPSE

Ellipse is the part of a point which moves so that the sum of its distance from two fixed points is constant.

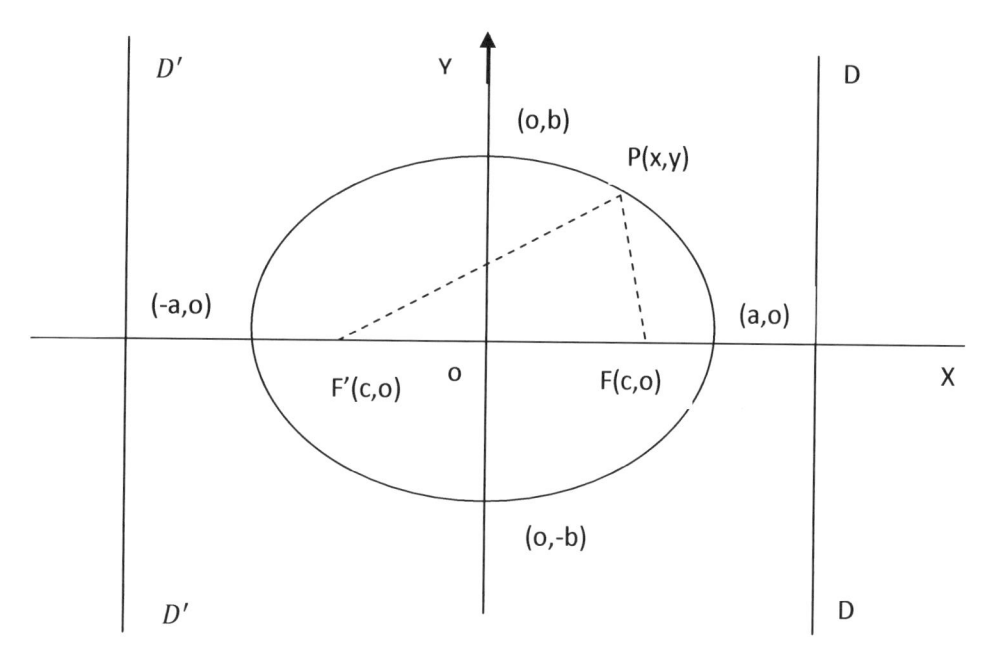

Consider the diagram above, where the two fixed points are F(c,o) and F'(-c,o) and the constant sum be 2a. Since PF + F'P = 2a, the distance formula becomes

$$\sqrt{(x+c)^2 + (y-0)^2} + \sqrt{(x-c)^2 + (y-0)^2} = 2a$$

$$\sqrt{(x+c)^2 + (y-0)^2} = 2a - \sqrt{(x-c)^2 + (y-0)^2}$$

$$(x+c)^2 + (y-0)^2 = \left[2a - \sqrt{(x-c)^2 + (y-0)^2}\right]^2$$

$$(x+c)^2 + (y-0)^2 = 4a^2 - 4a\sqrt{(x-c)^2 + (y-0)^2} + (x-c)^2 + (y-0)^2$$

$$(x+c)^2 + (y-0)^2 - [(x-c)^2 + (y-0)^2] = 4a^2 - 4a\sqrt{(x-c)^2 + (y-0)^2}$$

$$4cx = 4a^2 - 4a\sqrt{(x-c)^2 + (y-0)^2}$$

$$4cx - 4a^2 = -4a\sqrt{(x-c)^2 + (y-0)^2}$$

$$4(cx - a^2) = -4a\sqrt{(x-c)^2 + (y-0)^2} \rightarrow cx - a^2 = -a\sqrt{(x-c)^2 + (y-0)^2}$$

$[cx - a^2]^2 = (-a)^2[(x - c)^2 + (y - 0)^2] \rightarrow$

$c^2x^2 + a^4 - 2a^2cx = a^2[c^2 + x^2 - 2cx + y^2] = a^2c^2 + a^2x^2 - 2a^2cx + a^2y^2$

$(a^2 - c^2)x^2 + a^2y^2 = (a^2 - c^2)a^2$

Dividing by $(a^2 - c^2)a^2$

$\frac{x^2}{a^2} + \frac{y^2}{a^2 - c^2} = 1$

With a > c

$\frac{x^2}{a^2} + \frac{y^2}{b^2} = 1$

This is the standard form of the equation of an ellipse where a and b are respectively the semi major and semi minor axis.

Deductions

(i) It follows that if $x^2 > a^2$, y is not real. Similarly if $y^2 > b^2$, x is not real. Hence, there is no portion of the curve outside the limits.

(ii) The curve is symmetric. Thus, for every value of x such that $x^2 < a^2$, there are two equal and opposite values of y and every value of y such that $y^2 < b^2$, there are two equal and opposite values of x.

(iii) Eccentricity for an ellipse is less than one i.e e < 1 and it is given by

$e = \frac{c}{a} = \frac{\sqrt{a^2 - b^2}}{a}$

(iv) The origin of the coordinate system is the centre of the ellipse and it can be shown to bisect all chords passing through it.

(v) An ellipse has two foci and hence two directrices (DD and $D'D'$). The equation of the directrices is given by

$x + \frac{a}{e} = 0$ and $x - \frac{a}{e} = 0$, holds if the foci is on the x-axis as above

$y + \frac{a}{e} = 0$ and $y - \frac{a}{e} = 0$, holds if the foci is on the y-axis.

(vi) Length of the semi latus rectum of the ellipse.

From $\frac{x^2}{a^2} + \frac{y^2}{b^2} = 1$

When x = ae, $\frac{(ae)^2}{a^2} + \frac{y^2}{b^2} = 1 \rightarrow e^2 + \frac{y^2}{b^2} = 1 \rightarrow \frac{y^2}{b^2} = 1 - e^2$

From $b^2 = a^2(1 - e^2) \rightarrow \frac{b^2}{a^2} = 1 - e^2$. Inserting we have

$\frac{y^2}{b^2} = 1 - e^2 = \frac{b^2}{a^2} \therefore \frac{y^2}{b^2} = \frac{b^2}{a^2} \rightarrow b^4 = a^2 y^2 \rightarrow y^2 = \frac{b^4}{a^2} \therefore y = \sqrt{\frac{b^4}{a^2}} = \pm\frac{b^2}{a}$

Length of the latus rectum is $2y = 2\left[\frac{b^2}{a}\right]$

(vii) Change of origin: When the centre of the ellipse is at a point (x_1, y_1) such that the axis is parallel to either the x-axis or y-axis, the equation $\frac{x^2}{a^2} + \frac{y^2}{b^2} = 1$ becomes

$\frac{(x - x_1)^2}{a^2} + \frac{(y - y_1)^2}{b^2} = 1$ major axis parallel to x-axis

$\frac{(x - x_1)^2}{b^2} + \frac{(y - y_1)^2}{a^2} = 1$ major axis parallel to y-axis

In either case, the equation of the ellipse takes the form $Ax^2 + By^2 + Dx + Ey + F = 0$

(vii) Point of intersection of the line y = mx + c and the ellipse $\frac{x^2}{a^2} + \frac{y^2}{b^2} = 1$

Point of intersection is the simultaneous solution of both equations

y = mx + c   ....(i)

$\frac{x^2}{a^2} + \frac{y^2}{b^2} = 1$ ....(ii)

By substitution $\frac{x^2}{a^2} + \frac{(mx + c)^2}{b^2} = 1 \rightarrow \frac{x^2}{a^2} + \frac{m^2 x^2 + 2cmx + c^2}{b^2} = 1$

$\frac{b^2 x^2 + a^2 m^2 x^2 + 2a^2 cmx + a^2 c^2}{a^2 b^2} = 1 \rightarrow (b^2 + a^2 m^2)x^2 + 2a^2 mcx + a^2(c^2 - b^2) = 0$

As with all quadratic equations, the above equation has root which can either be complex, real or coincident.

For coincidence, $b^2 = 4ac \rightarrow (2a^2 mc)^2 = 4(b^2 + a^2 m^2)(a^2 c^2 - a^2 b^2)$

$4a^4 m^2 c^2 = 4a^2[(b^2 + a^2 m^2)(c^2 - b^2)] \rightarrow a^2 m^2 c^2 = [(b^2 + a^2 m^2)(c^2 - b^2)]$

$a^2m^2c^2 = b^2c^2 - b^4 + a^2m^2c^2 - a^2b^2m^2 \rightarrow b^2c^2 = b^4 + a^2b^2m^2$

$b^2(c^2) = b^2(b^2 + a^2m^2) \rightarrow c^2 = b^2 + a^2m^2 \therefore c = \pm\sqrt{b^2 + a^2m^2}$

Thus, for all values of m, the straight line y = mx $\pm\sqrt{b^2 + a^2m^2}$ are tangent to the ellipse.

(viii) Equation of chord to the ellipse $\frac{x^2}{a^2} + \frac{y^2}{b^2} = 1$

Since the points (x_1, y_1) and (x_2, y_2) lie on the ellipse, we have

$\frac{x_1^2}{a^2} + \frac{y_1^2}{b^2} = 1$ ....(i)

$\frac{x_2^2}{a^2} + \frac{y_2^2}{b^2} = 1$ ....(ii)

Subtracting, $\frac{x_1^2}{a^2} + \frac{y_1^2}{b^2} - \left[\frac{x_2^2}{a^2} + \frac{y_2^2}{b^2}\right] = 1 - 1 = 0 \rightarrow \frac{x_1^2 - x_2^2}{a^2} + \frac{y_1^2 - y_2^2}{b^2} = 0$

$\frac{(x_1 + x_2)(x_1 - x_2)}{a^2} = -\frac{(y_1 + y_2)(y_1 - y_2)}{b^2}$

With the line joining the points (x_1, y_1) and (x_2, y_2) given by $\frac{y - y_1}{x - x_1} = \frac{y_1 - y_2}{x_1 - x_1}$

The last expression becomes

$\frac{(x - x_1)(x_1 + x_2)}{a^2} = -\frac{(y - y_1)(y_1 + y_2)}{b^2} \rightarrow x\frac{(x_1 + x_2)}{a^2} - x_1\frac{(x_1 + x_2)}{a^2} = -y\frac{(y_1 + y_2)}{b^2} + y_1\frac{(y_1 + y_2)}{b^2}$

$\frac{xx_1}{a^2} + \frac{xx_2}{a^2} - \frac{x_1^2}{a^2} - \frac{x_1 x_2}{a^2} = -\frac{yy_1}{b^2} - \frac{yy_2}{b^2} + \frac{y_1^2}{b^2} + \frac{y_1 y_2}{b^2}$

$\frac{x[x_1 + x_2]}{a^2} + \frac{y[y_1 + y_2]}{b^2} = \frac{x_1 x_2}{a^2} + \frac{y_1 y_2}{b^2} + \frac{x_1^2}{a^2} + \frac{y_1^2}{b^2} = \frac{x_1 x_2}{a^2} + \frac{y_1 y_2}{b^2} + 1$

Since $\frac{x_1^2}{a^2} + \frac{y_1^2}{b^2} = 1$

$\therefore \frac{x[x_1 + x_2]}{a^2} + \frac{y[y_1 + y_2]}{b^2} = \frac{x_1 x_2}{a^2} + \frac{y_1 y_2}{b^2} + 1$

When $x_1 = x_2$ and $y_1 = y_2$, we have

$\frac{x[2x_1]}{a^2} + \frac{y[2y_1]}{b^2} = \frac{x_1^2}{a^2} + \frac{y_1^2}{b^2} + 1 = 1 + 1 \rightarrow 2\left[\frac{xx_1}{a^2} + \frac{yy_1}{b^2}\right] = 2$

$\frac{xx_1}{a^2} + \frac{yy_1}{b^2} = 1$

Which gives the equation of the tangent at (x_1, y_1)

(ix) Equation of tangent and normal to the ellipse $\dfrac{x^2}{a^2} + \dfrac{y^2}{b^2} = 1$

From $\dfrac{xx_1}{a^2} + \dfrac{yy_1}{b^2} = 1 \rightarrow \dfrac{yy_1}{b^2} = 1 - \dfrac{xx_1}{a^2} \rightarrow y = \dfrac{b^2}{y_1}\left[1 - \dfrac{xx_1}{a^2}\right] = \dfrac{b^2}{y_1} - \dfrac{xx_1 b^2}{a^2 y_1}$

The gradient of the straight line is $\dfrac{dy}{dx} = -\dfrac{x_1 b^2}{a^2 y_1}$

Since the tangent at the point (x_1, y_1) is perpendicular to the normal at the point

From $m_1 m_2 = -1$

$m_1 m_2 = -1 \rightarrow \dfrac{y - y_1}{x - x_1} \times \dfrac{y_2 - y_2}{x_2 - x_1} = -1 \rightarrow \dfrac{y - y_1}{x - x_1} \times \dfrac{dy}{dx} = -1 \rightarrow \dfrac{y - y_1}{x - x_1} \times \left[-\dfrac{x_1 b^2}{a^2 y_1}\right] = -1$

$\dfrac{y - y_1}{x - x_1} = \dfrac{a^2 y_1}{b^2 x_1} \rightarrow \dfrac{y - y_1}{a^2 y_1} = \dfrac{x - x_1}{b^2 x_1} \rightarrow (y - y_1)b^2 x_1 = (x - x_1)a^2 y_1$

$b^2 x_1 y - b^2 x_1 y_1 = a^2 y_1 x - a^2 x_1 y_1$

$\therefore (a^2 - b^2)x_1 y_1 = a^2 y_1 x - a^2 x_1 y_1$

(x) Parametric equation of the ellipse

From $\cos^2\theta + \sin^2\theta = 1$

Comparing with $\dfrac{x^2}{a^2} + \dfrac{y^2}{b^2} = 1$, $\cos^2\theta = \dfrac{x^2}{a^2}$, $\sin^2\theta = \dfrac{y^2}{b^2}$

Thus, $\left.\begin{array}{l} x = a\cos\theta \\ y = b\sin\theta \end{array}\right\}$

These are the parametric equations of an ellipse, where θ is the eccentric angle of the point P on the ellipse.

QUESTIONS

(28.1). The line $y + 2x = 3$ cuts the ellipse at P and Q. Find the coordinates of P and Q when the ellipse is given by $4x^2 + y^2 = 5$. Find the equation of the tangents and normals at the points P and Q.

Solution

$y = 3 - 2x$ ………(i)

$y^2 + 4x^2 = 5$ ……(ii)

Solving by substitution, $(3 - 2x)^2 + 4x^2 = 5 \rightarrow 9 - 12x + 4x^2 + 4x^2 = 5$

$9 - 5 - 12x + 4x^2 + 4x^2 = 0 \rightarrow 4 - 12x + 8x^2 = 0 \rightarrow 1 - 3x + 2x^2 = 0$

$2x^2 - 3x + 1 = 0 \rightarrow (2x - 1)(x - 1) = 0 \therefore x = 1/2$ or 1

Inserting values of x into (i)

$y = 3 - 2x \rightarrow y = 3 - 2(1) \therefore y = 1$

$y = 3 - 2x \rightarrow y = 3 - 2\left[\frac{1}{2}\right] \therefore y = 2$

Hence P = (1, 1) and Q = $\left[\frac{1}{2}, 2\right]$

The tangents of the ellipse are…..

From $4x^2 + y^2 = 5$

At point P $\rightarrow 4x(1) + y(1) = 5 \rightarrow 4x + y = 5$

At point Q $\rightarrow 4x\left[\frac{1}{2}\right] + y(2) = 5 \rightarrow 2x + 2y = 5$

The gradient of the tangents are

At P $\rightarrow y = 5 - 4x \therefore m = -4$

At Q $\rightarrow 2y = 5 - 2x \therefore m = -1$

The gradient of the normals are $\frac{1}{4}$ and 1

$\therefore$ Equation of the normals at P and Q are respectively

At P, $\frac{y-1}{x-1} = \frac{1}{4}$ → $4y - x - 3 = 0$

At Q, $\frac{y-2}{x-\frac{1}{2}} = 1$ → $2y - 2x - 3 = 0$.

(28.2). Find the equation of the tangent and normal to the ellipse $2x^2 + 9y^2 = 18$ at $\left[1, \frac{4}{5}\right]$.

Solution

$2x^2 + 9y^2 = 18$ → $\frac{x^2}{9} + \frac{y^2}{2} = 1$ ∴ $a^2 = 9, b^2 = 2$

Equation of tangent is given by $\frac{xx_1}{a^2} + \frac{yy_1}{b^2} = 1$

$\frac{x(1)}{9} + \frac{y\left[\frac{4}{5}\right]}{2} = 1$ → $\frac{x}{9} + \frac{4y}{10} = 1$ → $10x + 36y = 90$

The gradient of the tangent is → $y = 90 - \frac{10x}{36}$ ∴ $m = \frac{10}{36} = \frac{5}{18}$

The gradient of the normal is $\frac{18}{5}$

$\frac{y - \frac{4}{5}}{x - 1} = \frac{18}{5}$ → $\frac{5y - 4}{5x - 5} = \frac{18}{5}$ → $5(5y - 4) = 18(5x - 5)$ → $25y - 20 = 90x - 90$

$25y - 90x = -90 + 20 = 70$ ∴ $5y - 18x + 14 = 0$

(28.3). Determine if the pair of tangent from the point (3, 4) to the ellipse $\frac{x^2}{16} + \frac{y^2}{9} = 1$ are perpendicular.

Solution

From $\frac{x^2}{16} + \frac{y^2}{9} = 1$ → $a^2 = 16, b^2 = 9$

From $y = mx \pm \sqrt{b^2 + a^2 m^2}$ → $4 = 3m \pm \sqrt{9 + 16m^2}$
$4 - 3m = \pm\sqrt{9 + 16m^2}$ → $(4 - 3m)^2 = 9 + 16m^2$

$16 - 24m + 9m^2 = 9 + 16m^2$ → $7 - 7m^2 - 24m = 0$ → $7m^2 + 24m - 7 = 0$

For perpendicularity, product of the root of the above equation should = -1

∴ $\frac{c}{a} = \frac{-7}{7} = -1$

373

(28.4). Find the equation of the ellipse with its centre at (-1, -1), vertex (5, -1), e = $\frac{2}{3}$ and c = 4.

Solution

From given parameters,

$b^2 = a^2 - c^2 \rightarrow 36 - 16 = 20$, $e = \frac{c}{a} = \frac{4}{6} = \frac{2}{3}$

From $\frac{x^2}{a^2} + \frac{y^2}{b^2} = 1$

When centre is at (h, k) $\rightarrow \frac{(x+1)^2}{36} + \frac{(y+1)^2}{20} = 1$

(28.5). Given $4x^2 + 5y^2 - 24x - 20y + 36 = 0$. Determine the equation of the ellipse, (ii) coordinate of the centre, (iii) vertices of the ellipse, (iv) foci of the ellipse

Solution

$4x^2 + 5y^2 - 24x - 20y + 36 = 0 \rightarrow 4x^2 - 24x + 5y^2 - 20y + 36 = 0$

$4(x^2 - 6x) + 5(y^2 - 4y) + 36 = 0 \rightarrow$

$4(x^2 - 6x + 9 - 9) + 5(y^2 - 4y + 4 - 4) + 36 = 0$

$4(x^2 - 6x + 9) + 5(y^2 - 4y + 4) - 36 - 20 + 36 = 0$

$4(x - 3)^2 + 5(y - 2)^2 - 20 = 0$

$\frac{(x-3)^2}{5} + \frac{(y-2)^2}{4} = 1$

(ii) Coordinate of the centre = (3, -2)

(iii) Vertices are the four vertices i.e horizontal and vertical vertices

Vertices on the horizontal axis = $[b + x_1, 0 + y_1]$ and $[b + x_1, 0 + y_1]$

$= [\sqrt{5} + 3, 2]$ and $[\sqrt{5} + 3, 2]$

Vertices on the vertical axis $= [0 + x_1, a + y_1]$ and $[0 + x_1, -a + y_1]$

$= [3, 4]$ and $[3, 0]$

(iv) Foci: The two foci are given by $[0 + x_1, \ c + y_1]$ and $[0 + x_1, -c + y_1]$

With $b^2 = a^2 - c^2 \rightarrow c^2 = a^2 - b^2 = 5 - 4 = 1$

∴ *The foci are* $[3, \ 3]$ and $[3, \ 1]$

CHAPTER 29 CONIC SECTION: HYPERBOLA

Ellipse is the part of a point which moves so that the sum of its difference from two fixed points F(c, o) and F'(c, o) is 2a.

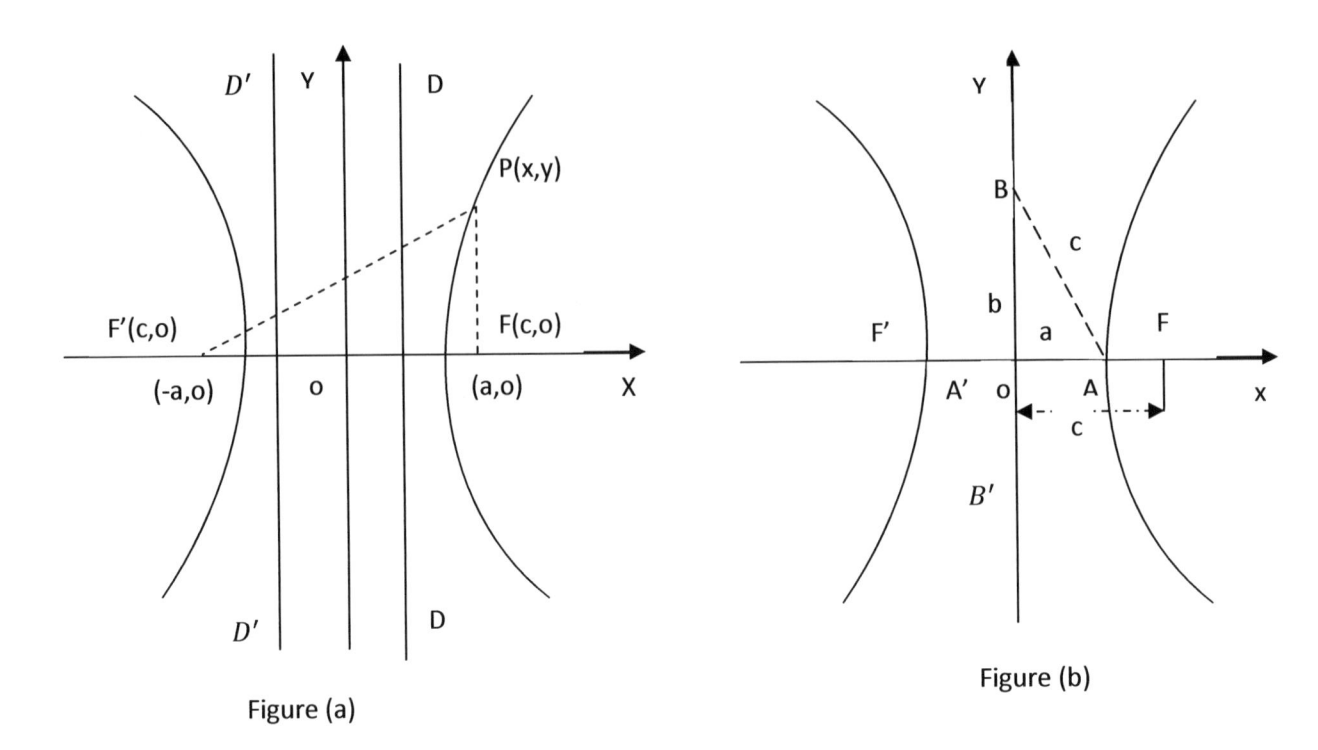

Figure (a)

Figure (b)

Consider the diagram above figure (a), where the two fixed points are F(c,o) and F'(-c,o) and the constant sum be 2a. Since $F'P - PF = 2a$, the distance formula becomes

$$\sqrt{(x+c)^2 + (y-0)^2} - \sqrt{(x-c)^2 + (y-0)^2} = 2a$$

$$\sqrt{(x+c)^2 + (y-0)^2} = 2a + \sqrt{(x-c)^2 + (y-0)^2}$$

$$(x+c)^2 + (y-0)^2 = \left[2a + \sqrt{(x-c)^2 + (y-0)^2}\right]^2$$

$$(x+c)^2 + (y-0)^2 = 4a^2 + 4a\sqrt{(x-c)^2 + (y-0)^2} + (x-c)^2 + (y-0)^2$$

$$(x+c)^2 + (y-0)^2 - [(x-c)^2 + (y-0)^2] = 4a^2 + 4a\sqrt{(x-c)^2 + (y-0)^2}$$

$$4cx = 4a^2 + 4a\sqrt{(x-c)^2 + (y-0)^2}$$

$$4cx - 4a^2 = +4a\sqrt{(x-c)^2 + (y-0)^2}$$

$$4(cx - a^2) = 4a\sqrt{(x-c)^2 + (y-0)^2} \to cx - a^2 = a\sqrt{(x-c)^2 + (y-0)^2}$$

$$[cx - a^2]^2 = (a)^2[(x-c)^2 + (y-0)^2] \to$$

$$c^2x^2 + a^4 - 2a^2cx = a^2[c^2 + x^2 - 2cx + y^2] = a^2c^2 + a^2x^2 - 2a^2cx + a^2y^2$$

$$(c^2 - a^2)x^2 - a^2y^2 = (c^2 - a^2)a^2$$

Dividing by $(c^2 - a^2)a^2$

$$\frac{x^2}{a^2} - \frac{y^2}{c^2 - a^2} = 1$$

With $c > a$

$$\frac{x^2}{a^2} - \frac{y^2}{b^2} = 1$$

This is the standard form of the equation of a hyperbola.

The general form of the equation with centre at the origin and foci on the coordinate axes is $Ax^2 - By^2 = \pm 1$, where positive sign occurs when focus is on x-axis and negative for y-axis.

Deductions

From $\frac{x^2}{a^2} - \frac{y^2}{b^2} = 1 \to -\frac{x^2}{a^2} + \frac{y^2}{b^2} = -1$

(i) It follows that if $x^2 > a^2$, there is no portion of the curve between $x = \pm a$ and the curve must contain two branches.

(ii) As $x \to \pm\infty, y \to \pm\infty$ and therefore the hyperbola extends towards infinity in both directions.

(iii) Eccentricity for an ellipse is greater than one i.e $e > 1$ and it is given by

$$e = \frac{c}{a} = \frac{\sqrt{a^2 + b^2}}{a}$$

(iv) A hyperbola has two foci and hence two directrices (DD and $D'D'$). The equation of the directrices is given by

$x = \pm \frac{a}{e}$, holds if the foci is on the x-axis as above

$y = \pm \frac{a}{e}$, holds if the foci is on the y-axis.

(v) From figure (b), the transverse axis is $A'A$, of length 2a while the conjugate axis is $B'B$, of length 2b.

(vi) Length of the semi latus rectum of the hyperbola.

From $\frac{x^2}{a^2} - \frac{y^2}{b^2} = 1$

When x = ae, $\frac{(ae)^2}{a^2} - \frac{y^2}{b^2} = 1 \rightarrow e^2 - \frac{y^2}{b^2} = 1 \rightarrow \frac{y^2}{b^2} = e^2 - 1$

From $b^2 = a^2(e^2 - 1) \rightarrow \frac{b^2}{a^2} = e^2 - 1$. Inserting we have

$\frac{y^2}{b^2} = e^2 - 1 = \frac{b^2}{a^2} \therefore \frac{y^2}{b^2} = \frac{b^2}{a^2} \rightarrow b^4 = a^2 y^2 \rightarrow y^2 = \frac{b^4}{a^2} \therefore y = \sqrt{\frac{b^4}{a^2}} = \pm \frac{b^2}{a}$

Length of the latus rectum is $2y = 2\left[\frac{b^2}{a}\right]$

(vi) Change of origin: When the centre of the hyperbola is at a point (x_1, y_1) such that the axis is parallel to either the x-axis or y-axis, the equation $\frac{x^2}{a^2} - \frac{y^2}{b^2} = 1$ becomes

$\frac{(x - x_1)^2}{a^2} - \frac{(y - y_1)^2}{b^2} = 1$ major axis parallel to x-axis

$\frac{(x - x_1)^2}{b^2} - \frac{(y - y_1)^2}{a^2} = 1$ major axis parallel to y-axis

In either case, the equation of the hyperbola takes the form $Ax^2 - By^2 + Dx + Ey + F = 0$

(vii) Point of intersection of the line y = mx + c and the hyperbola $\frac{x^2}{a^2} - \frac{y^2}{b^2} = 1$

Point of intersection is the simultaneous solution of both equations

y = mx + c   ....(i)

$\frac{x^2}{a^2} - \frac{y^2}{b^2} = 1$ ....(ii)

By substitution $\frac{x^2}{a^2} - \frac{(mx+c)^2}{b^2} = 1 \rightarrow \frac{x^2}{a^2} - \frac{m^2x^2 + 2cmx + c^2}{b^2} = 1$

$\frac{b^2x^2 - a^2m^2x^2 - 2a^2cmx - a^2c^2}{a^2b^2} = 1 \rightarrow (b^2 - a^2m^2)x^2 - 2a^2mcx - a^2(c^2 + b^2) = 0$

As with all quadratic equations, the above equation has root which can either be complex, real or coincident.

For coincidence, $b^2 = 4ac \rightarrow (2a^2mc)^2 = 4(b^2 + a^2m^2)(a^2c^2 - a^2b^2)$

$4a^4m^2c^2 = 4a^2[(b^2 + a^2m^2)(c^2 - b^2)] \rightarrow a^2m^2c^2 = [(b^2 + a^2m^2)(c^2 - b^2)]$

$a^2m^2c^2 = b^2c^2 - b^4 + a^2m^2c^2 - a^2b^2m^2 \rightarrow b^2c^2 = b^4 + a^2b^2m^2$

$b^2(c^2) = b^2(b^2 + a^2m^2) \rightarrow c^2 = b^2 + a^2m^2 \therefore c = \pm\sqrt{b^2 + a^2m^2}$

Thus, for all values of m, the straight line $y = mx \pm \sqrt{b^2 + a^2m^2}$ are tangent to the ellipse.

(vii) Equation of chord to the hyperbola $\frac{x^2}{a^2} - \frac{y^2}{b^2} = 1$

Since the points (x_1, y_1) and (x_2, y_2) lie on the ellipse, we have

$\frac{x_1^2}{a^2} - \frac{y_1^2}{b^2} = 1$ ....(i)

$\frac{x_2^2}{a^2} - \frac{y_2^2}{b^2} = 1$ ....(ii)

Following the same approach as in ellipse, we arrive at

$\frac{xx_1}{a^2} - \frac{yy_1}{b^2} = 1$

Which gives the equation of the tangent at (x_1, y_1)

(viii) Equation of tangent and normal to the hyperbola $\frac{x^2}{a^2} - \frac{y^2}{b^2} = 1$

From $\frac{xx_1}{a^2} - \frac{yy_1}{b^2} = 1 \rightarrow \frac{yy_1}{b^2} = \frac{xx_1}{a^2} - 1 \rightarrow y = \frac{b^2}{y_1}\left[\frac{xx_1}{a^2} - 1\right] = \frac{xx_1 b^2}{a^2 y_1} - \frac{b^2}{y_1}$

The gradient of the straight line is $\frac{dy}{dx} = \frac{x_1 b^2}{a^2 y_1}$

Since the tangent at the point (x_1, y_1) is perpendicular to the normal at the point

From $m_1 m_2 = -1$

$$m_1 m_2 = -1 \rightarrow \frac{y - y_1}{x - x_1} \times \frac{y_2 - y_2}{x_2 - x_1} = -1 \rightarrow \frac{y - y_1}{x - x_1} \times \frac{dy}{dx} = -1 \rightarrow \frac{y - y_1}{x - x_1} \times \left[\frac{x_1 b^2}{a^2 y_1}\right] = -1$$

$$\frac{y - y_1}{x - x_1} = -\frac{a^2 y_1}{b^2 x_1} \rightarrow \frac{y - y_1}{a^2 y_1} = -\frac{x - x_1}{b^2 x_1} \rightarrow$$

$$\frac{y - y_1}{x - x_1} = \frac{a^2 y_1}{b^2 x_1} \rightarrow \frac{y - y_1}{a^2 y_1} = \frac{x - x_1}{b^2 x_1} \rightarrow (y - y_1) b^2 x_1 = -(x - x_1) a^2 y_1$$

$$b^2 x_1 y - b^2 x_1 y_1 = -a^2 y_1 x + a^2 x_1 y_1 \rightarrow b^2 x_1 y + a^2 x y_1 = b^2 x_1 y_1 + a^2 x_1 y_1$$

$$\therefore b^2 x_1 y + a^2 x y_1 = (a^2 + b^2) x_1 y_1$$

(x) Parametric equation of the hyperbola

From $\sec^2 \theta - \tan^2 \theta = 1$

Comparing with $\frac{x^2}{a^2} - \frac{y^2}{b^2} = 1$, $\sec^2 \theta = \frac{x^2}{a^2}$, $\tan^2 \theta = \frac{y^2}{b^2}$

Thus, $\left. \begin{array}{l} x = a\sec\theta \\ y = b\tan\theta \end{array} \right\}$

These are the parametric equations of a hyperbola.

(xi) The rectangular hyperbola: A hyperbola is said to be rectangular if its asymptotes are perpendicular.

The asymptotes of the hyperbola $\frac{x^2}{a^2} - \frac{y^2}{b^2} = 1$ are $y = +\frac{b}{a}x$ and $y = -\frac{b}{a}x$

For perpendicularity $m_1 m_2 = -1 \rightarrow -\frac{b}{a} \cdot \frac{b}{a} = -1 \rightarrow \frac{b^2}{a^2} = 1 \therefore b^2 = a^2$

$b^2 = a^2(e^2 - 1) \rightarrow \frac{b^2}{a^2} = (e^2 - 1) \rightarrow 1 = (e^2 - 1) \rightarrow e^2 = 2 \therefore e = \sqrt{2}$

The equation is then $x^2 - y^2 = a^2$ and its asymptotes is $y = -x$ which bisects the angles between the axes.

QUESTIONS

(29.1). Find the equation of the tangent and the normal to the hyperbola $4x^2 - 9y^2 = 36$ at $(3\sqrt{2}, 2)$

Solution

From $4x^2 - 9y^2 = 36 \rightarrow \frac{x^2}{9} - \frac{y^2}{4} = 1 \therefore a^2 = 9, b^2 = 4$

Equation of tangent at $(3\sqrt{2}, 2)$

$\frac{x(3\sqrt{2})}{9} - \frac{y(2)}{4} = 1 \rightarrow \frac{x(\sqrt{2})}{3} - \frac{y}{2} = 1 \rightarrow 2x\sqrt{2} - 3y = 6$

Equation of normal at $(3\sqrt{2}, 2)$ is gotten from $a^2 x y_1 + b^2 x_1 y = (a^2 + b^2) x_1 y_1$

$9x(2) + 4(3\sqrt{2})y = (9 + 4)(3\sqrt{2})(2) \rightarrow 18x + 12\sqrt{2}\, y = 78\sqrt{2}$

(29.2). Find the point of intersection P, Q where the line $5y - 3x + 5 = 0$ cuts the hyperbola $4x^2 - 25y^2 - 15 = 0$. Also determine the equation of the tangents and normal to the hyperbola at the points P, Q.

Solution

Point of intersection implies solving both equations simultaneously

From $5y - 3x + 5 = 0 \rightarrow y = \frac{3x - 5}{5}$

By substitution, $4x^2 - 25 \left[\frac{3x - 5}{5}\right]^2 - 15 = 0 \rightarrow 4x^2 - 25\frac{(3x - 5)^2}{25} - 15 = 0$

$4x^2 - (3x - 5)^2 - 15 = 0 \rightarrow 4x^2 - (9x^2 - 30x + 25) - 15 = 0$

$4x^2 - 9x^2 + 30x - 25 - 15 = 0 \rightarrow -5x^2 + 30x - 40 = 0$

$-x^2 + 6x - 8 = 0 \rightarrow (x - 2)(x - 4) = 0 \therefore x = 2 \text{ or } 4$

Inserting into $x = 2$ or 4 into $y = \frac{3x - 5}{5}$

When $x = 2 \rightarrow y = \frac{3(2) - 5}{5} = \frac{1}{5}$

When $x = 4 \rightarrow y = \frac{3(4) - 5}{5} = \frac{7}{5}$

The points of intersection are $P\left[2, \frac{1}{5}\right], Q\left[4, \frac{7}{5}\right]$

The equation of the tangent at P is given by $\frac{xx_1}{a^2} - \frac{yy_1}{b^2} = 1$

Inserting values of x_1 and y_1 in the above equation yields

$4x(2) - 25y\left[\frac{1}{5}\right] - 15 = 0 \rightarrow 8x - 5y - 15 = 0$

Similarly, the equation of the tangent at Q is given by

$$4x(4) - 25y\left[\frac{7}{5}\right] - 15 = 0 \rightarrow 16x - 35y - 15 = 0$$

The gradient of the tangent is $\rightarrow y = \frac{8x}{5} - 3 \therefore m = \frac{8}{5}$

The gradient of the normal is $\rightarrow y = \frac{16x}{35} - \frac{15}{35} \therefore m = \frac{16}{35}$

$$\frac{y - \frac{1}{5}}{x - 2} = -\frac{5}{8} \rightarrow \frac{5y - 1}{5x - 10} = -\frac{5}{8} \rightarrow 8(5y - 1) = -5(5x - 10) \rightarrow$$

$$40y - 8 = -25x + 50$$

$$40y + 25x = 50 + 8 = 58 \therefore 40y + 25x - 58 = 0$$

$$\frac{y - \frac{7}{5}}{x - 4} = -\frac{35}{16} \rightarrow \frac{5y - 7}{5x - 20} = -\frac{35}{16} \rightarrow 16(5y - 7) = -35(5x - 20) \rightarrow$$

$$80y - 112 = -175x + 700$$

$$80y + 175x = 50 + 8 = 812 \therefore 80y + 175x - 812 = 0$$

CHAPTER 30 TRIGONOMETRY

This is a branch of mathematics that studies relationships involving lengths and angles of triangles. This includes, the trig ratio & relationship, types of applications

THE TRIG RATIO: This deals with ratio of sides related to a given related in a right angled triangle. The sides of the triangle are opposite, hypotenuse and adjacent

Opposite: side facing the required angle

Hypotenuse: the longest side of a triangle

Adjacent: the third side

1.

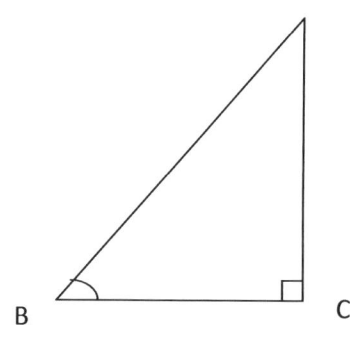

From the marked angle we have

Opposite = AC, Hypotenuse = AB adjacent = BC

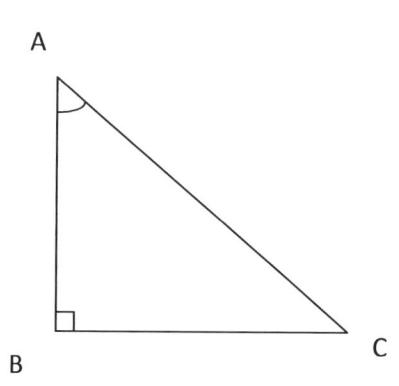

Opposite = BC, Hypotenuse = AC, Adjacent = AB

The frequently used trig ratio is SOH CAH TOA where

SOH: Sine = $\frac{Opp}{hyp}$, CAH : Cosine = $\frac{adj}{hyp}$, TOA = Tan = $\frac{Opp}{hyp}$

Other trigonometric ratios can be developed from these basic ratios e.g.

cosecant (Cosec), Secant (sec) and Cotangent (cot)

$$\text{Cosec} = \frac{1}{\text{sine}}, \quad \text{Sec} = \frac{1}{\text{cosine}}, \quad \text{Cot} = \frac{1}{\text{tan}}$$

Trig ratio of acute angles

This is simply the ratio of sides in a triangle with acute angles. It can also be regarded as ratio of sides in a triangle formed on the positive axis of y and x

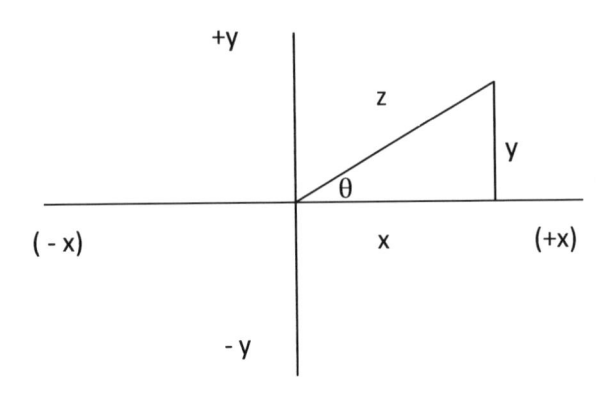

$$\text{Sin } \theta = \frac{\text{opp}}{\text{hyp}} = \frac{y}{z}, \quad \text{Cos}\theta = \frac{\text{adj}}{\text{hyp}} = \frac{x}{z}, \quad \text{Tan } \theta = \frac{\text{Opp}}{\text{adj}} = \frac{y}{x}$$

$$\text{Cosec } \theta = \frac{1}{\sin\theta} = \frac{1}{\text{opp/hyp}} = \frac{\text{hyp}}{\text{opp}} = \frac{z}{y}$$

$$\text{Sec } \theta = \frac{1}{\cos\theta} = \frac{1}{\text{adj/hyp}} = \frac{\text{hyp}}{\text{adj}} = \frac{z}{x}$$

$$\text{Tan } \theta = \frac{1}{\cot\theta} = \frac{1}{\text{adj/opp}} = \frac{1}{x/y} = \frac{y}{x}$$

Relationship between trigonometry ratios

Here we focus our attention on how to find the trig ratio in terms of the other.

This can be achieved by various way which include

1. Using the established relationship called identities

These are results of combining two or more of the ratios algebraically

They include

From Sine $= \frac{opp}{hyp} = \frac{O}{H}$ ....(a)   Cosine $= \frac{adj}{hyp} = \frac{A}{H}$ ......(b)

dividing a by b gives

$\frac{Sine}{Cosine} = \frac{O/H}{A/H} = \frac{O}{H} \div \frac{A}{H} = \frac{O}{H} \times \frac{H}{A} = \frac{O}{A} = \frac{opp}{adj}$

$\therefore \tan\theta = \frac{\sin\theta}{\cos\theta} = \frac{opp}{adj}$ ....(c)

Inverting c gives

$\frac{1}{\tan\theta} = \frac{\cos\theta}{\sin\theta} = \cot\theta$ ....(d)

Squaring a and b and adding gives

$\sin^2\theta + \cos^2\theta \to \left(\frac{O}{H}\right)^2 + \left(\frac{A}{H}\right)^2 = \frac{O^2}{H^2} + \frac{A^2}{H^2} = \frac{O^2 + A^2}{H^2} = \frac{H^2}{H^2} = 1$

$\therefore \sin^2\theta + \cos^2\theta = 1$ ....(e)

Dividing e by $\cos^2\theta$ gives

$\frac{\sin^2\theta}{\cos^2\theta} + \frac{\cos^2\theta}{\cos^2\theta} = \frac{1}{\cos^2\theta} \to \tan^2\theta + 1 = \sec^2\theta$

$\therefore \tan^2\theta + 1 = \sec^2\theta$ ....(f)

Dividing e also by $\sin^2\theta$ gives

$\frac{\sin^2\theta}{\sin^2\theta} + \frac{\cos^2\theta}{\sin^2\theta} = \frac{1}{\sin^2\theta} \to 1 + \cot^2\theta = \csc^2\theta$

$\therefore \cot^2\theta + 1 = \csc^2\theta$ ....(g)

Bringing together, we have

1. $\tan\theta = \frac{\sin\theta}{\cos\theta}$, $\cot\theta = \frac{\cos\theta}{\sin\theta}$
2. $\sin^2\theta + \cos^2\theta = 1$
3. $\tan^2\theta = \sec^2\theta - 1$
4. $\cot^2\theta = \csc^2\theta - 1$

2. Right angled triangle relationship

This involves application of Pythagoras's theorem and given trig ratio in a right angled triangle.

3. Using complementary property

Here we apply the relationship between the angles of right angle triangle. This is as shown below:

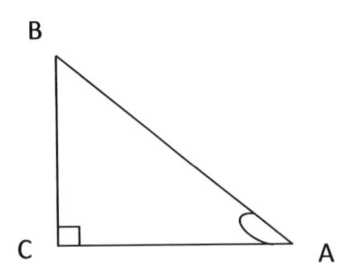

$\hat{A} + \hat{B} = 90^0 \rightarrow \hat{B} = 90 - \hat{A}$

$\sin A = \frac{BC}{AB}$ ……..(i)

$\cos A = \frac{AC}{AB}$ ………..(ii)

$\sin B = \frac{AC}{AB} \rightarrow \sin(90 - A) = \frac{AC}{AB}$ ………..(iii)

$\cos B = \frac{BC}{AB} \rightarrow \cos(90 - A) = \frac{BC}{AB}$ ………..(iv)

Comparing (i) and (iii)

$\sin A = \cos(90 - A) = \frac{BC}{AB}$

Comparing (ii) and (iv)

$\cos A = \sin(90 - A) = \frac{AC}{AB}$

Using same approach,

$\tan A = \cot(90 - A)$

$\sec A = \csc(90 - A)$

Trigonometry ratio of special acute angles

These are angles less than 90^0. They include

(i) 45^0: This can be produced from a square

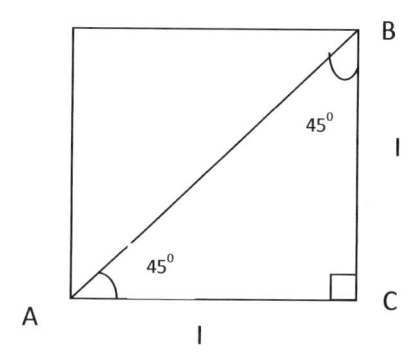

By Pythagoras $AB^2 = 1^2 + 1^2 = 1 + 1 = 2 \rightarrow AB = \sqrt{2}$

∴ $\sin 45 = \frac{1}{\sqrt{2}}$, $\cos 45 = \frac{1}{\sqrt{2}}$, $\tan 45 = \frac{1}{1} = 1$

(ii) 30^0 and 60^0: These can be produced from an equilateral triangle

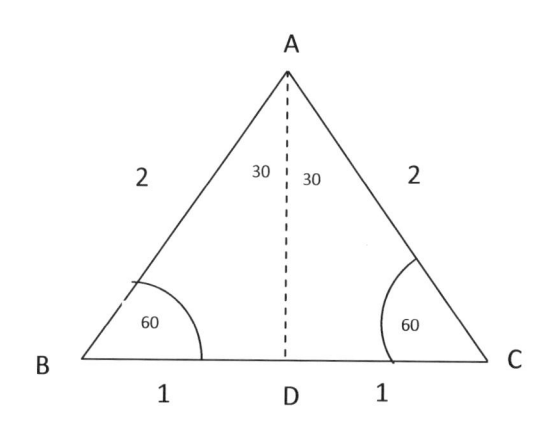

$AD^2 = 2^2 - 1^2 = 4 - 1 = 3 \rightarrow AD = \sqrt{3}$

Using any of the 30^0

$\sin 30 = \frac{1}{2}$, $\cos 30^0 = \frac{\sqrt{3}}{2}$, $\tan 30 = \frac{1}{\sqrt{3}}$

387

Using any of the 60^0

$Sin\ 60 = \frac{\sqrt{3}}{2}$, $Cos\ 60 = \frac{1}{2}$, $Tan\ 60 = \frac{\sqrt{3}}{1} = \sqrt{3}$

(*iii*) 0^0 and 90^0

$Sin\ 0 = 0$, $Cos\ 0 = 1$, $Tan\ 0 = \frac{Sin\ 0}{Cos\ 0} = \frac{0}{1}$

$Sin\ 90 = 1$, $Cos\ 90 = 0$, $Tan\ 90 = \frac{sin 90}{cos 90} = \frac{1}{0} = \infty$

Trigonometry ratio of negative angles

Here we simply add 360^0 or its multiples to the given angle until it become positive.

Trigonometry ratio of obtuse and reflex angles

Since obtuse and reflex angles are greater than 90^0 and all angles are measured from the positive side of x-axis on x-y plane trig ratio of angles other than acute are found by expressing them in form that contains an acute angle. The corresponding acute angle is obtained from a quadrant.

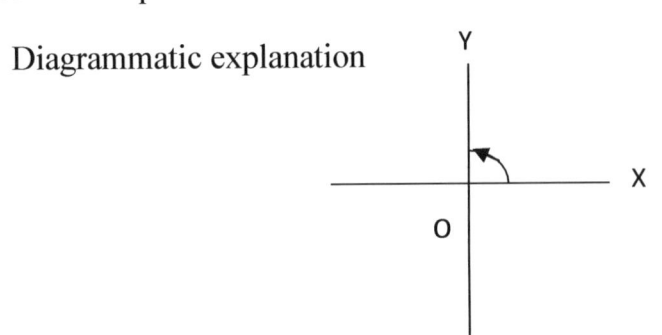

Diagrammatic explanation

measurement from the positive side of x–axis

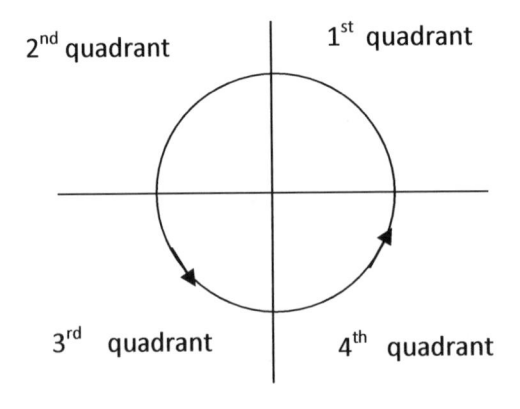

2nd quadrant | 1st quadrant

3rd quadrant | 4th quadrant

388

Various quadrants measured anti-clockwise

90 – 180	0 – 90
180 - 270	270 - 360

Angle in each quadrant

$180° - \theta$	θ
$180 - \theta$ or $\theta - 180$	$360 - \theta$

Formula for each quadrant

Thus,

(*i*) Determine the quadrant in which the given angle is located

(*ii*) Apply the formula for the quadrant ''taking note of the signs''

Note:

In the 1st quadrant – All are positive

In the 2nd quadrant – Only sine is positive others are negative

In the 3rd quadrant – Tan is positive others are negative

In the 4th quadrant – Cos is positive others are negative

Trigonometry ratio of allied angles

Allied angles are angles greater than 360^0. We simply subtracting 360^0 or its multiple from the angle and identifying the position of the remaining angle in the quadrant.

Trigonometry value of compound angles

Compound angles are angles that exist in parts other than the forms in quadrant E.g The quadrant has θ, 180 – θ, 180 + θ or θ - 180 and 360 – θ as its basic forms while examples of compound angles include: 45 + 30, 60 + 45, 70 – 20, 120 + 30 etc.

The Trigonometrical value of compound angle is found by characteristic expansion

Sin (A + B) = SinACosB + CosASinB

Sin (A – B) = SinACosB – CosAsinB

Cos (A + B) = CosACosB – SinASinB

Cos (A – B) = CosACosB + SinASinB

$$\text{Tan}(A + B) = \frac{Sin(A+B)}{Cos(A+B)} = \frac{SinACosB + CosASinB}{CosACosB - SinASinB} = \frac{tanA + tanB}{1 - tanAtanB}$$

$$\tan(A - B) = \frac{Sin(A-B)}{Cos(A-B)} = \frac{SinACosB - CosASinB}{CosACosB + SinASinB} = \frac{tanA - tanB}{1 + tanAtanB}$$

Applications of Compound angles

(*i*) Multiple angles: These can be obtained when the values are equal values i.e A = B

Sin 2A = Sin (A +A) = SinACosA + CosASinA = Sin 2A = 2sinACosA

Sin 3A = Sin (2A + A) = Sin2ACosA + Cos2ASinA

Sin 4 A = Sin(2A + 2A) = 2sin2Acos2A

$Cos\ 2A = Cos(A + A) = CosACosA - SinASinA = Cos^2A - Sin^2A = (1 - sin^2A) - Sin^2A = 1 - Sin^2A - Sin^2A = 1 - 2Sin^2A = 2Cos^2A - 1$

$Cos\ 3A = Cos(2A + A) = Cos\ 2A\ Cos\ A - Sin\ 2A\ Sin\ A$

$Cos\ 4A = Cos(2A + 2A) = 1 - 2Sin^2 2A$

(*ii*) Factor Formular: This is obtained when two compound angles are added or subtracted.

(*a*) $Sin(A + B) + Sin(A - B) = SinACosB + CosASinB + SinACosB - CosASinB$

$\therefore Sin(A + B) - Sin(A - B) = 2SinACosB$

(*b*) $Sin(A + B) - Sin(A - B) = SinACosB + CosASinB - (SinACosB - CosASinB)$

$SinACosB + CosASinB - SinACosB + CosASinB$

$\therefore Sin(A + B) - Sin(A - B) = 2CosASinB$

(*c*) $Cos(A + B) + Cos(A - B) = CosACosB - SinASinB + CosACosB + SinASinB$

$\therefore Cos(A + B) + Cos(A - B) = 2Cos\ A\ Cos\ B$

(*d*) $Cos(A + B) - Cos(A - B) = CosACosB - SinASinB - (CosACosB + SinASinB)$

$CosACosB - SinASinB - CosACosB - SinASinB$

$\therefore Cos(A + B) - Cos(A - B) = -2SinASinB$

The formula can be remembered as:

Sine + Sine = 2 Sin [(½ Sum) Cos(½ difference)]

Sine − Sine = 2 Cos [(½ Sum) Cos(½ difference)]

Cos + Cos = 2 Cos [(½ Sum) Cos(½ difference)]

Cos − Cos = 2 Sin [(½ Sum) Sin(½ difference)]

TRIGONOMETRICAL GRAPH

These graphs are obtained as the angle changes.

SINE GRAPHS

Case 1: When Y = sinθ

This is obtained by plotting sin θ against θ from θ to 360^0

When θ = 0   → y = sin 0 = 1

θ = 90^0 → y = sin 90 = 1

θ = 180^0 → y = sin 180 = 0

θ = 270^0 → y = sin 270 = -1

θ = 360^0 → y = sin 360 = 0

Thus the maximum and minimum amplitude are 1 and -1

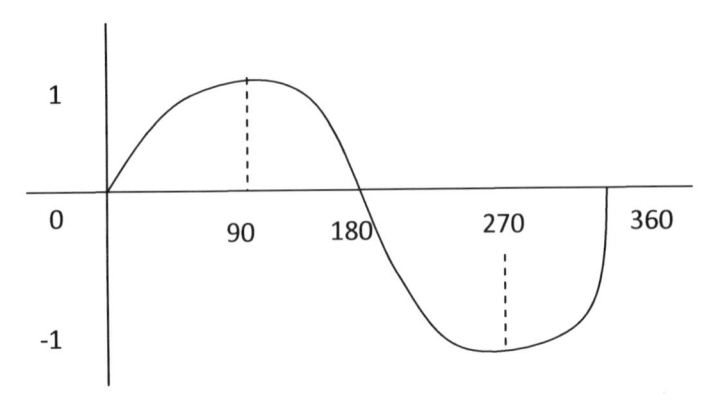

Sine graph for a complete revolution

Case 2: When Y = Asinθ

In this case, the graph takes the same shape as in case 1 but with the amplitude (A) (maximum and minimum value) changed.

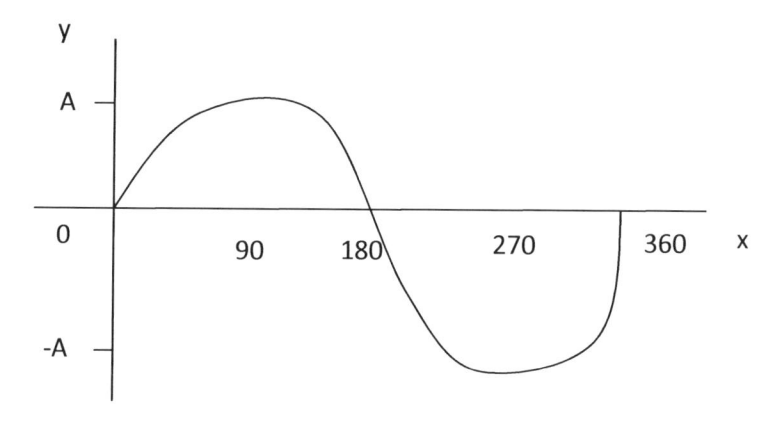

[Graph showing sine curve from 0 to 360 with amplitude A and -A]

Thus if Y = 2sinθ

Following the same procedure as in case 1, we find out that the maximum and minimum are 2 & - 2. So we retain the graph of case 1 and just replace the value of A.

To complete the angles along the curve, the number of points along the curve apart from the origin should be known. These are points on x–axis and the ones below and above.

Distance between the points $= \frac{360}{n}$

Where n is the no of points on the x–axis (above and below). Since the graph is always the same as case 1 with 2 points above and below

Distance between the points $= \frac{360}{4} = 90°$

∴ Distance between points for such case will always be 90°

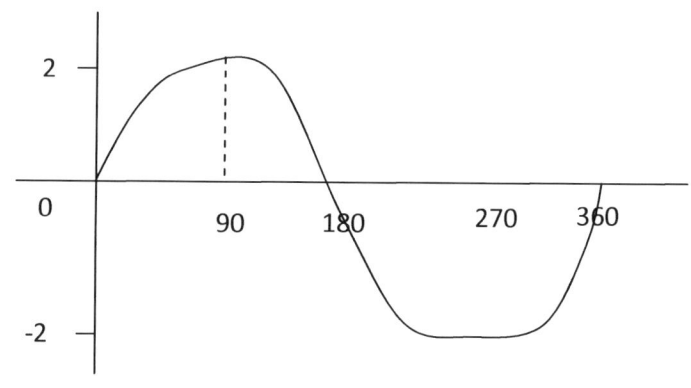

[Graph showing sine curve from 0 to 360 with amplitude 2 and -2]

i.e increase of 90^0 from 0 or decrease of 90^0 from 360^0

393

Case 3: When Y = sin$n$θ

For multiple angles, the maximum and minimum do not change (same with case 1) but the number of revolution or cycle changes. Thus the co-efficient of the given angle can be taken as the number of revolution or cycle in a particular curve.

If Y = sin 2θ

θ = 0, Y = sin 2(0) → sin 0 = 0. When θ = 45, Y = sin 2(45) = sin 90° = 0

θ = 90°, Y = sin 2(90) → sin 180 → sin (180 – 0) → sin 0 = 0

θ = 135, Y = sin 2(135) → sin 270° → sin (360 – 90) → sin 270 = -1

θ = 180, Y = sin 2(180) → sin 360 → sin (360 – 0) = sin 0 = 0

θ = 255, Y = sin 2(225) → sin 450 → sin (450 – 360) → sin (90) = 1

θ = 270, Y = sin 2 (270) → sin 540 → sin (540 – 360) → sin (180) = 0

θ = 315, Y = sin 2(315) → sin 630 → sin (630 – 360) → sin 270 = -1

θ = 360, Y = sin 2(360) → sin 720 → sin (720 – 360) → sin 360 = 0

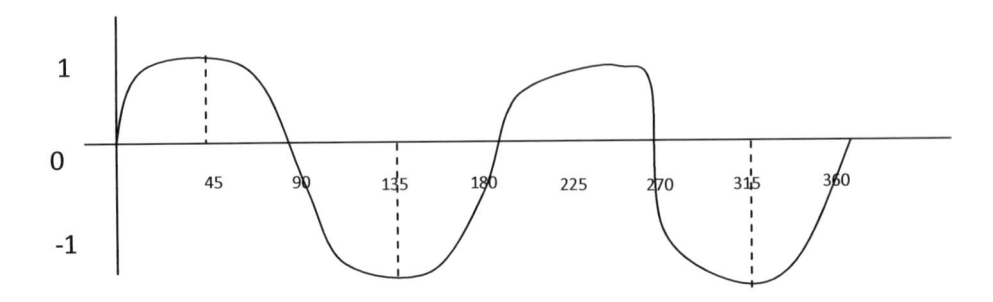

The number of revolution = the co-efficient of θ.

Distance between the points = $\frac{360}{4 \times 2}$ = 45°

∴ Distance between points for Y = sin2θ will always be 45°

If Y = sin 3θ

Distance between the points = $\frac{360}{6 \times 2}$ = 30°

∴ Distance between points for Y = sin3θ will always be 30°

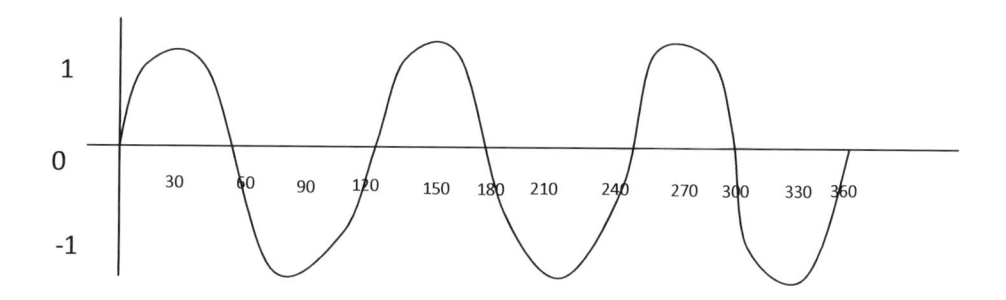

If Y = 3 sin2θ

Amplitude = 3

number of revolution between 0 and 360^0 = 2

Distance between the points = $\frac{360}{4 \times 2}$ = 45°

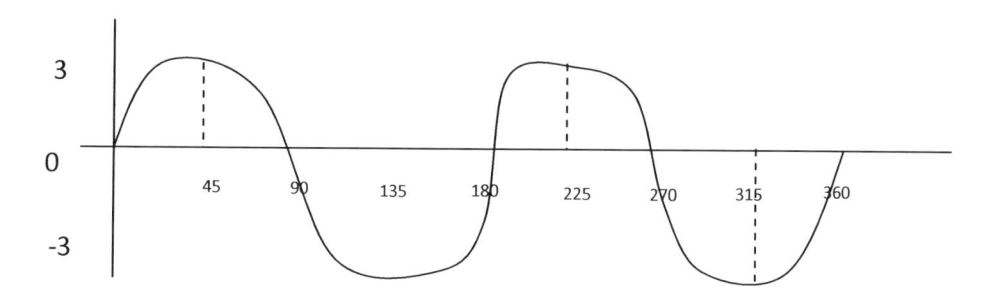

Case 4: When Y = k ± sinθ

In this case, k ± sinθ → k ± (case 1)

∴ we obtain new maximum and minimum values by adding and subtracting k from maximum and minimum values of case 1

Thus if Y = 3 + sinθ

$3 + \sin\theta = 3 \pm (1 \ \& \ -1) = (4, 2)$ are the new maximum & minimum values.

COSINE GRAPHS

This is also produced by plotting Cos θ from 0 to 360^0

Case 1: When Y = cosθ

When $\theta = 0 \rightarrow \cos 0 = 1$

$\theta = 90 \rightarrow \cos 90 = 0$

$\theta = 180 \rightarrow \cos 180 = -1$

$\theta = 270 \rightarrow \cos 270 = 0$

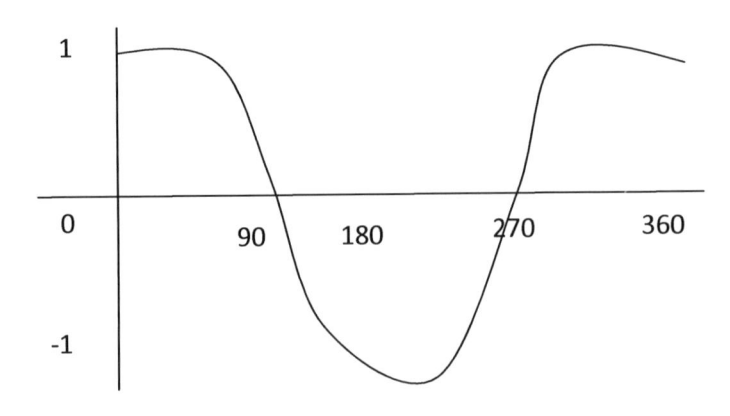

Case 2: When Y = Acosθ

In this case, the graph takes the same shape as in case 1 but with the amplitude (A) (maximum and minimum value) changed.

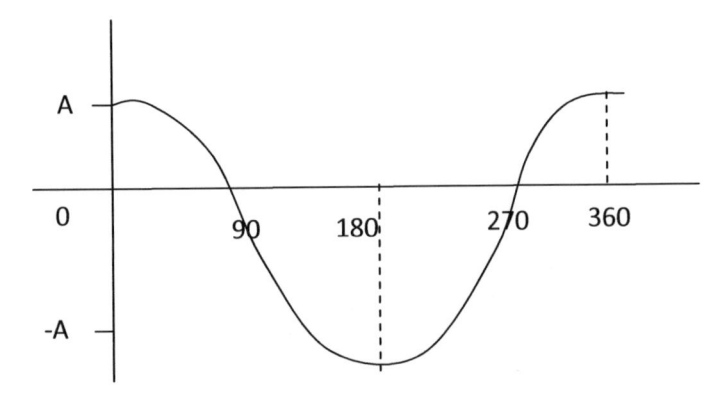

Thus if Y = 2cosθ

Following the same procedure as in case 1, we find out that the maximum and minimum are 2 & - 2. So we retain the graph of case 1 and just replace the value of A.

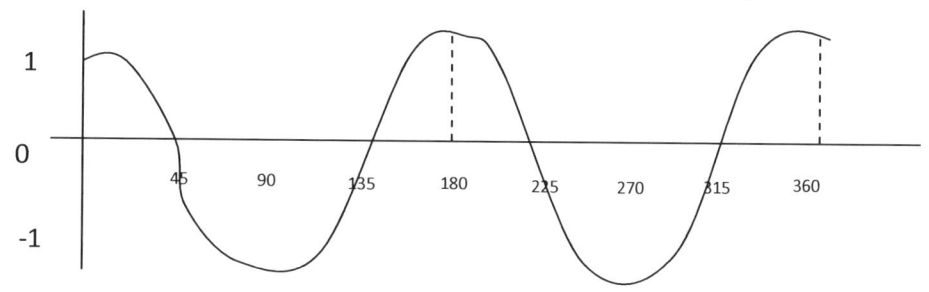

The number of revolution = the co-efficient of θ.

Distance between the points = $\frac{360}{4 \times 2}$ = 45°

∴ Distance between points for Y = sin2θ will always be 45°

Case 3: When Y = cosnθ

For multiple angles, the maximum and minimum do not change (same with case 1) but the number of revolution or cycle changes. Thus the co-efficient of the given angle can be taken as the number of revolution or cycle in a particular curve.

If Y = cos 2θ

θ = 0, Y = cos 2(0) = cos 0 = 1

θ = 45, Y = cos 2(45) = cos 90 = 0

θ = 90, Y = cos2(90) → cos 180 → cos(180 – 0) → - cos 0 = -1

θ = 135, Y = cos 2(135) → cos 270 → cos (360 – 90) → cos 90 = 0

θ = 180, Y = cos 2(180) → cos 360 → cos (360 – 0) → cos 0 = 1

θ = 225, Y = cos 2(225) → cos 450 → cos (450 – 360) → cos 90 = 0

θ = 270, Y = cos 2(270) → cos 540 → cos (540 – 360) → cos 180 = -1

θ = 315, Y = cos 2(315) → cos 630 → cos (630 – 360) → cos 270 = 0

θ = 360, Y = cos 2(360) → cos 720⁰ → cos(720 – 360) = cos 360

The number of revolution = the co-efficient of θ.

Case 4: When Y = k ± cosθ

In this case, $k \pm \cos\theta \rightarrow k \pm (case\ 1)$

∴ we obtain new maximum and minimum values by adding and subtracting k from maximum and minimum values of case 1

TANGENT GRAPH

When $\theta = 0 \rightarrow \tan\theta = \frac{\sin\theta}{\cos\theta} = \frac{0}{1} = 0$

When $\theta = 90^0 \rightarrow \tan 90^0 = \tan(90 - 0)$ or $\tan(90 + 0) = \cot 0 = \frac{1}{\tan 0} = \frac{1}{0} = \infty$

$\tan(90 + 0) = \tan(180 - 90) + 0) = \tan(180 - (90 - 0)) = -\tan(90 - 0) = -\cot 0 = -\infty$

∴ $\tan 90^0 = \pm\infty$

$\tan 180^0 = \tan(180 - 0)$ or $\tan(180 + 0)$

$\tan(180 - 0) = \tan 0 = 0$

$\tan(180 + 0) = \tan 0 = 0$

∴ $\tan 180^0 = 0$

$\tan 270^0 = \tan(180 + 90)$ or $\tan(360 - 90)$

$\tan(180 + 90) = 90^0 = \pm\infty$

$\tan(360 - 90) = -\tan 90^0 = -(\pm\infty) = \mp\infty$

∴ $\tan 270^0 = \pm\infty$ or $\mp\infty$

$\tan 360^0 = \tan(360 - 0) = -\tan 0 = 0$

+∞ means positive infinity which is a relatively number

- ∞ means negative infinity which is a relatively number

Thus + ∞ and - ∞ are largest and smallest numbers that can be obtained respectively

As Tan 0^0 = 0, Tan 90 = ±∞ , Tan 180 = 0,

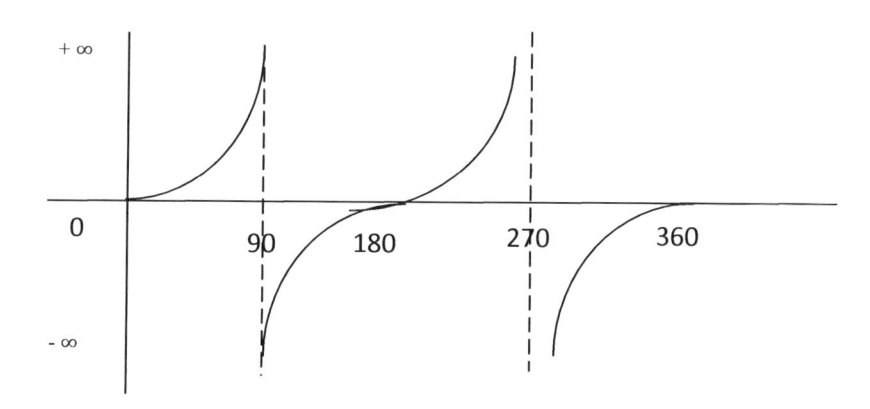

Tan 270 = ±∞, Tan 360 = 0

±∞ represented by dotted line.

From the graph above, it is observed that

i. From $0^0 – 90^0$, the value changes between 0 and ±∞. Thus from $0 – 90^0$, a curve moves (0 → +∞) i.e to a higher number, (remaining -∞).
ii. From $90 – 180^0$, a curve starts with the remaining (−∞ → 0).
iii. From 180 – 270, a curve moves from 0 to + ∞, leaving −∞.
iv. From 270 – 260, a curve moves from -∞ to 0 .

The lines through 90^0 and 270^0 i.e the infinity are called asymptotes.

QUESTIONS

(**30. 1**). The sketch represents the function of ?

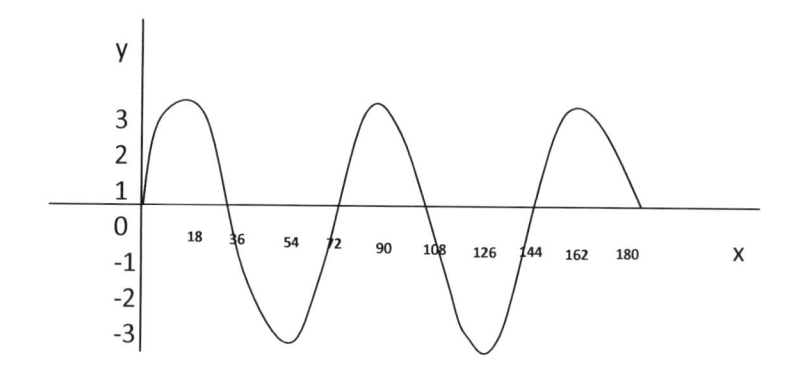

399

Solution

From the graph amplitude = 3

$$\frac{2^1/_2 \; revolution}{x \; revolution} = \frac{180}{360} \rightarrow x = \frac{360 \times 5}{2 \times 180} = 5 \; revolutions$$

∴ The graph = 3 sin 5x.

(30.2). Evaluate Sin 45Cos15 – Cos45Sin15 without using table.

Solution

From Sin A Cos B – Cos A Sin B = Sin (A – B)

Sin 45 Cos 15 – Cos 45 Sin 15 = Sin (45 – 15) → Sin 30° = ½.

(30.3). Evaluate Cos 30° sin 120° + Sin 30° Cos 120° without using mathematical tables.

Solution

From Sin (A + B) = Sin ACosB + CosASinB

Cos 30 Sin 120 + Sin 30 Cos 120 = Cos ASin B + Sin A Cos B

∴ Cos 30 Sin 120 + Sin 30 Cos 120 = Sin (30 + 120) = Sin150°

Sin (150) = Sin (180 – 30) = Sin 30 = ½

(30.4). Given that 2Sin(θ – 45) = Cos(θ + 45) find the value of tan θ.

Solution

Expanding we have

2Sin(θ - 45) = Cos(θ + 45)

2 (Sin θCos 45 – Cos θ Sin45) = CosθCos45 – Sinθ Sin45

$2\sin\theta\cos 45 - 2\cos\theta\sin 45 = \cos\theta\sin 45 + \sin\theta\cos 45$

$2\sin\theta\cos 45 + \sin\theta\cos 45 = \cos\theta\sin 45 + 2\cos\theta\sin 45^0$

$3\sin\theta\cos 45 = 3\cos\theta\sin 45 \rightarrow \sin\theta = \cos\theta \rightarrow \dfrac{\sin\theta}{\cos\theta} = \dfrac{\cos\theta}{\cos\theta}$

$\therefore \tan\theta = 1$

(30.5). If $\cos A = \dfrac{4}{5}$ and $\cos B = \dfrac{12}{13}$, both angles being acute, find the value of $\sin(A+B)$ without using tables.

Solution

From $\sin^2 A + \cos^2 A = 1$

$\cos A = \dfrac{4}{5}$, $\sin A = \sqrt{1 - \left(\dfrac{4}{5}\right)^2} \rightarrow \sqrt{1 - \dfrac{16}{25}} \rightarrow \sqrt{\dfrac{9}{25}} = \dfrac{3}{5}$

$\cos B = \dfrac{12}{13}$, $\sin B = \sqrt{1 - \left(\dfrac{12}{13}\right)^2} \rightarrow \sqrt{1 - \dfrac{144}{169}} \rightarrow \sqrt{\dfrac{25}{169}} = \dfrac{5}{13}$

$\sin(A+B) = \sin A\cos B - \cos A\sin B \rightarrow \dfrac{3}{5} \times \dfrac{12}{13} + \dfrac{4}{5} \times \dfrac{5}{13} = \dfrac{36}{65} + \dfrac{20}{65} = \dfrac{56}{65}$

(30.6). Find the value of $\cos 15^0$ in surd form.

Solution

$\cos 15 = \cos(45 - 30) = \cos 45\cos 30 + \sin 45\sin 30$

$\left(\dfrac{1}{\sqrt{2}} \cdot \dfrac{\sqrt{3}}{2}\right) + \left(\dfrac{1}{\sqrt{2}} \cdot \dfrac{1}{\sqrt{2}}\right) \rightarrow \dfrac{\sqrt{3}}{2\sqrt{2}} + \dfrac{1}{2\sqrt{2}} \rightarrow \dfrac{\sqrt{3}+1}{2\sqrt{2}} \rightarrow \dfrac{\sqrt{3}+1}{2\sqrt{2}} \cdot \dfrac{\sqrt{2}}{\sqrt{2}} \rightarrow \dfrac{\sqrt{2}(\sqrt{3}+1)}{2 \times 2} = \dfrac{\sqrt{2}(\sqrt{3}+1)}{4}$

(30.7). Evaluate $\sin 75 \cos 75$ without using table.

Solution

$2\sin A\cos A = \sin 2A = \sin(A+A) \rightarrow \sin A\cos A = \tfrac{1}{2}\sin(A+A)$

$\sin 75 \cos 75 = \dfrac{1}{2}\sin(75+75) \rightarrow \dfrac{1}{2}\sin 150^0 \rightarrow \dfrac{1}{2}\sin(180-30) \rightarrow \dfrac{1}{2}[\sin 30]$

$$\frac{1}{2} \times \frac{1}{2} = \frac{1}{4}$$

(30.8). Expressing $\sin 5\theta + \sin 3\theta$ in factors

Solution

For factors $\sin(A+B) + \sin(A-B) = 2\sin\left(\frac{1}{2}\text{sum}\right)\cos\left(\frac{1}{2}\text{difference}\right)$

$\therefore \sin 5\theta + \sin 3\theta = 2\sin\frac{(5\theta+3\theta)}{2}\cos\frac{(5\theta-3\theta)}{2} = 2\sin 4\theta \cos\theta$

(30.9). Express $\cos 2\theta - \cos 8\theta$ in factors

Solution

$\cos(A-B) - \cos(A+B) = 2\sin\left(\frac{1}{2}\text{sum}\right)\sin\left(\frac{1}{2}\text{difference}\right)$

$\cos 2\theta - \cos 8\theta = 2\sin\frac{(8\theta+2\theta)}{2}\sin\frac{(8\theta-2\theta)}{2} = 2\sin 5\theta \sin 3\theta$

(30.10). If $\sin\theta = \frac{15}{17}$, where θ is acute, find $\tan\theta$

Solution

Opposite = 15, Hypotenus = 17

$A^2 + O^2 = H^2 \rightarrow A^2 = H^2 - O^2 = 17^2 - 15^2 \rightarrow A^2 = 289 - 225 = 64 \therefore A = \sqrt{64} = 8$

$\tan\theta = \frac{opp}{adj} = \frac{15}{8}$

(30.11). The value of y in $\sin(90-y) = \cos(72°\,31')$ is ?

Solution

$\sin(90-y) = \cos y$

$\sin(90-y) = \cos(72°\,31') \therefore \cos y = \cos 72°\,31'$

$\therefore y = 72°\,31$

(30.12). If $\tan = \frac{5}{12}$, where B is an acute angle, evaluate $\frac{\cos B}{\sin B + \cos B}$

Solution

Given $\tan B = \dfrac{5}{12}$, $O = 5$, $A = 12$, $H = \sqrt{12^2 + 5^2} = \sqrt{169} = 13$

$\cos B = \dfrac{A}{H} = \dfrac{12}{13}$, $\sin B = \dfrac{O}{H} = \dfrac{5}{13}$

$\therefore \dfrac{\cos B}{\sin B + \cos B} = \dfrac{12/13}{\frac{5}{13}+\frac{12}{13}} \to \dfrac{\frac{12}{13}}{\frac{17}{13}} \to \dfrac{12}{13} \times \dfrac{13}{17} = \dfrac{12}{17}$

(30.13). If $\cos x = \sqrt{\dfrac{a}{b}}$ find $\csc x$

Solution

From $\cos x = \sqrt{\dfrac{a}{b}} \to \cos x = \dfrac{\sqrt{a}}{\sqrt{b}}$, $A = \sqrt{a}$, $H = \sqrt{b}$

$O^2 = H^2 - A^2 \to (\sqrt{b})^2 - (\sqrt{a})^2 = b - a \quad \therefore O = \sqrt{b-a}$

$\csc x = \dfrac{1}{\sin x} = \dfrac{\text{Hyp}}{\text{opp}} = \dfrac{\sqrt{b}}{\sqrt{b-a}} = \sqrt{\dfrac{b}{b-a}}$

(30.14). If $\tan \theta = \dfrac{m^2 - n^2}{2mn}$, find $\sec \theta$

Solution

From $\tan^2 \theta = \sec^2 \theta - 1 \to \sec^2 \theta = 1 + \tan^2 \theta$

$\sec^2 \theta = 1 + \left(\dfrac{m^2 - n^2}{2mn}\right)^2 \to 1 + \dfrac{(m^2 - n^2)^2}{4m^2 n^2} \to \dfrac{4m^2 n^2 + (m^2 - n^2)^2}{4m^2 n^2} \to \dfrac{4m^2 n^2 + m^4 + n^4 - 2m^2 n^2}{4m^2 n^2}$

$\to \dfrac{m^4 + n^4 + 2m^2 n^2}{4m^2 n^2} \to \dfrac{(m^2)^2 + 2m^2 n^2 + (n^2)^2}{4m^2 n^2} = \dfrac{(m^2 + n^2)^2}{4m^2 n^2}$

$\therefore \sec \theta = \sqrt{\dfrac{(m^2 + n^2)^2}{4m^2 n^2}} = \dfrac{m^2 + n^2}{2mn}$

(30.15). If $\cos^2 \theta + \dfrac{1}{8} = \sin^2 \theta$. Find $\tan \theta$

Solution

From $\sin^2 \theta + \cos^2 \theta = 1$

$1 - \sin^2 \theta + \dfrac{1}{8} = \sin^2 \theta \to 1 + \dfrac{1}{8} = \sin^2 \theta + \sin^2 \theta \to \dfrac{9}{8} = 2 \sin^2 \theta$

$\sin^2\theta = \frac{9}{16}$, $\sin\theta = \sqrt{\frac{9}{16}} = \frac{3}{4} = \frac{O}{H}$

$A^2 = H^2 - O^2 \to 4^2 - 3^2 \to 16 - 9 = 7 \therefore A = \sqrt{7}$

$\tan\theta = \frac{Opp}{Adj} = \frac{3}{\sqrt{7}} \to \frac{3}{\sqrt{7}} \cdot \frac{\sqrt{7}}{\sqrt{7}} = \frac{3\sqrt{7}}{7}$

(30.16). *Given* $4\sin^2 x - 3 = 0$, find x if $0 \le x \le 90^0$.

Solution

$0 \le x \le 90^0$ implies acute angle

$4\sin^2 x - 3 = 0 \to 4\sin^2 x = 3 \to \sin^2 x = \frac{3}{4} \therefore \sin x = \sqrt{\frac{3}{4}} = \frac{\sqrt{3}}{2}$

$x = \sin^{-1}\left[\frac{\sqrt{3}}{2}\right] = 60^0$

(30.17) Simplify $\cos^2 x(\sec^2 x + \sec^2 x \tan^2 x)$

Solution

$\cos^2 x(\sec^2 x + \sec^2 x \tan^2 x) \to \cos^2 x \sec^2 x (1 + \tan^2 x) \to \cos^2 x \sec^2 x(\sec^2 x)$

$\cos^2 x \cdot \frac{1}{\cos^2 x} \cdot \sec^2 x = \sec^2 x$

(30.18) Simplify the given expression $\sqrt{\frac{1 - \cos x}{1 + \cos x}}$

Solution

Rationalizing the denominator with the conjugate

$\sqrt{\frac{1 - \cos x}{1 + \cos x} \cdot \frac{(1 - \cos x)}{(1 - \cos x)}} = \sqrt{\frac{(1 - \cos x)^2}{(1 + \cos^2 x)}} = \sqrt{\frac{(1 - \cos x)^2}{\sin^2 x}} = \frac{1 - \cos x}{\sin x}$

(30.19). If $\sin\theta = \frac{\sqrt{3}}{2}$ and θ is less than 90^0. Calculate $\frac{\tan(90 - \theta)}{\cos^2\theta}$

Solution $\sin \theta = \frac{\sqrt{3}}{2}$

$\cos^2 \theta = 1 - \sin^2 \theta = 1 - \left(\frac{\sqrt{3}}{2}\right)^2 \to 1 - \frac{3}{4} = \frac{1}{4}$ $\therefore \cos \theta = \sqrt{1/4} = 1/2$

$\frac{\tan(90-\theta)}{\cos^2\theta} = \frac{\cot\theta}{\cos^2\theta} \to \frac{\frac{\cos\theta}{\sin\theta}}{\cos^2\theta} \to \frac{\cos\theta}{\sin\theta} \times \frac{1}{\cos^2\theta} = \frac{1}{\sin\theta \cos\theta} = \frac{1}{\frac{\sqrt{3}}{2} \times \frac{1}{2}} = \frac{1}{\frac{\sqrt{3}}{4}} = \frac{4}{\sqrt{3}}$

(30.20). If $\sin \theta = \frac{m-n}{m+n}$, find the value of $1 + \tan^2 \theta$

Solution

Given $\sin\theta = \frac{m-n}{m+n}$, Opposite = $m - n$, Hypotenuse = $m + n$

$A^2 = H^2 - O^2 \to (m+n)^2 - (m-n)^2 \to m^2 + 2mn + n^2 - (m^2 - 2mn + n^2)$

$m^2 + 2mn + n^2 - m^2 + 2mn - n^2 = 4mn$ $\therefore A = \sqrt{4mn} = 2\sqrt{mn}$

$1 + \tan^2\theta = 1 + \left[\frac{O}{A}\right]^2 \to 1 + \left(\frac{(m-n)}{\sqrt{4mn}}\right)^2 \to 1 + \frac{(m-n)^2}{4mn} \to$

$\frac{4mn + (m-n)^2}{4mn} = \frac{4mn + m^2 + n^2 - 2mn}{4mn} = \frac{m^2 + n^2 + 2mn}{4mn}$

(30.21). If $\sec^2\theta + \tan^2\theta = 3$, then the angle θ is equal to ?

Solution

$\sec^2\theta + \tan^2\theta = 3 \to \sec^2\theta + (\sec^2\theta - 1) = 3 \to 2\sec^2\theta = 3 + 1 = 4$

$\sec^2\theta = 2 \to \sec\theta = \sqrt{2} \to \frac{1}{\cos\theta} = \sqrt{2} \to \frac{\cos\theta}{1} = \frac{1}{\sqrt{2}}$

$\theta = \cos^{-1}\left(\frac{1}{\sqrt{2}}\right) = 45°$

(30.22). Given that $\cos z = L$, where z is an acute angle, find the expression for

$\frac{\cot z - \csc z}{\sec z + \tan z}$

Solution

Given $\cos z = \frac{L}{1}$, $A = L$, $H = 1$

405

$O^2 = H^2 - A^2 = 1^2 - L^2$, $O = \sqrt{1 - L^2}$

$\cot z - \text{cotsec } z = \frac{1}{\sqrt{1-L^2}} - \frac{1}{\sqrt{1-L^2}} = \frac{L-1}{\sqrt{1-L^2}}$

$\sec z + \tan z = \frac{1}{L} + \frac{\sqrt{1-L^2}}{L} = \frac{1 + \sqrt{1-L^2}}{L}$

$\frac{\cot z - \csc z}{\sec z + \tan z} = \frac{L-1}{\sqrt{1-L^2}} \times \frac{L}{1+\sqrt{1-L^2}} = \frac{L(L-1)}{\sqrt{1-L^2} \cdot (1+\sqrt{1-L^2})} = \frac{L(L-1)}{\sqrt{1-L^2} + 1 - L^2}$

(30.23). Evaluate $\frac{\sin^2 x}{1+\cos x} + \frac{\sin^2 x}{1-\cos x}$

Solution

$\frac{\sin^2 x}{1+\cos x} + \frac{\sin^2 x}{1-\cos x} \rightarrow \frac{\sin^2 x(1-\cos x) + \sin^2(1+\cos x)}{(1+\cos x)(1-\cos x)} \rightarrow \frac{\sin^2 x(1-\cos x + 1 + \cos x)}{(1+\cos x)(1-\cos x)}$

$\frac{2\sin^2 x}{1+\cos^2 x} \rightarrow \frac{2\sin^2 x}{\sin^2 x} = 2$

(30.24). Evaluate $\frac{\tan 45^0 + \cos 60^0}{\sin 150^0}$

Solution

With $\sin 150^0 = \sin(180 - 30) = \sin 30^0 = \frac{1}{2}$

$\therefore \frac{\tan 45^0 + \cos 60^0}{\sin 150^0} = \frac{\tan 45^0 + \cos 60^0}{\sin(180-150)} = \frac{\tan 45^0 + \cos 60^0}{\sin 30^0} = \frac{1+\frac{1}{2}}{\frac{1}{2}} = \frac{\frac{3}{2}}{\frac{1}{2}} = \frac{3}{2} \times \frac{2}{1} = 3$

(30.25). If $\sin \theta = -\frac{1}{2}$ and $0^0 < \theta < 270^0$, find θ.

Solution

From $\sin \theta = \frac{1}{2}$, $\theta = \sin^{-1}\left(\frac{1}{2}\right) = 30^0$

For $\sin \theta = -\frac{1}{2}$, θ is negative

$\sin \theta$ is negative in the third quadrant with formula $180 + \theta$ or $\theta - 180$

$\therefore 180 + 30 = 210^0$ or $\theta - 180 = 30$

$\theta = 30 + 180 = 210^0$

(30.26). The sine, cosine and tangent of 210^0 are respectively?

Solution

sine $210 = \sin(180 + 30) \to \sin 30 = -½$

$\cos 210 = \cos(180 + 30) \to -\cos 30 = \frac{\sqrt{3}}{2}$

$\tan 210 = \tan(180 + 30) \to \tan 30 = \frac{1}{\sqrt{3}} \to \frac{1}{\sqrt{3}} \times \frac{\sqrt{3}}{\sqrt{3}} = \frac{\sqrt{3}}{3}$

(30.27). If $\sin \theta = \cos \theta$, Find θ between 0 and 360

Solution

Given $\sin \theta = \cos \theta$

dividing through by $\cos \theta$

$\frac{\sin \theta}{\cos \theta} = \frac{\cos \theta}{\cos \theta} \to \tan \theta = 1 \to \theta = \tan^{-1}(1) = 45^0$

Also from $\tan \theta = 1$

Tangent is positive in 1st and 3rd quadrant

1st quadrant is acute i.e 45^0

3rd quadrant is $180 + \theta = 180 + 45 = 225^0$

$\therefore \theta = 45^0, 225^0$

(30.28). Solve the equation for all positive values of θ less than 360^0. $3\tan \theta + 2 = -1$

Solution

From $3\tan \theta + 2 = -1 \to 3\tan \theta = -3 \to \tan \theta = -1 \therefore \theta = \tan^{-1}(-1) = 45^0$

Since θ has a negative value.

Less than 360^0 means from the first to 4th quadrant.

Tangent is negative in 2nd and 4th with formula $180 - \theta$ and $360 - \theta$ rspectively

In 2nd quadrant, $180 - \theta = 180 - 45 = 135^0$

In 4th quadrant, $360 - \theta = 360 - 45 = 315^0$

∴ The angles 135^0 or 315^0

(30.29). Evaluate $\sin 1540^0$

Solution

By multiples → 360 x 4 = 1440

∴ sin1540 = sin (1540 – 1440) = sin (100)

(30.30). What is the value of $\sin(-690^0)$

Solution

By multiples $\sin(-690^0)$ = sin (360 x 2 + - 690) → sin (720 – 690) = $\sin 30^0$ = ½

(30.31). Evaluate $\frac{\sin(1440 - \theta)}{\sin(180 - \theta)}$

Solution

$\sin(1440 - \theta)$ = sin [(360 x 4) – θ] → $\sin(360 - \theta)$ = - sinθ

$\sin(180 - \theta) = \sin\theta$

∴ $\frac{\sin(1440 - \theta)}{\sin(180 - \theta)} = \frac{-\sin\theta}{\sin\theta} = -\frac{1}{1} = -1$

CHAPTER 31 APPLICATIONS OF TRIGONOMETRY

Trigonometry finds numerous applications in different branches of mathematics and allied courses. Here we consider some of its uses in mathematics.

(1) Derivation of the sine and cosine rule

Sine rule: This states that the ratio of a side of a triangle to its corresponding angle is constant for acute or obtuse angles.

Thus, sine rule can be used to solve problem involving triangles.

Using an acute triangle the sine rule can be derived as shown below

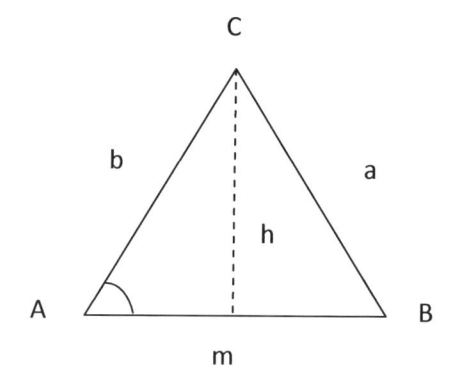

From the diagram

$\sin A = \dfrac{h}{b} \rightarrow h = b\sin A$

$\sin B = \dfrac{h}{a} \rightarrow h = a\sin B$

equating $b\sin A = a\sin B \rightarrow \dfrac{a}{\sin A} = \dfrac{b}{\sin B}$

Similarly, $\dfrac{a}{\sin A} = \dfrac{b}{\sin B} = \dfrac{c}{\sin C}$

This is the sine rule.

For obtuse triangle

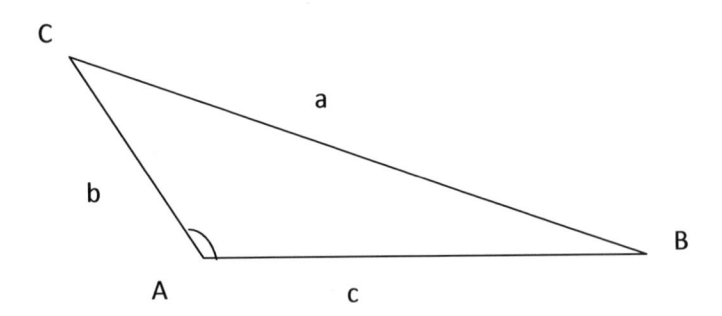

This can be produced and analyzed as shown below

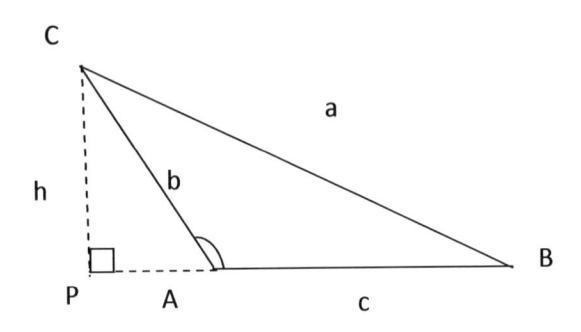

The right angled triangles are: CPB and CPA Also, CAP = 180 – A

In CPB, $\sin B = \dfrac{h}{a}$ → h = a sin B

In CPA, $\sin C\hat{A}P = \sin(180 - A) = \dfrac{h}{b}$

$\sin A = \dfrac{h}{b}$ → h = b sinA

equating bsinA = asinB → $\dfrac{a}{\sin A} = \dfrac{b}{\sin B}$

∴ $\dfrac{a}{\sin A} = \dfrac{b}{\sin B} = \dfrac{c}{\sin C}$

Using an acute triangle the cosine rule can be derived as shown below

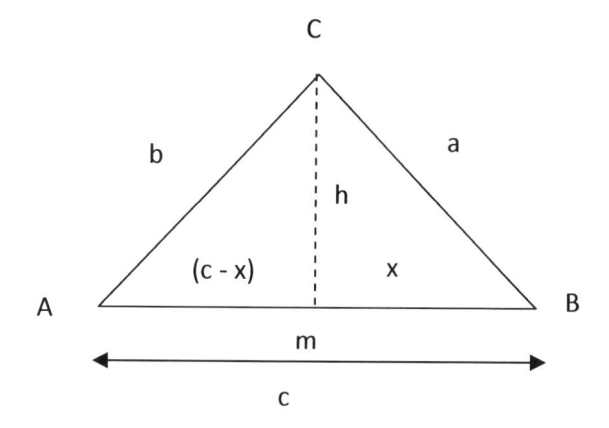

If MB = x, AM = (c − x)

Consider triangle ACM, by Pythagoras's theorem we have $b^2 = (c-x)^2 + h^2$

$b^2 = c^2 + x^2 - 2cx + h^2 \rightarrow b^2 = c^2 + x^2 + h^2 - 2cx$

Also in CMB → $a^2 = x^2 + h^2$ and $\cos B = \frac{x}{a} \rightarrow x = a \cos B$

∴ $b^2 = c^2 + x^2 + h^2 - 2cx \rightarrow b^2 = c^2 + a^2 - 2C(a\cos B)$

$b^2 = c^2 + a^2 - 2ac\cos B$

Similarly, $a^2 = b^2 + c^2 - 2bc\cos A$

$c^2 = a^2 + b^2 - 2ab\cos C$

And it is the same for obtuse triangle.

(2) **Angle of elevation and depression**

These are angles between the normal direction of vision and the line through an object placed above (elevation) or below (depression). We know consider various cases

(*a*) Elevation/Depression from the ground level: From the ground level, the following deduction can be made

A ----------------------

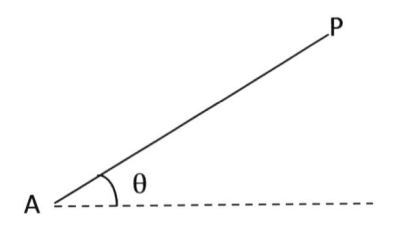

an observer at A looking
in the direction due East
in the normal vision.

an observer changing the normal direction
of vision to look at an object above it

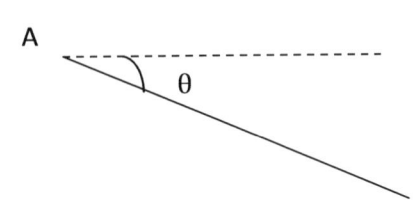

A ----------------------

An observer at A in a
direction of vision

an observer changing normal direction
of vision to look at an object below.

Drawing a vertical line to the above diagrams provides a triangle as the object is always at a vertical from the horizontal

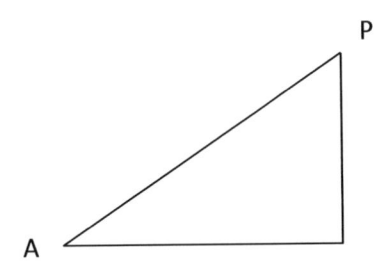

412

(b) Elevation or depression from a height

Here observation is made on top of a tower, cliff, or height

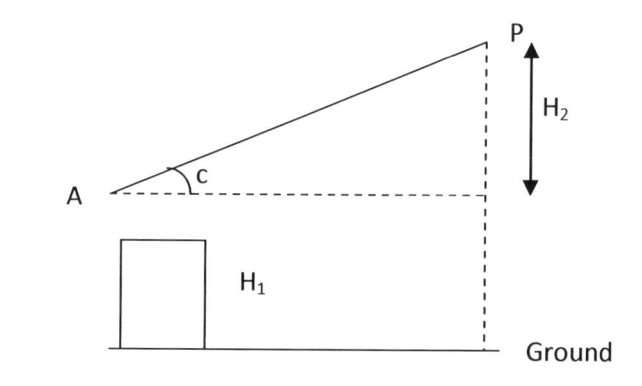

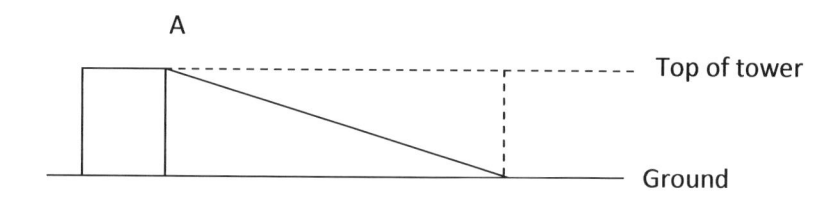

Total height of P above the ground = $h_1 + h_2$

where h_1 = height of the tower, h_2 = height above the tower

(c) Double elevation or depression on the same line and side with foot of an object

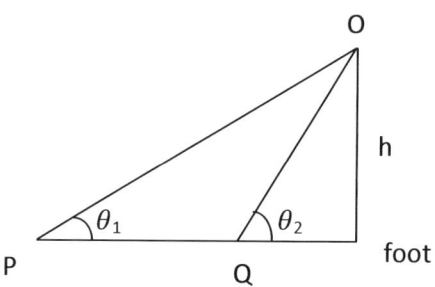

P, Q are points of observation of the same line and side with the foot. The characteristics of the diagram tells us the trig ratio to apply

(c) Double elevation/depression from two points on the same line and on opposite sides of the foot

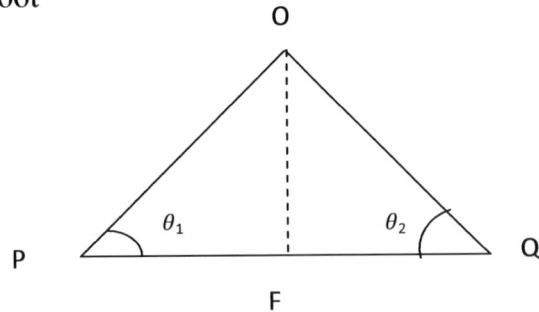

(d) Double elevation or depression from two points on the same plane with the foot of an object

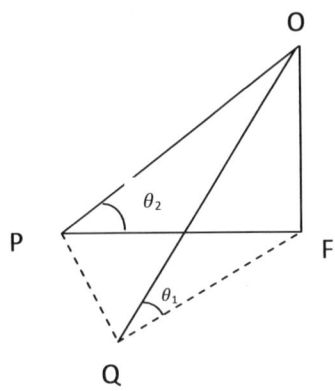

In the diagram above P and Q are on the same straight line, but not with the foot, F

Here the two points and the foot of the object are not on the same straight line. thus they will be combined by a triangle called plane.

(3) BEARING

Bearing is the direction of a line with respect to a North–South line measured clockwise from the north direction.

Forms of bearing

(a) 1-directional bearing: This is the bearing that involves only one direction. e.g. due South, due North, due East, or due West.

(*b*) **2-directional bearing:** This is the bearing that involves two bearings e.g. North and East, South and East etc. This is of two type's namely precise and referential bearing.

A *precise directional bearing* is one that gives the angle between the line, the first direction and the line that divides the two direction e.g.

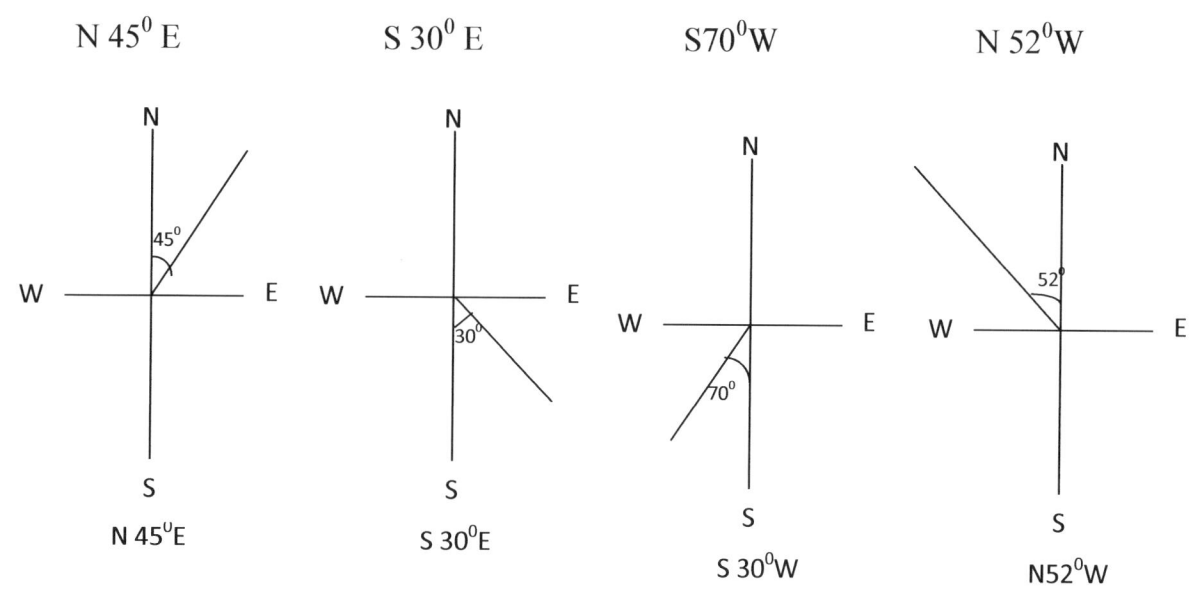

N 45° E   S 30° E   S70°W   N 52°W

N 45°E   S 30°E   S 30°W   N52°W

A refrential directional bearing is one in which the angle is given with respect to the last given direction i.e the angle usually comes before the two directions.

e.g. 60° North of East, 20° East of North etc

60° North of East implies with respect to East = E 60° N

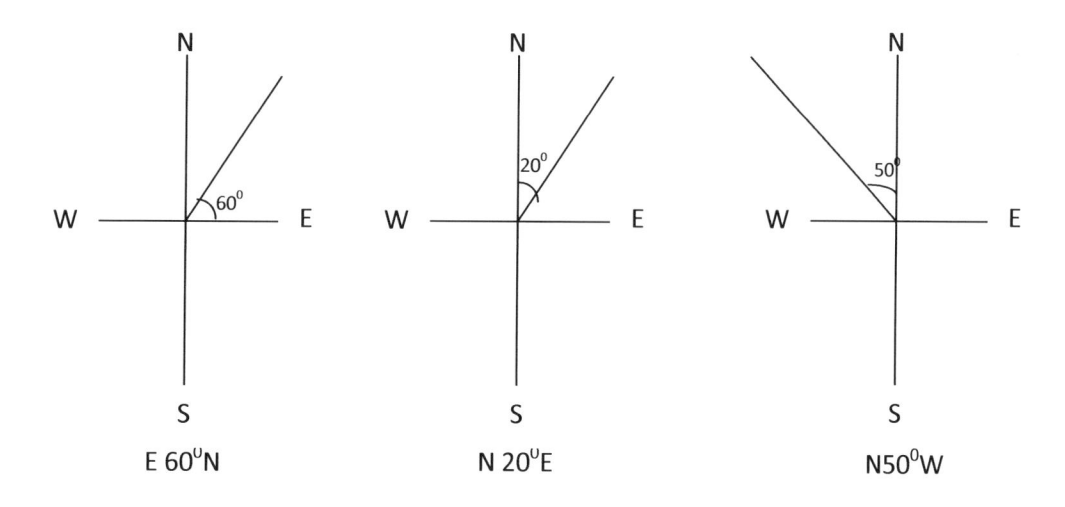

E 60°N   N 20°E   N50°W

(c) Whole circle bearing: This is the bearing measured clockwise from the North. it is a bearing in three figures e.g. 030^0, 120^0, 200^0 etc.

In this case, the bearing is located by the remaining angle when 90^0 or its multiples are counted off as quadrants from a given angle.

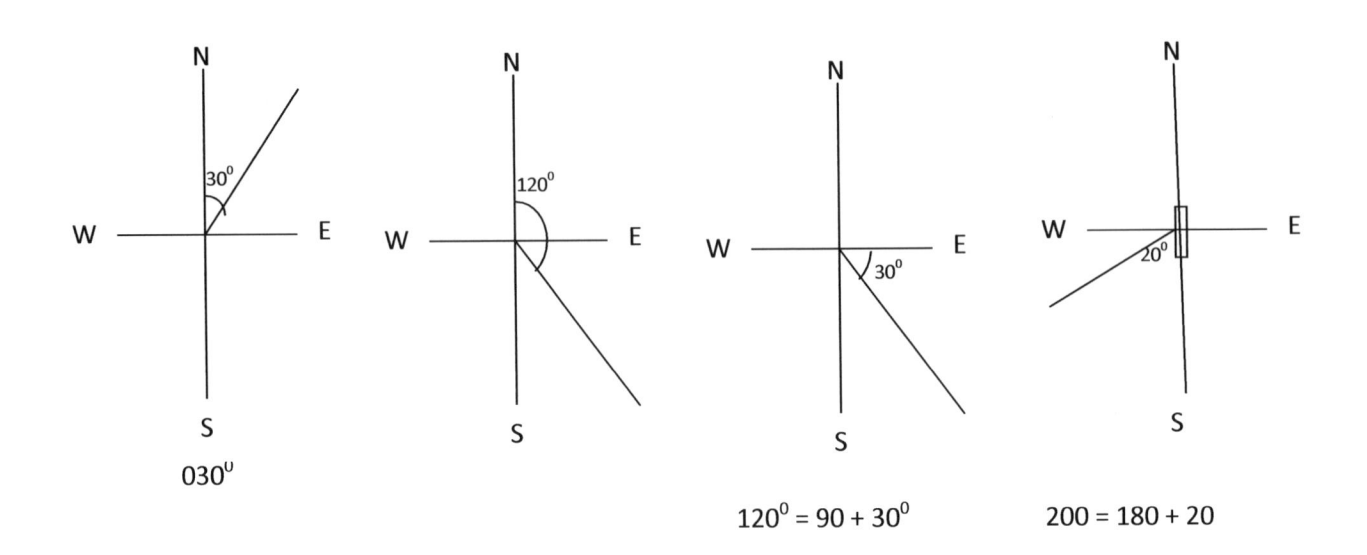

030⁰

$120^0 = 90 + 30^0$

$200 = 180 + 20$

Solution to bearing problems

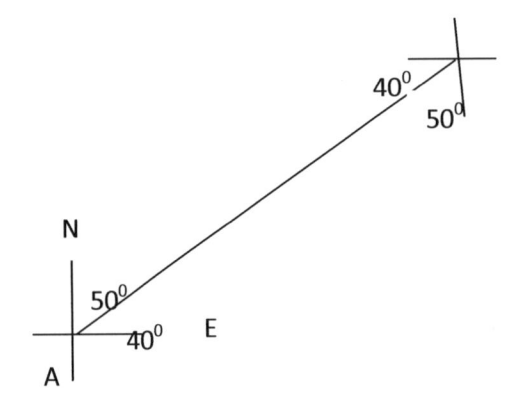

(i) Combine each bearing by drawing the angles alternate at its tip. e.g. Given N 50^0E at A is represented as

(*ii*) The length of the bearing line should be proportional to the distance given. A length of 4m should be longer than 3m. For example, if the bearing of A from B is 060^0 and the length is 3m and bearing of C from A is 130^0 with length 4m we have.

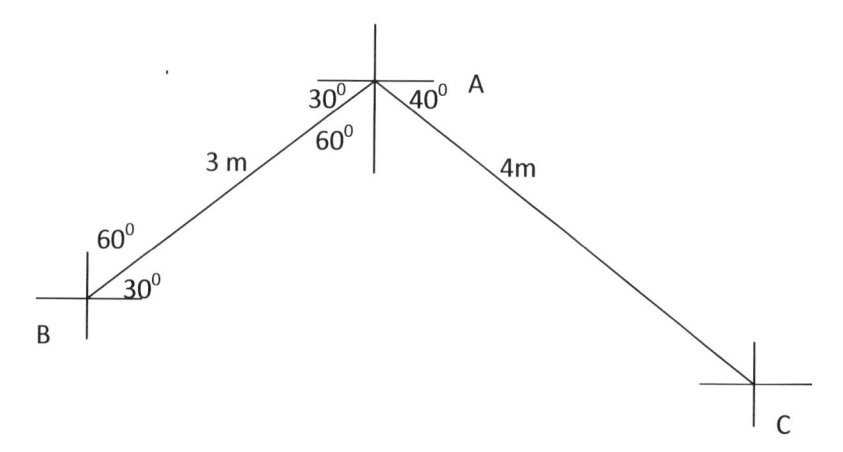

If the bearings of A and B from C are 060^0 and 140^0 respectively, this can be shown below:

(*iii*) If there is a connection between the starting and the ending point in terms of angle the tip angles are retained.

If there is no connection between the starting and the ending in terms of angle, the tip angles are excluded from the diagram.

The resultant diagram is used to solve the question

QUESTIONS

(**31. 1**). A girl walks 45 metres in the direction 050^0 from a point Q to a point X. She then walks 24 metres in the direction 140^0 X to a point Y. How far is she then from Q

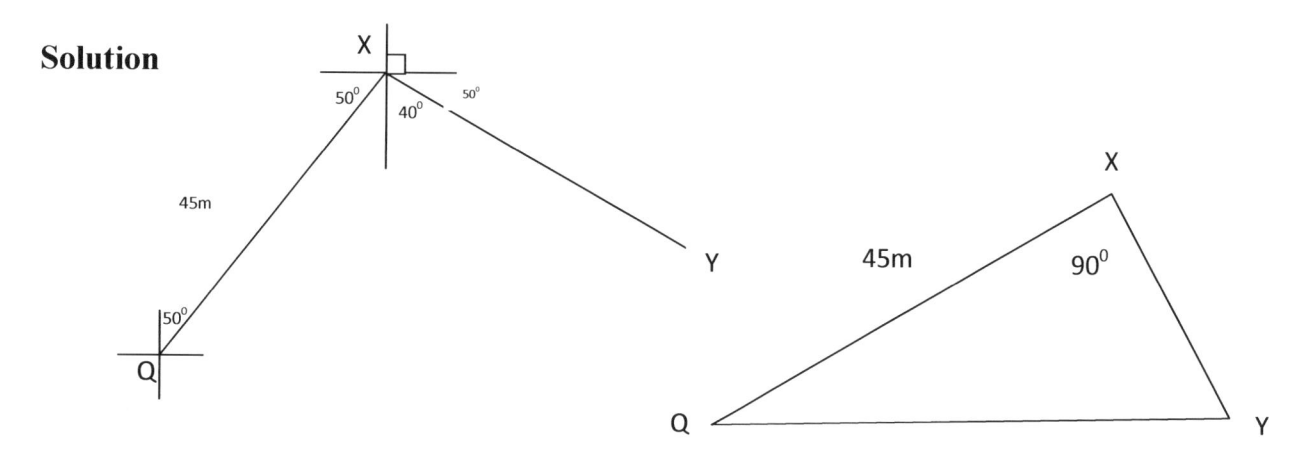

Solution

417

QXY is right angled triangle

$QY^2 = 45^2 + 24^2 \rightarrow 2025 + 576 = 2601$ ∴ $QY = \sqrt{2601} = 51m$

(31.2). A plane moves from a town X to town Y, 30 km apart in the direction 060^0 and then changes direction, moving to a point Z in the direction 120^0. If the point Z is due east of X, find the distance of the point Z from X

Solution

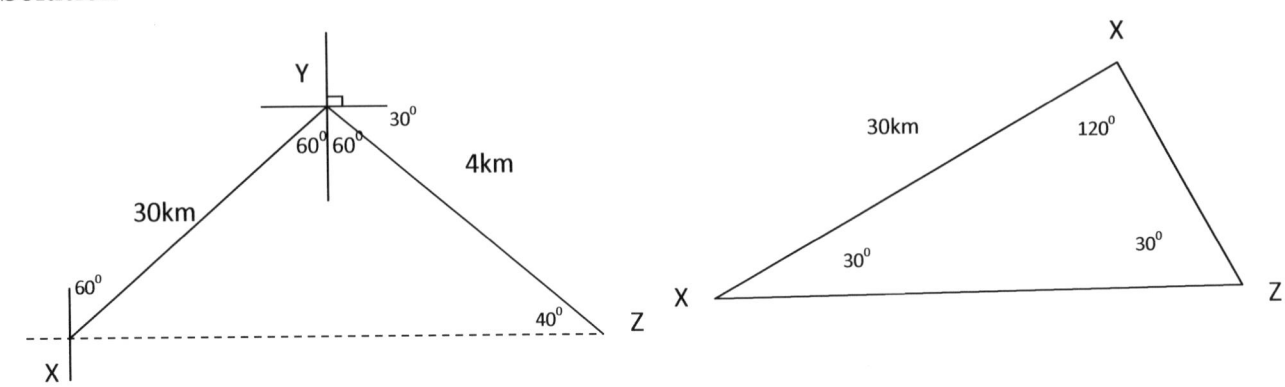

By sine rule

$\frac{ZX}{\sin 120} = \frac{30}{\sin 30} \rightarrow$ ZX sin 30 = 30 sin 120 = 30 sin (180 – 60)

ZX sin 30 = 30 sin60^0 → ZX = $\frac{30 \sin 60}{\sin 30} = \frac{30 \times \sqrt{3}/2}{1/2} = 30 \times \frac{\sqrt{3}}{2} \times \frac{2}{1} = 30\sqrt{3}$km

(31.3). An aeroplane leaves an airport and flies due North for 1 ½ hrs at 500 km/hr. It then flies 400km on a bearing 053^0. Calculate its final distance from the air port.

Solution

AB is 500km/hr, $1\frac{1}{2} hrs = \frac{3}{2} hrs$

From speed = $\frac{Distance}{Time}$ → Distance = Speed x Time = 500 x $\frac{3}{2}$ = 750km

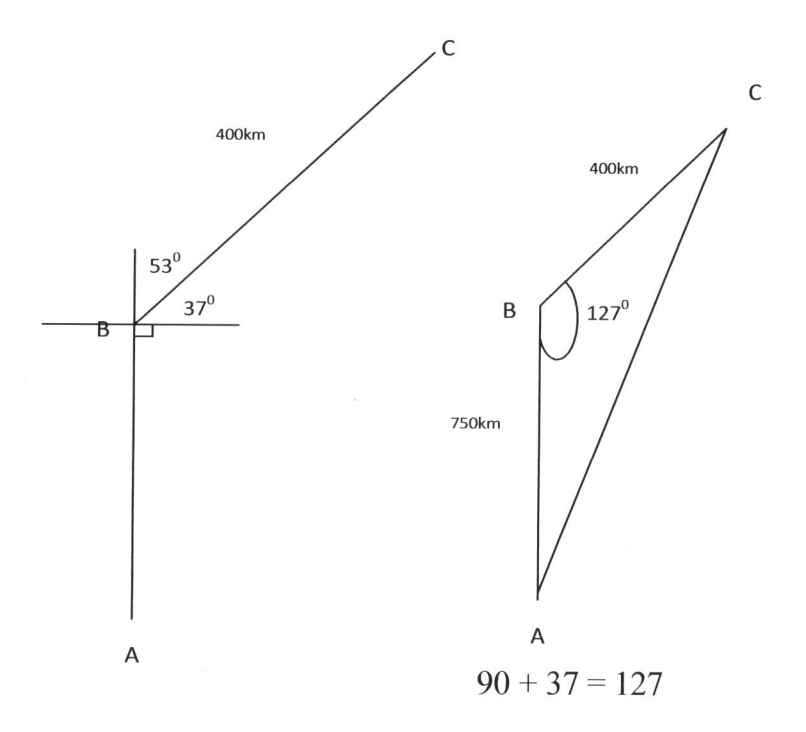

From cosine rule

$AC^2 = 750^2 + 400^2 - 2 \times 750 \times 400 \cos 127° \rightarrow 562500 + 160000 - 600000\cos(180 - 53)$

$722500 - 600000(-\cos 53) \rightarrow 722500 + 600000(0.6018) \rightarrow 722500 + 361080 = 1083580$

$AC = \sqrt{1083580} = 1040.95 = 1041 km$

(31.4). Two ships leave port at the same time, one steaming at 5km/hr on a bearing N $46°$E and the other at 9 km/hr on a bearing N $46°$ E and the other at 9km/hr on a bearing S $53°$E. How far apart are the ship after 2 hours?

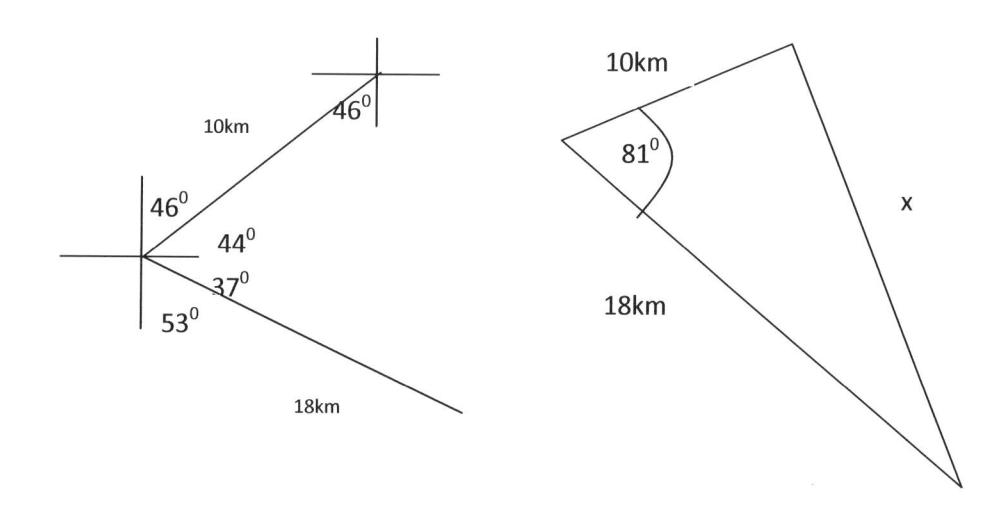

Solution

419

By cosine rule

$x^2 = 10^2 + 18^2 - 2 \times 10 \times 18 \times \cos 81 \rightarrow 100 + 324 - 360\cos 81 \rightarrow 424 - 260(0.1564)$

$x^2 = 424 - 56.304 = 367.696$ ∴ $x = \sqrt{367.696} = 19.18$

(31.5). The bearing of a bird on a tree from a hunter on the ground is N72°E. What is the bearing of the hunter from the bird?

Solution

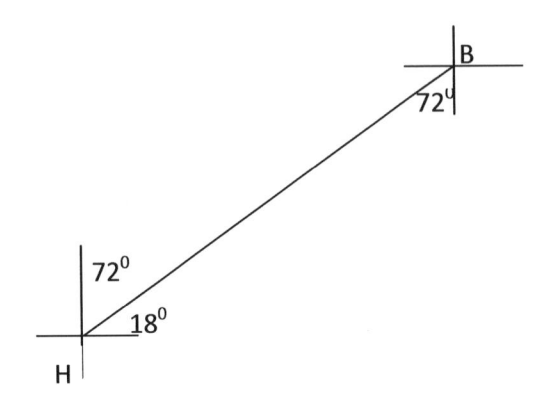

Bearing of hunter from the bird is at B i.e position of line HB from B

Bearing = S 72°W

(31.6). A ship H leaves a port P and sails 30km due south. Then it sails 60km due west. What is the bearing of H from P?

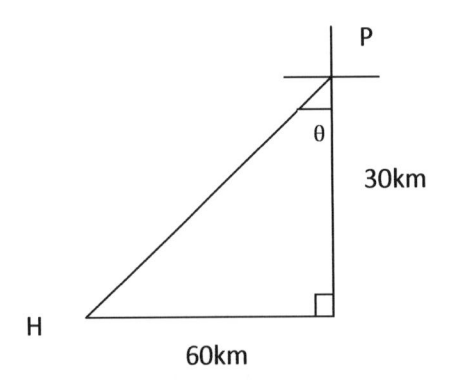

Solution

Bearing of H from P is at P. The bearing = $S\theta^0 W$

From the North, the bearing = $180 + \theta$

$\tan \theta = \frac{60}{30} = 2 \rightarrow \theta = \tan^{-1}(2) = 63.44^0 = 63^0 26^1$

The bearing = $180 + \theta = 180 + 63^0 26^1 = 243^0 26^1$

(31.7). X is a point due east of point Y on a coast. Z is another point on the coast but $6\sqrt{3}$ km due south of Y. If the distance ZX is 12km, calculating the bearing of Z from X.

Solution

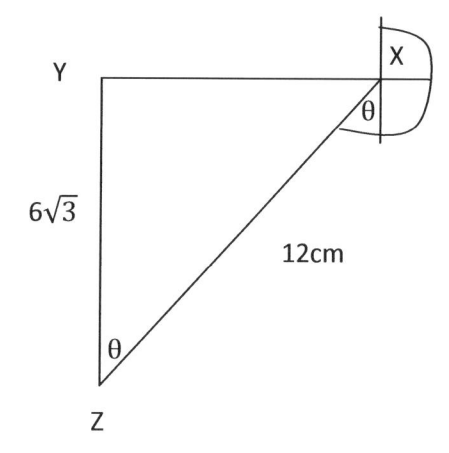

From the diagram Bearing of Z from X is angle from north of X to line XZ

$\cos \theta = \frac{6\sqrt{3}}{12} = \frac{\sqrt{3}}{2} \rightarrow \theta = \cos^{-1}\left(\frac{\sqrt{3}}{2}\right) = 30^0$

Bearing = $180 + 30 = 210^0$

(31.8). A man walks 2 km due east and then 4km due south. Find, correct to the nearest degree, his bearing from his original position.

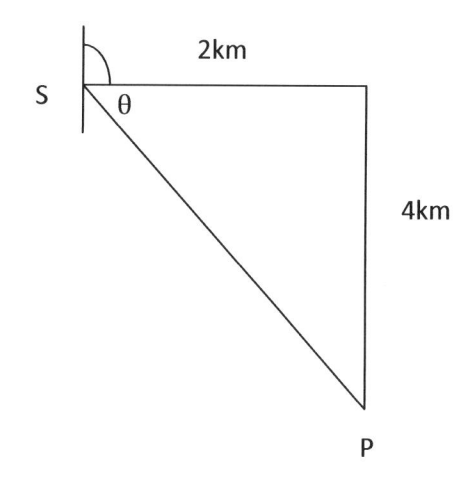

Solution

421

S = starting point or original position, P = final position

His bearing from the original position is angle at S to line SP.

The bearing = 90 + θ

$\tan \theta = \frac{4}{2} = 2 \rightarrow \theta = \tan^{-1}(2) = 63.4^0$

The bearing = $90 + 63.4^0 = 153.4^0$

The bearing = 153 (to nearest degree)

(31.9). From a point Z, 60 m north of X, a man walks $60\sqrt{3}$ east wards to another point Y. find the bearing of Y and X.

Solution

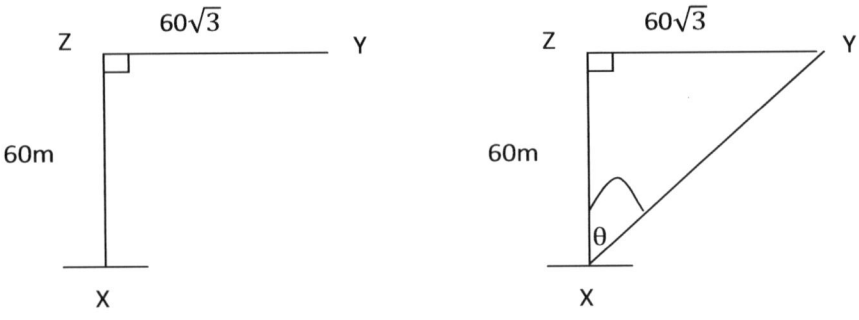

Bearing of Y from X is angle at X to line YX

$\tan \theta = \frac{60\sqrt{3}}{60} = \sqrt{3} \rightarrow \theta = \tan^{-1}(\sqrt{3}) = 60^0$

The bearing = 060^0

(31.10). Alero starts a 3km walk from P on a bearing 023^0. She then walks 4km on the bearing 113^0 to Q. what is the bearing of Q from P?

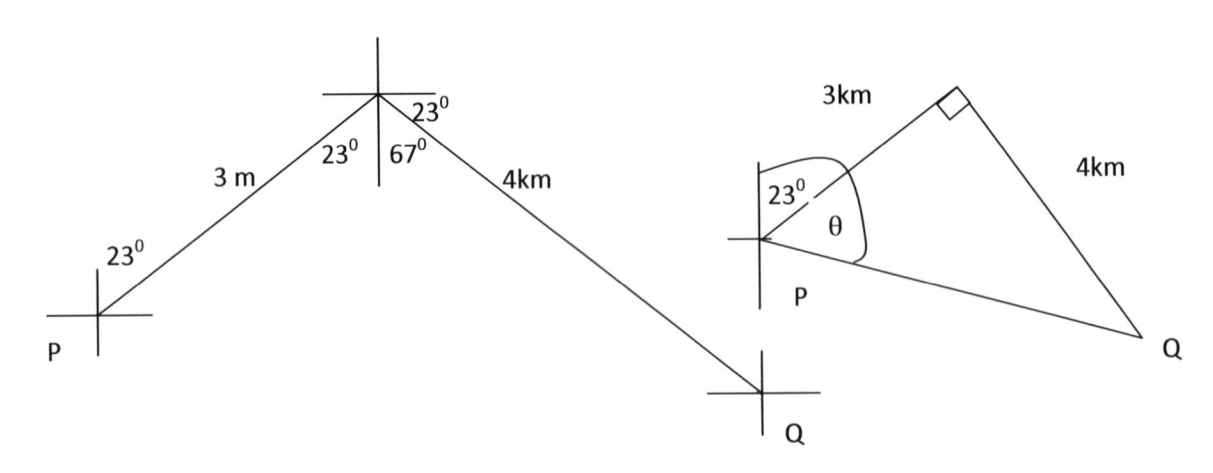

Bearing of Q from P is located at P joining PQ

From the diagram the diagram, bearing = 23 + θ.

$\tan θ = \frac{4}{3} = 1.333 \rightarrow θ = \tan^{-1}(1.333) = 53.13^0 = 53.8^1$

Bearing = $23 + 53^0 8^1 = 76^0 8^1$

(31.11). A walks 11km due North from A to B. he then walks 6.5km due East from B to C. Calculate. (a) The bearing of C from A (b) /AC/.

Solution

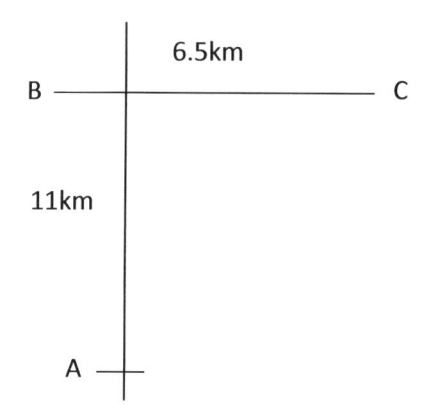

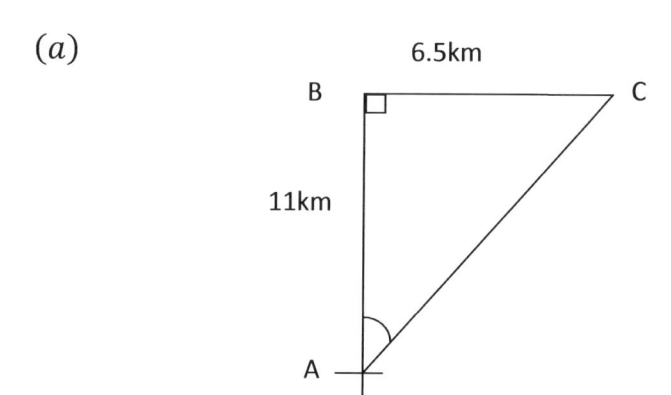

(a) The bearing is the angle from North of A to line AC

$\text{Tan A} = \frac{6.5}{11} = 0.5909 \rightarrow A = \tan^{-1}(0.5909) = 31^0$

the bearing of C from A is 031^0

(b) From the diagram above

By Pythagoras's $AC^2 = BC^2 + AB^2$ → $6.5^2 + 11^2$ → $42.25 + 121 = 163.5$

$AC = \sqrt{163.5} = 12.8$ ∴ Thus length $AC = 12.8km$

(12) An aeroplane flew from at G to city H on a bearing of 150^0. The distance between G and H is 300km. it then flew a distance of 450km to city J on a bearing of 060^0. Calculate, correct to reasonable degree of accuracy, (a) The distance from G to J (b) How far North of H is J (c) How far (west of H is G).

Solution

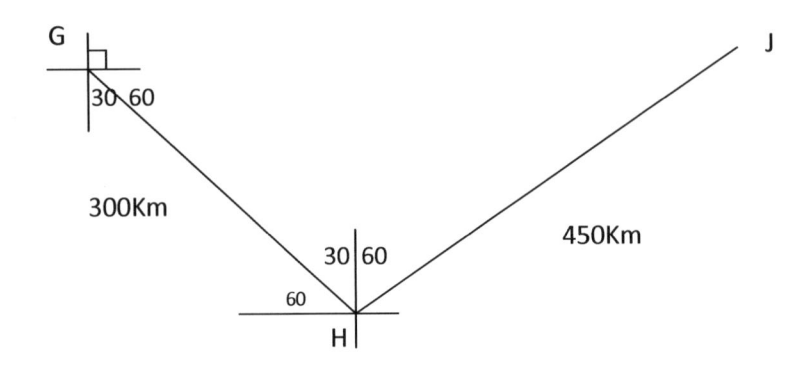

(a) Distance from G to J is the line joining G and J

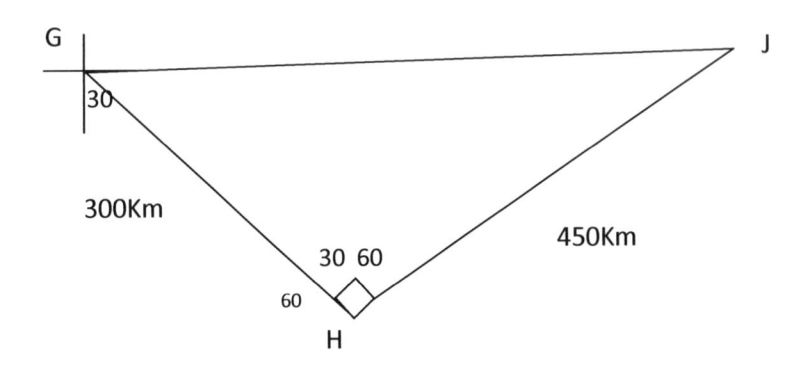

As the triangle is right angled by Pythagoras's gives

$GJ^2 = HG^2 + HJ^2$ → $300^2 + 450^2$ → $90000 + 202500 = 292500$

$GJ = \sqrt{292500} = 540.8km$

(b) How far North of H is J = J from North of H

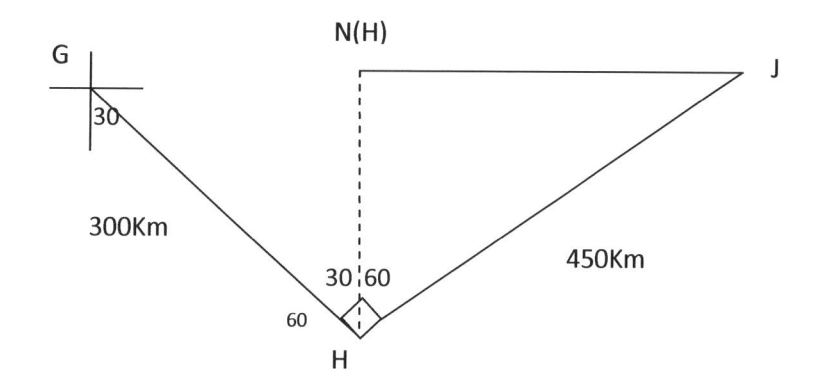

From the diagram $\sin 60 = \frac{x}{450}$ → x = 450sin 60 = 450 (0.8660) = 389.7 = 390 km (nearest km)

(c) How far west of H is G means distance between G and west of H. let this be y in the diagram below

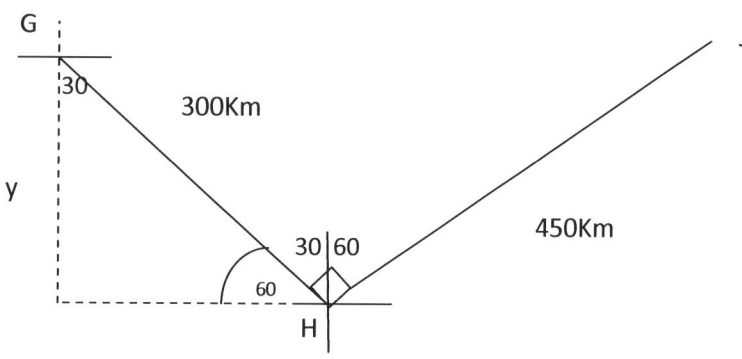

$\sin 60 = \frac{y}{300}$ → y = 300 sin 60 = 300 (0.8660) = 259.8

(31.13). A boy scout wishing to reach a point due east of him finds a lake between him and his objective. He therefore walks 220m on a bearing N 63°E and then straight to the point on a line bearing S 24° E. How far was he from his objective at first?

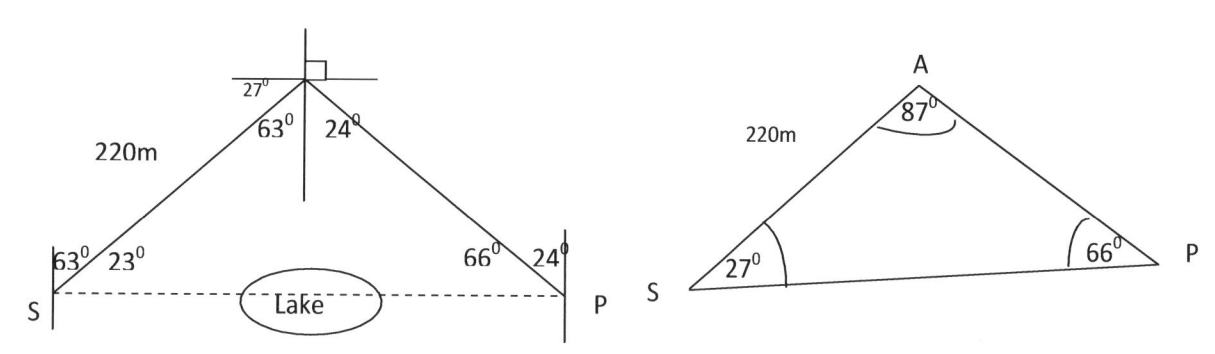

SP = The distance between the scout and his objective

By sine rule $\dfrac{SP}{\sin 87} = \dfrac{220}{\sin 66}$ → SP sin 60 = 220 sin 87° ∴ SP = $\dfrac{220\sin 87}{\sin 66}$ = 240.5km

(31.14). An aeroplane flies from a town X on a bearing of N 45°E to another town Y, a distance of 200km. It then changes courses and flies to another town Z on a bearing of S 60° E. If Z is directly east of X. calculate, correct to three significant figures.

(a) The distance from X to Z (b) The distance from Y to XZ.

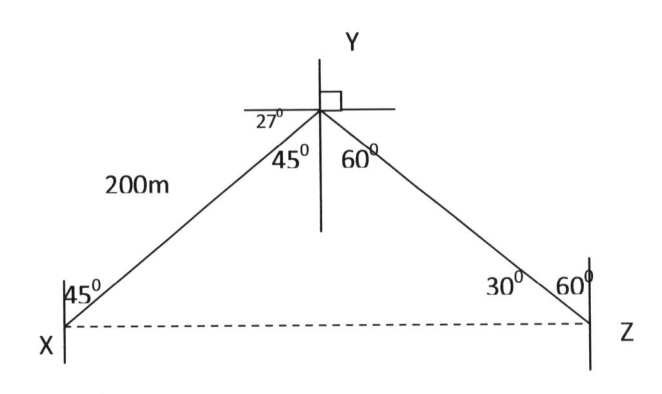

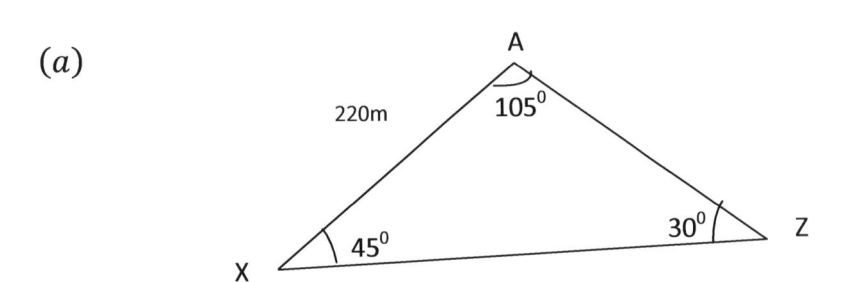

Solution

(a)

By sine rule: $\dfrac{XZ}{\sin 105} = \dfrac{200}{\sin 30}$ → XZ sin 30 = 200 sin 105

XZ = $\dfrac{200\sin 75}{\sin 30} = \dfrac{200\sin(180-105)}{\sin 30} = \dfrac{200\sin 75}{\sin 30}$

∴ XZ = 386.3 = 386 km

(*b*) Distance from Y to XZ is the line that joins XZ from Y as shown below:

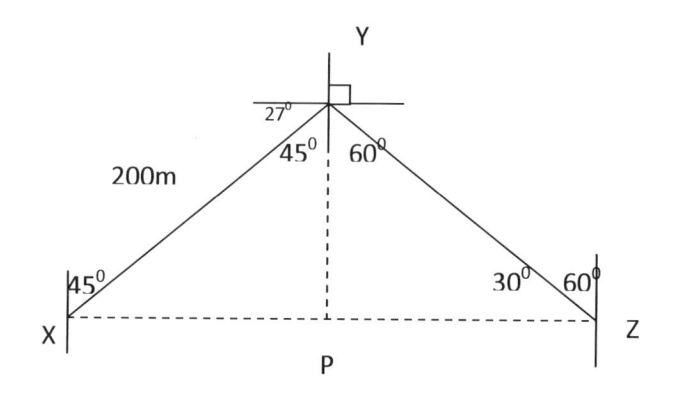

Drawing a straight line from Y, the line be YP.

From the diagram $\sin 45 = \dfrac{YP}{200}$ → YP = 200sin 45 = 200(0.7071) = 141.4 km

YM = 141km (to 3sfigures)

(**31.15**). A and B are two points 5km apart, the bearing of A from B being 052^0. It is required to fix a third point X, which is known to be exactly 10 km from B and on a Bearing of 152^0 from A. How far is X from A and what is the bearing of B from X?

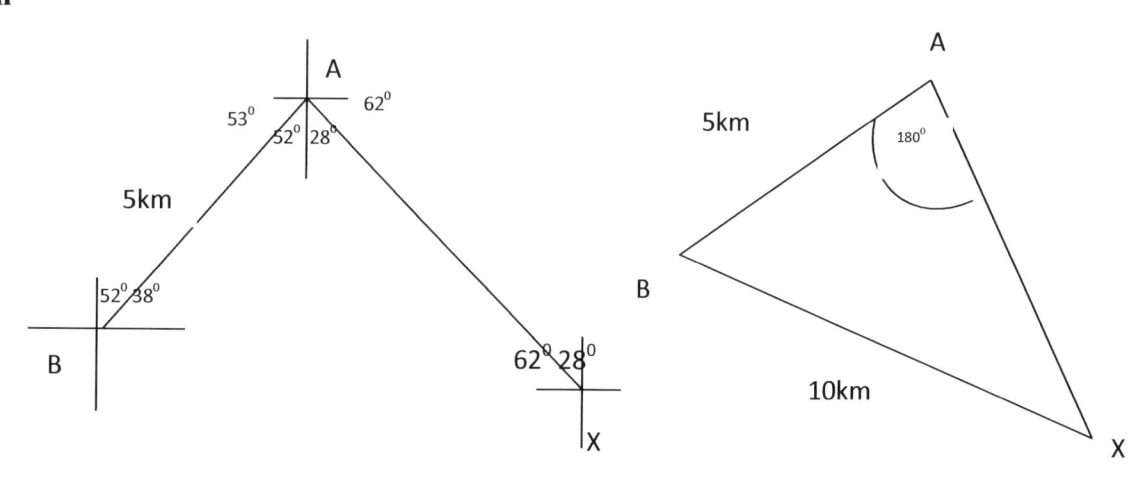

Solution

427

The distance between X and A is AX

By sine rule $\frac{10}{\sin 80} = \frac{5}{\sin X}$ → 10sinx = 5 sin 80 → $\sin x = \frac{5\sin 80}{10} = 0.5 \sin 80$

sin x = 0.5(0.9848) = 0.94924 → x = sin⁻¹ (0.4924) = 29.5⁰

B = 180 – (80 + 29.5) = 180 – 109.5 = 70.5

Also, $\frac{AX}{\sin 70.5} = \frac{10}{\sin 80}$ (by sine rule)

AX sin 80 = 10 sin 70.5 → $AX = \frac{10 \sin 70.5}{\sin 80} = 9.57$

Bearing of B from X is the angle marked from the North of X to the line BX as shown below

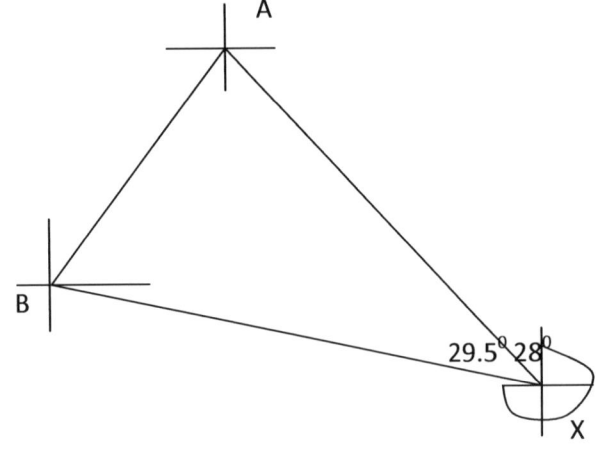

As the angle marked remains 29.5 and 28⁰ to complete 360⁰, the bearing = 360 – (29.5 + 28) = 360 – 57.5

The bearing of B from X = 302.5⁰

(31.16).

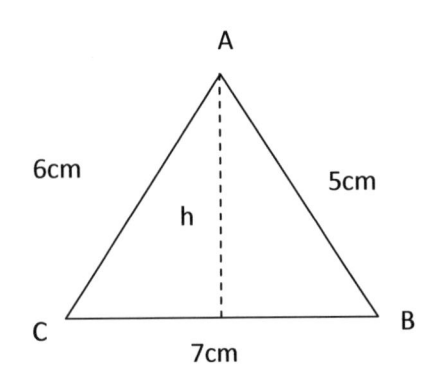

Find h in the diagram above

Solution

By Cosine rule

$\cos C = \dfrac{b^2 + a^2 - c^2}{2ba} \rightarrow \dfrac{6^2 + 7^2 - 5^2}{2 \times 6 \times 7} \rightarrow \dfrac{36 + 49 - 25}{84} \rightarrow \dfrac{60}{84} = \dfrac{5}{7}$

From $\cos^2 c + \sin^2 c = 1$

$\sin c = \sqrt{1 - \cos^2 c} \rightarrow \sqrt{1 - \left(\dfrac{5}{7}\right)^2} \rightarrow \sqrt{1 - \dfrac{25}{49}} = \sqrt{\dfrac{24}{49}}$

By trig ratio, $\sin C = \dfrac{h}{6} \rightarrow h = 6 \sin C \rightarrow 6x\sqrt{\dfrac{24}{49}} = 6\sqrt{\dfrac{4 \times 6}{7}} = \dfrac{6 \times 2\sqrt{6}}{7} = \dfrac{12}{7}\sqrt{6}$

(31.17). QRS is a triangle with QS = 12m, <RQS = 30⁰ and <QRS = 45⁰. Calculate the length of RS.

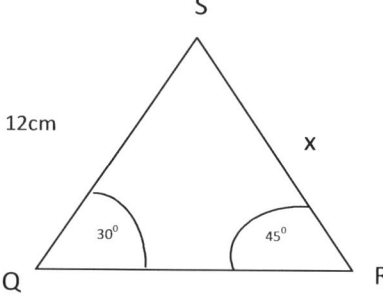

Solution

By Sine rule, $\dfrac{x}{\sin 30} = \dfrac{12}{\sin 45} \rightarrow x \sin 45 = 12 \sin 30 \rightarrow x = \dfrac{12 \sin 30}{\sin 45} = \dfrac{12\,(1/2)}{1/\sqrt{2}}$

$x = \dfrac{\frac{6}{1}}{\frac{1}{\sqrt{2}}} = \dfrac{6}{1} \times \dfrac{\sqrt{2}}{1} = 6\sqrt{2}$ m

(31.18). In a triangle PQR, /QR/ = 4cm, /RP/ = 3cm and /PQ/ = 2cm. find the cosine of angle QPR.

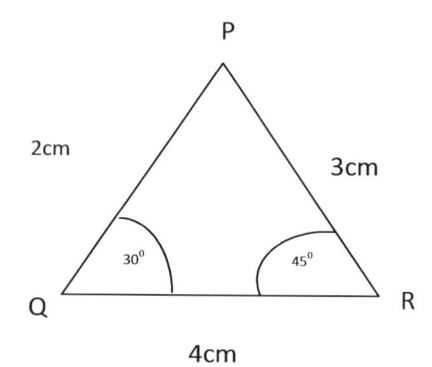

Solution

429

$$\text{Cos } Q\hat{P}R = Cos\ P = \frac{q^2 + r^2 - p^2}{2qr}$$

$$Cos\ P = \frac{3^2 + 2^2 - 4^2}{2 \times 3 \times 2} = \frac{9+4-16}{12} = \frac{-3}{12} = \frac{-1}{4}$$

(31.19).

In the diagram, PQR, is a right angled triangle, $<QPR = 30^0$, $<QSP = 60^0$ and PS = 20m. Calculate QR.

Solution

In triangle QPS

$<QSP = 180 - 60 = 120^0$ (angles on the straight line)

$<PQS = 180 - (30 + 120)$ (angles in a triangle)

$<PQS = 180 - 50 = 30^0$

By sine rule $\frac{QS}{\sin 30^0} = \frac{20}{\sin 30} \rightarrow QS = \frac{20 \sin 30}{\sin 30} = 20\ m$

In triangle QSR, $\sin 60 = \frac{QR}{QS}$

$QR = QS \sin 60 \rightarrow 20 \sin 60 \rightarrow 20 \frac{\sqrt{3}}{2} = 10\sqrt{3}$

(31.20). The angle of elevation of the sun is 45^0. A tree has a shadow 12m long. Find the height of the tree.

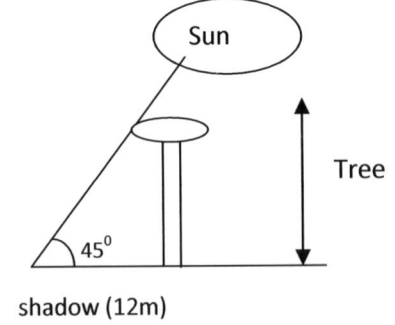

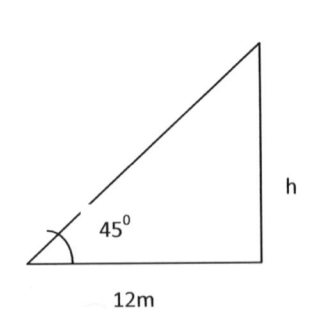

Solution

$\tan 45 = \frac{h}{12} \rightarrow h = 12 \tan 45^0 = 12m$

(31.21). The top of 75m ladder is made to rest against the top of a vertical wall. If the foot of the ladder is 21m away from the wall, how high is the wall?

Solution

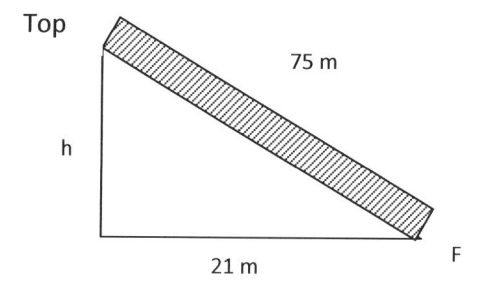

By Pythagoras's, $h^2 = 75^2 - 21^2 \rightarrow 5625 - 441 = \sqrt{5184} = 72m$

(31.22). A ladder resting on vertical wall makes an angle whose tangent is 2.4m with the ground. If the distance between the foot and the ladder and the wall is 50 cm. what is the lengh of the ladder?

Solution

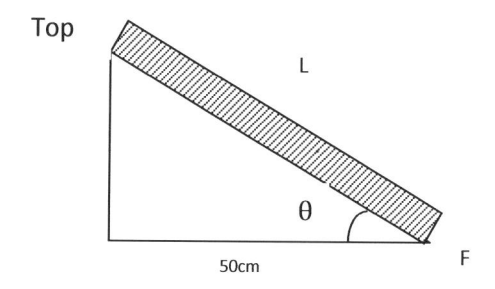

Given θ = angle whose tangent is 2.4

$\theta = \tan^{-1}(2.4) = 67.38^0$

$L = \frac{0.5}{\cos \theta} = \frac{0.5}{\cos 67.38} = 1.299 \, m = 1.3m$

(31.23). The angle of elevation of the top of a tower from a point on the horizontal ground, 80 m from the foot of the tower is 60^0. Find the height of the tower.

Solution

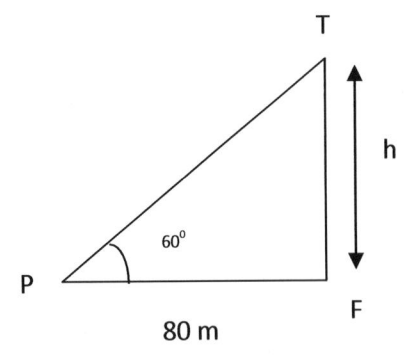

$\tan 60 = \dfrac{h}{80}$ → h = 80 tan 60 = 80 ($\sqrt{3}$)m

(31.24). The angle of depression of a boat from the top of a cliff 10 m high is 30^0. How far is the boat from the foot of the cliff.

Solution

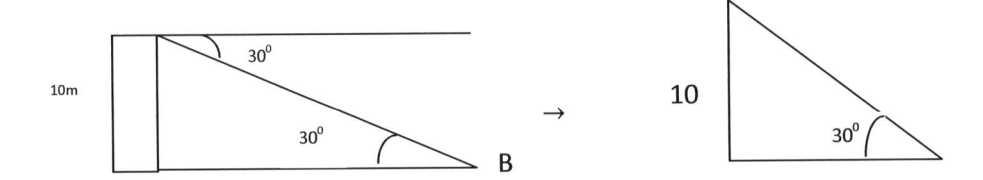

$\tan 30 = \dfrac{10}{x}$ → $x = \dfrac{10}{\tan 30}$ → $\dfrac{10}{1\sqrt{3}} = 10\sqrt{3}$m

(31.25). From a point $14\sqrt{3}$ metres away from a tree, a man discovers that the angle of elevation of the tree is 30^0. If the man measured this angle of elevation from a point 2 metres above the ground. How high is the tree?

Solution

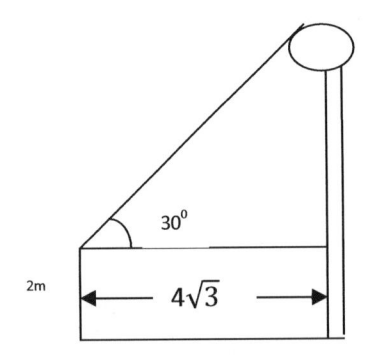

$$\tan 30 = \frac{h_a}{14\sqrt{3}}$$

$$h_2 = 14\sqrt{3} \tan 30 = 14\sqrt{3} \cdot \frac{1}{\sqrt{3}} = 14m$$

Total height $= h_1 + h_2 = 14 + 2 = 16$ m

(31.26). A man is standing in corridor of a 10 storey building and looking at a tall tree in front of the building. He sees the top of the tree at an angle of depression 30^0. If the tree is 200 m tall and the man's eyes are 300 m above the ground, calculate the angle of depression of the foot of the tree as seen by the man.

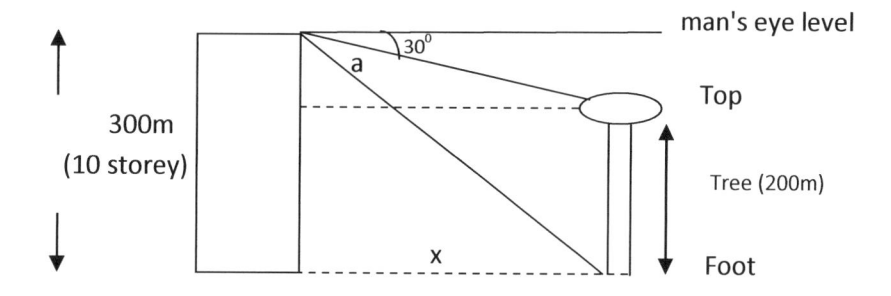

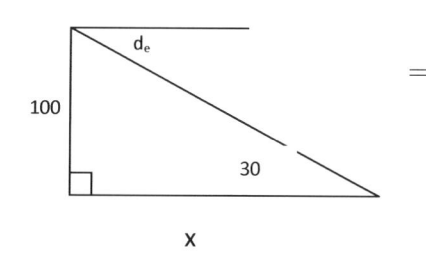

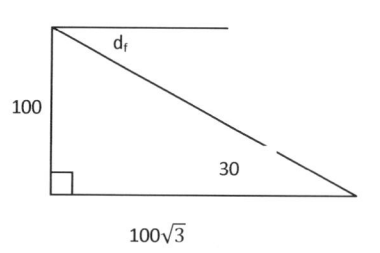

Solution

$$\tan 30 = \frac{100}{x} \rightarrow x = \frac{100}{\tan 30} = \frac{100}{1/\sqrt{3}} = 100\sqrt{3}$$

$$\tan d_f = \frac{300}{100\sqrt{3}} = \frac{3}{\sqrt{3}} \rightarrow d_f = \tan^{-1}(\sqrt{3}) = 60^0$$

433

(31.27). From two points X and Y, 8m apart and in line with a pole, the angle of elevation of the top of the pole are 30^0 and 60^0 respectively. Find the height of the pole assuming that X, Y, and foot of the pole of the pole are on the same horizontal plane and X and Y are on the same side of the pole.

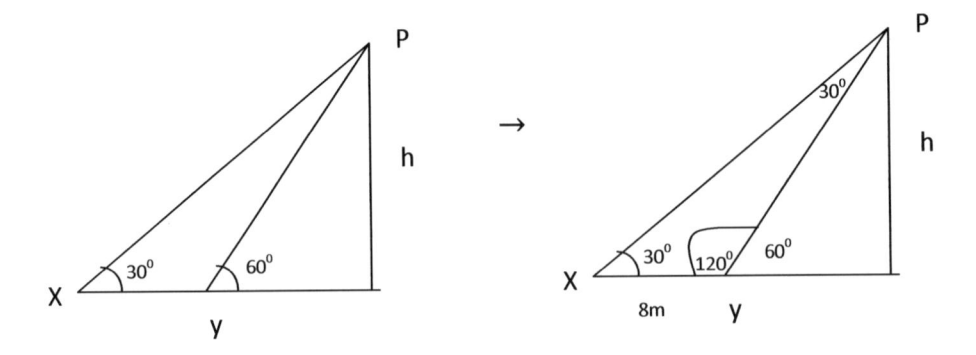

Solution

By sine rule → $\frac{Py}{\sin 30} = \frac{8}{\sin 30}$ → $Py = \frac{8 \sin 30}{\sin 30} = 8m$

Also $\sin 60 = \frac{h}{Py}$ → $h = Py \sin 60 = 8 \times \sin 60 = 4\sqrt{3}$

(31.28). The angle of elevation of the top of a vertical tower from a point A on the ground is 60^0. From a point B, 2 units distance further away from the foot of the tower, the angle of elevation of the top of the tower is 45^0. Find the distance of A from the foot of the tower.

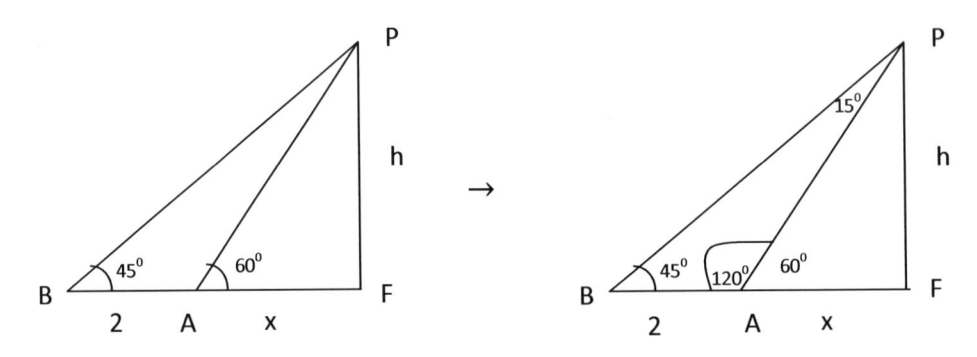

Solution

By sine rule → $\frac{PA}{\sin 45} = \frac{2}{\sin 15}$ → $PA = \frac{2 \sin 45}{\sin 15}$

Also $\cos 60 = \frac{x}{PA}$ → $x = PA \cos 60 = \frac{2 \sin 45 (\cos 60)}{\sin 15^0} = \frac{2 \times 1/\sqrt{2}}{\sin 15^0} \cdot \frac{1}{2} = \frac{1\sqrt{2}}{\sin 15}$

434

$$x = \frac{0.7070}{0.2588} = 2.732 = 1 + 1.732 = 1 + \sqrt{3}$$

(31.29). The angle of elevation of the top of a vertical tower 50 metres high from a point X on the ground is 30^0. From a point X on the ground is 30^0. From a point y on the opposite side of the tower, the angle of elevation of the top of the tower is 60^0. Find the distance between the point X and Y.

Solution

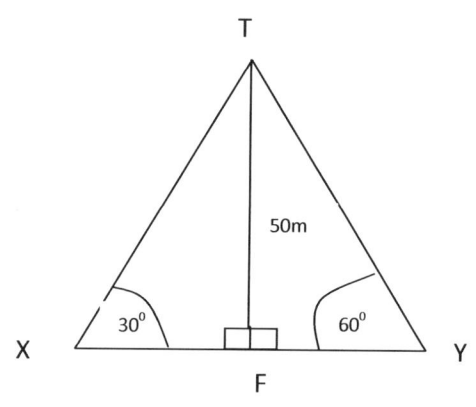

$$\tan 30 = \frac{50}{XF} \rightarrow XF = \frac{50}{\tan 30} = \frac{50}{1/\sqrt{3}} = 50\sqrt{3}$$

$$\tan 60 = \frac{50}{FY} \rightarrow FY = \frac{50}{\tan 60} = \frac{50}{\sqrt{3}} = \frac{50\sqrt{3}}{3}$$

$$XY = XF + FY = 50\sqrt{3} + \frac{50\sqrt{3}}{2} \rightarrow 50\sqrt{3}\left(1 + \frac{1}{3}\right) = 50\sqrt{3} \cdot \frac{4}{3} = \frac{200\sqrt{3}}{3} = \frac{200 \times 1.732}{3}$$

$$XY = 115.47$$

(31.30). A flag staff stands on the top of a vertical tower. A man standing 60 m away from the tower observes that the angles of elevation of the top and bottom of the flag staff the 64^0 and 62^0 respectively. Find the length of the flag staff.

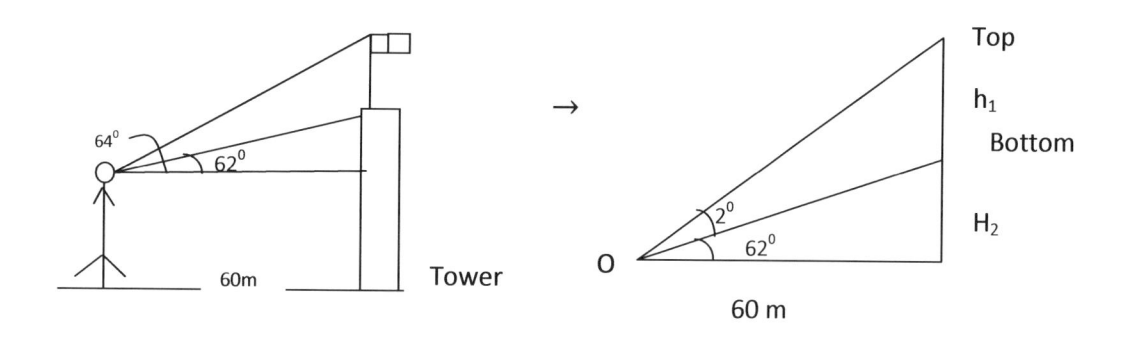

Solution

From the diagram

$\text{Tan } 62^0 = \frac{h_2}{60} \rightarrow h_2 = 60 \tan 62$ ....(i)

$\text{Tan } 64^0 = \frac{h_1 + h_2}{60} \rightarrow h_1 + h_2 = 60 \tan 64^0$ ....(ii)

Inserting (i) into (ii)

$h_1 + 60 \tan 62 = 60 \tan 64 \rightarrow h_1 = 60 \tan 64 - 60 \tan 62 = 60(\tan 64 - \tan 62)$

(31.31). The shadow of a post is 6m longer when the elevation of the sun is 30^0 than when it is 60^0. Calculate the height of the post.

Solution

Let the length of the shadow be x when the elevation is 60^0.

Hence the length of the shadow is (x + 6) when the elevation is 30^0.

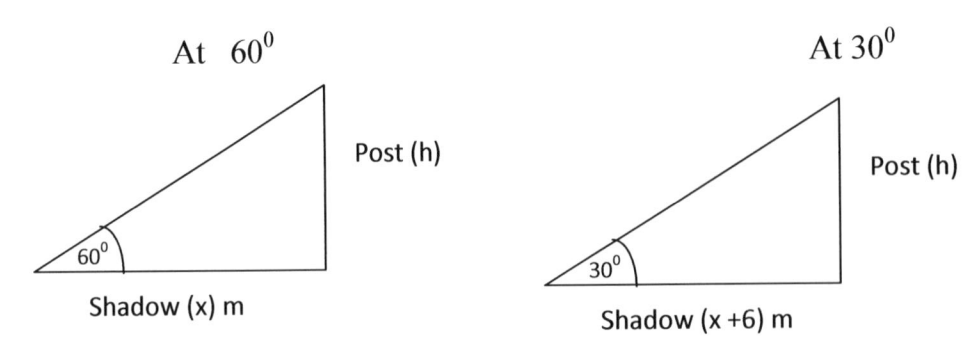

At 60^0 — Post (h), 60^0, Shadow (x) m

At 30^0 — Post (h), 30^0, Shadow (x +6) m

From (i) $\text{Tan } 60 = \frac{h}{x}$

$h = x \tan 60^0$

$h = x\sqrt{3}$

$x = \frac{h}{\sqrt{3}}$

From (ii) $\text{Tan } 30 = \frac{h}{x+6}$

$(x + 6) \tan 30 = h \rightarrow (x + 6)\frac{1}{\sqrt{3}} = h$

$(x + 6)\frac{1}{\sqrt{3}} = h \rightarrow (x + 6) = h\sqrt{3}$

substitute (i) and (ii) we have ;

$\frac{h}{\sqrt{3}} + 6 = h\sqrt{3} \rightarrow h + 6\sqrt{3} = h\sqrt{9} \rightarrow h + 6\sqrt{3} = 3h \rightarrow 3h - h = 6\sqrt{3}$

$2h = 6\sqrt{3}$ ∴ $h = \frac{6\sqrt{3}}{2} = (3\sqrt{3})m$

(31.32). The angle of elevation of the top of a vertical pole from a height 1.54m above a horizontal ground is 40^0. The foot of the pole is on the same horizontal ground and the point of observation is 20m from the pole. Calculate, correct to 3 significant figures

(*i*) The height of the pole (*ii*) The angle of depression of the foot of the pole from the point of observation.

Solution

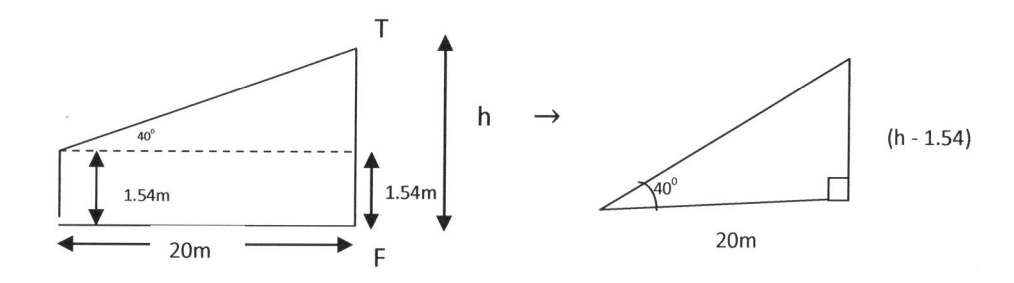

From, Total height of above the ground = $h_1 + h_2$ → $h_2 = Total\ height - h_1$

$\tan 40 = \frac{h - 1.54}{20}$ → h - 1.54 = 20tan 40^0 = 20(0.8391) = 16.78

h = 16.78 + 15 = 18.32 m = 18.3 m (to 3sf)

(ii)

$\tan d = \frac{1.54}{20} = 0.077$ → d = $\tan^{-1}$ (0.077) = 4.4^0

(31.33). A man whose eye is Y(m) above the ground stands X(m) away from the foot of a pole 6 m high on the same horizontal ground. He observes the angle of elevation of

437

the top of the pole to be 45^0 and the angle of depression of the bottom of the pole to be 60^0. Calculate, correct to 3 significant figures, the value of x.

Solution

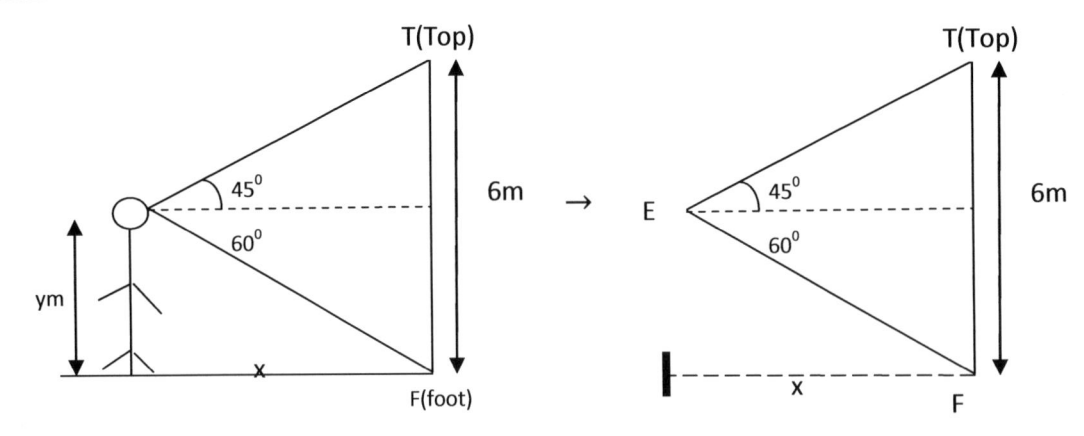

From the right angled triangle with 45^0

$\tan 45 = \frac{6-y}{x} \rightarrow 6 - y = x \tan 45 = x$ (1)

$6 - y = x, \quad y = 6 - x$ ....(i)

Also from the right angled triangle with 60^0

$\tan 60 = \frac{y}{x} \rightarrow y = x \tan 60^0 = x(\sqrt{3})$ ....(ii)

Substitute this in (i)

$x\sqrt{3} = 6 - x \rightarrow x\sqrt{3} + x = 6 \rightarrow x(\sqrt{3} + 1) = 6$

$x = \frac{6}{\sqrt{3}+1} = \frac{6}{1.732+1} = \frac{6}{2.732} = 2.196 = 2.20$ m

(31.34). The feet S and T of two vertical poles SR and TP are in line with a point Q on the same level ground. SR and TP are 5m and 9m respectively. S lies between Q and T is 25m from Q. The angle of elevation of P from R is 30^0. Calculate the (a) distance PR (b) distance QT. correct to two significant figures.

(c) Angle of elevation of P from Q, correct to one decimal place.

Solution

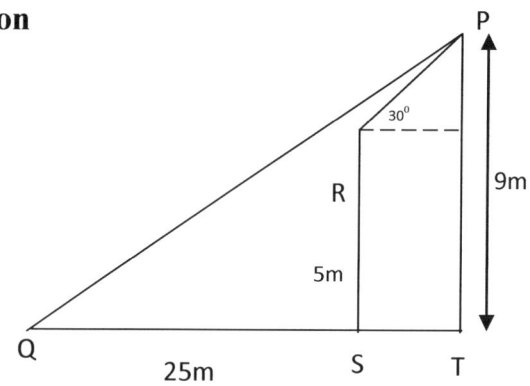

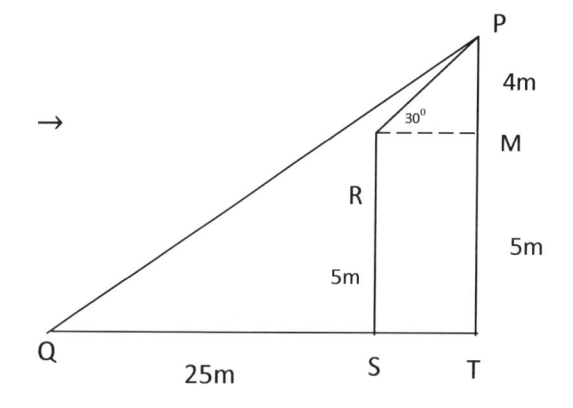

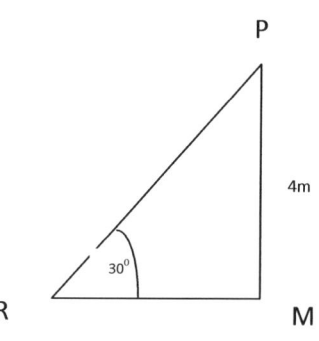

(a) $\sin 30 = \frac{4}{PR}$ → $PR \sin 30 = 4$ → $PR = \frac{4}{\sin 30} = \frac{4}{1/2} = \frac{4}{1} \times \frac{2}{1} = 8m$

(b) Distance QT = QS + ST where ST = RM

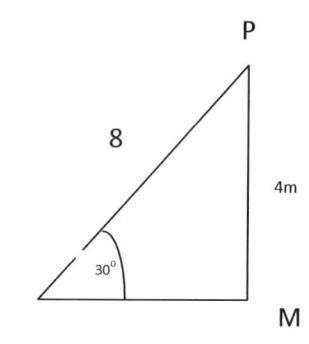

$\tan 30 = \frac{4}{RM}$ → $RM = \frac{4}{\tan 30} = \frac{4}{1\sqrt{3}} = 4\sqrt{3}$

sincde ST = RM = $4\sqrt{3}$

Distance QT = QS + ST → $25 + 4\sqrt{3}$ → $25 + 4(1.732) = 25 + 6.928 = 31.928$

QT = 32.00 m

(c) Angle of elevation of P from Q is $P\hat{Q}T$

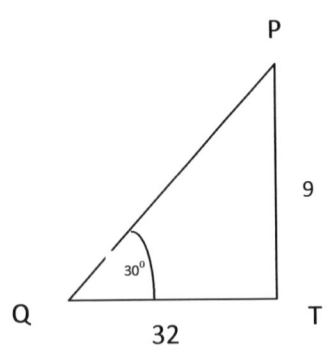

[Diagram: right triangle with P at top, Q at bottom-left, T at bottom-right; QT = 32, PT = 9, angle at T's area marked 30°]

$\tan \theta = \frac{9}{32} = 0.2819 \rightarrow \theta = \tan^{-1}(0.2571) = 15.71^0$

The angle of elevation of P from Q is 15.7^0

(31. 35). Two observers P and Q 15 metres apart observe a kite K in the same vertical plane and from the same side of the kite. The angles of elevation of the kite from P and Q are 35^0 and 45^0 respectively. Find the height of the kite to the nearest metre.

Solution

Let the height of the kite be h from a point A on the same as P and Q

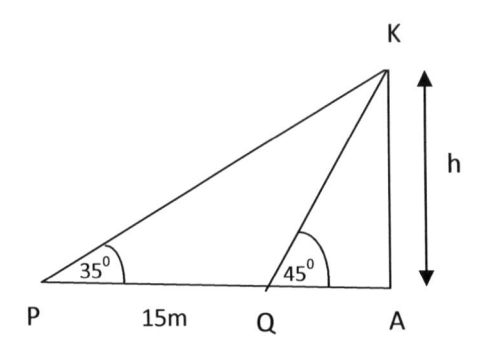

[Diagram: triangle with K at top, P at bottom-left with angle 35°, Q in middle with angle 45°, A at bottom-right; PQ = 15m, KA = h]

From the diagram, considering triangle KQA $\rightarrow \tan 45^0 = \frac{h}{QA} \rightarrow 1.00 = \frac{h}{QA} \therefore QA = h$

Also from triangle KPA, $\tan 35^0 = \frac{h}{PA} = \frac{h}{15 + QA} \rightarrow \tan 35 = \frac{h}{15 + h}$

$(15 + h) \tan 35 = h \rightarrow 15\tan 35 + h\tan 35 = h \rightarrow 15\tan 35 = h - h\tan 35$

$15\tan 35 = h(1 - \tan 35) \rightarrow h = \frac{15\tan 35}{1 - \tan 35} = \frac{15(0.7002)}{1 - 0.7002} = \frac{10.503}{0.2998} = 35.03$

440

Height of kite = 35 m.

(**31.36**). An aircraft is observed from two points A and B which are exactly 2km apart, the elevation of the aircraft from these points being $34°17'$ and $51°34'$. If the aircraft is vertical over the line $\overline{AB}$ and is between A and B, what is its height in metres?

Solution

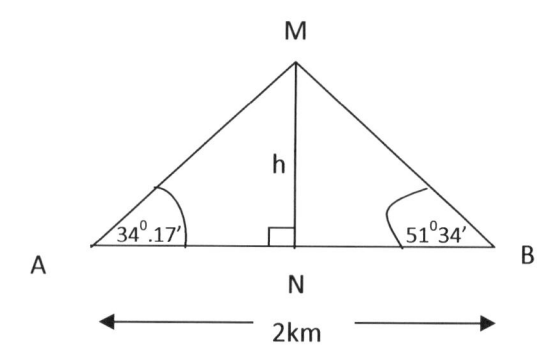

MN is the height of the aircraft

Working with the two triangles carefully,

From the diagram, $\tan 34° 17' = \frac{h}{x} \rightarrow x = \frac{h}{\tan 34°17'} = \frac{h}{0.6817}$ ......(i)

Also, $\tan 51° 34' = \frac{h}{2-x} \rightarrow 2 - x = \frac{h}{\tan 51°34'} = \frac{h}{1.2602}$ ∴ $x = 2 - \frac{h}{1.2602}$ .... (ii)

substitute (i) into (ii)

$2 - \frac{h}{1.2602} = \frac{h}{0.6817} \rightarrow 2 = \frac{h}{0.6817} + \frac{h}{1.2602} \rightarrow \frac{1.2602h + 0.6817h}{0.6817 \times 1.2602}$

$1.2602h + 0.6817h = 2 \times 0.6817 \times 1.2602$

$1.9419h = 1.7182$, $h = \frac{1.7182}{1.9419} = 0.8848$ km

h = 0.885 km = 0.885 x 1000 (in metres) ∴ h = 885m

(**31.37**). A tower and a building stand on the same horizontal level. From the point P at the bottom of the building, the angle of elevation of the top T, of the tower is $69°$. From the top Q of the building, the angle of elevation of the point T is $25°$. If the building is 20m high calculate the distance PT, Hence or otherwise, calculate the height of the tower.

Solution

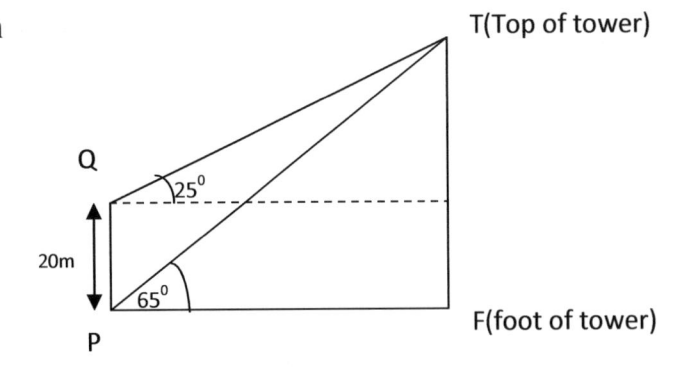

T(Top of tower)

Q 25°

20m

65°

P   F(foot of tower)

Let the distance between the building and the Tower be y and the height of the Tower above the building be x as shown below

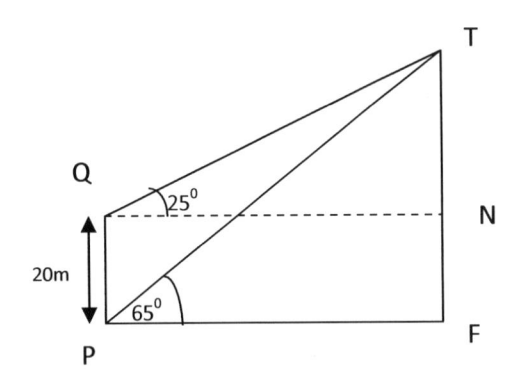

T

Q 25°   N

20m

65°

QN = y = PF   P   F

TN = x

Height of the Tower is x + 20

From right angled triangle TQN, $\tan 25 = \frac{x}{y}$ → $x = y \tan 25$ ……(i)

From right angled triangle TPF, $\tan 65^0 = \frac{TF}{PF} = \frac{20 + x}{y}$ → $20 + x = y \tan 65^0$ …..(ii)

putting (i) into (ii)

20 + ytan25 = y tan 65⁰ → ytan65 – ytan25 = 20 → y(tan65 – tan25) = 20

y(2.1445 – 0.4663) → y(1.6782) = 20

∴ $y = \frac{20}{1.6782} = 11.92 m$

In Triangle TPF,

442

Cos 65 = $\frac{PF}{TP}$ → TP = $\frac{11.92}{cos 65}$ = $\frac{11.92}{0.4226}$ = 28.21m

(b) Height of tower = TF = x + 20

But from equ (i) x = y tan 25^0 = 11.92 tan 25 = 11.92(0.4663) = 5.558 m

Height of the tower = 5.558 + 20 = 25.558 = 25.6 m

(31.38).

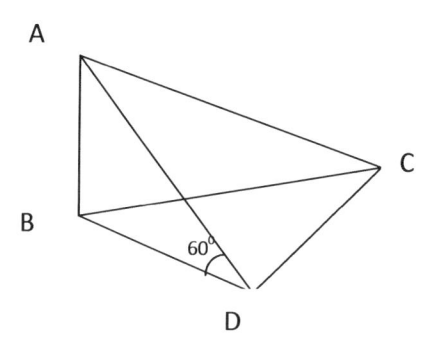

In diagram above, B, C and D are points on the same level ground; AB is a vertical tower 200 m high. The angles of depression of C and D from the top A of the tower are 30^0 and 60^0 respectively, if C is due east of B and < CBD = 60^0, Calculate

(*i*) /CB/, correct to 3 significant figures

(*ii*)The bearing of D from C, correct to the nearest degree.

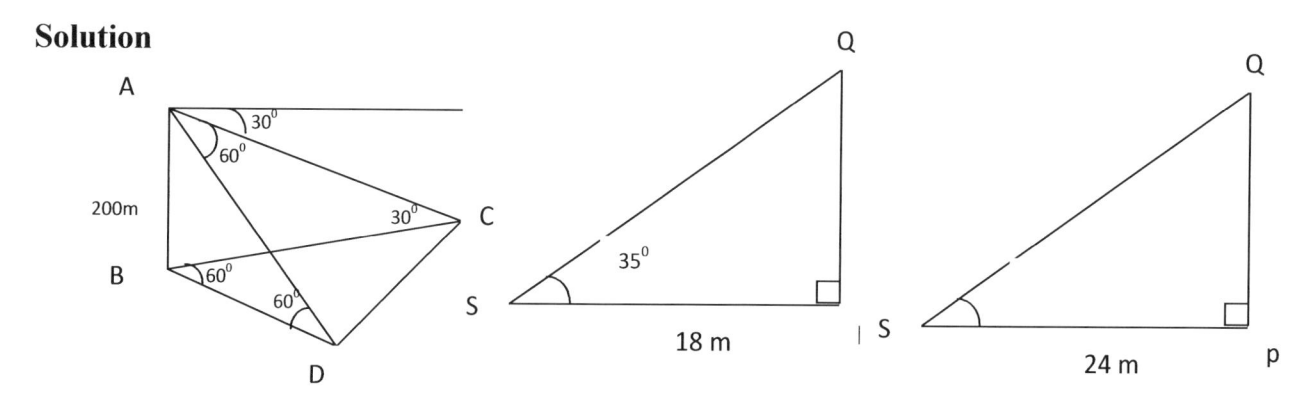

Solution

(*i*) From Triangle ABC,

tan 30 = $\frac{200}{BC}$ → BC tan 30 = 200

BC = $\frac{200}{Tan\ 30}$ = $\frac{200}{0.5774}$ = 346.38

∴ BC = 346m

(*ii*) The bearing D from C can be determined from the triangles as shown below.

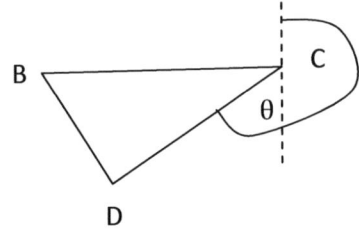

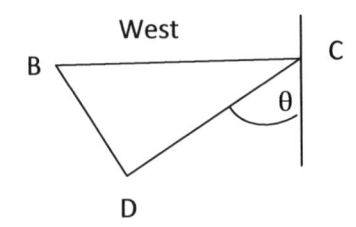

The bearing = $180 + \theta$ or $S\theta^0 W$

From triangle ABD

$\tan 60 = \dfrac{200}{BD} \rightarrow BD = \dfrac{200}{\tan 60} = \dfrac{200}{1.732} = 115.5 \cong 116m$

the angle between BC and BD is also 60^0, CD can be found by cosine rule

Thus $CD^2 = 346^2 + 116^2 - 2 \times 346 \times 116 \cos 60^0$

$CD^2 = 119716 + 1345 - 80272(0.5) = 133172 - 40136 = 93036$

$CD = \sqrt{93036} = 305.0 = 305$ m

In triangle BCD, sine rule gives $\dfrac{BD}{\sin C} = \dfrac{DC}{\sin B}$

$\dfrac{116}{\sin C} = \dfrac{305}{\sin 60} \rightarrow \sin c = \dfrac{116 \sin 60}{305} = \dfrac{116(0.866)}{305} = 0.3294$,

$C = 19.2^0 \cong 19^0$

Thus the bearing = $180 + 90 = 199^0$ or $S\ 19^0\ W$

(31.39). R and S are two observation posts on the same horizontal ground as the foot P of a vertical tower PQ. The tower is 18 m due North of S and 24m east of R. The angle of elevation of Q from S is 35^0. Calculate correct to 3 significant figures the:

(i) Height PQ (ii) distance RS (iii) angle of elevation of Q and R (iv) bearing of R from S

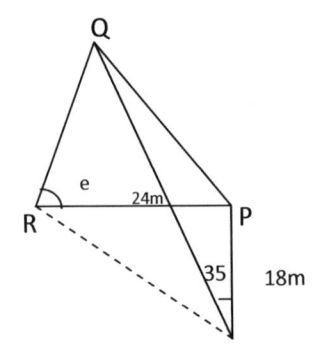

Solution

444

height PQ is perpendicular to the observation Points S and R , we obtain

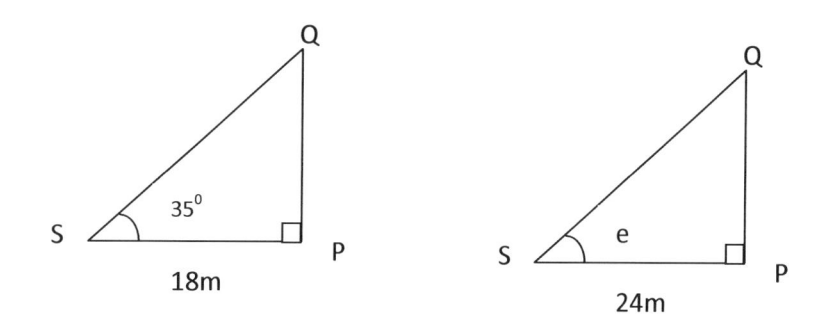

From triangle PQS,

Tan 35 = $\frac{PQ}{18}$ → PQ = 18 tan 35 = 18(0.7002) = 12.6036 = 12.6m

(ii) Distance RS is found from triangle RPS

By Pythagoras's Theorem, $RS^2 = RP^2 + PS^2$ → $RS^2 = 24^2 + 18^2 = 576 + 324 - 900$

∴ RS = $\sqrt{900}$ = 30m

(iii) Angle of elevation of Q from R is as represented in triangle RQP

Tan e = $\frac{PQ}{24} = \frac{12.6}{24}$ = 0.5250 → e = $tan^{-1} 0.5250$ ∴ e = 27.699 = 27.7

(iv) Bearing of R from S is as shown in the diagram below

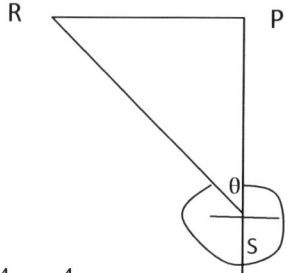

From triangles RPS, tan θ = $\frac{24}{18} = \frac{4}{3}$ = 1.333

θ = $tan^{-1} 1.333$ = 53.1°

Bearing = 360 − θ → 360 − 53.1 = 306.9°.

(31.40). Two boys A and B set out from the same point simultaneously. A goes due North and B run on a bearing of 046^0. When B has gone 440m, the boys are 400m apart. How far is A then from the starting point.

Solution

Let the common point and the boys be represented by P, A, and B respectively

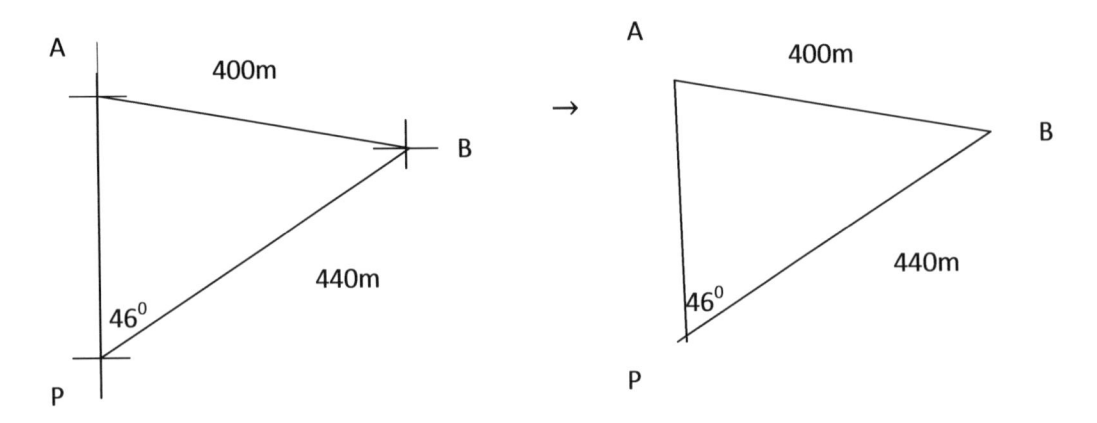

Distance between A and the starting point = AP

Thus, $\frac{400}{\sin 46} = \frac{400}{\sin A} = \frac{AP}{\sin S}$

$400 \sin A = 440 \sin 46 \rightarrow \sin A = \frac{440 \sin 46}{400} = 0.7912$, $A = \sin^{-1}(0.7912) = 52.3^0$

$B = 180 - (46 + 52.3) = 180 - 98.3 = 81.7^0$

using $\frac{440}{\sin 52.3} = \frac{AP}{\sin 81.7}$

$AP \sin 52.3^0 = 440 \sin 81.7 \rightarrow AP = \frac{440 \sin 81.7}{\sin 52.3} = 550.3m$

(31.41). An aeroplane flies due North from Ikeja Airport for 500km. It then flies on a bearing of 060^0 for a further distance of 300km before overflying a road junction. Calculate (i) The distance of the aeroplane from Ikeja Airport when it was directly above the road junction. (ii) Bearing of the aeroplane from Ikeja Airport at this instant.

Solution

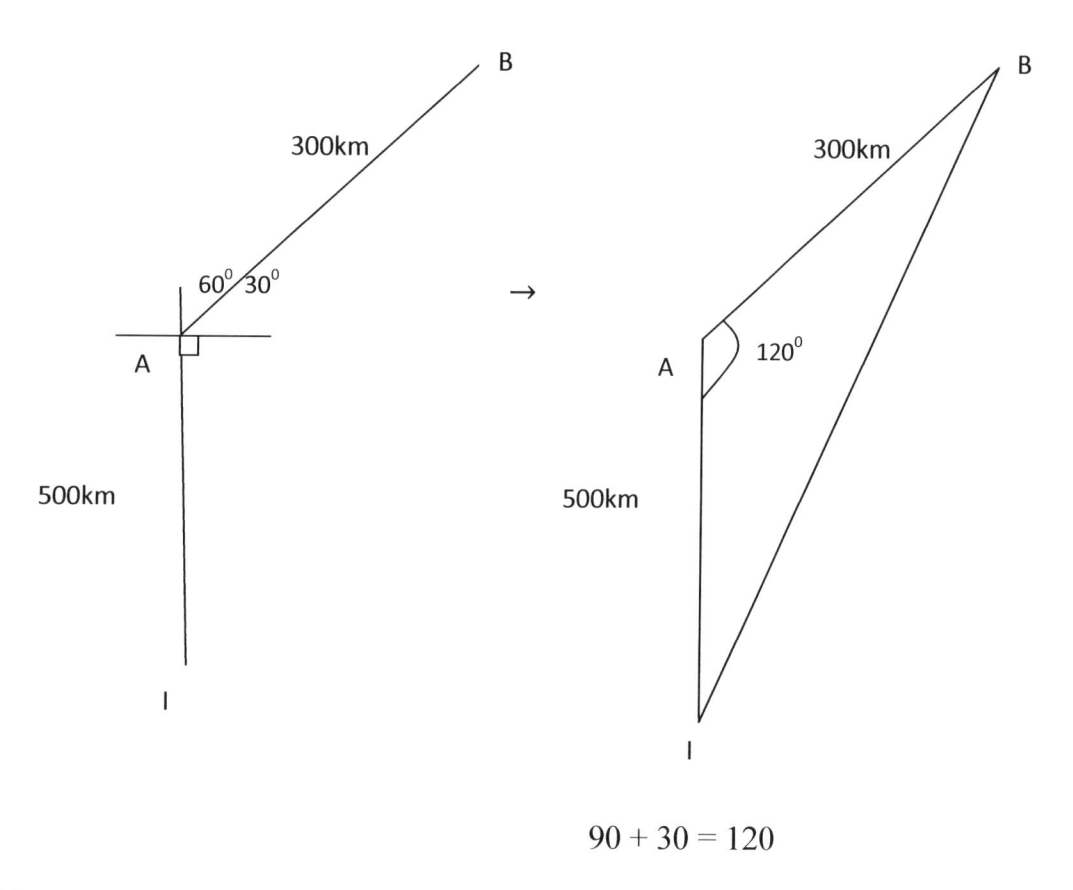

90 + 30 = 120

Distance of the aeroplane from ikeja Airport is IB

BY Cosine rule

$IB^2 = IA^2 + AB^2 - 2 \times IA \times AB \cos A$ → 250000 + 90000 – 300000 cos (180 – 120)

340000 – 300000 (- cos 60) → 340000 + 300000 (0.5) → 34000 + 150000 = 490000

IB = $\sqrt{490000}$ = 700km

(ii) Bearing of the aeroplane from Ikeja airport at this instance .

Thus the angle marked from the North of I to the line IB as shown below:

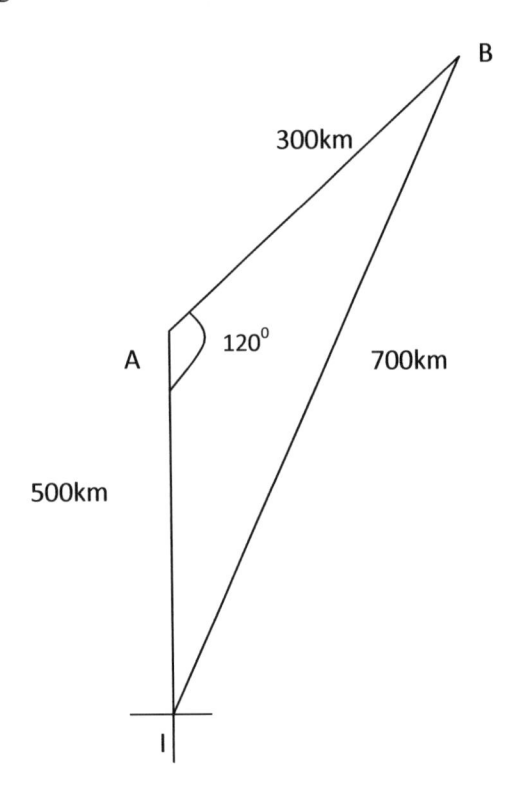

By sine rule: $\frac{300}{\sin I} = \frac{700}{\sin 120}$ → 700 sinI = 300sin120 → 700 sin I = 300 sin(180 – 120)

700 sin I = 300 sin 69 → Sin I = $\frac{300\sin 60}{700}$ ∴ I = $sin^{-1}\left[\frac{300\sin 60}{700}\right]$ = 21.8⁰

Thus the bearing of the aeroplane from Ikeja is 021.8⁰

(**31.42**). Two patrol boats Alpha and Beta leave the same time on two different straight courses. When Alpha travelled 8 nautical miles Beta has covered 10 nautical miles, the distance between the two patrols was found to be 4 nautical miles. Alpha was on a course of 079⁰ and Beta's course was the south side of Alpha's. Calculate Beta's course

Solution

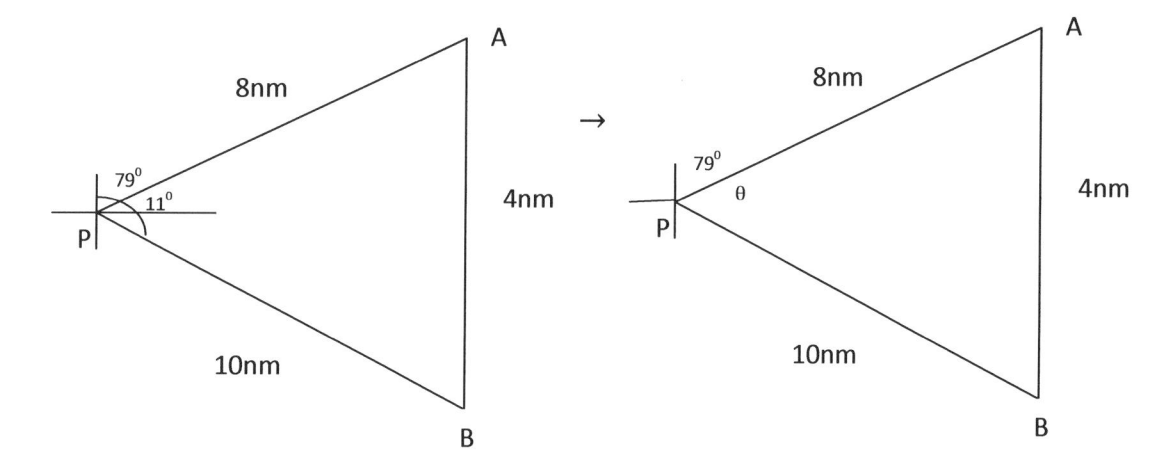

The bearing = 79 + θ where θ is the angle in the triangle at P

By cosine rule, $\cos P = \dfrac{b^2 + a^2 - p^2}{2ba}$

$\cos θ = \dfrac{8^2 + 10^2 - 4^2}{2 \times 8 \times 10} = \dfrac{64 + 100 - 16}{160} = \dfrac{148}{160} = 0.925$ ∴ $θ = \cos^{-1}(0.925) = 22.3^0$

Beta's course = $79 + 22.3^0 = 101.3^0$

(31.43). A boat sails round a quadrangular course ABCD, starting from A to B is 4km due east of A, C 3km due south of B and D 4km S 50^0 W from C. what is the distance and bearing of A from D?

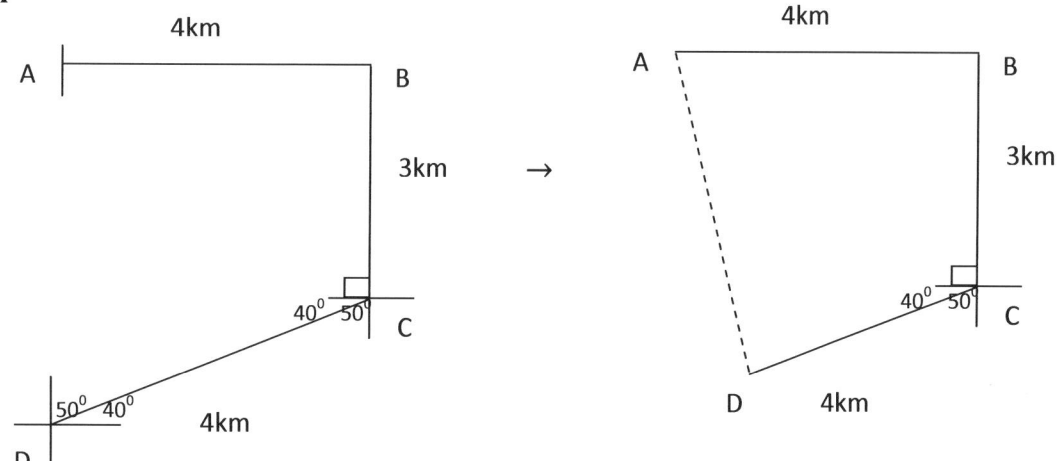

Solution

(*i*). Distance of A from D is AD

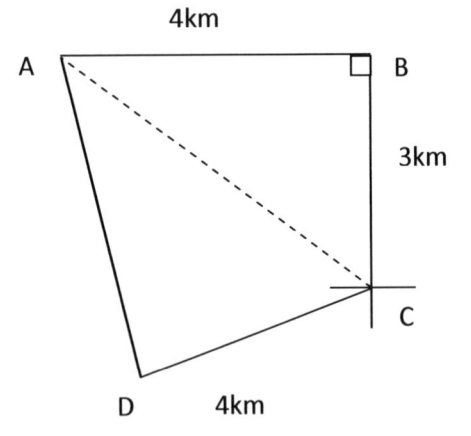

As ABC is right angled at B. Thus, $AC^2 = 4^2 + 3^2 = 16 + 9 = 25$

$AC = \sqrt{25} = 5$

Considering triangle ACB

Tan $A\hat{C}B = \frac{4}{3} = 1.3333 \rightarrow A\hat{C}B = \tan^{-1}(1.3333) = 53.1^0$

For triangle ACD two sides are known

$\therefore A\hat{C}B + 53.1 = 130 \quad \therefore A\hat{C}B = 130 - 53.1 = 76.9^0$

By cosine rule: $AD^2 = AC^2 + DC^2 - 2 \times AC \times DC \cos A\hat{C}D$

$AD^2 = 5^2 + 4^2 - 2 \times 5 \times 4\cos 76.9 \rightarrow 25 + 16 - 40(0.2267) = 41 - 9.068 = 31.93$

$AD = \sqrt{31.93} = 5.651 km$

(*ii*) The bearing A from D is the position occupied by the line AD with respect to D

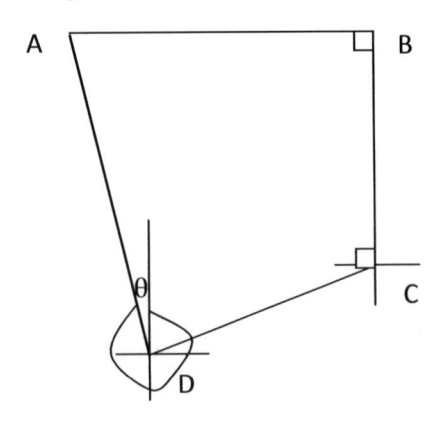

From the above diagram, the bearing is N θ⁰ W

(31.44). O, R and S are three points on the same horizontal plane. /QR/ = 20m and /OS/ = 32m. The bearings of R and S from O are 030⁰ and 135⁰ respectively. How far east of R is S?

Solution

How far east of R is S implies the bearing of S from R.

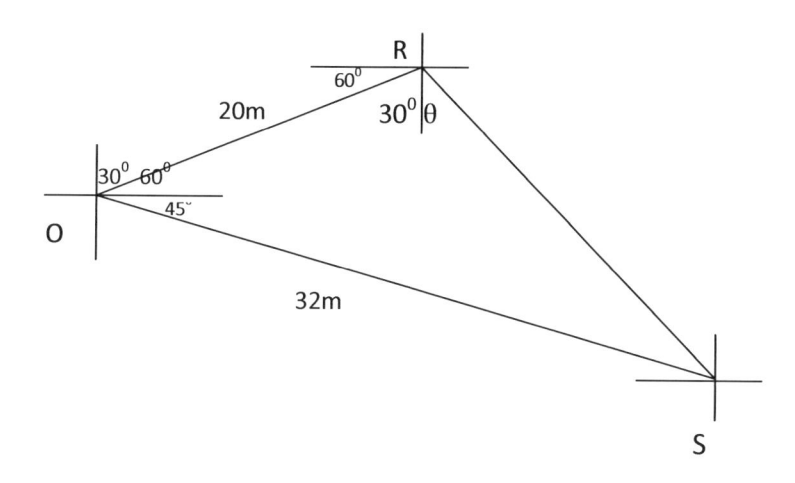

From the diagram above, the bearing is S θ⁰ E

By Cosine rule: $SR^2 = OR^2 + OS^2 - 2 \times OR \times OS \cos S\hat{O}R$

$SR^2 = 20^2 + 32^2 - 2 \times 20 \times 32 \cos 105^0$ → $400 + 1024 - 1280\cos(180 - 105)$

$1424 - 1280(-\cos 75)$ → $1424 + 1280\cos 75$ → $1424 + 1280(0.2588) = 1755.3$

$SR = \sqrt{1755.3} = 41.90m$

By sine rule $\frac{41.9}{\sin 105} = \frac{32}{\sin R}$ → $41.9 \sin R = 32 \sin 105$

$\sin R = \frac{32 \sin 105}{41.9}$ → $\frac{32 \sin(180 - 105)}{41.9}$ → $\frac{32 \sin 75}{41.9}$ → $\frac{32 \times 0.9659}{41.9} = 0.7377$

$R = \sin^{-1} 0.7377 = 47.5$

CHAPTER 32 CALCULUS 1: DIFFERENTIATION

Calculus is a branch of mathematics that studies the relationship between changes in quantities or variables.

DIFFERENTIATION

This is an aspect of calculus that deals with the ratio of the change in one quantity to the change in the other quantity to the nearest approximation.

Thus: if y and x are related, differentiation deals with the ratio of change in y to change in x to the nearest approximation.

Differentiation is $\frac{change\ in\ y}{change\ in\ x}$ (to nearest approximation)

Methods of differentiation

(1) *From* First principle: Here we simply find the ratio of the change in one quantity to the change in the other to the nearest approximation.

Thus if $y = 3x^2$ we let increase in x to be Δx and increase in y to be Δy

From $y = 3x^2 \rightarrow y + \Delta y = 3(x + \Delta x)^2 \rightarrow y + \Delta y = 3(x^2 + 2x\Delta x + \Delta x^2)$

$y + \Delta y = 3x^2 + 6x\Delta x + 3\Delta x^2 \rightarrow \Delta y = 3x^2 + 6x\Delta x + 3\Delta x^2 - y$

$\Delta y = 3x^2 + 6x\Delta x + 3\Delta x^2 - 3x^2$ (Where the value of y have been substituted)

$\Delta y = 6x\Delta x + 3\Delta x^2$

$\frac{\Delta y}{\Delta x} = \frac{6x\Delta x + 3\Delta x^2}{\Delta x} = \frac{(6x + 3\Delta x)\Delta x}{\Delta x} = 6x + 3\Delta x$

As $\Delta x = 0$

$\frac{\Delta y}{\Delta x} = \frac{dy}{dx} = 6x$

(2) Direct method: Here we simply apply

If $y = x^n$ $\quad \frac{dy}{dx}$ nx^{n-1}

For example, If $y = x^2 \rightarrow \frac{dy}{dx} = 2x^{2-1} = 2x^1 = 2x$

If $y = 6x^7 \to \frac{dy}{dx} = 7 \times 6 \, x^{7-1} = 42x^6$

Techniques of differentiation

(*i*) Differentiation of a constant

If y = k where k is a constant, then $\frac{dy}{dx} = 0$

This is because y = 2 can be written as $y = 2x^0$ from which $\frac{dy}{dx} = 0 \times 2x^{0-1} = 0$

(*ii*) Differentiation of a negative power

$$\text{If } y = \frac{6}{x^3}$$

By indices we can write $y = 6x^{-3}$ after which differentiation can be carried out to give

$\frac{dy}{dx} = -18x^{-4} = -\frac{18}{x^4}$

(*iii*) Fractional power differentiation

If $y = \sqrt{x}$

By indices we can write $y = x^{1/2}$ after which differentiation can be carried out to give

$\frac{dy}{dx} = \frac{1}{2}x^{-1/2} = \frac{1}{2x^{1/2}} = \frac{1}{2\sqrt{x}}$

(*iv*) Differentiation of function of a function: This is used when we want to differentiate anything of the form $y = (core)^n$, where n is the power which can be positive, negative or a fraction.

We apply $\frac{dy}{dx} = \frac{dy}{du} \times \frac{du}{dx}$ OR $n(core)^{n-1} \times derivative \, of \, the \, core$

Thus if $y = (4x^3)^8 \to \frac{dy}{dx} = 8(4x^3)^7 = (32)^7$

(*v*) Product rule differentiation: This is used when we what to differentiate anything of the form $y = (u)(v)$, where u and v is the first and second brackets respectively. To differentiate we apply

$\frac{dy}{dx} = v\frac{du}{dx} + u\frac{dv}{dx}$

For three brackets where $y = (u)(v)(w)$

$$\frac{dy}{dx} = uv\frac{dw}{dx} + uw\frac{dv}{dx} + vw\frac{du}{dx}$$

e.g. If $y = (x + 2)(3x - 5) \rightarrow \frac{dy}{dx} = (3x - 5)(1) + (x + 2)(3) = 3x - 5 + 3x + 6 = 6x + 1$

(*vi*) Quotient differentiation : This is used when we want to differentiate anything of the form $y = \frac{u}{v}$ where u and v is the numerator and denominator of the given fraction. Thus

$$\frac{dy}{dx} = \frac{v\frac{du}{dx} - u\frac{dv}{dx}}{v^2} = \frac{Bottom \times Differentiate\ top - Top \times differentiate\ bottom}{(Bottom)^2}$$

e.g. If $y = \frac{1}{2x} \rightarrow \frac{dy}{dx} = \frac{(2x)(0) \times - 1(2)}{(2x)^2} = \frac{-2}{4x^2} = \frac{-1}{2x^2}$

(*vii*) Trigonometry functions differentiation: There are six functions in trigonometry. Given below are the functions and their derivatives:

If $y = \sin x$, $\frac{dy}{dx} = \cos x$

If $y = \cos x$, $\frac{dy}{dx} = -\sin x$

If $y = \tan x$, $\frac{dy}{dx} = sec^2 x$

If $y = \operatorname{cosec} x$, $\frac{dy}{dx} = $ - cotan x cosec x

If $y = \operatorname{cotan} x$, $\frac{dy}{dx} = -cosec^2 x$

We can prove some using the quotient rule:

e.g. If $y = \tan x = \frac{\sin x}{\cos x}$

$$\frac{dy}{dx} = \frac{\cos x (\cos x) - \sin x(-\sin x)}{cos^2 x} = \frac{cos^2 x + sin^2 x}{cos^2 x} = \frac{1}{cos^2 x} = sec^2 x$$

(*viii*) Logarithmic differentiation: For logarithm function i.e logarithm to natural base e,

If $y = \log_e x$, $\frac{dy}{dx} = \frac{1}{x}$

(*ix*) Logarithmic function differentiation: For logarithm function

If $y = \frac{uv}{w}$ where u, v and w are also functions of x

454

$$ln y = \ln u + \ln v - \ln w \rightarrow \frac{1}{y}\frac{dy}{dx} = \frac{1}{u}\frac{du}{dx} + \frac{1}{v}\frac{dv}{dx} - \frac{1}{w}\frac{dw}{dx}$$

Solve for $\frac{dy}{dx}$

(x) Exponential function differentiation: For exponential function i.e natural base with power of variables

If $y = e^x$, $\frac{dy}{dx} = e^x$

(xi) Implicit differentiation: This is a differentiation in which we can't solve for y because the function is not in the form y = f(x). In this case all rules of differentiation should be obeyed.

(xii) Further/Higher derivatives: These are repeated derivatives e.g.

$\frac{dy}{dx} = 1^{st}$ derivative or result of differentiating once.

$\frac{d^2y}{dx^2} = 2^{nd}$ derivative or result of differentiating twice.

Thus, the power of d and x represent the number of repetition and have no mathematical effect on the left side.

Applications of differentiation

(1) Finding gradient at a point.

Gradient is defined as the ratio of change in y to change in x.

Thus, to get gradient simply find $\frac{dy}{dx}$ and substitute the value of x given in $\frac{dy}{dx}$

(2) Finding turning points: A turning point is a point at which $\frac{dy}{dx} = 0$. Turning points can be maximum, minimum or inflection point.

To find turning points find $\frac{dy}{dx}$, *equate to zero and solve for x,*

substitute the value of x gotten into the original function to get the corresponding value of y.

Generally after substitution:

i. If one point is produced, it is maximum for positive value and minimum for negative value.
ii. If two points are produced, the smaller is the minimum while the bigger is the maximum.

Alternatively, before substitution, the maximum and minimum are the smallest and biggest values respectively.

(3) Rate of change: rate of change are generally regarded as the ratio of the change in one quantity to the other. To solve for rate of change simply establish the relationship between the variables.

QUESTIONS

(32.1). If $y = \frac{4}{x^5} - \frac{2}{x^6} + \frac{3}{x^8}$ Find $\frac{dy}{dx}$

Solution

$y = 4x^{-5} - 2x^{-6} + 3x^{-8}$

$\frac{dy}{dx} = -20x^{-6} + 12x^{-7} - 24x^{-9} = -\frac{20}{x^6} + \frac{12}{x^7} - \frac{24}{x^9}$

(32.2). If $y = \frac{1}{x\sqrt{x}}$ Find $\frac{dy}{dx}$

Solution

$\frac{1}{x^{1+1/2}} \rightarrow \frac{1}{x^{3/2}} \rightarrow x^{-3/2}$

$\frac{dy}{dx} = -\frac{3}{2} x^{-3/2 - 1} \rightarrow -\frac{3}{2} x^{-5/2} \rightarrow -\frac{3}{2} \cdot \frac{1}{x^{5/2}} \rightarrow -\frac{3}{2} \cdot \frac{1}{x^2 x^{1/2}} = -\frac{3}{2} \cdot \frac{1}{x^2 \sqrt{x}}$

(32.3). If $y = \frac{2}{\sqrt{x}} - \frac{4}{\sqrt[3]{x}} + \frac{6}{5\sqrt{x}}$ Find $\frac{dy}{dx}$

Solution

$y = \frac{2}{x^{1/2}} - \frac{4}{x^{1/3}} + \frac{6}{x^{2/5}} \rightarrow 2x^{-1/2} - 4x^{-1/3} + 6x^{-2/5}$

$\frac{dy}{dx} = -\frac{1}{2}.2x^{-1/2 - 1} + \frac{1}{3}.4x^{-1/3 - 1} - \frac{2}{5}.6x^{-2/5 - 1} \rightarrow$

456

$$-x^{-3/2} + \frac{4}{3}\cdot x^{-4/3}\frac{12}{5}x^{-7/5} \to \frac{-1}{x^{3/2}} + \frac{\frac{4}{3}}{x^{4/3}} - \frac{\frac{12}{5}}{x^{7/5}}$$

(32.4). If $y = \frac{(2x+5)^2}{x^3}$ Find $\frac{dy}{dx}$

Solution

$$y = \frac{4x^2 + 20x + 25}{x^3} \to \frac{4x^2}{x^3} + \frac{20x}{x^3} + \frac{25}{x^3} \to \frac{4}{x} + \frac{20x}{x^2} + \frac{25}{x^3} \to 4x^{-1} + 20x^{-2} + 25x^{-3}$$

$$\frac{dy}{dx} = -4x^{-2} - 40x^{-3} - 75x^{-4} = -\frac{4}{x^2} - \frac{40}{x^3} - \frac{75}{x^4}$$

(32.5). If $y = (4x^3 - 6x^2 + 3x - 3)^8$ Find $\frac{dy}{dx}$

Solution

From $y = (core)^n \to \frac{dy}{dx} = n(core)^{n-1}$ x *derivative of the core*

$$\frac{dy}{dx} = 8[(4x^3 - 6x^2 + 3x - 3)^7](12x^2 - 12x + 3) \to$$

$$96x^2 - 96x + 24(4x^3 - 6x^2 + 3x - 3)^7$$

(32.6). If $y = \frac{1}{(4x^3 + 6x^2 - 7x + 3)^3}$ Find $\frac{dy}{dx}$

Solution

$$y = (4x^3 + 6x^2 - 7x + 3)^{-3}$$

$$\frac{dy}{dx} = -3[4x^3 + 6x^2 - 7x + 3)^{-4}](12x^2 + 12x - 7) = -3\frac{(12x^2+12x-7)}{[4x^3+6x^2-7x+3)^4]}$$

(32.7). If $y = (2x^3 - 4x^2 + 3x - 5)(3x^2 - 4x + 5)$. Find $\frac{dy}{dx}$

Solution

$$\frac{dy}{dx} = v\frac{du}{dx} + u\frac{dv}{dx} \to (3x^2 - 4x + 5)(6x^2 - 8x + 3x) + (2x^3 - 4x^2 + 3x - 5)(6x - 4)$$

$18x^4 - 24x^3 + 9x^2 - 24x^3 + 32x^2 - 12x + 30x^2 - 40x + 15 + 12x^4 - 8x^3 - 24x^3 + 16x^2 + 18x^2 - 12x - 30x + 20$

$30x^4 - 80x^3 + 105x^2 - 94x + 35$

(32.8). If $y = (x+2)(3x-5)^7$ Find $\frac{dy}{dx}$

Solution

$\frac{dy}{dx} = (x+2) \times 21(3x-5)^6 + (3x-5)^7 \times 1 \rightarrow (3x-5)^6[21(x+2) + (3x-5)]$

$(3x-5)^6[21x + 42 + 3x - 5] = (3x-5)^6[24x + 37]$

(32.9). If $y = \frac{5x^2 - 3x + 4}{4x - 2}$ Find $\frac{dy}{dx}$

Solution

$\frac{dy}{dx} = \frac{v \frac{du}{dx} - u \frac{dv}{dx}}{v^2} = \frac{\text{Bottom} \times \text{Differentiate top} - \text{Top} \times \text{differentiate bottom}}{(\text{Bottom})^2}$

$\frac{(4x-2)(10x-3) - (5x^2 - 3x + 4)4}{(4x-2)^2} \rightarrow \frac{40x^2 - 12x - 20x + 6 - 20x^2 + 12x - 16}{(4x-2)^2} = \frac{20x^2 - 20x - 10}{(4x-2)^2}$

(32.10). If $y = \frac{x^2}{(3x+5)^5}$. Find $\frac{dy}{dx}$

Solution

$\frac{dy}{dx} = \frac{(3x+5)^5 \times 2x - x^2 \times 15(3x+5)^4}{((3x+5)^5)^2} \rightarrow \frac{x(3x+5)^4[2(3x+5) - 15x]}{(3x+5)^{10}} \rightarrow \frac{x(6x + 10 - 15x)}{(3x+5)^6} = \frac{x(10 - 9x)}{(3x+5)^6}$

(32.11). If $y = \frac{2x - 4}{(3x^2 - 5x + 2)^4}$ Find $\frac{dy}{dx}$

Solution

$\frac{dy}{dx} = \frac{(3x^2 - 5x + 2)^4 \times 2 - (2x - 4) \times 4(3x^2 - 5x + 2)^3 \times (6x - 5)}{[(3x^2 - 5x + 2)^4]^2}$

$\rightarrow \frac{(3x^2 - 5x + 2)^3[2(3x^2 - 5x + 2) - (2x - 4)(24x - 20)]}{[(3x^2 - 5x + 2)^4]^2} \rightarrow \frac{(3x^2 - 5x + 2)^3[-42x + 126x - 76]}{(3x^2 - 5x + 2)^8} = \frac{[-42x + 126x - 76]}{(3x^2 - 5x + 2)^5}$

(32.12). If $y = (2x^3 - 4x^2 + 3x - 4)^3(3x^2 - 4x + 5)$. Find $\frac{dy}{dx}$

Solution

$\frac{dy}{dx} = v\frac{du}{dx} + u\frac{dv}{dx} \to (3x^2 - 4x + 5) \times 3(2x^3 - 4x^2 + 3x - 4)^2(6x^2 - 8x + 3) + (2x^3 - 4x^2 + 3x - 4)^3(6x - 4)$

$(2x^3 - 4x^2 + 3x - 4)^2[3(3x^2 - 4x + 5)(6x^2 - 8x + 3) + (2x^3 - 4x^2 + 3x - 4)^3(6x - 4)]$

(32.13). Find the limit of the function $\frac{x^2 - 4}{x + 2}$ as x tends to - 2

Solution

$\frac{x^2 - 4}{x + 2} \to \frac{x^2 - 2^2}{x + 2} \to \frac{(x-2)(x+2)}{(x+2)} \to (x - 2)$

As x tends to -2 we have $\to$ (-2 - 2) = - 4

(32.14). Find $\frac{dy}{dx}$ Simplify $\frac{1 - x^2}{x - x^2}$ where x ≠ 0

Solution

$\frac{1 - x^2}{x - x^2} \to \frac{1^2 - x^2}{x - x^2} \to \frac{(1 - x)(1 + x)}{x(1 - x)} \to \frac{(1+x)}{x}$

(32.15). Evaluate $\lim_{x \to 2} \frac{(x - 2)(x^2 + 3x - 2)}{x^2 - 4}$

Solution

$\frac{(x - 2)(x^2 + 3x - 2)}{x^2 - 4} \to \frac{(x - 2)(x^2 + 3x - 2)}{(x - 2)(x + 2)} \to \frac{x^2 + 3x - 2}{(x + 2)}$

As x tends to 2 $\to \frac{2^2 + 3(2) - 2}{(2 + 2)} \to \frac{4 + 6 - 2}{4} = \frac{8}{4} = 2$

(32.16). Find $\lim_{x \to 1} \frac{x - 1}{x^2 - 6x + 5}$

Solution

$x^2 - 6x + 5 = (x - 1)(x - 5)$

$\lim_{x \to 1} \frac{x-1}{x^2 - 6x+5} \to \lim_{x \to 1} \frac{x-1}{(x-1)(x-5)} \to \lim_{x \to 1} \frac{1}{x-5} = \frac{1}{1-5} = -\frac{1}{4}$

(32.17). Evaluate $\lim_{x \to \infty} \frac{5x^3 + 3}{2x^3 + 4x + 1}$

459

Solution $\lim_{x \to \infty} \dfrac{5 + \frac{3}{x^3}}{2 + \frac{4}{x^2} + \frac{1}{x^2}}$

As $x \to \infty$, $\dfrac{3}{x^3}, \dfrac{4}{x^2}$ and $\dfrac{1}{x^3} = 0 \to \dfrac{5+0}{2+0+0} = \dfrac{5}{2}$

(32.18). Calculate $\lim_{x \to 0} \dfrac{\cos x}{x - 2}$

Solution

$\lim_{x \to 0} \dfrac{\cos x}{x - 2} \to \dfrac{\cos 0}{0 - 2} \to \dfrac{1}{-2} = \dfrac{-1}{2}$

(32.19). Evaluate $\lim_{x \to 0} \dfrac{\cos x + 2 \sin x}{3 \cos x}$

Solution

$\lim_{x \to 0} \dfrac{\cos x + 2 \sin x}{3 \cos x} \to \dfrac{\cos 0 + 2 \sin 0}{3 \cos 0} \to \dfrac{1 + 0}{3} = \dfrac{1}{3}$

(32.20). If $y = 3t^2 + 2t^2 - 7t + 3$, find $\dfrac{dy}{dt}$ at $t = -1$

Solution

$\dfrac{dy}{dt} = 3.3t^2 + 2.2t^2 - 1(7)t^0 + 0 \to 9t^2 + 4t - 7$

When $t = -1$

$\dfrac{dy}{dt} = 9(-1)^2 + 4(-1) - 7 = 9 - 4 - 7 = -2$

(32.21). If $y = 2 \tan 3x + \cos 2x - \sin 5x$, find $\dfrac{dy}{dx}$

Solution

let $u = 3x$, $\dfrac{du}{dx} = 3$

$\therefore y = \tan u$

$\dfrac{dy}{du} = \sec^2 u$

$\dfrac{dy}{dx} = \dfrac{dy}{du} \times \dfrac{du}{dx} \to 3 \sec^2 u = 3\sec^2 3x$

For y = 2 tan 3x

$\frac{dy}{dx}$ = 2(3 sec² 3x) = 6 sec² 3x

For cos 2x, let u = 2x, $\frac{du}{dx}$ = 2

y = cos u, $\frac{dy}{du}$ = - sin u,

$\frac{dy}{dx} = \frac{dy}{du} \times \frac{du}{dx}$ → - 2sin u = - 2 sin 2x

For sin 5x

let u = 5x, $\frac{du}{dx}$ = 5

y = sin u, $\frac{dy}{du}$ = cos u

$\frac{dy}{dx}$ = 5 cos u = 5 cos 5x

∴ Total derivative = 6 sec² 3x - 2 sin 2x – 5 cos 5x

(32.22). If y = $\frac{1+x}{1-x}$ find $\frac{dy}{dx}$

Solution

$\frac{dy}{dx} = \frac{(1+x)^1(1-x)-(1-x)^1(1+x)}{(1-x)^2}$ → $\frac{1-x+1+x}{(1-x)^2}$ = $\frac{2}{(1-x)^2}$

(32.23). If y = $\frac{x}{(x^2-1)^{\frac{1}{2}}}$ find $\frac{dy}{dx}$

Solution

$\frac{dy}{dx} = \frac{(x)^1(x^2-1)^{\frac{1}{2}} - [((x^2-1)^{\frac{1}{2}}]^1(x)}{[(x^2-1)^{\frac{1}{2}}]^2}$ → $\frac{1(x^2-1)^{\frac{1}{2}} - \frac{1}{2}(x^2-1)^{\frac{-1}{2}} \cdot 2x \cdot (x)}{(x^2-1)}$ →

$\frac{(x^2-1)^{\frac{1}{2}} - x^2(x^2-1)^{\frac{-1}{2}}}{(x^2-1)}$ ....*

$(x^2-1)^{\frac{1}{2}} - x^2(x^2-1)^{-\frac{1}{2}}$ → $(x^2-1)^{\frac{1}{2}} - \frac{x^2}{(x^2-1)^{\frac{1}{2}}}$ → $\frac{(x^2-1)^{\frac{1}{2}}(x^2-1)^{\frac{1}{2}} - x^2}{(x^2-1)^{\frac{1}{2}}}$ →

$$\frac{(x^2-1) - x^2}{(x^2-1)^{\frac{1}{2}}} \to \frac{x^2 - 1 - x^2}{(x^2-1)^{\frac{1}{2}}} \to \frac{-1}{(x^2-1)^{\frac{1}{2}}}$$

∴ equation * becomes i.e $\frac{(x^2-1)^{\frac{1}{2}} - x^2(x^2-1)^{\frac{-1}{2}}}{(x^2-1)} = \frac{-1}{(x^2-1)(x^2-1)^{\frac{1}{2}}} = \frac{-1}{(x^2-1)^{\frac{1}{2}}}$

(32.24). Find with respect to x, the derivative of $\frac{\sin x}{1 - \cos x}$

Solution

$\frac{dy}{dx} = \frac{(\sin x)^1(1 - \cos x) - \sin x (1 - \cos x)^1}{(1-\cos x)^2} \to \frac{\cos x - \cos^2 x - \sin^2 x}{(1 - \cos x)^2} \to \frac{\cos x - (\cos^2 x + \sin^2 x)}{(1 - \cos x)^2}$

$\to \frac{\cos x - 1}{(1 - \cos x)^2} \to \frac{-(1 - \cos x)}{(1 - \cos x)(1 - \cos x)} = \frac{-1}{1 - \cos x}$

(32.25). The derivative of Cosec x is ?

Solution

$$\text{Cosec x} = \frac{1}{\sin x}$$

$\frac{1^1(\sin x) - (\sin x)^2}{(\sin x)^2} \to \frac{0(\sin x) - (\cos x)1}{(\sin x)^2} \to \frac{-\cos x}{\sin x \sin x} \to \frac{-\cos x}{\sin x} \cdot \frac{1}{\sin x} = -\cot x \csc x$

(32.26). If $y = x^3 + 3x^2$, find $2\frac{dy}{dx} - \frac{x d^2y}{dx^2}$

Solution

$\frac{dy}{dx} = 3x^2 + 6x, \quad \frac{d^2y}{dx^2} = 6x + 6$

∴ $2\frac{dy}{dx} - x\frac{d^2y}{dx^2} = 2(3x^2 + 6x) - x(6x + 6) \to 6x^2 + 12x - 6x^2 - 6x = 6x$

(32.27). If $y = x \sin x$, find $\frac{d^2y}{dx^2}$

Solution

$$y = x \sin x$$

$\frac{dy}{dx} = x' \sin x + (\sin x)' x \to (1)\sin x + (\cos x)x \to \sin x + x \cos x$

$\frac{d^2y}{dx^2} = \cos x + 1(\cos x) - (-\sin x)x \to \cos x + \cos x - x \sin x = 2\cos x - x\sin x$

(32.28). Find the point (x,y) on the Euclidean plane where the curve $y = 2x^2 - 2x + 3$ has 2 as gradient.

Solution $\quad y = 2x^2 - 2x + 3$

Gradient $= \frac{dy}{dx} = 2.2x^1 - 2 = 4x - 2$

with m = 2

$\therefore 4x - 2 = 2 \rightarrow 4x = 4 \therefore x = 1$

Putting x = 1 in the original function gives `

$y = 2x^2 - 2x + 3 \rightarrow 2(1)^2 - 2(1) + 3 = 2 - 2 + 3 = 3$

$\therefore$ The point (x, y) = (1, 3)

(32.29). Determine the turning point on the curve $y = x^2 + \frac{250}{x}$

Solution $\quad x^2 + \frac{250}{x} = x^2 + 250x^{-1}$

$\frac{dy}{dx} = 2x + -1(250)x^{-2} \rightarrow 2x - 250x^{-2} = 2x - \frac{250}{x^2}$

At turning point, $\frac{dy}{dx} = 0$

$\therefore 2x - \frac{250}{x^2} = 0 \rightarrow 2x^3 - 250 = 0 \rightarrow 2x^3 = 250 \rightarrow x^3 = 125 \therefore x = \sqrt[3]{125} = 5$

put x = 5 in y

$y = x^2 + \frac{250}{x} \rightarrow 5^2 + \frac{250}{5} = 25 + 50 = 75$

$\therefore$ the turning point = (x, y) = (5, 75)

(32.30). Find the minimum value of the function $2x^3 - 6x^2$.

Solution

Let $y = 2x^3 - 6x^2$

463

$\frac{dy}{dx} = 6x^2 - 12x$

At turning point $6x^2 - 12x = 0$

$\therefore 6x(x - 2) = 0 \rightarrow 6x = 0$ or $x - 2 = 0$ $\therefore x = 0$ or $x = 2$

(32.31). A swimming pool is treated periodically to control harmful bacterial growth. The concentration of bacterial per cm^3 after t days is given by $c(t) = 30t^2 - 240t + 500$.

How many days after a treatment will the concentration be minimal?

Solution

$C = 30t^2 - 240t + 500$

$\frac{dc}{dt} = 60t - 240$

At minimum or maximum, $\frac{dc}{dt} = 0$

$\therefore 60t - 240 = 0 \rightarrow 60t = 240$ $\therefore t = 4$ days

Thus, the concentration is minimal after 4 days.

(32.32). For what value of x is the tangent to the curve $y = x^2 - 4x + 3$ parallel to the x-axis?

Solution from $y = x^2 - 4x + 3$, $\frac{dy}{dx} = 2x - 4$

When tangent is parallel to x–axis, then the gradient is 0 i.e $\frac{dy}{dx} = 0$

$\therefore 2x - 4 = 0 \rightarrow 2x = 4$ $\therefore x = 2$

(32.33). The minimum point on the curve $y = x^2 - 6x + 5$ is at?

Solution

$y = x^2 - 6x + 5$, $\frac{dy}{dx} = 2x - 6$

at minimum, $\frac{dy}{dx} = 0$

$\therefore 2x - 6 = 0 \rightarrow 2x = 6$ $\therefore x = 3$

Putting x = 3 in the original question

$y = 3^2 - 6(3) + 5 \rightarrow 9 - 18 + 5 = -4$

the minimum point = (3, -4)

(32.34). The minimum value of y in the equation $y = x^2 - 6x + 8$ is?

Solution

$y = x^2 - 6x + 8 \rightarrow \frac{dy}{dx} = 2x - 6$

at minimum $\frac{dy}{dx} = 0$

$\therefore 2x - 6 = 0 \rightarrow 2x = 6 \therefore x = 3$

Put x = 3 into the original question

$y = 3^2 - 6(3) + 8 \rightarrow 9 - 18 + 8 = -1$

(32.35). At what value of x is the function $y = x^2 - 2x - 3$ minimum?

Solution

$y = x^2 - 2x - 3, \frac{dy}{dx} = 2x - 2$

at minimum $\frac{dy}{dx} = 0$

$\therefore 2x - 2 = 0 \rightarrow 2x = 2 \therefore x = 1$

(32.36). The sum of two numbers is 20. Find their greatest possible product.

Solution

a + b = 20 or a = 20 – b

product = ab = (20 – b)b

$P = (20 - b)b = 20b - b^2$

Greatest possible product = maximum product

$\frac{dP}{db} = 20 - 2b$

∴ 20 − 2b = 0, 2b = 20, b = 10

From P = (20 − b)b → P = (20 − 10)10 → 10(10) = 100

(32.37). The sum of two numbers is 4P. Find their greatest possible product.

Solution

Let the two numbers be x and y

x + y = 4p → x = 4p − y

product = xy → (4p − y)y → 4py − y²

$\frac{dP}{dy}$ = 4p − 2y = 0 → y = 2p

Greatest possible product = 4py − y² → 4p(2p) − (2p)² → 8p² − 4p² = 4p²

(32.38). A rectangle has a perimeter of 60m. Find their greatest possible area.

Solution

Perimeter = 2(L + B) = 60 → L + B = 30 → L = (30 − B)

Area = length x breadth → (30 − B)B = 30B − B²

Greatest area = maximum area

∴ $\frac{dA}{dB}$ = 30 − 2B

30 − 2B = 0 → 2B = 30 → B = 15

A = (30 − B)B → (30 − 15)15 = 225m²

(32.39). ABC is a triangle right angle at B. The length of AC is 4cm. Find the greatest possible area of the triangle ABC.

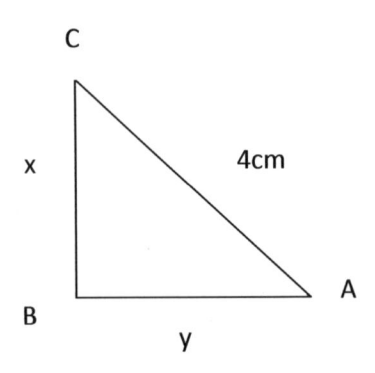

466

by Pythagoras's $y = \sqrt{4^2 - x^2}$

$A = \frac{1}{2}xy \rightarrow \frac{1}{2}.x\left(\sqrt{16-x^2}\right) = \frac{1}{2}.x(16-x^2)^{\frac{1}{2}}$

Greatest possible area occurs if $\frac{dA}{dx} = 0$

$\frac{dA}{dx} = \frac{1}{2}.x.\left[\frac{1}{2}(16-x^2)^{\frac{-1}{2}}\right].(-2x) + \frac{1}{2}(16-x^2)^{\frac{1}{2}} \rightarrow$

$-\frac{1}{2}x^2(16-x^2)^{-\frac{1}{2}} + \frac{1}{2}(16-x^2)^{\frac{1}{2}} = 0$

$\frac{1}{2}(16-x^2)^{\frac{1}{2}} = \frac{1}{2}x^2(16-x^2)^{\frac{-1}{2}} \rightarrow \sqrt{16-x^2} = \frac{x^2}{\sqrt{16-x^2}}$
$\rightarrow \sqrt{16-x^2}\sqrt{16-x^2} = x^2 \rightarrow 16 - x^2 = x^2 \rightarrow 16 = 2x^2$

$x^2 = 8 \therefore x = \sqrt{8}$

$A = \frac{1}{2}xy \rightarrow \frac{1}{2}.\sqrt{8}.\sqrt{16-8} \rightarrow \frac{1}{2}.\sqrt{8}.\sqrt{8} \rightarrow \frac{8}{2} = 4\text{cm}^2$

(32.40). A solid rectangular body has a sphere base. Given that the volume is 8m³, find its least possible surface area.

Solution

Surface area = base area + face area = $2L^2 + 4LH$

But $L^2H = 8 \rightarrow H = \frac{8}{L^2}$

$\therefore A = 2L^2 + 4L\left(\frac{8}{L^2}\right) = 2L^2 + 32L^{-1}$

Least possible area is found where $\frac{dA}{dL} = 0$

$\frac{dA}{dL} = 4L - 32L^{-2} = 0 \rightarrow 4L = 32L^{-2} \rightarrow L = 8L^{-2} = \frac{8}{L^2} \rightarrow L^3 = 8 \therefore L = 2$

$A = 2L^2 + 32L^{-1} \rightarrow 2(2)^2 + 32(2)^{-1} \rightarrow 8 + \frac{32}{2} \rightarrow 8 + 16 = 24 \text{ m}^3$

(32.41). A solid rectangular body has a sphere base. Given that its total surface area is 216cm², find its greatest possible volume.

Solution

Total area $(A) = 2L^2 + 4Lh = 216 \rightarrow L^2 + 2Lh = 108 \therefore h = \left(\frac{108 - L^2}{2L}\right)$

Volume $= L \cdot b \cdot h = L^2 h \rightarrow L^2\left(\frac{108-L^2}{2L}\right) \rightarrow \frac{L(108-L^2)}{2L} \rightarrow \frac{108L}{2} - \frac{L^3}{2} \rightarrow 54L - \frac{1}{2}L^3$

Greatest possible volume occurs when $\frac{dV}{dL} = 0$

$\frac{dV}{dL} = 54 - \frac{3}{2}L^2 = 0 \rightarrow 54 = \frac{3}{2}L^2 \rightarrow L^2 = \frac{54 \times 2}{3} = 36 \therefore L = 6$

$V = 54L - \frac{L^3}{2} = 54(6) - \frac{6^3}{2} = 324 - 108 = 216$

(32.42). A solid cylinder has a volume of $16\pi\text{cm}^3$. Find the least possible surface area.

Solution

Total surface area of cylinder $= 2\pi r^2 + 2\pi rh = 2\pi r(r + h)$

Volume of the cylinder $= \pi r^2 = 16\pi \rightarrow h = \frac{16}{r^2}$

$\therefore A = 2\pi r^2 + 2\pi r \left(\frac{16}{r^2}\right) = 2\pi r^2 + 32\pi r^{-1}$

$\frac{dA}{dr} = 4\pi r + -32\pi r^{-2} = 0 \rightarrow 4\pi r = \frac{32\pi}{r^2} \rightarrow r^3 = 8 \therefore r = 2$

$A = 2\pi r^2 + 32\pi r^{-1} \rightarrow 2\pi(2)^2 + 32\pi(2)^{-1} \rightarrow 8\pi + \frac{32\pi}{2} \rightarrow 8\pi + 16\pi = 24\pi\text{cm}^2$

(32.43). If $V = 4\pi r^2$, what is the rate of change of volume with respect to r?

Solution

$V = 4\pi r^2$,

$\therefore \frac{dV}{dr} = 2.4\pi r^1 = 8\pi r$

(32.44). The formular $Q = 1.5 + 0.5b$ gives the cost Q (in naira) of feeding n people for a week. Find in kobo the extra cost of feeding one additional person.

Solution

cost of feeding one addition person is given by

$Q = 1.5 + 0.5n$

$\frac{dQ}{dn} = 0 + 0.5 = 0.5$ (in naira)

∴ In kobo → 0.5 x 100k = 50k

(32.45). Water is pumped into a circular cylinder of radius 7 cm and height h at the rate 44cm³/s. Find the rate at which the water is rising in the cylinder ($\pi = 22/7$).

Solution

r = 7cm, $\frac{dv}{dt} = 44$cm³/s, height = h,

$\frac{dv}{dt} = \frac{dv}{dh} \cdot \frac{dh}{dt}$ → $\frac{dh}{dt} = \frac{dv/dt}{dv/dh}$

Volume of cylinder = $\pi r^2 h$ $\frac{dv}{dh} = \pi r^2$

$\frac{dh}{dt} = \frac{dv/dt}{dv/dh} = \frac{44}{\pi r^2}$ → $\frac{44}{\frac{22}{7} \times 7^2}$ → $\frac{44}{154} = \frac{2}{7}$

(32.46). The volume of a sphere is increased at the rate of 40.8cm³/s. Calculate, correct to 3 sig. figures, the rate at which the surface area is increasing when the radius is 3.2cm.

Solution

$\frac{dV}{dt} = 40.8$cm³/s, r = 3.2cm, $\frac{dA}{dt} = ?$

$\frac{dV}{dt} = \frac{dA}{dt} \cdot \frac{dr}{dA} \cdot \frac{dV}{dr}$ → $\frac{dA}{dt} = \frac{\frac{dv}{dt}}{\left(\frac{dr}{dA}\right)\left(\frac{dv}{dr}\right)}$

For sphere, A = $4\pi r^2$ → $\frac{dA}{dr} = 8\pi r$ ∴ $\frac{dr}{dA} = \left(\frac{1}{8\pi r}\right)$

Volume = $\frac{4}{3}\pi r^3$ → $\frac{dV}{dr} = 3.\frac{4}{3}\pi r^2 = 4\pi r^2$

∴ $\frac{dA}{dt} = \frac{dv/dt}{\left(\frac{dr}{dA}\right)\left(\frac{dv}{dr}\right)} = \frac{40.8}{\frac{1}{8}\pi r \times 4\pi r^2} = \frac{40.8}{\frac{r}{2}}$ → $\frac{81.6}{r}$ → $\frac{81.6}{3.2} = 25.5$ cm²/s

(32.47). At what rate is the area of a circle decreasing when radius is 4cm and decreasing at the rate of 0.2 cm/s?

Solution

$\frac{dA}{dt} = ?$, $r = 4cm$, $\frac{dr}{dt} = 0.2 cm/s$

Area of circle $= \pi r^2$, $\frac{dA}{dr} = 2\pi r$

$\therefore \frac{dA}{dt} = \frac{dr}{dt} \cdot \frac{dA}{dr}$ → $0.2 \times 2\pi r$ → $0.2 \times 2 \times \pi r^2$ → $0.2 \times 2 \times \pi \times 4 = 1.6\pi cm^2/s$

(32.48). The length of each side of a cube is expanding at the rate of 0.02m/s. At what rate is the volume increasing when each side is 0.25m long?

Solution

$\frac{dL}{dt} = 0.02 m/s$, $\frac{dV}{dt} = ?$, $L = 0.25m$

Volume of a cube $= L^3$

$\therefore \frac{dV}{dL} = 3L^2$

$\frac{dV}{dt} = \frac{dL}{dt} \cdot \frac{dV}{dL}$ → $0.02 \times 3L^2$ → $0.2 \times 3 \times (0.25)^2$ → $0.00375 = 3.75 \times 10^{-3} m^3/s$

(32.49). If $y = e^{(x^2 - 4x + 5)}$ find $\frac{dy}{dx}$

Solution

$\frac{dy}{dx} = (2x - 4)e^{(x^2 - 4x + 5)}$

(32.50). If $y = e^{\cos x}$ find $\frac{dy}{dx}$

Solution

$\frac{dy}{dx} = -\sin x e^{\cos x}$

(32.51). If $y = e^{3x^4}$ find $\frac{dy}{dx}$

Solution

Let $u = 3x^4$, $\frac{du}{dx} = 12x^3$

$y = e^u$

$\frac{dy}{dx} = \frac{dy}{du} \times \frac{du}{dx} \rightarrow 12x^3 e^{3x^4}$

(32.52). If $y = \log_a(4x^2 - 3x + 2)$ find $\frac{dy}{dx}$

Solution

$\frac{dy}{dx} = \frac{derivative}{original\ function} = \frac{8x - 3}{4x^2 - 3x + 2}$

(32.53). If $y = \ln 3x^2$ find $\frac{dy}{dx}$

Solution

$\frac{dy}{dx} = \frac{derivative}{original\ function} = \frac{6x}{3x^2} = \frac{2}{x}$

(32.54). If $y = x^4 e^{3x} \tan x$ find $\frac{dy}{dx}$

Solution

$\ln y = \ln u + \ln v + \ln w \rightarrow \frac{1}{y}\frac{dy}{dx} = \frac{1}{x^4} 4x^3 + \frac{1}{e^{3x}} 3e^{3x} + \frac{1}{\tan x} \sec^2 x$

$\frac{1}{y}\frac{dy}{dx} = \frac{4}{x} + 3 + \frac{\sec^2 x}{\tan x} \rightarrow \frac{dy}{dx} = y\left[\frac{4}{x} + 3 + \frac{\sec^2 x}{\tan x}\right] \rightarrow x^4 e^{3x} \tan x \left[\frac{4}{x} + 3 + \frac{\sec^2 x}{\tan x}\right]$

(32.55). If $y = \frac{x^4 \sin x}{\cos 2x}$ find $\frac{dy}{dx}$

Solution

$\frac{1}{y}\frac{dy}{dx} = \frac{1}{x^2} 2x + \frac{1}{\sin x}\cos x - \frac{1}{\cos 2x}(-2\sin 2x) \rightarrow \frac{dy}{dx} = y\left[\frac{2}{x} + \cot x + 2\tan 2x\right]$

$\rightarrow \frac{x^4 \sin x}{\cos 2x}\left[\frac{2}{x} + \cot x + 2\tan 2x\right]$

(32.56). If $y = \frac{e^{4x}}{x^3 \cosh 2x}$ find $\frac{dy}{dx}$

Solution

$\frac{1}{y}\frac{dy}{dx} = \frac{1}{e^{4x}} 4e^{4x} - \frac{1}{x^3} 3x^2 - \frac{1}{\cosh 2x}(2\sinh 2x) \rightarrow \frac{dy}{dx} = y\left[4 - \frac{3}{x} - 2\tanh 2x\right]$

$\frac{dy}{dx} = \frac{e^{4x}}{x^3 \cosh 2x}\left[4 - \frac{3}{x} - 2\tanh 2x\right]$

(32.57). Differentiate $x^2 + y^2 + 3x - 3y - 38 = 0$.

Solution

Implicit differentiation gives

$$2x + 2y\frac{dy}{dx} + 3 - 3\frac{dy}{dx} = 0 \to 2y\frac{dy}{dx} - 3\frac{dy}{dx} = -2x - 3 \to$$

$$\frac{dy}{dx}[2y - 3] = 2x - 3 \to \frac{dy}{dx} = \frac{-(2x+3)}{2y-3}$$

(32.58). Differentiate $x^3y^5 + 3x = 8y^3 + 1$.

Solution

$$3x^2y^5 + 5x^3y^4\frac{dy}{dx} + 3 = 24y^2\frac{dy}{dx} \to 3x^2y^5 + 3 = 24y^2\frac{dy}{dx} - 5x^3y^4\frac{dy}{dx} \to$$

$$3x^2y^5 + 3 = [24y^2 - 5x^3y^4]\frac{dy}{dx} \to \frac{dy}{dx} = \frac{3x^2y^5+3}{24y^2 - 5x^3y^4}$$

(32.59). Differentiate $x^2 \tan y + y^{10} \sec x = 2x$.

Solution

$$2x\tan y + x^2\sec^2 y\frac{dy}{dx} + 10y^9\frac{dy}{dx}\sec x + y^{10}\sec x \tan x = 2$$

$$[x^2\sec^2 y + 10y^9\sec x]\frac{dy}{dx} = 2 - y^{10}\sec x \tan x - 2x\tan y$$

$$\frac{dy}{dx} = \frac{2 - y^{10}\sec x \tan x - 2x\tan y}{x^2\sec^2 y + 10y^9\sec x}$$

(32.60). Differentiate $e^{2x+3y} = x^2 - \ln(xy^3)$.

Solution

$$e^{2x+3y}\left[2 + 3\frac{dy}{dx}\right] = 2x - \frac{y^3 + 3xy^2\frac{dy}{dx}}{xy^3} \to 2e^{2x+3y} + 3\frac{dy}{dx}e^{2x+3y} = 2x - \frac{y^3}{xy^3} - \frac{3xy^2\frac{dy}{dx}}{xy^3}$$

$$2e^{2x+3y} + 3\frac{dy}{dx}e^{2x+3y} = 2x - \frac{1}{x} - \frac{3\frac{dy}{dx}}{y} \to$$

$$[3e^{2x+3y} + 3y^{-1}]\frac{dy}{dx} = 2x - x^{-1} - 2e^{2x+3y} \to \frac{dy}{dx} = \frac{2x - x^{-1} - 2e^{2x+3y}}{3e^{2x+3y} + 3y^{-1}}$$

CHAPTER 33 CALCULUS 2 : INTEGRATION

Integration is the inverse of differentiation. In differentiation, a function is given to find the rate of change called derivative. Thus in integration, the function is found from the derivative. The function found is also called an integral.

Techniques of integration

(i) Direct method; If $y = x^n \rightarrow \int x^n = \frac{x^{n+1}}{n+1}$

(ii) Trigonometry functions integration: There are six functions in trigonometry. Given below are the integral:

If $y = \sin x$, $\int \sin x \, dx = -\cos x$

If $y = \cos x$, $\int \cos x \, dx = \sin x$

If $y = \sec^2 x$ $\int \sec^2 x \, dx = \tan x$

(iii) For functions where the derivative of the denominator is the same as the value of the numerator, the integral is simply the logarithm (Natural) of the denominator.

(iv) Integration by partial fraction:

This is used when a fraction is not in its simplest form. The reader should consult partial fraction for necessary foundation.

(v) Integration by substitution: This is applied when direct integration is not possible.

Nature of integral

The result of integration, called integral can be indefinite or definite.

Indefinite integral: Here the limit of integration is not given. After integration an arbitrary constant must be added:

$\int x^2 dx = \frac{x^3}{3} + c$ or $\frac{x^3}{3} + k$

Where k is constant to be determined from the boundary conditions.

Definite integral: Here the limit of integration is given. After integration no arbitrary constant is added.

e.g. $\int_b^a x^2 dx$ means integral of x^2 between $x = a$ and $x = b$

where a = upper limit, b = lower limit

$$\int_b^a x^2 = \left[\frac{x^3}{3}\right]_b^a = \left[\frac{a^3}{3} - \frac{b^3}{3}\right]$$

APPLICATIONS OF INTEGRATION

(*i*) *Integration of* areas and volumes of solids.

(*ii*) Determination of a function from a given derivative.

(*i*) **Integration of Areas**

Given a line with a curve, we simply determine the type of turning point.

If the curve is maximum (if the curve is above the line)

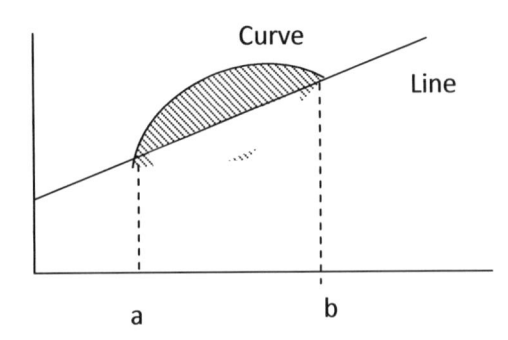

$$Area = \int_a^b (curve - line) dx$$

If the curve is minimum (if the curve is below the line)

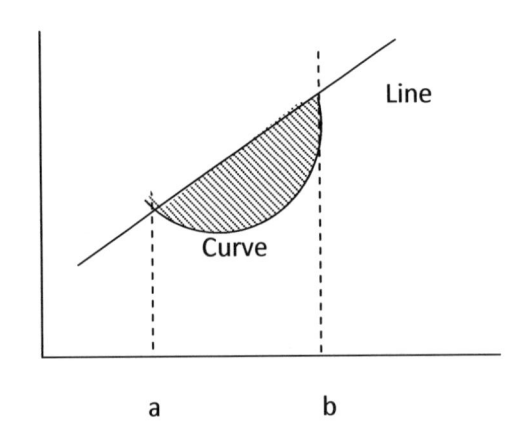

474

$$Area = \int_a^b (Line - curve)dx$$

For both cases, do the following:

(i) Equate line and curves function to get the limit of integration. (ii) Test the turning point. (iii) Apply the formula.

If two curves are given

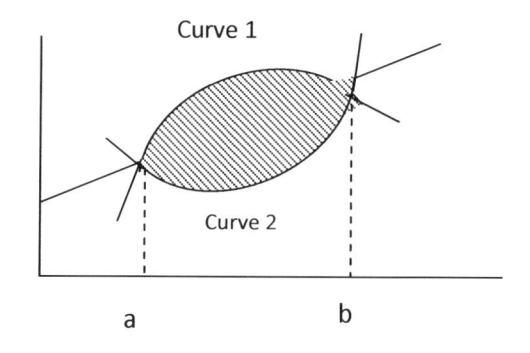

Do the following:

(i) Equating both curves to get the limit of integration.

(ii) Next determine which curve is bigger by inserting any value between the limits into the two curves.

(iii) $Area = \int_a^b (bigger\ curve - smaller\ curve2)dx$

(ii) **Integration of Volumes**

If the revolution is along the x-axis

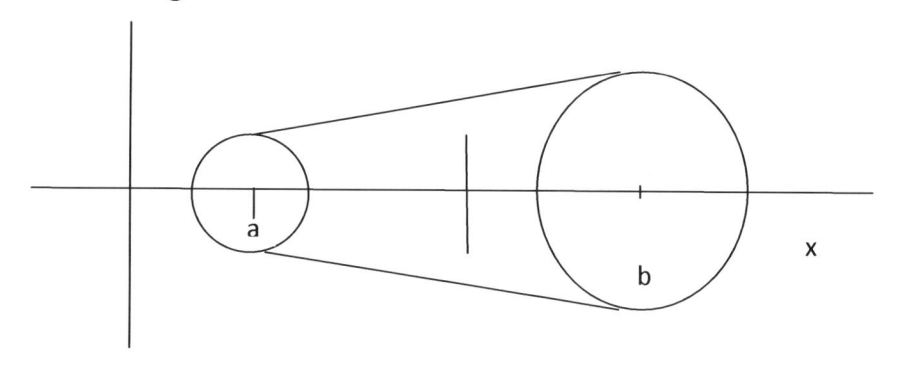

$$Volume = \int_a^b \pi y^2 dx$$

If the revolution is along the y-axis

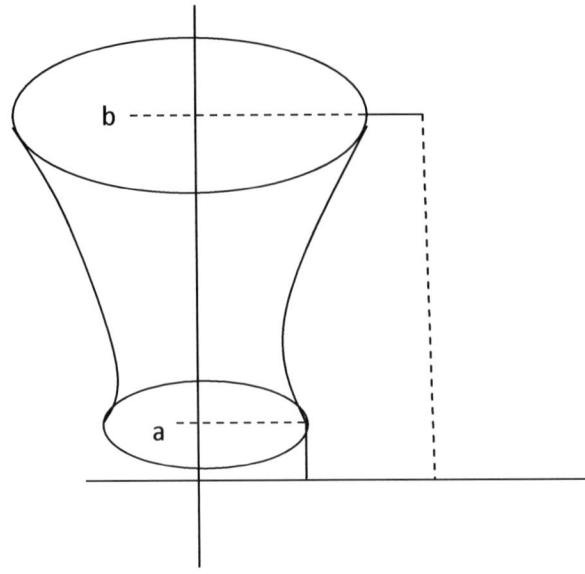

$$Volume = \int_a^b \pi x^2 dy$$

QUESTIONS

(33.1). Evaluate $\int \frac{2x+3}{(x-1)(x-2)(2x-3)} dx$.

Solution

$$\frac{2x+3}{(x-1)(x-2)(2x-3)} \rightarrow \frac{A}{(x-1)} + \frac{B}{(x-2)} + \frac{C}{(2x-3)}$$

Solving by partial fraction we find A = 5, B = 7 and C = - 24

$$\int \frac{2x+3}{(x-1)(x-2)(2x-3)} dx \rightarrow \int \frac{5}{(x-1)} dx + \frac{7}{(x-2)} dx - \frac{24}{(2x-3)} dx$$

$$5\ln(x-1) + 7\ln(x-2) - 12\ln(2x-3) + c \rightarrow \ln \frac{(x-1)^5 (x-2)^7}{(2x-3)^{12}} + c.$$

(**33.2**). Evaluate $\int \frac{3x^2+1}{x^4-1}dx$.

Solution

By factorization $x^4 - 1 = (x^2)^2 - (1^2)^2 = (x^2+1)(x+1)(x-1)$

$\int \frac{3x^2+1}{x^4-1}dx \rightarrow \int \frac{3x^2+1}{(x+1)(x-1)(x^2+1)}dx$

$\frac{3x^2+1}{(x+1)(x-1)(x^2+1)} = \frac{A}{(x+1)} + \frac{B}{(x-1)} + \frac{Cx+D}{(x^2+1)}$

Solving by partial fraction we find A = -1, B = 1 and C = 0 and D = 1

$\int \frac{3x^2+1}{x^4-1}dx \rightarrow \int \frac{-1}{(x+1)}dx + \int \frac{1}{(x-1)}dx + \int \frac{1}{(x^2+1)}dx$

$ln(x-1) - ln(x+1) + tan^{-1}x + c \rightarrow ln\frac{(x-1)}{(x+1)} + tan^{-1}x +$

(**33.3**). Evaluate $\int \frac{x+2}{x^2+4x+1}dx$.

Solution

Differentiating the denominator $x^2 + 4x + 1$ gives the numerator $x + 2$

$\therefore \int \frac{x+2}{x^2+4x+1}dx \rightarrow \frac{1}{2}ln(x^2+4x+1)$

(**33.4**). Evaluate $\int 3\sqrt{4x-1}\,dx$.

Solution

Let u = $4x - 1 \rightarrow \frac{du}{dx} = 4 \rightarrow dx = \frac{du}{4}$

$\int 3\sqrt{4x-1}\,dx \rightarrow \int 3u^{1/2}\frac{du}{4} \rightarrow \frac{3}{4}\int u^{1/2}du \rightarrow \frac{3}{4}\cdot\frac{u^{3/2}}{3/2} \rightarrow \frac{6}{12}u^{3/2} \rightarrow$

$\frac{1}{2}(4x-1)^{3/2} + c$

(**33.5**). Evaluate $\int_{\frac{\pi}{4}}^{\frac{\pi}{3}} tan^2 x\,sec^2 x\,dx$.

Solution

Let u = tan x $\rightarrow \frac{du}{dx} = sec^2 x \rightarrow dx = \frac{du}{sec^2 x}$

$$\int_{\frac{\pi}{4}}^{\frac{\pi}{3}} tan^2 x sec^2 x \, dx \to \int_{\frac{\pi}{4}}^{\frac{\pi}{3}} u^2 sec^2 x \cdot \frac{du}{sec^2 x} \to \int_{\frac{\pi}{4}}^{\frac{\pi}{3}} u^2 \, du \to \left[\frac{u^3}{3}\right]_{\frac{\pi}{4}}^{\frac{\pi}{3}} \to \frac{1}{3}[tan^3 x]_{\frac{\pi}{4}}^{\frac{\pi}{3}}$$

With $\frac{\pi}{3} = 60°$ and $\frac{\pi}{4} = 45°$

$$\int_{\frac{\pi}{4}}^{\frac{\pi}{3}} tan^2 x sec^2 x \, dx = \frac{1}{3}[tan^3 60 - tan^3 45]_{\frac{\pi}{4}}^{\frac{\pi}{3}} \to \frac{1}{3}[(\sqrt{3})^3 - 1^3]$$

(33.6). Evaluate $\int 2x \sin x^2 \, dx$.

Solution

Let $u = x^2 \to \frac{du}{dx} = 2x \to dx = \frac{du}{2x}$

$\int 2x \sin x^2 \, dx \to \int 2x \sin u \frac{du}{2x} \to \int \sin u \, du \to -\cos u = -\cos x^2 + c$

(33.7). Two variables x and y are such that $\frac{dy}{dx} = 4x - 3$ and y = 5 when x = 2. Find y in terms of x.

Solution

$\frac{dy}{dx} = 4x - 3 \to dy = (4x - 3)dx$

Integrating both sides

$\int dy = \int (4x - 3)dx \to y = \frac{4x^2}{2} - 3x + c \to y = 2x^2 - 3x + c$

When y = 5, x = 2

$5 = 2(2)^2 - 3(2) + c \to 5 = 8 - 6 + c \to 5 = 2 + c \therefore c = 3$

The equation is $y = 2x^2 - 3x + 3$

(33.8). Ice forms in a refrigerator ice-box at the rate of (4 – 0.6t)g per minute after t minutes. If initially there are 2g of ice in the box, find the mass of ice formed in 5 minutes.

Solution

Rate = mass per time $\therefore \frac{dm}{dt} = 4 - 0.6t$

Integrating we have $\int dm = \int(4 - 0.6t)dt \to m = 4t - \frac{0.6t^2}{2} \to 4t - 0.3t^2 + c$

When m = 2, t = 0

$2 = 4(0) - 0.3(0) + c \therefore 2 = c$

$\therefore m = 4t - 0.3t^2 + 2$

When t = 5 minutes

$m = 4(5) - 0.3(5)^2 + 2 \to 20 - 7.5 + 2 = 14.5g$

(33.9). A student blows a balloon and its volume increases at a rate of $\pi(20 - t^2) cm^3/s$ after t seconds. If the initial volume is $0 cm^3$, find the volume of the balloon after 2 seconds.

Solution

rate of increase = $\frac{dv}{dt} = \pi(20 - t^2) \to dv = \pi(20 - t^2) dt \to \int dv = \pi \int 20 - t^2 dt$

$v = \pi\left(20t - \frac{t^3}{3} + c\right)$

at the initial time, t = 0 and v = 0

$\therefore 0 = \pi\left[20(0) - \frac{0^3}{3} + c\right] \to 0 = \pi(0 - 0 + c) \therefore c = 0$

With c = 0, $V = \pi\left(20t - \frac{t^3}{3}\right)$

When t = 2

$V = \pi\left(20(2) - \frac{2^3}{3}\right) \to \pi\left(40 - \frac{8}{3}\right) \to \pi\left(40 - 2\frac{2}{3}\right) \to \pi\left(37\frac{1}{3}\right) = \pi(37.33)$

(33.10). The gradient of a curve which passes through the point (1, 1) is given by 2x. Find the equation of the curve.

Solution

Gradient = $\frac{dy}{dx} \to \frac{dy}{dx} = 2x \to dy = 2xdx \to \int dy = \int 2x \, dx \to y = \frac{2x^2}{2} + c,$

$y = x^2 + c$

From (1,1) → x = 1, y = 1

∴ $y = x^2 + c$ → $1 = 1^2 + c$ → $1 = 1 + c$ ∴ c = 0

The equation is $y = x^2$

(33.11). Find the area under the curve y = 2x + 3 and the coordinates x = 1 and x = 3.

Solution

$A = \int_1^3 (2x + 3) \, dx$ → $\left[\frac{2x^2}{2} + 3x\right]_1^3$ → $[x^2 + 3x]_1^3$ → $[3^2 + 3(3)] - [(1^2 + 3(1)]$ →

18 – 4 = 14 units

(33.12). Find the area under the curve $y = 2x^2 + 3x$ between the coordinates x = 1 and x = 2.

Solution

$A = \int_1^2 y \, dx = \int_1^2 2x^2 + 3x = \left[\frac{2x^3}{3} + \frac{3x^2}{2}\right]_1^2$

$A = \left[\frac{2(2)^3}{3} + \frac{3(2)^2}{2}\right] - \left[\frac{2(1)^3}{3} + \frac{3(1)^2}{2}\right]$ → $\left[\frac{16}{3} + 6\right] - \left[\frac{2}{3} + \frac{3}{2}\right]$ → $\frac{16}{3} - \frac{2}{3} + 6 - \frac{3}{2}$

→ $\frac{32 - 4 + 36 - 9}{6}$ → $\frac{55}{6} = 9\frac{1}{6}$

(33.13). Find the area between the curve y = sin x, x axis and x = 0 and x = 2π.

Solution

The limit is 0 and 2π → 0 and 2(180) i.e 0 & 360°

$A = 2\int y \, dx$ → $2 \int (\sin x) \, dx$ → $2(-\cos x)_0^\pi$ → $2[(-\cos 180) - (-\cos 0)]$

→ 2(1 + 1) = 4 units

(33.14). Find the area enclosed by y = cos x, the x-axis and $0 \leq x \leq \frac{1}{2\pi}$.

Solution

The limit is $0 \leq x \leq \frac{1}{2\pi}$

$\frac{1}{2\pi} = \frac{1}{2}(180) = 90°$

$A = \int_0^{\frac{\pi}{2}} y\, dx \rightarrow \int_0^{\frac{\pi}{2}} \cos x \rightarrow (\sin x)_0^{\frac{\pi}{2}} \rightarrow \left(\sin \frac{\pi}{2} - \sin 0\right) \rightarrow \sin 90^0 - \sin 0$

$1 - 0 = 1$ unit

(33.15). Find the area between the line y = x and the curve y = 4x².

Solution

Equating the line and curve i.e

Line = curve $\rightarrow x = 4x^2 \rightarrow 4x^2 - x = 0 \rightarrow x(4x - 1) = 0 \therefore x = 0, x = ¼$

The limit is x = 0, x = ¼

Testing the turning point

$\frac{dy}{dx} = 8x, \frac{d^2y}{dx^2} = 8 \rightarrow \therefore$ It's a minimum

$Area = \int_a^b (Line - curve) dx \rightarrow \int_0^{\frac{1}{4}} x\, dx - \int_0^{\frac{1}{4}} 4x^2\, dx \rightarrow \left(\frac{-x^2}{2}\right)_0^{\frac{1}{4}} - \left(\frac{4x^3}{3}\right)_0^{\frac{1}{4}}$

$\frac{\left[\frac{1}{4}\right]^2}{2} - \frac{4\left[\frac{1}{4}\right]^3}{3} \rightarrow \frac{1}{32} - \frac{1}{48} = \frac{1}{96}$

(33.16). Find the area included between the parabolas y² = 4x and x² = 4y.

Solution

Given curve 1: $y^2 = 4x \rightarrow y = \sqrt{4x} \rightarrow 2\sqrt{x} = 2x^{1/2}$

Given curve 2: $x^2 = 4y \rightarrow y = \frac{x^2}{4}$

Equating both curves to get the limit of integration i.e

$\sqrt{4x} = \frac{x^2}{4} \rightarrow 4x = \frac{x^4}{16} \rightarrow 64x = x^4 \rightarrow x^4 - 64x = 0 \rightarrow x(x^3 - 64) = 0$

x = 0 or x³ − 64 = 0

$x^3 - 64 = 0 \rightarrow x^3 = 64 \rightarrow x = \sqrt[3]{64} = 4$

∴ the limit is between x = 0 and x = 4

Next determine which curve is bigger by inserting any value between the limits (0/4) into the two curves.

Inserting x = 3

In $y^2 = 4x \to y^2 = 4(3) \to y^2 = 12 \therefore y = \sqrt{12}$

In $x^2 = 4y \to 3^2 = 4y \to y = \frac{9}{4}$

Since $\sqrt{12} > \frac{9}{4} \therefore y^2 = 4x$ is greater than $x^2 = 4y$

For two curves

$Area = \int_a^b (above\ curve - below\ curve)dx \to \int_0^4 \sqrt{4x}\ dx - \int_0^4 \frac{x^2}{4} dx$

$\int_0^4 2x^{1/2} dx - \int_0^4 \frac{x^2}{4} dx \to \left[\frac{2x^{\frac{3}{2}}}{\frac{3}{2}} - \frac{1}{4}\frac{x^3}{3}\right]_0^4 \to \frac{2(4^{\frac{3}{2}})}{3/2} - \frac{1}{4}\left(\frac{4^3}{3}\right) \to \frac{32}{3} - \frac{16}{3} = \frac{16}{3}$

(33.17). The area of the finite region bounded by the curve $y = kx^2 + 4$, x axis, lines x = 2 and x = 4 is 36 units. Find the value of the constant.

Solution

$A = \int_2^4 ydx \to \int_2^4 kx^2 + 4 \to \left[\frac{kx^3}{3} + 4x\right]_2^4 \to \left[\frac{k(4)^3}{3} + 4(4)\right] - \left[\frac{k(2)^3}{3} + 4(2)\right]$

$\frac{64k}{3} + 16 - \frac{8k}{3} - 8 \to \frac{56}{3}k + 8$

$A = 36 = \frac{56k}{3} + 8 \to 56k + 24 = 108 \to 56k = 108 - 24 = 84$

$K = \frac{84}{56} = \frac{12}{8} = \frac{3}{2}$

(33.18). Find the volume generated by rotating the curve $y = x + 1$ from x = 1 to x = 2 completely round the x – axis.

Solution

For revolution along the x–axis $V = \pi \int y^2 dx$

$V = \pi \int y^2 dx \to \pi \int_1^2 (x+1)^2 dx \to \pi \int_1^2 (x^2 + 2x + 1)\ dx \to$

$\pi \left(\frac{x^2}{3} + \frac{2x^2}{2} + 1\right)_1^2 \to \pi\left[\left(\frac{2^3}{3} + 2^2 + 2\right) - \left(\frac{1^3}{3} + 1^3 + 1\right)\right]$

$\pi\left[\frac{8}{3} + 4 + 2 - \frac{1}{3} - 1 - 1\right] \to \pi\left[\frac{8}{3} - \frac{1}{3} + 4\right] \to \pi\left[\frac{7}{3} + 4\right] = \frac{19\pi}{3}$ cubic unit

(33.19). The area under the curve $y^2 = x - 1$, the y – axis and the line $y = \pm 2$ is rotated about the y – axis. Find the volume of the solid so formed.

Solution

For revolution along the y-axis $V = \pi \int x^2 dy$

From $y^2 = x - 1 \rightarrow x = y^2 + 1$

$V = \pi \int x^2 dy \rightarrow \pi \int (y^2 + 1)^2 dy \rightarrow \pi \int (y^4 + 2y^2 + 1) dy = \pi \left[\frac{y^5}{5} + \frac{2y^3}{3} + y\right]_{-2}^{2}$

$\left[\frac{2^5}{5} + \frac{2(2^3)}{3} + 2\right] - \left[\frac{(-2)^5}{5} + \frac{2(-2)^3}{3} + (-2)\right] \rightarrow \pi \left[\frac{32}{5} + \frac{16}{3} + 2\right] - \pi \left[\frac{-32}{5} - \frac{16}{3} - 2\right]$

$\pi \left[\frac{32}{5} + \frac{16}{3} + 2 + \frac{32}{5} + \frac{16}{3} + 2\right] \rightarrow \pi \left[\frac{64}{5} + \frac{32}{3} + 4\right]$

$\rightarrow \pi \left[\frac{192 + 160 + 60}{15}\right] = \frac{412\pi}{15}$ *cubic unit*

(33.20). A bowl is designed by resolving completely the area enclosed $y = x^2 - 1$, $y = 0$, $y = 3$ and $x \geq 0$ around the y-axis. What is the volume of the bowl?

Solution

$V = \pi \int x^2 dy \rightarrow \int x^2 dy \rightarrow \int (y + 1) dy \rightarrow \left[\frac{y^2}{2} + y\right]_0^3 \rightarrow \left[\frac{3^2}{2} + 3\right] = \frac{15\pi}{2}$

(33.21). Evaluate $\int 2^{secx} secx\, tanx\, dx$

Let $u = sec\, x \rightarrow \frac{du}{dx} = secx\, tanx \rightarrow dx = \frac{du}{secx\, tanx}$

$\int 2^{secx} secx\, tanx\, dx \rightarrow \int 2^u secx\, tanx \frac{du}{secx\, tanx} \rightarrow \int 2^u du \rightarrow \frac{2^u}{\ln 2} \rightarrow \frac{2^{secx}}{\ln 2} + c$

(33.22). Evaluate $\int x\sqrt{x+1}\, dx$.

Solution

Let $u = \sqrt{x+1} \rightarrow u^2 = x+1 \rightarrow x = u^2 - 1 \rightarrow \frac{du}{dx} = 2u$

$\int x\sqrt{x+1}\, dx \rightarrow \int (u^2 - 1) u2u\, du \rightarrow 2\int (u^4 - u^2) du \rightarrow 2\left[\frac{u^5}{5} - \frac{u^3}{3}\right]$

$\frac{2u^5}{5} - \frac{2u^3}{3} \rightarrow \frac{2(\sqrt{x+1})^5}{5} - \frac{2(\sqrt{x+1})^3}{3} \rightarrow \frac{2}{5}(x+1)^{5/2} - \frac{2}{5}(x+1)^{3/2} + c$

(33.23). Evaluate $\int 2^{-x} \tan 2^{1-x} dx$.

Let $u = 2^{1-x} \to \frac{du}{dx} = 2^{1-x} \ln 2 \to dx = \frac{du}{2^{1-x}\ln 2}$

$\int 2^{-x}\tan 2^{1-x} dx \to \int 2^{-x} \tan u . \frac{du}{2^{1-x}\ln 2} \to \int 2^{-1} \tan u . \frac{du}{\ln 2} \to -\frac{1}{2\ln 2}\int \tan u du$

$\frac{\ln 2}{2} \int \tan u du$

(33.24). Evaluate $\int \frac{1-x}{x^3} dx$.

Solution

$\frac{1-x}{x^3} = \frac{1}{x^3} - \frac{x}{x^3} = x^{-3} - x^{-2}$

$\int \frac{1-x}{x^3} dx = \int (x^{-3} - x^{-2}) dx \to \frac{x^{-3+1}}{-3+1} - \frac{x^{-2+1}}{-2+1} \to \frac{x^{-2}}{-2} - \frac{x^{-1}}{-1} \to \frac{-x^{-2}}{2} + x^{-1}$

$\to x^{-1} - \frac{1}{2}x^{-2} = \frac{1}{x} - \frac{1}{2x^2}$

$\int \frac{1-x}{x^3} = \frac{1}{x} - \frac{1}{2x^2} + c.$

(33.25). $\int 2x(2x2 - 3x + 4) dx$.

Solution

$2x(2x^2 - 3x + 4) \to 4x^3 - 6x^2 + 8x$

$\int 2x(2x^2 - 3x + 4) = \int 4x^3 - 6x^2 + 8x \to \frac{4x^4}{4} - \frac{6x^3}{3} + \frac{8x^2}{2} \to x^4 - 2x^3 + 4x^2.$

(33.26). Evaluate $\int_2^6 \frac{3}{x^2} dx$.

Solution

$\int \frac{3}{x^2} dx \to \int 3x^{-2} dx = 3\int x^{-2} dx \to 3.\frac{x^{-2+1}}{-2+1} \to \frac{3x^{-1}}{-1} \to -3x^{-1} = \frac{-3}{x}$

$\int_2^6 \frac{3}{x^2} = \left[\frac{-3}{x}\right]_2^6 \to \left(\frac{-3}{6}\right) - \left(\frac{-3}{2}\right) \to \frac{-1}{2} + \frac{3}{2} = \frac{-1+3}{2} = 1.$

(33.27). Evaluate $\int_{-1}^{1} (2x+1)^2 dx$.

Solution

$\int (2x+1)^2 \to \int 4x^2 + 4x + 1 \to \frac{4x^3}{3} + \frac{4x^2}{2} + x$

$\int_{-1}^{1}(2x+1)^2 \to \left[\frac{4(1)^3}{3} + 2(1)^2 + (1)\right] - \left[\frac{4(-1)^3}{3} + 2(-1)^2 + (-1)\right]$

$\left(\frac{4}{3} + 2 + 1\right) - \left(\frac{-4}{3} + 2 - 1\right) \to \frac{4}{3} + 2 + 1 + \frac{4}{3} - 2 + 1 \to \frac{8}{3} + 2 \to 2\frac{2}{3} + 2 = 4\frac{2}{3}$.

(**33.28**). Evaluate $\int_0^1 \frac{2}{1+2x} dx$.

Solution

Differentiating the denominator $1 + 2x$ gives the numerator 2

$\int_0^1 \frac{2}{1+2x} dx \to ln[1 + 2x]_0^1 \to ln[1 + 2(1)] - ln[1 + 2(0)] \to$

$ln[3] - ln[1] = ln[3]$.

(**33.29**). Evaluate $\int_1^{-2}(3x^2 + 4)\,dx$.

Solution

$\int 3x^2 + 4 \to \int 3x^2 + 4x^0 \to \frac{3x^3}{3} + \frac{4x^{0+1}}{0+1} \to \frac{3x^3}{3} + \frac{4x^1}{1}$

$\int_1^{-2}(3x^2 + 4)\,dx \to |x^3 + 4x|_1^2 \to [2^3 + 4(2)] - [1^3 + 4(1)]$

$\to (8 + 8) - (1 + 4) = 16 - (5) = 11$.

(**33.30**). If $\frac{dy}{dx} = x^3 - 2x^2 - 3x + 1$ then y is?

Solution

$\int dy = \int (x^3 - 2x^2 - 3x + 1)dx \to y = \frac{x^4}{4} - \frac{2x^3}{3} - \frac{3x^2}{2} + x + c$.

(**33.31**). Simplify $\int \frac{x^2 + 3x + 2}{(x+1)} dx$.

Solution

$\int \frac{x^2 + 3x + 2}{(x+1)} \to \int \frac{(x+1)(x+2)}{(x+1)} \to \int x + 2 \to \frac{x^2}{2} + 2x + c$.

(**33.32**). Evaluate $\int \frac{x+3}{\sqrt{2x+4}} dx$.

485

Solution

Let $u = 2x + 4 \to dx = \frac{du}{2}$, $x = \frac{1}{2}(u-4)$

$\int \frac{x+3}{\sqrt{2x+4}} dx \to \int \frac{\left(\frac{1}{2}(u-4)+3\right)}{u^{1/2}} \cdot \frac{du}{2} \to \int \frac{\left(\frac{1}{2}u - 2 + 3\right)}{u^{1/2}} \cdot \frac{du}{2} \to \frac{1}{2}\int \frac{\left(\frac{1}{2}u + 1\right)}{u^{1/2}} du$

$\frac{1}{2}\int \frac{\frac{1}{2}u}{u^{1/2}} + \frac{1}{u^{1/2}} du \to \frac{1}{2}\int \frac{1}{2}u^{1-1/2} + u^{-1/2} du \to \frac{1}{2}\int \frac{1}{2} u^{1/2} + u^{-1/2} du \to$

$\frac{1}{2}\left[\frac{1}{2} \frac{u^{\frac{1}{2}+1}}{\frac{1}{2}+1} + \frac{u^{-\frac{1}{2}+1}}{-\frac{1}{2}+1}\right] \to \frac{1}{2}\left[\frac{1}{2} \cdot \frac{u^{\frac{3}{2}}}{\frac{3}{2}} + \frac{u^{\frac{1}{2}}}{\frac{1}{2}}\right] \to \frac{1}{2}\left[\frac{1}{2} \cdot \frac{2}{3} \cdot u^{\frac{3}{2}} + 2u^{\frac{1}{2}}\right] \to \frac{1}{6}u^{\frac{3}{2}} + u^{\frac{1}{2}} =$

$\frac{1}{6}(2x+4)^{\frac{3}{2}} + (2x+4)^{\frac{1}{2}}.$

(33.33). Evaluate $\int (x^2 + 3x - 9)^7 (2x+3) dx$.

Solution

Let $u = x^2 + 3x - 9$, $\frac{du}{dx} = 2x + 3 dx \to dx = \frac{du}{2x+3}$

$\int (x^2 + 3x - 9)^7 (2x + dx) dx \to \int u^7 (2x+3) \cdot \frac{du}{2x+3} \to \int u^7 du \to \frac{u^8}{8} + k$

$\frac{(x^2+3x-9)^8}{8} + k.$

(33.34). $\int \cos^5 x \sin x \, dx$.

Solution

Let $u = \cos x \to \frac{du}{dx} = -\sin x \to dx = \frac{du}{-\sin x}$

$\int \cos^5 x \sin x \, dx \to \int u^5 \sin x \cdot \frac{du}{-\sin x} \to -\int u^5 du \to -\left[\frac{u^6}{6}\right] \to -\frac{\cos^6 x}{6} + c.$

(33.35). Evaluate $\int_0^1 x(x^2 + 1)^2 dx$.

Solution

Let $u = x^2 + 1$, $\frac{du}{dx} = 2x \to dx = \frac{du}{2x}$

$\int_0^1 x(x^2+1)^2\, dx \rightarrow \int x \cdot u^2 \cdot \frac{du}{2x} \rightarrow \frac{1}{2}\int u^2 du \rightarrow \frac{1}{2}\left[\frac{u^3}{3}\right] \rightarrow \frac{u^3}{6} \rightarrow \left|\frac{(x^2+1)^3}{6}\right|_0^1 \rightarrow$

$\frac{(1^2+1)^3}{6} - \frac{(0^2+1)^3}{6} \rightarrow \frac{2^3}{6} - \frac{1^3}{6} \rightarrow \frac{8}{6} - \frac{1}{6} = \frac{7}{6}.$

(33.36). Evaluate $\int \frac{\sin^3 x}{\cos^2 x}\, dx$.

Solution

$u = \cos x,\ \frac{du}{dx} = -\sin x \rightarrow dx = -\frac{du}{\sin x}$

$\int \frac{\sin^3 x}{\cos^2 x}\, dx \rightarrow \int \frac{\sin^3 x}{u^2} \cdot \frac{du}{-\sin x} \rightarrow \int \frac{\sin^2 x}{u^2} du \rightarrow \int \frac{(1-\cos^2 x)}{u^2} du \rightarrow \int \frac{(1-u^2)}{u^2} du$

$\int \left[\frac{1}{u^2} - \frac{u^2}{u^2}\right] du \rightarrow \int (u^{-2} - 1) du \rightarrow \frac{u^{-2+1}}{-2+1} - u \rightarrow \frac{u^{-1}}{-1} - u \rightarrow \frac{-1}{u} - u \rightarrow \frac{-1}{\cos x} - \cos x.$

(33.37). $\int_2^\pi (\sec^2 x - \tan^2 x)\, dx.$

Solution

$\tan^2 \theta + 1 = \sec^2 \theta$

$\int_2^\pi (\tan^2 \theta + 1 - \tan^2 x)\, dx \rightarrow \int_2^\pi 1\, dx \rightarrow [x]_2^\pi = (\pi - 2).$

CHAPTER 34 SET THEORY

A set is the collection of objects that are classified together.

Forms of set

(*i*) Tabular form: In this case the element or members are listed e.g. A = {1, 2, 3}.

(*ii*) Builder form: In this case the element or members are not listed but the properties with which they can be determined are given e.g. The set of even integers {2, 4, 6, 8..}.

Terms associated with set

(1) Element: Each members of a set is called an element and they written in curly brackets {}. Set are normally represented by capital letters and elements by small letters.

If "a" is an element of a set A, we write a ∈ A (read as "a belongs to A").

If "a" is not an element of set A, we write a ∉ A.

(2) Singleton: A set containing only one element is called a singleton set.

e.g. : B = {3}

(3) Universal Set: The totality of object under consideration is called universal set. The universal set is known to contain all other sets and is normally denoted by U.

(4) Subset: This is a set that contains element that are part of a bigger set. e.g. a class is a subset of the students in a school.

Consider sets A and B in universal set U. If set A is the collection of all elements contained in set B (i.e set A contains all elements of set B), then we say B is a subset of A and is denoted by B ⊆ A

(5) Superset: This is a set that contains another set. e.g If B is a subset of A, then A is a superset of B

(6) Complement of a set: The complement of a set A with respect to universal set U is the set of elements belonging to U but not to A and is denoted by A^C or A'

e.g. IF U = {8,10,12,1,2,3,4,5,6,7,9,11} and A = {3,5,2,8}

∴ A^C or A' = {1,4,6,7,9,10,11,12}

(7) Power set: This is a list of all possible subsets. It is given by $P = 2^n$

Where n = no of elements

(8) Equality of sets: sets A and B are said to be equal if A is a subset of B and B is a subset of A i.e A = B if A $\subseteq$ B and B $\subseteq$ A. That is, if all elements of set A are all the elements of another set B, the A = B

e.g. Given A = {8, 2, 4} and B = {2, 8, 4}

∴ A $\subseteq$ B and B $\subseteq$ A

Hence, A = B

(9) Unions of sets: This is obtained when the elements between two or more sets are arranged in a definite order without repetition. It is denoted by A ∪ B.

e.g. Given A = {5,1,8,6,3} and B = {5,7,2,4} ∴ A ∪ B = {1,2,3,4,5,6,7,8}

(10) Intersection of sets: This is the collection of elements common to both A and B. it is denoted by A ∩ B

e.g. : If A = {3,5,6,8} and B = {2,5,3,6,9}   ∴ A ∩ B = {3,5,6}

(11) Disjoint set: Two sets A and B are said to be disjoint sets if A ∩ B = ∅.

e.g. If V = set of all vowels and C = set of all constants.

∴ V ∩ C = ∅. Hence, V and C are disjoint sets.

Also If A and B be the sets of male and females students in a class respectively, then A ∩ B = ∅.

(12) Difference of sets: The difference of two sets A and B is the set of the elements belonging to A but not to B i.e set of elements belonging to A only

e.g. If = A {1, 3, 5, 6} and B = {1,3,8,4} ∴ A – B = {5,6} and B – A = {8, 4}

(13) Venn diagram: This is the representation of set information with circles drawn within a rectangle

Venn diagram representation for a two sets

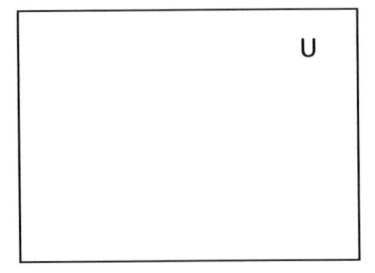

Represents the Universal

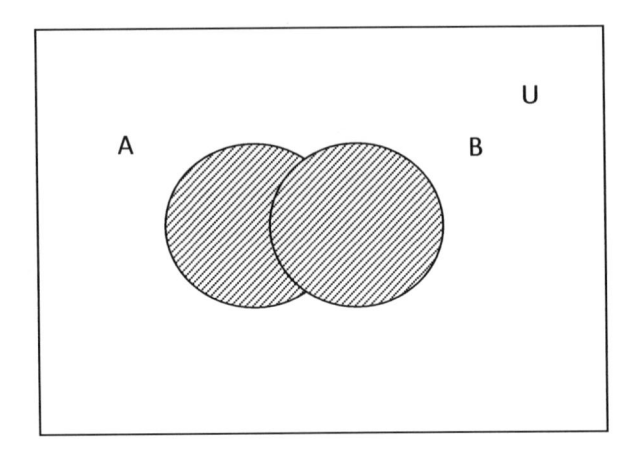

The shaded portion represents A ∪ B

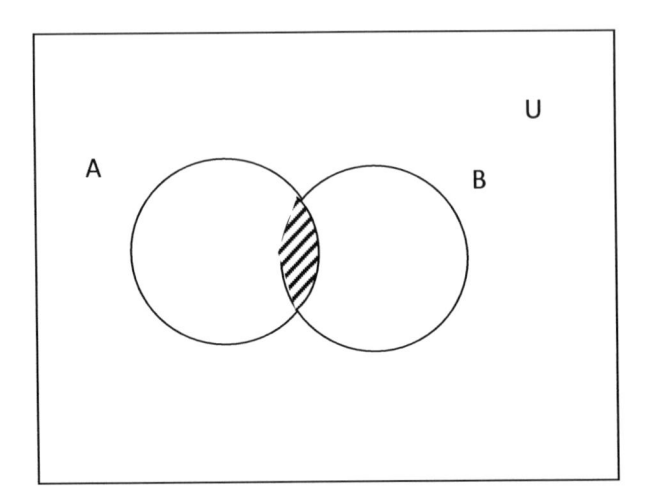

The shaded portion represent A ∩ B

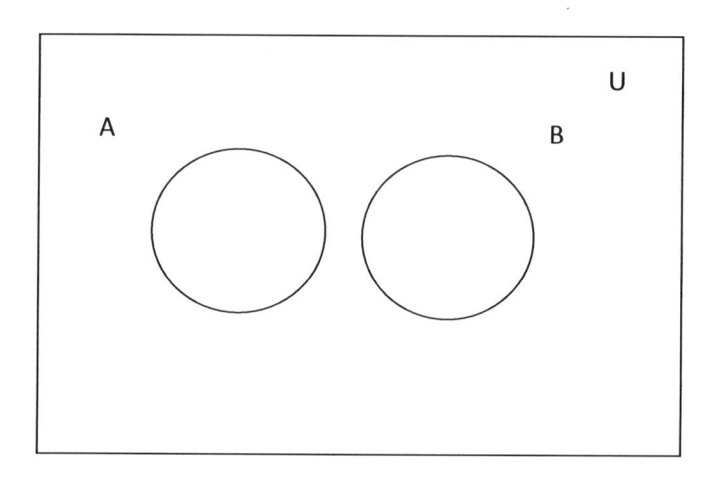

Shaded portion represents Disjoint set A ∩ B = ∅

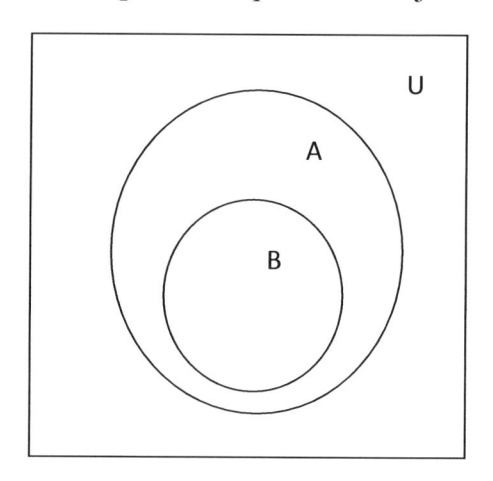

Represent the subset, B ⊆ A

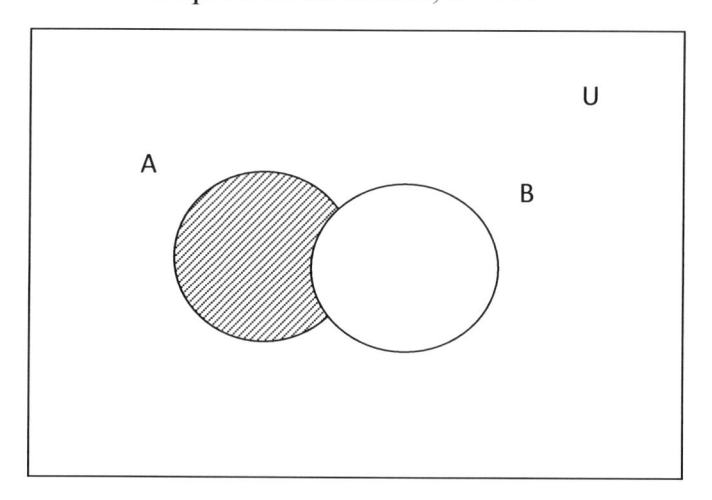

The shaded portion represents (A − B)

From the diagram $A - B = A \cap B' = A - A \cap B$

Venn diagrams representation for a three sets relationship

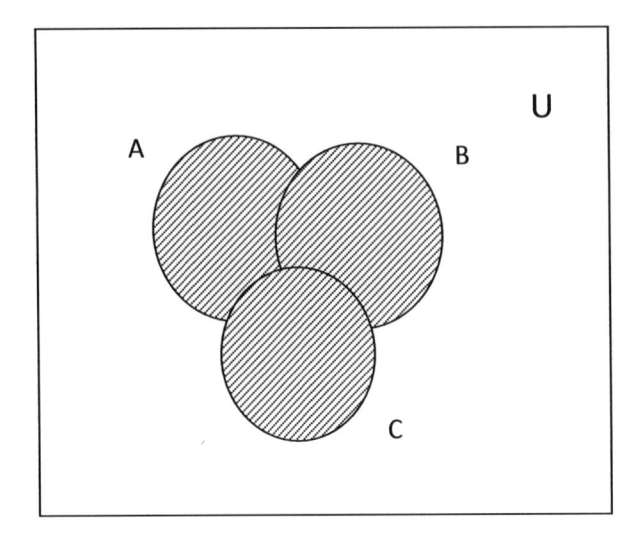

The shaded portion represent A ∪ B ∪ C

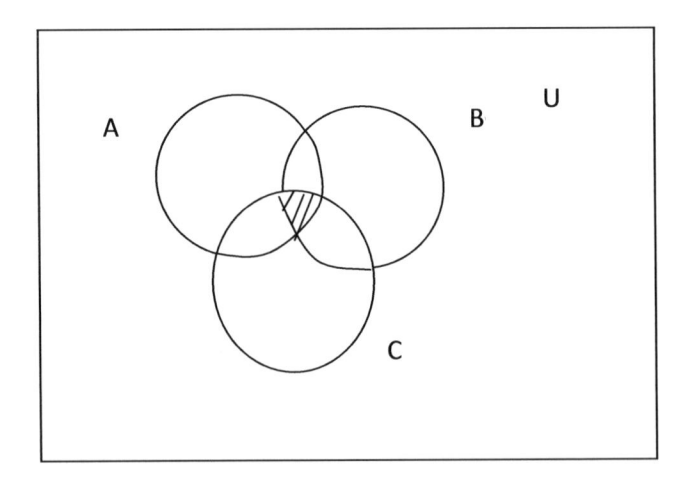

The shaded portion represents A ∩ B ∩ C

Shaded portion represents disjoint set A ∩ B ∩ C = ∅

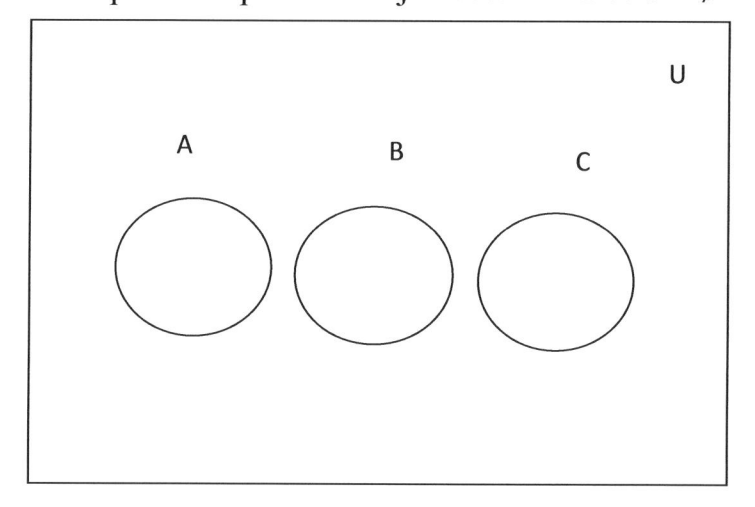

Represent the subset, C ⊆ B ⊆ A

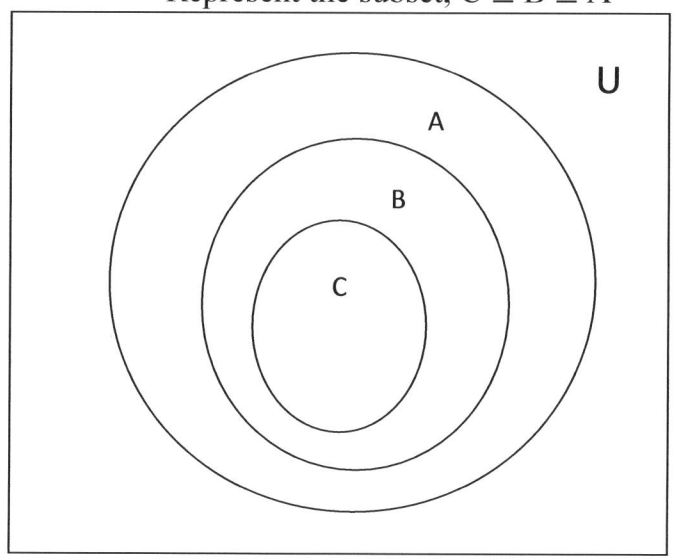

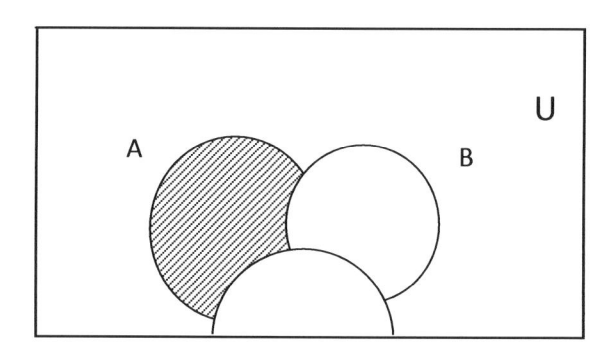

The shaded portion represents A − (B ∪ C)

Deductions from a two set relationship

Here we focus on possible deductions/questions that can be asked from a two set relationship

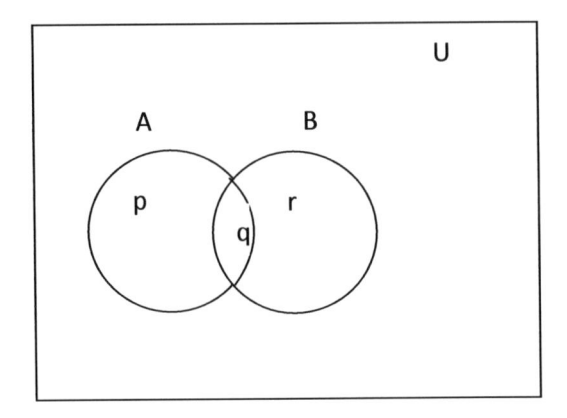

(1) Elements in A only

From the diagram above $p + q = A$

$p + q = A \rightarrow p = A - q \rightarrow n(A \cap B') = n(A) - n(A \cap B)$

(2) Elements in B only

From the diagram above $q + r = B$

$q + r = B \rightarrow r = B - q \rightarrow n(A' \cap B) = n(B) - n(A \cap B)$

(3) At least one of the two = $(A \cup B)$

$n(A \cup B) = n(A) + n(B) - n(A \cap B)$

(4) Only one type of $= n(A' \cap B) + n(A \cap B')$

$n(A' \cap B) + n(A \cap B') = U - n(A \cap B) - n(A \cup B)'$

(5) *The universal set* U

$U = n(A) + n(B) - n(A \cap B) + n(A \cup B)'$

$ = (A \cup B) + n(A \cup B)'$

Note: $A' \cap B' = (A \cup B)'$

Deductions from a three set relationship

Here we focus on possible deductions/questions that can be asked from a three set with a commom intersection.

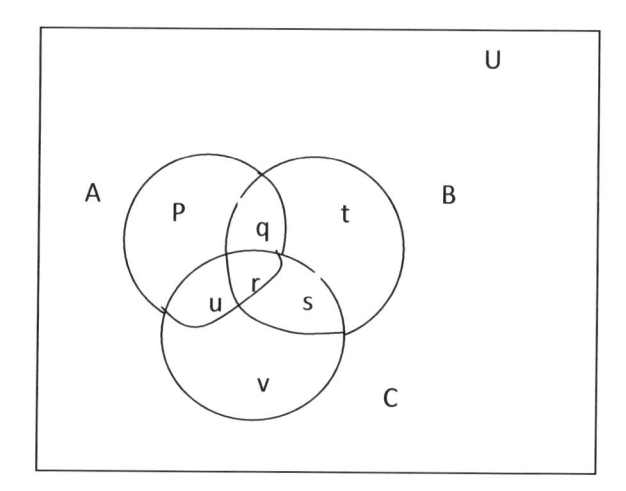

(1) Elements in A only

From the diagram above $p + q + r + u = A$

$p = A \cap B' \cap C' = A - (q + r + u)$ →

495

$A \cap B' \cap C' = n(A) - n(A \cap B) - n(A \cap C) + n(A \cap B \cap C)$

(2) Elements in B only

From the diagram above $t + q + r + s = B$

$t = A' \cap B \cap C' = B - (q + r + s) \rightarrow$

$A' \cap B \cap C' = n(B) - n(B \cap C) - n(B \cap A) + n(A \cap B \cap C)$

(3) Elements in C only

From the diagram above $u + r + s + v = C$

$v = A' \cap B' \cap C = C - (u + r + s) \rightarrow$

$A' \cap B' \cap C = n(C) - n(A \cap C) - n(C \cap B) + n(A \cap B \cap C)$

(4) Elements in A and C only

$u + r = A \cap C \rightarrow u = A \cap C - r \rightarrow n(A \cap C) - n(A \cap B \cap C)$

$A \cap B' \cap C = n(A \cap C) - n(A \cap B \cap C)$

(5) Elements in B and C only

$r + s = B \cap C \rightarrow s = A \cap C - r \rightarrow n(B \cap C) - n(A \cap B \cap C)$

$A' \cap B \cap C = n(B \cap C) - n(A \cap B \cap C)$

(6) Elements in A and B only

$q + r = A \cap B \rightarrow q = A \cap B - r \rightarrow n(A \cap B) - n(A \cap B \cap C)$

$A \cap B \cap C' = n(A \cap B) - n(A \cap B \cap C)$

(7) The universal set

$U = n(A) + n(B) + n(C) - n(A \cap B) - n(B \cap C) - n(A \cap C) + n(A \cap B \cap C)$
$\quad + n(A \cup B \cup C)'$

$\quad = n(A \cup B \cup C) + n(A \cup B \cup C)'$

Here we focus on possible deductions/questions that can be asked from a three set with no common intersection.

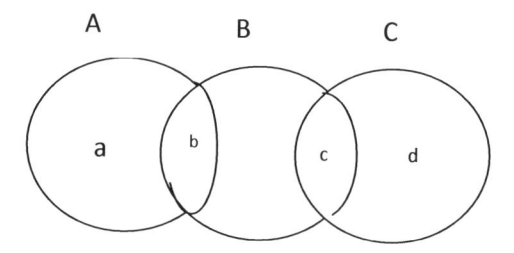

From the diagram we have a = $A \cap B'$, c = $C \cap B'$

$U = A \cap B' + B + C \cap B'$

FOUR SET RELATIONSHIP

This involves groups with distinct either/or categories [male/female, blue/white etc] The approach to such case is to form a grid with the information given as shown below.

	C	D	Total
A			
B			
Total			

SET LAWS

Idempotent Law: $A \cup A = A$, $A \cap A = A$

Commutative Laws: $A \cup B = B \cup A$, $A \cap B = B \cap A$

Associative Laws: $(A \cup B) \cup C = A \cup (B \cup C)$, $(A \cap B) \cap C = A \cap (B \cap C)$

Distributive Laws: $A \cup (B \cap C) = (A \cup B) \cap (A \cup C)$

Identity Laws: $A \cup \emptyset = A$, $A \cup U = U$, $A \cap \emptyset = \emptyset$, $A \cap U = A$

Complementary Laws: $A \cup A' = U$, $(A')' = A$, $A \cap A' = \emptyset$, $(U) = \emptyset$, $\emptyset = U$

De-Morgan's Laws: $(A \cup B)' = A' \cap B'$, $(A \cap B)' = A' \cup B'$

(34.1). There are 150 people at an international medical conference. 40 are Africans, 70 are women and 110 are doctors. 12 of the women are African, 46 of the doctors are women and 31 of the African men are not doctors. (*i*) How many of the women are doctors (*ii*) How many of the men are neither African nor doctors

Solution

n(ε) = 150, n(A) = 40, n(W) = 70, n(D) = 110, n(W ∩ A) = 12, n(D∩W) = 46

n(A∩ D) = 31, n(A ∩ M ∩ D') = 5

As man is not in the data given, we infer that men = those that are not women M = W'

∴ $n(A \cap M \cap D') = n(A \cap W' \cap D') = 5$

(*i*) African women that are doctors = $n(A \cap W \cap D)$

From $n(A \cap W' \cap D') = n(A) - n(A \cap W) - n(A \cap D) + n(A \cap W \cap D)$

$5 = 40 - 12 - 31 + n(A \cap W \cap D) \rightarrow n(A \cap W \cap D) = 5 - 40 + 12 + 31 = 8$

(*ii*) Men that are neither African nor Doctors is $n(W' \cap A' \cap D') = n(W \cap A \cap D)'$

From n(ε) = $n(A \cup WD) + n(A \cup W \cup D)'$

$n(\varepsilon) = n(A) + n(W) + n(D) - n(A \cap W) - n(A \cap D) - n(W \cap D) + n(A \cap W \cap D) + n(W' \cap A' \cap D')$

$150 = 40 + 70 + 110 - 12 - 31 - 46 + 8 + n(W' \cap A' \cap D') \rightarrow$

$150 = 139 + n(W' \cap A' \cap D') \rightarrow n(W' \cap A' \cap D') = 150 - 139 = 11$

(34.2). In a certain examination, 72 candidates offered mathematics, 64 English and 62 french. 18 offered both mathematics and English, 24 mathematics and French and 20 English and French. 8 candidates offered all three subjects, How many candidates were there for the examinations.

Solution

498

$$\varepsilon = n(A) + n(B) + n(C) - n(A \cap B) - n(B \cap C) - n(A \cap C) + n(A \cap B \cap C) + n(A \cup B \cup C)'$$

$$\varepsilon = 72 + 64 + 62 - 18 - 24 - 20 + 8 + 0 = 144$$

(34.3). The ministry of Education has 25 vacancies for tutors in its institutions. There are 15 for English tutors, 14 for Geography and 12 for French. It is required that of these 8 have to be able to teach both English and Geography, 6 both Geography and French and 5 English and French. Calculate: (i) How many must be able to teach all three subjects (ii) How many tutors of French only could be employed (iii) How many tutors of English and Geography but not French are required.

Solution

$\varepsilon = 25, E = 15, G = 14, F = 12, (E \cap G) = 18, (G \cap F) = 6, (E \cap F) = 5$

(i) $\varepsilon = n(E) + n(G) + n(F) - n(E \cap G) - n(G \cap F) - n(E \cap F) + n(E \cap G \cap F) + n(E \cap G \cap F)'$

$25 = 15 + 14 + 12 - 8 - 6 - 5 + x \rightarrow x = 3$

(ii) $(E' \cap G' \cap F) = n(F) - n(E \cap F) - n(F \cap G) + n(E \cap G \cap F)$

$= 12 - 5 - 6 + 3 = 4$

(iii) $(E \cap G \cap F') = n(E \cap G) - n(E \cap G \cap F) \rightarrow 18 - 3 = 15$

(34.4). In a pantry there are 28 cans of vegetables. Eight of these have labels with white lettering, 18 have labels with green lettering, and 8 have labels with neither white nor green. How many cans have both white and green lettering?

Solution

$W(8), G(8), (G \cap W)' = 8, \varepsilon = 28$

$\varepsilon = n(G) + n(W) - n(G \cap W) + n(G \cup W)' \rightarrow 28 = 18 + 8 - x + 8$

$28 = 34 - x \therefore x = 6$

(34.5). A maths class has 27 students in it. Of those students, 14 are also enrolled in history and 17 are enrolled in English. What is the minimum percent of the students in maths class who also enrolled in history and English?

Solution

M(27), $m \cap H = 14, M \cap E = 17$

If H + E = 14 + 17 = 31, and M = 27

H + E - m = 31 – 27 = 4

∴ 4 students were enrolled for the 3 subjects

$minimum\ percentage = \frac{4}{27} \times \frac{100}{1} = 15\%$

(34.6). At a certain professional conference with 130 attendees, 94 of the attendees are doctors and the rest are dentists. If 48 of the attendees are women and ¼ of the dentists in attendance are women. How many of the attendees are male doctors?

Solution

	Doctors	Dentists	Total
Male	55	27	82
Female	39	9	48
Total	94	36	130

Male doctors = 55

(34.7). Out of a total of 1,000 employees at a certain corporation, 52 percent are femake and 40 percent of these female work in research. If 60 percent of the total number of employees work in research. How many male employees do not work in research?

Solution

Male = M, Female = F, Research = R, Total = 100

Female = $\frac{52}{100} \times 1000 = 520$

Female in research = $\frac{40}{100} \times 520 = 208$

Research = $\frac{60}{100} \times 1000 = 600$

Male = 1000 – Female = 1000 – 520 = 480

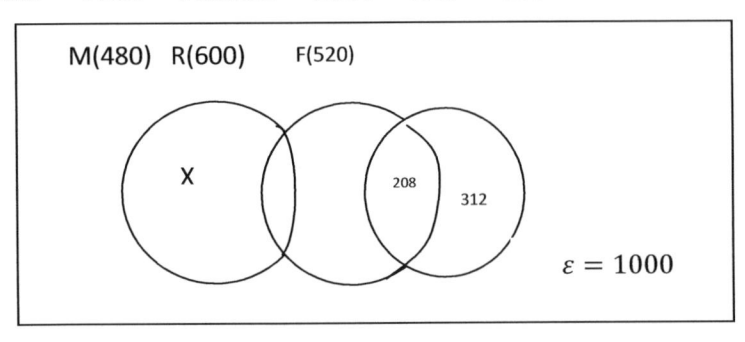

M(480) R(600)   F(520)

X   208   312

$\varepsilon = 1000$

$\varepsilon = A \cap B' + B + C \cap B' \rightarrow 312 + 600 + x = 1000$

$x = 1000 - 912 = 88$

(34.8). One–fifth of the eight switches produced by a certain factory are defective. Fourth-fifth of the detective switches are rejected and $\frac{1}{25}$ of the non defective switches are rejected by mistake. If all the switches not rejected are sold, what percent of the switches sold by the factory are defective?

Solution

Defective = D, Non- defective = N, Sold = s, Rejected = R

Let total be 100

$D = \frac{1}{5} \times 100 = 20$, ND = 80

$RD = \frac{4}{5} \times 20 = 16$, $RN = \frac{1}{20} \times 80 = 4$

Since Total Non rejected = Total sold

	D	N	Total
S	4	76	80
R	16	4	20
T	20	80	100

$\% = \frac{4}{80} \times 100 = 5\%$

(34.9). If 75 percent of all Nigerian own an automobile, 15 percent of Nigerians bicycle and 20 percent of all Nigerians own neither an automobile nor a bicycle, what percent of Nigerian own both an automobile and a bicycle.

Solution

$A = \frac{75}{100} \times 100$, $B = \frac{15}{100} \times 100 = 15$, $(A \cup B)' = \frac{20}{100} \times 100$

$\varepsilon = n(B) + n(A) - n(B \cap A) + n(A \cap B)' \rightarrow 100 = 15 + 75 - x + 20$

$x = 110 - 100 = 10$

$\% = \frac{10}{100} \times 100 = 10\%$

(34. 10). At a certain school, 60% of the sensor class is female, if among the members of the senior class, 70% of the female and 90% of the males are going on the senior trip, then what percentage of the senior class is going on the senior trip?

Solution

$Female = F = \frac{60}{100} \times 100 = 60, Male = m = \frac{40}{100} \times 100 = 40$

$Female = senior\ trip = \frac{70}{100} \times 60 = 42, Male - Senior\ trip = \frac{90}{100} \times 40 = 36$

Senior trip = 42 + 36 = 78

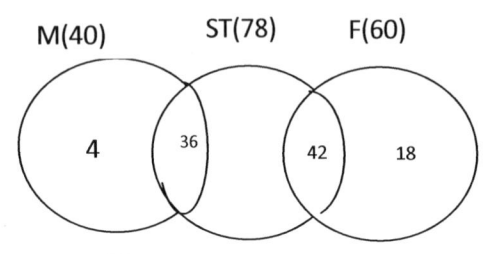

$Percentage = \frac{78}{100} \times 100 = 78\%$

(34. 11). In a company X, 30 percent of the employees live over 10 miles, from work and 60 percent of the employees who live over ten mile from work are in car pools. If 40 percent of the employees of company X are in car pools, what percent of the employees of company x live ten miles or less from work and are in car pools.

Solution

Let A = Employees living 10 miles from work

B = Employees living 10 miles less from work

C = Employees of company X in car pools over 10 miles

D = Employees of company X in no car pools

Let total employees = 100

$A = \frac{30}{100} \times 100 = 30, B = \frac{70}{100} \times 100 = 70, C = \frac{60}{100} \times 30 = 18$

$C = \frac{40}{100} \times 100 = 40$, $D = \frac{60}{100} \times 100 = 60$

	A	B	Total
C	18	22	40
D	12	48	60
Total	30	70	100

% of employees of company X which live ten miles or less from work and are in car pools = 22%

(34.12). In a certain company, 55% of the workers are men. If 30% of the workers are full – time employees and 60% of these are women, what percentage of the full-time workers in the company are men?

Solution

Let total workers = 100

$M = \frac{55}{100} \times 100 = 55$, $W = \frac{45}{100} \times 100 = 45$

$F = \frac{30}{100} \times 100 = 30$, $P = \frac{70}{100} \times 100 = 70$

$FW = \frac{60}{100} \times 30 = 18$

	M	W	Total
F	12	18	30
P	43	27	70
Total	55	45	100

$\% = \frac{12}{30} \times 100 = 40\%$

(34.13). In a class of 40 students, each student offers at least one of physics and chemistry. If the no of students that offer physics is three times the number that offer both subjects and the number that offer chemistry is twice the number that offer physics. Find the number of students that offer physics only.

Solution

$\varepsilon = 40, \varepsilon = n(P) + n(C) - n(P \cap C) + n(P \cup C)' \ldots \ldots (i)$

$n(P \cap C) = x$, $n(P) = 3\, n(P \cap C) = 3x$, $n(C) = 2n(P) = 2.3x = 6x$

inserting into (1) gives

$40 = 3x + 6x - x \rightarrow 8x = 40 \therefore x = 5$

Physics only $\rightarrow n(P \cap C') = n(P) - n(P \cap C) \rightarrow 3x - x = 2x = 10$

(34.14). A magazine's survey of its subscribers finds that 20 percent are male. If 70 percent of the subscribers are married, and 10 percent of these are male, what percent of the male subscribers are not married?

Solution

	Married	Unmarried	Total
Male	7	13	20
	63	17	80
Total	70	30	100

Let total be 100

Married $= \frac{70}{100} \times 100 = 70$, Male married $= \frac{10}{100} \times 70 = 7$

Male $= \frac{20}{100} \times 100 = 20$, Male unmarried $= \frac{13}{20} \times 100 = 60\%$

(34.15). Evaluate $[P' \cap (Q \cup Q')]'$.

Solution

$[P' \cap (Q \cup Q')]' \rightarrow (P')' \cap' (Q \cup Q')' \rightarrow P \cup (Q' \cap Q) = P \cup \emptyset$

(34.16). Evaluate $(P \cup Q) \cap (P \cup Q')$.

Solution

$(P \cup Q) \cap (P \cup Q') \rightarrow [(P \cup Q) \cap P] \cup [(P \cup Q) \cap Q'] \rightarrow [(P \cap P) \cup (P \cap Q)] \cup [(Q' \cap P) \cup (Q' \cap Q)] \rightarrow [P \cup (P \cap Q)] \cup [(P \cap Q')] \cup \emptyset] \rightarrow P \cup (P \cap Q') = P$

(34.17). Evaluate $[P \cap (P \cap Q)']'$

Solution

$[P \cap (P \cap Q)']' \rightarrow P' \cap' \cup [(P \cap Q)']' \rightarrow P' \cup (P \cap Q) \rightarrow (P' \cup P) \cap (P' \cup Q)$
$\rightarrow \varepsilon \cap (P' \cap Q) = (P' \cap Q)$

(34.18). Evaluate $[P \cap (P' \cap Q')]'$.

Solution

$[P \cap (P' \cap Q')]' \rightarrow P' \cup (P \cup Q) \rightarrow (P' \cap P) \cup Q \rightarrow \varepsilon \cup B = \varepsilon$

(34.19). If the universal set U = {x: x is a natural number and $1 \leq x \leq 9$}.

P = {x: $1 \leq x \leq 4$} and Q = {2, 4, 6, 8}. Find $(P \cup Q)'$

Solution

Since the sign $\leq$ is given numbers including the extreme is used

U = {1, 2, 3, 4, 5, 6, 7, 8, 9}, P = {1, 2, 3, 4} $P \cup Q$ = {1, 2, 3, 4, 6, 8}

$\therefore (P \cup Q)'$ = universal set - $P \cup Q$ = {5, 7, 9}

(34.20). P and Q are subsets of the universal set U defined as

U = {x: x is an integer and $1 < x < 15$}

P = {x: x is odd}, Q = {x: x is prime}. Find $n(P' \cap Q')$

Solution

Since the sign $<$ is given the numbers within the limit only is used

U = {2, 3, 4, 5, 6, 7, 8, 9, 10, 11, 12, 13, 14,}, P = {3, 5, 7, 9, 11, 13}, Q = {2, 3, 7, 11, 13}, P' = {2, 4, 6, 8, 10, 12, 14}, Q' = {4, 6, 8, 9, 10, 12, 14},

$P' \cap Q'$ = {4, 6, 8, 10, 12, 14} $\therefore n(P' \cap Q')$ = *no of element in* $(P' \cap Q') = 6$

CHAPTER 35 PROBABILITY

Probability can be defined as a measure of likelihood of an event occurring. It is dependent on the chance. Example: The chance of head turning up when a coin is tossed once.

Terms associated with Probability

(i) Statistical experiment: It is the process of performing an act, which is not in any way related to laboratory experiments. Examples are tossing of coins, balloting, throwing of dice.

(ii) Sample space: Is the collection of all possible outcomes of statistical experiment and it is normally denoted by S and referred to as Universal set in set theory.

(iii) Sample point: Each member of a sample space is called sample point.

A necessary condition of a sample space is that a given experiment must produce a result correspondent to exactly one of the points in the sample space Ω

(iv) Event: Any subset of the sample space is called an event. This is called a sigma field in Algebra

(v) Simple event: This is an event that consists of exactly one outcome.

Example: If a coin is tossed twice, event A can be defined as an event of having exactly two heads which is a subset of the Sample space S.

(vi) Compound event: This is an event that consists of more than one outcome Example: when two dice are tossed there are 36 possible outcomes, so there are 36 simple events

(vii) Joint Event: is an event that relates two or more characteristics of interest

e.g. The collection of Nigerian National team. The collection of the falcons is a joint event. The first characteristic is a Nigerian National team and the second characteristic is the female.

($viii$) Complement of an event: Given that an event A is contained in the Sample space, S, then the complement of event A denoted by A' is a collection of elements in the Sample space, S but not in event A.

(ix) Outcomes: This is the result of a statistical experiment.

(x) Non-equiprobable events: These are events with items having different numbers of element .e.g. students in a class.

(xi) Equiprobable events: This are events with items having equal number of elements e.g. An unbiassed die, A well shuffled pack of cards and a fair coin

(xii) Independent events: This are events where the probability of one does not influence the other e.g. Tossing two dice, throwing two coins, a coin and die etc

($xiii$) Dependent Events: This are events where the probability of one affects the other e.g. in selecting two balls one after the other from a basket, the total number is reduced by 1 once a draw is made.

(xiv) Mutually exclusive events: This are events that cannot occur simultaneously e.g. The occurrence of head and tail is not possible in a toss of one coin

(xv) Mutually inclusive events: This are events where either one or both of the events can occur.

(xvi) Compound events: A combination of two simple events results in compound event. e.g. tossing a coin and a die at the same time.

($xvii$) Tree diagrams: This is a diagram used for determine the probability of compound events.

($xviii$) Sampling is the act of selecting a sample

(xix) Trial: This is the act of performing a random experiment

(xix) Odd in favour of an event: This reflects the likelihood that a particular event will take place. Mathematically, Odd in favour $= \dfrac{Number\ of\ success}{Number\ of\ failure}$

(xx) Odd against an event: This reflects the likelihood that a particular event will not take place Odd in favour. Mathematically, $= \dfrac{Number\ of\ failure}{Number\ of\ success}$

We know focus our attention to detailed analysis of probability for various events

PROBABILITY OF COINS

The sample space for tossing a coin is given by the following

Tossing a coin once

Sample space, S = $\begin{Bmatrix} H \\ T \end{Bmatrix}$, where H = head and T = Tail

Tossing a coin twice.

2nd Toss

		H	T
1st Toss	H	HH	HT
	T	TH	TT

Tossing a coin three times

3rd Tosss

		HH	HT	TH	TT
	H	HHH	HHT	HTH	HTT
	T	THH	THT	TTH	TTT

Thus, for a coin No of Possible outcomes is given by 2^n

n = number of tosses

PROBABILITY OF DICE

The sample space for tossing a die is given by the following

Tossing a single die

Sample space, S = {1, 2, 3, 4, 5, 6 }

Tossing a die twice

2nd Throw

	1	2	3	4	5	6
1	(1,1)	(1,2)	(1,3)	(1,4)	(1,5)	(1,6)
2	(2,1)	(2,2)	(2,3)	(2,4)	(2,5)	(2,6)
3	(3,1)	(3,2)	(3,3)	(3,4)	(3,5)	(3,6)
4	(4,1)	(4,2)	(4,3)	(4,4)	(4,5)	(4,6)
5	(5,1)	(5,2)	(5,3)	(5,4)	(5,5)	(5,6)
6	(6,1)	(6,2)	(6,3)	(6,4)	(6,5)	(6,6)

Note that (1,2) is an outcome where 1 comes from first throw and 2 from second throw, while (2,1) is an outcome where 2 comes from the first throw and 1 from the second throw of die.

If the outcomes are added we have

+	1	2	3	4	5	6
1	2	3	4	5	6	7
2	3	4	5	6	7	8
3	4	5	6	7	8	9
4	5	6	7	8	9	10
5	6	7	8	9	10	11
6	7	8	9	10	11	12

If the outcomes are subtracted we have

-	1	2	3	4	5	6
1	0	1	2	3	4	5
2	1	0	1	2	3	4
3	2	1	0	1	2	3
4	3	2	1	0	1	2
5	4	3	2	1	0	1
6	5	4	3	2	1	0

Thus, for a dice no of Possible outcomes is given by 6^n

n = number of throw

PROBABILITY OF CARDS

The sample space for drawing a well-shuffled pack of cards is given by the following

	Red cards ♥ Heart ↓	♦ Diamond ↓	Black cards ♠ Spade ↓	♣ Club ↓	Total
Kings	K	K	K	K	4
Queen	Q	Q	Q	Q	4
Jack	J	J	J	J	4
Ace	A	A	A	A	4
	2	2	2	2	4
	3	3	3	3	4
	4	4	4	4	4
	5	5	5	5	4
	6	6	6	6	4
	7	7	7	7	4
	8	8	8	8	4
	9	9	9	9	4
	10	10	10	10	4
Total by Type	13	13	13	13	
Total by colour	26		26		52

Probability Laws

Multiplication Law: This applies to independent and dependent events i.e events combined by ''and/both''.

For independent event identified by ''and''

$P(A \text{ and } B) = P(A \cap B) = P(A) \times P(B)$

For dependent event identified by ''Given''

$P(A \text{ and } B) = P(A \cap B) = P(A) \times P\left[\dfrac{B}{A}\right]$

$P\left[\dfrac{B}{A}\right]$ = probability of B given that A has occurred.

Addition Law: This applies to mutually exclusive and mutually inclusive events i.e events combined by "or/either".

For mutually exclusive events:

P(A or B) = P(A ∪ B) = P(A) + P(B)

For mutually inclusive Events

P(A or B) = P(A∪ B) = P(A) + P(B) – P(A ∩ B)

Note: Probability is related to set. It is important to understand what the phrase either, at most, at least etc means.

QUESTIONS

(35. 1). The probability of selecting a figure which is a parallelogram from a square, a rectangle, a rhombus, a kite and a trapezium is?

Solution

Parallelogram = Square, rectangle and rhombus

$P = \frac{3}{5}$

(35. 2). Find the total number of possible outcomes in a throw of three dice.

Solution

Total number of possible outcomes for a die = $6^n = 6^3 = 216$

(35. 3). If two dice are thrown together, what is the probability of obtaining at least a score of 10?

Solution

For addition the sample space is as shown below

```
+ | 1  2  3  4  5    6
--|------------------------
1 | 2  3  4  5  6    7
2 | 3  4  5  6  7    8
3 | 4  5  6  7  8    9
4 | 5  6  7  8  9   10*
5 | 6  7  8  9 10*  11*
6 | 7  8  9 10* 11* 12*
```

P (at least a score of 10) → 10 and above

∴ P(at least a score of 10) $= \frac{6}{36} = \frac{1}{6}$

(35.4). Two perfect dice are thrown together. Determine the probability of obtaining a total score of 8.

Solution

```
+ | 1  2  3  4  5  6
--|------------------
1 | 2  3  4  5  6  7
2 | 3  4  5  6  7  8*
3 | 4  5  6  7  8* 9
4 | 5  6  7  8* 9 10
5 | 6  7  8* 9 10 11
6 | 7  8* 9 10 11 12
```

∴ P(a score of 8) $= \frac{5}{36}$

(35.5). A fair die with faces 1,2,3,4,5,6 is rolled twice. Find the probability of NOT getting 7 or 11.

Solution

```
+ | 1  2  3  4   5   6
--|--------------------
1 | 2  3  4  5   6   7*
2 | 3  4  5  6   7*  8
3 | 4  5  6  7*  8   9
4 | 5  6  7* 8   9  10
5 | 6  7* 8  9  10  11*
6 | 7* 8  9 10  11* 12
```

Total or sum of 7 or 11 = 8 numbers

Numbers that are not sum of 7 or 11 = (36 – 8) = 28

P (obtaining a total not 7 or 11) = $\frac{28}{36} = \frac{7}{9}$

(35.6). When two dice are thrown, what is the probability that the sum of the scores shown is divisible by 5.

Solution

+	1	2	3	4	5	6
1	2	3	4	5*	6	7
2	3	4	5*	6	7	8
3	4	5*	6	7	8	9
4	5*	6	7	8	9	10*
5	6	7	8	9	10*	11
6	7	8	9	10*	11	12

Sum scores divisible by 5 = 7 numbers

∴ P (sum of scores divisible by 5) = $\frac{7}{36}$

(35.7). Find the probability of selecting a prime number from the integers between 1 and 10 inclusive.

Solution

Numbers between 1 and 10 inclusive = 1, 2, 3, 4, 5, 6, 7, 8, 9, 10

Prime numbers = (2, 3, 5, 7) = 4 numbers

∴ P(selecting a prime) = $\frac{4}{10}$

(35.8). A number is selected at random between 20 and 30 both numbers inclusive. Find the probability that the number is a prime.

Solution

Numbers between 20 and 30 inclusive are 20, 21, 22, 23, 24, 25, 26, 27, 28, 29, 30

Numbers that are prime = (23, 29)

P (selecting a prime) = $\frac{2}{11}$

(35.9). All the digits 0, 1, 2,…, 9 are kept in a bag and one is drawn at random. What is the chance of it being Odd?

Solution

Digit comprises of 0,1,2,3,4,5,6,7,8,9 = 10 numbers

Odd digits are 1, 3, 5, 7, 9 = 5 numbers

P(drawing on Odd) = $\frac{no\ of\ odd}{Total} = \frac{5}{10} = \frac{1}{2}$

(35.10). The probability of a footballer being selected for a club team is 0.1, for a National team is 0.05 and for both teams is 0.02. What is the probability of his being selected for at least one of the teams?

Solution

P(at least one of the teams) = P(C ∪ N) = P(C) + P(N) − P(C ∩ N)

$P(C \cup N) = 0.1 + 0.05 - 0.025 = 0.125$

(35.11). In a survey, it was observed that 20 students read newspaper and 35 read novels, if 40 of the students read either newspapers or novels, what is the probability of the students who real both newspapers and novels?

Solution

n(P) = 20, n(N) = 35, n(P ∪ N) = 40

From set theory → n(ε) = n(P ∪ N) = n(P) + n(N) - n(P ∩ N)   40 = 20 + 35 - n(P∩N)

$n(P \cap N) = 20 + 35 - 40 = 15$

P(students that read Newspaper and Novel) = $\frac{15}{40} = \frac{3}{8}$

(35.12). Find the probability that a number selected at random from 40 to 50 is a prime.

Solution

Numbers from 40 to 50 = 40, 41, 42, 43, 44, 45, 46, 47, 48, 49, 50 = 11 numbers

Number that are prime = 41, 43, 47 = 3 numbers

P (selecting a prime) = $\frac{no\ of\ prime}{Total}$ = $\frac{3}{11}$

(35.13). A man kept 6 black, 5 brown and 7 purple shirts in a drawer. What is the probability of his picking a purple shirt with his eyes closed?

Solution

Black shirts = 6, Brown shirts = 5, Purple shirts = 7, Total = 18

P (Purple shirt) = $\frac{no\ of\ purple}{Total\ no\ of\ shirts}$ = $\frac{7}{18}$

(35.14). The letters of the word "SOPHISCATED" are put in a bag and one is picked at random. What is the chance of getting an "S" in the first draw?

Solution

From the word SOPHISCATED

P (getting an S) = $\frac{no\ of\ s}{Total\ no\ of\ letters}$ = $\frac{2}{13}$

(35.15). A bag contains three red, two while and four green balls. If one is chosen at random, what is the chance of not picking a green ball?

Solution

Not picking green means picking red or white

P(Not green) = 1 − P(G) = 1 − $\frac{4}{9}$ = $\frac{5}{9}$

(35.16). A Crate of soft drinks contains 10 bottles of coca-cola, 8 of fanta and 6 of sprite. If one bottle is selected at random, what is the probability that it is NOT a Coca-cola bottle?

Solution

Coca–Cola = 10, Fanta = 8, Sprite = 6, Total = 24

$P(C') = 1 - P(C) = 1 - \frac{10}{24} = \frac{14}{24} = \frac{7}{12}$

(35.17). The probability of carrots for launch is $\frac{3}{4}$. The probability of rice pudding for launch is $\frac{1}{10}$ and the probability of both is $\frac{3}{40}$. Find the probability of carrots but not rice?

Solution

$P(C) = \frac{3}{4}$, $P(R) = \frac{1}{10}$, $P(C \cap R) = \frac{3}{40}$

Carrots but not Rice means carrots only i.e parts of total carrots i.e C ∩ R'

$C \cap R' = C - C \cap R \rightarrow \frac{3}{4} - \frac{3}{40} = \frac{30 - 3}{40} = \frac{27}{40}$

(35.18). The letters of the word 'MATRICULATION' are cut and put into a box. One letter is drawn at random from a box. Find the probability of drawing a vowel.

Solution

P(drawing a vowel) = $\frac{no\ of\ vowels}{Total\ no\ of\ letters} = \frac{6}{13}$

(35.19). Find the probability that a number selected at random from 41 to 56 is a multiple of 9.

Solution

Numbers from 41 to 56 = 41,42,43,44,45,46,47,48,49,50,51,52,53,54,55,56 = 16

Numbers that are multiples of 9 are (45, 54) = 2 numbers

∴ P (selecting a multiple of 9) = $\frac{2}{16} = \frac{1}{8}$

(35.20). A bag contains seven balls, 4 of which are yellow and the rest black. What is the probability of picking either a yellow or black ball at random?

Solution

Total balls = 7, Yellow = 4, Black = 7 – 4 = 3

P(yellow or black) = $P(Y \cup B) = P(Y) + P(B) = \frac{4}{7} + \frac{3}{7} = 1$

(35.21). A football coach remarked that the Odds in favour of his team winning the next game were 5 to 3. The swimming Coach Commented that the Odds in favour of the swimming team winning the next competition were 3 to 1. What is the probability that both team will win their next competition.

Solution

P(Football winning) = P(FW) = $\frac{5}{5+3} = \frac{5}{8}$

P(Swimming winning) = P(SW) = $\frac{3}{3+1} = \frac{3}{4}$

P(Both winning) = multiplication law = P(FW) x P(SW) = $\frac{5}{8} \times \frac{3}{4} = \frac{15}{32}$

(35.22). A box contains 36 balls, some white, some yellow and some blue. If a ball is chosen at random, the probability of getting a white ball is $\frac{1}{18}$ and that of getting a yellow ball is $\frac{1}{3}$. How many blue balls are in the box?

Solution

Total number of balls = 36

P(W) = $\frac{1}{18}$, P(Y) = $\frac{1}{3}$

Total probabilities = P(W) + P(Y) + P(B) = 1

P(B) = 1 – P(W) – P(Y) → $1 - \frac{1}{18} - \frac{1}{3} = \frac{18-1-6}{18} = \frac{11}{18}$

P(B) = $\frac{\text{No of blue balls}}{\text{Total no of balls}}$ → No of blue balls = P(B) x Total no of balls = $\frac{11}{18} \times 36 = 22$

(35.23). A number is selected from the set (4, 5, 6, 7, 8, 9, 11, 12, 13) with equal probabilities. What is the probability that the number chosen is either less than 10 or is even?

Solution

The set (4, 5, 6, 9, 11, 12, 13) = 7 numbers

Number less than 10 = (4, 5, 6, 9) = L

Number that are even = (4, 6, 12) = E

Number less than 10 or even = (L ∪ E) = (4, 5, 6, 9, 12) = 5 numbers

P(selecting a number less than 10 or even) = $\frac{5}{7}$

(35.24). Bola chooses at random a number 1 and 300. What is the probability that the number is divisible by 4?

Solution

Number between 1 and 300 = 1, 2, 3,.....300

Numbers divisible by 4 = 4, 8, 12,... 300

From arithmetic progression

a = 4, d = 4, L = 300

L = a + (n -1)d → L – a = (n -1)d → n – 1 = $\frac{L-a}{d}$ ∴ n = $\frac{L-a}{d}$ + 1

$\frac{300-4}{4}$ + 1 = $\frac{296}{4}$ + 1 = 74 + 1 = 75

P(choosing a number divisible by 4) = $\frac{75}{300}$ = $\frac{1}{4}$ = 0.25

(35.25). The probability of an event P is $\frac{3}{4}$ while that of another event Q is $\frac{1}{6}$. If the probability of both P and Q is $\frac{1}{12}$, what is the probability of either P or Q?

Solution

Probability of OR is addition law

P(P or Q) = P(P ∪ Q) = P(P) + P(Q) – Pr(P ∩ Q)

Pr(P or Q) = $\frac{3}{4}$ + $\frac{1}{6}$ – $\frac{1}{12}$ → $\frac{9+2-1}{12}$ → $\frac{10}{12}$ = $\frac{5}{6}$

(35.26). The probability that a person stopping at a gas station will ask to have his tyres checked is 0, 12, the probability that he will ask to have his oil checked is 0.29 and the probability that he will ask to have them both checked is 0.07. (a) What is the probability that a person stopping at this station will have either his tyres or his oil checked? (b)

What is the probability that a person stopping at a gas station will have neither his tyres nor oil checked?

Solution

(a) P(either tyres or oil checked) = $P(T \cup O) = P(T) + P(O) - P(T \cap O)$

$= 0.12 + 0.29 - 0.07 = 0.34$

(b) P(neither tyres nor oil checked) → $P(Neither) = 1 - P(Either)$

$= 1 - 0.34 = 0.66$

(35.27). What is the probability that a number chosen at random from the integers between 1 and 10 inclusive is either a prime or multiple of 3?

Solution

Number between 1 and 10 inclusive = 1, 2, 3, 4, 5, 6, 7, 8, 9, 10 = 10 number

Prime numbers, P = 2, 3, 5, 7, Multiples of 3, M = 3, 6, 9

Prime number or multiple of 3 = P ∪ M = 2, 3, 5, 6, 7, 9 = 6 numbers

P(Prime or multiple) = $\frac{6}{10} = \frac{3}{5}$

(35.28). Each evening, a man either watches television or reads a book. The probability that he watches television is $\frac{4}{5}$. If he watches television, there is a probability of $\frac{3}{4}$ that he will fall asleep. If he reads a book, there is a probability of $\frac{1}{4}$ that he will fall asleep. Find the probability that he falls asleep.

Solution

By tree diagram

```
                        ¾        Asleep
               T ●
         4/5   
      ●         1 − ¾ = ¼   Not Asleep
         1 − 4/5 = 1/5
                                Asleep
               R ●
                  1 − 3/4 = 1/4
                            Not Asleep
```

From the tree diagram above

Falling Asleep could be DT & TA or DR & RA

P(falling asleep) = $\left(\frac{4}{5} \times \frac{3}{4}\right) + \left(\frac{1}{5} \times \frac{1}{4}\right) = \frac{3}{5} + \frac{1}{20} = \frac{13}{20}$

(35.29). A man travel to work either by car or by train. There is a probability or ¾ that he will travel by car the next day. if he travels by car on any one day, there is a probability of 5/6 that he will travel by train the next day. Find the probability that he travel (i) by car on Tuesday (ii) by train on Tuesday (iii) by car on Wednesday (iv) by train on Wednesday

Solution

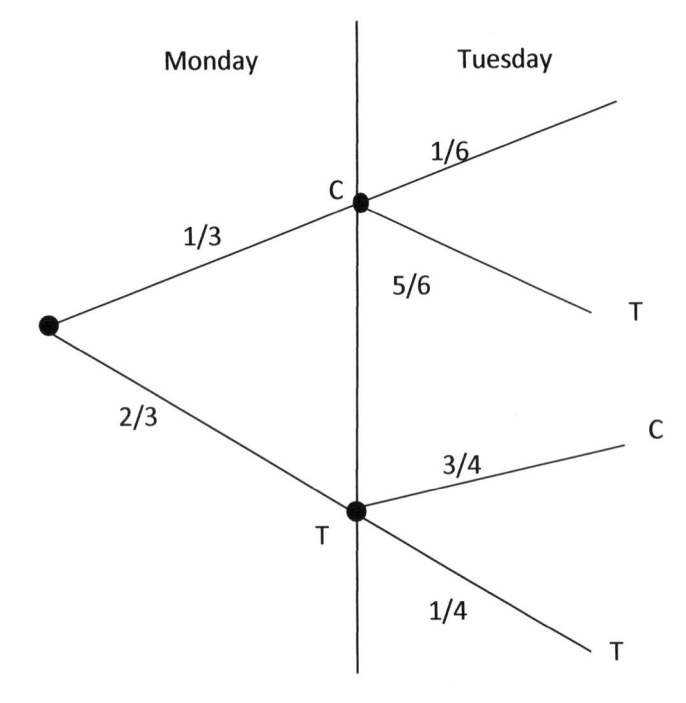

(*i*) P(car on Tuesday) could be (DC & CC or DT & TC) = $\frac{1}{3} \times \frac{1}{6} + \frac{2}{3} \times \frac{3}{4}$

= $\frac{1}{18} + \frac{1}{2} \rightarrow \frac{1+9}{18} \rightarrow \frac{10}{18} = \frac{5}{9}$

(*ii*) P(train on Tuesday) could be P(DT & TT or DC & CT) = $\left(\frac{2}{3} \times \frac{1}{4} + \frac{1}{3} \times \frac{5}{6}\right)$

= $\frac{1}{6} + \frac{5}{18} = \frac{4}{9}$

(*iii*) For the Wednesdays we continue from Tuesdays

Car on Wednesday could be:

(*a*) Car on Tue and Car on Wed $= \frac{5}{9} \times \frac{1}{6} = \frac{5}{54}$

(*b*) Train on Tue and Car on Wed $= \frac{4}{9} \times \frac{3}{4} = \frac{1}{3}$

P(car on Wednesday) $= \frac{5}{54} + \frac{1}{3} = \frac{23}{24}$

(*iv*) Train on Wednesday could be

(*a*) Car on Tuesday and Train on Wed $= \frac{5}{9} \times \frac{5}{6} = \frac{25}{54}$

(*b*) Train on Tuesday and Train on Wed $= \frac{4}{9} \times \frac{1}{9} = \frac{1}{9}$

P(Train on Wednesday) $= \frac{1}{9} + \frac{25}{54} = \frac{31}{54}$

(35.30). The chances of three independent events X, Y, Z occurring are $\frac{1}{2}, \frac{2}{3}, \frac{1}{4}$ respectively. What are the chances of Y and X only occurring?

Solution

Chances of Y and Z only occurring from three means Y occurs, Z occurs and X does not occur

P(Y and Z only) = P(Y ∩ Z ∩ X′) = P(Y) x P(Z) x (P X′) = P(Y) x P(Z) x [1 − P(X)]

P(Y and Z only) $= \frac{2}{3} \times \frac{1}{4} \times \frac{1}{2} = \frac{1}{12}$

(35.31). The chances of Adbulahi, Ngozi and Bola winning a lottery are $\frac{3}{5}, \frac{4}{5},$ and $\frac{7}{10}$ respectively. What is the probability that only Bola wins the lottery?

Solution

P(Bola winning only) = P(B) x P(A′) x P (N′) = P(B) x [1 − P(X)] x [1 − P(N)]

P(B) $= \frac{7}{10}$, P(A) $= \frac{3}{5}$, P(N) $= \frac{4}{5}$, P(A′) $= 1 - \frac{3}{5} = \frac{2}{5}$, P(N′) $= 1 - \frac{4}{5} = \frac{1}{5}$

∴ P (Bola winning only) = $\frac{7}{10} \times \frac{2}{5} \times \frac{1}{5} = \frac{7}{125}$

(35.32). Consider the experiment of tossing a coin three times. Find the probability of getting: (*i*) Exactly two heads (*ii*) No head (*iii*) At least two heads (*iv*) Exactly one head (*v*) At most one head

Solution

	HH	HT	TH	TT
H	HHH	HHT	HTH	HTT
T	THH	THT	TTH	TTT

Let x = Number of heads. Also number of outcomes = $2^n = 2^3 = 8$

(*i*) Exactly two heads → P(X = 2) = $\frac{1}{8} + \frac{1}{8} + \frac{1}{8} = \frac{3}{8}$

(*ii*) No head → P(X = 0) = $\frac{1}{8}$

(*iii*) At least two heads → P(X ≥ 2) = P(X = 2) + P(X = 3) = $\frac{3}{8} + \frac{1}{8} = \frac{4}{8} = \frac{1}{2}$

(*iv*) Exactly one head → P(X = 1) = $\frac{1}{8} + \frac{1}{8} + \frac{1}{8} = \frac{3}{8}$

(*v*) At most one head → P(X ≤ 1) = P(X = 0) + P(X = 1) = $\frac{1}{8} + \frac{3}{8} = \frac{4}{8} = \frac{1}{2}$

(35.33). Consider a bag containing 5 yellow balls, 2 blue balls and 3 green balls. If a ball is selected at random, what is the probability that it is:

(*i*) Yellow or Blue (*ii*) Green or Yellow (*iii*) Green or Blue (*iv*) Blue

(*v*) Yellow (*vi*) Green

Solution

Let Y = Yellow ball, B = Blue ball, G = Green ball.

This is a mutually exclusive event

(i) P(Y or B) → P(Y ∪ B) = P(Y) + P(B) − P(Y∩B) → $\frac{5}{10} + \frac{2}{10} - 0 = \frac{7}{10}$

(ii) P(G or Y) → P(G ∪ Y) = P(G) + P(Y) − P(G∩Y) → $\frac{3}{10} + \frac{5}{10} - 0 = \frac{8}{10}$

(iii) P(G or B) → P(G ∪ B) = P(G) + P(B) − P(G∩B) = $\frac{3}{10} + \frac{2}{10} - 0 = \frac{5}{10} = \frac{1}{2}$

(iv) P(B) = $\frac{2}{10} = \frac{1}{5}$ (v) P(Y) = $\frac{5}{10} = \frac{1}{2}$ (vi) P(G) = $\frac{3}{10}$

(35.34). Suppose a bag contains 5 blue balls, 6 yellow balls, and 9 green balls. Two balls are selected at random one after the other (i) with replacement (ii) without replacement

What is the probability that (i) One is Blue and one is Yellow (ii) One is Green and one is Blue (iii) The two balls are green (iv) The two balls are of the same colour (v) The first is blue and other is yellow.

Solution

Let B ≡ Blue ball, Y ≡ Yellow ball, G ≡ Green ball.

For with replacement

(i) P(One is Blue and one is Yellow) = P(1st Blue and 2nd Yellow) + P(1st yellow and 2nd blue)

$P(B_1 \cap Y_2) + P(Y_1 \cap B_2) = P(B_1) \times P(Y_2) + P(Y_1) \times P(B_2) = \left[\frac{5}{20} \times \frac{6}{20}\right] + \left[\frac{6}{20} \times \frac{5}{20}\right] = \frac{60}{400}$

(ii) P(one is Green and one is Blue) = P(1st green and 2nd blue) + P(1st blue and 2nd green)

$P(G_1 \cap B_2) + P(B_1 \cap G_2) = P(G_1) \times P(B_2) + P(B_1) \times P(G_2) = \left[\frac{9}{20} \times \frac{5}{20}\right] + \left[\frac{5}{20} \times \frac{9}{20}\right] = \frac{90}{400}$

(iii) P(The two balls are green) = P(1st green and 2nd green)

$P(G_1 \cap G_2) = P(G_1) \times P(G_2) = \frac{9}{20} \times \frac{9}{20} = \frac{81}{400}$

(iv) P(the two balls are of the same colour) = P(The two balls are blue or yellow or green) = P(The two balls are blue) + P(The two balls are yellow) + P(The two balls are green)

$P(B_1 \cap B_2) + P(Y_1 \cap Y_2) + P(G_1 \cap G_2) = P(B_1) \times P(B_2) + P(Y_1) \times P(Y_2) + P(G_1) \times P(G_2)$

$\left[\dfrac{5}{20} \times \dfrac{5}{20}\right] + \left[\dfrac{6}{20} \times \dfrac{6}{20}\right] + \left[\dfrac{9}{20} \times \dfrac{9}{20}\right] = \dfrac{25}{400} + \dfrac{36}{400} + \dfrac{81}{400} = \dfrac{142}{400}$

(*v*) P(The 1st is blue and other is yellow) = $P(B_1 \cap Y_2) = P(B_1) \times P(Y_2) = \dfrac{5}{20} \times \dfrac{6}{20} = \dfrac{30}{400}$

For without replacement

(*i*) P(One is Blue and one is Yellow) = P(1st Blue and 2nd Yellow) + P(1st yellow and 2nd blue)

$P(B_1 \cap Y_2) + P(Y_1 \cap B_2) = P(B_1) \times P(Y_2 / B_1) + P(Y_1) \times P(B_2 / Y_1)$

$\left(\dfrac{5}{20} \times \dfrac{6}{19}\right) + \left(\dfrac{6}{20} \times \dfrac{5}{19}\right) = \dfrac{60}{380}$

(*ii*) P(one is Green and one is Blue) = P(1st green and 2nd blue) + P(1st blue and 2nd green)

$P(G_1 \cap B_2) + P(B_1 \cap G_2) = P(G_1) \times P(B_2 / G_1) + P(B_1) \times P(G_2 / B_1)$

$\left(\dfrac{9}{20} \times \dfrac{5}{19}\right) + \left(\dfrac{5}{20} \times \dfrac{9}{19}\right) = \dfrac{90}{380}$

(*iii*) P(The two balls are green) = P(1st green and 2nd green)

$P(G_1 \cap G_2) = P(G_1) \times P(G_2 / G_1) = \dfrac{9}{20} \times \dfrac{8}{19} = \dfrac{72}{380}$

(*iv*) P(the two balls are of the same colour) = P(The two balls are blue or yellow or green) = P(The two balls are blue) + P(The two balls are yellow) + P(The two balls are green)

$P(B_1 \cap B_2) + P(Y_1 \cap Y_2) + P(G_1 \cap G_2) \rightarrow P(B_1) \times P(B_2 / B_1) + P(Y_1) \times P(Y_2 / Y_1) + P(G_1) \times P(G_2 / G_1)$

$\left(\dfrac{5}{20} \times \dfrac{4}{19}\right) + \left(\dfrac{6}{20} \times \dfrac{5}{19}\right) + \left(\dfrac{9}{20} \times \dfrac{8}{19}\right) = \dfrac{122}{380}$

(*v*) P(The first is blue and other is yellow) = $P(B_1 \cap Y_2) = P(B_1) \times P(Y_2 / B_1)$

$\dfrac{5}{20} \times \dfrac{6}{19} = \dfrac{30}{380}$

(**35.35**). Consider a box containing 3 defective bulbs and 5 non-defective bulbs. If the bulbs are selected at random (i) With replacement (ii) without replacement

What is the probability that (i) Both bulbs are defective (ii) The first bulb selected is defective and the second bulb is non–defective

Solution

Let D_1 be the event that the first bulb selected is defective.

Let D_2 be the event that the second bulb selected is defective.

Let N_1 be the event that the first bulb selected is non- defective.

Let N_2 be the event that the second bulb selected is non – defective.

For with replacement

(*i*) P(Both bulbs are defective) = $P(D_1 \cap D_2) = P(D_1) \times P(D_2) = \frac{3}{8} \times \frac{3}{8} = \frac{9}{64}$

(*ii*) P(1st is defective and 2nd non-defective) = $P(D_1 \cap N_2) = P(D_1) \times P(N_2) = \frac{3}{8} \times \frac{5}{8} = \frac{15}{64}$

For without replacement:

(*i*) P(Both bulbs are defective) = $P(D_1 \cap D_2) = P(D_1) \times P(D_2 / D_1) = \frac{3}{8} \times \frac{2}{7} = \frac{6}{56}$

(*ii*) P(1st is defective and 2nd is non-defective) = $P(D_1 \cap N_2) = P(D_1) \times P(N_2 / D_1)$

$\frac{3}{8} \times \frac{5}{7} = \frac{15}{56}$

(**35.36**). The probability that Philip will be alive in 10 years to come is 0.6 and the probability that his wife will be alive in 10 years time is 0.7. what is the probability that in the next 10 years (*i*) Both will be alive (*ii*) Only Philip will be alive (*iii*) Only the wife will be alive (*iv*) Neither of the two will be alive (*v*) Either of the two will be alive.

Solution

Let A be the event that Philip will be alive in the next 10 years.

B be the event that Mr. Philip's wife will be alive in the next 10 years

P(A) = 0.6, P(W) = 0.7

(*i*) P(Both will be alive) = P(Philip is alive and his wife is alive)

$P(A \cap W) = P(A) \times P(W) \rightarrow 0.6 \times 0.7 = 10.42$

525

(*ii*) P(only Philip will be alive) = P(Philip is alive and his wife is dead)

$P(A \cap W) = P(A) \cdot P(W) \rightarrow 0.6 \times \left[1 - \frac{7}{10}\right] \rightarrow 0.6 \times 0.3 = 0.18$

(*iii*) P(Only the wife will be alive) = P(Philip is dead and his wife is alive)

$P(A \cap W) = P(A) \cdot P(W) \rightarrow \left[1 - \frac{6}{10}\right] \times 0.7 \rightarrow 0.4 \times 0.7 = 0.28$

(*iv*) P(Neither of the two will be alive) = P(Philip is dead and his wife dead)

$P(A' \cap W') = P(A) \cdot P(W) \rightarrow (1 - 0.6).(1 - 0.7) \rightarrow 0.4 \times 0.3 = 0.12$

(*v*) P(Either of the two will be alive) = P(Philip is alive or his wife is alive)

$P(A \cup W) = P(A) + P(W) - P(A \cap W) \rightarrow 0.6 + 0.7 - (0.6 \times 0.7) \rightarrow 1.3 - 0.42 = 0.88$

(*vi*) P(Either of the two will not be alive) = P(Philip is not alive or his wife is not alive)

$P(A' \cup W') = P(A') + P(W') - P(A' \cap W') \rightarrow 0.4 \times 0.3 - 0.12 = 0.58$

(**35.37**). Consider a well shuffled pack of cards. If card is selected at random from the pack, what is the probability that it is (*i*) Heart or Ace (*ii*) Jack or club (*iii*) Black card or Spade (*iv*) Red card or Ace (*v*) Red card or Diamond?

Solution

Observer that each of the card selected are from different row and Column and there is an intersection between them thus, it a non-mutually exhaustive event.

Let H represents Heart Card.

Let A represents Ace Card.

Let J represents Club Card.

Let C represents Club Card.

Let B represents Black Card.

Let R represents Red Card.

Let D represents Diamond Card.

Let S represents Spade Card.

a. P(Heart or Ace) = P (H or A) = P(H ∪ A) = P(H) + P(A) − P(H ∩ A)
$= \frac{13}{52} + \frac{4}{52} - \frac{1}{52} = \frac{16}{52}$

b. P(Jack or Club) = P(J or C) = P(J ∪ C) = P(J) + P(C) − P(J ∩ C)
$= \frac{4}{52} + \frac{13}{52} - \frac{1}{52} = \frac{16}{52}$

c. P(Black Card or Spade) = P(B or S) = P(B ∪ S) = P(B) + P(S) − P(B ∩ S)
$= \frac{26}{52} + \frac{13}{52} - \frac{13}{52} = \frac{26}{52}$

d. P(Red Card or Ace) = P(R or A) = P(R ∪ A) = P(R) + P(A) − P(R ∩ A)
$\frac{26}{52} + \frac{4}{52} - \frac{2}{52} = \frac{28}{52}$

e. P(Red Card or Diamond Card) = P(R or D)
$= \frac{26}{52} + \frac{13}{52} - \frac{13}{52} = \frac{26}{52}$

(35.38). Consider a well shuffled pack of cards. If card is selected at random from the pack, what is the probability that it is (*i*) Ace or queen (*ii*) Spade or diamond (*iii*) King or jack (*iv*) Red card or club (*v*) Red card (*vi*) Club.

Solution

Observer that each of the card selected are from same row and column without any intersection between them thus, it a mutually exhaustive event.

a. P(Ace or queen) = P (A or Q) = P(A ∪ Q) = P(A) + P(Q) − P(A ∩ Q)
$= \frac{4}{52} + \frac{4}{52} - 0 = \frac{2}{13}$

b. P(Spade or Diamond) = P(S or D) = P(S ∪ D) = P(S) + P(D) − P(S ∩ D)
$= \frac{13}{52} + \frac{13}{52} - 0 = \frac{26}{52}$

c. P(King or Jack) = P(K or J) = P(K ∪ J) = P(K) + P(J) − P(K ∩ J)
$= \frac{4}{13} + \frac{4}{13} - 0 = \frac{8}{13}$

d. P(Red Card or Club) = P(R or C) = P(R ∪ C) = P(R) + P(C) − P(R ∩ C)
$\frac{26}{52} + \frac{13}{52} - 0 = \frac{39}{52}$

e. P(Red Card) = P(R)
$= \frac{26}{52}$

f. P(Club Card) = P(C)
$= \frac{13}{52}$

CHAPTER 36 PERMUTATION AND COMBINATION

Permutation relates to arrangement of items where the order is important.

Thus the following key word implies permutation sitting, standing or lining, ways of movements, placement of objects and formation of digit numbers

n! = factorial = n(n - 1)(n - 2) …………..(n – r + 1)

n!! = super factorial = 1!2!3! n! = $1^n \, 2^{n-1} \, 3^{n-2} \ldots\ldots (n-1)^2 n$

Note that 0! = 1

(*i*) Permutation of n different object is given by $n!$

(*ii*) Permutation of n different object taking r at a time $n_{P_r} = \dfrac{n!}{(n-r)!}$

(*iii*) Permutation of n different object with repetition is given by $\dfrac{n!}{r_1! \, r_2! r_3!}$

(*iv*) Permutation of n different object taking r at a time when one particular object must be included in each arrangement is given by r x $\left[n-1_{P_{r-1}}\right]$

(*v*) Permutation of n different object taking r at a time when one particular object must be excluded from the arrangement is given by $n-1_{P_r}$

(*vi*) Permutation of n different object round a circle is given by $(n-1)!$

(*vii*) Permutation of n different object where a particular object must occupy a given position (fixed position) is given by $(n-r)!$ r = no of fixed position

(*viii*) Permutation of n different letters with r object being together is given by

$(n-r+1)!$

Where n = total number of persons, r = total number who are together

(*ix*) Permutation of n different letters with r object being separate is given by

Not together = Total permutation without restriction - Permutation of being together

$$= \dfrac{n!}{r!r!r!} - (n-r+1)!$$

(*x*) Permutation of n different objects with r object being separate is given by

528

Not together = $(group\ with\ no\ restriction)! \times (n-1)(n-2)(n-3)\ldots\ldots(n-r)$

The group that must not be together determines were to stop

(xi) How many n-digit numbers can be formed by using the digits if no digit may be repeated = multiply each of the digit given n number of times starting from the biggest

(xii) How many n-digit numbers can be formed by using the digits if repetition of digits is allowed = multiply the number of digit given n number of times

(xiii) How many n-digit odd/even no can be formed by using the digits if no digit may be repeated = Total no of odd/even numbers x $(n-1)(n-2)(n-3)\ldots\ldots(n-r)$
where n = total no of digits given

(xiv) How many n-digit odd/even numbers can be formed by using the digits if repetition of digit is allowed = Total no of odd/even numbers x $n \times n \times n \ldots\ldots$

where n = total no of digits given

Combination: relates to selection of items where the order is not important.

Thus the following key word implies combination pairing, handshakes and formation of committees. The following

(i) Combination of n different object taking r at a time is given by

$$n_{C_r} = \frac{n!}{(n-r)!r!} = \frac{n_{P_r}}{r!}$$

Relationships between permutation and combination

These are useful relations which makes evaluation easy. They include..

(i) $n_{P_r} = (n-1)(n-2)(n-3)\ldots\ldots(n-r+1)$

(ii) $n_{C_r} = \frac{(n-1)(n-2)(n-3)\ldots\ldots(n-r+1)}{r!}$

(iii) $n_{C_r} = \frac{n_{P_r}}{r!}$

(iv) $n_{C_r} = n_{C_{n-r}}$

(v) $n_{C_r} + n_{C_{r+1}} = n+1_{C_{r+1}}$

LAWS OF PERMUTATION & COMBINATION

Addition Law: Applies to permutation or combination that involves "or"

Multiplication Law: Applies to permutation or combination that involves "and"

Formation of groups in combination

Case 1:

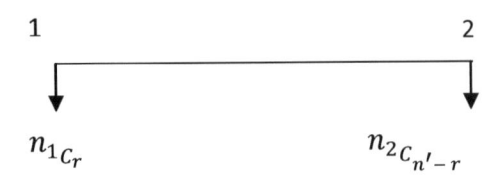

$$\underset{n_1 C_r}{1} \qquad \underset{n_2 C_{n'-r}}{2}$$

Group 1 controls Group 2.

n' = Total number of committee required, n_1 = Total number of first group

n_2 = Total number of second group

Group 1 is the first group mentioned in the question

(i) If r for group 1 is given, substitute into the equation above and solve since that is the value of r that will be used for both groups.

(ii) If r for group 2 is given, then apply T = A + B and solve for A.

The value of A becomes the value of r that will be used for both groups.

(iii) If r value for group 1 and group 2 are given, ignore r value for group 2 and solve with r value of group 1.

We now consider various cases

(1) No restriction: In this case, the formula becomes $n_1 + n_2 C_{n'}$

(2) When the phrase ''either all r (for group 1) or all (group 2)'' is used. The formula becomes $n_1 C_{n'} + n_2 C_{n'}$

(3) When the phrase ''equal number of r (for group1) and (group2)'' is used: In this

530

$n' \to \frac{n'}{2}$ ∴ The formula becomes $n_1C_{\frac{n'}{2}} \cdot n_2C_{\frac{n'}{2}}$

(4) When probability is required

$$\text{Probability} = \frac{Combination\ of\ Case\ required}{Combination\ of\ (No\ restriction)}$$

(5) When the phrase ''at least'' is used: Here we apply T = A + B with the total number of committee needed (n') telling you where to stop.

If at least A or B is asked, and the total committee needed is 5 we write 5 = A + B the at least value must not exceed 5 i.e the values of A or B is dependent on the total committee needed and not the number where they are selected from "it must not exceed it"

Insert the value of A or B

Formation of Two group

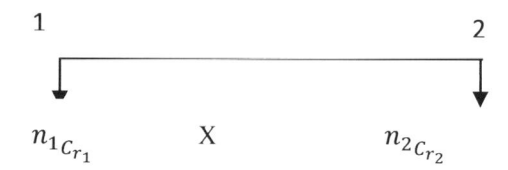

```
        1                           2
        |                           |
        ↓                           ↓
    n₁C_{r₁}         X          n₂C_{r₂}
```

n_1 = Total number of first group, n_2 = Total number of second group

r_1 = no of first group needed, r_2 = no of second group needed

We now consider various cases

(1) No restriction: In this case apply the formula above like that

(2) Certain number of persons from group 1 or group 2 <u>MUST</u> be selected: In this case we reduce the value of n_1, n_2 and r_1, r_2 or both depending on the number of person that must be selected i.e the value of n and r must be changed.

(3) Certain number of persons from group 1 or group 2 <u>MUST NOT</u> be selected: In this case we reduce the value of n_1 or n_2 or both depending on the number of persons that must not be selected leaving the r's like that i.e the value of r remains unchanged.

(3) When the phrase ''at least'' is used: Here the value of n_1 and n_2 is constant while the values of the r's varies. To determine the values of r_1 and r_2 to be used we apply

T = A + B

T = Total no of committee to be formed

A and B are r_1 and r_2 values to be used.

QUESTION

(36.1). In how many ways can 8 people sit at a round table.

Solution

From formula (vi)

$(n-1)! \rightarrow (8-1)! = 7! = 5040$

(36.2). How many three digit odd numbers can be formed from the digits, 1, 2, 3, 4, 5. If it is permitted to use any the digits more than once?

Solution

From (xiii) → How many n-digit odd no = Total no of odd numbers x $n \times n \times n$ ......

$= 3 \times 5 \times 5 = 75$

(36.3). In how ways can the 1st, 2nd and 3rd prizes be awarded in a class of 20.

Solution

From formula (ii) → $20_{P_3} = 6840$

(36.4). Find the number of arrangement using any three letters of the words CHEMISTRY.

Solution

From formula (ii) → $9_{P_3} = 504$

(36.5). How many 4 digit number can be formed using the digits 1,2,3,4,5 if no digit must be repeated.

Solution

From formula (x) → $5 \times 4 \times 3 \times 2 = 120$

(**36.6**). How many numbers can be formed using three digits 1, 2, 3. If (a) no digit can be repeated (b) any digits can be used more than once.

Solution

(a) From formula (x) → 3 x 2 x 1 = 6 ways

(b) From formula (xi) → 3 x 3 x 3 = 27

(**36.7**). In how many ways can 6 pupil be lined up, if 3 of them insist on following one another?

Solution

From formula (viii) → $(n - r + 1)! = (6 - 3 + 1)! = 4! = 24$ ways

(**36.8**). How many distinct arrangement can be made using all the letters of the word MALARIA?

Solution

From formula (iii) → $\frac{7!}{3!} = \frac{7 \times 6 \times 5 \times 4 \times 3!}{3!} = 840$

(**36.9**). In how many ways can the letters of the word "BEGINNING" be arranged?

Solution

From "BEGINNING", B= 1, E = 1, G = 2, I = 2, N = 3

From formula (iii) → $\frac{9!}{2!2!3!} = \frac{9 \times 8 \times 7 \times 6 \times 5 \times 4 \times 3!}{4 \times 3!} = 15120$

(**36.10**). In how many ways can the word "MATHEMATICS" be arranged?

Solution

From formula (iii) → $\frac{n!}{r_1! \, r_2! r_3!} = \frac{11!}{2! \, 2! \, 2!}$

(**36.11**). In how many ways can 4 books be arranged on a shelf if two particular books are to be next to each other?

Solution

From formula (viii) → $(n - r + 1)! = (4 - 2 + 1)! = 3! = 6$ ways

(36.12). Five people are to be arranged in a row for a group photograph. How many arrangements are there if a married couple in the group insists on sitting next to each other.

Solution

From formula (viii) → $(n - r + 1)! = (5 - 2 + 1)! = 4! = 24$

(36.13). In how many ways can seven balls (yellow, blue, brown, green, grey, pink and white) be arranged in threes such that we have yellow ball as member of each arrangements?

Solution

Since yellow ball is required to be in the collection, the yellow balls have three ways of appearing in the collection.

from

$r \times [n - 1_{P_{r-1}}] \rightarrow 3 \times {}^{7-1}P_{3-1} \rightarrow 3 \times ({}^{6}P_2) \rightarrow 3 \times \frac{6!}{(6-2)!} \rightarrow 3 \times \frac{6!}{4!} = 90 \; ways$

(36.14). Out of the seven questions set by a physics lecturer, students are required to answer five questions, of which question three is compulsory. Determine the number of ways in which the questions can be attempted.

Solution

$5 \times ({}^{7-1}P_{5-1}) \rightarrow 5 \times ({}^{6}P_4) \rightarrow 5 \times \frac{6!}{(6-4)!} \rightarrow 5 \times \frac{6!}{2!} = 1800 \; ways$

(36.15). In how many ways can three people be seated on eight seats in a row?

Solution

From formula (ii) → $8_{P_3} = \frac{8!}{(8-3)!} = \frac{8!}{5!} = \frac{8 \times 7 \times 6 \times 5!}{5!} = 336$

(36.16). Five students were late to a class and only three vacant seats were available. In how many ways can the seats be occupied?

Solution

From formula (ii) → $5_{P_3} = 60 \; ways$

(36.17). How many four-digits odd numbers can be formed from the digits 1, 2, 3, 4, 5, 6 If no repetition of digits is allowed?

Solution

From formula (xiii) → Total no of odd no x $(n-1)(n-2)(n-3)\ldots\ldots(n-r)$

$$= 3 \times 5 \times 4 \times 3 = 180$$

(36.18). In how many ways can the letters of the word "CHEMISTRY" be arranged if the vowels must always be together

Solution

Vowels are E, I = 2

From formula (viii) → $(9-2+1)! = 8! = 40320$ ways

(36.19). There are three different ways of going from A to B and 4 different ways going from B to C. How many possible routes are there from A to C via B?

Solution

Going from A to C = 3 x 4 = 12

(36.20). A boy has 6 double sided pop records. In how many different orders can he play them?

Solution

A double sided record has 2 faces = 12!

(36.21). How many numbers greater than 100 can be formed using the digits 1,2,3,4,5 if no digit may be repeated?

Solution

From 1,2,3,4,5 number > 100 can be formed from a3 digits number, 4 digit number and 5 digit number

3 digit number = 3 from 5 = 5 x 4 x 3 = 60

4 digit number = 4 from 5 = 5 x 4 x 3 x 2 = 120

5 digit number = 5 from 5 = 5 x 4 x 3 x 2 x 1 = 120

Number > 100 = 60 + 120 + 120 = 300

(36.22). Find the number of arrangements of the letters of the word "PERCENTAGE" if the E 's must be placed next to each other.

Solution

P = 1, E = 3, R = 1, C = 1, N = 1, T = 1, A = 1, G = 1

From formula (viii) → (10 − 3 + 1)! = 8! = 40320 ways

(36.23). Find the number of ways in which the letters of the word "SHALLOW" can be arranged if the two L's must not come together

Solution

From formula (ix) → Not coming together = $\frac{n!}{r!r!r!}$ - $(n - r + 1)!$

$= \frac{7!}{2!}$ - $(7 − 2 + 1)!$ → 2520 - 720 = 1800

(36.24). How many arrangements can be made of the letters in the word "TROTTING"?

Solution

T = 3, R = 1, O = 1, I = 1, N = 1, G = 1

From formula (iii) → $\frac{n!}{r!} = \frac{8!}{3!} = \frac{8 \times 7 \times 6 \times 5 \times 4 \times 3!}{3!} = 6720$

(36.25). How many arrangement are there of the letters of the word "LETTERS"?

Solution

L = 1, E = 2, T = 2, R = 1, S = 1, Total = 7

From formula (iii) → $\frac{n!}{r_1! \, r_2!} = \frac{7!}{2!2!} = \frac{7 \times 6 \times 5 \times 4 \times 3 \times 2!}{2! \times 2!} = 1260$

(36.26). In how many years can one place 3 white balls, 2 green balls and 1 black ball in a line.

Solution

White = 3, Green = 2, Black = 1, Total = 6

From formula (iii) → $\dfrac{n!}{r_1! \, r_2!} = \dfrac{6!}{3!2!} = \dfrac{6 \times 5 \times 4 \times 3 \times 2!}{6 \times 2!} = 60$

(**36.27**). In how many different ways can the letters of the word "SALOON" be arranged If (a) the two O's must not come together (b) If the consonants and vowels must occupy alternate places.

Solution

(a) From formula (ix) → Not coming together = $\dfrac{n!}{r!r!r!}$ - $(n - r + 1)!$

$= \dfrac{6!}{2!}$ - $(6 - 2 + 1)!$ → 360 - 120 = 240

(b) Consonants are: S, L, N = 3, Vowels are: A, O, O = 3

Arranging constants = 3!, Arranging vowel = 3!

Arranging constant and vowels separately = 3! × 3! = 36

(**36.28**). The letters of the word "DIGIT" are to be permuted. In how many of these permutations (a) do the I's come together (b) are the I's separated

Solution

(a) From formula (viii) → $(5 - 2 + 1)! = 4! = 24$

(b) From formula (ix) → Not together = $\dfrac{n!}{r!}$ - $(n - r + 1)!$ → $\dfrac{5!}{2!} - 24 = 60 - 24 = 36$

(**36.29**). In how many ways can 8 books be arranged on a shelf if 3 particular books are to be together?

Solution

From formula (viii) → $(8 - 3 + 1)! = 6! = 720$

(**36.30**). Evaluate $x_{C_8} = x_{C_{12}}$

Solution From $x_{C_{x-r}} = x_{C_r}$

$x - r = 8$, $r = 12$ ∴ $x = 12 + 8 = 20$

(**36.31**). If $8_{C_n} : 6_{C_{n-1}} = \dfrac{56}{15}$ find n

Solution

$$8_{C_n} = \frac{(n-1)(n-2)(n-3)\ldots(n-r+1)}{r!} \rightarrow \frac{8 \times 7 \ldots (8-n+1)}{n!} \rightarrow \frac{8 \times 7 \ldots (9-n)}{n!}$$

$$6_{C_{n-1}} = \frac{(n-1)(n-2)(n-3)\ldots(n-r+1)}{r!} \rightarrow \frac{6 \times 5 \ldots (6-(n-1)+1)}{(n-1)!} \rightarrow \frac{6 \times 5 \ldots (8-n)}{(n-1)!}$$

$$8_{C_n} : 6_{C_{n-1}} = \frac{56}{15} \text{ becomes}$$

$$\frac{8 \times 7 \ldots (9-n)}{n!} : \frac{6 \times 5 \ldots (8-n)}{(n-1)!} = \frac{56}{15}$$

$$\frac{\frac{8 \times 7 \ldots (9-n)}{n!}}{\frac{6 \times 5 \ldots (8-n)}{(n-1)!}} = \frac{56}{15} \rightarrow \frac{8 \times 7 \ldots (9-n)}{n!} \times \frac{(n-1)!}{6 \times 5 \ldots (8-n)} = \frac{56}{15}$$

$$\frac{8 \times 7 \times 6 \times 5 \ldots (9-n)}{n(n-1)!} \times \frac{(n-1)!}{6 \times 5 \ldots (8-n)} = \frac{56}{15}$$

since $8 \times 7 = 56$ and cancelling we are left with

$$\frac{1}{n} \times \frac{1}{(8-n)} = \frac{1}{15} \rightarrow n(8-n) = 15 \rightarrow 8n - n^2 = 15 \rightarrow n^2 - 8n + 15 = 0$$

$$n(n-3) - 5(n-3) = 0 \therefore n = 3 \text{ or } 5$$

(36.32). If $n_{P_3} = 6[n_{C_5}]$ find n

Solution

$$n_{C_5} = \frac{n(n-1)(n-2)(n-3)(n-4)}{5!}, \quad n_{P_3} = n(n-1)(n-2)$$

$$n_{P_3} = 6[n_{C_5}] \rightarrow n(n-1)(n-2) = 6\left[\frac{n(n-1)(n-2)(n-3)(n-4)}{5!}\right]$$

$$5! = 6(n^2 - 7n + 12) \rightarrow \frac{120}{6} = (n^2 - 7n + 12) = 20$$

$$n^2 - 7n - 8 = 0 \rightarrow (n+1)(n-8) = 0 \therefore n = 8 \text{ or } -1$$

(36.33). Given $\frac{n_{P_3}}{n_{C_4}} = 6$ find n

Solution

$$\frac{n(n-1)(n-2)}{\frac{n(n-1)(n-2)(n-3)}{4!}} = 6 \rightarrow \frac{4 \times 3 \times 2}{n-3} = 6 \rightarrow 24 = 6n - 18 \therefore n = 7$$

(36.34). In a class of 6 boys and 4 girls, 3 boys and 2 girls are to be selected. In how many ways can this be done if (i) there is no restriction (ii) a particular boy must be selected (iii) a particular boy and a particular girl must be selected (iv) a particular boy and a particular girl must not be selected.

Solution

From 1 → 2

$n_1 C_{r_1}$ X $n_2 C_{r_2}$

(i) Boys   Girls

6_{C_3} x 4_{C_2} = 20 x 6 = 120 ways

(ii) 5_{C_2} x 4_{C_2} = 10 x 6 = 60 ways

(iii) 120 - 30 = 90 ways

(36.35). Given $m_{P_6} = 90 m_{P_4}$. Evaluate $2m_{P_4}$ If m is positive.

Solution

$m_{P_6} = 90 m_{P_4} \rightarrow \frac{m!}{(m-6)!} = \frac{90 m!}{(m-4)!} = \frac{90 m!}{(m-4)(m-5)(m-6)!}$

$1 = \frac{90}{(m-4)(m-5)} \rightarrow (m-4)(m-5) = 90 \rightarrow m^2 - 9m + 20 = 90 \rightarrow m^2 - 9m - 70 = 0$

$m^2 - 14m + 5m - 70 = 0 \rightarrow m(m-4) + 5(m-14) \rightarrow (m+5)(m-14) = 0$

$m + 5 = 0 \rightarrow m = -5, m - 14 = 0 \rightarrow m = 14$

∴ positive value of m = 14

$2m_{P_4} = 2 \times 14P_2 = 28P_2 = \frac{28!}{(28-2)!} = \frac{28!}{26!} = 756$

(36.36). For what value of K is $kC_3 = kP_2$

Solution

$$\frac{k!}{(k-3)!\,3!} = \frac{k!}{(k-2)!} \to k!(k-2)! = k!(k-3)!\,3! \to (k-2)! = (k-3)!\,3!$$

$$(k-2)(k-3)! = 3!(k-3)! \to (k-2) = 6 \quad \therefore k = 8$$

(36.37). Evaluate $8C_{r+2}$ if $\frac{C_r}{6P_r} = \frac{1}{24}$

Solution

From $\frac{6C_r}{6P_r} = \frac{1}{24} \to 24 \cdot 6C_r = 6P_r \to 24 \times \frac{6!}{(6-r)!\,r!} = \frac{6!}{(6-r)!} \to 24 = r! \to 4! = r! \quad \therefore r = 4$

$$8C_{r+2} = 8C_{4+2} = 8C_6 = \frac{8!}{(8-6)!6!} = \frac{8!}{2!6!} = 28$$

(36.38). If $6P_r = 6$, Evaluate $12C_{r+2} + 8P_{r+3}$

Solution

From $6P_r = 6 \to \frac{6!}{(6-r)!\,r!} = 6 \to \frac{6!}{6} = (6-r)! \to \frac{720}{6} = (6-r)! \to 120 = (6-r)$

$5! = (6-r)! \to 5 = 6-r \quad \therefore r = 1$

$12C_{r+2} + 8P_{r+3} \to 12C_{1+2} + 8P_{1+3} \to {}^{12}C_3 + {}^8P_4 \to \frac{12!}{(12-3)!3!} + \frac{8!}{(8-4)!} = 220 + 1680 = 1900$

(36.39). A committee consisting of five members is to be formed out of six men and four women, how many ways can the committee be formed in such a way that we have (i) Two men (ii) Four men (iii) Three men and two women (iv) At least three men (v) At least one woman (vi) No woman (vii) No restriction.

Solution

```
        1                    2
        ↓                    ↓
      n1Cr                 n2Cn'-r
```

From the diagram above

$F(r) = \binom{6}{r}\binom{4}{5-r}$

Total = M + W

540

(i) When w = 2 → Total = M + W → 5 = m + 2 ∴ m = 3

$F(r) = \binom{6}{r}\binom{4}{5-r}$ → $\binom{6}{3}\binom{4}{2}$ → 20 x 6 = 120 ways

(ii) When $m = 4$ → $\binom{6}{4}\binom{4}{1}$ → 15 x 4 = 60 ways

(iii) When $m = 3$ and $W = 2$. we use only value of M

→ $\binom{6}{3}\binom{4}{2}$ = 20 x 6 = 120 ways

(iv) At least three men r ≥ 3 , m = 3, 4, 5 and correspondence value for W are 2, 1 and 0

∴ $\binom{6}{3}\binom{4}{2} + \binom{6}{4}\binom{4}{1} + \binom{6}{5}\binom{4}{0}$ → 20(6) + 15(4) + 6(1) = 120 + 60 + 6 = 186 ways

(v) At least one woman. Substituting w = 1, 2, 3, 4, 5 into the formula we obtain corresponding value for m = 4, 3, 2, 1

$\binom{6}{4}\binom{4}{1} + \binom{6}{3}\binom{4}{2} + \binom{6}{2}\binom{4}{3} + \binom{6}{1}\binom{4}{4}$ → 15(4) + 20(6) + 15(4) + 6(1) = 246 ways

Note: Nothing like $^4C_5$

(vi) No woman. Here w = 0 → T = m + 0 ∴ m = 5

$\binom{6}{5}\binom{4}{0}$ → 6(1) = 6 ways

(vii) Without restriction $^{10}C_5$ = 252 ways

(36.40). From six boys and four girls, five people have been selected for admission to Harvard university. In how many ways can these be done if there must be exactly two girls?

Solution

T = B + G → 5 = B + 2 ∴ B = 3

$6C_r \times 4C_{5-r}$ → $6C_3 \times 4C_2$ = 20 x 6 = 120 ways

(36.41). Out of ten consonants and four vowels, how many words can be formed from six consonants and three vowels?

Solution

$10C_6 \times 4C_3$ → 210 x 40 = 840 ways

(36.42). Jane must select three different items for each dinner she will serve. The items are to be chosen from among five different vegetarian and four different meat selection. If at least one of the selection must be vegetarian, how many different dinners could Jane create?

Solution

$5C_r \times 4C_{n'-r}$

At least one vegetarian implies

$5C_1 \times 4C_{3-1} + 5C_2 \times 4C_{3-2} + 5C_3 \times 4C_{3-3} \rightarrow 5C_1 \times 4C_2 + 5C_2 \times 4C_1 + 5C_3 \times 4C_0$

$30 + 40 + 10 = 80$

(36.43). If $n_{C_3} = n_{P_2}$. Evaluate $2nC_{n+1} + 3nP_{n-1}$

Solution

$n_{C_3} = n_{P_2} \rightarrow \dfrac{n!}{(n-3)!3!} = \dfrac{n!}{(n-2)!} \rightarrow n!(n-2)! = n!(n-3)!\,3! \rightarrow (n-2)! = (n-3)!3!$

Since $(n-2)! = (n-2)(n-2-1)! = (n-2)(n-3)!$

$\therefore (n-2)(n-3)! = (n-3)!\,3! \rightarrow n-2 = 3! = 6 \therefore n = 8$

(36.44). For what value of n is $n+1_{C_3} = 7(n_{C_2})$?

Solution

From $n+1_{C_{r+1}} = n_{C_r} + n_{C_{r+1}}$

$r + 1 = 3 \therefore r = 2$

$n+1_{C_3} = 7(n_{C_2}) \rightarrow n_{C_3} + n_{C_2} = 7(n_{C_2}) \rightarrow n_{C_3} = 7(n_{C_2}) - n_{C_2} = 6(n_{C_2})$

$n_{C_3} = 6(n_{C_2}) \rightarrow \dfrac{n(n-1)(n-2)}{3!} = 6\left[\dfrac{n(n-1)}{2!}\right] \rightarrow (n-2) = \dfrac{6 \times 3!}{2!} = \dfrac{6 \times 3 \times 2 \times 1}{2!}$

$(n-2) = 18 \therefore n = 20$

(36.45). Evaluate $\dfrac{n_{P_3}}{n_{C_2}} + n_{C_0}$

Solution

From $n_{C_r} = \dfrac{n_{P_r}}{r!} \to n_{P_r} = n_{C_r} \cdot r!$

$\dfrac{n_{P_3}}{n_{C_2}} + n_{C_0} \to \dfrac{(n_{C_3})3!}{n_{C_2}} + n_{C_0}$

With $(n_{C_3})3! = \dfrac{n(n-1)(n-2)3!}{3!} = n(n-1)(n-2)$ and $n_{C_2} = \dfrac{n(n-1)}{2!}$

$\dfrac{(n_{C_3})3!}{n_{C_2}} + n_{C_0} \to \dfrac{n(n-1)(n-2)}{\frac{n(n-1)}{2!}} + n_{C_0} \to 2(n-2) + 1 \to 2n - 4 + 1 = 2n - 3$

CHAPTER 37 THE BINOMIAL THEOREM

Consider the expansion of the following

$(x + y)^0 = 1$

$(x + y)^1 = 1x + 1y$

$(x + y)^2 = 1x^2 + 2xy + 1y^2$

$(x + y)^3 = 1x^3 + 3x^2y + 3xy^2 + 1y^3$

$(x + y)^4 = 1x^4 + 4x^3y + 6x^2y^2 + 4xy^3 + 1y^4$

The coefficients of x and y when extracted can be displaced in the form of

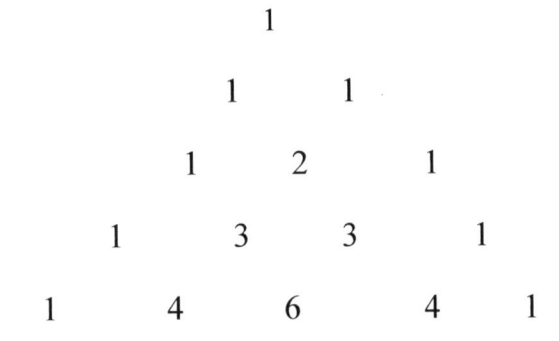

```
            1
          1   1
        1   2   1
      1   3   3   1
    1   4   6   4   1
```

And so on

The above representation is called Pascal's triangle. It is used to determine the coefficients of the terms of the powers of a binomial expression.

Features of a Pascal triangle

(i) While the power of x is in decreasing order, the power of y is in increasing order.

(ii) Each line of coefficient is symmetrical.

(iii) Each line of coefficient can be obtained from the line of coefficient immediately preceding it.

(iv) The number of terms increases by $n + 1$

The Binomial Expansion Formula

Recall the expansions carried out earlier. What happens if we what to expand

$(x + y)^{50}$. That would take days to be done. Hence the binomial expansion formula for positive, negative, integral or rational value of n was derived. It is given by

$$(x + y)^n = x^n + n_{C_1}x^{n-1}y + n_{C_2}x^{n-2}y^2 + \ldots n_{C_r}x^{n-r}y^r + \ldots y^n$$

From $n_{C_r} = \frac{n!}{(n-r)!r!} = \frac{n(n-1)(n-2)\ldots(n-r+1)(n-r)!}{(n-r)!r!} = \frac{n(n-1)(n-2)\ldots(n-r+1)}{r!}$

Hence,

$$(x + y)^n = x^n + nx^{n-1}y + \frac{n(n-1)}{2!}x^{n-2}y^2 + \frac{n(n-1)(n-2)}{3!}x^{n-3}y^3 \ldots$$
$$\frac{n(n-1)(n-2)\ldots(n-r+1)}{r!}x^{n-r}y^r + \ldots y^n$$

Provided there is restriction on the values of x and y in the expansion $(x + y)^n$

The above expression holds!

$(r + 1)th$ term $= n_{C_r}a^{n-r}b^r$

QUESTIONS

(37.1). Find the eight term in the expansion $(2x - y)^{10}$

Solution

$(r + 1)th$ term $= n_{C_r}a^{n-r}b^r$

$r + 1 = 8 \rightarrow r = 8 - 1 = 7$, $a = 2x$, $b = -y$, $n = 10$

$n_{C_r}a^{n-r}b^r \rightarrow 10_{C_7}(2x)^{10-7}(-y)^7 \rightarrow \frac{10!}{(10-7)!\,7!}(2x)^3(-y)^7 \rightarrow \frac{10!}{3!7!}$ x $8x^3$ x $(-y)^7 =$ 120 x $8x^3$ x $(-y)^7 = -960x^3y^7$

(37.2). Evaluate the coefficient of x^3y^4 in the expansion of $(2x - 3y)^7$

Solution

$a = 2x$, $b = -3y$, $n = 7$

$n_{C_r}a^{n-r}b^r \rightarrow n_{C_r}(2x)^{n-r}(-3y)^r \rightarrow n_{C_r}$ x $(2)^{n-r}$ x $(x)^{n-r}$ x $(-3)^r$ x y^r

Comparing we have

545

$x^3 y^4 = (x)^{n-r} \times y^r \rightarrow n - r = 3$ and $r = 4$

$n = 3 + r \rightarrow 3 + 4 = 7$

Evaluating the coefficient

$n_{C_r} \times (2)^{n-r} x\ y^r \rightarrow 7_{C_4} \times 2^{7-4} \times (-3)^4 = 35 \times 8 \times 81 = 22680$

(37.3). Find the value of the co-efficient of x^7 in the expansion of $(1 + 2x)^{10}$.

Solution

$(r+1)th$ term $= n_{C_r} a^{n-r} b^r$

$a = 1,\ b = 2x,\ n = 10$

$10_{C_r}(1)^{10-r}(2x)^r \rightarrow 10_{C_r} \cdot 2^r \cdot x^r$

Comparing $x^r = x^7 \therefore r = 7$

$10_{C_r} \cdot 2^r \cdot x^r \rightarrow \dfrac{10!}{(10-7)!7!} \times 2^7 = 120 \times 128 = 1536$

(37.4). Find the value of P if the coefficient of x^3 in the expansion of $(1 + px)^4 (2 - x)^3$ is $32p^3 - 1$

Solution

$(1 + px)^4 = 1 + 4px + 6p^2 x^2 + 4p^3 x^3 + p^4 x^4$

$(2 - x)^3 = 8 - 12x + 6x^2 - x^3$

$(1 + px)^4 (2 - x)^3 = [1 + 4px + 6p^2 x^2 + 4p^3 x^3 + p^4 x^4 x)(8 - 12x + 6x^2 - x^3)$

Expanding gives

$8 - 12x + 6x^2 - x^3 + 32 - 48x^2 p + 24x^3 p - 4x^4 p + 48p^2 x^2 - 72x^3 p^2 + 36x^4 p^2 - 6x^5 p^2 + 32x^3 p^3 - 48x^4 p^3 + 24x^5 p^3 - 4x^6 p^3 + 8x^4 p^4 - 12x^5 p^4 + 6x^6 p^4 - x^5 p^4$

terms in x^3 will result from

$24x^3 p - x^3 - 72x^3 p^2 + 32x^3 p^3 \rightarrow [24p - 1 - 72p^2 + 32p^3]x^3 = 32p^3 - 1$

$32p^3 - 72p^2 + 24p - 1 = 32p^3 - 1 \rightarrow -72p^2 + 24p = 0 \rightarrow p[24 - 72p] = 0$

either $24 - 72p = 0$ or $p = 0$

$24 = 72p \rightarrow p = \frac{24}{72} = \frac{1}{3}$ ∴ $p = \frac{1}{3}, 0$

(37.5). Find the term which when simplified contains x^{-4} in the binomial expansion of $\left(x - \frac{2}{x^2}\right)^8$

Solution

$(x - 2x^{-2})^8$

$(r + 1)$th term $= {}^nC_r\, a^{n-r}\, b^r$

$a = x,\ b = -2x^{-2},\ n = 8$

$8_{C_r}(x)^{8-r}.(-2x^{-2})^r \rightarrow 8_{C_r}.x^{8-r}.-(2)^r(x)^{-2r} \rightarrow -\left[8_{C_r}.x^{8-r-2r}.(2)^r\right]$

$-\left[8_{C_r}.x^{8-3r}.(2)^r\right]$

Comparing $x^{-4} = x^{8-3r} \rightarrow 8 - 3r = -4 \rightarrow 3r = 12$ ∴ $r = 4$

Evaluating

$8_{C_r}.x^{8-3r}.(2)^r \rightarrow 8_{C_r}.(-2)^r.x^{8-3r} \rightarrow 8_{C_r}.(-2)^r \rightarrow 8_{C_4}.(-2)^4 = \frac{8!}{(8-4)!4!}$ x 16

16 x 70 = $1120x^{-4}$ and it's the 5th term

(37.6). Find the co-efficient of x^3 in the expansion of $(1 + x + x^2)^3$

Solution

$(1 + x + x^2)^3 \rightarrow (1 + x + x^2)(1 + x + x^2)(1 + x + x^2)$

$(1 + x + x^2)[1 + x + x^2 + x + x^2 + x^3 + x^2 + x^3 + x^4]$

$(1 + x + x^2)(1 + 2x + 3x^2 + 2x^3 + x^4)$

$1 + 2x + 3x^2 + 2x^3 + x^4 + x + 2x^2 + 3x^3 + 2x^4 + x^5 + x^2 + 2x^3 + 3x^4 + 2x^5 + x^6$

$\rightarrow 1 + 3x + 6x^2 + 7x^3 + 6x^4 + 3x^5 + x^6$

∴ The coefficient of x^3 is 7

(37.7). Calculate a if the co-efficient of x^3 in $(a + 2x)^5$ is 320

Solution

(r + 1)th term = $^nC_r \, a^{n-r} \, b^r$

a = a, b = 2x, n = 5

$5_{C_r}(a)^{5-r}(2x)^r \to 5_{C_r} \cdot 2^r \cdot x^r \cdot a^{5-r}$

Comparing $x^r = x^3 \therefore r = 3$

$5_{C_3} \cdot a^{5-3} 2^3 \to \dfrac{5!}{(5-3)!3!} \times 8a^2 = 120 \times 128 = 1536$

$8a^2 = 320 \to a^2 = \dfrac{320}{80} = 4 \therefore a = \sqrt{4} = \pm 2$

(37.8). Let p be the coefficient of x^4 in the expansion of $(1 + 2x)^7$ and q be the coefficient of x^3 in the expansion of $(1 - 2x)^8$. Find 2pq

Solution

(r + 1)th term = $n_{C_r} \, a^{n-r} \, b^r$

For $(x + 2x)^7 \to n = 7, \ a = 1, \ b = 2x$

$7_{C_r} \cdot 1^{n-r} \cdot (2x)^r \to 7_{C_r} \cdot 1^{n-r} \cdot 2^r \cdot x^r$

Comparing $x^r = x^4 \therefore r = 4$

$7_{C_r} \cdot 1^{n-r} \cdot 2^r \cdot x^r$ becomes $7_{C_4} \cdot 1^{7-4} \cdot 2^4 = 35 \times 16 = 560$

For $(1 - 2x)^8 \to n = 8, \ a = 1, \ b = -2x$

$8_{C_r} \cdot 1^{8-r} \cdot (-2x)^r \to 8_{C_r} \cdot 1^{8-r} \cdot (-1)^r \cdot 2^r \cdot x^r$

Comparing $x^r = x^3 \therefore r = 3$

$8_{C_r} \cdot 1^{8-r} \cdot (-1)^r \cdot 2^r \to 8_{C_3} \cdot (-1)^3 \cdot 2^3 = -36 \times 8 = -448$

∴ P = 560, q = - 448

2pq = 2 x 500 x (- 448) = - 501760

CHAPTER 38 STATISTICS

Statistics is the study of the collection, organization, analysis, interpretation and presentation of data.

Terms associated with statistics

(i) Data: This is the lowest level of abstraction from which information and knowledge are derived.

Data are classified as either discrete or continuous.

A discrete data is one that deals with countable objects

A continuous data is one that deals with uncountable objects.

(ii) Grouped data: This is the representation of large data into classes using a table to show the frequency distribution of the variables.

(iii) Ungrouped data: This is a data that has not been organized into groups. It is just a list of numbers.

(iv) Class Limits: These are lower and upper value of a class.

Thus in 1 – 4, 1 is the lower limit while 4 is the upper limit.

(v) Class widths: This is the difference between the class limits

Thus in 1 – 4, class width = 4 – 1 = 3

(vi) Class boundaries: These are regions where the class limits can be extended to. They are found by averaging the class limit and the one before or next.

(vii) Class Marks: This is the average or midpoint of the class limit.

($viii$) Class interval: This is the height of a class. It depends on the range of the data and the number of classes.

Class interval = $\frac{Range}{number\ of\ class}$

(ix) Ogive: This is a cumulative frequency curve. It is drawn by plotting the cumulative frequencies against the upper class boundaries or against the class mark.

Representation of data

Data are usually represented in various ways. Common examples includes

(*i*) Pictogram: In this graph with picture of objects are plotted against the frequency

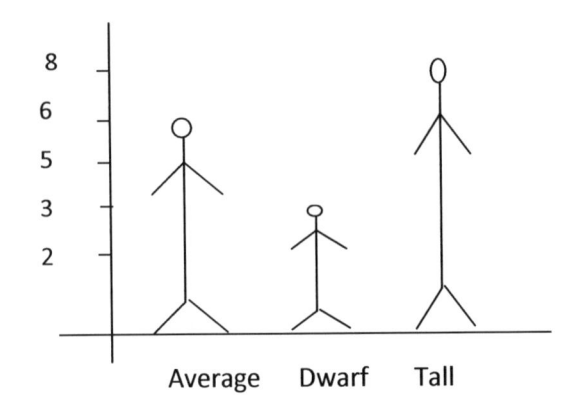

(*ii*) Pie chart: This is a circular chart divided into sectors called pie illustrating numerical proportion. The arc length of each sector is proportional to the quantity it represents.

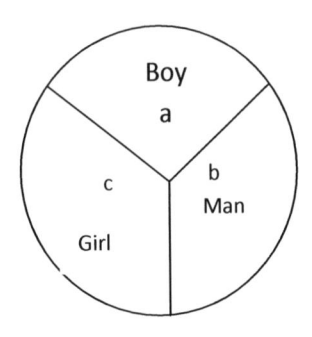

The relation $\frac{Sectorial\ angle}{360} \times Total$ can be used to solve.

(*iii*) Bar chart: This is a chart with rectangular bars with lengths proportional to the values that they represent. The bars can be plotted vertically or horizontally.

Types of bar chart

Simple bar chart: A bar chart is simple when it expresses single information.

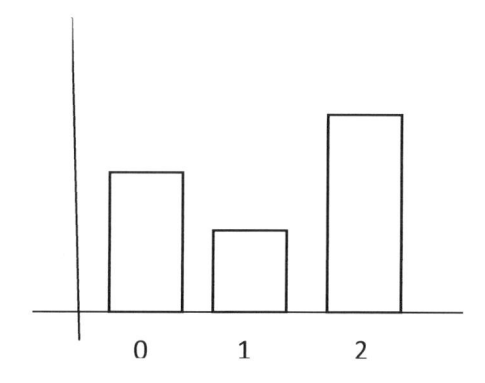

Component bar chart: A bar chart is component when each bar is divided in two sections whose sizes are proportional to the quantities. e.g. rainfall for the first five months of the year for two years

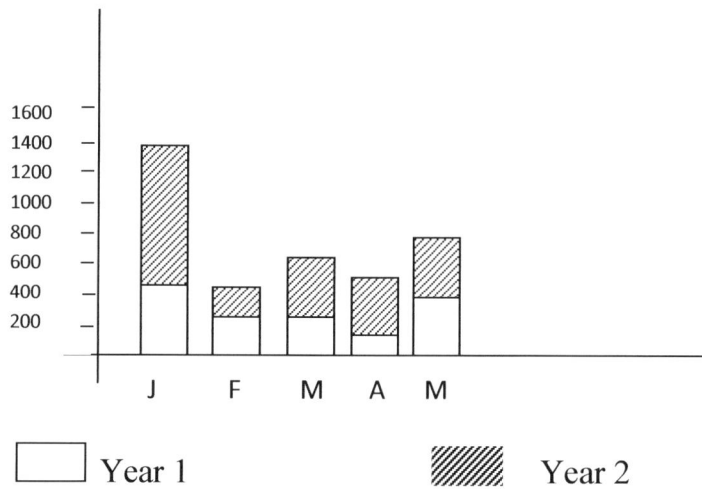

☐ Year 1   ▨ Year 2

Multiple bar chart: A bar chart is multiple when the components of each rectangle or bars are drawn besides each other. e.g. rainfall for the first five months of the year for two years.

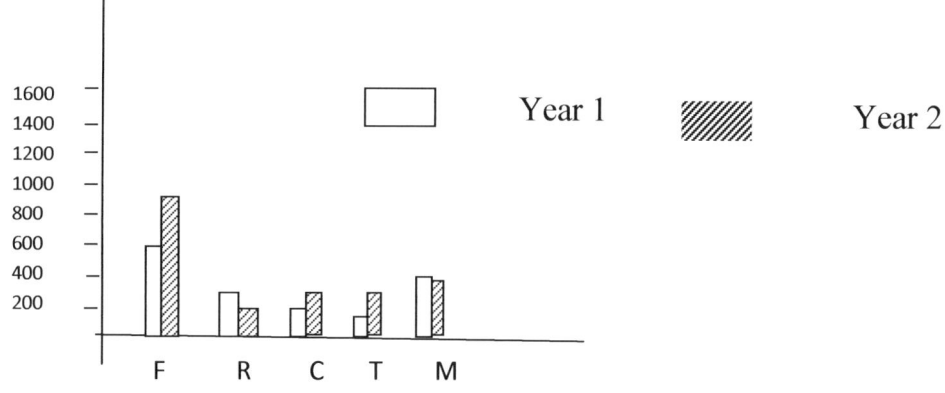

☐ Year 1   ▨ Year 2

(*iv*) **Line Graph:** This is one in which the bars of a bar chart are replaced by a single line.

(*v*) **Frequency:** This is the number of times a particular data occurs

(*vi*) **Frequency Distribution:** This is a table used for reducing a large data into quantities that can be handled using how often they occur e.g.

0, 1, 0, 2, 1, 2, 1, 1, 2, 2, 1, 2, 2 can be represented as:

x	0	1	2
f	2	5	6

(*vii*) **Histogram:** This is a graphical representation of tabulated frequencies shown as adjacent rectangles or square erected over discrete intervals with an area proportional to the frequency of the observation

For an ungrouped data: the quantities are plotted directly against the frequency.

For a grouped data: the bars are drawn with the frequency against the class mark or class upper limits. e.g.

Number of goal	0	1	2	3	4
Frequencies	8	12	14	10	5

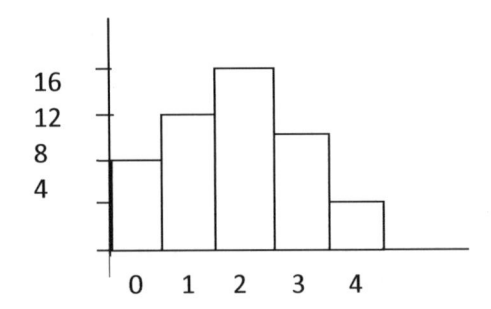

Measures of central tendencies

Is the tendency of a quantitative data to cluster around some central value. The most common measures of central tendency are the mean, median and the mode.

MEAN

This is the sum of a collection of numbers divided by the numbers in the collection. It is given by the following

(**1**) In the absence of frequency $\bar{x} = \frac{\sum x}{N}$

(**2**) In the presence of frequency $\bar{x} = \frac{\sum Fx}{\sum F}$

(**3**) In the presence of assumed mean $\bar{x} = \frac{\sum Fd}{\sum F} + A$

A = assumed value, d = deviation and d = x - A

Advantages of the mean

(1) It is unique as it exist always.

(2) It is easy to understood.

(3) It can be determined without arrangement.

(4) It has the least deviation from the elements in a data.

Disadvantages of the mean

(1) It is affected by extreme values.

(2) It is sensitive to changes.

(3) It cannot be determined without calculation.

MEDIAN

This is the middle score of a data when the data is arranged in ascending or descending order. It is given by the following

(i) In the absence of frequency and total numbers is even:

$$\text{Median} = \frac{\text{sum of two middle numbers}}{2}$$

(ii) In the absence of frequency and total numbers is odd: Median = middle number

In order to determine the median, the median position is first determined.

(iii) In the presence of frequency: we first determine the median position

Median position is given by $\left[\frac{N+1}{2}\right]$th

(iv) From a grouped data: $\dfrac{L_m + \left[\frac{N}{2} - CF_b\right]i}{F}$

L_m = Lower class boundary of the median class.

CF_b = Cumulative frequency before the median class.

N = total frequency, i = class interval, F = frequency of the median class

Note: The answer gotten should fall within the range of the median class.

(v) From a histogram: is found as a point on the horizontal axis where the bars of the histogram are divided into two parts. This is found as the bar that occupies the median position when the frequencies of the bars drawn are added or cumulated

Advantages of the median

(1) It is unique as it exist always.

(2) It is easy to compute.

(3) It is not affected by extreme values.

Disadvantages of the median

(1) It does not involve all the elements in a the data.

Quartiles

These are obtained when we divide the cumulative frequency curve into quarters. The value at the lower quarter is referred to as the lower quartile, the value at the middle gives the median and the value at the upper quarter is the upper quartile.

If N = cumulative frequency

Lower quartile = $\left[\dfrac{N+1}{4}\right]$

Upper quartile = $3\left[\dfrac{N+1}{4}\right]$

Inter quartile range → Upper quartile – lower quartile = $Q_3 - Q_1$

Semi inter quartile range → $\dfrac{Q_3 - Q_1}{2}$

Deciles

These are obtained when we divide a data into ten.

$\dfrac{1}{10}$ of a data is called first Decile = D_1

$\dfrac{3}{10}$ of a data is called third Decile = D_3

$\dfrac{5}{10} = \dfrac{1}{2}$ of a data is called fifth Decile = Median

Percentile

These are obtained when we divide a data into hundred.

$\dfrac{1}{100}$ of a data is called first percentile = P_1

$\frac{2}{100}$ of a data is called second percentile = P_2

$\frac{50}{100} = \frac{1}{2}$ of a data is called fifty percentile = P_{50} = $median$

Mode

This is the most frequent element in a data.

(1) From an ungrouped data, it is taken as the number with the highest frequency

(2) From a grouped data, it is obtained from

$$L_m + \left(\frac{\Delta_1}{\Delta_1 + \Delta_2}\right)i$$

L_m = Lower class boundary of the modal class.

f_m = frequency of the modal class

Δ_1 = Change between frequencies of the modal class and the one before it i.e $f_m - f_b$

Δ_2 = Change between frequencies of the modal class and the one above it i.e $f_m - f_a$

i = Class interval

(3) From a histogram: Here we join the edges of the tallest bar alternatively to the ones on both sides and tracing the point of intersection to the horizontal axis.

Advantages of the mode

(1) It is easy to understand.

(2) It is easy to determine.

(3) It can be located graphically.

(4) It can be useful for qualitative data.

Disadvantages of the mode

(1) It is not well defined.

(2) It is not based on all the values.

Measures of Dispersion

This is a measure of the spread of a data about the mean. It includes..

(1) Range: This is the difference between the smallest and the greatest number in a data.

Range = Greatest - Lowest

Mean deviation: This is the average of the set of distance between the element in a data and the mean. It is found by treating all the distances as though, they were positive ignoring, the sign of the negative distances.

$$\bar{d} = \frac{\sum |(x-\bar{x})|}{N}$$

Variance

This is the average of the squared distances of mean from the elements in a data.

(1) For a group data it is given by $\frac{\sum d^2}{N-1} = \frac{\sum (x-\bar{x})^2}{N-1}$

(2) For ungrouped data it is given by $\frac{\sum d^2}{N} = \frac{\sum (x-\bar{x})^2}{N}$

(3) In the presence of frequency it is given by $\left(\frac{\sum fx^2}{\sum f}\right) - \left(\frac{\sum fx}{\sum f}\right)^2$

Standard deviation

This is the positive square of the variance.

Mathematically, $S.D = k\sqrt{V} \rightarrow k = \frac{S.D}{V} \therefore \frac{S.D_1}{\sqrt{V_1}} = \frac{S.D_2}{\sqrt{V_2}}$

(1) For a group data it is given by $\sqrt{V} = \sqrt{\frac{\sum (x-\bar{x})^2}{N-1}}$

(2) For ungrouped data it is given by $\sqrt{V} = \sqrt{\frac{\Sigma d^2}{N}} = \sqrt{\frac{\Sigma(x-\bar{x})^2}{N}}$

(**38.1**). Find the mean deviation of the set of numbers 4, 5, 9

Solution

$\bar{x} = \frac{\Sigma x}{N} \rightarrow \frac{4+5+9}{3} \rightarrow \frac{18}{9} = 6$

Mean deviation $= \Sigma \frac{|d|}{N} \rightarrow \frac{|4-6|+|5+6|+|9-6|}{3} \rightarrow \frac{2+1+3}{3} = \frac{6}{3} = 2$

(**38.2**).

Score	1	2	4	5	6
Frequency	3	3	4	5	5

Find the mean deviation of the scores in the table above

Solution

x	f	fx
1	3	3
2	3	6
4	4	16
5	5	25
6	5	30

d = x - $\bar{x}$	Fd
3.0	9.0
2.0	6.0
0.0	0.0
1.0	5.0
2.0	10.0

$\bar{x} = \frac{\Sigma fx}{\Sigma f} = \frac{80}{20} = 4.0$

$mean\ deviation = \frac{\Sigma fd}{\Sigma f} = \frac{30.0}{20} = 1.50$

(**38.3**). Calculate the mean deviation of the data shown below

No. of tomatoes	21 - 25	26 - 30	31 – 35	36 - 40	41 – 45
No. of baskets	10	12	5	4	2

Solution

Reproducing the table

x	x_m	f	fx	$\bar{x}$	x - $\bar{x}$	fd
21 – 25	23	10	230	$\bar{x} = \frac{\Sigma fx}{\Sigma f}$	6.4	64
26 – 30	28	12	336	$\bar{x} = \frac{969}{33}$	1.4	16.8
31 – 35	33	5	165		3.6	18.0
36 – 40	38	4	152	$\bar{x} = 29.4$	8.6	34.4
41 – 45	43	2	86		13.6	27.2
		33	969			160.4

Mean deviation = $\frac{160.4}{33}$ = 4.86

(38.4). If the mean of the number 0, x + 2, 3x + 6, and 4x + 8 is 4. Find their mean deviation.

Solution

$\bar{x} = \frac{0 + (x+2) + (3x+6) + (4x+8)}{4} = 4 \rightarrow \frac{8x+16}{4} = 4 \rightarrow 8x + 16 = 16 \therefore x = 0$

Mean deviation = $\frac{|0-4| + |2-4| + |6-4| + |8-4|}{4} \rightarrow \frac{4+2+2+4}{4} = \frac{12}{4} = 3$

(38.5). Find the variance of 3, 5, 7, 9, 11.

Solution

Variance = $\frac{\Sigma d^2}{N} \rightarrow \frac{\Sigma(x-\bar{x})^2}{N} \rightarrow \frac{\Sigma x^2}{N} - \Sigma\left(\frac{x}{N}\right)^2$

$\Sigma x^2 = 9 + 25 + 49 + 81 + 121 = 284$

Variance = $\frac{285}{5} - \left(\frac{35}{5}\right)^2 \rightarrow 57 - (7)^2 \rightarrow 57 - 49 = 8$

(38.6).

x	1	2	3	4	5
f	2	1	2	1	2

Find the variance of the frequency distribution above.

Solution

With frequency present

x	1	2	3	4	5
f	2	1	2	1	2
x^2	1	4	9	16	25
fx	2	2	6	4	10

$\sum fx = 24, \sum fx^2 = 90, \sum f = 8$

Variance $= \left(\frac{\sum fx^2}{\sum f}\right) - \left(\frac{\sum fx}{\sum f}\right)^2 \rightarrow \frac{(90)}{8} - \left(\frac{24}{8}\right)^2 \rightarrow \frac{90}{8} - (3)^2 \rightarrow \frac{90}{8} - 9$

$\frac{90 - 72}{8} = \frac{18}{8} = \frac{9}{4}$

(38.7). If the scores of 3 students in a test are 5, 6, and 7. Find the standard deviation of their scores.

Solution

$S.D = \sqrt{V} = \sqrt{\frac{\sum fx^2}{\sum f} - \left(\frac{\sum fx}{\sum f}\right)^2}$

$\sum x^2 = 5^2 + 6^2 + 7^2 = 25 + 36 + 49 = 110$

$\sum x = 5 + 6 + 7 = 18$

$S.D = \sqrt{\frac{110}{3} - \left(\frac{18}{3}\right)^2} \rightarrow \sqrt{\frac{110}{3} - \frac{324}{9}} \rightarrow \sqrt{\frac{320 + 324}{9}} \rightarrow \sqrt{\frac{6}{9}} = \sqrt{\frac{2}{3}}$

(38.8). Find the positive value of x if the standard deviation of the number 1, x + 1, 2x + 1, is $\sqrt{6}$

Solution

$S.D = \sqrt{\frac{\sum x^2}{N} - (\bar{x})^2} = \sqrt{6}$

$$\bar{x} = \frac{\Sigma x}{N} \to \frac{1 + (x+1) + (2x+1)}{3} \to \frac{3 + 3x}{3} = 1 + x$$

$$\frac{\Sigma x^2}{N} = \frac{1 + (x+1)^2 + (2+1)^2}{3}$$

Squaring both sides $\frac{\Sigma x^2}{N} - (\bar{x})^2 = 6 \to \frac{1 + (x+1)^2 + (2+1)^2}{3} - (x+1)^2 = 6$

$$\frac{1 + (x^2 + 2x + 1) + (4x^2 + 4 + 1)}{3} - (1 + 2x + x^2) = 6$$

$$1 + x^2 + 2x + 1 + 4x^2 + 4x + 1 - 3 - 6x - 3x^2 = 18$$

$$x^2 + 4x^2 - 3x^2 + 2x + 4x - 6x + 1 + 1 + 1 - 3 = 18$$

$$2x^2 = 18 \to x^2 = 9 \therefore x = 3$$

(38.9).

Class	1 – 3	4 – 6	7 – 9
Frequency	5	8	5

Find the standard deviation of the data using the table above.

Solution

Class	1 – 3	4 – 6	7 – 9
Frequency	5	8	5
x	2	5	8
fx	10	40	40

Where x = class mark i.e $\frac{1+3}{2}, \frac{4+6}{2}, \frac{7+9}{2}$

$$\Sigma f = 5 + 8 + 5 = 18$$

$$\Sigma f x^2 = (5 \times 2^2) + (8 \times 5^2) + (5 \times 8^2) \to 20 + 200 + 320 = 540$$

$$\Sigma f x = (5 \times 2) + (8 \times 2) + (5 \times 8) \to 10 + 40 + 40 = 90$$

$$S.D = \sqrt{\frac{\Sigma fx^2}{\Sigma f} - \left(\frac{\Sigma fx}{\Sigma f}\right)^2} \to \sqrt{\frac{540}{18} - \left(\frac{90}{18}\right)^2} \to \sqrt{30 - 5^2} \to \sqrt{30 - 25} = \sqrt{5}$$

(38.10). Calculate the variance of the following quantities (x – 2), (x + 1), (x + 2) and (x + 3)

Solution

$$\frac{\Sigma x^2}{N} = \frac{(2)^2 + 1^2 + 2^2 + 3^2}{4} = \frac{18}{4} = 4\frac{1}{2}$$

$$\frac{\Sigma x}{N} = \frac{-2 + 1 + 2 + 3}{4} = \frac{4}{4} = 1$$

$$V = \left(\frac{\Sigma fx^2}{\Sigma f}\right) - \left(\frac{\Sigma fx}{\Sigma f}\right)^2 \rightarrow 4\frac{1}{2} - 1^2 \rightarrow = 3\frac{1}{2}$$

(38.11). Find the variance of the numbers, k, k + 1, k + 2

Solution

$$\bar{x} = \frac{k + 1 + k + 2 + k + 3}{3} \rightarrow \frac{3k + 3}{3} \rightarrow k + 1$$

$$(x - \bar{x}) \rightarrow k - (k + 1) + k + 1 - (k + 1) + k + 2 - (k + 1) = -1, 0 \text{ and } 1$$

$$variance(\sigma) = \frac{\Sigma(x - \bar{x})^2}{N} \rightarrow \frac{(-1)^2 + (0)^2 + (1)^2}{3} \rightarrow \frac{2}{3}$$

(38.12). The table below gives the distribution of scores of 80 students.

Scores	10 – 19	20 – 29	30 – 39	40 – 49	50 – 59
No. of students	4	20	28	16	12

(38.13). What is the lower class boundary of the fifth class?

Solution

Lower class boundary = average of lower limit and the preceding upper limit.

Fifth class = 50 – 59

Lower class boundary = $\frac{49 + 50}{2}$ = 49.5

(38.14).

Marks Interval	1 – 5	6 – 10	11 - 15	16 – 20	21 – 25
Frequency	2	4	12	8	4

What is the upper boundary of the fifth class?

Solution

Fifth class = 21 – 25

Lower boundary → $\frac{20 + 21}{2} = \frac{41}{2} = 20.5$

With the boundary increasing by 0.5

Upper boundary = 25.5

(38.15).

Height (cm)	Number of students
155 – 159	5
160 – 164	6
165 – 169	10
170 – 174	8
175 – 179	6
180 - 184	5

Using the information above what is the upper class limit of the second class.

Solution

Second class is 160 – 164. Upper class limit is 164

(38.16). Using the information above determine the class boundaries of the fourth class

Solution

Fourth class is 170 -174

lower classs boundary $= \frac{169 + 170}{2} = 169.5$

upper class boundary $= \frac{174 + 175}{2} = 174.5$

The class boundaries are 169.5 – 174.5

(38.17).

Marks	30 – 39	40 – 49	50 – 59	60 – 69	70 – 79
Frequency	1	8	15	19	7

Using the information above what is the lower class boundary of the modal class.

Solution

Modal class = class with highest frequency i.e 60 – 69

Lower class boundary $= \frac{59+60}{2} = 59.5$

(38.18). What is the class mark of the median class

Solution

Marks	30 – 39	40 – 49	50 – 59	60 – 69	70 – 79
Frequency	1	8	15	19	7
CF	1	9	24	43	50

$CF = 50, \frac{1}{2}CF = 25$

Median class is class with cumulative frequency of 25 i.e 60 – 69

Class mark = class average $= \frac{60 + 69}{2} = \frac{129}{2} = 64.5$

(38.19).

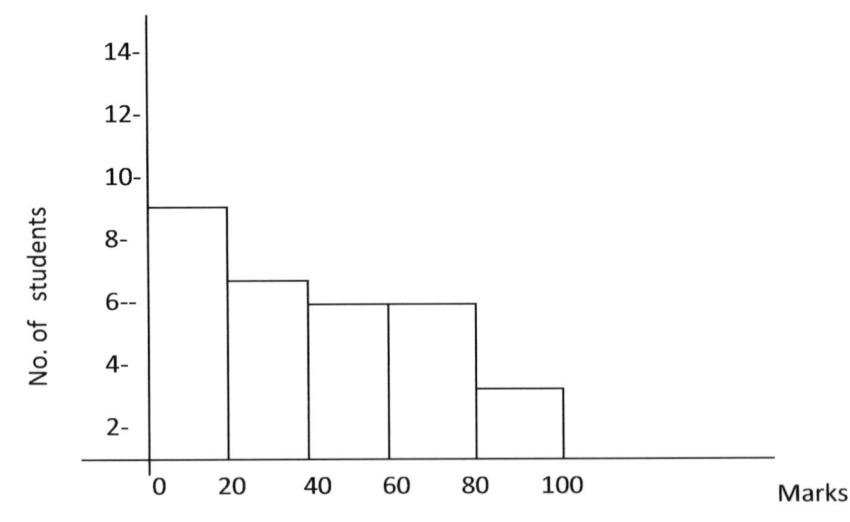

In a class of 30 students, the mark scored in an examination are displayed in the following histogram. What percentage of the students scored more than 40%.

Solution

Those that scored more than 40% are those that scored 40 – 60, 60 – 80 and 80 – 100.

From the diagram we have 6 + 6 + 2 = 14 students

Percentage → $\frac{14}{30}$ x 100 = $46\frac{2}{3}$%

(38.20).

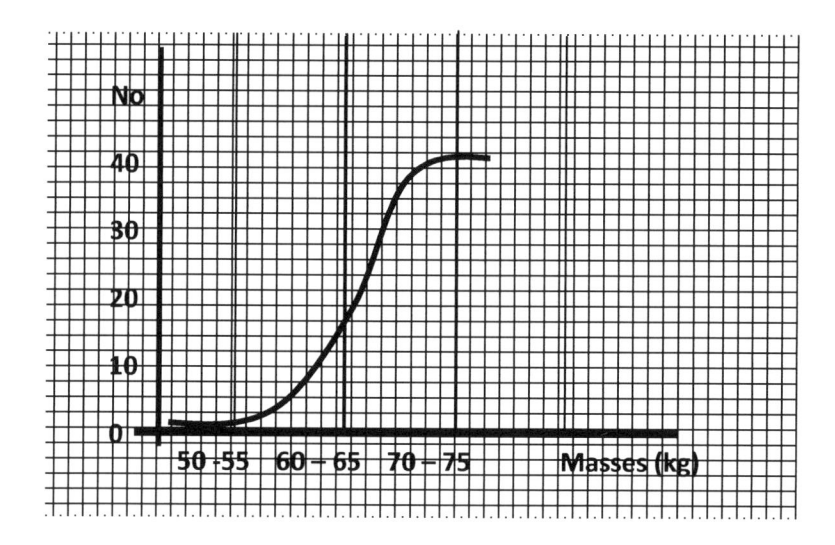

The graph shows a cumulative frequency curve of a distribution of masses of 40 students in a class. Find the 80th percentile.

Solution

$\Sigma f = 40$

80th percentile position = $\frac{80}{100}$ (40) = 32

Tracing this from the vertical axis to the horizontal axis as shown below.

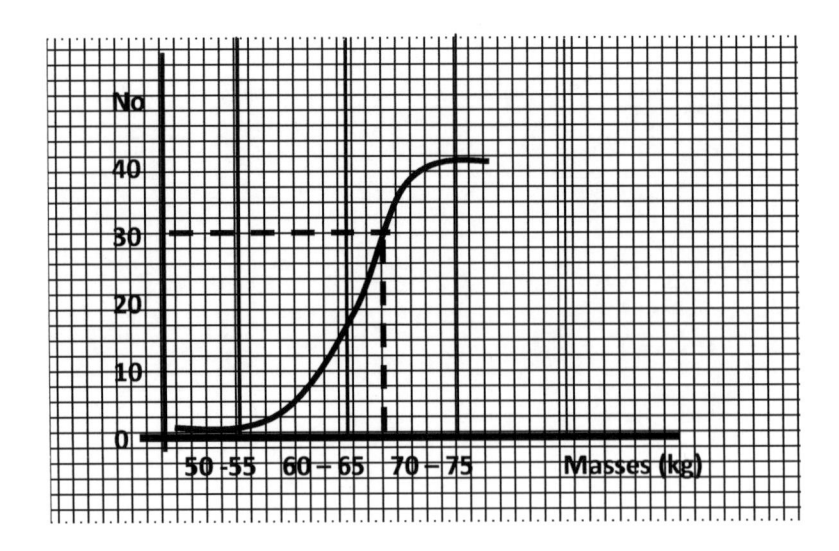

80th percentile $= 65 + 2 = 67$kg

(**38.21**). The cumulative frequency function of the data below is given by the equation $y = cf(x)$. What is $cf(5)$?

Scores (n)	Frequency (f)
3	30
4	32
5	30
6	35
8	20

Solution

Scores	Frequency	Cf
3	30	30
4	32	62
5	30	92
6	35	127
8	20	147

$Cf(5) = 92$

(38.22). Below are the scores of a group of students in music test

Scores	1	2	3	4	5	6	7	8	9
No of students	3	6	10	8	6	5	2	4	12

If $Cf(x)$ is the number of students with scores less than or equal to x, find $Cf(6)$

Solution

Scores	F	Cf
1	3	3
2	6	9
3	10	19
4	8	27
5	6	33
6	5	38
7	2	40
8	4	44
9	12	46

$Cf(6) = 38$

(38.23). Find $Cf(2) + Cf(6)$ if the cumulative frequency function of the data below is given by the equation $m = Cf(n)$

Scores	2	3	4	5	6	7
Frequency	2	15	10	5	20	10

Solution

$Cf(2) = 2$, $Cf(6) = 2 + 15 + 10 + 5 + 20 = 52$

$Cf(2) + Cf(6) = 2 + 52 = 54$

(38.24). Marks scored by some children in an arithmetic test are 5, 3, 6, 9, 4, 7, 8, 6, 2, 7, 8, 4, 5, 2, 1, 0, 6, 9, 0, 8 The arithmetic mean of the mark is?

Solution

$\bar{x} = \frac{\Sigma x}{N} \rightarrow \frac{5+3+6+9+4+7+8+6+2+7+8+4+5+2+1+0+6+9+0+8}{20} = \frac{100}{20} = 5$

(38.25).

x	1	2	3	4	5
f	y + 2	y - 1	2y - 3	y + 4	3y - 4

The table above shows the frequency distribution of a data. If the mean is $\frac{43}{14}$, find y.

Solution

x	1	2	3	4	5
f	y + 2	y - 1	2y - 3	y + 4	3y - 4
fx	y + 2	2y - 2	6y - 9	4y + 16	15y – 2y

In the presence of frequency

$\bar{x} = \frac{\Sigma Fx}{\Sigma F} \rightarrow \frac{43}{14} = \frac{28y - 13}{8y - 2} \rightarrow 14(28y - 13) = 43(8y - 2) \rightarrow 392y - 182 = 344y - 86$

$392y - 344y = 182 - 86 \rightarrow 48y = 96 \quad \therefore y = 2$

(38.26). The median of the set of number 4, 9, 4, 13, 17, 14, 10, 17 is ?

Solution
Arranging the numbers, we have

4, 4, 7, 9, 10, 13, 14, 17

Median $= \frac{9 + 10}{2} = \frac{19}{2}$

(38.27). Find the median of the numbers:

110, 116, 113, 119, 118, 127, 118, 117 and 113

Solution

Arranging the numbers in order, we have 110, 113, 113, 116, 117, 118, 118. 119. 127

Counting equal numbers from the left and right, median = 117

(38.28). What is the median of the distribution below

Speed	0	1	2	3	4	5	6	7	8	9	10
Freq	4	6	6	5	9	10	2	3	3	5	1

Solution

Speed	0	1	2	3	4	5	6	7	8	9	10
Freq	4	6	6	5	9	10	2	3	3	5	1
CF	4	10	16	21	30	40	42	45	48	53	54

Median position is given by $\left[\frac{N+1}{2}\right]$th $\rightarrow \left[\frac{54+1}{2}\right] = 27.5$ th

27.5 th position is between 27th & 28th which corresponds to 4

∴ median = 4

(38.29). Find the median of the distribution given below :

x	1	2	3	4	5	6	7	8	9
f	1	2	2	1	2	2	1	3	1

Solution

x	1	2	3	4	5	6	7	8	9
f	1	2	2	1	2	2	1	3	1
CF	1	3	5	6	8	10	11	14	15

Median position is given by $\left[\frac{N+1}{2}\right]$th $\rightarrow \left[\frac{15+1}{2}\right] = 8th\ position$

8th position corresponds to 5

∴ median = 5

(38.30).

Class	Frequency
1 – 5	2
6 – 10	4
11 – 15	5
16 – 20	2
21 – 25	3
26 – 30	2
31 – 35	1
36 – 40	1

Find the median of the observation in the table

Solution

For a grouped data: median is given by $\dfrac{L_m + \left[\frac{N}{2} - CF_b\right]i}{F}$

The class marks is gotten from $\dfrac{1+5}{2}$, $\dfrac{6+10}{2}$

$N = 20, F = \dfrac{1}{2}(20) = 10$

The median class = 11 – 15, The lower class boundary $L_1 = \dfrac{10 + 11}{2} = 10.5$

Cumulative frequency before the median class, $CF_b = 2 + 4 = 6$

Frequency of median class, $F_m = 5$, Class interval i = 6 – 1, or 10 – 5 = 5

Substituting gives $10.5 + \dfrac{(10 - 6)}{5} \times 5 = 14.5$

And it falls with the range (11 – 15)

(38.31).

Class interval	1 – 5	6 – 10	11 – 15	16 – 20	21 – 25
Frequency	6	15	20	7	2

Estimate the median of the frequency distribution

Solution

N = 50, Median class = ½(50) = 25th position i.e 11 – 15

L_1 = 10.5, CF_b = 6 + 15 = 21

Median = $10.5 + \frac{(25-21)}{20} \times 5$ → $10.5 + \frac{4}{4}$ → 10.5 + 1 = 11.5

Which falls within the range (11 – 15)

(38.32).

Class	10 – 14	15 – 19	20 – 24	25 – 29	30 – 34	35 – 39	40 – 49
Freq	4	10	12	12	8	6	2

Calculate the median score of the grouped frequency distribution shown in the table above.

Solution

N = 54, F = ½ (54) = 27 which is the 25 – 29 class when the CF is added to the table.

$L_1 = \frac{24+25}{2} = 24.5$, $Cf_b = 4 + 10 + 12 = 26$

Median = $24.5 = \frac{(27-26)}{12} \times 5$ → 24.5 + 0.417 = 24.91

Which does not fall within the range of the median class (25 – 29).

F is calculated from $\frac{1}{2}(N+1)$ → $\frac{1}{2}(54+1) = 27.5$

Median → $24.5 + \frac{(27.5-26)}{12} \times 5$ → $24.5 + \frac{7.5}{12}$ → 24.5 + 0.624 = 25.125

(38.33).

x	1 -10	11 – 20	21 – 30	31 - 40	41 – 60
f	5	8	15	12	7

Find the median of the distribution

Solution

N = 47   F = ½(N + 1) → ½(47 + 1) = 24

Median position = class with Cf = 24 i.e 21 – 30

Median = $20.5 + \frac{(24-13)}{15} \times 10 \rightarrow 20.5 + \frac{11}{15} \times 10 = 20.5 + 7.31 = 27.83$

(38.34).

The table below gives the ages of students in a university

Age	31 - 35	36 - 40	41 - 45	46 - 50	51 - 55	56 – 60
frequency	5	16	7	8	10	9

Find the median of the distribution.

Solution

$N = 55, F = ½(N + 1) \rightarrow ½(55 + 1) = 28$

If a cumulative frequency is added to the table above, 28 is with 41 – 45

Median class = 41 – 45

(38.35). The weights of 30 new born babies are given as follows:

6,9,5,7,6,7,5,8,9,5,7,5,8,7,8,7,5,6,5,7,6,9,9,7,8,8,7,8,9,8 The mode is

Solution

x	5	6	7	8	9
f	6	4	8	7	5

Mode = 7

(38.36).

Score	3	4	5	6	7
Frequency	1	5	4	2	1

The table above gives the distribution of scores obtained by thirteen candidates in a test find the mode.

Solution   Mode = 4

(38.37).

Weight (g)	0 - 10	10 – 20	20 - 30	30 – 40	40 – 50
No of counts	10	27	19	6	2

Estimate the mode of the frequency distribution above.

Solution

Class interval = $(10 – 0)$ or $(20 – 10) = 10$

Modal class is the class with the highest frequency = 10 – 20

$L_m = \frac{10+10}{2} = 10$

$Mode = L_m + \left(\frac{\Delta_1}{\Delta_1+\Delta_2}\right)i \rightarrow 10 + \left(\frac{(27-10)}{(27-10)+(27-19)}\right) \times 10 \rightarrow 10 + \frac{17 \times 10}{(17+8)}$

$10 + \frac{170}{25} = 10 + 6.8 = 16.8g$

(38.38).

Class interval	Frequency	Class boundaries	Class m.p
1.5 – 1.9	2	1.45 – 1.95	1.7
2.0 – 2.4	1	1.95 – 2.45	2.2
2.5 – 2.9	4	2.45 – 2.95	2.7
3.0 – 3.4	15	2.95 – 3.45	3.2
3.5 – 3.9	10	3.45 – 3.95	3.7
4.0 – 4.4	5	3.95 – 4.45	4.2
4.5 – 4.9	3	4.45 – 4.95	4.7

Use the table above find the mode of the distribution.

Solution

Difference between corresponding limit $\rightarrow 2 - 1.5 = 0.5$

Modal class = $(3.0 – 3.4)$

$$Mode = L_m + \left(\frac{\Delta_1}{\Delta_1+\Delta_2}\right)i \rightarrow 2.95 + \left(\frac{15-4}{(15-4)+(15-10)}\right) \times 0.5 \rightarrow 2.95 + \left(\frac{11}{16}\right) \times 0.5$$

$2.95 + 1.375 = 4.4$

(38.39). The median of the distribution is?

Solution

N = 40, F = ½(40) = 20 i.e class (3.0 – 3.4)

Median $= 2.95 + \frac{(13)}{15} 0.5 = 2.95 + 0.43 = 3.38$

(38.40). In a soccer competition in one season, a club had the following goals, 2, 0, 3, 3, 2, 1,4,0,0,5,1,0,2,2,1,3,1,4,1 and 1

The mean, median and mode are respectively?

Solution

x	0	1	2	3	4	5
f	4	6	4	3	2	1

$$\bar{x} = \frac{\Sigma fx}{\Sigma f} \rightarrow \frac{(0 \times 4) + (1 \times 6) + (2 \times 4) + (3 \times 3) + (4 \times 2) + (5 \times 1)}{4+6+4+3+2+1} = \frac{36}{20} = 1.8$$

$N = 20$

$F = \frac{1}{2}(N+1) = ½(20+1) = 10.5$

Median is the value of x between 10th and 11th position i.e $\frac{1+2}{2} = 1.5$

Mode = 1

mean, median and mode are respectively 1.8, 1.5 and 1

(38.41). For the set of numbers 2, 3, 5, 6, 7, 7, 8. The mean, median and mode are respectively?

Solution

For number 2, 3, 5, 6, 7, 7, 8

$$\overline{X} = \frac{\sum x}{N} = \frac{2+5+6+7+7+8}{7} = \frac{38}{7} = 5.4$$

Median = 6, Mode = 7

mean, median and mode are respectively 5.4, 6 and 7

(38.42). The scores of 16 students in mathematics tests are

65 65 55 60 60 65 60 70 75 70 65 70 60 65 65 70

The sum of the median and modal score is?

Solution

x	55	60	65	70	75
f	1	4	6	4	1

mode = 65

N = 16

Median position → ½(16 + 1) = 8.5th position

If CF is added to the table above number occupying the 8th and 9th position = 65

sum of median and mode = 65 + 65 = 130

(38.43).

Score	0 - 9	10 - 19	20 - 29	30 – 39	40 - 49	50 – 59
freq	35	83	98	75	44	25

From the table above. how many students made a score of 30 and above?

Solution

Students that made score of 30 = 75 + 44 + 25 = 144

(**38.44**). The bar chart below shows the marks out of 10 obtained by a class of students.

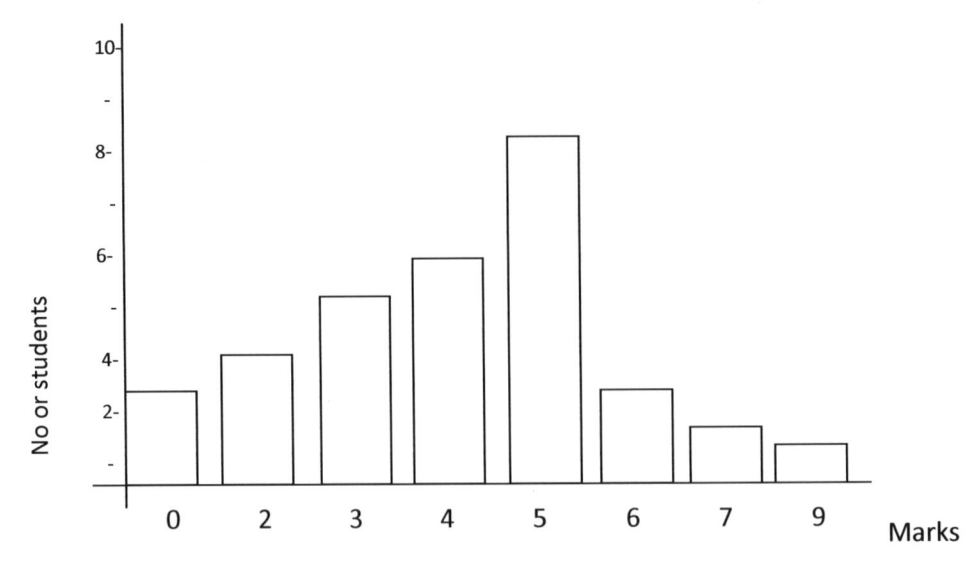

Using the bar chart above how many student took the test ?

Solution

Number of students that took the test = sum of the frequency

$3 + 4 + 6 + 7 + 9 + 3 + 2 + 1 = 35$

(**38.45**). Using the bar chart above what is the modal mark?

Solution

Modal mark is the mark of the highest bar in the chart = 5

(**38.46**). Calculate the mean mark for the test.

Solution

$$\bar{X} = \frac{\Sigma fx}{\Sigma f} = \frac{140}{35} = 4$$

(**38.47**). How many students scored less than half marks?

Solution

Mark out of 10 implies total score is 10.

half marks are those who scored less than 5 marks i.e those that scores 0, 2, 3 and 4 from the chart we have $3 + 4 + 5 + 7 = 20$

(38.48). The shaded and unshaded bars represent the performance of girls and boys respectively in a class test.

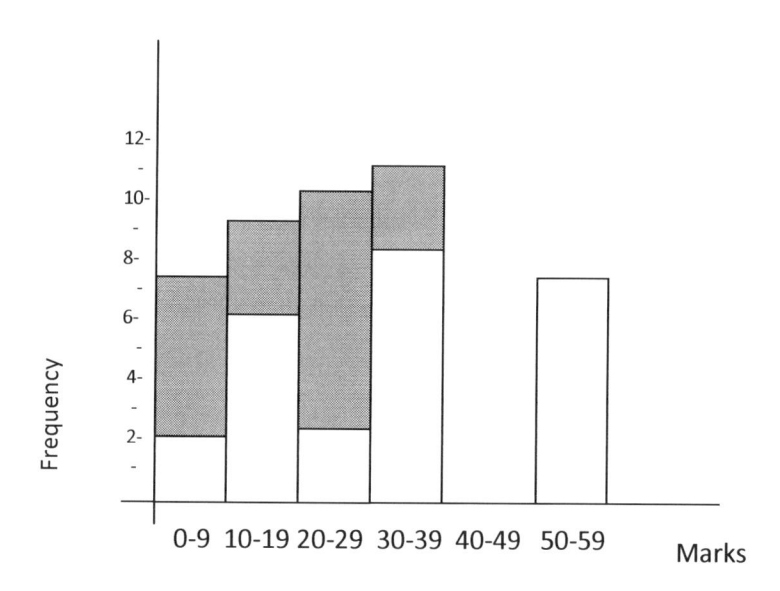

Using the chart above find the number of students who took the test.

Solution

Number of students that took the test = sum of the frequency

$7 + 9 + 10 + 11 + 8 = 45$

(38.49). If the pass mark is 30, find the ratio of the number of girls who failed to the number of boys who passed the test

Solution

Number of girls that failed = height of shaded bars before 30 – 39

No. of girls that failed = $(7 - 2) + (9 - 6) + (10 - 4) = 5 + 3 + 6 = 14$

Number of boys that passed = heights of unshaded bars after 20 – 29

Number of boys that passed = $8 + 8 = 16$

∴ Ratio of girls that failed to the boys that passed is $\frac{14}{16} = \frac{7}{8}$

(38.50). The histogram gives the distribution of 100 students according to the scores they obtained in a test

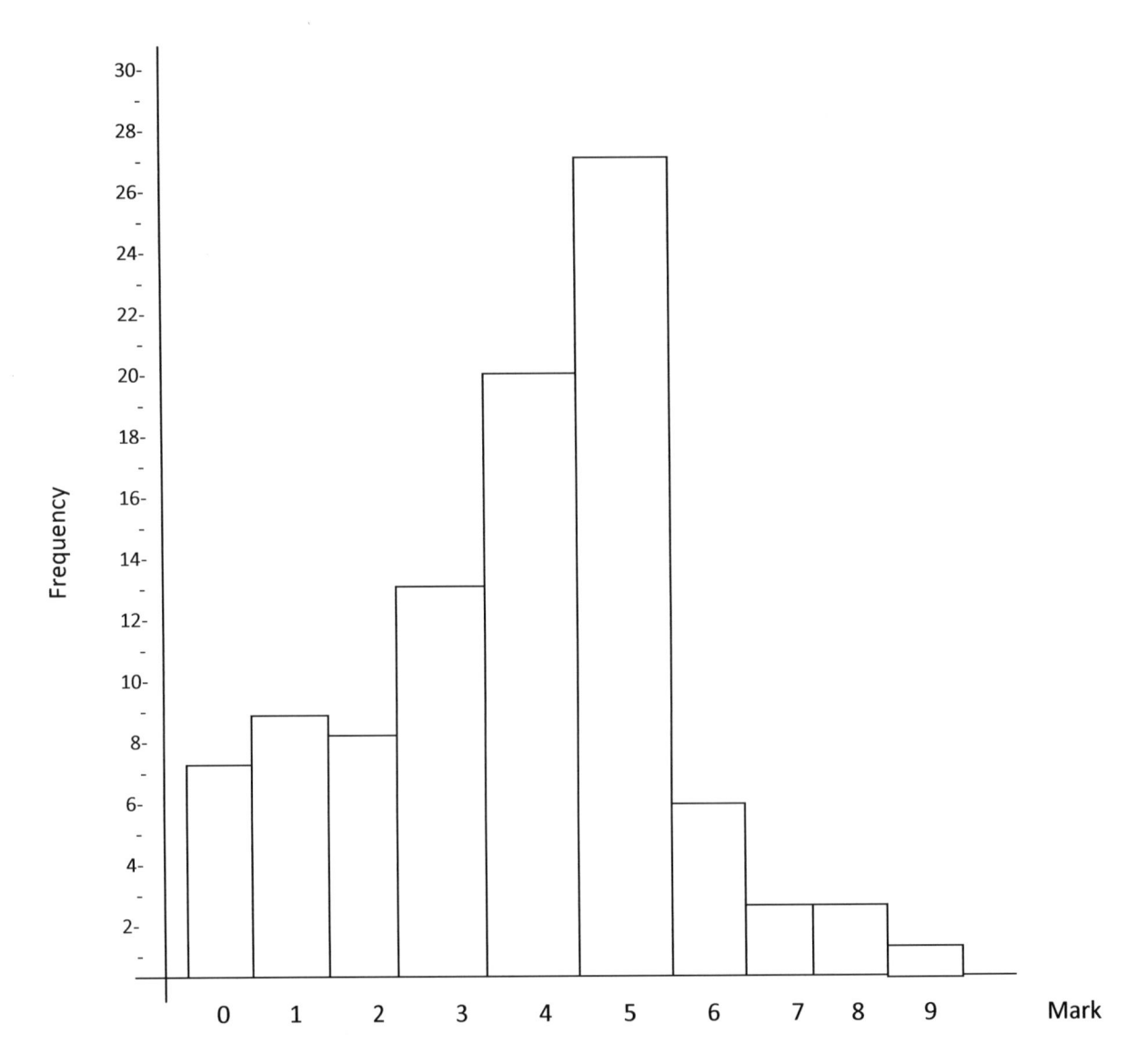

(38.51). What is the median of this distribution.

Solution

Median position = ½(30 + 1) th = 15.5th position i.e 15th and 16th position, a line through 15.5 the frequency axis meets the bar with score 4

Median = 4

(38.52). How many students scored below 4 marks?

Solution

student that scored below 4 marks are students that scores 0,1,2 or 3

These are $7 + 10 + 8 + 13 = 38$

(38.53). If distinction is seven and above, what percentage had distinction?

Solution

Those that had distinction are those that scored, 7, 8, and 9

These are $3 + 3 + 1 = 7$

∴ Percentage of those that had distinction $= \dfrac{7}{100}$

(38.54).

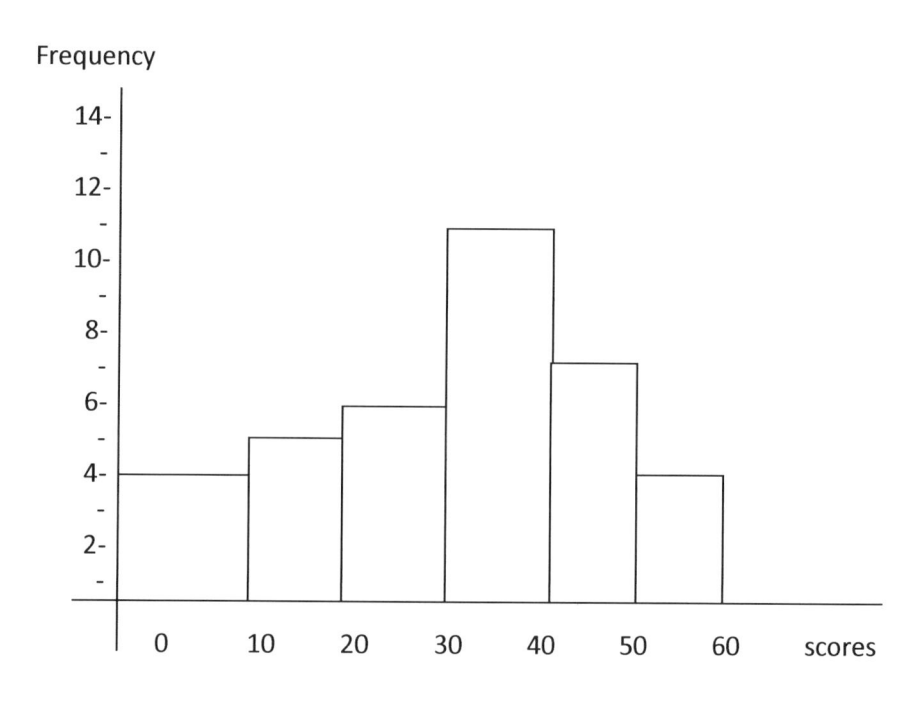

Frequency

```
14-
  -
12-
  -
10-
  -
 8-
  -
 6-
  -
 4-
  -
 2-
  -
    0   10   20   30   40   50   60   scores
```

Use the histogram above to estimate the mode:

Solution

Frequency

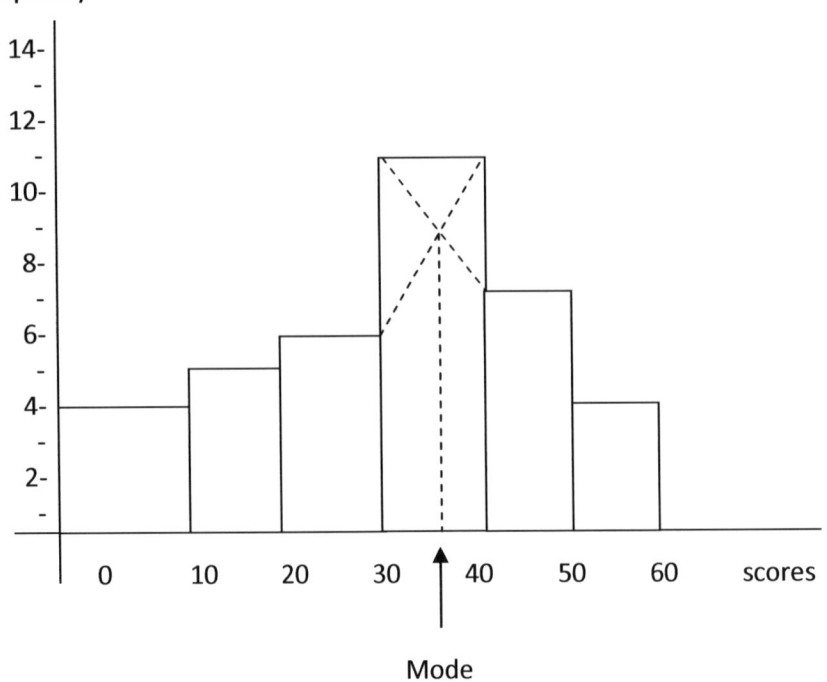

[Histogram with bars showing frequencies 4, 5, 6, 11, 7, 4 across intervals 0-10, 10-20, 20-30, 30-40, 40-50, 50-60. Dashed lines from top corners of tallest bar (30-40) intersect at Mode point between 30 and 40.]

the gap is between 30 and 40

∴ Mode = 30 + 6 = 36

(**38.55**).

Days	350-359	360-369	370-379	380-389	390-399	400-499	410-419	420-429	430-439
Freq	1	3	3	7	12	11	6	5	2
Cf	1	4	7	14	26	37	43	48	50

Estimate the semi-quartile range.

Solution

N = 50

Semi-inter quartile range = $\frac{Q_3 - Q_1}{2}$

1st Quartile position = $\frac{1}{4}$(N) → $\frac{1}{4}$ x 50 = 12.5 i.e (380 - 399)

From the median formula

$Q_1 = 379.5 + \frac{(12.5-7)}{7} \times 10 = 379.5 + \frac{55}{7} = 386.6$

3rd Quartile position $= \frac{3}{4}(N) \rightarrow \frac{3}{4} \times 50 = 37.50$ i.e (410 - 499)

$Q_3 = 409.5 + \frac{(37.5-37)}{6} \times 10 \rightarrow 409.5 + \frac{5}{6} = 410.3$

Substituting,

Semi-inter quartile range $\frac{Q_3 - Q_1}{2} \rightarrow \frac{410.3 - 386.6}{2} = 11.85$

(**38.56**). Find the median of the data shown below:

Centre of interval	60	80	100	120	140	160	180	200	Tot
Frequency	2	5	14	28	25	18	7	1	100

Solution

Centre of interval is the same as class mark which implies it is a grouped data.

class interval i = 80 – 60 or 100 – 80 = 20, $N = 100$

Frequency of median position, F = ½(N) → ½(100) = 50

∴ The median class is the class with mark 140

The lower class boundary $= \frac{120+140}{2} = 130$

Median $= 130 + \frac{(50-49)}{25} \times 20 = 130 + \frac{20}{25}$

Median $= 130 + 0.8 = 130.8$

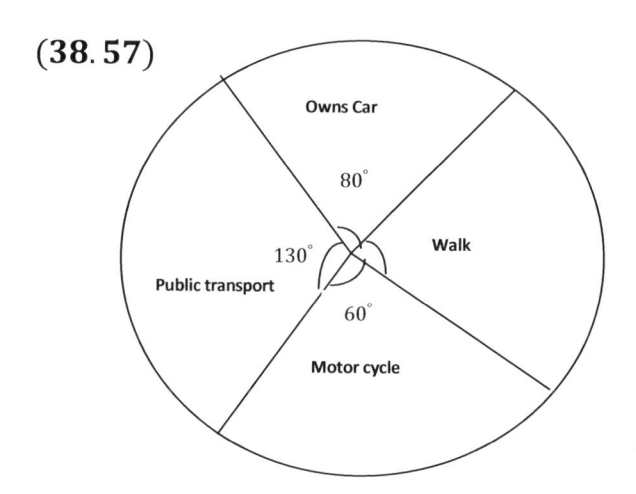

(**38.57**)

581

The pie chart shows the distribution of how 900 workers in a factor go to work.

How many go to work by motor cycle?

Solution

1 revolution = 360

$\frac{60}{360}$ x 900 = 150

(38.58). *U*sing the diagram above what percentage of the workers go to work by public transport?

Solution

1 revolution = 360

$\frac{13}{360}$ x 900 = 325

% of workers → $\frac{x}{100}$ x 900 = 325 ∴ $x = \frac{100 \times 325}{900} = 36\%$

(38.59).

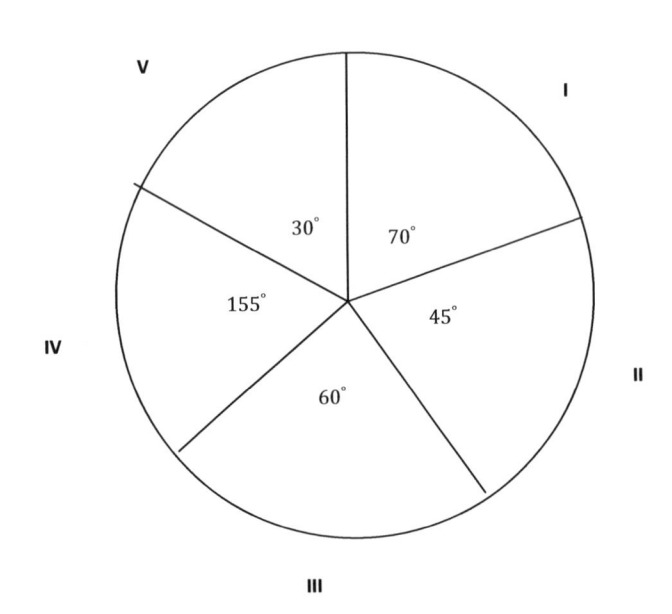

The pie chart shows the distribution of sales by a pharmacist shop during a five day period. If the sales during period II amounts to $135. What was the value of the sales during period IV.

Solution

Applying ratio

$\frac{45}{155} = \frac{135}{x} \rightarrow 45x = 155 \times 135 \therefore x = \$465$

(**38.60**). If the combined sales during period II and period IV is $600. Find the total sales of the day.

Solution

II + IV = 155 + 55 = 200

$360 = \$x \rightarrow x = \frac{600 \times 360}{200} = \$1,080$

200 = $600

(**38.61**).

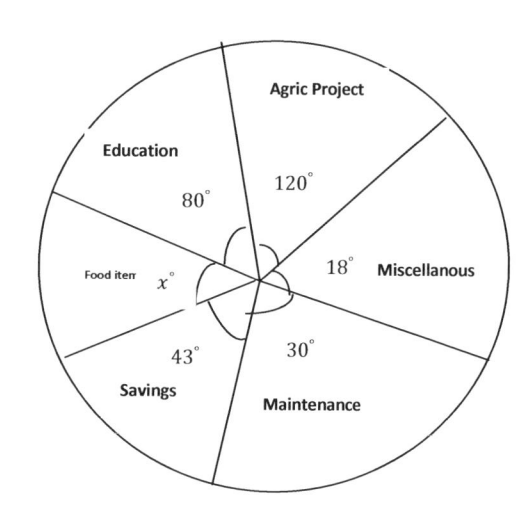

Mr Jamiu Mohammed annual salary was $12000. He spent it on education, agricultural project, savings, food item, maintenance and miscellaneous as shown in the chart above. How much did he spend on food item.

Solution

$x° + 80° + 120° + 18° + 30° + 43° = 360° \rightarrow x = 360 - 291 = 69°$

(**38.62**). How much money did he spent on agricultural project?

Solution

$12000 = 360 \rightarrow x = \dfrac{12000 \times 120}{360} = \$4000$

$x = 120$

(38.63). The variance of the sample 6, 8, 11, 5, 6, 9 is 5.1. Find the variance of 18, 24, 33, 15, 18, 27.

Solution

Sample 1: 6, 8, 11, 5, 6, 9

Sample 2: 18, 24, 33, 15, 18, 27 = 3(6, 8, 11, 5, 6, 9)

$\therefore \bar{x}_2 = 3\bar{x}_1$ also $SD_2 = 3SD_1$

From $\dfrac{SD_1}{\sqrt{V_1}} = \dfrac{SD_2}{\sqrt{V_2}} \rightarrow \sqrt{V_2} = \sqrt{V_1} \times \dfrac{SD_2}{SD_1} \rightarrow V_2 = \left[\sqrt{V_1} \times \dfrac{SD_2}{SD_1}\right]^2 \rightarrow V_1 \times \left[\dfrac{SD_2}{SD_1}\right]^2$

$V_2 = 5.1 \times [3]^2 = 45.9$

(38.64). The variance of the numbers – 3, - 2, 0, k, 4, 5 is $\dfrac{26}{3}$. Find the standard deviation of - 6, - 4, 0, 2k, 8, 10

Solution

Sample 1: – 3, - 2, 0, k, 4, 5

Sample 2: - 6, - 4, 0, 2k, 8, 10 = 2(– 3, - 2, 0, k, 4, 5)

$\therefore \bar{x}_2 = 2\bar{x}_1$ also $SD_2 = 2SD_1$

From $SD_1 = \sqrt{V_1}$

$SD_2 = 2SD_1 \rightarrow SD_2 = 2\sqrt{V_1} = 2\sqrt{\dfrac{26}{3}}$

(38.65). The mean of 12 numbers is 18. If each of the numbers is increased by 5, what is the new mean?

Solution

$\bar{x}_1 = \dfrac{x_1 + x_2 + \ldots}{n} = 18$

When each of x_1, x_2 is increased by 5 we have $\bar{x}_2 = \frac{(x_1+5) + (x_2+5) .....}{n}$

$\therefore \bar{x}_2 = \bar{x}_1 + 5 = 18 + 5 = 23$

(38.66). Given that the mean of the numbers $x_1, x_2, x_3, ... x_n$ is k, find the mean of the numbers $(3x_1 + 2), (3x_2 + 2) ...... 3x_n + 2$

Solution

Sample 1: $x_1, x_2, x_3, ... x_n$

Sample 2: $(3x_1 + 2), (3x_2 + 2) ...... 3x_n + 2$

Close observation reveals that the 3 is multiplied to the original numbers and 2 added

$\bar{x}_2 = 3k + 2$

(38.67). The variance of the numbers 9, 7, 8, 5, 7, 6 is $1\frac{2}{3}$. Find the standard deviation of 12, 10, 11, 8, 10, 9.

Solution

Sample 1: 9, 7, 8, 5, 7, 6

Sample 2: 12, 10, 11, 8, 10, 9 = addition of 3 to each numbers of Sample 1

For addition only the mean increases by 3 while others are constant

From $SD_1 = \sqrt{V_1} \rightarrow SD_1 = \sqrt{\frac{5}{3}}$

(38.68). The standard deviation of the numbers 1, 2, 3, 4, 5, 6, 7, 8, 9 is 2.58. What is the standard deviation of the numbers 101, 102, 103, 104, 105, 106, 107, 108, 109.

Solution

Sample 1: 1, 2, 3, 4, 5, 6, 7, 8, 9

Sample 2: 101, 102, 103, 104, 105, 106, 107, 108, 109 = addition of 100 to each numbers of Sample 1

For addition only the mean increases by 100 while others are constant

From $\frac{SD_1}{\sqrt{V_1}} = \frac{SD_2}{\sqrt{V_2}} \rightarrow SD_2 = SD_1 \times \frac{\sqrt{V_2}}{\sqrt{V_1}} \rightarrow SD_2 = SD_1 = 2.58$

Since $\frac{\sqrt{V_2}}{\sqrt{V_1}}$ is constant.

CHAPTER 39 PROBABILITY DISTRIBUTIONS

Probability distribution is a table or an equation that links each outcome of a statistical experiment with its probability of occurrence.

Terms associated with probability distributions

(i) Random variable: This is a real-value defined on the sample space. It can either be qualitative or quantitative.

(ii) Discrete variable: These are quantitative variables that can take distinct values.

(iii) Continuous variable: These are quantitative variables that take values within a given range.

(iv) Probability mass function: This is the distribution of a discrete random variable.

Discrete distributions are our focus here, we there consider each in details.

(1) BINOMIAL DISTRIBUTION

Binomial distribution is the discrete probability distribution of the number of success in a sequence of n independent yes/no experiments which yields success with probability p.

Mathematically, it is represented as

$$P(X = x) = \begin{cases} \begin{bmatrix} n \\ x \end{bmatrix} [p]^x [q]^{n-x} & x = 0, 1, 2, \ldots, n \\ & \text{Other wise} \end{cases}$$

Properties of Binomial Distribution

The outcomes can be classified into mutually exclusive and collectively exhaustive events usually called success and failure.

The probability of outcomes classified is p and constant from outcome to the other. Hence, the probability of an outcome classified failure is $1 - p$, which is also constant.

Characteristics of Binomial Distribution

When the parameters n and p are specified, a particular model can be generated.

The curve of a binomial distribution can be symmetrical or skewed

It is symmetrical when p = 0.5 and not skewed when p ≠ 0.5

Therefore the closer p is to 0.5, the less skewed the distribution will be.

It has a mean given by $\mu = np$

It has a variance given by $\sigma^2 = np(1-p) = npq$. Where q = (1 − p)

It has a central moment given by $npq[1 + 3(n-2)pq]$

It has a recurrence relation given by $P(r+1) = \frac{n-r}{r+1} \frac{p}{q} \cdot P(r)$

(2) POISSON DISTRIBUTION

This is a discrete probability distribution that expresses the probability of a given number of event occurring in a fixed interval of time.

Mathematically, it is given by

$$P(X = x) = \begin{cases} \frac{e^{-\lambda}\lambda^x}{x!} & x = 0,1,2,\ldots\ldots,\infty \\ 0 & \text{Other wise} \end{cases}$$

Where x = number of success per unit

λ = expected number of successes, e = exponential value 2.71828

Characteristics of Poisson Distribution

It has a mean given by λ

It has a variance given by λ

It has a recurrence relation given by $P(r+1) = \frac{\lambda}{r+1} P(r)$

(3) NORMAL DISTRIBUTION

This is continuous distribution that tells the probability that any real observation will fall between any two real limits as the curve approaches zero on either side. It is given as:

$$F(x) = \begin{cases} \dfrac{1}{\sigma\sqrt{2\pi}} e^{-\dfrac{(x-\mu)^2}{2\sigma^2}} & -\infty < x < \infty \\ & -\infty < \mu < \infty \\ & \sigma > 0 \\ 0 & \text{Other wise} \end{cases}$$

With Standard score given by $Z = \dfrac{x - \mu}{\sigma}$

From $Z = \dfrac{x - \mu}{\sigma} \rightarrow Z\sigma = x - \mu$ inserting into the function above we have

$$\dfrac{1}{\sigma\sqrt{2\pi}} e^{-\dfrac{(Z\sigma)^2}{2\sigma^2}} \rightarrow \dfrac{1}{\sigma\sqrt{2\pi}} e^{-\dfrac{Z^2\sigma^2}{2\sigma^2}} \rightarrow \dfrac{1}{\sqrt{2\pi}} e^{-\dfrac{Z^2}{2}}$$

$$F(x) = \begin{cases} \dfrac{1}{\sqrt{2\pi}} e^{-\dfrac{Z^2}{2}} & -\infty < Z < \infty \\ 0 & \text{Other wise} \end{cases}$$

$\mu = mean, \sigma = standard\ deviation$

Characteristics of the Normal distribution

It has a variance equal to σ^2

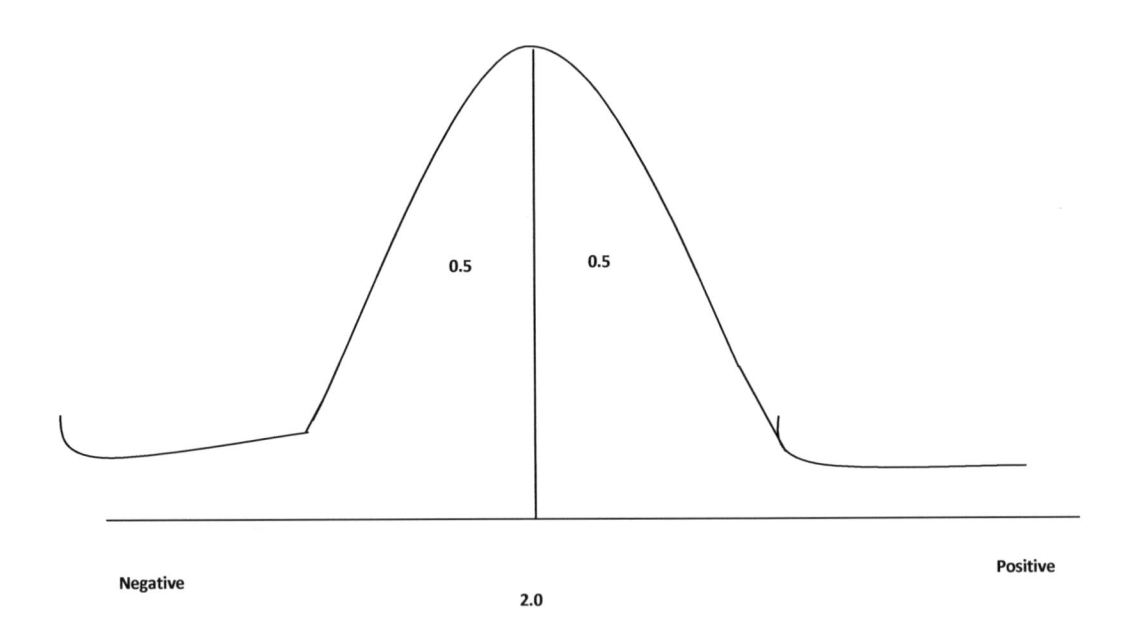

Characteristics of the Normal curve

(i) It has a mean, median and mode are all equal to μ

(ii) The curve is maximum at point $Z = 0$

(iii) The area under the curve is 1 i.e 0.5 to the left and 0.5 to the right

(iv) The curve is symmetrical i.e one side is the mirror image of the other

(v) The curve is maximum at point $Z = 0$

(vi) The curve is asymptotic to the x-axis at both directions

Deductions from Normal curve

We consider the following cases

(i) Case 1: If $P(Z < Z_1)$

If $Z_1 > 0$ $\rightarrow$ $0.5 + T(Z_1)$

If $Z_1 < 0$ $\rightarrow$ $0.5 - T(Z_1)$

If $Z_1 = 0$ $\rightarrow$ 0.5

(ii) Case 2: If $P(Z > Z_1)$

If $Z_1 > 0$ $\rightarrow$ $0.5 - T(Z_1)$

If $Z_1 < 0 \rightarrow 0.5 + T(Z_1)$

(*iii*) Case 3: If $P(Z_1 < Z < Z_2)$

If $Z_1 < 0$ *and* $Z_2 > 0 \rightarrow T(Z_1) + T(Z_2)$

If $Z_1 > 0$ *and* $Z_2 > 0 \rightarrow T(Z_2) - T(Z_1)$

QUESTIONS

(39.1). Consider the experiment of tossing a coin five times. Find the probability of obtaining (*i*) Exactly 3 heads. (*ii*) No head. (*iii*) At least 4 heads. (*iv*) At most 1 head. (*v*) At least 2 heads. (*vi*) At most 4 heads. (*vii*) Between 1 and 4 heads. (*viii*) *Between 2 and 4 heads inclusive.*

Solution

$n = 5, \ p = P(H) = \frac{1}{2}, q = (1-p) = \frac{1}{2}, \ X = Number\ of\ heads\ in\ five\ tosses$

$$P(X = x) = \begin{cases} \binom{5}{x} \left[\frac{1}{2}\right]^x \left[\frac{1}{2}\right]^{5-x} & x = 0,1,2,3,4,5 \\ & \text{Other wise} \end{cases}$$

(*i*) $P(X = 3) = \binom{5}{3} \left[\frac{1}{2}\right]^3 \left[\frac{1}{2}\right]^2 \rightarrow (10)\left[\frac{1}{2}\right]^5 = \frac{10}{32}$

(*ii*) $P(X = 0) = \binom{5}{0} \left[\frac{1}{2}\right]^0 \left[\frac{1}{2}\right]^5 \rightarrow (1)(1)\left[\frac{1}{2}\right]^5 = \frac{1}{32}$

(*iii*) At least 4 implies 4 and above. $P(X \geq 4) = P(X = 4) + P(X = 5)$

$P(X \geq 4) = \binom{5}{4} \left[\frac{1}{2}\right]^4 \left[\frac{1}{2}\right]^1 + \binom{5}{5} \left[\frac{1}{2}\right]^5 \left[\frac{1}{2}\right]^0 \rightarrow (5)\left[\frac{1}{2}\right]^5 + (1)\left[\frac{1}{2}\right]^5 = \frac{6}{32}$

(*iv*) At most 1 implies 1 and below. $P(X \leq 1) = P(X = 0) + P(X = 1)$

$P(X \leq 1) = \binom{5}{0}\left[\frac{1}{2}\right]^0\left[\frac{1}{2}\right]^5 + \binom{5}{1}\left[\frac{1}{2}\right]^1\left[\frac{1}{2}\right]^4 \rightarrow (1)(1)\left[\frac{1}{2}\right]^5 + (5)\left[\frac{1}{2}\right]^5 = \frac{6}{32}$

(v) At least 2 implies 2 and above. $P(X \geq 2) = 1 - P(X \leq 1)$

$P(X \geq 2) = 1 - [P(X=0) + P(X=1)] \rightarrow 1 - \frac{6}{32}$

It is important to note the technique employed saves a great deal of time under examination conditions. If each were computed the same answer would be gotten.

(vi) At most 4 implies 4 and above. $P(X \leq 4) = 1 - P(X=5)$

$P(X \leq 4) = 1 - \binom{5}{5}\left[\frac{1}{2}\right]^5\left[\frac{1}{2}\right]^0 \rightarrow 1 - (1)\left[\frac{1}{2}\right]^5 = 1 - \frac{1}{32} = \frac{31}{32}$

(vii) Between 1 and 4 implies $P(1 < X < 4) = P(X=2) + P(X=3)$

$\binom{5}{2}\left[\frac{1}{2}\right]^2\left[\frac{1}{2}\right]^3 + \binom{5}{3}\left[\frac{1}{2}\right]^3\left[\frac{1}{2}\right]^2 \rightarrow (10)\left[\frac{1}{2}\right]^5 + (10)\left[\frac{1}{2}\right]^5 = \frac{20}{32}$

(viii) Between 2 and 4 inclusive implies $P(2 \leq X \leq 4) = P(X=2) + P(X=3) + P(X=3)$

$\binom{5}{2}\left[\frac{1}{2}\right]^2\left[\frac{1}{2}\right]^3 + \binom{5}{3}\left[\frac{1}{2}\right]^3\left[\frac{1}{2}\right]^2 + \binom{5}{4}\left[\frac{1}{2}\right]^4\left[\frac{1}{2}\right]^1 \rightarrow (10)\left[\frac{1}{2}\right]^5 + (10)\left[\frac{1}{2}\right]^5 + (5)\left[\frac{1}{2}\right]^5 = \frac{25}{32}$

(39.2). Consider the experiment of throwing a die eight times. Find the probability that a 3 will show (i) Exactly 2 times. (ii) At least seven times. (iii) At least once.

Solution

$n = 8, \ p = P(X) = p(getting\ a\ three\ from\ a\ die) = \frac{1}{6}, q = (1-p) = \frac{5}{6}$

$X = Number\ of\ three\ in\ each\ throw$

$P(X = x) = \begin{cases} \binom{8}{x}\left[\frac{1}{6}\right]^x\left[\frac{5}{6}\right]^{8-x} & x = 0,1,2,3,4,5,6,7,8 \\ & \\ & Other\ wise \end{cases}$

(*i*) Getting 3 exactly 2 times

$$P(X=2) = \binom{8}{2} \left[\frac{1}{6}\right]^2 \left[\frac{5}{6}\right]^6 \to (28)\frac{5^6}{6^8} = 0.2604$$

(*ii*) Getting 3 at least seven times implies 7 and above.

$$P(X \geq 7) = P(X=7) + P(X=8) \to \binom{8}{7}\left[\frac{1}{6}\right]^7\left[\frac{5}{6}\right]^1 + \binom{8}{8}\left[\frac{1}{6}\right]^8\left[\frac{5}{6}\right]^0 \to$$

$$(8)\left[\frac{1}{6}\right]^7 \left[\frac{5}{6}\right]^1 + (1)\left[\frac{1}{6}\right]^8 = \frac{41}{6^8}$$

(*ii*) Getting 3 at least once implies 1 and above.

$$P(X \geq 1) = 1 - [P(X=0)] \to 1 - \left[\binom{8}{0}\left[\frac{1}{6}\right]^0 \left[\frac{5}{6}\right]^8\right] \to 1 - \left[\frac{5}{6}\right]^8$$

(39.3). Past experience shows that 7% of all luncheon vouchers are in error. If a random sample of 5 vouchers are selected, what is the probability that (*i*) Exactly two will have an error. (*ii*) At least two will have error. (*iii*) At most one will have error.

Solution

$n = 5, p = 7\% = 0.07, q = (1-p) = 1 - 0.07 = 0.93$

$X = Number\ of\ luncheon\ vouchers\ having\ error$

$$P(X=x) = \begin{cases} \binom{5}{x}[0.07]^x [0.93]^{5-x} & x = 0,1,2,3,4,5 \\ & \\ & \text{Other wise} \end{cases}$$

(*i*) $P(X=2) = \binom{5}{2}[0.07]^2 [0.93]^3 \to (10)[0.07]^2 [0.93]^3 = 0.03941$

(*ii*) At least two will have error implies 2 and above.

$P(X \geq 2) = 1 - [P(X=0) + P(X=1)]$

$\to 1 - \left[\binom{5}{0}[0.07]^0 [0.93]^5 + \binom{5}{1}[0.07]^1 [0.93]^4\right] \to 1 - [0.6569 + 0.26182] \to$

$1 - 0.95751 = 0.04249$

(*iii*) At most one will have error implies one and below

P(X ≤ 1) = P(X = 0) + P(X = 1)

P(X ≤ 1) = $\binom{5}{0}$ [0.07]⁰ [0.93]⁵ + $\binom{5}{1}$ [0.07]¹ [0.93]⁴ → 0.6956 + 0.26182

= 0.9575

(39.4). The average number of days schools are closed due to industrial strike in a year in Nigeria is 4. What is the probability that the schools will be closed for (*i*) 6 days (*ii*) At least 2 days (*iii*) (*iii*) At most a day (*iv*) Between 2 and 5 days inclusive (*v*) Between 2 and 5 days

Solution

$$P(X = x) = \begin{cases} \dfrac{e^{-\lambda}\lambda^{x}}{x!} & x = 0,1,2,\ldots,\infty \\ 0 & \text{Other wise} \end{cases}$$

(*i*) P (Exactly 6 days) = P (X = 6) = $\dfrac{e^{-4}4^{6}}{6!}$ → $\dfrac{\frac{1}{(2.7182)^{4}} \cdot 4^{6}}{6!}$ → $\dfrac{\frac{4096}{54.59}}{720}$ = 0.1042

(*ii*) P (At least 2 days) = P (X ≥ 2) = 1 - P(X ≤ 1) → [P(X = 0) + P(X = 1)]

$1 - \left[\dfrac{e^{-4}4^{0}}{0!} + \dfrac{e^{-4}4^{1}}{1!}\right]$ → 1 − (0.01832 + 0.36788) → 1 − 0.3862 = 0.6138

(*iii*) P (At most 1 day) = P (X ≤ 1) = [P(X = 0) + P(X = 1)]

$\left[\dfrac{e^{-4}4^{0}}{0!} + \dfrac{e^{-4}4^{1}}{1!}\right]$ → (0.01832 + 0.36788) = 0.3682

(*iv*) P (Between 2 and 5 days inclusive) = P (2≤ X ≤ 5)

P(X = 2) + P(X = 3) + P(X = 4) + P(X = 5) → $\dfrac{e^{-4}4^{2}}{2!} + \dfrac{e^{-4}4^{3}}{3!} + \dfrac{e^{-4}4^{4}}{4!} + \dfrac{e^{-4}4^{5}}{5!}$ = 0.6937

(*v*) P (Between 2 and 5 days) = P (2< X < 5) → [P(X = 3) + P(X = 4)]

$\dfrac{e^{-4}4^{3}}{3!} + \dfrac{e^{-4}4^{4}}{4!}$ = 0.3908

(39.5). A researcher has found that the probability that a dwarf is born by a Nigerian woman is 10^{-14}. What is the probability that the next 1000 children born in Nigeria (by Nigerian mothers) is of most 2.

Solution

$\lambda = np \rightarrow 10^{-14} \times 1000 = 1 \times 10^{-11}$

$$\frac{e^{-(1 \times 10^{-11})} \cdot (1 \times 10^{-11})^2}{2!} \rightarrow \frac{3.68 \times 10^{-12} \times 1 \times 10^{-22}}{2} = 1.84 \times 10^{-34}$$

(39.6). The average number of claims per hour made to a particular insurance company for damages incurred is 3.5. Determine the probability that in any given hour (*i*) Less than three claims will be made (*ii*) Exactly two claims will be made (*iii*) At least three claims will be made (*iv*) More than three claims will be made

Solution

$$P(X = x) = \begin{cases} \dfrac{e^{-(3.5)}(3.5)^x}{x!} & x = 0,1,2,\ldots,\infty \\ 0 & \text{Other wise} \end{cases}$$

(*i*) P(Less than three claims) = $P(X < 3) = P(X \leq 2) = P(X = 0) + P(X = 1) + P(X = 2)$

$$\frac{e^{-3.5}(3.5)^0}{0!} + \frac{e^{-3.6}(3.5)^1}{1!} + \frac{e^{-3.5}(3.5)^2}{2!} = 0.3208$$

(*ii*) P(Exactly two claims) = $P(X = 2) = \dfrac{e^{-3.5}(3.5)^2}{2!} = 0.1850$

(*iii*) P(At least three claims) = $P(X \geq 3) = 1 - P(X \leq 2) = 1 - [P(X = 0) + P(X = 1) + P(X = 2)]$

$$1 - \left[\frac{e^{-3.5}(3.5)^0}{0!} + \frac{e^{-3.6}(3.5)^1}{1!} + \frac{e^{-3.5}(3.5)^1}{2!}\right] \rightarrow 1 - 0.3208 = 0.6792$$

(39.7). In a certain factory producing cycle tyres, there is a small chance of 1 in 500 tyres to be defective. The tyres are supplied in lots of 10. Using Poisson distribution, calculate number of lots containing (i) No defective (ii) One defective (iii) Two defective tyres in a consignment of 10,000 lots.

Solution

$\lambda = np \rightarrow 10 \times \dfrac{1}{500} = \dfrac{1}{50} = 0.02$

(i) P(No defective) = P(X = 0) $\rightarrow \dfrac{e^{-0.02}(0.02)^0}{0!} = 0.9802$

Number of lots containing no defective = 10000 × 0.9802 = $9802 \; lots$

(ii) P(One is defective) = P(X = 1) $\rightarrow \dfrac{e^{-0.02}(0.02)^1}{1!} \rightarrow \dfrac{e^{-0.02} \times (0.02)}{1!} = 0.019604$

Number of lots containing one defective = 10000 × 0.019604 = $196 \; lots$

(iii) P(Two is defective) = P(X = 2) $\rightarrow \dfrac{e^{-0.02}(0.02)^2}{2!} = 0.00019604$

Number of lots containing two defectives = 10000 × 0.00019604 = $2 \; lots$

(39.8). The grade point average of 1000 university students are normally distributed with mean 2.89 and standard deviation 0.4. If a university student is selected at random, what is the probability that the student (i) Has a grade point between 2.05 and 3.04 (ii) Has a grade point below 2.15 (iii) Has a grade point above 2.00 (iv) Has a grade point that allow him win the university scholarship. A student wins the scholarship, if his grade point is at least 3.3.

Solution

From $Z = \dfrac{x - \mu}{\sigma} \rightarrow \dfrac{x - 2.89}{0.4}$

(i) P(Has a grade point between 2.05 and 3.04) = P(2.05 < X < 3.04)

$P(2.05 < X < 3.04) \rightarrow P\left[\dfrac{2.05 - 2.89}{0.4} < \dfrac{x - 2.89}{0.4} < \dfrac{3.04 - 2.89}{0.4}\right] \rightarrow P(-2.1 < Z < 0.375)$

This is similar to $P(Z_1 < Z < Z_2)$

From, If $Z_1 < 0$ and $Z_2 > 0 \rightarrow T(Z_1) + T(Z_2)$

$\therefore P(-2.1 < Z < 0.375) = T(-2.1) + T(0.375)$

From normal distribution table $T(-2.1) + T(0.375) = 0.1443 + 0.0019 = 0.1462$

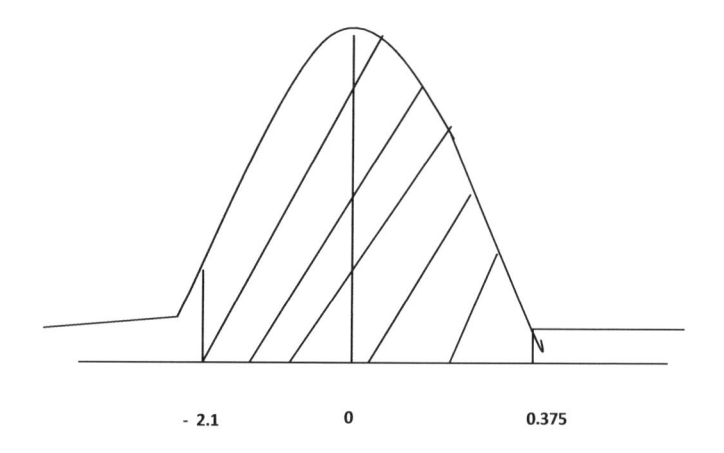

                    -2.1   0   0.375

(*ii*) P(Has a grade point below 2.15) = P(X < 2.15)

P(X < 2.15) → $P\left[\frac{x - 2.89}{0.4} < \frac{2.15 - 2.89}{0.4}\right]$ → P(Z < −1.85)

This is similar to $P(Z < Z_1)$

From, If $Z_1 < 0$ → $0.5 - T(Z_1)$

∴ P(X < 2.15) = $0.5 - T(-1.85)$

From normal distribution table $T(-1.85) = 0.4678$

∴ P(X < 2.15) → $0.5 - 0.4678 = 0.0322$

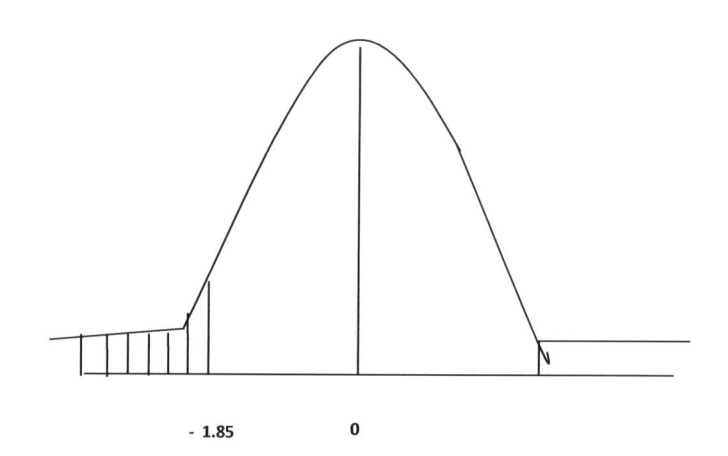

                   -1.85   0

(*iii*) P(Has a grade point above 2.00) = P(X > 2.00)

P(X > 2.00) → $P\left[\frac{x - 2.89}{0.4} < \frac{2 - 2.89}{0.4}\right]$ → P(Z > −2.225)

This is similar to $P(Z < Z_1)$

From, If $Z_1 < 0 \rightarrow 0.5 - T(Z_1)$

∴ $P(X > 2.00) = 0.5 + T(-2.225)$

From normal distribution table $T(-2.225) = 0.4870$

∴ $P(X > 2.15) \rightarrow 0.5 + 0.4678 = 0.9870$

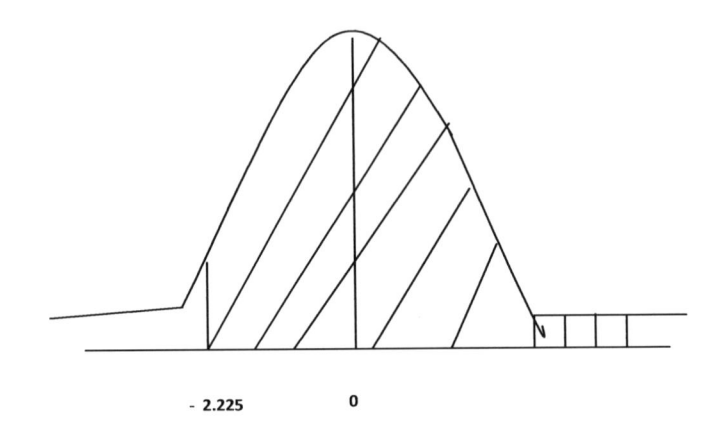

- 2.225   0

(iv) P(Has a grade point above 3.3) = $P(X > 3.3)$

$P(X \geq 3.3) \rightarrow P\left[\frac{x - 2.89}{0.4} < \frac{3.3 - 2.89}{0.4}\right] \rightarrow P(Z > 1.025)$

This is similar to $P(Z > Z_1)$

From, If $Z_1 > 0 \rightarrow 0.5 - T(Z_1)$

∴ $P(X > 3.3) = 0.5 - T(1.025)$

From normal distribution table $T(1.025) = 0.3473$

∴ $P(X > 3.3) \rightarrow 0.5 - 0.3473 = 0.1527$

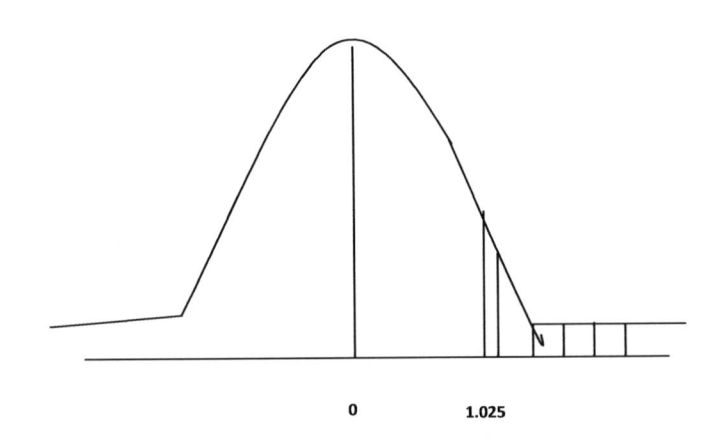

0   1.025

(39.8). The time lag between the billing and paying of bills in a bank is approximately normally distributed with a mean of 20 days and standard deviation of 5 days. what is the probability that the bill will be paid (*i*) Between 13 and 21 days (*ii*) Between 22 and 28 days (*iii*) In less than 10 days (*iv*) In 13 or more days.

Solution

From $Z = \dfrac{x - \mu}{\sigma} \rightarrow \dfrac{x - 20}{5}$

(*i*) P(Between 13 and 21 days) = $P(13 < X < 21)$

$P(13 < X < 21) \rightarrow P\left[\dfrac{13 - 20}{5} < \dfrac{x - 20}{5} < \dfrac{21 - 20}{5}\right] \rightarrow P(-1.4 < Z < 0.2)$

This is similar to $P(Z_1 < Z < Z_2)$

From, If $Z_1 < 0$ and $Z_2 > 0 \rightarrow T(Z_1) + T(Z_2)$

$\therefore P(-1.4 < Z < 0.2) = T(-1.4) + T(0.2)$

From normal distribution table $T(-1.4) + T(0.2) = 0.4192 + 0.0793 = 0.4985$

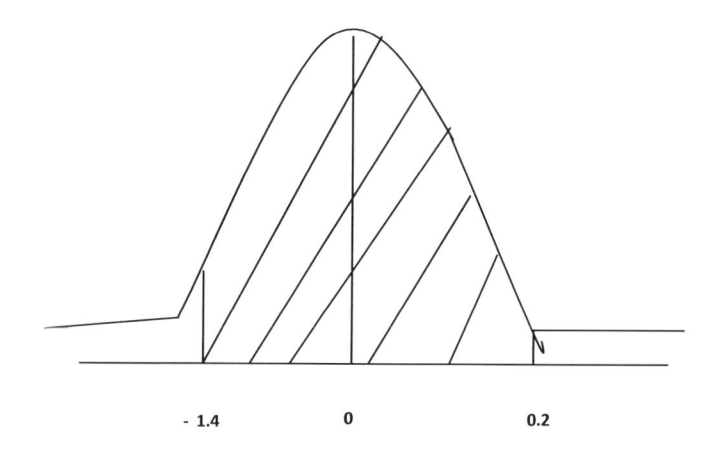

(*ii*) P(Between 22 and 28 days) = $P(22 < X < 28)$

$P(22 < X < 28) \rightarrow P\left[\dfrac{22 - 28}{5} < \dfrac{x - 20}{5} < \dfrac{28 - 20}{5}\right] \rightarrow P(0.4 < Z < 1.6)$

$\therefore T(1.6) - T(0.4)$

From normal distribution table $T(1.6) = 0.4452, T(0.4) = 0.1554$

∴ $T(1.6) - T(0.4) \rightarrow 0.4452 - 0.1554 = 0.2898$

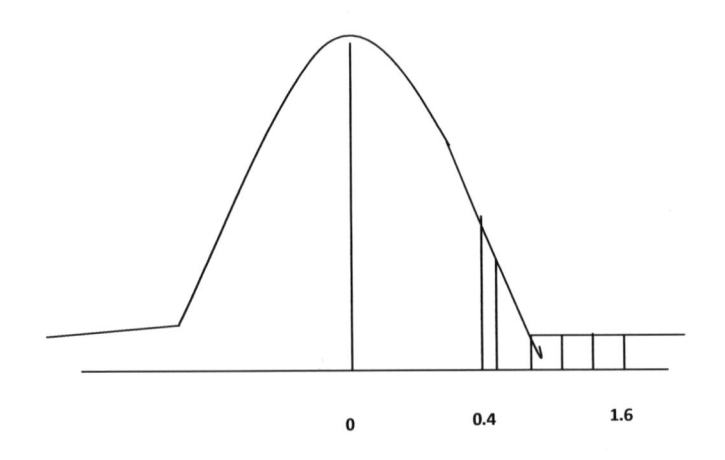

(iii) In less than 10 days = $P(X < 10)$

$P(X < 10) \rightarrow P\left[\dfrac{x - 20}{5} < \dfrac{10 - 20}{5}\right] \rightarrow P(Z < -2.0)$

∴ $P(X < 10) = 0.5 - T(-2.0)$

From normal distribution table $T(2.0) = 0.4775$

∴ $P(X < 10) \rightarrow 0.5 - 0.4775 = 0.0225$

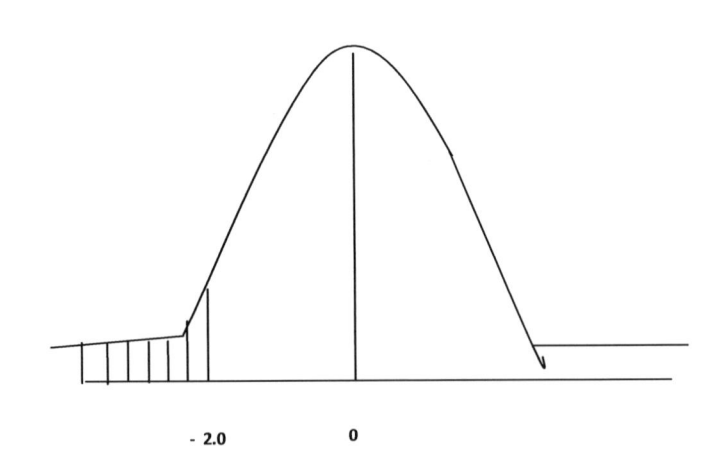

(iv) In 13 or more days = $P(X \geq 13)$

$P(X < 10) \rightarrow P\left[\frac{x-20}{5} < \frac{13-20}{5}\right] \rightarrow P(Z > -1.4)$

From normal distribution table $T(1.4) = 0.4192$

$\therefore P(X \geq 13) \rightarrow 0.5 + 0.4192 = 0.9192$

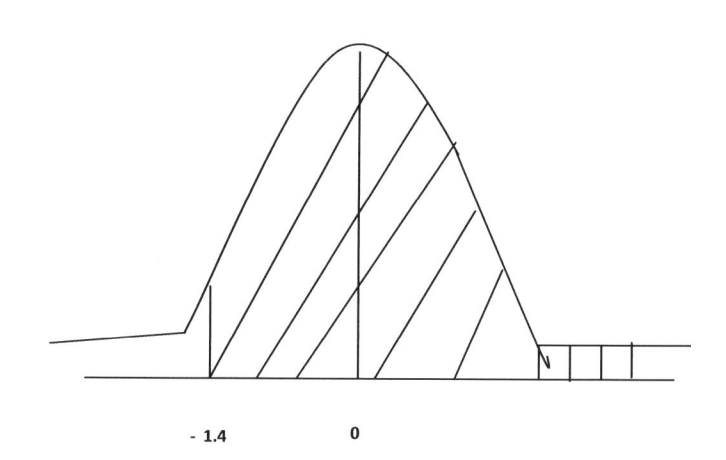

IMPORTANT QUOTES

I have had my results for a long time: but I do not yet know how I am to arrive at them. **Carl Friedrich Gauss**

In mathematics you don't understand things. You just get used to them. - **John Von Neumann**

Let no one ignorant of mathematics enter here. -**Plato**

The day a man discovers himself is the day he starts living purposefully. - **Jude Onicha**

REFERENCES

Schaums Outline Series	-	**On Geometry**
Integrated Mathematics	-	**J R. Afolabi**
JAMB	-	**Past Questions on Mathematics**
WAEC/NECO	-	**Past Questions on Mathematics/Further mathematics**
Wikipedia	-	**Important definitions**

Made in the USA
Lexington, KY
13 February 2015